FIFTH EDITION

THE LAW AND SPECIAL EDUCATION

Mitchell L. Yell
University of South Carolina

 Pearson

330 Hudson Street, NY NY 10013

Director and Publisher: *Kevin M. Davis*
Content Producer: *Janelle Rogers*
Portfolio Management Assistant: *Casey Coriell*
Executive Field Marketing Manager: *Krista Clark*
Executive Product Marketing Manager: *Christopher
Barry*
Procurement Specialist: *Carol Melville*
Full Service Project Management: *Kathy Smith, SPi
Global*

Cover Designer: *Carie Keller, SPi Global*
Cover Image: © *pixhook/Getty Images*
Composition: *SPi Global*
Printer/Binder: *LSC Communications*
Cover Printer: *LSC Communications*
Text Font: *Garamond 3 LT Std*

Library of Congress Cataloging-in-Publication Data
Names: Yell, Mitchell L., author.
  Title: The law and special education / Mitchell L. Yell, University of South Carolina.
    Description: Fifth edition. | New York, NY : Pearson, [2019] | Includes bibliographical references
and index.
  Identifiers: LCCN 2018018369| ISBN 9780135175002 | ISBN 0135175003
  Subjects: LCSH: Children with disabilities--Education--Law and legislation--United States. | Special
education--Law and legislation--United States.
  Classification: LCC KF4210 .Y45 2019 | DDC 344.73/0791--dc23
LC record available at https://lccn.loc.gov/2018018369

16 2021

ISBN-10:   0–13–517536–4
ISBN-13: 978–0–13–517536–1

*This book is dedicated to the memory of my mother and father,
Vonnet and Erwin; to my in-laws, Vern and Delores Quam; and to my wife,
Joy, and three sons, Nick, Eric, and Alex.*

About the Author

Mitchell Yell, Ph.D., is the Fred and Francis Palmetto Chair in Teacher Education and Professor in Special Education in the College of Education at the University of South Carolina in Columbia. For the past 26 years, Dr. Yell has conducted extensive research and presented numerous workshops on developing individualized education programs (IEPs), formulating legally correct special education policies, and adopting best practices in educating students with disabilities. His primary goal has been to extrapolate principles from legislation and litigation; communicate them to parents, teachers, and administrators in clear, "nonlegalese" language; and assist teachers and school districts in the use of legally sound research-based policies and practices.

Prior to coming to the University of South Carolina, Dr. Yell was a special education teacher in Minnesota for 16 years. During this time, he taught in elementary, middle, and secondary school classrooms and in special schools for students with learning disabilities, emotional and behavioral disorders, and autism.

He has published 112 articles and 30 book chapters, and has conducted numerous workshops on special education law and classroom management. He is the author of four textbooks published by Pearson, titled *The Law and Special Education, Evidence-Based Practices for Educating Students with Emotional and Behavioral Disorders,* and *No Child Left Behind: A Guide for Professionals,* and is the coauthor of *A Teacher's Guide to Preventing Behavior Problems in the Elementary Classroom* with Stephen Smith.

Preface

Federal laws mandating the provision of special education and related services to students with disabilities have been in effect since 1975. To understand the field of special education, it is essential that we be familiar with the history and development of these laws. Because special education has become a highly litigated area, it is important that special education teachers, administrators, and associated staff know the requirements of these laws. Moreover, the laws are in a constant state of development and refinement; therefore, we need to be able to locate the necessary information to keep abreast of these changes. Thus, the purpose of this text is threefold: (a) to acquaint readers with the legal development of special education, (b) to expose readers to the current legal requirements in providing a free appropriate public education to students with disabilities, and (c) to assist readers in understanding the procedures involved in obtaining legal information in law libraries and on the Internet and to guide them in conducting legal research using a variety of sources.

NEW TO THIS EDITION

The Fifth Edition retains the same structure but updates and adds content. Additionally, this edition contains the following new information:

- Coverage of the U.S. Supreme Court's 2017 ruling in *Endrew. F. v. Douglas County Schools* has been added throughout the textbook.
- Coverage of the U.S. Supreme Court's 2017 ruling in *Fry v. Napoleon Community Schools* has been added to the textbook.
- Coverage of a number of new policy letters from the Office of Civil Rights and the Office of Special Education and Rehabilitative Services in the U.S. Department of Education have been added to the textbook.
- Chapter 7 has been rewritten to include complete coverage of the Every Student Succeeds Act of 2015.
- Coverage of charter schools and students with disabilities has been added to the final chapter of the textbook.
- Coverage of cases on the implementation of IEPs has been added to Chapters 8 and 10.
- A section of standards-based IEPs was added to Chapter 10.
- The Fifth Edition includes a number of new cases and policy letters from the U.S Department of Education.

This textbook is written in the style of an educational textbook rather than a legal textbook. That is, rather than including passages from selected cases, legal principles from these cases will be presented. However, exposure to the written opinions is important, and readers are urged to locate and read them in a law library or on the Internet. Readers should note the wealth of materials on the Internet described in Chapter 2. For ease of use, references are presented in accordance with the format described in the *Publication Manual of the American Psychological Association* (Sixth Edition) rather than in the standard legal format. Finally, legal terms are kept to a minimum, explained when used, and defined in the glossary.

A unique feature of this textbook is a Special Education Law blog, which is available at http://spedlawblog.com. The primary purpose of the blog is to provide readers and instructors using the text with frequent updates regarding legal developments in special education.

Acknowledgments

In writing this book I benefited from the help of many friends and colleagues. Thanks go to all of them. Terrye Conroy, the law librarian at the University of South Carolina, did a fabulous job in co-writing Chapters 1 and 2. David Rogers and Elisabeth Lodge Rogers, director of special services, intermediate district #287, Plymouth, MN, did great work in Chapter 4. Thanks also to the reviewers of this text for their timely and helpful reviews: Iffat Jabeen, University of Texas at San Antonio; Carl Lashley, UNC Greensboro; and Gretchen Robinson, University of NC at Pembroke. This is a better textbook because of their efforts. A hearty thank you goes to Joseph Cross of the University of South Carolina law library, who was extremely helpful, and Delys Nast, who generously contributed her considerable talents. A special thank you goes to Ken Heinlein of the University of Wyoming for his insightful editorial comments. Thanks also to Erik Drasgow and Bill Brown of the University of South Carolina for their helpful editorial feedback, and to Antonis Katsiyannis of Clemson University and the many readers who made useful suggestions for this edition. I would also like to thank Kevin Davis, who has guided me through this endeavor with enormous skill, patience, and sound advice. Thanks also go to the giants on whose shoulders I perched, Frank Wood and the late Stan Deno of the University of Minnesota. Thank you to Barbara Bateman, whose writing and work has been an inspiration to me. Finally, I want to thank my wife, Joy, and our three sons, Nick, Eric, and Alex, for their love and our lives together.

Brief Contents

Contents

Chapter 3

The History of the Law and Children with Disabilities 36

Chapter 4

The Individuals with Disabilities Education Act 53

Chapter 5

Section 504 of the Rehabilitation Act of 1973 83

Chapter 8

Free Appropriate Public Education 158

Chapter 9

Identification, Assessment, and Evaluation 195

Chapter 12

Chapter 13

Chapter 14

APPENDICES

Chapter 1

Introduction to the American Legal System

Mitchell L. Yell, Ph.D., and Terrye Conroy, J.D., M.L.I.S.

> (Laws are) rules of civil conduct prescribed by the state ... commanding what is right and prohibiting what is wrong.
>
> BLACKSTONE (1748)

Learner Objectives

At the end of the chapter, students will be able to

1.1 Describe federalism and how it underlies our system of laws.

1.2 Describe the four sources of law: constitutional law, statutory law, regulatory law, and case law.

1.3 Describe how law is created in the federal system.

1.4 Describe the hierarchy of the federal court system.

1.5 Describe precedence and its importance in the court system.

1.6 Describe the parts of a judicial opinion.

1.7 Describe the evolution of special education law.

Laws ensuring the provision of special education to students with disabilities are based on constitutional principles, written and enacted by legislatures, enforced by administrative agencies, and interpreted by the courts. It is through the interaction of the various components of the legal system, legislative and judicial, that special education law evolves. The purpose of this chapter is to examine the workings of the American legal system.

THE AMERICAN LEGAL SYSTEM

Federalism

The American system is a federal system. That is, the government of the United States is composed of a union of states joined under a central federal government. Federalism represents the linkage of the American people and the communities in which they live through a unique political arrangement. The federal government protects the people's rights and liberties and acts to achieve certain ends for the common good while simultaneously sharing authority and power with the states (Elazar, 1984). The U.S. Constitution delineates the nature of this arrangement in the 10th Amendment (see Appendix B for selected provisions of the U.S. Constitution) by limiting excessive concentration of power in the national government while simultaneously limiting full dispersal of power to the states. The national government, therefore, has specific powers granted to it in the Constitution; those powers not granted to the national government are the province of the states.

The Constitution does not contain any provisions regarding education. According to Alexander and Alexander (2012), this is not because the nation's founders had no strong beliefs regarding education. Rather, they believed the states should be sovereign in matters as important as education. Education, therefore, is governed by the laws of the 50 states.

Nevertheless, federal involvement has been an important factor in the progress and growth of education. The government's role provided under the authority given Congress by the Constitution's general welfare clause (Article I, Section 8) has, however, been indirect. In the earliest method of indirect federal involvement in education, the federal government made grants of land to the states for the purpose of creating and aiding the development of public schools. In addition to the federal land grants creating public schools, Congress in the Morrill Act of 1862 provided grants of land to each state to be used for colleges. In the land grants, the federal government had no direct control of education in the public schools or colleges.

The federal government has continued to indirectly assist states with education through categorical grants. The purposes of the categorical grants have been to provide supplementary assistance to the state systems of education and to shape educational policy in the states. States have the option of accepting or rejecting the categorical grants offered by the federal government. If states accept the categorical grants, they must abide by the federal guidelines for the use of these funds. Examples of categorical grants include the National Defense Education Act of 1958, the Higher Education Facilities Act of 1963, the Vocational Education Act of 1963, the Elementary and Secondary Education Act of 1965, and the Education for All Handicapped Children Act of 1975 (now the Individuals with Disabilities Education Act). The role of the federal government in guiding educational policy has increased greatly through the categorical grants (Alexander & Alexander, 2012).

Sources of Law

There are four sources of law: constitutional law, statutory law, regulatory law, and case law. These sources exist on both the federal and state level. The supreme laws are contained in federal and state constitutions (i.e., constitutional law), and these constitutions empower legislatures to create law (i.e., statutory law). Legislatures in turn delegate lawmaking authority to regulatory agencies to create regulations that implement the law (i.e., regulatory law). Finally, courts interpret laws through cases, and these interpretations of law accumulate to form case law. Figure 1.1 illustrates the sources of law.

Constitutional Law   The U.S. Constitution is the basic source of law in our legal system. The Constitution (a) defines the fundamental rules by which the American system functions, (b) sets the parameters for governmental action, and (c) allocates power and responsibility among the legislative, executive, and judicial branches of government (Berring & Edinger, 2005). The Constitution further defines the separation of powers between the legislative, executive, and judicial branches. Figure 1.2 illustrates the branches of government and their powers as created by the Constitution.

FIGURE 1.1 ▪ The Sources of Law

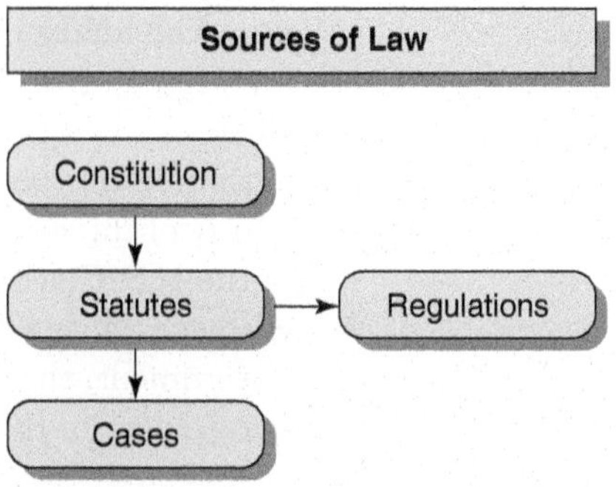

FIGURE 1.2 ■ The Branches of Government

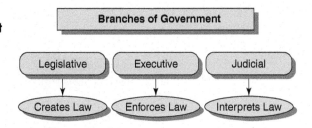

Provisions in the U.S. Constitution authorize federal statutes. The specific section of the Constitution that is the basis for special education laws (e.g., the Individuals with Disabilities Education Act and Section 504 of the Rehabilitation Act of 1973) is the provision that allows spending money to provide for the general welfare (Article 1, Section 8).

The Constitution can be amended by Congress and the states. Thus far, the Constitution has been amended only 27 times. The first 10 amendments, known as the Bill of Rights, describe the basic rights of individuals. The 14th Amendment is important because it has become the constitutional basis for special education. This amendment holds that no state can deny equal protection of the law to any person within its jurisdiction. Essentially, the equal protection clause requires states to treat all similarly situated persons alike (Alexander & Alexander, 2012). The 14th Amendment also states that persons may not be deprived of life, liberty, or property without due process of law. This amendment has played an important role in the right-to-education cases that will be explained in Chapter 3.

All 50 states have their own state constitutions. Like the U.S. Constitution, state constitutions establish the principle of separation of powers by establishing a lawmaking body (legislature), a chief executive officer (governor), and a court system. State constitutions tend to be more detailed than the federal Constitution. Often they address the day-to-day operations of the state government in addition to ensuring the rights of the state's citizens (Berring & Edinger, 2005). States cannot deny persons the rights found in the U.S. Constitution, but they can provide additional rights not found in the federal document. That is, they can provide more rights, but they cannot provide fewer.

There is no constitutional mandate regarding the provision of education by the federal government and, therefore, no constitutional right to an education afforded by the U.S. Constitution. The states thus have the authority to mandate the provision of an education for their citizens. All states have educational mandates in their constitutions.

Statutory Law   The U.S. Constitution gives Congress the authority to make laws. The laws passed or enacted by Congress and state legislatures are referred to as *statutes*. The process of enacting laws is long and complicated. In Congress, the formal process begins with the introduction of a bill by a senator or representative. The bill is assigned a number that reflects where it originated (House or Senate) and the order of introduction. The bill is then referred to the appropriate House or Senate committee. Most bills never pass this stage; some bills merely die, while some pass one house but not the other. If a bill passes both the House and the Senate but in different forms, a conference committee comprising House members and senators is appointed to develop a compromise bill. The compromise bill is then voted on again. If both the House and the Senate initially pass the same bill, the conference committee is bypassed. The final version of the bill is sent to the president, who either signs or vetoes it. The House and Senate can override the veto with a two-thirds vote in each house. The website Congress. gov provides a graphic with links to videos explaining each stage of how federal laws are made. Figure 1.3 illustrates this process.

The enacted law (also called an act), if intended to apply generally, is designated as a public law (P.L.). In addition to the name given to the law (e.g., the Individuals with Disabilities Education Act, the The Every Student Succeeds Act), the law is also given a number. The number reflects the number of the Congress in which it was passed and the number assigned to the bill.

FIGURE 1.3 ■
Creation of Law in the American Legal System

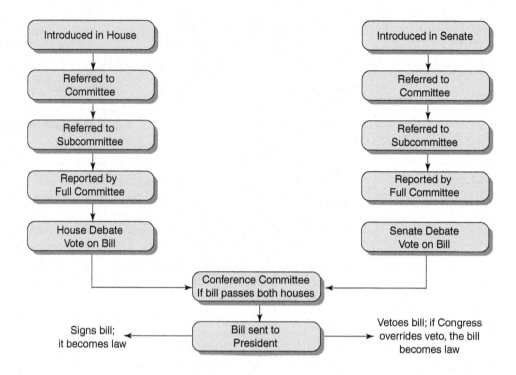

For example, P.L. 94-142, the public law number of the Education for All Handicapped Children Act, means that this public law was the 142nd law passed by the 94th Congress. Federal laws are published chronologically at the end of each congressional session (referred to as session laws) in the *United States Statutes at Large*. They are then arranged by subject (codified) into 54 titles that comprise the *United States Code*. For example, Public Law 94-142 (the Education for All Handicapped Children Act) was published in volume 89 beginning on page 773 of the *United States Statutes at Large* (89 Stat. 773). It was codified (as amended by subsequent acts) in Title 20 (Education) of the *United States Code* (20 U.S.C. § 1400 *et seq.*). Et seq. is an abbreviation for the Latin term *et sequentes*, meaning "and the following."

State statutes or laws may have different designations or names, but they are created and enacted in a manner similar to that of federal statutes. For the most part, bills are introduced and passed by state legislative bodies and published chronologically as session laws before being arranged by subject (codified) (Barkan, Mersky, & Dunn, 2009). Most statutes concerning matters of education are state rather than federal laws.

Regulatory Law   When Congress passes a law, it cannot possibly anticipate the many situations that may arise under that law (Berring & Edinger, 2005). Moreover, members of Congress do not have expertise in all areas covered by the laws they pass. The statutes passed by Congress, therefore, tend to be broad and general in nature. To fill in the details of the law, Congress delegates power to the appropriate administrative agencies to create specific regulations to implement the laws. These agencies are part of the executive branch of government. The regulations, also called *rules*, that they create supply specifics to the general content of the law and provide procedures by which the law can be enforced. For instance, many of the procedural safeguards contained in the regulations implementing the Individuals with Disabilities Education Act are codified in Title 34 Part 300 of the *Code of Federal Regulations* (34 C.F.R. pt. 300 (2013). Regulations have the force of law. A violation of a regulation, therefore, is as serious as a violation of the law.

In addition to promulgating regulations, most administrative agencies have a quasi-judicial function, which means they can make rulings regarding compliance with their regulations. These judgments may take the form of formal hearings or rulings on written inquiries. The U.S. Department of Education is a cabinet-level agency in the executive branch of the U.S. government. The agencies within the Department of Education that often rule on special education matters are the Office of Special Education and Rehabilitative Services (OSERS) and the Office of Special Education Programs (OSEP). The Office of Civil Rights (OCR) of the Department of Education investigates and issues findings on claims of violation of Section 504 of the Rehabilitation Act, and therefore often investigates matters relating to special education.

Case Law   Case law refers to the published opinions of judges that arise from court cases where they often interpret statutes, regulations, and constitutional provisions. This aggregate of published opinions forms a body of jurisprudence distinct from statutes and regulations (Garner, 2014). The American legal system relies heavily on the value of these decisions and the legal precedents they establish.

The American emphasis on case law comes to us from the English tradition known as *common law.* English common law was developed as a set of customs, rules, and traditions that were handed down through generations and reflected in the reports of decisions of the courts. Once a legal principle or precedent was established, it would be applied to cases with similar facts by subsequent courts. This process of following precedent is based upon the doctrine of *stare decisis,* a Latin phrase meaning, "to stand by things decided" (Garner, 2014).

Over time, legislation has become more important in our system, with most judicial opinions today interpreting statutes or administrative regulations. Legislation has been used to create new areas of law, fill gaps in the common law, and change laws established by the courts. However, the American judicial system continues to have great precedential power (Barkan et al., 2009; Berring & Edinger, 2005).

Sources of Judicial Power

To understand the role of case law in the American legal system, it is necessary to become familiar with the sources of judicial power. Judicial power emanates from two sources; the first has been referred to as horizontal, the second vertical (Reynolds, 2003).

Horizontal Power   There are essentially two types of horizontal power (Reynolds, 2003). The first is supreme power. In some areas of decision making, the power of the judiciary is virtually supreme. This is when the courts, especially the U.S. Supreme Court, act as the ultimate interpreter of the Constitution. The second type of horizontal power is limited power. Virtually all judicial decisions involve the interpretation of the laws of the legislative branch. The power is limited because the legislature has the final say as to the content of the law. If the legislature disagrees with a court's interpretation, it can change or alter the law or write another law. Figure 1.4 represents the horizontal power of the courts.

FIGURE 1.4 ▪ The Horizontal Power of the Courts

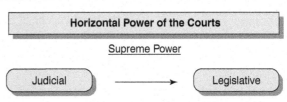

When courts acts as the interpreter of the U.S. Constitution, they are virtually supreme.

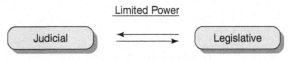

When the courts interpret the laws created by the legislative branch, the legislature may change or alter the law or write another law if legislators disagree with the court's interpretation.

An example of horizontal power is the passage of the Handicapped Children's Protection Act (1986) following the Supreme Court's decision in *Smith v. Robinson* (1984). The Education for All Handicapped Children Act originally contained no mention of parents being able to collect attorney's fees if they sued schools to obtain what they believed to be their rights under the law. Undaunted by this problem, attorneys for parents sued school districts for these rights and also brought suit under other federal statutes to collect attorney's fees. In 1984, however, the U.S. Supreme Court held that because the EAHCA did not contain a provision for attorney's fees, fees were not available. In his dissent, Justice Brennan argued that parents should not be required to pay when they had to go to court to obtain the rights given to them in the law. He further suggested that Congress revisit the issue and write attorney's fees into the law. Congress did, and in 1986 passed the Handicapped Children's Protection Act (IDEA 20 U.S.C. § 1415(i)(3)(B)(I)), which made possible the award of attorney's fees under the EAHCA and overturned *Smith v. Robinson*.

Vertical Power   The vertical power of the courts lies in the hierarchical nature of the system. The hierarchy in most jurisdictions consists of a trial court, an intermediate appellate court, and a court of last resort. The vertical power of the courts is illustrated in Figure 1.5.

The first level of courts is the trial court level. Within the federal system, the trial courts are called district courts. The role of the trial court is essentially fact-finding. Litigants (i.e., participants in a lawsuit) may appeal the decision of the trial court to the next highest level of court, the intermediate appellate court. The decision of an intermediate appellate court is binding on all trial courts in its jurisdiction. The next level of appeal is to the court of last resort, which is called the Supreme Court in most states and on the federal level. Decisions of a court of last resort are binding on all lower courts, trial and appellate.

There are 51 separate jurisdictions in the United States: the federal courts and the 50 state courts. While the names of the courts may differ, the equivalent of the generic system described previously can be found in all 51 systems. A line of authority exists within the system, such that the inferior courts are expected to follow the decisions of courts superior to them. This line of authority is within a jurisdiction but does not cross jurisdictional lines. Therefore, a trial court in a certain jurisdiction is not obligated to follow the ruling of an appellate court in another jurisdiction. For example, a trial court in Minnesota is not obligated to adhere to an appellate court's ruling that is authority in South Carolina. A trial court in South Carolina, however, is obligated to follow a ruling of the appellate court with authority in South Carolina. Because lines of authority run only within a jurisdiction, it is important to know in which jurisdiction a particular decision occurs.

FIGURE 1.5 ■ The Vertical Power of the Courts

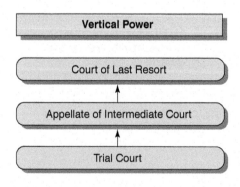

Court Structure

The generic model of the hierarchy of courts applies to both the federal system and the state jurisdictions. Figure 1.6 illustrates the generic model when applied to the federal judicial system.

In some states, the number of levels varies slightly, although the model is essentially the same. Questions involving state law are brought before the state courts, and questions involving federal law and the U.S. Constitution are usually brought before the federal courts. Most special education cases have been heard in the federal court system because most have concerned the application of federal law (e.g., the Individuals with Disabilities Education Act and Section 504 of the Rehabilitation Act). The administrative office of the U.S. courts maintains a website at uscourts.gov that explains the federal court system.

Trial Court   The trial court is the first level in the court system, the level at which the fact-finding process takes place. A judge or jury hears matters of dispute, and the issues of fact are determined. When the facts have been determined, they remain constant. This means that if the case goes to the appellate court or the court of last resort, the facts as determined by the trial court do not change, unless a higher court finds a procedural problem or bias in the fact-finding process. The facts of the case, once determined, cannot be appealed.

In addition to the facts of the case, issues of law arise at the trial court level. The judge makes determinations concerning the issues of law and applies them to the facts of the case. The rulings of the judge on the law, however, can be appealed to a higher court.

There are close to 100 trial courts in the federal judicial system. The federal trial courts are called U.S. District Courts. The geographic distribution of the district courts is based on state boundaries, with all states having between one and four district courts. All judicial districts have at least one and as many as three judges to share the federal district court caseload.

The role of the federal district court differs slightly in special education cases. Because the fact-finding process takes place during the administrative review process (i.e., the due process hearing or hearing by the state educational agency), the trial court takes on more of an appellate role and determines if the administrative agency or due process hearing officer correctly applied the law.

Intermediate Appellate Court   Usually litigants have the right to appeal the trial court decision to the intermediate appellate court in that jurisdiction. In an appeal, the appellate court reviews the decision of the trial court on the issues of law. The role of the appellate court is to ensure that the trial court did not err and to guide and develop the law within the jurisdiction (Reynolds, 2003). The appellate court determines whether the trial court's judgment should be affirmed, reversed, or modified. If the appellate court concludes that the

FIGURE 1.6 ■ The Federal Court System

Federal Court System

United States Supreme Court

↑

United States Courts of Appeals

↑

United States District Court

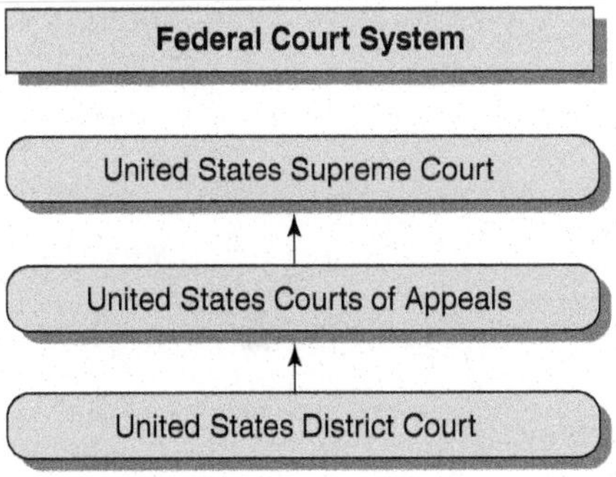

lower court did not properly apply the law, the court may reverse the trial court's decision. If the appellate court determines that the law was not applied properly, but that the error was of a minor nature and did not affect the outcome, it may affirm the decision. Decisions of the appellate court develop law through the creation of precedents.

Because the facts are determined at the trial court level, the appellate court does not retry the case. The facts as determined by the trial court, therefore, are accepted by the appellate court. The primary concern of the appellate court is whether the trial court applied the principles of law correctly.

There is no jury at the appellate level, only the judges or justices. Typically, the attorneys for each party exchange written briefs. Oral arguments may also be heard. An appellate court will usually consist of three or more judges who will then vote on the disposition of the dispute.

Each federal appellate court is composed of 12 judges, but typically cases will be heard by only 3 judges. By dividing judges in this manner, the courts can hear more cases. Occasionally all of the judges on the appellate court will hear a case. A hearing by the full court is referred to as *en banc*, or "on the bench" (Garner, 2014). When an opinion is issued by an appellate court without designating the particular judge who wrote it, it is called a *per curiam* opinion (Garner, 2014).

There are 13 U.S. Courts of Appeals in the federal court system. The First Circuit through the Eleventh Circuit cover three or more states each; a Twelfth Circuit covers the District of Columbia; and a Thirteenth Circuit, called the *Federal Circuit*, hears appeals from throughout the country on specialized matters (e.g., patents and international trade). The courts of appeals hear cases from trial courts in their respective jurisdictions where their decisions become binding authority.[i]

Figure 1.7 shows the geographic jurisdictions of the federal appellate courts.

FIGURE 1.7 ■ The Federal Judicial Circuits Alaska and Hawaii are in the U.S. Court of Appeals for the Ninth Circuit. Puerto Rico is in the U.S. Court of Appeals for the First Circuit. The U.S. Court of Appeals for the Third Circuit has appellate jurisdiction over the Virgin Islands. *Source:* United States Courts.

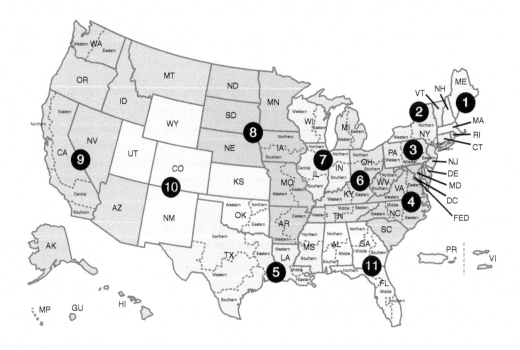

---

[i] The U.S. Court of Appeals for the Eleventh Circuit was created in 1981 by taking Florida, Georgia, and Mississippi from the Fifth Circuit. Because there was no case law prior to that date, no controlling authority to guide court decisions (except decisions of the U.S. Supreme Court) was available in the Eleventh Circuit. To remedy this problem, in the first case heard before the Eleventh Circuit Court, *Bonner v. Alabama* (1981), an en banc court ruled that all decisions of the U.S. Court of Appeals for the Fifth Circuit decided prior to September 30, 1981, would be controlling in the Eleventh Circuit.

Court Of Last Resort   Litigants may file an appeal with the court of last resort. The court of last resort is called the Supreme Court in most jurisdictions. Because the courts of last resort are extremely busy, they cannot hear every case that is appealed. The courts therefore have the power to determine which cases they will hear.

The court of last resort reviews the decision of the intermediate appellate court to determine if the law has been correctly applied. As with the intermediate appellate court, the court of last resort is not a forum for retrying the case. The decision of the court of last resort will be binding on all lower courts (trial and appellate) in its jurisdiction. The decisions of a court of last resort are thus important sources of law.

The U.S. Supreme Court is the highest court in the land. The Court has nine Justices, one designated as the Chief Justice. If a litigant decides to appeal a decision of an appellate court to the Supreme Court, the litigant files a petition for a writ of certiorari, usually called a *petition for cert*. This petition for cert essentially asks the Court to consider the case. The Justices review the petitions, and if four of the nine Justices decide to grant the petition, a writ of certiorari will be issued and the case will be heard. This is usually referred to as *granting cert*. If the Court decides not to hear the case, it will deny cert. When the Court denies cert, it does not have to explain why it is doing so. Because a denial can be for any of a number of reasons, it has no precedential value. If the high court denies cert, the lower court decision stands and may still exert controlling and persuasive authority.

The U.S. Supreme Court grants cert to only a small number of cases, less than 1%. Cases that the Court hears present important questions of constitutional or federal law and often involve issues that have split the appellate courts. In the latter case the Supreme Court acts to resolve the conflict. The U.S. Supreme Court has resolved several conflicts among the federal circuits since the Education for All Handicapped Children Act (now the Individuals with Disabilities Education Act) was passed in 1975.

Precedent

The American system of law follows the doctrine of stare decisis. According to stare decisis, also referred to as *precedent*, courts are expected to follow the decisions of courts in similar cases. When a higher court applies the law to a specific set of facts, its decision controls decisions in similar cases within its jurisdiction. If the court does not follow the precedent, it must explain why that precedent does not apply or control in the particular case. Courts are not absolutely locked to every precedent, however, and can abandon earlier doctrines that are no longer useful (Valente & Valente, 2005). This doctrine helps to ensure efficiency, predictability, and uniformity or fairness in court decisions (Reynolds, 2003).

A decision by a higher court controls the disposition of lower courts in the same jurisdiction. The lower court cannot make a decision contrary to decisions by the higher court. This is referred to as *controlling authority*. The decision of the court of last resort, typically the Supreme Court, in a jurisdiction controls the decisions of all lower courts (Reynolds, 2003). The U.S. Supreme Court is the highest authority in the United States on questions of constitutional or federal law (Barkan et al., 2009).

Another type of authority may come from a court that is not controlling (e.g., a court in a different jurisdiction). This type of authority is called *persuasive authority*. A court is not bound to follow the precedent but does so because it is persuaded by the decision (Reynolds, 2003). For example, the decision of an appellate court in Minnesota will not control the decision of a court (even a lower court) in South Carolina, because they are in different jurisdictions. The court in South Carolina may find the decision in the Minnesota court to be persuasive, however, and use similar reasoning in arriving at its decision. An example of a special education ruling that has been extremely persuasive is the decision of the U.S. Court of Appeals for the Fifth Circuit in *Daniel R.R. v. State Board of Education* (1989). The reasoning in the Fifth Circuit's decision regarding the determination of the least restrictive environment for children in special education has been accepted by the U.S. Courts of Appeals in a number of other circuits (see Chapter 12).

Holding and Dicta

The holding of the case is the portion of the decision that controls decisions of lower courts in the same jurisdiction. The holding of the case is the actual ruling on a point or points of law. Judicial comments, illustrations, speculations, and so on that do not directly relate to the holding in a case are referred to as *dicta*, the plural form of *dictum*. Dicta are not controlling but can be persuasive. They do not have value as precedent.

The Opinion

One of the judges of the appellate court or court of last resort will usually be appointed to write an opinion stating the ruling of the court and the court's reasoning for arriving at the decision. A written opinion typically contains a summary of the case, a statement of the facts, an explanation of the court's reasoning, and a record of the decision. The opinion of the court also lists the author's name and the names of judges or justices who agree with it (the majority). A court's opinion may contain a concurring opinion, a dissenting opinion, or both. A concurring opinion is written when a judge (or judges) agrees with the majority of the court on the ruling but does not agree with the reasoning used to support the ruling. A dissenting opinion is a statement of a judge or justice who does not agree with the results reached by the majority.

Dissents can be important. Because dissents are typically circulated among the justices hearing a case prior to writing a final opinion, they can serve to dissuade the majority justices from judicial advocacy, encourage judicial responsibility, and appeal to outside audiences (e.g., Congress) for correction of perceived mistakes by the majority (Reynolds, 2003). They can also serve as general appeals or appeals to higher courts or legislators to correct a perceived judicial error. Although dissents carry no controlling authority, they can be persuasive.

Dissents are sometimes used to appeal to a higher court or legislature to correct the court's action. An example of the latter is Justice Brennan's dissent in *Smith v. Robinson* (1984), discussed earlier. In his dissent, Justice Brennan disagreed with the Supreme Court's ruling that attorney's fees were not available in special education cases and appealed to Congress to revisit P.L. 94-142 and correct the Court's error. Congress did revisit the issue and passed the Handicapped Children's Protection Act in 1986.

INTERPRETATIONS OF FEDERAL LAW

Agencies in the federal government occasionally issue guidance that interpret laws. Such guidance may be in the form of question and answer documents, memos, or public letters. These memos, letters, which are often referred to as "Dear Colleague Letters" (DCLs), and question and answer documents provide guidance on meeting obligations under the law. The U.S. Department of Education has issued many DCLs that have provided guidance in a number of areas. Letters that address the IDEA are issued by OSEP, and OCR issues letters that interpret Section 504. When federal agencies send DCLs they do not create law; neither do DCLs add requirements to existing law; rather, DCLs inform recipients about how the agencies interpret the legal obligations under the law by covered entities. Additionally, because they may have persuasive legal authority, DCLs may be cited in hearings or court cases. The Department of Education maintains websites that collect the letters of guidance. Guidance letters from OSEP and OSERS can be found at www2.ed.gov/policy/speced/guid/idea/memosdcltrs/index.html. In later chapters, we will occasionally address DCLs that have been issued by OSEP and OCR.

THE LAW AND SPECIAL EDUCATION

The four branches of law—constitutional, legislative, regulatory, and case law—often interact. Laws are sometimes made by one branch of government in response to developments in another branch. This can be seen clearly in the development of special education law.

Actions by the courts, such as *Mills v. Board of Education* (1972) and *Pennsylvania Association of Retarded Citizens (PARC) v. Commonwealth of Pennsylvania* (1972), recognized the right to a special education for children with disabilities under the 14th Amendment to the Constitution. Congress reacted to this litigation by passing legislation to ensure the educational rights of children with disabilities (P.L. 94-142). Regulations were promulgated to implement and enforce the law by the then Department of Health, Education, and Welfare. In response to the federal law, all 50 states eventually passed state laws and created state regulations ensuring the provision of special education to qualified children. The inevitable disputes that arose concerning the special education rules and regulations led to a flood of federal litigation to interpret the special education law. Some of this litigation, such as *Smith v. Robinson* (1984), led to more legislation. In *Smith v. Robinson,* the Supreme Court ruled that attorney's fees were not available under the EAHCA. Thus, parents who had to hire an attorney and go to court regarding their child's special education had to bear the cost of their attorney. In 1986, Congress passed new legislation, the Handicapped Children's Protection Act (HCPA), to overturn the effects of *Smith v. Robinson* by allowing a student's parents to collect attorney's fees when they prevail in a special education lawsuit. This legislation, in turn, has led to more litigation to interpret it. Thus, the development of law is cyclical. Through the interaction of the various sources of law, special education law evolves. This interaction of the sources of law is depicted in Figure 1.8.

FIGURE 1.8 ■ The Evolution of Law

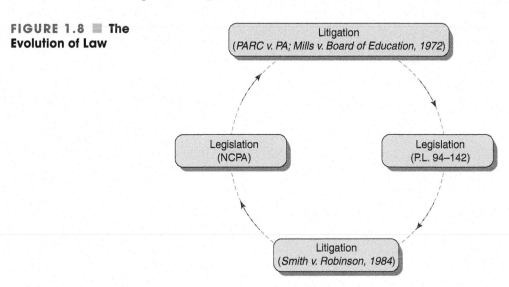

SUMMARY

An elaborate and extensive body of statutes, regulations, and court decisions governs special education. The U.S. Constitution and the state constitutions provide the foundations for special education. Congress and the state legislatures write statutes or laws that mandate and guide the provision of special education. These laws are implemented through the promulgation of regulations issued by administrative agencies such as the state and federal Departments of Education.

Finally, the courts interpret laws and regulations. The role of the courts is to apply the principles of the law to settle disputes. Although the courts do not enact laws, their published decisions may result in judicially created principles known as *case law.* Legislation and litigation in special education have rapidly increased in the last decade. The effect of these judicial and legislative actions is that special education continues to evolve.

Enhanced eText **Application Exercise 1.1:** *Smith v. Robinson,* 468 U.S. 992 (1984).

FOR FURTHER INFORMATION

Bonfield, L. (2006). *American law and the American legal system in a nutshell.* St. Paul, MN: Thomson/West.

Carp, R.A., Stidham, R., Manning, K.L., & Holmes, L.M. (2017). *Judicial process in America* (10th ed.). Los Angeles, CA: CQ Press/Sage.

Congress.gov: Available at www.congress.gov.

Davis, J. (2007). *Legislative law and process in a nutshell* (3rd ed.). St. Paul, MN: Thomson/West.

Elias, S. (2012). *Legal research: How to find and understand the law* (16th ed.). Berkeley, CA: Nolo.

Gellhorn, E., & Levin, R. M. (2006). *Administrative law and process in a nutshell* (5th ed.). St. Paul, MN: Thomson/West.

Lehman, J., & Phelps, S. (2005). *West's encyclopedia of American law.* Detroit: Thomson/Gale.

Reynolds, W. L. (2003). *Judicial process in a nutshell* (3rd ed.). St. Paul, MN: Thomson/West.

United States Courts: Court Role and Structure. Available at www.uscourts.gov/about-federal-courts/court-role-and-structure

REFERENCES

Alexander, K., & Alexander, M. D. (2012). *American public school law* (8th ed.). Belmont, CA: Wadsworth Cengage Learning.

Barkan, S. M., Mersky, R. M., & Dunn, D. J. (2009). *Fundamentals of legal research* (9th ed.). New York: Foundation Press.

Berring, R. C., & Edinger, A. E. (2005). *Finding the law* (12th ed.). St. Paul, MN: Thomson/West.

Bonner v. Alabama, 661 F.2d 1206 (11th Cir. 1981).

Daniel R.R. v. State Board of Education, 874 F.2d 1036 (5th Cir. 1989).

Elazar, D. J. (1984). Federalism. In *The guide to American law: Everyone's legal encyclopedia* (Vol. 5, pp. 190–198). St. Paul, MN: West Publishing.

Garner, B. A. (Ed.). (2014). *Black's law dictionary* (10th ed.). St. Paul, MN: Thomson Reuters.

Handicapped Children Protection Act of 1986, Pub. L. No. 99-372, 100 Stat. 796 (1986).

Hilyerd, W. A. (2004). Using the law library: A guide for educators—Part I: Untangling the legal system. *Journal of Law and Education, 33*(2), 213–224.

Individuals with Disabilities Education Act, 20 U.S.C. § 1400 *et seq.* (2012).

Mills v. Board of Education, 348 F. Supp. 866 (D.D.C. 1972).

Pennsylvania Association of Retarded Citizens (PARC) v. Commonwealth of Pennsylvania, 343 F. Supp. 279 (E.D. Pa. 1972).

Reynolds, W. L. (2003). *Judicial process in a nutshell* (3rd ed.). St. Paul, MN: Thomson/West.

Smith v. Robinson, 468 U.S. 992 (1984).

Valente, W. D., & Valente, C. (2005). *Law in the schools* (6th ed.). Upper Saddle River, NJ: Merrill/Pearson Education.

Pennsylvania Association of Retarded Citizens (PARC) v. Commonwealth of Pennsylvania (1972), to see a video on www.youtube.com/watch?v=QtFmp3XduaQ

Chapter 2

Legal Research

Mitchell L. Yell, Ph.D., and Terrye Conroy, J.D., M.L.I.S.
University of South Carolina

> The key to becoming a successful legal researcher is to stay abreast of the vast array of available print and online legal resources so that you may learn to apply them effectively to any given situation.
>
> CONROY, T. (2016)

Learner Objectives

At the end of the chapter, students will be able to

2.1 Describe primary sources for legal research.

2.2 Describe the United States Code (USC) and citations to laws in the code.

2.3 Describe the Code of Federal Regulations (CFR) and citations to regulations.

2.4 Describe the federal court system.

2.5 Describe how cases can be located using case citations.

2.6 Describe the parts of a judicial opinion.

2.7 Describe the evolution of special education law.

Legal research is the process of finding laws that govern activities in our society (Cohen & Olson, 2013). It involves finding statutes and regulations and the cases that interpret them. It also involves consulting sources that explain and analyze the particular laws you find. Special education is governed by statutes and regulations at the national and state levels and is among the most frequently litigated areas in education. The result is an extensive body of case law interpreting special education laws and regulations. Through legal research, educators will better understand the principles of special education law, the facts giving rise to these principles, and the application of these principles to various situations they may encounter.

The purpose of this chapter is to describe the legal research process. Legal research requires an understanding of a variety of resources. Legal resources include primary sources, secondary sources, and finding tools. Legal resources differ in their authority. Some are controlling or mandatory, others are persuasive only, and still others are useful tools for finding mandatory and persuasive authorities. We will begin this chapter by explaining the primary sources: statutes, regulations, and cases, and how to find them. Next, we will examine secondary sources that both explain the law and serve as finding tools. We will also discuss legal research using online subscription databases and free Internet sources. We will end by presenting a strategy for conducting legal research.

PRIMARY SOURCES

Primary sources are actual statements of the law. There are three categories of primary source material: statutes or laws passed by either federal or state legislatures and signed into law, regulations promulgated by administrative agencies to implement the statutes, and judicial decisions that interpret the statutes and regulations.

Enormous amounts of primary source materials are issued chronologically rather than by subject. Resources used to locate these primary authorities are referred to as *finding tools*. Finding tools include indexes, annotated codes, case digests, and citators (discussed throughout this chapter).

Federal Statutes

The *United States Code*
Federal statutes are organized by topic and published in a series of volumes called the United States Code (U.S.C.). The 54 numbered titles in the *United States Code* are divided into chapters and sections. Each title contains the statutes that cover a specific subject. For example, the Individuals with Disabilities Education Act (IDEA) can be found in Title 20 of the *United States Code*, which contains statutes on education. Section 504 of the Rehabilitation Act of 1973 can be found in Title 29, which contains labor statutes. The Americans with Disabilities Act (ADA) is in Title 42, which contains public health and welfare statutes. Some titles are published in one volume, while others comprise many volumes. A revised edition of the *United States Code* is issued every six years, with hardbound supplements issued during the interim years. Prepared and published by the Office of the Law Revision Counsel of the U.S. House of Representatives and printed by the U.S. Government Publishing Office (GPO), the *United States Code* is considered the official version of federal statutes. The *United States Code* is accessible on the website of the Office of Law Revision Counsel of the U.S. House of Representatives and the GPO's Federal Digital System website, known as FDsys (soon to be called govinfo). The *United States Code* is also available on nongovernmental websites such as Cornell Law School's Legal Information Institute (LII) and FindLaw's Cases and Codes. Table 2.1 lists the web addresses for federal statutes.

All Internet versions allow you to access the *United States Code* by citation to a particular title and section; to browse the code by title, chapter, and section; to browse or search the code by popular name; and to search the full text of the code. Both the official print and Internet versions of the *United States Code* are un-annotated.

Annotated Codes
There are two annotated versions of the *United States Code*. The first, published by West, a Thomson Reuters business, is the *United States Code Annotated*

TABLE 2.1 ▓ Websites for Federal Statutes

Website Names	URL
Congress.gov	congress.gov/
Cornell's Legal Information Institute (LII)	www.law.cornell.edu/uscode
FindLaw's United States Code-Unannotated	Codes.findlaw.com/us
GPO's Federal Digital System (FDsys; soon to become govinfo)	www.gpo.gov/fdsys/ www.govinfo.gov
U.S. House of Representatives	www.house.gov/
U.S. House of Representatives Office of the Law Revision Counsel	uscode.house.gov/
U.S. Senate	www.senate.gov/

(U.S.C.A.); the second is the *United States Code Service* (U.S.C.S.), published by LexisNexis®. Annotated versions are useful because in addition to the actual text of the *United States Code*, they contain research references pertaining to each statute. Both the official un-annotated code (U.S.C.) and unofficial annotated versions of the *United States Code* (U.S.C.A. and U.S.C.S.) include references to each statute's authority and history as well as cross-references to related statutes.

In addition, the U.S.C.A. and U.S.C.S. includes references to relevant federal regulations; references to secondary sources such as legal encyclopedias, treatises, and journal articles; and summaries of court decisions that have interpreted each statute. Because annotated versions of the *United States Code* have information that is more useful than simply the text of the statute, many researchers prefer to use the U.S.C.A. or U.S.C.S. rather than the official government code. Annotated codes are also updated more frequently than the official *United States Code*.

Once you locate statutes relevant to the legal issue at hand, you may wish to consult the annotations to both the U.S.C.A. and U.S.C.S., if available, because the cases and secondary authorities included by each publisher may differ (Cohen & Olson, 2013).

Updating Federal Statutes

Because federal statutes are frequently changed (amended or repealed), it is important to locate the most recent versions. The annotated codes are published in hardcover editions, which are only reissued occasionally. In the back of each volume, however, is a paper supplement called a pocket part that updates the hardcover book annually. It is important to check the most recent pocket part to see if the statute being researched has been changed. When amendments to federal statutes cannot be contained in a single annual pocket part, a separate softbound supplement is issued (this volume sits next to the hardcover volume). Pocket parts may reprint only the sections of the statute that have been changed. If a particular section has not changed, the reader may be referred to the hardcover volume for the text of that section. It is also important to check the pocket part or softbound supplement to the main volume for current cases interpreting the statute being researched. Although pocket parts and supplements are published annually, they cumulatively update the bound volumes, which may not be reprinted for some years. The annual pocket parts and supplements may also include current references to secondary sources, such as legal encyclopedias and law review articles that analyze the statute being researched.

Recently enacted statutes will not be available in the annual pocket parts. Between publication of the annual pocket parts, both the U.S.C.A. and U.S.C.S. are updated by interim pamphlets that accompany each set of annotated codes. The annotated U.S.C.A. and U.S.C.S. are available electronically through the subscription databases Westlaw (U.S.C.A.) and Lexis Advance (U.S.C.S.). Both are very current, eliminating the necessity to check pocket parts or supplements. Law schools typically subscribe to both databases. Academic institutions can provide access to legal resources such as annotated codes for all students and faculty by subscribing to the academic versions of Westlaw (Westlaw Campus Research) or LexisNexis (Nexis Uni). Federal statutes may be further updated and validated (checked for amendments or repeal) by consulting a print or an online citator. Citators, which allow you to verify the authority of primary sources and to find additional sources relating to the legal issues they represent, are discussed in detail later in this chapter.

Pending Federal Legislation

The status, history, and text of pending federal legislation (bills) and laws currently passed by Congress (public laws), before they are codified in the *United States Code*, are available through the Library of Congress's Congress.gov website. Bills and public laws for several congresses are accessible by number and by keyword search. The House and Senate and their various congressional committees also maintain websites containing information on pending legislation. Websites like Govtrack are available for researchers to track pending federal legislation. Table 2.2 lists web addresses for finding and tracking federal legislation.

TABLE 2.2 ■ Websites for Federal Regulations

Website Names	URL
Building the Legacy: IDEA 2004	idea.ed.gov/
Cornell's Legal Information Institute (LII)	www.law.cornell.edu/cfr/
e-CFR (Electronic Code of Federal Regulations)	www.ecfr.gov
GPO's Federal Digital System (FDsys)	www.gpo.gov/fdsys/
(Soon to become govinfo)	www.govinfo.gov
IDEA: U.S. Dept. of Education	https://sites.ed.gov/idea
U.S. Dept. of Education Office of Special Education and Rehabilitative Services (OSERS): U.S. Department of Education	www2.ed.gov/about/offices/list/osers/ osep/index.html
Parallel Table of Authorities and Rules	www.gpo.gov/help/parallel_table.pdf
Regulations.gov	www.regulations.gov
The Unified Agenda	www.reginfo.gov/public/do/ eAgendaMain
USA.gov: A-Z Index of U.S. Government Departments and Agencies	www.usa.gov/federal-agencies

Finding Federal Statutes

Several methods can be used to find federal statutes in print. The first method is to use the citation; the second is to use the popular name; the third is to use the table of contents, and the fourth, when you know only the subject, is to use the code indexes.

By Citation   A reference to a primary law source is a citation. The citation tells where the law source is located. Citations are always written in standard form. Figure 2.1 is a citation to a section of the IDEA. The first number, 20, is the title number. The letters following the title number refer to the particular code; in this case, U.S.C. refers to the *United States Code*. The numeral 1401 is the section number (§ is the symbol for section). The (29) after 1401 is the subsection.

In the *United States Code*, the text of the IDEA begins at § 1400 and ends at § 1482. Title and section numbers will be constant in all three sources (i.e., the IDEA will appear in Title 20, §§ 1400–1482, in U.S.C., U.S.C.A., and U.S.C.S.). To locate the federal statute (section of the IDEA) represented in Figure 2.1, find the maroon set of books labeled U.S.C. or U.S.C.A. or the black set of books labeled U.S.C.S. On the spine of the volumes, look for the title number 20. Below the title number on the spine of each volume is the subject of that title (Education) and the section numbers contained in that volume. To find a statute with a citation to a particular title, section, and subsection, such as 20 U.S.C.A. § 1401(29) (the definition of *special education* under the IDEA), find the volume that contains Title 20 and section (1401) and turn to the subsection you need (29).

By Table of Contents   The sections within each title are arranged numerically. Each volume of the U.S.C., U.S.C.A., and U.S.C.S. includes a table of contents listing the subjects covered by the chapters within that title. For instance, Chapter 33 of Title 20 addresses Education of Individuals with Disabilities and begins with Section 1400. Although the chapter

FIGURE 2.1 ■ **Citation for a Section within the IDEA Statute**

20 U.S.C. § 1401(29)

Title Number   United States Code   Section Number   Subsection number is not included in a citation for the *United States Code* (only the title and section), it is useful to know where a particular subject (chapter) is arranged within a certain title of the code.

By Popular Name

If the citation for a federal law is not available but its popular name (e.g., IDEA) is known, the statutes can be found using a *Popular Name(s) Table*. In most law libraries, the *Popular Name(s) Table* is placed after the codes (U.S.C., U.S.C.A., and U.S.C.S.) and provides the following information: the law's popular name, public law number and *United States Statutes at Large* citation, date of passage, and the title and code section(s) where the statutes that fall under the act are published (codified) in the *United States Code*.

By Subject Using an Index

If you do not know a statute's citation or popular name, you can use an index to locate the statute by subject. For example, if the citation and popular name for the IDEA were not available, you could use the General Index at the end of the U.S.C.S. and search under the topic "EDUCATION" for the entry "Special education, 20 §§ 1400 to 1482." The annotated codes also include an index for each title in the back of the final volume for that title. If you know that statutes relating to education are codified (arranged by subject) in Title 20 of the *United States Code*, you can begin by searching the index at the end of that title in the U.S.C.A. or U.S.C.S.

Federal Statutes Online

Online subscription databases, like Westlaw and Lexis Advance, allow you to access their annotated versions of the *United States Code* by citation and by popular name. Westlaw and Lexis Advance also provide a table of contents and an index, as well as the ability to search the full-text version or individual titles of the *United States Code*.

Most free Internet versions include options to retrieve sections by citation or popular name; to browse by title, chapter, and section; or to search the full-text version or individual titles of the *United States Code* (Table 2.1). The un-annotated Internet versions of the *United States Code*, however, do not include citators to alert you to pending legislation and recent amendments to individual code sections. Citators are discussed later in this chapter.

Federal Regulations

The *Code of Federal Regulations*

Federal administrative agencies, such as the U.S. Department of Education, promulgate regulations to implement and enforce federal statutes (e.g., the IDEA). Proposed and final federal regulations are published daily in the *Federal Register*. Final regulations are codified by agency and subject and published annually in the *Code of Federal Regulations* (C.F.R.). Both are published by the Office of the Federal Register, National Archives and Records Administration (NARA) and printed by the GPO. The *Federal Register* and *Code of Federal Regulations* are both available on the GPO's FDsys website, soon to be called govinfo (see Table 2.2).

Statutory Authority

Each of the 54 titles in the C.F.R. covers a general subject area. Titles in the C.F.R. and *United States Code* do not always correspond. For example, the subject of Title 20 of the *United States Code* is education, but the subject of Title 20 of the C.F.R. is employee benefits. Regulations regarding education are found in Title 34. Along with the text of the regulations, the C.F.R. provides references to the statutes that authorize them (authority) and the date of their publication in the *Federal Register* (source). The *Index and Finding Aids* volume accompanying the C.F.R. set contains a *Parallel Table of Authorities and Rules* that allows you to identify regulations enacted pursuant to a particular statute. The current *Parallel Table of Authorities and Rules* is also available on the GPO's FDsys website (soon to be called govinfo). Both annotated versions of the *United States Code* also include cross-references to regulations.

Finding Federal Regulation

Federal regulations may be located by citation, by subject, and on relevant federal agency websites.

Finding Regulations by Citation

Regulations, like statutes, have citations that are written in a standard form directing you to where a regulation is located. Figure 2.2 is the citation for a section of the IDEA.

The first number, 34, is the title number. C.F.R. stands for the *Code of Federal Regulations*. The number 300 is the part of Title 34 where the regulation can be found. The 300.39 is the specific section of the IDEA regulations that further describes the term *special education*. To locate this federal regulation in a law library, find the paperbound set of books labeled *Code of Federal Regulations*. Every year the colors of the C.F.R. volumes are changed. The revision year included in the citation in Figure 2.2 appears on the front cover of each volume of regulations in the C.F.R. The title number (34) can be found on the spine of the volumes. Section numbers of regulations contained in each volume are listed under the title number. You may also retrieve a regulation by citation from GPO's FDsys website (govinfo) and other nongovernmental websites (Table 2.2). There is a table of contents at the beginning of each part within a title of the C.F.R. that helps you quickly find specific sections within that part.

Finding Regulations by Subject

If the citation for a federal regulation is unavailable, you may consult the annually revised *CFR Index and Finding Aids* volume of the *Code of Federal Regulations* to locate regulations by subject. You can also find regulations by subject through a keyword search of the entire *Code of Federal Regulations* or by searching an individual title on GPO's FDsys website (govinfo) and on nongovernmental websites (Table 2.2).

Federal Agency Websites

A federal agency's website can be a great resource for identifying regulations governing a particular area of law (e.g., special education), along with the statutes authorizing that agency to promulgate and enforce those regulations. For instance, the U.S. Department of Education's ED.gov website hosts the IDEA webpage, which contains resources related to the IDEA and its implementing regulations. USA.gov maintains an A-Z Listing of U.S. Government Departments and Agencies (Table 2.2).

Updating Regulations

Individual titles of the C.F.R. are revised annually. For example, Title 34 of the C.F.R. is revised each year on July 1. Like statutes, however, regulations are often changed in some way. To determine if a regulation has changed since the annual print volume for that title was last revised, you should consult the most recent monthly pamphlet entitled *Code of Federal Regulations List of Sections Affected* (LSA) and the back pages of the most recent *Federal Register* for C.F.R. parts affected during that month.

The GPO's FDsys website (govinfo) includes the most current *List of CFR Sections Affected (LSA)* and *Federal Register*. GPO's FDsys (govinfo) now also offers the unofficial Electronic Code of Federal Regulations, or *e-CFR*, which incorporates amendments from the *LSA* and *Federal Register* within a few days (Table 2.2).

Citators, discussed in detail later in this chapter, alert you to newly proposed amendments to regulations and help you locate cases and secondary sources that have cited a particular regulation.

FIGURE 2.2 ■ Citation for the Individuals with Disabilities Education Act (regulations)

34 C.F.R. § 300.39(a)(1)

Title Number   Code of Federal Regulations   Section Number   Subsection Letter & Number

Tracking Regulations   You may also consult websites like Regulations.gov, which are designed for citizens to track and comment on proposed regulations before they become final and codified in the *Code of Federal Regulations*. There is also a semiannual *Unified Agenda* that summarizes the proposed and final regulations each agency expects to issue during the next year (Table 2.2).

Federal Regulations Online   As discussed earlier, the *Federal Register* and *Code of Federal Regulations* are available for free on the Internet through the GPO's FDsys website (govinfo). You may also search the *Federal Register* and annotated versions of the *Code of Federal Regulations* by citation or full-text search using subscription databases such as West-law and Lexis Advance, which are current within a few days. Many colleges and universities subscribe to academic versions of Westlaw (Westlaw Campus Research) or LexisNexis (Nexis Uni™) as well as to HeinOnline. HeinOnline offers scanned images of the *Federal Register* and *Code of Federal Regulations* from their first day of publication, along with indexes for both publications.

State Statutes and Regulations

State Statutes   Some states organize their statutes in volumes according to subject by name (e.g., education, health), while most states assign a title or chapter and section number to each subject, similar to the *United States Code*. Citations for state statutes typically refer to the name, title, or chapter within which the statute is arranged, along with section numbers and the publication date of the volume(s) where the statute is published. All states have at least one annotated code containing summaries of cases and references to secondary sources that cite individual statutes. Many collections of state statutes include general indexes for all laws as well as indexes for each subject. State annotated codes often include popular name(s) tables.

State statutes, like federal statutes, are often amended and can be repealed. The hardcover volumes of state statutes are updated by annual pocket parts, and some states publish interim pamphlets as well. State annotated codes are available on Westlaw and Lexis Advance to retrieve statutes by citation or full-text search. Westlaw also includes an index for each state code. State statutes may be validated (checked for amendments or repeal) using a citator (discussed later in this chapter).

All states now have the typically unofficial and un-annotated versions of their codes available on the Internet in some format. State legislative websites generally allow you to search by keyword and to browse by title, chapter, or section. Some include popular name(s) tables and indexes. For access to legislative websites for all states, consult the website for the National Conference of State Legislatures and other state resource websites maintained by entities such as FindLaw and Cornell's LII. Their web addresses are provided in Table 2.3.

State Regulations   State regulations can be difficult to locate in print. In many states, regulations are published in looseleaf formats by the promulgating agency, while some are published as part of their state codes. Law libraries may carry only the regulations for their

TABLE 2.3 ■ Websites for All State Statutes and Regulations

Website Names	URL
ACR: AdministrativeRules.com	www.administrativerules.org/
Cornell: Law by Source: State	www.law.cornell.edu/states/listing.html
FindLaw: State Resources	caseline.findlaw.com
LLSDC (Law Librarians' Society of Washington, DC)	www.llsdc.org/state-legislation
National Conference of State Legislatures	www.ncsl.org/

state. Some state regulations are annotated with case summaries and secondary sources. Usually, special education regulations are included under the broader category of education regulations. This is because special education regulations are typically promulgated by the state's department of education. Like federal regulations, proposed and final state regulations are first published in state registers. You may also use a citator to validate a particular state regulation and to locate primary and secondary sources that cite that regulation (discussed later in this chapter). Westlaw and Lexis Advance include current databases for all available state regulations.

Typically, unofficial and unannotated state regulations and registers are also available on state government websites and can generally be browsed by section, chapter, or title and searched by keyword. Links to all state regulations available on the Internet are included on the Administrative Codes and Registers (ACR) website (a section of the National Association of Secretaries of State). FindLaw, Cornell's LII, and the Law Librarians' Society of Washington, DC also provide links to all available state regulations.

State government websites, accessible through FindLaw and Cornell's LII, include links to department of education websites for each state, which should include information on the special education laws and regulations that state enforces (Table 2.3).

Case Law

An important part of legal research is finding court opinions (i.e., cases) that interpret statutes and regulations. Cases are published in volumes called *reporters* by the level of court where decided for federal courts, and by geographical regions and sometimes level of court for state courts. Print reporters are available in major law libraries that have the funding to maintain such large collections, while many libraries provide access to state and federal court opinions via electronic databases (discussed later in this chapter).

Federal Cases

There are no official publications by the government for federal district or appellate court opinions. With the exception of electronic databases, the only source for decisions of the lower federal courts is the print reporters published by West (a division of Thomson Reuters). The published decisions of the U.S. District Courts (federal trial courts) are collected in a series of reporters called the *Federal Supplement* (abbreviated F. Supp.). West began publication of the *Federal Supplement, Second Series* (abbreviated F. Supp. 2d) in 1998 *and the Federal Supplement, Third Series* (abbreviated F. Supp. 3d) in 2014. Decisions by the U.S. District Courts are appealed to federal courts of appeals, which are organized by circuits. Decisions by the U.S. Courts of Appeals are published in a series of reporters called the *Federal Reporter*. In 1924 the *Federal Reporter, Second Series*, began. This series (abbreviated F.2d) ran until 1994, when volume 1 of the *Federal Reporter, Third Series* (abbreviated F.3d) was issued.

Appeals from the U.S. Courts of Appeals and from state courts of last resort are to the U.S. Supreme Court. Opinions of the U.S. Supreme Court are published in three different sources. The *United States Reports* (abbreviated U.S.) is the official report because it is printed by the U.S. government. The reporter published by Thomson Reuters (West) is called the *Supreme Court Reporter* (abbreviated S.Ct.). A third reporter, *United States Supreme Court Reports, Lawyers' Edition* (abbreviated L.Ed. and now in its second series), is published by Matthew Bender, a member of the LexisNexis Group. The three reporters contain the same cases, but the latter two unofficial publications include editorial enhancements. The *Supreme Court Reporter* is part of West's complete legal reference system called the National Reporter System, which arranges headnotes at the beginning of cases by topic and key number, while *United States Supreme Court Reports, Lawyers' Edition* provides editorial comments about each case and annotations referring to other cases on the same subject. Table 2.4 lists abbreviations for the federal court reporters.

TABLE 2.4 ■ Federal Court Reporters

Reporter	Coverage	Abbreviation
Federal Supplement (1933-1998)	U.S. District Courts	F. Supp.
Federal Supplement, Second Series (1998–2014)	U.S. District Courts	F. Supp.2d
Federal Supplement, Third Series (2014-present)	U.S. District Courts	F. Supp. 3d
Federal Reporter (1880-1923)		F.
Federal Reporter, Second Series (1924–1993)	U.S. Courts of Appeals	F.2d
Federal Reporter, Third Series (1994–present)	U.S. Courts of Appeals	F.3d
United States Reports	U.S. Supreme Court	U.S.
Supreme Court Reporter	U.S. Supreme Court	S.Ct
United States Supreme Court Reports, Lawyers' Edition	U.S. Supreme Court	L.Ed
United States Supreme Court Reports, Lawyers' Edition, Second Series	U.S. Supreme Court	L.Ed.2d

There is a lag between the date a case is decided and the publication of that case in a hardcover reporter. During this lag period, new cases can be found in paperback updates called *advance sheets*, located on the shelf at the end of the hardcover reporters.

However, current opinions are accessible daily from official federal court websites on a daily basis. The United States Courts website provides links to the U.S. Supreme Court and all U.S. Courts of Appeals and U.S. District Court websites. The official U.S. Supreme Court website not only publishes slip opinions, but also includes bound volumes of decisions from 1991 forward, transcripts of oral arguments, and briefs. In addition, the Oyez Project website provides digital audio recordings of oral arguments before the U.S. Supreme Court as well as links to the full-text versions of opinions dating back from 1793 forward. Table 2.5 lists web addresses for federal court opinions.

Keep in mind, however, that federal and state court opinions accessible on the Internet will not include the editorial enhancements (e.g., synopses and headnotes with topics and key numbers) that the bound volumes of West's National Reporter System provide (see the following discussion under Finding Cases).

Online subscription databases such as Lexis Advance and Westlaw include comprehensive databases for all federal and state cases with many editorial enhancements and citators (discussed below) to check the validity of a case and to locate primary and secondary sources that cite it. Many colleges and universities subscribe to academic versions of Westlaw (Westlaw Campus Research) or LexisNexis (Nexis Uni™).

TABLE 2.5 ■ Websites for Federal and State Court Opinions

Website Names	URL
Cornell's Legal Information Institute (LII)	www.law.cornell.edu/
FindLaw's Cases and Codes	Caselaw.findlaw.com
Google Scholar	https://scholar.google.com/
Justia	www.justia.com/courts
Oyez	www.oyez.org/
Public Library of Law	www.plol.org/
Supreme Court of the United States	www.supremecourt.gov
United States Courts	www.uscourts.gov

State Cases   The published appellate court opinions for each state can be found in that state's official report or in regional reporters published by Thomson Reuters (West). Many states have, in fact, discontinued their official reports and rely solely upon West's regional reporters to publish their appellate court decisions.

West's regional reporters contain opinions for each state and the District of Columbia. West divides the country into seven regions and publishes the appellate decisions of certain states together. Table 2.6 lists the states as they are arranged by region in West's National Reporter System. Separate reporters are published for California and New York. Advance sheets containing recent opinions before the publication of the next hardbound volume are also provided for the regional reporters. State appellate courts now typically publish their slip opinions immediately on their judicial websites.

Several free websites also provide access to court opinions for all states. For example, Cornell's LII maintains links to all state judicial websites and Google Scholar enables researchers to search federal and state cases individually or together. See Table 2.5 for web addresses for federal and state court opinions.

Finding Cases

Federal and state court decisions are published in reporters chronologically rather than by subject. Major academic law libraries may contain millions of reported cases. Without a means of accessing these cases, however, research would be a hopeless endeavor. Therefore, finding tools that enable researchers to access opinions by citation, by case name, and by subject becomes essential.

Finding Cases by Citation   Every published decision includes a citation to where it is located in a reporter. Case citations follow a standard format. Figure 2.3 is a citation to a special education case.

The first item in the citation is the name of the case (*Daniel R.R. v. State Board of Education*). The name of the case will usually be two names separated by "v." (versus). The first name will be the plaintiff or the appellant. The plaintiff is the party that initially brought the suit seeking a remedy from the court. In the case of an appeal, the appellant is the party that appeals the decision of the lower court, whether the party was the original plaintiff or the defendant. The plaintiff in this case was Daniel R.R. The second name is that of the defendant (the party who has been sued and is responding to the complaint of the plaintiff). If the defendant appeals the ruling of the lower court, in most states that party will become the appellant and will then be listed first. The defendant in this case was the State Board of

TABLE 2.6 ■ West's Regional Reporters

Reporter	States and Courts
Atlantic Reporter	CT, DC, DE, MD, ME, NH, NJ, PA, RI, VT
Northeastern Reporter	IL, IN, MA, NY, OH
Northwestern Reporter	IA, MI, MN, NE, ND, SD, WI
Pacific Reporter	AK, AZ, CA, CO, HI, ID, KS, MT, NM, NV, OK, OR, UT, WA, WY
Southeastern Reporter	GA, NC, SC, VA, WV
Southern Reporter	AL, FL, LA, MS
Southwestern Reporter	AR, KY, MO, TN, TX
New York Supplement	New York Court of Appeals, Appellate Division of the State Supreme Court, and additional state courts (The highest court in New York is the Court of Appeals; the intermediate court is called the Supreme Court.)
California Reporter	California Supreme Court and intermediate appellate courts

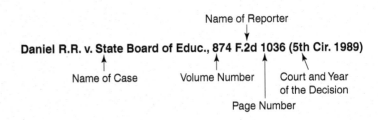

Education of Texas. Cases sometimes only have a phrase and one name, such as *In Re Gary B*. The phrase in re is Latin and means "in the matter of." Usually this means there was no opponent in the court proceeding. You can access citations to court opinions by case name using the Table of Cases volumes included with print digests (discussed later in this chapter) and using online resources.

The second element in the citation is the volume number of the reporter in which the case appears. The volume number of the *Daniel R.R.* case is 874. The third element of the citation is the name of the reporter. The reporter in which *Daniel R.R.* can be found is the *Federal Reporter, Second Series*, written as F.2d (called "Fed second"). The F.2d contains cases heard by the U.S. Courts of Appeals; therefore, *Daniel R.R.* was heard by a federal appellate court. The fourth element of the citation is the page number on which the case starts. Thus, the *Daniel R.R.* decision can be found on page 1036 of volume 874 of the F.2d reporter.

The final element of the citation is the year of the decision. In researching cases, it is important to include the most recent ones. In federal cases, the level of court deciding the case will appear along with the year of the decision. *Daniel R.R.* was decided by the U.S. Court of Appeals for the Fifth Circuit in 1989. If the decision is from a federal district court, the state and judicial district of the case will be included. For example, the court that decided *Hayes v. Unified School District*, 699 F. Supp. 1519 (D. Kan. 1987) was the U.S. District Court for the District of Kansas, while *Espino v. Besteiro*, 520 F. Supp. 905 (S.D. Tex. 1981), was decided by the U.S. District Court for the Southern District of Texas. If cases can be found in more than one reporter, the names of all the reporters may be included in the citation. For example, a case decided by the U.S. Supreme Court will appear in all three reporters (U.S., S.Ct., and L.Ed.) and all three "parallel" cites may be included in its citation. The landmark decision *Brown v. Board of Education* is often cited to include all three reporters as follows: *Brown v. Board of Education*, 347 U.S. 483, 74 S.Ct. 686, 98 L.Ed. 873 (1954). State court rules often require parallel citations to include both the official state reports and West regional reporter cites for that states' appellate court opinions.

Finding Cases by Subject

Several finding tools are designed to help researchers locate primary sources, particularly cases. Finding tools discussed here include annotated codes, case digests, citators, and *American Law Reports* (ALR).

The Annotated Codes   The annotated versions of the *United States Code—United States Code Annotated* (U.S.C.A.) and *United States Code Service* (U.S.C.S.)—are powerful research tools. In addition to the statutory language contained in the *United States Code*, the annotated codes include a wealth of information useful to researchers. For example, West's U.S.C.A. contains information on legislative history; cross-references to other federal statutes and regulations; references to the West topics and key numbers (discussed below); citations to West's legal encyclopedias (*American Jurisprudence 2d* [Am Jur 2d] and *Corpus Juris Secundum* [CJS]) as well as other secondary sources, such as law reviews; and notes with citations to relevant court decisions. The "Notes of Decisions" following the statutes in the U.S.C.A. consist of abstracts of relevant cases that have interpreted the statute. The most current annotations are contained in the pocket parts to each volume and the interim pamphlets that update the annotated codes. Both annotated codes are available through the subscription databases, Westlaw (U.S.C.A.) and Lexis Advance (U.S.C.S.).

The West Digest System   Another useful tool for locating cases is West's digest system. West's digests are alphabetical indexes to case law published in West's state, regional, and federal reporters, arranging headnotes of cases by topics and key numbers. To access the West digest system, you must understand the topic and key number system.

The West Topic and Key Number System   An opinion published in a West reporter follows a standard format. Figure 2.4 is the first page of the *Daniel R.R. v. State Board of Education* opinion. The first item on the page is the name of the case: *Daniel R.R. v. State Board of Education*. Daniel R.R. is listed as the plaintiff-appellant and the Board of Education is the defendant. Following the title is the docket number (No. 88-1279), the court in which the case was heard (U.S. Court of Appeals for the Fifth Circuit), and the date the court's decision was handed down (June 12, 1989). Following this information is the synopsis of the decision, written by an editor at West.

Next is the headnote section. A headnote is a one-sentence summary of a legal issue arising in a case. The headnotes are not part of the judicial opinion but are an editorial enhancement. Editors at West review judicial opinions and write the headnotes by isolating the individual issues of law that appear in each decision. Often opinions contain a number of legal issues and will therefore have a number of headnotes. *Daniel R.R.* contains 16 headnotes. Each headnote will appear as a boldface number (e.g., 2), followed by a topic (e.g., Schools), an illustration of a key, and a number (e.g., 148[2]) (see Figure 2.4).

The headnote numbers (e.g., the boldface 2) are in order and are used as a table of contents to the case. Numbers corresponding to the headnotes appear in the text of the case at the point where that legal issue is discussed. The term or phrase after the number (e.g., Schools) is the topic where West has classified that legal issue. Following the image of a key is the key number (148[2]), which represents a subsection of that legal topic.

For example, in headnote number 2 of the 16 headnotes in *Daniel R.R.* is *Schools 148(2)*. "Schools" is a topic area. The number 148 refers to the subtopic "Nature of right to instruction in general." The number 2 in parentheses represents a subtopic of 148, entitled "Handicapped children and special services therefore." There are over 400 topics and numerous subtopics in the West digest system. At the beginning of each topic in a West digest is an outline of all of its subtopics and corresponding key numbers.

In whichever West digest you use (e.g., federal, state, or regional), cases addressing instruction and special services for children with disabilities will appear under the topic and key number *Schools 148(2)*. Therefore, you can use West's print digests or Westlaw to find all state and federal cases published on that topic.

Using the Digest System

When using West digests to find cases, it is preferable to begin with the one that is narrowest in scope. Special educators will usually be interested in federal special education cases, so the appropriate digest will be the *Federal Practice Digest* (now in its fifth series). It contains headnotes from every case appearing in West's *Supreme Court Reporter* (S.Ct.), *Federal Reporters* (F.2d and F.3d), and *Federal Supplement* (F. Supp. and F. Supp.2d).

To find relevant cases using a digest, you must first determine the relevant topic and key number(s) (e.g., Schools 148[2]). In the topical volumes of a digest, headnotes are arranged under each topic and key number by jurisdictions in chronological order, beginning with the most recent. The topic and key number system is uniform in every West digest.

FIGURE 2.4 ■ **First Page of the *Daniel R.R.* Case in a West Reporter**

Source: Reprinted from the Federal Reporter 2d, with permission of Thomson Reuters.

1036   874 FEDERAL REPORTER, 2d SERIES

In that situation, it is certainly not clear that, as a matter of law, the protection which would have been afforded by a warning line and at least one monitor—which the employer would have had to have anyway for employees working near the edge—was no safer than the two monitors and no warning line which the employer actually provided.

Accordingly, I respectfully dissent.

DANIEL R.R., Plaintiff-Appellant,

v.

STATE BOARD OF EDUCATION, et al., Defendants,

El Paso Independent School District, Defendant-Appellee.

No. 88-1279.

United States Court of Appeals, Fifth Circuit.

June 12, 1989.

Parents of handicapped child brought action against school district alleging violations of Education of the Handicapped Act. The United States District Court for the Western District of Texas, Lucius Desha Bunton, III, Chief Judge, entered judgment in favor of school district, and parents appealed. The Court of Appeals, Gee, Circuit Judge, held that: (1) issues raised on appeal were not moot; (2) district did not violate Act's procedural requirements; and (3) district adequately complied with Act's mainstreaming requirement.

Affirmed.

1. Federal Courts ⬅13.30

Challenge to school officials' individualized education plan for handicapped child under Education of Handicapped Act was not moot although two years had passed since plan was developed and child had since been placed in private school, since there was reasonable expectation that conduct giving rise to suit would recur every school year, yet evade review during nine-month academic term. Education of the Handicapped Act, § 601 et seq., as amended, 20 U.S.C.A. § 1400 et seq.

2. Schools ⬅148(2)

School district gave handicapped child's parents proper notice of proposed change in child's individualized educational plan, as required by Education of the Handicapped Act; notice apprised parents that child's placement would be changed by removing him from regular education classes, and placing him in self-contained classroom, and stated that board would not change educational plan. Education of the Handicapped Act, § 601 et seq., as amended, 20 U.S.C.A. § 1400 et seq.

3. Schools ⬅148(2)

School district's failure to evaluate handicapped child before removing him from regular education did not violate Education of the Handicapped Act, where child's parents agreed with prior evaluation and refused to consent to new evaluation because they felt it was not necessary. Education of the Handicapped Act, § 601 et seq., as amended, 20 U.S.C.A. § 1400 et seq.

4. Schools ⬅148(2)

School district sufficiently provided continuum of educational services for handicapped child as required by Education of the Handicapped Act regulations; district experimented with variety of alternative placements and supplementary services, including mixed placement that allocated child's time equally between regular and special education. Education of the Handicapped Act, § 601 et seq., as amended, 20 U.S.C.A. § 1400 et seq.

5. Schools ⬅148(2)

School district's decision to remove handicapped child from regular education

The easiest way to find cases using a digest is to begin with headnotes from a case on point. In Figure 2.5 the *Daniel R.R. v. State Board of Education* decision is used as an example of how to access West's digest system using the topic and key numbers from a relevant case. Whatever case is used, the method of using the West digest system will be the same.

Cases can also be located by subject using the descriptive word indexes, by case name using the table of cases volumes, and by specific terms interpreted by courts using the words and phrases volumes. All of these volumes are located at the end of each digest set. You may also find cases using the topical outlines at the beginning of each topic within the digest volumes. Digests are updated with recent headnotes by pocket parts and softcover supplements.

FIGURE 2.5 ■ Using West's Digest System

Step 1: Locate the Daniel R.R. decision at 874 F.2d 1036 in the F.2d reporter.

Step 2: Read the headnotes at the beginning of the case and note the topic and key numbers. If the researcher is interested in the issue of law raised in headnote 2, locate Schools 148(2) in the appropriate digest.

Step 3: Whenever possible use the more specific digest; therefore, locate the Federal Practice Digest in the library.

Step 4: Locate the volume of the Fourth Series that contains the topic Schools, key number 148(2). The correct volume number is 84.

Step 5: Turn to the page that begins with headnotes that are keyed 148(2). Headnotes with the key number 148(2) from all federal court cases will be listed by jurisdictions in reverse chronological order (most recent first).

Step 6: Check the pocket part and white softcover supplements for the most recent cases.

In Westlaw, you can find cases on a particular topic by clicking on a relevant topic and key number in a case and choosing the appropriate jurisdiction(s). You may also search or browse the West Key Number System in Westlaw. Lexis Advance has also developed its own topic and headnote system for researchers using its online subscription database to find cases relevant to a particular topic. You can browse topics in Lexis Advance as well.

Citators   Citators help you validate and expand your research. After you identify a relevant case, it is critical to ensure that the case is currently valid. That is, does it still have precedential value, or has it been overruled or reversed or even highly criticized by the courts? Citators use a system of flags and signals to alert you that a case has been reversed or overruled and to show how it has been treated by other courts. You may also use citators to locate cases and secondary sources that have cited a case. Citators are available for other primary authorities (e.g., statutes and regulations) as well and for some secondary sources.

Shepard's® Citations, which is owned by LexisNexis, is available in print and through LexisNexis online databases. Many colleges and universities subscribe to Nexis Uni™, which allows you to Shepardize® state and federal cases online; thus eliminating the necessity for academic libraries to maintain print versions of Shepard's®. West's citator is called *KeyCite®*. KeyCite® performs the same verification and research functions as Shepard's and is available exclusively online through Westlaw. Bloomberg Law, which is rapidly becoming a third major online legal research database, has developed its own citator called BCite.

Citators indicate by a system of symbols or signals whether a case has been overruled or reversed by a higher court and help you find other cases that have dealt with similar issues. Citators list the cases that have cited a particular case. For example, if you are interested in least restrictive environment cases and have the citation for *Daniel R.R. v. State Board of Education*, you can use a citator to locate other federal decisions that have cited the case. Because *Daniel R.R.* has proved to be a persuasive case, most subsequent federal cases on least restrictive environment have cited it. However, other least restrictive environment cases that do not cite *Daniel R.R.* will not be listed. Researchers can find those cases using the topic and key numbers found in the headnotes in *Daniel R.R.* to consult *West's Federal Practice Digest* in print or on Westlaw or using the headnotes in Westlaw or Lexis Advance.

American Law Reports (ALR) Annotations   ALR, which is published by Thomson/West, is an excellent resource for finding cases. Each annotation begins with a court decision addressing a particular legal issue. The opinion is reprinted in the ALR followed by suggested secondary sources for further research on the topic covered in the case and a comprehensive survey of cases from across the country addressing the same legal issues. ALR annotations are published in print volumes that are updated annually by pocket parts. The

ALR Index lists ALR annotations by subject and includes a table of annotations by federal and state laws, rules, and regulations. ALR annotations are also accessible online through Westlaw and Lexis Advance.

SECONDARY SOURCES

Secondary sources are materials that describe and explain the law. Because secondary materials are not actual statements of law, they have no formal authority. They may, however, have significant persuasive authority.

In conducting legal research, it is often easier to begin with secondary sources. Secondary sources have two primary functions: They introduce the researcher to a particular area of the law by explaining the issues involved, and they provide citations to primary source material, e.g., statutes, regulations, and cases. Of the many secondary sources available, included are citation guides, legal dictionaries, legal encyclopedias, books and treatises, law review and journal articles, and topical services. Many secondary sources are fully searchable through electronic databases such as Westlaw, Lexis Advance, Bloomberg Law, and HeinOnline. The following discussion will focus on the secondary source materials that may be of greatest use to the educator.

Legal Dictionaries and Encyclopedias

Legal Dictionaries
Common words can take on special meaning when used in the law; in addition, there are many terms and phrases, often in Latin, that are unique to the legal field. To better understand the language of the law, you may use legal dictionaries such as *Black's Law Dictionary* and *Ballentine's Law Dictionary*. There are also dictionaries for specialized areas of law, such as *Education and the Law: A Dictionary*. Although not as comprehensive or authoritative, several other legal dictionaries are available on the Internet, including *The People's Law Dictionary* on Law.com and *Nolo's Free Dictionary of Law Terms and Legal Definitions*. Table 2.7 lists secondary source websites.

Citation Guides
The legal field has its own citation style, with numerous unique abbreviations. The standard citation guide for legal materials is *The Bluebook: A Uniform System of Citation*. Many legal writers, however, prefer the Association of Legal Writing Directors' *ALWD Citation Manual*. Cornell's LII publishes an online guide entitled *Introduction to Basic Legal Citation*, which includes examples for both citation styles (Table 2.7).

TABLE 2.7 ▪ Websites for Secondary Sources

Website Names	URL
ABA's Free Full-Text Online Law Review/Law Journal Search Engine	www.americanbar.org/groups/ departments_offices/legal_ technology_resources/resources/ free_journal_search.html
Georgetown Law Library Treatise Finder	www.law.georgetown.edu/library/ research/treatise-finders/
Google Scholar	https://scholar.google.com/
Harvard's Legal Treatises by Subject	https://guides.library.harvard.edu/ legaltreatises
Introduction to Basic Legal Citation	www.law.cornell.edu/citation/
The People's Law Dictionary	https://dictionary.law.com/
Nolo's Free Dictionary of Law Terms and Legal Definitions	www.nolo.com/dictionary/
WorldCat	www.worldcat.org/

Legal Encyclopedias   Two national legal encyclopedias help researchers understand the law: *American Jurisprudence* 2d (Am Jur 2d) and *Corpus Jurus Secundum* (CJS). Both multivolume sets are published by Thomson/West and are arranged in alphabetical order by topic and section numbers. Each set has its own annual set of *General Indexes*, including a *Table of Laws and Rules*. Both are updated using annual pocket parts. CJS is available on Westlaw. Am Jur 2d is available on Westlaw, Lexis Advance, and Lexis Uni. Am Jur 2d and CJS include extensive footnotes to cases for each topic as well as references to West's topics and key numbers for locating more cases using the West Digest system. Neither publication cites state statutes, but both cover federal laws. For example, Am Jur 2d and CJS discuss the IDEA under the topics "Schools" and "Schools and School Districts," respectively. *West's Encyclopedia of American Law*, which is geared more toward a general audience, can be found in many libraries. Encyclopedias are also available on specialized legal topics, for example, the *Encyclopedia of Education Law*.

Books and Treatises

Books and treatises help researchers identify relevant primary source materials (statutes, regulations, and cases) on particular legal topics. Books and treatises also help you gain a better understanding of the legal issues involved in an area of law. Books on education law and special education law range in complexity from nutshells, which are a series of paperbacks published by West in a simple and straightforward manner on a range of legal topics (e.g., *The Law of Schools, Students, and Teachers in a Nutshell*), to hornbooks, which are single-volume hardback books that cover the key issues involved in a specific area of legal study (e.g., *Disability Civil Rights Law and Policy*), to multivolume treatises. A treatise is an exhaustive treatment of a field of law by a legal scholar or practitioner that can span multiple volumes. Treatises may be published in bound volumes or looseleaf binders (e.g., *Special Education Law and Litigation Treatise*) and are usually updated annually. Many are available online on Westlaw, Lexis Advance, Bloomberg Law sites, and as stand-alone databases.

Searching the Catalog   You should always check your library's online catalog for dictionaries, encyclopedias, books, and treatises on the topic you are researching. The catalog record will indicate whether a resource is available in print, online, or is restricted to specific users via password. Colleges and universities can also borrow books from other academic institutions through interlibrary loan programs; therefore, you may wish to consult the online catalog WorldCat, which searches the collections of libraries around the world for books as well as articles. Law school libraries such as Harvard and Georgetown also maintain websites that list treatises by subject (Table 2.7).

Law Review and Journal Articles

Because of their extensive coverage and footnoting to primary authorities and other secondary sources, law review articles can "introduce the researcher to a universe of legal information" (Berring & Edinger, 2005, p. 319). It is not unusual to encounter pages in law review articles containing just a few lines of commentary and the rest footnotes, making them excellent case-finding tools. All accredited law schools in the United States produce law reviews. Law reviews are periodicals that contain articles on legal developments, legal issues, historical research, and empirical studies. Law reviews are usually edited by law students and include lengthy articles written by law professors, scholars, and practitioners along with shorter notes and comments authored by law students. Law review articles are often cited by legal scholars as well as by the courts and can have great persuasive authority. Student notes and comments, while not as prestigious, can be helpful sources for legal research.

Many law schools publish one or more specialized academic journals in addition to general law reviews, such as the *Journal of Law & Education*, edited by the University of South Carolina School of Law and the University of Louisville's Louis D. Brandeis School of Law.

Indexes

H.W. Wilson Company's *Index to Legal Periodicals Retrospective: 1908–1981* and *Index to Periodicals Full Text: 1981–Forward* are available to colleges and universities through the EBSCOhost.com website. Both cover hundreds of legal periodicals and offer basic and advanced searching. The Gale Group began publishing the *Current Law Index* (CLI) in 1980. The CLI provides access to hundreds of legal periodicals and is available online to libraries as *LegalTrac*. Both the *Index to Legal Periodicals* (ILP) and *LegalTrac* provide the full text of some articles, and libraries may link researchers to other online databases such as Nexis Uni™ and HeinOnline to retrieve the full-text versions of articles not included.

Online Databases   Several online databases allow college and university students and faculty to search and retrieve the full-text versions of journal articles by citation, by author, and by subject. Two specific databases on law reviews and legal journals are Nexis Uni™ and HeinOnline. HeinOnline can include digital images of articles from their first to the most current issues.

Open Source   Many law reviews across the country are now maintaining a web presence, and a growing number are including the full-text versions of articles on their websites. In fact, in the decade of the 1990s and 2000s there has been a growing movement in favor of "open access" to legal information both primary and secondary (e.g., law review articles). Law review and legal journal articles are not only accessible to browse, but are full-text searchable on such websites as Google Scholar and the American Bar Association's (ABA) Free Full-Text Online Law Review/Law Journal Search Engine (Table 2.7).

Citators   Online citators such as Shepard's® on Lexis Advance and Nexis Uni™ and KeyCite® through Westlaw can be used both to find journal articles that cite a particular primary source of law and to locate legal resources that cite a particular law review. HeinOnline's *ScholarCheck* provides links to articles in its database that cite the article that you are reading via a link titled "Articles that cite this document."

Looseleaf or Topical Services

Looseleaf services contain analyses of legal issues and reprints of primary source material in specific subject areas. A looseleaf service therefore may serve as both a secondary source and as a finding tool for primary authorities.

The traditional looseleaf service is a publication that is issued in a binder with removable pages. The publisher monitors legal developments in the subject area the service covers and regularly issues new pages to keep the publication current. The primary advantages of looseleaf services are that the information is current (updated frequently) and that much of the information needed to conduct research on a particular topic has already been compiled for the researcher, including authorities not published in West's National Reporter System, such as decisions of trial courts and state and federal administrative agencies.

Looseleaf services that were once published only in binders in print are now also available online as stand-alone databases or on Lexis Advance and Westlaw or both. An example of a special education looseleaf service is the *Individuals with Disabilities Education Law Report*® (IDELR), published by LRP Publications in print and through its online database Special Ed Connection.

You may consult the publication *Legal Looseleafs in Print* to identify looseleaf services currently published on a particular legal topic, for example, education law or special education law. *Legal Looseleafs in Print* indexes looseleaf services by subject, publisher, and title and indicates whether each looseleaf service listed is available as part of an online database or on the Internet.

No two looseleaf services or online databases (referred to as topical services) are the same; therefore, the key to using such a valuable service for legal research is to become familiar with its unique finding aids and indexing system.

Treatises on a particular area of law or legal topic may also be published in looseleaf format for ease of updating. One example is *Legal Rights of Persons with Disabilities*: *An Analysis of Federal Law*, also published by LRP Publications.

News and Current Awareness

With the availability of online access to legal information today through legal newspapers, newsletters, blogs, and even Facebook and Twitter, you can learn about a new development in an area of law almost immediately.

Newspapers   Online legal journal indexes (e.g., LegalTrac) and databases (e.g., Lexis Advance, Westlaw, and Bloomberg Law) provide access to legal news articles. Several legal news sources are also available on the Internet. For example, FindLaw, Law.com, and Jurist offer daily legal news, including information on key court decisions across the country and around the world. Table 2.8 lists websites for current awareness in special education law.

Newsletters   Newsletters are also published for specialized areas of law and may be available in print, as part of an online topical database, or via the Internet. Many newsletters are part of a looseleaf or topical service, which may be available in print, online, or both. For example, the *Individuals with Disabilities Education Law Report*® (IDELR) looseleaf service, published by LRP Publications, includes a biweekly newsletter (*Highlights*) that provides updates on recent decisions and rulings in special education law. IDELR is also available online through Special Ed Connection, which includes Special Ed e-news via weekly e-mails. You may also subscribe to electronic newsletters on the Internet published by governmental agencies, for example, the U.S. Department of Education's ED.gov website, or by experts in special education law.

Blogs   Blogs allow attorneys, law professors, and education professionals to report and comment on developments in special education law as they occur, from state-level due process hearings to cases on appeal to the U.S. Supreme Court. The blog developed for readers of this textbook, www.spedlawblog.com, also reports on developments in special education

TABLE 2.8 ■ Websites for Current Awareness in Special Education Law

Website Names	URL
ABA Blawg Directory	www.abajournal.com/blawgs/topic/education+law
BlawgSearch	https://blawgsearch.justia.com/
ED.gov newsletters	www2.ed.gov/news/newsletters/index.html
FindLaw for Legal Professionals	lp.findlaw.com
Jurist	www.jurist.org/paperchase/
Law.com	www.law.com
The Law and Special Education	http://spedlawblog.com

law. Blogs and blawgs, which are blogs about the law, are so prevalent today that directories and search engines have developed to locate blogs by author, title, region, and subject (e.g., special education law) and to search blog postings. Examples include the ABA's Blawg Directory and Justia's BlawgSearch (Table 2.8). Bloggers also include lists called blogrolls on their blogs directing researchers to other blogs they read.

ELECTRONIC LEGAL RESEARCH

As noted throughout this chapter, many legal resources that were once available only in print are now accessible to researchers electronically through pay databases and increasingly for free via the Internet. Electronic legal research has not, however, replaced traditional legal research. Rather, it is used most effectively in combination with print resources available in the library.

Two major electronic legal research services, Westlaw and Lexis Advance, are used by law firms, government entities, and law students across the country. For students and faculty in other disciplines, for example, education, colleges and universities generally subscribe to Nexis Uni™ or Westlaw's Campus Research. Although the academic versions of Lexis Advance and Westlaw contain fewer databases, they enable students and faculty to access a wide range of legal resources, including state and federal cases, statutes, regulations and constitutions, and secondary sources such as law review articles and legal encyclopedias.

Two primary advantages of electronic legal research services through LexisNexis and Westlaw are the enormous amounts of information they contain and the speed with which you can access their databases and navigate between them. Westlaw and Lexis Advance are very current, and their databases are updated constantly. Both systems contain full libraries of cases, statutes, and regulations from all jurisdictions, as well as a variety of finding tools and secondary source materials. Both include editorial enhancements such as annotated codes and headnotes for cases that are unmatched by other systems. Another benefit offered by Lexis Advance and Westlaw is the ease with which you can move from one primary or secondary source to another through hypertext links to materials cited within the various search results.

These and many other electronic research services allow you to retrieve legal resources by citation, to browse tables of contents and indexes, and to search the full-text versions of distinct databases by keyword. You choose the database you wish to search (e.g., U.S. Supreme Court decisions), then enter specific keywords (e.g., "special education" or "least restrictive environment") designed to retrieve the desired information.

The key to successful full-text searching is to choose the smallest database possible, for example, U.S. Supreme Court cases instead of all federal and state cases, and to use the tools within a particular database to filter or narrow your results. No two electronic research services are the same and new databases and upgrades are constantly being added for more efficient searching. Therefore, for optimal search results, you should take advantage of the many tutorials, "Help" pages, and research tips available for the various research systems and databases.

THE INTERNET AND LEGAL RESEARCH

Throughout this chapter, the fee-based electronic research services were introduced along with specific Internet versions of print resources available at no cost. The Internet is particularly useful because all researchers can access information quickly for free. For example, if the U.S. Supreme Court or a U.S. Court of Appeals announces a decision in an area of special education, it may be days before the final court opinion is available in a law library, and months before analyses of the decision appear in scholarly journals. Using the Internet, however, one can access the full opinion on the court's website within hours after it is announced. Analyses of the decision may be available almost as quickly. Similarly, when Congress passed the Individuals with Disabilities Education Improvement Act of 2004 reauthorizing the Individuals with Disabilities Act, the text of the new legislation was posted on the U.S. Library of Congress's Congress.gov website that same day, and within days the Council for Exceptional Children (CEC) had posted summaries, analyses, and a link to the new bill on its website.

The Internet has become increasingly more valuable as a free resource for legal information. However, it is not a substitute for the law library. For instance, although all state and federal appellate court systems maintain websites and many post their decisions daily, these opinions may date back only 10 years or so and do not include the editorial enhancements contained in the print reporters and subscription databases. The same is true of state and federal statutes available online. The Internet versions of these laws typically do not include annotations that direct the legal researcher to regulations implementing them, nor will they provide cases that interpret them. Although the availability of e-books for legal materials is increasing and many legal treatises are accessible through electronic subscription databases such as Westlaw, Lexis Advance, and Bloomberg Law, many books and treatises on special education law remain in print. Additionally, although peer-reviewed law reviews and legal journals are beginning to post recent issues on the Internet, you must be prepared to evaluate the credibility and usefulness of the host of other information available on the World Wide Web. With any research, but especially legal research, information must be evaluated for its authenticity, objectivity, comprehensiveness, accuracy, and currency. Given the ease of publication on the Internet, applying these criteria to websites as potential resources for legal research is essential. Table 2.9 lists web addresses for legal research websites, including The People's Law Library of Maryland's *Evaluating Legal Websites*, which offers a detailed description of the "10 signs of excellence in a legal website."

Used appropriately, the Internet offers valuable and timely access to primary and secondary legal resources and offers today's researcher immediate access to information needed to stay abreast of developments in the law.

Although various websites for primary and secondary legal resources are mentioned throughout this chapter, the next section discusses specific legal research tools available via the Internet.

TABLE 2.9 ■ Legal Research Websites

Website Names	URL
Cornell's Legal Information Institute (LII)	www.law.cornell.edu/
Education Information Resource Center (ERIC)	www.eric.ed.gov/
FindLaw for Legal Professionals	http://lp.findlaw.com/
Georgetown Law Library Research Guides, Treatise Finders, & Tutorials	guides.ll.georgetown.edu/home
GPO's FDsys (soon to become govinfo)	www.gpo.gov/fd /
Justia	www.justia.com/
The People's Law Library of Maryland: Evaluating Legal Websites	www.peoples-law.org/evaluating-legal-websites
UCLA's Online Legal Research: Beyond Lexis & Westlaw	libguides.law.ucla.edu/onlinelegalresearch

INTERNET RESEARCH TOOLS

Government Websites

The U.S. government is a rich source of primary legal authority. Many useful websites for researchers interested in special education law are either sponsored in whole or part by the federal government or are produced by the federal government for the purpose of providing government information to citizens.

The Government Printing Office's FDsys website (govinfo) includes resources (statutes, regulations, and cases) for all three branches of the federal government. The USA.gov website offers an A-Z Index of U.S. Government Departments and Agencies.

The United States Courts website provides links to official court websites for opinions from the U.S. Supreme Court, U.S. Courts of Appeals, and U.S. District Courts. All states provide links to their judicial departments from their official government websites for access to their appellate court opinions.

The U.S. government also supports access to secondary source research materials through projects such as the Education Resource Information Center (ERIC), which is an online digital library sponsored by the Institute of Education Sciences (IES) of the U.S. Department of Education to support the use of education research. The ERIC database indexes over 1 million journals, books, reports, and other education-related materials by title, author, and keyword, with links to articles available in full-text versions (Table 2.9).

Legal Directories and Search Engines

In addition to the many Internet resources recommended throughout this chapter for access to specific primary (federal and state cases, statutes, and regulations) and secondary (dictionaries, encyclopedias, law review articles, etc.) legal resources, legal directories and search engines enable researchers to search both primary and secondary legal resources available on the Internet by topic.

Directories divide websites into categories and subcategories, allowing you to continue clicking to narrow a search. Search engines index pages from the web and enable researchers to search using keywords and advanced searching techniques. Several websites for legal research serve as both a directory and a search engine. Two examples are FindLaw and Justia. Also of note is Google Scholar for searching legal opinions and journal articles (Table 2.9).

Legal Research Guides

Legal research guides available on the Internet from academic law libraries can serve as great starting points for identifying key print and online resources on a specific legal topic (e.g., education law, legal research). An excellent example is Georgetown Law Library's Research Guides website. Law school libraries (e.g., Georgetown and UCLA) are also beginning to create guides for free and low-cost legal research (Table 2.9).

Information and Advocacy

Information and advocacy websites can also serve as tools for special education law research. The Center for Parent Information and Resources (CPIR) is a national information and referral center for disabilities and disability-related issues funded by the Office of Special Education Programs (OSEP) of the U.S. Department of Education.

Wrightslaw.com is a website maintained by Pete and Pam Wright, who teach special education law and advocacy at William and Mary Law School and have co-authored several books on the subject. Wrightslaw's online advocacy and law libraries link to articles, cases, and other resources on special education law by topic. The website also offers an electronic newsletter and blog. Wrightslaw is a great resource for accessing both primary and secondary special education law resources and for staying abreast of developments in the law.

LEGAL RESEARCH STRATEGIES

This chapter has introduced the essential tools of legal research—primary sources, secondary sources, and finding tools—both in print and online. In addition to knowing the legal resources available, a method for conducting legal research is required. The following three-step model may be useful.

Step 1: Analyze the Problem

The first task of a legal researcher is to analyze the problem and determine the most efficient manner in which to proceed. In the problem-analysis phase, Johnson, Berring, and Woxland (Johnson, Berring, & Woxland, 2009) suggest that the researcher (a) think about the answer that is needed for the research problem, (b) determine what it is that the research is to accomplish, and (c) decide what the ideal final product will look like. After analyzing the problem, you must decide what legal sources will be needed to answer that question. Will the research question require information from statutes, regulations, current cases, historical information, an analysis of the law, or some combination of these? Will primary source material (i.e., statements of the law), secondary sources (i.e., interpretations of the law), or both be required? Answers to these questions will help you focus your research and decide on a research strategy.

Step 2: Conduct the Research

Next, you must locate relevant primary source materials. If a statute citation is available, you can find case citations by looking up the statute in the annotated codes (e.g., U.S.C.A.) and reading the abstracts of relevant cases. A citation to regulations implementing a statute may also be available.

Perhaps the most important element of step 2 is to identify one good case on the subject you are researching. Once you have one good case, you can use the West's topics and key numbers in that case's headnotes to find additional cases on the same topic. You can also use citators, such as Shepards® and KeyCite® to find cases and secondary sources that cite the cases you find.

If a statute, regulation, or relevant case citation is not available, you should begin with secondary sources (e.g., to locate a law review article on the subject). Law review articles are replete with statutory, regulatory, and case citations. Print looseleaf or online topical services are also useful in locating primary source material. In addition to references to primary sources, the secondary source materials provide you with commentary and analyses of the law.

The ability to move between the sources of law and pull together the relevant information is critical in this stage of research. Analysis of legal issues requires the integration of both primary and secondary resources.

Step 3: Evaluate the Results

The final step of the legal research process is to evaluate your results. Have you obtained enough information? Are the materials current? Is the analysis logically based on the legal sources located? Because the law is constantly changing, it is critically important that your legal research be current. Updating your research, therefore, should be a continuous part of the process, which is also a distinct final step in evaluating the results of your research (Olson, 2009).

SUMMARY

Law refers to the rules that govern activities in society. Legal research is the process of finding these laws. It involves locating actual statements of the law (i.e., primary sources) as well as explanations and analyses of the law (i.e., secondary sources).

The primary sources include statutes, regulations, and cases. To varying degrees, the primary sources are the controlling authority; that is, these sources are the laws that courts in a given jurisdiction must follow. These sources are available on both the federal and state level.

Finding tools are resources for locating primary sources. The purpose of finding tools is to allow you to access the enormous body of primary and secondary sources. Examples of finding tools include the annotated codes (i.e., U.S.C.A. and U.S.C.S.), West's digests, citators, and ALR annotations.

Secondary materials discuss and analyze the primary sources. Although secondary sources do not have controlling authority, they are useful explanations of the law and may serve as persuasive authority. Books and treatises, law review articles, and looseleaf or online topical services are examples of secondary sources. Electronic databases such as Westlaw and Lexis Advance assist you in retrieving both primary and secondary legal resources using full-text keyword searching. The Internet is also becoming increasingly more useful as a legal research tool.

Legal research requires the ability to understand, locate, and use both print and electronic legal resources, including primary sources, secondary sources, and finding tools. You must also approach legal problems with a strategy. Although personal strategies vary, they will often include problem analysis, methods for systematically conducting the research, and an evaluation and updating phase.

FOR FURTHER INFORMATION

Barkan, S. M., Bintliff, B.A, & Whisner, M. (2015). *Fundamentals of legal research* (10th ed.). St. Paul, MN: Foundation Press.

Berring, R. C. (2016). *Legal research* (2nd ed.). St. Paul, MN: West Academic (Sum & Substance series).

Berring, R. C., & Edinger, A. E. (2005). *Finding the law* (17th ed.). St. Paul, MN: Thomson/West.

Elias, S. (2015). *Legal research: How to find & understand the law* (17th ed.). Berkeley, CA: Nolo.

Johnson, N. P., Berring, R. C., & Woxland, T. A. (2009). *Winning research skills*. St. Paul, MN: Thomson/West.

Olson, K. C. (2015). *Principles of legal research* (2nd ed.). St. Paul, MN: West Academic.

Osbeck, M. K. (2016). *Impeccable research: A concise guide to mastering legal research skills* (2nd ed.). St. Paul, MN: West Academic.

Sloan, A. E. (2017). *Researching the law: Finding what you need when you need it* (2nd ed.). New York: Wolters Kluwer Law & Business.

For more information on online legal research services, visit the following websites:

Bloomberg Law: www.bloomberglaw.com/

Nexis Uni™: www.lexisnexis.com/en-us/products/nexis-uni.page

Campus Research by Thomson Reuters: http://legalsolutions. thomsonreuters.com/law-products/westlawnext/campus-research

REFERENCES

Berring, R. C., & Edinger, E. A. (2005). *Finding the law* (12th ed.). St. Paul, MN: Thomson/West.

Cohen, M. L., & Olson, K. C. (2013). *Legal research in a nutshell* (11th ed.). St. Paul, MN: West®.

Daniel R .R. v. State Board of Education, 874 F.2d 1036 (5th Cir. 1989).

Johnson, N. P., Berring, R. C., & Woxland, T. A. (2009). *Winning research skills* (2nd ed.). St. Paul, MN: Thomson/West.

Olson, K. C. (2009). *Principles of legal research*. St. Paul MN: Thomson/West.

Chapter 3

The History of the Law and Children with Disabilities

Mitchell L. Yell,
University of South Carolina

David Rogers,
Retired Special Education Professor

Elisabeth Lodge Rogers,
Director of Special Services and Education Programs,
Immediate District 287, Plymouth, MN

> In these days, it is doubtful that any child may reasonably be expected to succeed in life if he is denied the opportunity of an education. Such an opportunity, where the state has undertaken to provide it, is a right that must be made available to all on equal terms.
>
> CHIEF JUSTICE EARL WARREN, *BROWN V. BOARD OF EDUCATION* (1954, P. 493)

Learner Objectives

At the end of the chapter, students will be able to

3.1 Describe the history of excluding students with disabilities from public education.

3.2 Describe the history and effect of parental advocacy in the development of special education.

3.3 Describe how the civil rights movement affects special education.

3.4 Describe the equal opportunity cases.

3.5 Describe the history of federal involvement in special education.

3.6 Describe the major laws affecting students with disabilities in the United States.

3.7 Describe and explain the meaning of the phrase "from access to accountability" as it pertains to the development of special education laws.

The educational rights of children and youth with disabilities were gained largely through the tireless efforts of parents and advocacy groups in the courts and legislatures of this country. The purpose of this chapter is to provide a brief chronology of these efforts. The history of special education law will be examined from the initiation of compulsory attendance laws to inclusion of students with disabilities. The effects of the civil rights movement on special education will be discussed, with particular attention paid to *Brown v. Board of Education* (1954) and the landmark cases of the equal opportunity movement.

The manner in which these cases led inexorably to the legislation that ensured the educational rights of children and youth with disabilities will be explained. Finally, federal legislative mandates from Section 504 of the Rehabilitation Act of 1973 to P.L. 108-446, the Individuals with Disabilities Education Improvement Act of 2004, will be briefly examined.

COMPULSORY ATTENDANCE

In our country, public education is viewed as a birthright. Public education leads to an educated electorate, which is necessary for a democracy to be viable (Levine & Wexler, 1981). A common misconception regarding public education is that the U.S. Constitution guarantees it. In fact, education is not mentioned in the Constitution. According to the 10th Amendment to the U.S. Constitution, powers that are not specifically granted to the federal government in the Constitution are reserved to the states. Education, therefore, is the responsibility of the individual states.

Massachusetts was the first state to pass a compulsory education law in 1852; Vermont passed the second in 1867, with other states following suit. By 1918 compulsory education laws were in place in all states. Despite the enactment of compulsory education laws, however, children with disabilities were often excluded from public schools.

THE EXCLUSION OF STUDENTS WITH DISABILITIES

The continued exclusion of students with disabilities, notwithstanding the compulsory education laws enacted by the states, was upheld in the courts. For example, in 1893 the Massachusetts Supreme Judicial Court ruled that a child who was "weak in mind" and could not benefit from instruction, was troublesome to other children, made "unusual noises," and was unable to take "ordinary, decent, physical care of himself" could be expelled from public school (*Watson v. City of Cambridge,* 1893). Twenty-six years later, the Wisconsin Supreme Court, in *Beattie v. Board of Education* (1919), ruled that school officials could exclude a student with disabilities, even though that student had attended public school until the fifth grade. The student's condition caused drooling, facial contortions, and speech problems. School officials claimed this condition nauseated the teachers and other students, required too much teacher time, and negatively affected school discipline and progress. School officials expelled the student from school and suggested he attend a day school for students who were deaf.

In 1934, the Cuyahoga County Court of Appeals in Ohio ruled that the state statute mandating compulsory attendance for children ages 6 through 18 gave the State Department of Education the authority to exclude certain students (Winzer, 1993). This ruling was indicative of the contradiction between compulsory attendance and the exclusion of students with disabilities, a contradiction that was frequently present in legal rulings of the time on students with disabilities. The court stated that students have a right to attend school, and it noted the importance of education as evidenced by the compulsory education statute. Although the court acknowledged the conflict between compulsory education and the exclusionary provisions, it did not rule to resolve this conflict.

Despite compulsory attendance laws, states continued to enact statutes that specifically authorized school officials to exclude students with disabilities. As recently as 1958 and 1969, the courts upheld legislation that excluded students who school officials judged would not benefit from public education or who might be disruptive to other students. In 1958 the Supreme Court of Illinois, in *Department of Public Welfare v. Haas,* held that the state's existing compulsory attendance legislation did not require the state to provide a free public education for the "feeble minded" or to children who were "mentally deficient" and who, because of their limited intelligence, were unable to reap the benefits of a good education. In 1969, the State of North Carolina made it a crime for parents to persist in forcing the attendance of a child with disabilities after the child's exclusion from public school (Weber, 2008).

PARENTAL ADVOCACY

Parents led the way in seeking educational rights for their children with disabilities. In fact, Dr. Edwin Martin (2013), a commissioner of the Bureau of Education of the Handicapped and the first Assistant Secretary of Education for Special Education and Rehabilitative Services in the U.S. Department of Education, observed that "parents had provided the energy and will to create special education programs wherever they occurred... there would be little, if any, special education if the parents had not created it, directly or through political persuasion" (Martin, 2013, p. 22).

The parental advocacy movement reflected changes in the social climate of this country at the turn of the 20th century. The nation, having long ignored individuals with disabilities, focused on the need to humanely treat and educate these individuals, particularly children. In order to understand the impact parents had on legislation to protect the rights of children with disabilities, it is helpful to become aware of the evolution of special education in the first three decades of that century.

The White House Conference of 1910

The first White House Conference on Children in 1910 focused national attention on children and youth with disabilities. A primary goal of this conference was to define and establish remedial programs for children with disabilities or special needs. This goal reflected a broader societal shift in perspective on the treatment of children with disabilities. The conference led to an increased interest in educating children with disabilities in public school settings rather than institutionalizing them. As children with disabilities were moved from institutions to public schools, permanent segregated classes were formed in public schools to meet their needs. According to Winzer (1993), the move from institutions to public school settings resulted in changing primary placements of students with disabilities from isolated settings to segregated settings.

Public School Programming

The number of special segregated classes and support services in public schools increased significantly from 1910 to 1930 (Winzer, 1993). Public school educators believed that the segregated classes were beneficial to the children with disabilities because (a) smaller class size would allow more individualized instruction, (b) homogeneous grouping would facilitate teaching, and (c) the less competitive nature of these classes would improve the children's self-esteem.

A few states began to adopt laws requiring public schools to educate students with disabilities. The first states passing such laws were New Jersey in 1911, New York in 1917, and Massachusetts in 1920. However, enforcement of these laws was ineffective (Colker, 2013).

Despite the increase in the numbers of special education classrooms and the presence of state laws, many children and youth with disabilities remained unidentified and continued to struggle in regular classrooms. Furthermore, many students with disabilities did not benefit from public school education because they had dropped out of school, had been expelled or excluded from school, or were considered unteachable (Winzer, 1993). These problems led to a decrease in the growth of special education programs in the 1930s.

Many factors contributed to this decline in support for and provision of special education classes for students with disabilities. The country was in the midst of the Great Depression, and many, including public entities, were struggling with the resulting financial constraints. The public school system had been developed as an ideal for a democratic society. Compulsory education laws resulted in an increasingly heterogeneous student population, leading to a conflict between the democratic ideal and maintenance of order and high standards in public schools. The result of this conflict was to further separate children with special needs from the mainstream. Under increasingly grim conditions, the special classroom placements became as restrictive and custodial as placements in institutions had been (Winzer, 1993).

The Organization of Advocacy Groups

In response to the poor educational programming that their children with special needs had to endure in school as well as the increasing exclusion of children with disabilities from school, parents began to band together to advocate for their children's education rights. They came together to support one another and to work for change. In 1933, the first such group formed in Cuyahoga County, Ohio. The Cuyahoga County Ohio Council for the Retarded Child consisted initially of five mothers of children with mental retardation (now termed *intellectual disability*) who banded together to protest the exclusion of their children from school (Levine & Wexler, 1981; Turnbull, Turnbull, Erwin, Soodak, & Shogren, 2011; Winzer, 1993). Their efforts resulted in the establishment of a special class for their children, sponsored by the parents themselves. Similar types of local groups were established throughout the nation during the 1930s and 1940s, although they did not begin to band together at the national level until the 1950s. These local organizations served several purposes. They provided an avenue of support for parents, offered a means to unite to make change locally, and set the stage for national advocacy movements on behalf of children and youth with disabilities.

The advocacy movement was critical to the development of special education services. The activities of interest groups were critical in terms of providing information, stimulus, and support to Congress when considering, developing, and acting on legislation. Congress cannot function without such interest groups (Levine & Wexler, 1981). Let's briefly trace the development of a few national groups that advocated for the rights of individuals with disabilities.

The National Association for Retarded Citizens
The National Association for Retarded Citizens (now ARC/USA, the Association for Retarded Citizens) was organized in Minneapolis, Minnesota, in September 1950. Forty-two parents and concerned individuals from 13 local and state organizations met to establish what has become a powerful and significant organization of parents, families, and other persons with an interest in improving services for individuals with mental retardation. ARC's mission is to (a) provide information to concerned individuals, (b) monitor the quality of services for individuals with mental retardation, and (c) advocate for the rights and interests of individuals with mental retardation. The ARC's website is www.thearc.org.

The Council for Exceptional Children
The Council for Exceptional Children (CEC) is a professional organization concerned with the education of children with special needs. It was founded in 1922 by Elizabeth Farrell and 10 of her students at Teachers College, Columbia University, in New York (Kode, 2017). Elizabeth Farrill was elected the first president of the CEC. At the meeting, the group identified the three major aims of the CEC:

- "Emphasize the education of the 'special child'—rather than his identification or classification
- Establish professional standards for teachers in the field of special education
- Unite those interested in the educational problems of the 'special child'" (Kode, 2017, p. 47).

CEC has been a longtime advocate for the educational rights of children and youth with disabilities, and has been a leader in the movement to obtain these rights at the federal and state levels. The membership of CEC exceeds 60,000 people. The organization is a major force in (a) the development of innovative educational programming, (b) preservice and in-service teacher education, and (c) policymaking and lobbying efforts for children and youth with special needs. The CEC's website is www.cec.sped.org.

The Association for Persons with Severe Handicaps

The Association for Persons with Severe Handicaps (TASH) is another organization that has provided strong support for individuals with disabilities. TASH was established in 1974 and comprises teachers, parents, administrators, and related service providers. TASH disseminates information on best practices, publishes research reports, and supports the rights and humane treatment of individuals with severe and multiple disabilities through active involvement in court cases (Siegel-Causey, Guy, & Guess, 1995). TASH's website is www.tash.org.

Additional Advocacy Groups

Other advocacy groups founded primarily by and for parents and families of individuals with disabilities include the United Cerebral Palsy Association, Inc. (founded in 1949), the National Society for Autistic Children (1961), the National Association for Down Syndrome (1961), and the Association for Children with Learning Disabilities (ACLD) (1964). More recently, the Federation of Families for Children's Mental Health was formed after a group of 60 parents and professionals interested in children and youth with emotional, behavioral, and mental disorders met in 1988 (Turnbull et al., 2011).

The progress made in special education can be attributed in great part to the success of parents as advocates for their children. Parents have worked together, and continue to do so, at the local level by pushing local school boards, administrators, teachers, and legislators to provide appropriate educational programming for their children. Parent groups such as ARC and ACLD banded together with professional organizations to challenge state and federal governments in the courts and ultimately to establish federal legislation that mandated a free and appropriate education for all children with disabilities.

THE CIVIL RIGHTS MOVEMENT AND *BROWN V. BOARD OF EDUCATION*

Every year hundreds of thousands of people immigrate to the United States. Many are escaping war or economic and political persecution. Many come not to avoid hardship, but to seek the promise of greater individual rights that is provided for the citizens of the United States under its Constitution. The civil rights that are protected under the Constitution and enforced by legislation, however, have not always been provided to all citizens on an equal basis.

In the 1950s and 1960s, the civil rights movement, which sought changes in society that would allow minorities, particularly African Americans, equality of opportunity, led to litigation and changes in legislation. This legislation provided greater constitutional protection for minorities, and eventually for individuals with disabilities.

A landmark case, *Brown v. Board of Education* (1954, hereinafter *Brown*), was a major victory for the civil rights movement and became the major underpinning for further civil rights action. The *Brown* decision not only had a tremendous impact on societal rights for minorities, but also affected many aspects of educational law and procedure (Turnbull, Stowe, & Huerta, 2007). Although it took time, the precedents set in *Brown* resulted in sweeping changes in the schools' policies and approaches to students with disabilities.

 Enhanced eText Video Example 3.1:
To view an excellent **video** on the *Brown v. Board of Education* decision, go to www.youtube.com/watch?v=TTGHLdr-iak

State-mandated segregation of the races in the schools denied black students admission to schools attended by white students. The plaintiffs maintained that the practice of segregating schools was inherently damaging to the educational opportunities of minorities, that segregated public schools were not—and could not be made—equal, and that segregated public schools violated black students' constitutional rights under the equal protection clause of the 14th Amendment. As an extension of this argument, the Court maintained that state-required or state-sanctioned segregation solely on the basis of an individual's unalterable characteristics (e.g., race or disability) was unconstitutional. The high court also determined that segregation solely on the basis of race violated equal protections and denied children from minority backgrounds equal educational opportunity. This decision opened a number of legal avenues for those seeking redress for students with disabilities.

In *Brown*, the high court reasoned that because of the importance of education in our society, the stigmatizing effects of racial segregation, and the negative consequences of racial segregation on the education of those against whom segregation was practiced, segregated public schools denied students equal educational opportunities. This basic truth was considered by many to be equally applicable to those denied equal opportunity to an education because of a disability.

Parental Advocacy in the Wake of Brown

An outcome of the *Brown* case was that the equal protection doctrine was extended to a "class" of people, in this case racial minorities (Turnbull et al., 2007). Advocates for students with disabilities, citing *Brown*, claimed that students with disabilities had the same rights as students without disabilities. Advocates based their arguments on two main premises. First, they pointed out that there was an unacceptable level of differential treatment within the class of children with disabilities. Second, they argued that some students with disabilities were not furnished with an education, whereas all students without disabilities were provided an education. Thus, *Brown* became a catalyst for the efforts to ensure educational rights for children and youth with disabilities because if segregation by race was a denial of equal educational opportunity for black children, then certainly the total exclusion of children and youth with disabilities was also a denial of equal educational opportunity (Huefner & Herr, 2011). On the basis of the *Brown* decision, a series of court cases was brought on behalf of children and youth with disabilities by advocates and individuals with disabilities in which they both challenged and sought redress for similar inequities.

THE EQUAL OPPORTUNITY CASES

The *Brown* decision was important for students with disabilities because the concept of equal opportunity was applicable to them as well as to students of minority background. Sixteen years after the *Brown* decision, two seminal federal district court cases applied the concept of equal opportunity to children with disabilities. The two landmark decisions in which action was brought against state statutes and policies that excluded students with disabilities were *Pennsylvania Association for Retarded Citizens (PARC) v. Commonwealth of Pennsylvania* (1972) and *Mills v. Board of Education of the District of Columbia* (1972).

Pennsylvania Association for Retarded Children (PARC) v. Pennsylvania, 1972

In January 1971, the Pennsylvania Association for Retarded Children brought a class action suit (hereafter referred to as *PARC*) against the Commonwealth of Pennsylvania in a federal district court. Specifically, the suit named the state's secretaries of Education and Public Welfare, the state Board of Education, and 13 school districts. The plaintiffs argued that students with mental retardation were not receiving publicly supported education because the state was delaying or ignoring its constitutional obligations to provide a publicly supported education for these students, thus violating state statute and the students' rights under the equal protection of the laws clause of the 14th Amendment to the U.S. Constitution. Witnesses for the plaintiffs established four critical points. The first was that all children with mental retardation are capable of benefiting from a program of education and training. Second, education cannot be defined as only the provision of academic experiences for children (this legitimizes experiences such as learning to clothe and feed oneself as outcomes for public school programming). A third point was that, having undertaken to provide all children in the Commonwealth of Pennsylvania with a free public education, the state could not deny students with mental retardation access to free public education and training. A final stipulation was that the earlier students with mental retardation were provided education, the greater the amount of learning that could be predicted, a point related to denying preschoolers with retardation access to preschool programs available to children without disabilities (Levine & Wexler, 1981; Zettel & Ballard, 1982).

PARC was resolved by consent decree specifying that all children with mental retardation between the ages of 6 and 21 must be provided a free public education, and that it was most desirable to educate children with mental retardation in a program most like the programs provided for their peers without disabilities (Levine & Wexler, 1981; Zettel & Ballard, 1982). The decree, which was amended a year later, set the stage for continued developments regarding the educational rights of students with disabilities.

Mills v. Board of Education, *1972*

Soon after the *PARC* decision, a class-action suit was filed in the Federal District Court for the District of Columbia. This suit, *Mills v. Board of Education* (1972; hereafter *Mills*), was filed against the District of Columbia's Board of Education on behalf of all out-of-school students with disabilities. The action was brought by the parents and guardians of seven children who presented a variety of disabilities, including behavior problems, hyperactivity, epilepsy, mental retardation, and physical impairments. These seven children were certified as a class, thereby representing more than 18,000 students who were denied or excluded from public education in Washington, D.C. The suit, which was based on the 14th Amendment, charged that the students were improperly excluded from school without due process of law (Zettel & Ballard, 1982). The court held that because segregation in public education on the basis of race was unconstitutional, the total exclusion of students with disabilities was also unconstitutional. *Mills* resulted in a judgment against the defendant school board mandating that the board provide all children with disabilities a publicly supported education. In addition, the court ordered the district to provide due process safeguards. Moreover, the court clearly outlined due process procedures for labeling, placement, and exclusion of students with disabilities (Zettel & Ballard, 1982). The procedural safeguards included the following: the right to a hearing, with representation, a record, and an impartial hearing officer; the right to appeal; the right to have access to records; and the requirement of written notice at all stages of the process. These safeguards became the framework for the due process component of the Education for All Handicapped Children Act (EAHCA).

Additional Cases

The *PARC* and *Mills* decisions set precedent for similar cases to be filed across the country. In the 2½ years following the *PARC* and *Mills* decisions, 46 right-to-education cases were filed on behalf of children with disabilities in 28 states (Zettel & Ballard, 1982). The outcomes of these cases were consistent with those established in *Mills* and *PARC*. Notwithstanding the judicial success, many students with disabilities continued to be denied an appropriate public education (Zettel & Ballard, 1982). School districts continued to argue that sufficient funds did not exist, that facilities were inadequate, and that instructional materials and adequately trained teachers were unavailable. By the early 1970s, the majority of states had passed laws requiring that students with disabilities receive a public education. These laws, however, varied substantially and resulted in uneven attempts to provide education to these students. Additionally, Congress was well aware of the decisions in which courts held that the constitutional rights of students with disabilities were being violated by their exclusion from schools or by receiving an inferior education in segregated classrooms. For these and other reasons, it became obvious to many that some degree of federal involvement was necessary.

FEDERAL INVOLVEMENT

Early Federal Involvement

The first significant federal involvement in the education of students with disabilities occurred in the late 1950s and early 1960s. Some of these early efforts included the Education of Mentally Retarded Children Act of 1958, in which Congress appropriated funds to train teachers of children with mental retardation, and the Training of Professional Personnel Act of 1959, which helped train leaders to educate children with mental retardation. In these laws, Congress appropriated funds to encourage the development for students with disabilities.

The Elementary and Secondary Education Act of 1965
In 1965, the Elementary and Secondary Education Act (ESEA) was passed and signed by President Lyndon Johnson as an important component of the war on poverty. This law was the first time the federal government provided direct funding to the states to assist in educating certain groups of students. As such, it was a precursor of direct aid for students with disabilities. The purpose of the ESEA was to provide federal money to states to improve educational opportunities for disadvantaged children, including students with disabilities who attended state schools for the deaf, blind, and retarded.

Enhanced eText **Video Example 3.2:**
Pictures and recorded remarks of President Johnson's signing of the ESEA on April 4, 1965, are available at www.youtube.com/watch?v=QQzCV1UdPLc

According to Martin, Martin, and Terman (1996), advocates for children with disabilities had three important goals. First, they wanted a single federal agency that would coordinate federal efforts for children with disabilities. This was achieved when the Bureau for the Education of the Handicapped (BEH) in the U.S. Office of Education was mandated in Title VI of the ESEA, which was passed in 1966. Second, they sought increased categorical funding to educate students with disabilities. This goal was partially achieved in Title VI of the ESEA, which also added funding for pilot programs to develop promising programs for children with disabilities. Title IV was titled the Education of the Handicapped Act. The third goal, an enforceable entitlement for educating students with disabilities, was seemingly being achieved through the courts and state legislatures.

The Education of the Handicapped Act of 1970
In 1970, Title VI of the ESEA was replaced by the Education of the Handicapped Act (EHA). This law was to become the basic framework for much of the legislation that was to follow. The purpose of the EHA was to consolidate and expand the previous federal grant programs and to continue funding pilot projects at the state and local levels. The EHA provided funding to states if they would initiate, expand, or improve programs and projects for students with disabilities. The law also provided funding to institutions of higher education to develop programs to train teachers of students with disabilities. Funds were also authorized for the development of regional resource centers to provide technical assistance to state and local school districts. The EHA, however, did not contain extensive substantive rights (Colker, 2013). It was, nevertheless, a very important step because it (a) was the first freestanding special education law, (b) mandated that students with disabilities be educated, and (c) required that students with disabilities should receive the special education and related services they needed to progress (Colker, 2013).

In the early 1970s it became apparent to many legislators, advocates, and parents that states were failing in their efforts to educate all of their children with disabilities (Martin, 2013). Congress's approach to addressing these problems: a nondiscrimination approach through Section 504 of the Rehabilitation Act of 1973 and an educational grant approach through the Education for All Handicapped Children Act of 1975 (Martin, et al. 1996).

Section 504 of the Rehabilitation Act of 1973

In 1973 Congress passed P.L. 93-112, the Rehabilitation Act of 1973. Section 504, a short provision of this act, was the first federal civil rights law to protect the rights of individuals with disabilities. Section 504 states:

> No otherwise qualified handicapped individual in the United States… shall solely by reason of his handicap, be excluded from the participation in, be denied the benefits of, or be subject to discrimination under any activity receiving federal financial assistance.
> (Section 504, 29 U.S.C. § 794[a])

In both language and intent, Section 504 mirrored other federal civil rights laws that prohibited discrimination by federal recipients on the basis of race (Title VI of the Civil Rights Act of 1964) and sex (Title IX of the Education Amendments of 1972). A "handicapped" person was defined as any person who has a physical or mental impairment that substantially limits one or more of that person's major life activities, or a person who has a record of such an impairment or who is regarded as having such an impairment.

The primary purpose of Section 504 was to prohibit discrimination against an individual with a disability by any agency receiving federal funds. These agencies are any that receive funds, personnel services, and interests in property, whether receiving these benefits directly or through another recipient. Section 504 requires agencies that are the recipients of federal financial assistance to provide assurances of compliance, to take corrective steps when violations are found, and to make individualized modifications and accommodations to provide services that are comparable to those offered to individuals without disabilities.

The Education Amendments of 1974

The Education Amendments of 1974, P.L. 93-380, were amendments to the EHA. The law was greatly influenced by the *PARC* and *Mills* decisions. The amendments authorized the creation of the National Advisory Council on Handicapped Children. The purpose of the 1974 amendments was to require that each state receiving federal special education funding establish a goal of providing full educational opportunities for all children with disabilities.

P.L. 93-380 was significant legislation for both children with disabilities and children who are gifted and talented (Weintraub & Ballard, 1982). The amendment acknowledged the right of students with disabilities to an education, created procedural safeguards, provided funds for programs for the education of students with disabilities under Title IV-B, specified due process procedures, and addressed the issue of least restrictive environment. The law, however, was not sufficiently enforceable in the eyes of many advocates for students with disabilities (Weber, 2008).

The Education for All Handicapped Children Act of 1975

Prior to 1975, the access of students with disabilities to educational opportunities was limited in two major ways (Katsiyannis, Yell, & Bradley, 2001; Yell, Drasgow, Bradley, & Justesen, 2004). First, many students were completely excluded from public schools. In fact, congressional findings in 1974 indicated that more than 1.75 million students with disabilities did not receive educational services. Second, more than 3 million students with disabilities who were admitted to school did not receive an education that was appropriate to their needs (Yell et al., 2004). To address these problems, President Gerald Ford signed into law the most significant increase in the role of the federal government in special education to date on November 29, 1975—the *Education for All Handicapped Children Act* (EAHCA).

The EAHCA, often called P.L. 94-142, combined an educational bill of rights with the promise of federal financial incentives. The EAHCA contained administrative and funding provisions providing that states develop policies assuring all qualified students with disabilities a special education. The EAHCA required participating states to provide a free appropriate public education for all qualified students with disabilities between the ages of 3 and 18 by September 1, 1978, and for all students up to age 21 by September 1, 1980. Furthermore, P.L. 94-142 mandated that qualified students with disabilities had the right to (a) nondiscriminatory testing, evaluation, and placement procedures; (b) education in the least restrictive environment; (c) procedural due process, including parent involvement; (d) a free education; and (e) an appropriate education, as developed by a group of persons, including a student's parents, in an individualized education program (IEP).

The EAHCA delineated the educational rights of students with disabilities and also provided the promise of federal funding to the states. Funding would flow from the federal government to the state education agencies (SEAs) and, finally, the local education agencies (LEAs). To receive the funds, states had to submit plans meeting the federal requirements. Local school districts, in turn, had to have programs meeting the state requirements. Federal funding was to supplement state and local dollars and could not be used to supplant these funds. Additionally, 75% of the federal funds were to flow through the state to the local school districts. By 1985 all states had complied with the requirements of this act.

When the EAHCA was first enacted in 1975, the primary issue driving the passage of the law was access to education (Katsiyannis et al., 2001; Yell et al., 2004). That is, far too many students with disabilities were (a) excluded from education, (b) segregated from their same-age nondisabled peers, or (c) placed in educational programs that were not appropriate for their unique needs. The EAHCA was successful in ameliorating these problems. Today the right to access education for students with disabilities is assured. Clearly, the original purposes of the law have been met.

The Handicapped Children's Protection Act of 1986

Prior to 1984, there was no provision regarding attorney's fees in the EAHCA. This meant that parents could not collect attorney's fees under the EAHCA when they had to sue school districts to ensure their rights under the law. Typically, attorneys who brought actions for parents under the law had to collect attorney's fees by using other laws (e.g., 42 U.S.C. 1983 and Section 504) to recover fees. The U.S. Supreme Court stopped this practice in the *Smith v. Robinson* (1984) decision. The high court held that because the EAHCA was the sole source for relief in cases brought under law, attorneys could not sue under other laws to collect their fees. The decision effectively made the recovery of attorney's fees impossible because the EAHCA contained no attorney's fees provision. Less than two years later, President Ronald Reagan signed the Handicapped Children's Protection Act of 1986 (HCPA; P.L. 99-372) into law. The HCPA amended the EAHCA, thereby granting courts the authority to award attorney's fees to parents or guardians if they prevailed in their actions pursuant to the law. The HCPA also overturned the Court's decision that the EAHCA was the sole source of legal relief and allowed the HCPA to be applied retroactively to cases pending or brought after the 1984 *Smith v. Robinson* decision. (For elaborations on attorney's fees, see Chapter 14.)

The Education of the Handicapped Amendments of 1986

Congress recognized the importance of early intervention for young children when it passed the Education of the Handicapped Amendments in 1986. This law, which became a subchapter of the IDEA (Part H), made categorical grants to states contingent on providing services to children with developmental disabilities from birth to their third birthday. The amendment required participating states to develop and implement statewide interagency programs of early intervention services for infants and toddlers with disabilities and their families (IDEA, 20 U.S.C. § 1471[B] [1]). With the consolidation of the IDEA in the amendments of 1997, Part H became Part C.

In the law, infants and toddlers with disabilities were defined as children from birth to their third birthday who needed early intervention services because they were experiencing developmental delays. Additionally, children were eligible who had a diagnosed physical or mental condition that put them at risk of developing developmental delays.

Early intervention services were defined as developmental services provided at public expense and under public supervision that were designed to meet the child's physical, cognitive, communication, social or emotional, and adaptive needs (IDEA, 20 U.S.C. § 1472[2]). Early intervention services may include family training, counseling, home visits, speech pathology, occupational therapy, physical therapy, psychological services, case management services, medical services (for diagnostic or evaluation purposes only), health services, social work services, vision services, assistive technology devices and services, and transportation, along with related costs (IDEA, 20 U.S.C. § 1472[2][E]). To the maximum extent appropriate, these services must be provided in natural environments (e.g., home and community settings) in which children without disabilities participate.

The infants and toddlers program did not require that the SEA assume overall responsibility for the early intervention programs. The agency that assumes responsibility was referred to as the lead agency. The lead agency could be the SEA, the state welfare department, the health department, or any other unit of state government. Many states chose to provide Part C services through multiple state agencies (Weber, 2008). In these cases, an interagency coordinating council was the primary planning body to work out the interagency agreements concerning jurisdiction and funding.

The centerpiece of the infants and toddlers section of the law was the individualized family services plan (IFSP). In states that receive Part C funds, all infants or toddlers with disabilities must have an IFSP. The plan is developed by a multidisciplinary and interagency team that includes the parents, other family members, the case manager (i.e., coordinator of the process), the person or persons conducting the evaluation, and other persons who will be involved in providing services (IDEA Regulations, 34 C.F.R. § 303.340). The IFSP must be reviewed and evaluated every six months and revised every year if necessary.

The IFSP must contain

1. A statement of the infant's or toddler's present levels of physical development, cognitive development, communication development, social or emotional development, and adaptive development, based on acceptable objective criteria,
2. A statement of the family's resources, priorities, and concerns related to enhancing the development of the family's infant with a disability,
3. A statement of the major outcomes expected to be achieved for the infant or toddler and the family, and the criteria, procedures, and timelines used to determine the degree to which progress toward achieving the outcomes is being made and whether modifications or revisions of the outcomes or services are necessary,
4. A statement of the specific early intervention services necessary to meet the unique needs of the infant or toddler and the family, including the frequency, intensity, and the method of delivering services,
5. A statement of the natural environments in which the early intervention services shall appropriately be provided,
6. The projected dates for initiation of services and the anticipated duration of such services,
7. The name of the case manager ... from the profession most immediately relevant to the infant's or toddler's or family's needs ... who will be responsible for the implementation of the plan and coordination with other agencies and persons, and
8. The steps to be taken supporting the transition of the toddler with a disability to [special education] services. (IDEA, 20 U.S.C. § 1477[d])

The infants and toddlers section of the law contained procedural safeguards similar to those in Part B. For example, written consent of the parents is required prior to providing services. The primary area of differences between Part C and the rest of the IDEA, however, is that Part C had a more flexible definition of eligible children, focused on the family, and provided for coordinated interagency efforts.

The 1986 infants and toddlers amendments also created financial incentives for states to make children with disabilities eligible for special education at age 3. If a state lowered the age of eligibility, children with disabilities from age 3 to 5 would be entitled to receive all the procedural and substantive protections of Part B of the IDEA (Weber, 2008).

The Individuals with Disabilities Education Act of 1990

The 1990 amendments to P.L. 94-142, P.L. 101-476, renamed the EAHCA the Individuals with Disabilities Education Act (IDEA). The IDEA amendments of 1990 substituted the term *disability* for the term *handicap* throughout the law. The law also used "people first" language (e.g., "student with a disability" rather than "disabled student") to emphasize that the individual should precede the category of disability. The 1990 amendments added two disability categories, autism and traumatic brain injury. The law also added and clarified types of related services, assistive technology, and rehabilitation services.

IDEA 1990 also required that individualized transition planning be included in the individualized education programs (IEPs) of students with disabilities who were 16 years of age or older. The provision of transition services was a significant addition to the IDEA. Transition services refer to a

> coordinated set of activities for a student, designed within an outcome-oriented process, that promotes movement from school to post-school activities, including postsecondary education, vocational training, [and] integrated employment (including supported employment, continuing and adult education, adult services, independent living, or community participation).
>
> (IDEA Regulations, 34 C.F.R. § 300.18 *et seq.*)

Transition activities must be based on students' individual needs and take into account their preferences and interests. Transition services include instruction, community experience, the development of employment and adult living objectives, and acquisition of daily living skills and a functional vocational evaluation. Transition services may be either special education or related services.

Recent Federal Involvement

The IDEA Amendments of 1997

The Individuals with Disabilities Education Act Amendments of 1997, P.L. 105-17, were passed to reauthorize and make improvements to the IDEA. In passing the amendments, Congress noted that the IDEA had been successful in ensuring access to a free appropriate public education and improving educational results for students with disabilities. Nevertheless, the implementation of the IDEA had been impeded by low expectations for students with disabilities, an insufficient focus on translating research into practice, and too great an emphasis on paperwork and legal requirements at the expense of teaching and learning.

To improve the IDEA, Congress passed the most significant amendments to the law since the original passage of P.L. 94-142 in 1975. The changes were seen as the next vital step in providing special education services by ensuring that students with disabilities received a quality public education through emphasizing the improvement of student performance. By adopting the 1997 amendments to the IDEA, Congress indicated that the goal of the amendments was to improve the effectiveness of special education by requiring demonstrable improvements in the educational achievement of students with disabilities. According to Eyer (1998), with the passage of these amendments, providing a quality education for each student with disabilities became the new goal of IDEA.

The No Child Left Behind Act

No Child Left Behind (NCLB) was signed into law by President George W. Bush on January 8, 2002. The law was the most recent reauthorization of the ESEA. No Child Left Behind, which was a reaction to low academic achievement of America's students, dramatically expanded the role of the federal government in public education by holding states, school districts, and schools accountable for producing measurable gains in students' achievement in reading and mathematics (Yell & Drasgow, 2005). The purpose of NCLB was to increase the achievement of students in America's public schools. The law required states to establish rigorous systems that hold school districts and schools accountable for measurably improving student achievement. Moreover, the law required states and school districts to use numerical data to provide evidence of improved student outcomes (Yell, Drasgow, & Lowrey, 2005). Specifically, NCLB mandated that all public schools bring every student up to state standards in reading and math within a certain period of time, thus closing the achievement gap based on race, ethnicity, language, and disability.

Students with disabilities were included in NCLB. Specifically, Congress and President Bush believed that to ensure that instruction and achievement for students with disabilities would be improved, and students with disabilities would not be left behind, they had to be included in NCLB's accountability requirements. They also believed that if students with disabilities were excluded from schools' accountability systems, these students would be ignored and not receive the academic attention they deserved. This means that all students with disabilities must be assessed and the results of these assessments must be included in the data used to determine if a school and school district meet accountability requirements under the law. By including students with disabilities in NCLB's assessment and accountability systems, Congress made certain that schools would be held accountable for the educational performance of these students.

The President's Commission on Excellence in Special Education

In October 2002, President Bush created the President's Commission on Excellence in Special Education. The purpose of the commission was to recommend reforms to improve special education and to bring it into alignment with NCLB by requiring special education to be accountable for results and to rely on scientifically based programming. Accountability for results would mean that special education would be driven by increases in academic achievement and improved results for students with disabilities. Scientifically based programming would mean that special educators would only use instructional strategies and methods that were based on solid evidence.

The commission held 13 public hearings in which parents, teachers, administrators, researchers, and representatives of organizations testified about the state of special education. The commission concluded that special education had created an important base of civil rights and legal protections for students with disabilities; nevertheless, special education needed fundamental changes, a shift in priorities, and a new commitment to individual student needs. According to the commission, accountability for results must guide special educators, and the ultimate goal of special education must be to close the achievement gap with nondisabled peers.

The commission issued its findings in a report titled *A New Era: Revitalizing Special Education for Children and Their Families*. The commission issued three major recommendations. First, special education must focus on results rather than process and be judged by the outcomes students achieve. Second, special education must embrace a model of prevention, not a model of failure. That is, rather than waiting for a child to fail before identifying a student as eligible and intervening, reforms must move the system toward early identification and swift intervention using scientifically based strategies and methods. Third, because special education and general education share responsibility for children with disabilities, both systems must work together to provide strong teaching and effective interventions using scientifically based instruction and strategies. The report of the President's Commission and the requirements of NCLB were important influences on Congress during work to reauthorize the IDEA.

The Individuals with Disabilities Education Improvement Act of 2004

On December 3, 2004, President Bush signed the Individuals with Disabilities Education Improvement Act (hereafter IDEIA 2004), P.L. 108-446, into law. The IDEA 2004 builds on NCLB by emphasizing increased accountability for student performance at the classroom, school, and school district levels. The changes were codified in the IDEA.

The changes in IDEA 2004 are significant. Among the most important of these are changes in the IEPs, discipline, and identification of students with learning disabilities. Additionally, IDEA 2004 requires that all special education teachers must be certified in special education and meet the highly qualified teacher requirements of NCLB. The IDEA 2004 also adopted NCLB's requirement regarding the use of instructional strategies and methods that are grounded in scientifically based research. (See Chapter 4 for a description of the changes in IDEIA 2004.)

Table 3.1 depicts the five most recent amendments to the IDEA.

TABLE 3.1 ■ Case Law and Legislation That Shaped Special Education

Date	Case Law and Legislation	Description
1954	*Brown v. Board of Education*	• Prohibited segregation in public schools on the basis of race
1965	Elementary and Secondary Education Act (P.L. 89-10)	• Provided federal funding to assist states in educating students as part of the war on poverty
1966	Amendments to the ESEA, Title VI (P.L. 89-750)	• Provided federal funding to assist states to expand programs for children with disabilities
1970	Education of the Handi-capped Act (P.L. 91-230)	• Expanded state grant programs for children with disabilities • Provided grants to institutions of higher education to train special education teachers • Created regional resource centers
1972	*PARC v. Commonwealth of Pennsylvania*	• Required the State of Pennsylvania to provide students with mental retardation with a free appropriate public education
1972	*Mills v. Board of Education of the District of Columbia*	• Held that because segregation in public schools by race was illegal, it would be unconstitutional for the D.C. Board of Education to deprive students with disabilities from receiving an education
1973	Section 504 of the Rehabilita-tion Act (P.L. 93-112)	• Prohibited discrimination against otherwise qualified individuals with disabilities in programs that receive federal funding
1974	Education Amendments (P.L. 93-380)	• Incorporated the rights from *PARC* and *Mills* into the law
1975	Education for All Handicapped Children Act (P.L. 94-142)	• Provided federal funding to states that agree to educate eligible students with disabilities as required in the EAHCA • Established the rights of eligible students with disabilities to a free appropriate public education in the least restrictive environment • Required schools to develop an IEP • Established procedural safeguards
1986	The Handicapped Children's Protection Act (P.L. 99-372)	• Allowed parents to recover attorney's fees if they prevail in a due process hearing or court case
1986	Education of the Handi-capped Amendments (P.L. 99-457)	• Created federal financial incentives to educate infants (birth through age 2) using early intervention strategies • Required IFSPs for eligible children and their families • Extended the EAHCA's Part B programs to 3- to 5-year-olds in participating states
1990	Individuals with Disabili-ties Education Act (P.L. 101-476)	• Renamed the EAHCA the IDEA • Added traumatic brain injury and autism as new disability categories under the IDEA • Added a transition requirement to the IEP for students age 16 or older • Added language that states were not immune from lawsuits under the 11th Amendment for violations of the IDEA • Changed to "people first" language
1997	Individuals with Disabilities Education Act Amendments (P.L. 105-17)	• Added new IEP contents and changed the IEP team • Added new disciplinary provisions • Required states to offer mediation to parents prior to due process hearings • Reorganized the structure of the IDEA
2004	Individuals with Disabilities Education Improvement Act (P.L. 108-446)	• Defined a "highly qualified" special education teacher • Removed the short-term objectives requirement from IEPs, except for students with severe disabilities • Prohibited states from requiring school districts to use a discrepancy formula for determining eligibility of students with learning disabilities • Encouraged the use of a response-to-intervention model to determine if students were learning disabled

The Every Student Succeeds Act of 2015   The Every Student Succeeds Act (ESSA), P.L. 114-95 was signed into law by President Barack Obama on December 10, 2015. The ESSA, which eliminated many of NCLB's requirements and retained but altered others, is the most recent reauthorization of the ESEA. The law scaled back much of the role given to the U.S. Department of Education in NCLB and gave leeway to the states to implement the new requirements of ESSA. Additionally, the ESSA also eliminated many of the controversial requirements of NCLB such as the adequate yearly progress, accountability provisions, and sanctions. The new law gave the states discretion in designing accountability systems and addressing the needs of low-performing schools.

The ESSA retained the requirements that state departments of education submit state plans and conduct annual testing for students between the third and eighth grades. The reauthorized law also retained the requirement that school districts disaggregate subgroups of students, including students with disabilities, and report on the subgroups' results on the state tests. As was the case under NCLB, students with disabilities will still be required to take statewide assessments, with or without modifications. Students with more severe disabilities may take alternate achievement tests. The ESSA allows school districts to test 1% of their students using alternate achievement tests.

STATE EDUCATION STATUTES

Education is the business of the states; however, with the passage of the EAHCA, special education became essentially federally controlled. States were not required to follow the EAHCA requirements, but by choosing not to adhere to the strictures of the law, a state would forfeit federal funding for special education. All states have chosen to comply with the federal regulations based on the EAHCA. States with special education programs in place were required to revise state law to comply with the EAHCA, and states that were not providing special education programs for children with disabilities were required to develop them. Some states developed statutes and regulations that expanded the federal special education requirements. The inclusion of children who are gifted and talented as eligible for special education services is one such example of states (such as Kansas and New Mexico) going beyond the requirements of the EAHCA. States set their own laws, codes, and regulations specifying teacher certification regulations, teacher-to-pupil ratios, transportation time, and age-span requirements in the classroom. (Readers can access their state's education laws at either the website of their state Department of Education or at the website of the National Conference of State Legislators: www.plol.org/Pages/Search.aspx). In addition, states were allowed some flexibility in funding mechanisms. States were required to distribute 75% of the federal funds to local education agencies; however, they could exceed the 75% allocation if they so desired. As the examples indicate, state statutes and regulations must meet the federal requirements as outlined in the EAHCA, though they may go beyond these requirements.

THE HISTORY OF SPECIAL EDUCATION LAW: FROM ACCESS TO ACCOUNTABILITY

The early history of special education law spans from the efforts of parents and advocacy groups to ensure that children with disabilities were not excluded from public schools through the early court decisions and legislation. This history can be characterized as a struggle to ensure equal access for students with disabilities. These court decisions and the early legislation, culminating in the EAHCA in 1975, were profoundly successful. This law succeeded in securing access to public education for students with disabilities.

Building on these successes, legislation in the late 1990s and early 2000s began to focus on a new issue: ensuring that students with disabilities received beneficial and meaningful educational programs. Moreover, these laws required that schools and school districts be accountable for providing quality programming. Thus, the history of special education can fairly be characterized as a movement from access to quality and accountability. As President Bill Clinton aptly stated on the 25th anniversary of the signing of the EAHCA (U.S. Department of Education, 2000):

> Today I join millions of Americans in celebrating the 25th anniversary of the Individuals with Disabilities Education Act (IDEA)—a landmark law that opens the doors to education and success for more than six million American children each year. As we recognize this milestone, we know that education is the key to our children's future, and it is the IDEA that ensures all children with disabilities have access to a free appropriate public education. We have seen tremendous progress over the past 25 years—students with disabilities are graduating from high school, completing college, and entering the competitive workforce in record numbers—and we must continue this progress over the next 25 years and beyond.

PRESIDENT BILL CLINTON, NOVEMBER 29, 2000

SUMMARY

By the early 1900s, all of the states had compulsory education laws, yet the exclusion of children with disabilities was still widely practiced. The educational rights of children with disabilities were gained largely through the efforts of parents and advocacy groups. The civil rights movement, specifically the U.S. Supreme Court's decision in *Brown v. Board of Education* (1954), provided the impetus for subsequent legislation and litigation granting students with disabilities the right to a free appropriate public education. Two seminal cases in securing these rights were *PARC v. Pennsylvania* (1972) and *Mills v. Board of Education* (1972). The early 1970s witnessed a number of federal legislative efforts to improve the education of students with disabilities. The major pieces of legislation to emerge in this decade were Section 504 of the Rehabilitation Act of 1973 and the Education for All Handicapped Children Act of 1975. The years following the passage of the EAHCA saw Congress attempting to improve the EAHCA through a number of amendments, such as the Handicapped Children's Protection Act and the Individuals with Disabilities Education Act. In 1997, the Individuals

with Disabilities Education Act Amendments made significant changes to the IDEA. Recent federal legislation that have made important changes in special education requirements includes the No Child Left Behind Act, the Every Student Succeeds Act, and the Individuals with Disabilities Education Improvement Act of 2004.

In this chapter, we have provided a brief examination of the historical development of special education through case law and legislation. The struggle for equal educational opportunity for children and youth with disabilities has been arduous and, for the most part, successful. The history of special education law can be characterized as a movement to ensure access to education to one that seeks to ensure quality of educational programming. Although tremendous progress has been made in the early 21st century, much remains to be accomplished. Individuals with disabilities, their advocates, teachers, and all individuals who desire fair and equitable treatment must continue to work toward attaining the goal of delivering a meaningful education for all children and youth with disabilities.

> **Enhanced eText Application Exercise 3.1:** *The Pennsylvania Association for Retarded Children et al., Plaintiffs, v. Commonwealth of Pennsylvania et al., Defendants*

FOR FURTHER INFORMATION

Ballard, J., Ramirez, B., & Weintraub. F. (Eds.). (1982). *Special education in America: Its legal and governmental foundations*. Reston, VA: Council for Exceptional Children.

Levine, E. L., & Wexler, E. M. (1981). *P.L. 94-142: An act of Congress*. New York: Macmillan.

Kode, K. (2017). *Elizabeth Farrell and the history of special education*. Arlington, VA: The Council for Exceptional Children.

Martin, E.W. (2013). *Breakthrough: Special education legislation 1965-1981*. Sarasota, FL: Bardolf & Company.

Winzer, M. A. (1993). *History of special education from isolation to integration*. Washington, DC: Gallaudet Press.

REFERENCES

Beattie v. Board of Education, 172 N. W. 153 (Wis. 1919).

Brown v. Board of Education, 347 U.S. 483 (1954).

Civil Rights Act of 1964, 42 U.S.C. § 2000d.

Colker, R. (2013). *Disabled education: A critical analysis of the Individuals with Disabilities Education Act*. New York: NYU Press.

Department of Public Welfare v. Haas, 154 N.E.2d 265 (Ill. 1958).

Education Amendments of 1972, 20 U.S.C. § 1681 *et seq.*

Education Amendments of 1974, Pub. L. No. 93-380, 88 Stat. 580.

Education for All Handicapped Children Act of 1975, 20 U.S.C. § 1401 *et seq.*

Education of the Handicapped Act of 1970, Pub. L. No. 91-230, §§ 601–662, 84 Stat. 175. of 1986, 20 U.S.C. § 1401 *et seq.*

Elementary and Secondary Education Act of 1965, Pub. L. No. 89-10, 79 Stat. 27.

Elementary and Secondary Education Act, amended by Pub. L. No. 89-750. § 161 [Title VI], 80 Stat. 1204 (1966).

Eyer, T. L. (1998). Greater expectations: How the 1997 IDEA Amendments raise the basic floor of opportunity for children with disabilities. *Education Law Report, 126,* 1–19.

Handicapped Children's Protection Act of 1986, 20 U.S.C. § 1401 *et seq.*

Huefner, D. S., & Herr, C. M. (2011). *Navigating special education law and policy*. Verona, WI: Attainment.

Individuals with Disabilities Education Act of 1990, 20 U.S.C. § 1401 et seq.

Individuals with Disabilities Education Act Amendments of 1997, 20 U.S.C. § 1401 *et seq.*

Individuals with Disabilities Education Act Regulations, 34 C.F.R. § 300.1 *et seq.*

Katsiyannis, A., Yell, M. L., & Bradley, R. (2001). Reflections on the 25th anniversary of the Individuals with Disabilities Education Act. *Remedial and Special Education, 22,* 324–334.

Kode, K. (2017). *Elizabeth Farrell and the history of special education*. Arlington, VA: The Council for Exceptional Children.

Levine, E. L., & Wexler, E. M. (1981). *P.L. 94-142: An act of Congress*. New York: Macmillan.

Martin, E.W. (2013). *Breakthrough: Special education legislation 1965-1981*. Sarasota, FL: Bardolf & Company.

Martin, E. W., Martin, R., & Terman, D.L. (1996). The legislative and litigation history of special education. In *The future of children: Special education for students with disabilities*, 6 (1), 25-39. Princeton: Princeton University Press.

Mills v. Board of Education of the District of Columbia, 348 F. Supp. 866 (D.D.C. 1972).

No Child Left Behind Act, 20 U.S.C. § 16301 *et seq.*

Pennsylvania Association for Retarded Children (PARC) v. Commonwealth of Pennsylvania, 343 F. Supp. 279 (E.D. Pa. 1972).

Rehabilitation Act of 1973, Section 504, 29 U.S.C. § 794.

Siegel-Causey, E., Guy, B., & Guess, D. (1995). Severe and multiple disabilities. In E. L. Meyen & T. M. Skrtic (Eds.), *Special education and student disability, an introduction: Traditional, emerging, and alternative perspectives* (4th ed., pp. 415–448). Denver: Love Publishing.

Smith v. Robinson, 468 U.S. 992 (1984).

Turnbull, A. P., Turnbull, H. R., Erwin, E. J., Soodak, L. C., & Shogren, K. A. (2011). *Families, professionals, and exceptionality: Positive outcomes through partnerships and trust* (6th ed.). Upper Saddle River, NJ: Merrill/Pearson Education.

Turnbull, H. R., Stowe, M. J., & Huerta, N. E. (2007). *Free appropriate public education: The law and children with disabilities* (7th ed.). Denver: Love Publishing.

U.S. Department of Education. (2000, November 29). Education department celebrates IDEA 25th anniversary; progress continues for students with disabilities. Available at www.ed.gov/PressRe-leases/11-2000/112900.html.

Watson v. City of Cambridge, 32 N.E. 864 (Mass. 1893).

Weber, M. C. (2008). *Special education law and litigation treatise* (3rd ed). Horsham, PA: LRP Publications.

Weintraub, F. J., & Ballard, J. (1982). Introduction: Bridging the decades. In J. Ballard, B. Ramirez, & F. Weintraub (Eds.), *Special education in America: Its legal and governmental foundations* (pp. 1–10). Reston, VA: Council for Exceptional Children.

Winzer, M. A. (1993). *History of special education from isolation to integration*. Washington, DC: Gallaudet Press.

Yell, M. L., & Drasgow, E. (2005). *No Child Left Behind: A guide for professionals*. Upper Saddle River, NJ: Merrill/Pearson Education.

Yell, M. L., Drasgow, E., Bradley, R., & Justesen, T. (2004). Critical legal issues in special education. In A. McCray Sorrells, H. J. Reith, & P. T. Sindelar (Eds.), *Issues in special education* (pp. 16–37). Boston: Allyn & Bacon.

Yell, M. L., Drasgow, E., & Lowrey, K. A. (2005). No Child Left Behind and students with autism spectrum disorders. *Focus on Autism and Other Developmental Disorders, 22,* 148–160.

Zettel, J. J., & Ballard, J. (1982). The Education for All Handicapped Children Act of 1975 (P.L. 94-142): Its history, origins, and concepts. In J. Ballard, B. Ramirez, & F. Weintraub (Eds.), *Special education in America: Its legal and governmental foundations* (pp. 11–22). Reston, VA: Council for Exceptional Children.

Chapter 4

The Individuals with Disabilities Education Act

> We must recognize our responsibility to provide education for all children (with disabilities) which meets their unique needs. The denial of the right to education and to equal opportunity within this nation for handicapped children—whether it be outright exclusion from school, the failure to provide an education which meets the needs of a single handicapped child, or the refusal to recognize the handicapped child's right to grow—is a travesty of justice and a denial of equal protection under the law.
>
> SENATOR HARRISON WILLIAMS, PRINCIPAL AUTHOR OF THE EDUCATION FOR ALL HANDICAPPED
> CHILDREN ACT, *CONGRESSIONAL RECORD* (1974, P. 15, 272)

Learner Objectives

At the end of the chapter, students will be able to

4.1 Describe the historical development of the Individuals with Disabilities Education Act (IDEA) from early court rulings and legislation to the enactment of the IDEA.

4.2 Describe the four parts of the IDEA: Parts A, B, C, and D.

4.3 Describe the purpose of the IDEA.

4.4 Describe the reauthorizations of the IDEA.

4.5 Describe the major principles of the IDEA.

4.6 Describe the mechanisms for funding the IDEA.

4.7 Describe the monitoring and enforcement provisions of the IDEA.

On November 29, 1975, while traveling to China on Air Force One, President Gerald Ford signed the Education for All Handicapped Children Act (EAHCA). The EAHCA, often referred to as P.L. 94-142, was enacted to meet the educational needs of students with disabilities. The law was actually an amendment to the Education of the Handicapped Act and became Part B of that law. Part B offered federal funding to states in exchange for the states offering educational services to specified categories of students with disabilities. Moreover, the educational services states offered had to be provided in conformity with the requirements of the EAHCA. Amendments to the EAHCA enacted in 1990, P.L. 101-476, changed the name of the act to the Individuals with Disabilities Education Act (IDEA). Amendments to the IDEA added in 1997 and 2004 further clarified, restructured, and extended the law. In this chapter I will provide an overview of the IDEA. First, I review

 Enhanced eText Video Example 4.1: To view an excellent video issued by the U.S. Department of Education celebrating the 35th anniversary of the IDEA, go to the following link: www.youtube.com/watch?v=DUn6luZQaXE

the historical developments that led to the passage of the IDEA. Second, I examine the purpose, goals, and structure of the law. Third, I consider the major principles of the IDEA and how they affect the education of students with disabilities. Finally, I will examine the changes in the Individuals with Disabilities Education Improvement Act (IDEIA) of 2004.

THE DEVELOPMENT OF THE IDEA

The genesis of the IDEA can be found in the (a) advocacy of various coalitions for children with disabilities, (b) litigation in the federal courts, and (c) federal and state legislation during the 1950s and 1960s (see Chapter 3). Many of the principles that were eventually incorporated into the IDEA can be traced to these court decisions and this legislation. As we have seen, advocacy groups played a major role in securing the principle of an equal educational opportunity for students with disabilities. The advocacy of these groups was aided through the support of national figures such as President John F. Kennedy and Senator Hubert H. Humphrey.

Early Court Rulings and Legislation

Until the 1960s, the cost of educating students with disabilities was borne by state and local governments. During this period, very few teachers were being trained to work with students with disabilities, and extremely small amounts of funds were available to universities to support research (Levine & Wexler, 1981). With the passage of the Elementary and Secondary Education Act (ESEA) in 1965, and amendments to the ESEA in 1966 and 1968, the federal government began to provide funding to states to assist efforts to educate students with disabilities through various grant programs.

In 1970, the Education of the Handicapped Act (EHA) was signed into law. The EHA (a) consolidated the earlier grant programs under one law, (b) provided additional federal money to fund pilot projects in the states, (c) funded institutions of higher education to develop teacher training programs in special education, and (d) funded regional resource centers to provide technical assistance to state and local school districts.

The two seminal court cases in 1972, *Pennsylvania Association for Retarded Citizens (PARC) v. Pennsylvania* and *Mills v. Board of Education District of Columbia*, resulted in requirements that the Pennsylvania and D.C. public schools provide access to public education for students with disabilities. Moreover, these cases resulted in basic procedural rights being granted to students with disabilities. These cases influenced the federal government to amend the EHA in 1974. The Education Amendments to the EHA required each state that received federal funding to provide (a) full educational opportunities, (b) procedural safeguards, and (c) education in the least restrictive environment for students with disabilities. Nonetheless, advocacy groups believed that the law was not sufficiently enforceable and neither parents nor advocacy groups would be able to ensure that local school districts and states were meeting their obligations under the law.

Additionally, by the early 1970s, many states had their own statutes and regulations regarding the education of students with disabilities. Unfortunately, the efforts across states were uneven, and many believed that a more enforceable federal standard was needed. In fact, in late 1975 Congress reported that during this period approximately 1.75 million students with disabilities were excluded from public schools and 2.2 million were educated in programs that did not meet their needs. In response to these problems, four bills were introduced in the Senate regarding the education of students with disabilities: S.896, introduced by Senator Jennings Randolph, to extend the life of the Education of the Handicapped Act for 3 years; S.34, introduced by Senator Ernest Hollings, to fund research on the problems of children with autism; S.808, introduced by Senator Mike Gravel, to provide federal funds for screening preschool children for the presence of learning disabilities; and S.6, introduced by Senator Harrison Williams, a comprehensive bill for the education of students with disabilities based on the *Mills* and *PARC* cases. The purpose of Williams's bill was to mandate that a free appropriate public education be available to all students with disabilities by 1976. These four bills were the subject of Senate hearings held in 1973. Eventually, conference committees agreed on a bill that would be known as the Education of the Handicapped Amendments of 1974, P.L. 93-380. The 93rd Congress, however, failed to act on this bill before adjournment.

The Passage of the IDEA

Because bills pending at the end of a final session of Congress die, Senator Williams had to reintroduce his bill, S.6, the Education for All Handicapped Children Act (EAHCA), in the next session. In April 1973, the Senate Subcommittee on the Handicapped held hearings on this bill in Newark, New Jersey; Boston, Massachusetts; Harrisburg, Pennsylvania; St. Paul, Minnesota; and Columbia, South Carolina. Even though the years since the passage of Title VI of the ESEA in 1966 had seen progress in the education of students with disabilities, the hearings on Senator Williams's bill indicated that significant problems remained.

The Senate passed S.6, and the House passed a similar bill, H.7217. When bills are passed in both houses of Congress, a conference committee is appointed to write a final bill by combining the two bills and ironing out any differences between them. In this situation, the conference committee resolved differences in the House and Senate bills and sent one bill, the EAHCA, to both houses of Congress. The Senate and the House approved the bill and sent it to the president for signing. On November 29, 1975, President Gerald Ford signed the 142nd bill passed by the 94th Congress, the EAHCA, into law. Federal regulations implementing the law took effect on August 23, 1977.

President Ford had serious reservations about the EAHCA; however, he signed the bill into law, perhaps because the bill had veto-proof majorities in the House and the Senate. President Ford believed that the law promised more than the federal government could deliver and that it gave the federal government too much control over state and local matters. Concerning the signing of EAHCA, Ford stated:

> Unfortunately, this bill promises more than the Federal Government can deliver, and its good intentions could be thwarted by the many unwise provisions it contains. Everyone can agree with the objective stated in the title of this bill—educating all handicapped children in our Nation. The key question is whether the bill will really accomplish that objective.... Despite my strong support for full educational opportunities for our handicapped children, the funding levels proposed in this bill will simply not be possible if Federal expenditures are to be brought under control and a balanced budget achieved over the next few years. There are other features in the bill which I believe to be objectionable and which should be changed. It contains a vast array of detailed, complex, and costly administrative requirements which would unnecessarily assert Federal control over traditional State and local government functions. It establishes complex requirements under which tax dollars would be used to support administrative paperwork and not educational programs.

PRESIDENT GERALD FORD, DECEMBER 2, 1975

The EAHCA provided federal funding to states to assist them in educating students with disabilities. States wanting to receive federal funding were required to submit a state plan to the Bureau of Education for the Handicapped. The purpose of the plan was to describe the state's policies and procedures to educate students with disabilities in accordance with the procedures contained in the EAHCA. If the bureau approved the plan, the state was obligated to guarantee a free appropriate public education to students with disabilities in return for the federal funding it would receive. The federal funding that states received would be based on an annual count of all children and youth served under the law. The EAHCA made the federal government a partner with the states in educating students with disabilities who were covered by the law.

All but one state, New Mexico, submitted a plan for federal funding under P.L. 94-142. New Mexico decided not to implement the EAHCA nor to accept the federal funds. An advocacy group for citizens with disabilities in New Mexico, the New Mexico Association for Retarded Citizens, sued the state for failing to provide an appropriate education for students with disabilities in the case *New Mexico Association for Retarded Citizens v. New Mexico* (1982). The association sued under Section 504 of the Rehabilitation Act of 1973, which prevents entities that receive federal funds from discriminating against individuals with disabilities. The association maintained that the state discriminated against individuals with disabilities by denying them an appropriate education. (For elaborations on Section 504, see Chapter 5.) The association prevailed. The decision indicated that even though a state did not accept federal funding and the requirements attached to the funds (adherence to P.L. 94-142), it would still have to comply with Section 504, a civil rights law that contained no funding provisions. New Mexico, therefore, was required to provide a free appropriate public education to students with disabilities even though the state received no federal funding under the IDEA. New Mexico subsequently submitted a state plan to the Bureau of Education for the Handicapped, opting to implement the law and accept the federal funding. Following this action, all 50 states were participants in federal funding through the EAHCA.[1]

THE PURPOSE AND STRUCTURE OF THE IDEA

The IDEA was enacted to assist states in meeting the educational needs of students with disabilities via federal funding of state efforts. According to the U.S. Supreme Court, however,

> Congress did not content itself with passage of a simple funding statute. Rather the [IDEA] confers upon disabled students an enforceable substantive right to public education ... and conditions federal financial assistance upon states' compliance with substantive and procedural goals of the Act. (*Honig v. Doe*, 1988, p. 597)

Purpose of the IDEA

In 1975 Congress stated that:

> Disability is a natural part of the human experience and in no way diminishes the right of individuals to participate in or contribute to our society. Improving educational results for children with disabilities is an essential element of our national policy of ensuring equality of opportunity, full participation, independent living, and economic self-sufficiency for individuals with disabilities.

(20 U.S.C. § 1401[c][1])

Nonetheless, Congress also found that prior to the enactment of the EAHCA in 1975, the educational needs of millions of children with disabilities were not being met because many (a) children with disabilities were excluded from public schools; (b) children with disabilities who did attend public schools often did not receive an education that was appropriate for their needs; (c) children with disabilities were not diagnosed, which prevented them from receiving a successful educational experience; and (d) states and local school districts lacked adequate resources, which forced families to find services outside the public school system.

---

[1]In 1990, Congress changed the name of the EAHCA to the Individuals with Disabilities Education Act (IDEA). For the remainder of this chapter, I will refer to the law as the IDEA.

The purpose of the IDEA is to

> ensure that all children with disabilities have available to them a free appropriate public education that emphasizes special education and related services designed to meet their unique needs and prepare them for further education, employment, and independent living, to ensure that the rights of children with disabilities and parents of such children are protected, to assist states, localities, educational service agencies, and Federal agencies to provide for the education of all children with disabilities.

(IDEA, 20 U.S.C. § 1400[d])

Rather than establishing substantive educational standards to ensure that the goal of the IDEA was fulfilled, Congress created an elaborate set of procedural safeguards. The purpose of these safeguards was to allow parental input into a school's decisions and to maximize the likelihood that children with a disability would receive a free appropriate public education.

Who Is Protected?   Students meeting the IDEA's definition of a student with disabilities receive the procedural protections of the law. Students with disabilities, determined to be eligible in accordance with the provisions of the IDEA, are entitled to receive special education and related services. The determination of eligibility is made on an individual basis by the multidisciplinary team in accordance with guidelines set forth in the law. The IDEA uses a categorical approach to define students with disabilities by setting forth categories of disabilities. Not all students with disabilities are protected; only those students with disabilities included in the IDEA, and only if those disabilities have an adverse impact on their education, are eligible to receive a special education. The IDEA categories are exhaustive.

Categories of Disabilities   The IDEA disability categories (see Figure 4.1) and regulations defining them can be found at 20 U.S.C. § 1401(a) and 34 C.F.R. § 300.7(a)(1)–(b)(13). The Office of Special Education Programs (OSEP) solicited public comments regarding the possible addition of a category for attention deficit hyperactivity disorder (ADHD) in the 1990 amendments to the IDEA. ADHD was not made a separate category; however, OSEP did issue a policy memo stating that students with ADHD could be eligible for special education under the categories of specific learning disability, serious emotional disturbance, or other health impairment (Joint Policy Memorandum, 1991). Students with ADHD may also be eligible for services under Section 504 of the Rehabilitation Act.

In the IDEA Amendments of 1997, the terminology "serious emotional disturbance" was changed to "emotional disturbance." The reason for this change was to eliminate the pejorative connotation of the term *serious*. The change was not intended to have substantive or legal significance (Senate Report, 1997).

FIGURE 4.1
Categories of Disabilities

Autism
Deaf-blindness
Deafness
Hearing impairment
Intellectual disability
Multiple disabilities
Orthopedic impairments
Other health impairment
Emotional disturbance
Specific learning disability
Speech or language impairment
Traumatic brain injury
Visual impairment, including blindness

In October 2010 President
Barack Obama signed Rosa's law,
which required the federal government to replace the term "mental
retardation" with the term "intellectual disability" in the IDEA and all
other federal health, education, and

Enhanced eText **Video Example 4.2:**
To view an excellent **video** on this law
and on the successful campaign to
eliminate the word "retarded," go to the
following website:
www.youtube.com/watch?v=bdx95EnWkms

labor laws. The law was named for Rosa Marcello, a child with Down syndrome.

States are required to provide services to students who meet the criteria in the IDEA.
This does not mean that states must adopt every category exactly as specified in the IDEA.
States may combine categories (e.g., many states combine deafness and hearing impairment),
divide categories (e.g., many states divide the category of intellectual disabilities in two or
more categories, such as mild, moderate, and severe), use different terminology (e.g., *serious
emotional disturbance* goes by a number of different terms, such as *emotionally and behaviorally
disordered* or *emotionally disabled*), or expand the definitions (e.g., Minnesota does not exclude
students identified as socially maladjusted in its definition of emotional or behavioral disorders, as does the federal definition). At a minimum, however, all students with disabilities
who meet the appropriate criteria as defined in the IDEA categories must receive services.

Age Requirements

The IDEA requires that a program of special education and related
services be provided to all eligible students with disabilities between the ages of 3 and 21.
States are required to identify and evaluate children from birth to age 21, even if the state
does not provide educational services to students with disabilities in the 3-to-5 and 18-to-
21 age groups (IDEA Regulations, 34 C.F.R. § 300.300, comment 3). The duty to provide
special education to qualified students with disabilities is absolute between the ages of 6 and
17. If states do not require an education for students without disabilities between ages 3 to
5 and 18 through 21, they are not required to educate students in those age groups (IDEA,
20 U.S.C. § 1412[2][B]).

If a special education student graduates with a diploma, successfully completes an appropriate individualized education program (IEP) leading to graduation, or voluntarily drops
out of school, the school's obligation to the student ends (*Wexler v. Westfield*, 1986). If the
graduation is merely used to terminate a school district's obligation, however, the district
can be required to supply compensatory education, such as educational services beyond the
age of 21 (*Helms v. Independent School District #3*, 1985).

Infants and Toddlers

An amendment to the IDEA, passed in the Education of the
Handicapped Amendments of 1986 (P.L. 99-457), was the infants and toddlers program.
This law was codified in the IDEA. This amendment was originally added to the then
EAHCA as Part H. Part H, which became Part C in the IDEA Amendments of 1997,
provided incentive grants to states that provide special education and related services to
children with disabilities from birth through age 2. At age 3, a child with a disability is
entitled to receive services under Part B. When a child who receives early intervention
services turns 3 years of age, the state is required to convene a transition meeting with the
Part C lead agency, the local educational agency (LEA), and the parents to ensure that a
smooth transition takes place.

The purpose of the law was to (a) enhance the development of infants and toddlers with
disabilities and to minimize their potential for delay, (b) reduce educational costs by mini-
mizing the need for special education and related services after infants and toddlers with
disabilities reach school age, (c) minimize the likelihood of institutionalization of individuals with disabilities, and (d) enhance the capacity of families to meet the special needs of
infants and toddlers. This amendment is codified at 20 U.S.C. §§ 1541–1585. Regulations
implementing this section of the IDEA are codified at 34 C.F.R. §§ 303.1–303.653. Part C
requires that participating states develop a statewide system of multidisciplinary interagency

programs to provide early intervention services. The populations targeted for this program are infants and toddlers who:

1. Are experiencing developmental delays … in one or more of the following areas:
   (i) Cognitive development.
   (ii) Physical development, including vision and hearing.
   (iii) Communication development.
   (iv) Social or emotional development.
   (v) Adaptive development; or
2. Have a diagnosed physical or mental condition that has a high probability of resulting in developmental delay.

   (a) The term may also include, at a state's discretion, children from birth through age 2 who are at risk of having substantial developmental delays if early intervention services are not provided.

(IDEA Regulations, 34 C.F.R. § 303.16)

Infants and toddlers may be designated as developmentally delayed and receive special education services. It is not required that the children fit into a category of disabilities included in the IDEA to receive services.

States have an option of submitting plans to participate in Part C funding. To determine if a state has submitted a plan and is obligated under Part C, consult state statutes and regulations.

Structure of the IDEA

The IDEA is codified at 20 U.S.C. §§ 1400–1485. Originally the law was divided into eight subchapters (Parts A through H). In the IDEA Amendments of 1997, the law was restructured into four subchapters. The structure of the IDEA is depicted in Table 4.1.

Title I of the IDEA

Title I consists of four parts. Of these four parts, Part B contains the requirements that school personnel must be most concerned with when developing programs for students in special education. I next review the four parts of Title I.

TABLE 4.1 ■ The Four Parts of the IDEA

Part	Purpose	Contents
Part A	General provisions	Part A contains findings of fact regarding the education of students with disabilities that existed when the IDEA was passed. This section also contains definitions of terms that are used throughout the IDEA.
Part B	Assistance for education of all children with disabilities	Part B contains the information regarding the state grant program in which states submit plans that detail how the state will ensure a free appropriate public education to all qualified children and youth with disabilities who live in the state.
Part C	Infants and toddlers with disabilities	Part C provides categorical grants to states contingent on states adhering to the provisions of law, which requires participating states to develop and implement statewide interagency programs of early intervention services for infants and toddlers with disabilities and their families.
Part D	National activities to improve education of children with disabilities	Part D contains support or discretionary programs that support the implementation of the IDEA and assist states in improving the education of students with disabilities. Supporting research, personnel preparation, and professional development are especially important goals of Part D.

Part A of the IDEA   Part A is the section of the law in which Congress justifies the IDEA (Yell, Drasgow, Bradley, & Justesen, 2004). It contains findings of fact regarding the education of students with disabilities that existed when the IDEA was passed. This section also contains definitions of terms that are used throughout the IDEA. These definitions are crucial. For example, the requirements necessary to be a highly qualified special education teacher are listed in Part A. The goals of the IDEA are also included in this part.

Part B of the IDEA   Part B addresses educational requirements for students ages 3 through 21 and thus is the section with which special education teachers and administrators should be most familiar. Part B contains the information regarding the state grant program in which states submit plans that detail how they will ensure a free appropriate public education to all qualified children and youth with disabilities who live in the state. If the plan is approved, the state receives federal financial assistance. Part B also contains the procedural safeguards designed to protect the interests of children and youth with disabilities.

The IDEA was originally enacted to address the failure of states to meet the educational needs of students with disabilities. The method chosen to accomplish this goal is federal funding for states submitting special education plans that meet the IDEA's requirements. After the plan is approved, the state assumes the responsibility for meeting the provisions of the law. In addition to setting the formulas by which states can receive funds, the IDEA contains provisions to ensure that all qualifying students with disabilities receive a free appropriate education and that procedural protections are granted to students and their parents. These provisions are as follows: (a) zero reject, (b) identification and evaluation, (c) free appropriate public education, (d) least restrictive environment, (e) procedural safeguards, (f) technology-related assistance, (g) personnel development, and (h) parental participation.

Readers should note that even though some scholars have divided Part B into major principles for discussion purposes (e.g., Katsiyannis, Yell, & Bradley, 2001; Turnbull, Turnbull, Erwin, Soodak, & Shogren, 2010; Turnbull, Turnbull, & Wehmeyer, 2009), neither the IDEA's statutory language nor OSEP recognizes the division of the law into these principles (Yell et al., 2004). It is, however, a useful tool for facilitating a thorough understanding of the law.

Zero Reject   According to the zero-reject principle, all students with disabilities eligible for services under the IDEA are entitled to a free appropriate public education. This principle applies regardless of the severity of the disability. According to the U.S. Court of Appeals for the First Circuit, public education is to be provided to all students with educational disabilities, unconditionally and without exception (*Timothy W. v. Rochester, New Hampshire, School District*, 1989).

The state must assure that all students with disabilities, from birth to age 21, residing in the state who are in need of special education and related services or are suspected of having disabilities and needing special education are identified, located, and evaluated (IDEA Regulations, 34 C.F.R. § 300.220). These requirements include children with disabilities attending private schools. This requirement is called the *child find system*. States are free to develop their own child find systems (IDEA, 20 U.S.C. § 1414[a][1][A]). The state plan must identify the agency that will coordinate the child find tasks, the activities it will use, and the resources needed to accomplish the child find. School districts are usually responsible for conducting child find activities within their jurisdiction. The child find applies to all children and youth in the specified age range, regardless of the severity of the disability. Furthermore, the child find requirement is an affirmative duty, because parents do not have to request that a school district identify and evaluate a student with disabilities. In fact, parents' failure to notify a school district will not relieve a school district of its obligations (Norlin, 2014). It is up to the school district to find these students. When students are identified in the child find, the school district is required to determine whether they have a disability under the IDEA.

A school district's child find system can take many forms. One method is the general public notice. School districts are obligated to notify the public as a means of locating children with disabilities. Additional methods that may be used to locate and identify children with disabilities include referrals, public meetings, door-to-door visits, home and community visits, brochures, speakers, contacting pediatricians, contacting day-care providers, kindergarten screening, and public awareness efforts. If a school district becomes aware of or suspects that a student may need special education, an evaluation is required.

Identification and Evaluation   In hearings on the original EAHCA, Congress heard testimony indicating that many schools were using tests inappropriately and therefore were making improper placement decisions (Turnbull et al., 2010). Sometimes schools placed students in special education based on a single test, administered and placed students using tests that were not reliable or valid, or used tests that were discriminatory. To remedy these problems, the IDEA includes protection in evaluation procedures (PEPs). A fair and accurate evaluation is extremely important to ensure proper placement and, therefore, an appropriate education. The PEPs were incorporated into the IDEA to address abuses in the assessment process (Salvia, Ysseldyke, & Bolt, 2013).

The IDEIA made a few changes in the initial evaluation process. The statutory language makes it clear that a child's parents, the state educational agency (SEA), or LEA may request an initial evaluation. Moreover, when an LEA decides to evaluate a child for special education services and seeks consent from the child's parents, it must determine eligibility within 60 days of receiving consent or within the timeline that the state allows, if it is less than 60 days. The timeline does not apply, however, if the parents repeatedly fail to produce the child for the evaluation. (For elaborations on the identification of students with disabilities, see Chapter 9.)

Free Appropriate Public Education   The IDEA requires that states have policies assuring all students with disabilities the right to a free appropriate public education (FAPE). The FAPE requirement has both procedural and substantive components (Yell, Katsiyannis, Ennis, & Losinsky, 2013). The procedural components are the extensive procedural protections afforded to students and their parents. These protections ensure the parents' right to meaningful participation in all decisions affecting their child's education. The substantive right to a FAPE consists of

> special education and related services which (A) have been provided at public expense, under public supervision and direction, and without charge, (B) meet standards of the state educational agency (SEA), (C) include an appropriate preschool, elementary, or secondary school education in the state involved, and (D) are provided in conformity with the Individualized Education Program.

(IDEA 20 U.S.C. § 1401[18][C])

Special education is defined in the statutory language as "specially designed instruction, at no charge to the parents or guardians, to meet the unique needs of a child with a disability" (IDEA, 20 U.S.C. § 1404[a][16]). Related services are any developmental, corrective, or supportive services that students need to benefit from special education (IDEA, 20 U.S.C. § 1404[a][17]).

Public schools must provide special education and related services to eligible students at no cost. If a student is placed out of the school district by a school district, the home district retains financial responsibility. This includes tuition fees and related service charges. The only fees that schools may collect from parents of children with disabilities are those fees that are also imposed on the parents of children without disabilities (e.g., physical education fees, lunch fees).

The IDEA also acknowledges the rights of states to set standards for a FAPE. The IDEA requires that local school districts meet states' special education standards. These standards may exceed the minimum level of educational services provided for in the IDEA. For example, Massachusetts requires that schools provide a FAPE that will assure a student's maximum possible development (Massachusetts General Laws Annotated, 1978), a standard greater than that contained in the IDEA. State standards may not, however, set lower educational benefits than those contained in the IDEA. (See Chapter 8 for an extensive discussion of the FAPE mandate.)

One of the most crucial aspects of the substantive component is that the special education and related services must be provided in conformity with the IEP. An IEP must be developed for all students in special education. (See Chapter 10 for elaborations of IEP requirements.) The school district is responsible for providing the student's education as described in the IEP. The IEP must be in effect at the beginning of the school year and be reviewed at least annually (IDEA, 20 U.S.C. § 1414[a][5]).

Least Restrictive Environment   The IDEA mandates that students with disabilities are educated with their peers without disabilities to the maximum extent appropriate (IDEA Regulations, 34 C.F.R. § 300.550[b][1]). Students in special education can only be removed to separate classes or schools when the nature or severity of their disabilities is such that they cannot receive an appropriate education in a general education classroom with supplementary aids and services (IDEA Regulations, 34 C.F.R. § 300.550[b][2]). When students are placed in segregated settings, schools must provide them with opportunities to interact with their peers without disabilities where appropriate (e.g., art class, physical education).

To ensure that students are educated in the least restrictive environment (LRE) that is appropriate for their needs, school districts must ensure that a complete continuum of alternative placements is available. This continuum consists of regular classes, resource rooms, special classes, special schools, homebound instruction, and instruction in hospitals and institutions (IDEA Regulations, 34 C.F.R. § 300.551). (For a discussion of LRE, see Chapter 11.)

Procedural Safeguards   A central part of the IDEA is the procedural safeguards designed to protect the interests of students with disabilities. The IDEA uses an extensive system of procedural safeguards to ensure that parents are equal participants in the special education process (IDEA Regulations, 34 C.F.R. § 300.500 *et seq.*). These safeguards consist of four components: general safeguards, the independent educational evaluation, the appointment of surrogate parents, and dispute resolution (i.e., state complaint resolution system, mediation, resolution session, and the due process hearing).

The general safeguards for parents and students consist of notice and consent requirements. Specifically, notice must be given to parents a reasonable amount of time prior to the school's initiating or changing or refusing to initiate or change the student's identification, evaluation, or educational placement (IDEA Regulations, 34 C.F.R. § 300.504[a] *et seq.*). Informed consent must be obtained from a student's parents prior to conducting a preplacement evaluation and again prior to initial placement in a special education program (IDEA Regulations, 34 C.F.R. § 300.504[b] *et seq.*).

When the parents of a child with disabilities disagree with the educational evaluation of the school, they have a right to obtain an independent evaluation at public expense (IDEA Regulations, 34 C.F.R. § 300.503). The school has to supply the parents, on request, with information about where the independent educational evaluation may be obtained. When the parents decide to have the evaluation done independently, the district must pay for the cost of the evaluation or see that it is provided at no cost to the parents. If, however, the school believes its evaluation was appropriate, the school may initiate a due process hearing. If the result of the hearing is that the school's evaluation was appropriate, the parents do not have the right to receive the evaluation at public expense. Parent-initiated independent evaluations, when done at the parents' own expense, must be considered by the school. Results may also be presented as evidence at a due process hearing. Finally, a hearing officer can request an independent evaluation as part of a hearing; in this case, the cost must be borne by the school.

When a child's parents cannot be located or the child is a ward of the state, the agency is responsible for appointing surrogate parents to protect the rights of the child. Employees of the school or individuals with conflicts of interest cannot serve as surrogate parents. The method of selecting a surrogate parent must be in accordance with state law. The actual selection and appointment methods, therefore, are not determined by the IDEA. The IDEA does require that the surrogate parent must represent the child in all matters relating to the provision of special education to the child (IDEA Regulations, 34 C.F.R. § 300.514 *et seq.*).

When parents and the school disagree about identification, evaluation, placement, or any matters pertaining to the FAPE, either party may request a due process hearing. For example, if the parents refuse consent for evaluation or initial placement, the school may use the due process hearing to conduct an evaluation or place the child (IDEA Regulations, 34 C.F.R. § 300.504[b][3]). The IDEA Amendments of 1997 require that states offer parents the option of resolving their disputes through the mediation process prior to going to a due process hearing. The mediation process is voluntary and must not be used to deny or delay parents' right to a due process hearing. A trained mediator who is knowledgeable about the laws and regulations regarding the provision of special education and related services conducts the mediation. A mediator has no decision-making powers as do impartial due process hearing officers. Rather, the mediator attempts to facilitate an agreement between the parents and school officials regarding the matter in dispute. If attempts to mediate and reach agreement are not successful, either party may request an impartial due process hearing.

Either the SEA or the LEA that is responsible for the education of the student must conduct the due process hearing. A due process hearing is a forum in which both sides present their arguments to an impartial third party, the due process hearing officer. During the hearing, the student must remain in the program or placement in effect when the hearing was requested. A school district cannot unilaterally change placement or program during the pendency of the due process hearing or judicial action. The IDEA provision that mandates the student's placement or program must not be changed without the agreement of both parties is referred to as the *stay-put provision* (IDEA Regulations, 34 C.F.R. § 300.513). The stay-put provision may be abrogated in situations where a student with disabilities brings a weapon to school, uses or sells illegal drugs, or presents a danger to other students or to staff. (See Chapter 13 for elaborations on the stay-put provision and students with disabilities.)

Any party in the hearing has the right to be represented by counsel, present evidence, compel the attendance of witnesses, examine and cross-examine witnesses, prohibit the introduction of evidence not introduced five days prior to the hearing, obtain a written or electronic verbatim record of the hearing, and be provided with the written findings of fact by the hearing officer. Additionally, the parent may have the child present and may open the hearing to the public. Following the hearing, the hearing officer announces the decision. This decision is binding on both parties. Either party, however, may appeal the decision. In most states, the appeal is to the SEA. The decision of the agency can then be appealed to the state or federal court.

The IDEA also includes an alternative to using the due process hearing for resolving disputes. A student's parents may file a state complaint with the state administrative agency regarding an alleged denial of appropriate services. Under this system each state educational agency must have a system for resolving complaints. This system includes a procedure for filing a complaint, investigating the complaint, and mandating remedies when a denial of appropriate services is found. (For elaboration on procedural safeguards, see Chapter 12.)

Technology-Related Assistance   The pervasive impact of technology on the lives of individuals with disabilities was recognized in a report issued by the Federal Office of Technology Assessment in 1982 (Gibbons, 1982). The report identified a lack of comprehensive, responsive, and coordinated mechanisms to deliver and fund technology to improve the lives of individuals with disabilities. In 1988, Congress passed the Technology-Related Assistance for

Individuals with Disabilities Act (29 U.S.C. §§ 3001–3007). The purpose of the law, which was reauthorized in 1994, was to establish a program of federal grants to states to promote technology-related assistance to individuals with disabilities. Assistive technology, as defined in the law, includes both technological devices and services. Congress further recognized the importance of technology in the lives of children and youth with disabilities by incorporating the definitions of assistive technology devices and services from the Technology Act into the IDEA:

> The term "assistive technology device" means any item, piece of equipment, or product system, whether acquired commercially off the shelf, modified, or customized, that is used to increase, maintain, or improve functional capabilities of [children] with disabilities.
>
> The term "assistive technology service" means any service that directly assists a [child] with a disability in the selection, acquisition, or use of an assistive technology device. Such a term includes—
>
> A. the evaluation of the needs of a [child] with a disability including a functional evaluation of the [child] in the [child's] customary environment;
> B. purchasing, leasing, or otherwise providing for the acquisition of assistive technology devices by [children] with disabilities;
> C. selecting, designing, fitting, customizing, adapting, applying, retaining, repairing, or replacing of assistive technology devices;
> D. coordinating and using other therapies, interventions, or services with assistive technology devices;
> E. training or technical assistance for a [child] with disabilities or, where appropriate, the family of a [child] with disabilities; and
> F. training or technical assistance for professionals.

(IDEA, 20 U.S.C. § 1401, 25–26)

These definitions were included in the IDEA; however, nothing in the law mandated that participating states provide assistive technology devices or services to students. Julnes and Brown (1993) noted that this was because assistive technology devices and services were implicitly required by the EAHCA prior to the inclusion of the assistive technology definitions in 1990. Regulations implementing these definitions support this contention. The regulations provide that:

> Each public agency shall ensure that assistive technology or assistive technology services, or both ... are made available to a child with a disability if required as part of the child's—
>
> A. Special education under § 300.17;
> B. Related services under § 300.16; or
> C. Supplementary aids and services under § 300.550(b)(2).

(IDEA Regulations, 34 C.F.R. § 300.308)

The regulations indicate that assistive technology devices and services should be included in the IEP if necessary to provide a FAPE as a special education service or a related service or to maintain children and youth with disabilities in the LRE through the provision of supplementary aids and services.

The IDEA Amendments of 1997 added a requirement regarding technology and special education to the IEP. IEP teams are now required to consider whether students with disabilities, regardless of category, need assistive technology devices and services. In the IDEIA, however, Congress added a section on related services that specifically stated that schools did not have to provide or maintain surgically implanted devices (e.g., cochlear implants). Because such a device is medical in nature, it cannot be considered an assistive technology device.

In 2004, President George W. Bush signed the Assistive Technology Act of 2004. The purpose of the law was to expand access to technology for individuals with disabilities. The law assisted students with disabilities in several ways. First, it required that schools use assistive technology resources when they are necessary to improve transitions for students with disabilities. Second, it ensured that students with disabilities have better information and support when they apply for loans for assistive devices. Third, it helped to raise public awareness about the importance of assistive technology devices.

Personnel Development   States are required to submit a plan to the U.S. Department of Education that describes the kind and number of personnel needed in the state to meet the goals of the IDEA. To receive funding from the state, school districts must also provide a description of the personnel they will need to ensure a FAPE to all students with disabilities.

The original EAHCA required states to develop and implement a Comprehensive System of Personnel Development plan that ensured that an adequate supply of special education and related services personnel was available and that these individuals received adequate and appropriate preparation. The IDEIA eliminated the language requiring a comprehensive system of personnel development in each state. Instead it substituted the term *state personnel development grant* and required that states ensure that special education teachers and related services personnel meet state-approved or state-recognized certification/licensure requirements. Additionally, districts had to use 100% of their funding under these grants for personnel preparation and professional development activities. The purpose of the professional development activities, according to the IDEIA, was to enable teachers to deliver scientifically based academic instruction and behavioral interventions to their students.

States had to ensure that by the end of the 2005–2006 school year, all special education teachers would meet the highly qualified requirements of No Child Left Behind (NCLB), the 2001 reauthorization of the Elementary and Secondary Education Act (see Chapter 7 on the Every Students Succeeds Act). The NCLB requirements were also incorporated into the IDEA. Furthermore, the highly qualified requirements of NCLB and IDEA did not allow emergency, temporary, or provisional certification or licenses to be issued in lieu of full state special education certification/licensing requirements; and state certification requirements could not be waived. Additionally, states had to have a policy that required school districts to have measurable goals to recruit, hire, train, and retain highly qualified personnel. The Every Student Succeeds Act (ESSA) of 2015 eliminated the highly qualified teacher requirements of NCLB and IDEA. The ESSA and now the IDEA requires that special education teachers at the elementary, middle, and secondary levels have a bachelor's degree, hold full state special education licensure or pass a special education licensing examination, and have a special education teaching license (IDEA, 20 U.S.C. § 1412[a][14][c]). Special education teachers cannot meet the IDEA's requirements if their certification or licensure is waived on an emergency, temporary, or provisional basis (Gamm, 2017).

To ensure that these requirements were met, states had to delineate current and projected needs for special education and related services personnel, and coordinate efforts among school districts, colleges, and universities to see that personnel needs were met and that professional development activities were offered. Grants are also made available to colleges and universities to train special education teachers (IDEA Regulations, 34 C.F.R. § 381).

The states also needed procedures for adopting promising practices, materials, and technology (IDEA Regulations, 34 C.F.R. § 382). Furthermore, states had to disseminate knowledge derived from research and demonstration projects to special educators. Finally, school districts needed to provide a description of special education personnel to the state to receive special education funding.

Parent Participation   Since the early days of special education litigation, the parents of students with disabilities have played an important role in helping schools to meet the educational needs of their children. Key provisions of the IDEA that require parental participation are scattered throughout the law. Parents must be involved in evaluation, IEP meetings, and placement decisions. The IDEA Amendments of 1997 also required that schools give progress reports to the parents of students with disabilities as frequently as they give reports to the parents of students without disabilities. The goal of this principle is to have parents play a meaningful role in the education of their children and to maintain a partnership between schools and families. Parental involvement is crucial to successful results for students. Indeed, this provision has been one of the cornerstones of the IDEA.

Part C of the IDEA   Congress recognized the importance of early intervention for young children when it passed the Education of the Handicapped Amendments in 1986, P.L. 99-457 (IDEA, 20 U.S.C. §§ 1471–1485). This law, which became subchapter H of the IDEA, made categorical grants to states contingent on states adhering to the provisions of the law, which required participating states to develop and implement statewide interagency programs of early intervention services for infants and toddlers with disabilities and their families. With the consolidation of the IDEA in the amendments of 1997, Part H became Part C.

Part C is a discretionary or support program. In addition to extending Part B protections to infants and toddlers with disabilities and strengthening incentives for states to provide services to infants and toddlers (birth to age 3), this section also created a variety of national activities to improve the education of children with disabilities through investments in areas including research, training, and technical assistance (Yell et al., 2004).

The IDEA defines infants and toddlers as children from birth through age 2 who need early intervention services because they are experiencing developmental delays or have a diagnosed physical or mental condition that puts them at risk of developing developmental delays. States may include infants and toddlers who are at risk of having substantial developmental delays if they do not receive early intervention services. Early intervention services can be any developmental services, which are provided at public expense and under public supervision, that are designed to meet the physical, cognitive, communication, social or emotional, and adaptive needs of the child. Early intervention services may include family training, counseling, home visits, speech pathology, occupational therapy, physical therapy, psychological services, case management services, medical services (for diagnostic or evaluation purposes only), health services, social work services, vision services, assistive technology devices and services, transportation, and related costs. To the maximum extent appropriate, these services must be provided in natural environments (e.g., home and community settings) in which children without disabilities participate.

The infants and toddlers program does not require that the SEA assume overall responsibility for the early intervention programs. The agency that assumes responsibility is referred to as the *lead agency*. The lead agency may be the SEA, the state welfare department, the health department, or any other unit of state government. Many states provide Part C services through multiple state agencies. In these cases, an interagency coordinating council is the primary planning body that works out the agreements between the agencies regarding jurisdiction and funding.

Part D of the IDEA   Part D is also a discretionary or support program. This section of the law contains provisions that are vitally important to the development of special education in the United States. The activities funded by Part D have also had a great effect on students in regular education and on the lives of all individuals with disabilities. The purpose of Part D is to fund activities that improve the education of children and youth with disabilities. Figure 4.2 lists some of the congressional findings and goals regarding the Part D programs.

According to OSEP (2000), Part D programs account for less than 1% of the national expenditure on programs to educate students with disabilities. Nevertheless, programs funded by Part D have played a crucial role in identifying, implementing, evaluating, and

FIGURE 4.2 ■
Congressional Findings on Part D of the IDEA

1) The federal government has an ongoing obligation to support activities that contribute to positive results for children and youth with disabilities, thus enabling those children to lead productive and independent lives.

2) Systematic change that benefits all students, including students with disabilities, will require the involvement of states, local education agencies, parents, individuals with disabilities and their families, teachers, and other service providers so that they may develop and implement strategies that improve educational results for children and youth with disabilities.

3) An effective educational system serving students with disabilities should—

   a) maintain high academic achievement standards and clear performance goals for students with disabilities. Moreover, these standards and goals should be consistent with the standards and expectations for all students in the educational system and provide for appropriate and effective strategies and methods to ensure that all children and youth with disabilities have the opportunity to achieve those standards and goals;

   b) clearly define, in objective, measurable terms, the school and post-school results that children and youth with disabilities are expected to achieve; and

   c) promote transition services and coordinate interagency services so that they effectively address the full range of student needs. This is particularly important for children and youth with disabilities who need significant levels of support to participate and learn in school and the community.

4) The availability of an adequate number of qualified personnel is critical—

   a) to serve effectively children with disabilities;

   b) to assume leadership positions in administration and direct services;

   c) to provide teacher training; and

   d) to conduct high-quality research to improve special education.

5) High-quality, comprehensive professional development programs are essential to ensure that the persons responsible for the education or transition of children with disabilities possess the skills and knowledge necessary to address the unique needs of those children.

6) Models of professional development should be scientifically based and reflect successful practices, including strategies for recruiting, preparing, and retaining personnel.

7) Continued support is essential for the development and maintenance of a coordinated and high-quality program of research to inform successful teaching practices and model curricula for educating children with disabilities.

8) Training, technical assistance, support, and dissemination activities delivered in a timely manner are necessary to ensure that Parts B and C are fully implemented and achieve high-quality early intervention, educational, and transitional results for children with disabilities and their families.

9) Parent training and information activities are of particular importance in—

   a) playing a vital role in creating and preserving constructive relationships between parents and schools;

   b) ensuring the involvement of parents in planning and decision making; and

   c) assisting parents in the development of skills that allow them to participate effectively in the child's education.

10) Support is needed to improve technological resources and integrate technology, including universally designed technologies, into the lives of children and youth with disabilities and their parents.

disseminating information about effective practices in educating students with disabilities. Essentially, Part D programs support the other 99% of the federal expenditures to educate students with disabilities (OSEP, 2000). In the IDEIA, three major Part D programs were authorized.

Subpart 1—State Personnel Development Grants Because personnel development and professional development are necessary to improve results for children and youth with disabilities, this subpart provides federal support for assisting state education agencies to reform and improve their personnel preparation and professional development systems. This subpart authorizes funds for competitive grants to states to develop and implement personnel preparation and professional development. Personnel preparation and professional development are especially important goals of Part D. In fact, one of the primary purposes of the IDEA, listed in Part A, is

> Supporting high-quality, intensive preservice preparation and professional development for all personnel who work with children with disabilities in order to ensure that such personnel have the skills and knowledge necessary to improve the academic achievement and functional performance of children with disabilities, including the use of scientifically based instructional practices.

> (IDEA, 20 U.S.C. § 1401 [c][5][E])

This subpart also authorizes formula grants that are given to states that apply and meet the requirements of the subpart. To apply for these grants, states must establish partnerships with school districts and institutions of higher education. The personnel preparation and professional development activities that are supported by these grants must (a) improve the knowledge of special and regular education teachers of the academic and functional needs of students with disabilities; (b) improve the knowledge of special and regular education teachers of effective instructional strategies and methods; and (c) provide training in the methods of positive behavioral interventions and supports, scientifically based reading instruction, including early literacy instruction, effective instruction for children with low-incidence disabilities, and classroom-based procedures to assist struggling children prior to referral to special education; and (d) provide training to special education personnel and regular education personnel in planning, developing, and implementing effective and appropriate IEPs. Additionally, these grants can be used for developing and implementing programs to recruit and retain highly qualified special education teachers.

Subpart 2—Personnel Preparation, Technical Assistance, Model Demonstration Projects, and Dissemination of Information   This subpart provides federal support for (a) training personnel to work with students with disabilities using scientifically based instructional practices; (b) providing technical assistance to state and local education agencies; (c) developing and implementing model demonstration projects to promote the use of scientifically based instructional practices; (d) conducting research to improve educational programs for students with disabilities; (e) conducting evaluations of exemplary programs for students with disabilities; (f) funding national programs that provide for technical assistance, dissemination, and implementation of scientifically based research; and (g) investigating and implementing interim alternative educational settings, preventing problem behavior by using positive behavioral interventions and supports, and employing systematic schoolwide approaches and interventions.

Subpart 3—Supports to Improve Results for Children with Disabilities   This subpart provides federal support for (a) establishing parent training and information centers, (b) establishing community parent resource centers, (c) providing technical support to parent training and information centers, and (d) developing, demonstrating, and utilizing devices and strategies to make technology accessible and usable for students with disabilities.

Part D programs are often referred to as *support programs* because the primary purpose of these programs is to support the implementation of the IDEA and to assist states in improving the education of students with disabilities. The Part D programs, even though they constitute a small amount of the total federal expenditure for the IDEA, help to ensure that the field of special education will continue to move forward by translating research to practice and improving the futures of students with disabilities (Yell et al., 2004).

In 1976 the Department of Health, Education, and Welfare promulgated regulations implementing the IDEA. With every amendment to the law these regulations have been clarified, added to, or changed. The extensive regulations can be found at 34 C.F.R. §§

300.1–300.754. Regulations implementing the original Part C—early intervention programs for infants and toddlers with disabilities—can be found at 34 C.F.R. §§ 303.1–303.670.

Title II of the IDEA   When the IDEA was reauthorized and amended in 2004, Congress added Title II, which established the National Center on Special Education Research. The center is located within the Institute of Education Sciences (IES) in the U.S. Department of Education. The center's mission is to sponsor research that (a) expands the knowledge base in special education, (b) improves services under the IDEA, and (c) evaluates the implementation and effectiveness of the IDEA.

A commissioner selected by the director of the IES heads the center. The commissioner of the center, along with the assistant secretary of the Office of Special Education and Rehabilitation Services (OSERS), develops a research plan. This plan is to be submitted to the IES director. This research plan is to serve as a blueprint for all of the center's research activities.

A central goal of the center is to identify scientifically based educational practices that support learning and improve academic achievement, functional outcomes, and educational results for students with disabilities. Additionally, the center seeks to sponsor research that will improve the preparation of special education personnel. Finally, the center synthesizes and disseminates research findings through the National Center for Educational Evaluation and Regional Assistance.

THE IDEA AND THE REAUTHORIZATION PROCESS

When Congress passes statutes that appropriate money, it may fund the statutes on either a permanent or a limited basis. If a law is funded on a permanent basis, the funding will continue as long as the law remains unchanged—that is, unless the law is amended to remove funding or is repealed. Part B, the section of the IDEA that creates the entitlement to a FAPE and provides federal funding to the states, is permanently authorized. Congress may also appropriate funds for a statute on a limited basis. In this case, the funding period will be designated in the statute. When this period of time expires, Congress has to reauthorize funding or else let funding expire. The discretionary or support programs of the IDEA—Parts C and D—are authorized on a limited basis. In the past, funding for these programs has been authorized for periods of 4 or 5 years. Approximately every 4 or 5 years, therefore, Congress has had to reauthorize the IDEA, with the exception of Parts A and B.

Amendments to the IDEA

Since the passage of the original EAHCA in 1975, there have been numerous changes to the law. Some of these changes have been minor; for example, P.L. 100-630 in 1988 altered some of the statute's language, and P.L. 102-119 in 1991 modified parts of the infants and toddlers program. Some of the amendments, however, have made important changes to the law. These changes have expanded the procedural and substantive rights of students with disabilities protected under the IDEA. Four acts that made significant changes to the then EAHCA were the Handicapped Children's Protection Act (P.L. 99-372), the Infants and Toddlers with Disabilities Act (P.L. 99-457), the Individuals with Disabilities Education Act of 1990 (P.L. 101-476), the Individuals with Disabilities Education Act Amendments of 1997 (P.L. 105-17), and the Individuals with Disabilities Education Improvement Act of 2004 (P.L. 108-446). As amendments, the changes were incorporated into the act and are not codified as separate laws. The last two reauthorizations were perhaps the most significant changes to the law since its original passage in 1975. The following sections briefly review these two reauthorizations.

The IDEA Amendments of 1997

The IDEA Amendments of 1997 (hereafter IDEA 1997) added several significant provisions to the law. Additionally, the IDEA was restructured by consolidating the law from eight parts to four, and significant additions were made in the following areas: (a) strengthening the role of parents, ensuring access to the general education curriculum; (b) emphasizing student progress toward meaningful educational goals through changes in the IEP process; (c) encouraging parents and educators to resolve differences by using nonadversarial mediation; and (d) allowing school officials greater leeway in disciplining students with disabilities by altering aspects of the IDEA's procedural safeguards. Additionally, these amendments required states to develop performance goals and indicators, such as dropout and graduation rates.

The Individualized Education Program

Congress believed that the IDEA had been extremely successful in improving students' access to public schools, and the critical issue in 1997 was to improve the performance and educational achievement of students with disabilities in both the special education and general education curricula. To this end, Congress mandated a number of changes to the IEP and the inclusion of students with disabilities in state- and district-wide assessments. Regarding the IEP, changes include the requirement that a statement of measurable annual goals, including benchmarks or short-term objectives, that would enable parents and educators to accurately determine a student's progress be included in the IEP. The primary difference in the statement of goals from that of the original IDEA is the emphasis on accurately measuring and reporting a student's progress toward the annual goals. The core IEP team was expanded to include both a special education teacher and a general education teacher. The original IDEA mandated that the child's teacher be a member of the IEP team but did not specify if the teacher should be in special or general education.

The 1997 amendments required that students with disabilities be included in state- and district-wide assessments of student progress. The amendments also required that the IEP team be the forum to determine if modifications or accommodations were needed to allow a student to participate in these assessments. The IEP, therefore, requires a statement regarding a student's participation in these assessments and what, if any, modifications to the assessment are needed to allow participation.

Disciplining Students In Special Education

Another significant addition of IDEA 1997 was a section addressing the discipline of students with disabilities. In hearings prior to the reauthorization, Congress heard testimony regarding the lack of parity school officials faced when making decisions about disciplining students with and without disabilities who violated the same school rules (Senate Report, 1997). To address these concerns, Congress added a section to the IDEA in an attempt to balance school officials' obligation to ensure that schools were safe and orderly environments conducive to learning and the school's obligation to ensure that students with disabilities received a FAPE.

To deal with behavioral problems in a proactive manner, IDEA 1997 required that if a student with disabilities had behavior problems, regardless of the student's disability category, the IEP team should consider strategies—including positive behavioral interventions, strategies, and supports—to address these problems. In such situations a proactive behavior management plan, based on functional behavioral assessment, was to be included in the student's IEP. Furthermore, if a student's placement was changed following a behavioral incident and the IEP did not contain a behavioral intervention plan, a functional behavioral assessment and a behavioral plan had to be completed no later than 10 days after changing the placement.

School officials were allowed to discipline a student with disabilities in the same manner as they disciplined students without disabilities, with a few notable exceptions. If necessary, school officials could unilaterally change the placement of a student for disciplinary purposes to an appropriate interim setting, move the student to another setting, or suspend the student to the extent that these disciplinary methods were used with students without disabilities. The primary difference is that with students who had disabilities, the suspension or placement change could not exceed 10 school days. School officials could unilaterally place a student with disabilities in an interim alternative educational setting (IAES) for up to 45 days if the student brought a weapon to school or a school function or knowingly possessed, used, or sold illegal drugs or controlled substances at school or a school function. The interim alternative educational setting had to be determined by the IEP team. Additionally, a hearing officer could order a 45-day change in placement if school officials had evidence indicating that maintaining the student with disabilities in the current placement was substantially likely to result in injury to the student or others and that school officials had made reasonable efforts to minimize this risk of harm.

The Manifestation Determination

If school officials sought a change of placement, suspension, or expulsion in excess of 10 school days, a review of the relationship between a student's disability and his or her misconduct had to be conducted within 10 days. This review, called a *manifestation determination*, must be conducted by a student's IEP team and other qualified personnel. If a determination was made that no relationship existed between the misconduct and disability, the same disciplinary procedures as would be used with students without disabilities could be used on a student with disabilities. Educational services, however, had to be continued. The parents of the student could request an expedited due process hearing if they disagreed with the results of the manifestation determination. The student's placement during the hearing would be in the IAES. (For elaborations on the manifestation determination and the IAES, see Chapter 13.)

Dispute Resolution

Congress also attempted to alleviate what was believed to be the overly adversarial nature of special education by encouraging parents and educators to resolve differences by using nonadversarial methods. Specifically, IDEA 1997 required states to offer mediation as a voluntary option to parents and educators as an initial process for dispute resolution. The mediator had to be trained or qualified to conduct mediation sessions and knowledgeable regarding special education law. Furthermore, the mediator could not be an employee of the LEA or SEA and could not have any personal or professional conflict of interest. The results of mediation sessions had to be put in writing and were confidential. If mediation was not successful, either party could request an impartial due process hearing.

Attorney's Fees

The 1997 amendments also limited the conditions under which attorneys could collect fees under the IDEA. Attorney's fees for participation in IEP meetings were eliminated unless the meeting was convened because of an administrative or judicial order. Similarly, attorney's fees were not available for mediation sessions prior to a party filing for a due process hearing. Attorney's fees could also be reduced if the parents' attorney did not provide the appropriate information to the school district regarding the possible action. Finally, parents had to notify school district officials of the problem and proposed solutions prior to filing for a due process hearing if they intended to seek attorney's fees.

Special Education and Adult Inmates

The 1997 amendments also allowed states to opt not to provide special education services to individuals with disabilities in adult prisons if they were not identified as IDEA-eligible prior to their incarceration. If these individuals had been identified and received special education services when attending school, however, states had to continue their special education while they were in prison.

Charter Schools

The 1997 amendments also required school districts to serve students with disabilities who attended charter schools just as they would serve students attending the district's schools. Charter schools may not be required to apply for IDEA funds jointly with LEAs. Finally, school districts had to provide IDEA funds to charter schools in the same manner as they provided funds to other schools.

The Individuals with Disabilities Education Improvement Act of 2004

On December 3, 2004, President George W. Bush signed the IDEIA into law. The bill had almost unanimously passed both the U.S. House of Representatives and the U.S. Senate. Figure 4.3 depicts the process that resulted in passage of the new law. Appendix A contains a table that depicts the major changes of the IDEIA.

An important congressional goal in passing the IDEIA was to align the IDEA with the Elementary and Secondary Education Act (ESEA; formerly referred to as No Child Left Behind [NCLB]), thereby increasing accountability for improving student performance. Thus, the IDEIA included measures to increase academic results for students with disabilities, such as requiring the use of scientifically based practices. The law also defines highly qualified special education teachers in line with the definition in NCLB. Additionally, Congress sought to reduce the paperwork burden on teachers, expand options for parents, and reduce litigation.

Congress stated that the IDEA had successfully ensured access to educational services for millions of children and youth with disabilities. Nevertheless, implementation of the IDEA had been impeded by low expectations and an insufficient focus on applying scientifically based research on proven methods of teaching children and youth with disabilities. Specifically, Congress stated that having high expectations for students with disabilities and ensuring their access to the general education curriculum would assist them to be prepared to lead productive and independent lives. Moreover, the IDEIA sought to support high-quality, intensive preservice preparation and professional development based on scientific research. Congress, in passing the IDEIA, also sought to encourage schools to develop schoolwide approaches to reduce the need to label children as disabled and to provide assistance to all children who need it. Indeed, one of the major purposes of the IDEIA was:

> providing incentives for whole-school approaches, scientifically based early reading program, positive behavioral interventions and supports, and services to reduce the need to label children as disabled in order to address the learning and behavioral needs of such children.

(IDEA, 20 U.S.C. § 1401[c][5][F])

FIGURE 4.3 ■
Passage of the IDEIA

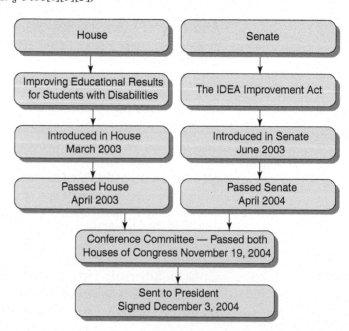

In the IDEIA, Congress made significant changes to the law. Some of the areas affected included: early intervening services, IEP, discipline, eligibility, attorney's fees, "highly qualified" teachers, scientifically based instruction, and funding. The U.S. Department of Education regulations implementing the law were made available in 2006.

The Individualized Education Program   Congress altered the IEP process to (a) ease the process for IEP teams, (b) decrease paperwork and meetings, and (c) increase accountability.

Changes in the IEP Development Process   The IDEIA required that the IEP team must, at a minimum, include (a) the student's parents; (b) the special education teacher; (c) a general education teacher (at least one, if a student has multiple general education teachers); (d) a representative of the local educational agency (i.e., school) who can provide, or supervise the provision of, special education services; (e) an individual who can explain the instructional implications of the evaluation results; and (f) others at the discretion of the student's parents or the school. The IDEIA, however, allowed a member of the IEP team whose attendance was not necessary because his or her area of curriculum or related services was not being modified or discussed at the meeting to be excused from attending the IEP meeting or other meetings if the student's parents and the LEA agreed that the person's presence was not necessary. To be excused from the meeting the team member must submit a request in writing to the parents and the IEP team, and the parents and IEP team must agree with excusing the team member. This purpose of this change was to make it easier to schedule meetings.

Changes in the IEP Document   The federal law no longer required that benchmarks or short-term objectives be included in the IEP, except for students with severe disabilities who take alternate assessments. Rather, the IDEIA emphasized the importance of writing measurable annual goals and then measuring progress toward each goal during the course of the year. Teachers were required to inform students' parents of their progress toward each annual goal at least every 9 weeks. If students were not making sufficient progress to enable them to reach their goals by the end of the year, instructional changes were to be made to their instructional program.

Changes in the IEP Modification Process   According to the IDEIA, when changes are proposed to a student's program after the annual IEP meeting has been held, the IEP team and a student's parents could agree to make the changes in a written document rather than reconvening the IEP team to make the changes. These modifications would then become part of the IEP. This was a significant change because previously an IEP team had to be reconvened to revise a student's special education program. Congress believed this would allow teachers to spend less time having to schedule, prepare for, and attend IEP meetings.

Three-Year IEPs   The IDEIA allowed up to 15 states to develop and implement 3-year IEPs. If the states applied to the U.S. Department of Education and were accepted for the pilot program, they could offer parents the option of developing a comprehensive 3-year IEP designed to coincide with natural transition points in their child's education (e.g., preschool to kindergarten, elementary school to middle school, middle school to high school). Parents had to agree to this option. States that did not apply for this pilot program are still required to develop and implement 1-year IEPs. No state applied for the three year IEP, therefore, this provision was never implemented.

IEPs for Transfer Students   When a special education student transfers from an in-state or out-of-state school district to a new school district, the accepting school is required to continue to provide the student with a FAPE. In other words, the new school must continue to provide services comparable to those described in the student's previous IEP. Moreover, the accepting school is required to consult with the student's parents regarding the services. If the student is from out of state, the new school is required to conduct an evaluation and, if appropriate, develop a new IEP.

Disciplining Students in Special Education

Congress made changes in the IDEIA designed to provide schools with greater flexibility to maintain safe educational environments while protecting the disciplinary safeguards that were extended to students with disabilities in the IDEA Amendments of 1997.

The Manifestation Determination

The IDEIA keeps the manifestation determination mandate that required LEAs to determine if a student's misbehavior leading to a suspension was related to the student's disability whenever schools suspend students with disabilities for more than 10 school days. This provision simplified and strengthened the manifestation determination standard because a behavior could be determined to be a manifestation of a student's disability only if the conduct in question was "caused by" or has a "direct and substantial relationship" to the student's disability. Additionally, if a school failed to implement a student's IEP, a direct relationship would also exist. Many educators believed the new standard made it easier for IEP teams to find that there was no relationship between a student's misbehavior and disability, thus subjecting a student with disabilities to the regular school disciplinary policies regarding suspensions and expulsions. Additionally, when a student with disabilities was suspended in excess of 10 school days or expelled, the law required that he or she must continue to receive educational services.

Behaviors That Can Lead to a 45-Day Disciplinary Removal

The IDEA Amendments of 1997 listed behaviors that could result in a student with disabilities being removed to an IAES for up to 45 calendar days, even in situations where the behavior is a manifestation of a student's disability. The IDEIA adds the offense of committing serious bodily injury upon another person to drugs and weapons offenses that were previously included as behaviors allowing a 45-day removal. Additionally, the law changes the time that a student could be in an IAES from 45 calendar days to 45 school days.

If a student with disabilities, therefore, engages in behavior that causes serious bodily injury to another person while at school, on school grounds, or at a school function, the school can place the student in an interim alternative setting for up to 45 school days. This can be done even when the misbehavior is related to his or her disability.

Stay-Put Provision

Under the previous IDEA, when a student was disciplined and his or her parents filed for due process, the student had to stay put in his or her previous educational setting during the hearing. The IDEIA changed the requirement so that the stay-put placement is no longer the previous setting; rather, it is the IAES. Congress believed this change would remove the temptation for parents to litigate or file for due process, which was created by the old stay-put provision because it allowed students to remain in the prediscipline placement during the hearing except in situations involving drugs or weapons.

Dispute Resolution

Congress attempted to reduce litigation in special education in two major ways when it enacted the IDEIA. First, the law limited the time that parents can request due process hearings to 2 years from the date they knew or should have known about the issues that led to the due process request, and it imposed a 90-day limit for filing appeals. Second, the law created a resolution session that school districts are required to hold in an attempt to settle the complaint that led the parents to request a due process hearing. This session must be held within 15 days of the request for the due process hearing. A representative of the school district is required to be at the meeting. A school district cannot send an attorney to the session unless the parents also have an attorney. If the school district and parents decide to go to mediation and bypass the resolution session, they must agree to this in writing. If the school district and parents decide to go ahead with the process and reach an agreement regarding the issue, both parties most sign a binding settlement agreement.

Attorney's Fees   The IDEIA altered the attorney's fees provision, included in the IDEA in 1986, by not allowing attorneys to be reimbursed for any actions or proceedings performed before a written settlement is made by the school district. Attorneys also are not allowed to receive reimbursement for attending IEP meetings, unless a hearing officer orders the meeting. The law also allows courts to award attorney's fees to school districts, when parents' attorneys (a) file a complaint that is frivolous, unreasonable, or without foundation; (b) continue to litigate after the case is shown to be frivolous, unreasonable, or without foundation; or (c) bring a complaint or action to harass, cause delay, or increase the costs to the school district.

Eligibility   The IDEIA included three new requirements regarding eligibility for special education services. First, a student's parents, the SEA, other state agency, or the LEA could request an initial evaluation. Furthermore, eligibility determinations had to be made within 60 days of consent for evaluation or, if the state has a timeframe for evaluation, within that timeframe. Second, a school's multidisciplinary team could not determine that a student had a disability under the IDEA if the student's fundamental problem resulted from the lack of (a) scientifically based instruction in reading, including in the essential components of reading instruction (e.g., phonemic awareness, phonics, vocabulary development, reading fluency, and reading comprehension strategies); (b) lack of appropriate teaching in math; or (c) limited English proficiency. This requirement meant that IEP teams had to examine the programming that a student had received in general education to ensure that poor programming was not the cause of the student's problems. Third, when determining whether a child had a specific learning disability, the SEA could no longer require that school districts use a discrepancy formula for determining whether a student has a learning disability (IDEA Regulations, 34 C.F.R. § 300.307[a][1]). The regulations that implemented IDEA 1997, which were published in 1999, required that states use a discrepancy formula to determine if a student has a learning disability. Although there are a few different ways to determine a discrepancy, the formula most frequently used involved (a) assessing a student's ability, most often with an intelligence test; (b) measuring a student's level of achievement, usually by administering a standardized achievement test; and (c) comparing the difference between the scores using a discrepancy formula. States were prohibited from requiring that school districts use a discrepancy formula; instead, states could allow or require that schools use a process that determined whether a student responded to scientific, research-based interventions. This procedure, which became known as **response to intervention (RTI)**, was adopted by many states and school districts. (For elaborations on RTI, see Chapter 14.) When schools develop RTI systems they must include the following components: (a) procedures to determine that students were provided with appropriate scientific-research-based instruction in general education (IDEA Regulations, 34 C.F.R. § 300.306[b][1][i–ii] and IDEA Regulations, 34 C.F.R. § 300.309[b][1]); (b) data-based progress monitoring system to continually track how students are responding to instruction (IDEA Regulations, 34 C.F.R. § 300.309[b][2]); (c) scientific-research-based interventions for addressing the needs of students who do not respond to instruction and are placed in special education (IDEA Regulations, 34 C.F.R. § 300.320[a][3]); and (d) procedures for informing students' parents about the amount and nature of student performance data that are collected, information about general education services, and research-based strategies that will be used to increase a student's rate of learning (IDEA Regulations, 34 C.F.R. § 300.311[a][7][ii][A & B]).

Funding   The IDEIA gave states greater flexibility in their use of IDEA funds. For example, states were allowed to use their IDEA funds for technical assistance and direct services to provide supplemental educational services to students with disabilities who attended schools that have failed to make adequate yearly progress for three years in a row. However, these schools must have been identified for improvement solely because of the performance of the subgroup of students with disabilities.

States could also establish risk pools by setting aside 10% of their reserve funds. The purpose of the state risk pools was to help schools pay for the high cost of teaching students with the most serious disabilities or because of unexpected increases in student enrollments.

Early Intervening Services

The IDEIA allowed school districts to spend up to 15% of their IDEA Part B funds on early intervening services (EIS) for students in kindergarten through grade 12, with an emphasis on students in kindergarten through grade 3, who have *not* been identified as needing special education or related services but who need additional academic and behavioral support to succeed in the general education environment (IDEA 20 U.S.C. § 613[f][1]). Furthermore, if a school district had "significant disproportionality" in its special education programs, the district must use 15% of its IDEA Part B funds to establish EIS.

The purpose of EIS was to identify young students who were at risk for developing academic and behavioral problems while they were still in general education settings, and then to address these problems by delivering interventions in a systematic manner by using research-based academic and behavioral interventions along with progress monitoring systems.

The IDEIA also required that when school district officials delivered EIS, they should (a) provide schoolwide academic and behavioral assessments for all students; (b) implement schoolwide academic and behavioral services to students identified as needing additional services, including scientifically based reading instruction and positive behavior support systems; and (c) offer professional development activities to teachers and other school staff to enable them to deliver scientifically based academic and behavioral interventions. Thus, to provide EISs, school district personnel had to screen all general education students within a school to determine which students were at risk for developing significant academic or behavior problems. School personnel also had to implement scientifically based academic and behavioral programs and adopt a method to determine which students were failing to respond to the research-based interventions. If students were failing to progress, school-based personnel had to provide additional, and more intense, research-based interventions with these students.

Additionally, school district officials who used IDEA funds for EISs had to describe the services that they were providing to general education students in a report to the respective SEAs. Furthermore, the district officials had to report on the number of students who were served in their EISs and the number of students in the services who were eventually found eligible for special education services. The advantages of an early intervening model included (a) identifying students early in their school careers using a risk rather than a deficit model, (b) emphasizing research-based practices in intervention, and (c) focusing on student outcomes rather than services received (Lane, Kalberg, & Menzies, 2009).

Highly Qualified Teachers

The IDEIA defined a highly qualified special education teacher according to standards developed in NCLB. The IDEIA required that all new special education teachers (a) obtain a bachelor's degree, (b) be certified by the state as a special education teacher, and (c) demonstrate competency of subject matter. Additionally, special education teachers could not be classified as highly qualified if they held an emergency, temporary, or provisional certification.

Demonstrating subject matter knowledge for an elementary special education position required that teachers pass a rigorous state test of knowledge in the basic elementary curriculum. Demonstrating subject matter knowledge for a special education teacher who taught a number of different subjects required that the teacher pass a rigorous state test in the core academic subjects that he or she taught. Teachers of students with severe disabilities, who would be assessed by using an alternative achievement measure, could demonstrate subject matter competency by passing an elementary test, if their students learn at the level of elementary school students, or by passing a test at their students' level of instruction. This level would be determined by individual states. The highly qualified teacher requirements were eliminated and replaced by the new requirements of the ESSA of 2015. (For elaborations on the ESSA, see Chapter 7).

FUNDING OF THE IDEA

The federal government, through the IDEA, provides funding to assist SEAs with special education costs. To receive IDEA funds, SEAs must submit a state special education plan to the U.S. Department of Education. This plan must show that an SEA is providing free appropriate special education services to all students with disabilities residing in the state from the ages of 3 through 21 in accordance with the procedures set forth in the IDEA (this includes students with disabilities who have been suspended or expelled from school). States that meet the IDEA requirements receive federal funding.

A large portion of the federal IDEA funds received by the SEA must be distributed to school districts, or LEAs. The federal funds do not cover the entire cost of special education, but rather are intended to provide financial assistance to the states. Congress originally intended to fund 40% of states' costs in providing special education services through the IDEA. The actual level of funding to the states, however, has never reached this amount. In the first years following passage of the IDEA, federal funding reached approximately 12% of the total state expenditures on special education. From the late 1980s to late 1990s the federal IDEA expenditures equaled approximately 7% to 8% of total expenditures. The Omnibus Consolidated Appropriations Act Fiscal Year 1997, enacted in 1996, raised the federal contribution to close to 10%. With the passage of IDEIA and the subsequent appropriations, funding levels reached approximately 19% of state expenditures.

In the IDEIA, Congress announced that federal funding from 2004 to 2010 would increase each year so that the IDEA would be fully funded in accordance with the original promise that Congress made in 1975. Readers should note that full funding means that the IDEA will reach the original funding goal of 40% of state costs. Additionally, the funding targets announced in the IDEIA were not mandatory.

Federal expenditures are computed on a state-by-state basis in accordance with the number of students with disabilities served (no adjustments are made either for the category of disability or for the setting in which a student is served). A state is responsible for counting the number of students with disabilities educated in special education. This is called the *child count*. The number is multiplied by 40% of the average per-student expenditure in public schools in the United States. The federal government caps the number of students in special education in each state that federal sources will fund. States cannot receive federal IDEA funding for more than 12% of the total number of school-age students in the state.

The funding formula remains based on the child count until federal appropriations reach $4.9 billion. Federal appropriations above that level will be allocated according to a population-based formula with an adjustment for poverty rates. When the trigger of $4.9 billion is reached, the new formula, based on the state's population (85%) and poverty level (15%), will apply to all excess appropriations. Congress capped the total increases a state could receive under this formula as no more than 1.5% over the federal funding from the previous year. Neither can states receive less than they did in fiscal 1997. The purpose of the caps and floors is to limit the increase in federal monies to states that gain from the formula change and to prevent large decreases in states that receive less under the new formula.

The federal money states receive must not be used to supplant state funds but to supplement and increase funding of special education and related services. This requirement, often referred to as the nonsupplanting requirement of the IDEA, ensures that states will not use IDEA funds to relieve themselves of their financial obligations, but that the funds will increase the level of state expenditures on special education. The state is ultimately responsible for ensuring the appropriate use of funds. IDEA regulations also grant school districts the authority to use other sources of funding to pay for special education services (IDEA Regulations, 34 C.F.R. § 300.600[c]).

The IDEA also requires that 75% of the federal funds received by the states be directed to the local schools and that 25% may be used at the state level. The majority of federal funding, therefore, flows from the federal to the state government and in turn to local school districts. To receive state funds, local school districts must have programs that meet the state requirements. States are required to establish management and auditing procedures to ensure that federal funds will be expended in accordance with IDEA provisions. States must also set up systems of fund allocation. The amount of flow-through funds given to an LEA is in proportion to the district's contribution to the state total of students in special education.

The 25% of the federal monies that may be set aside for state agency activities may be used for administration and supervision, direct and supportive services for students with disabilities, and monitoring and complaint investigation (IDEA Regulations, 34 C.F.R. § 300.370[a]). States may, however, use only 5% of the federal funds they receive for administrative purposes. The states' administrative activities may include technical assistance to local education agencies, administering the state plan, approval and supervision of local activities, and leadership activities and consultative services (IDEA Regulations, 34 C.F.R. § 300.621). The IDEA Amendments of 1997 capped the actual dollar amount of the 5% that may be used for administrative purposes at the fiscal 1997 level. States will also be given increases equal to the inflation rate or the increase in federal expenditures, whichever is less. If inflation is lower than the percentage increase in federal appropriations, states are required to spend the difference on improvements in services to students with disabilities.

States may also use up to 10% of the federal funds they retain to establish risk pools to reimburse school districts for the cost of educating students who require high-cost services (e.g., residential placement, medically related services). For a school district to qualify for the reimbursement through the risk pool, the cost of serving a student must be three times greater than the school district's average per-pupil expenditure and must represent a significant proportion of the district's overall budget.

The IDEIA also gave school districts greater flexibility in determining how they would spend new federal special education funding. For example, districts were allowed to divert much of their new special education funding under certain programs to other programs under the ESEA. Additionally, states could spend a portion of the federal funds on special education activities such as administrative case management, early intervening services, and programming for at-risk students even if they are not in special education.

MONITORING AND ENFORCING THE IDEA

The U.S. Department of Education is the federal government agency responsible for monitoring and enforcing the IDEA. The Office of Special Education and Rehabilitative Services (OSERS) is the specific department within the Department of Education that assumes these responsibilities. A subdivision within OSERS, the Office of Special Education Programs

(OSEP), is responsible for (a) writing regulations that implement the IDEA, (b) conducting many of the activities authorized by Part D of the IDEA, (c) monitoring and enforcing the provisions of the law, and (d) providing technical assistance to states. Moreover, this agency is responsible for approving states' special education plans and releasing IDEA funds to the states.

Enhanced eText **Video Example 4.3:** OSEP has produced an interesting video in which Ruth Rider and Greg Corr, from OSEP, discuss the monitoring, technical assistance, and enforcement of the IDEA.

One of the most important functions of OSERS and OSEP is to draft the regulations that implement the IDEA. The regulations that implement Part B of the IDEA can be found at 34 C.F.R. Part 300. When the IDEA is changed during the reauthorization process, the regulations are rewritten. Prior to rewriting the final regulations, OSEP must have a public comment period. Additionally, the role of any agency that drafts regulations is to be consistent with the statute. In areas in which the statute is vague, the agency has authority to fill in missing details and clarify the law so that it can be implemented. As we discussed in Chapter 1, regulations have the force of law.

OSEP also interprets the IDEA, often through the issuance of policy letters and interpretive guidance. In this respect, OSEP acts in a policy-making role. OSEP accomplishes this by issuing documents that provide guidance on how to follow the law. For example, in 1999, OSEP issued policy guidance on disciplining students with disabilities. OSEP also issues memoranda to explain particular issues or topics. Finally, OSEP will answer specific questions about the IDEA. Any interested person can send a question to OSEP, which will review the question and issue an opinion. These legal interpretations are not legally binding. Nevertheless, they are important. In fact, Zirkel (2003) asserted that in special education cases, OSEP policy letters will be considered by hearing officers and judges. Pitasky (2000) noted that these interpretations are highly valuable to the special education community and should be studied carefully. She also stated that because of the issues of regulations and interpretation, OSEP has led the way in shaping and influencing special education law.

OSEP monitors states to determine if (a) states and local school districts are complying with the strictures of the IDEA, and (b) IDEA funds are being spent in an appropriate manner. States may be forced to return funds that were spent improperly. Federal monies, once disbursed, can be withheld by the U.S. Department of Education if the state fails to comply with IDEA provisions. If the department withholds funds, this decision is subject to judicial review. The department also has the power to issue an administrative complaint requesting a cease-and-desist order and may enter into compliance agreements with a state that the federal agency believes is violating the IDEA.

The amendments to the IDEA in 2004 required that each state develop a State Performance Plan (SPP) to evaluate a state's efforts to implement the IDEA and describe efforts to improve implementation. The SPP for Part B required that states include baseline data, measurable and rigorous targets, and improvement activities for 18 performance indicators. The indicators on which officials must monitor their state school district's performance are as follows:

1. Percent of students with IEPs who graduate from high school with a regular diploma.

2. Percent of students with IEPs who drop out of high school.

3. Participation and performance of students with IEPs on statewide assessments, including (a) percent of districts with a disability subgroup that meets the minimum "n" size that meet the state's adequate yearly performance (AYP) targets for the disability subgroup.

4. Rates of suspension and expulsion of students with IEPs.

5. Percent of students with IEPs aged 6 through 21 served (a) inside the regular class 80% or more of the day, (b) inside the regular class less than 40% of the day, or (c) in separate schools, residential facilities, or homebound/hospital placements.

6. Percent of students aged 3 through 5 with IEPs attending a (a) regular early childhood program and receiving the majority of services in that program, or (b) attending a separate special education class, separate school, or residential facility.

7. Percent of preschool students aged 3 through 5 with IEPs who demonstrate improved (a) positive social-emotional skills, (b) acquisition and use of knowledge and skills, and (c) use of appropriate behavior to meet their needs.

8. Percent of parents with a child receiving special education services who report that school-facilitated parent involvement as a means of improving services and results for children with disabilities.

9. Percent of districts with disproportionate representation of racial and ethnic groups in special education that is the result of inappropriate identification.

10. Percent of districts with disproportionate representation of racial and ethnic groups in specific disability categories that is the result of inappropriate identification.

11. Percent of students who were evaluated within 60 days of receiving parental consent for initial evaluation or, if the state establishes a timeframe within which the evaluation must be conducted, within that timeframe.

12. Percent of children referred by Part C prior to age 3, who are found eligible for Part B, and who have an IEP developed and implemented by their third birthday.

13. Percent of students with IEPs aged 16 and above with an IEP that includes appropriate measurable postsecondary education goals that are updated annually and based upon an age appropriate transition assessment, transition services, including courses of study, that will reasonably enable the student to meet those postsecondary education goals, and annual IEP goals related to the student's transition services needs. There also must be evidence that the student was invited to the IEP team meeting where transition services are to be discussed and evidence that, if appropriate, a representative of any participating agency was invited to the IEP team meeting with the prior consent of the parent or student who has reached the age of majority.

14. Percent of youth who are no longer in secondary school, had IEPs in effect at the time they left school, and were (a) enrolled in higher education within 1 year of leaving high school, (b) enrolled in higher education or competitively employed within 1 year of leaving high school, or (c) enrolled in higher education or in some other postsecondary educational program, or competitively employed, or in some other employment within 1 year of leaving high school.

15. General supervision system (including monitoring, complaints, hearings, etc.) identifies and corrects noncompliance as soon as possible but in no case later than 1 year from identification.

16. Percent of hearing requests that went to resolution sessions that were resolved through resolution session settlement agreements.

17. Percent of mediations held that resulted in mediation agreements.

18. State reporting data (e.g., state Performance Plans and Annual Performance Reports) are timely and accurate.

States are required to report to the U.S. Department of Education's Office of Special Education and Rehabilitative Services (OSERS) on their performance under the SPP. This report, called the Annual Performance Report (APR), includes data on a state's progress in meeting the measurable targets established in the SPP. The U.S. Department of Education reviews the state's APRs and issues annual determination letters to each state on its progress in meeting the SPP targets. These letters determine whether a state (a) meets the requirements and purposes of the IDEA, (b) needs assistance in implementing the requirements of the IDEA, (c) needs intervention in implementing the requirements of the IDEA, or (d) needs substantial intervention in implementing the requirements of the IDEA. Information on OSERS accountability system and states' APRs are available at www2.ed.gov/fund/data/report/idea/sppapr.html.

States are also required to monitor local school districts' use of funds. If a school district has failed to comply with the IDEA or the state law mandating a FAPE, the state may withhold funds until the district comes into compliance. If the school district wishes to contest the decision, it may request a hearing.

States must also have procedures to receive and resolve complaints regarding possible violations of the IDEA. Organizations or individuals can file complaints, and states must investigate these complaints. Written complaint procedures help to fulfill federal requirements that states ensure that all special education programs conform to federal law.

SUMMARY

In 1975, President Gerald Ford signed P.L. 94-142, the Education for All Handicapped Children Act. The law, renamed the Individuals with Disabilities Education Act in 1990, provides funding to states to assist them in providing an appropriate education, consisting of special education and related services, to students with disabilities. The IDEA uses a categorical approach to delineate students covered by the law by setting forth 13 categories of disabilities covered by the act. Only those students with disabilities covered by the IDEA are protected by the act. Additionally, the disability must adversely affect the student's education.

The IDEA sets forth several principles that states must follow in providing a special education to students with disabilities. The primary objective of the law is to ensure that all eligible students with disabilities receive a free appropriate public education specifically designed to meet their unique needs. The U.S. Department of Education maintains a webpage on the IDEA that is a useful resource and addresses many of the aspects of the law that have been examined in this chapter: https://sites.ed.gov/idea/.

> **Enhanced eText Application Exercise 4.1:** *Mills v. Board of Education,* 348 F. Supp. 866 (D.D.C. 1972).

FOR FURTHER INFORMATION

The following book gives an analysis of special education law:
Norlin, J. (2014). *What do I do when: The answer book on special education law* (6th ed.). Horsham, PA: LRP Publications.
The following books explain the beginnings of governmental involvement in special education, offer an account of the IDEA from inception to passage, and provide interesting examinations of how a bill becomes law:

Ballard, J., Ramirez, B. A., & Weintraub, F. J. (Eds.). (1982). *Special education in America: Its legal and governmental foundations.* Reston, VA: Council for Exceptional Children.
Levine, E. L., & Wexler, E. M. (1981). *P.L. 94-142: An act of Congress.* New York: Macmillan.

REFERENCES

Education Amendments of 1974, Pub. L. No. 93-380, 88 Stat. 580.

Education for All Handicapped Children Act of 1975, 20 U.S.C. § 1401 *et seq.*

Education of the Handicapped Act of 1970, Pub. L. No. 91-230, §§ 601–662, 84 Stat. 175. of 1986, 20 U.S.C. § 1401 *et seq.*

Elementary and Secondary Education Act, amended by Pub. L. No. 89-750. § 161 [Title VI], 80 Stat. 1204 (1966).

Every Student Succeeds Act, 20 U.S.C. § 6301 *et seq.*

Ford, Gerald R. (1975, December 2). Education for All Handicapped Children Act, signing statement. Ford Presidential Library and Museum, Grand Rapids, MI. Available at www.ford.utexas.edu/library/speeches/750707.htm.

Gamm, S. (2017). *ESSA and IDEA: Assessment and accountability rules made simple.* Palm Beach Garden, FL: LRP Publications.

Gibbons, J. (1982). *Technology and handicapped people.* Washington, DC: Office of Technology Assessment.

Helms v. Independent School District #3, 750 F.2d 820 (10th Cir. 1985).

Honig v. Doe, 479 U.S. 1084 (1988).

Individuals with Disabilities Education Act, 20 U.S.C. § 1400 *et seq.*

Individuals with Disabilities Education Act Amendments of 1997, Pub. L. No. 105-17, 105th Cong., 1st sess.

Individuals with Disabilities Education Act Regulations, 34 C.F.R. § 300.1 *et seq.*

Joint Policy Memorandum, 18 IDELR 118 (1991).

Julnes, R. E., & Brown, S. E. (1993). The legal mandate to provide assistive technology in special education programming. *Education Law Reporter, 82,* 737–749.

Katsiyannis, A., Yell, M. L., & Bradley, R. (2001). Reflections on the 25th anniversary of the Individuals with Disabilities Education Act. *Remedial and Special Education, 22,* 324–334.

Lane, K. L., Kalberg, J. R., & Menzies, H. M. (2009). *Developing school-wide programs to prevent and manage problem behaviors: A step-by-step approach.* New York: Guilford Press.

Levine, E. L., & Wexler, E. M. (1981). *P.L. 94-142: An act of Congress.* New York: Macmillan.

Massachusetts General Laws Annotated, Chapter 71B § 3 (West, 1978).

Mills v. Board of Education, 348 F. Supp. 866 (D.D.C. 1972).

New Mexico Association for Retarded Citizens v. New Mexico, 678 F.2d 847 (10th Cir. 1982).

Norlin, J. W. (2014). *What do I do when: The answer book on special education law* (6th ed.). Horsham, PA: LRP Publications.

Office of Special Education Programs. (2000). IDEA 25th anniversary website. Available at www.ed.gov/offices/OSERS/IDEA 25th.html.

Omnibus Consolidated Appropriations Act, FY97, Senate Joint Resolution, N. 63, 104th Cong., 2d session, *Congressional Record,* S12327 (1996).

Pennsylvania Association of Retarded Citizens (PARC) v. Commonwealth of Pennsylvania, 343 F. Supp. 279 (E.D. Pa. 1972).

Pitasky, V. M. (2000). *The complete OSEP handbook.* Horsham, PA: LRP Publications.

Rehabilitation Act of 1973, Section 504, 29 U.S.C. § 794.

Salvia, J., Ysseldyke, J. E., & Bolt, S. (2013). *Assessment* (12th ed.). Independence, KS: Cengage.

Senate Report of the Individuals with Disabilities Act Amendments of 1997. (1997). Available at http://wais.access.gpo.gov.

Technology-Related Assistance for Individuals with Disabilities Act, 29 U.S.C. § 2201 *et seq.*

Timothy W. v. Rochester, New Hampshire, School District, 875 F.2d 954 (1st Cir. 1989).

Turnbull, A. P., Turnbull, H. R., Erwin, E. J., Soodak, L., & Shogren, K. A. (2010). *Families, professionals, and exceptionality: Positive outcomes through partnerships and trust* (6th ed.). Upper Saddle River, NJ: Merrill/Pearson.

Turnbull, A. P., Turnbull, R., & Wehmeyer, M. L. (2009). *Exceptional lives: Special education in today's schools* (6th ed.). Upper Saddle River, NJ: Merrill/Pearson.

Wexler v. Westfield, 784 F.2d 176 (3d Cir. 1986).

Yell, M. L., Drasgow, E., Bradley, R., & Justesen, T. (2004). Critical legal issues in special education. In A. McCray Sorrells, H. J. Reith, & P. T. Sindelar (Eds.), *Issues in special education* (pp. 16–37). Boston: Allyn & Bacon.

Yell, M. L., Katsiyannis, A., Ennis, R. P., & Losinski, M. (2013). Avoiding procedural errors in IEP development. *Focus on Exceptional Children, 56,* 56–64.

Zirkel, P. (2003). Do OSEP policy letters have legal weight? *Education Law Reporter, 171,* 391–396.

Chapter 5

Section 504 of the Rehabilitation Act of 1973

> (Section 504) is the civil rights declaration of the handicapped. It was greeted with great hope and satisfaction by Americans who have had the distress of physical or mental handicaps compounded by thoughtless or callous discrimination. These Americans have identified (Section) 504 with access to vital public services, such as education ... they consider it their charter ... it is a key to, and a symbol of, their entry as full participants in the mainstream of national life.
>
> SENATOR HUBERT H. HUMPHREY, PRINCIPAL SENATE AUTHOR OF SECTION 504,
>
> *CONGRESSIONAL RECORD* (APRIL 26, 1977, P. 12, 216)

Learner Objectives

At the end of the chapter, students will be able to

5.1 Describe the origins of Section 504 of the Rehabilitation Act.

5.2 Describe the purpose of Section 504 of the Rehabilitation Act.

5.3 Describe the structure of Section 504 of the Rehabilitation Act.

5.4 Describe eligibility of individuals with disabilities under Section 504 of the Rehabilitation Act.

5.5 Describe the effect of the Americans with Disabilities Act Amendments of 2008 on Section 504 of the Rehabilitation Act.

5.6 Describe school district responsibilities under Section 504 of the Rehabilitation Act.

5.7 Describe the U.S. Supreme Court decision in *Fry v. Napoleon Community School District* (2017).

Section 504 of the Rehabilitation Act of 1973 is a brief but powerful civil rights law that prohibits discrimination against individuals with disabilities in programs and activities that receive federal financial assistance. Section 504 is codified at 29 U.S.C § 794 (Section 504). The U.S. Department of Education regulations for Section 504 are promulgated at 34 C.F.R. § 104.1 to 104.61. With respect to schools, Section 504 protects students, parents with disabilities, and employees.

Discrimination in schools occurs when students with disabilities (or parents and employees with disabilities) are excluded from participation or receive inferior or different treatment because they have a disability. The statute holds that:

> No otherwise qualified individual with a disability in the United States ... shall, solely by reason of his or her disability, be excluded from the participation in, be denied the benefits of, or be subjected to discrimination under any program or any activity receiving Federal financial assistance.

(Section 504, 29 U.S.C. § 794[a])

This law covers public preschools, school districts, technical colleges, and universities that receive federal financial assistance. Additionally, Section 504 also covers private schools and religious schools that receive any type of federal financial assistance. Protection from discrimination includes, and extends beyond, the school's provision of an education to such areas as the provision of related services, participation in extracurricular and nonacademic activities, and architectural accessibility. For example, bullying or harassment on the basis of a disability is also a form of discrimination (U.S. Department of Education, 2010). In addition to covering students in preschool, elementary, secondary, and postsecondary schools and institutions, Section 504 also applies to school district programs such as day care, afterschool care, and summer recreation programs (Office of Civil Rights Senior Staff Memorandum, 1990). Extracurricular programs such as athletic teams are also covered (U.S. Department of Education, 2013). Unlike the Individuals with Disabilities Education Act (IDEA), no federal funds are available under Section 504 to help school districts meet the requirements of the law.

Although Section 504 became law prior to the enactment of the IDEA, it seems that only in the last decade or so have educators taken notice of the statute. Champagne (1995) believed that the struggle of educators to stay abreast of rules and developments of the IDEA's many procedures made it difficult to enlarge their scope to Section 504. Additionally, because there was no federal funding, school personnel may have felt little motivation to meet the requirements of the law (Smith & Patton, 1998).

Parents and advocates for children and youth with disabilities, however, began requesting that schools provide their children with educational services and protection under Section 504, which forced educators to become familiar with the law (Smith, 2001). An additional factor that may have influenced parents to request services under Section 504 is that their children may have had disabilities that were not included under the IDEA (e.g., attention deficit hyperactivity disorder), but would be covered under Section 504. Moreover, the increased activity of the Office of Civil Rights (OCR) of the U.S. Department of Education regarding school district compliance with Section 504 and increased litigation demanded that school district personnel and educators pay attention to the requirements of this law.

The purposes of this chapter are to (a) provide an overview of Section 504 and (b) examine the effects of Section 504 on public elementary, secondary, postsecondary, and vocational schooling. First, I review the historical developments that led to the passage of Section 504. Second, I examine the purpose, goals, and structure of the law. Finally, I consider the major principles of Section 504 and how they affect the education of students with disabilities.

THE DEVELOPMENT OF SECTION 504

In 1973, the first major effort to protect individuals with disabilities against discrimination based on their disabilities took place when Congress passed Section 504 of the Rehabilitation Act. President Richard Nixon signed the act into law on September 26, 1973. Section 504 was seemingly out of place, located in a labor statute titled the Rehabilitation Act. Additionally, Section 504 had an interesting and sometimes turbulent beginning to its existence.

What was to eventually become Section 504 was originally proposed in 1972 as an amendment to the Civil Rights Act of 1964 by Rep. Charles Vanik of Ohio and Sen. Hubert Humphrey of Minnesota. Section 504 was passed later that year as an amendment to the revision of the Rehabilitation Act. The Rehabilitation Act provided for federally assisted rehabilitation programs for individuals with disabilities. President Nixon, however, vetoed the law twice. The following year, the law was rewritten and passed, and this time the president signed it.

Section 504 was written in the same antidiscrimination language as Title VI of the Civil Rights Act of 1964, which prohibits discrimination based on race and national origin, and Title IX of the Education Amendments of 1972, which prohibits discrimination based on sex. It was not clear, however, what protections were actually extended to individuals with disabilities through the statute. Many believed the purpose of Section 504 was merely to correct problems in the rehabilitation of individuals with disabilities, while others understood the law to be an extension of the Civil Rights Act of 1964. Because Congress failed to include any means to eliminate discrimination based on disability in Section 504, such as civil or criminal remedies, it seemed that the law was not a civil rights statute.

Amendments to Section 504 in 1974 and the Rehabilitation, Comprehensive Services, and Developmental Disabilities Act of 1978 clarified these ambiguities (Schoenfeld, 1980). The result of these clarifications was to extend civil rights protection to individuals with disabilities by including all of the remedies, procedures, and rights contained in the Civil Rights Act of 1964.

The issuance of regulations to implement and enforce Section 504 took an interesting route. Because of confusion over the original intent of Congress in passing Section 504, as well as political concerns, there was a four-year delay in promulgating regulations to implement the law. A lawsuit was filed protesting the government's failure to issue the regulations under Section 504. In 1976, in *Cherry v. Matthews*, the Federal District Court of Washington, D.C., held that the Secretary of Health, Education, and Welfare (HEW)[1] was required to issue the regulations implementing the Act. In the opinion, the court sarcastically noted that Section 504 was certainly not intended to be self-executing.

Because of the importance of Section 504, the HEW secretary for the Gerald Ford administration, David Matthews, felt that the incoming Jimmy Carter administration should assume responsibility for writing the regulations implementing the law. Matthews, therefore, left HEW without issuing the Section 504 regulations. The secretary of HEW in the Carter administration, Joseph Califano, also appeared to some to be stalling on the issuance of the regulations for political reasons. Angered at this lack of interest in moving the law forward through the issuance of regulations, advocacy groups for individuals with disabilities began to exert political pressure on the new secretary. Demonstrations and sit-ins were held at regional HEW offices, and advocacy groups blocked Secretary Califano's driveway and various regional HEW offices with their wheelchairs. The weight of litigation and political pressure finally led to the issuance of the Section 504 regulations. According to Gerry and Benton (1982), "on May 4, 1977 the political system finally gave life to the promise of equal opportunity made in September 1973" (p. 47).

THE PURPOSE AND STRUCTURE OF SECTION 504

The Purpose of Section 504

Enhanced eText **Video Example 5.1:** This short **video** provides an overview of Section 504. www.youtube.com/watch?v=LrUorokVgm8

Section 504 is a civil rights law that prohibits discrimination against individuals with disabilities in programs and activities that receive federal financial assistance. The U.S. Department of Education maintains a website of frequently asked questions about Section 504 and the education of students with disabilities that briefly but thoroughly addresses the purpose and major components of the law (www2.ed.gov/about/offices/list/ocr/504faq.html).

Discrimination, in this case, is the unequal treatment of individuals with disabilities solely because of their disability. Discrimination can occur in many ways, but it typically involves exclusion or inferior treatment of some sort. Discrimination need not be deliberate. In fact, the U.S. Supreme Court noted that discrimination is "most often the product, not of invidious animus, but rather of thoughtlessness and indifference—of benign neglect" (*Alexander v. Choate*, p. 239).

---

[1] In 1979, President Jimmy Carter divided the U.S. Department of Health, Education, and Welfare into the the U.S. Department of Health and Human Services and the U.S. Department of Education.

In addition to ensuring that students with disabilities are not subject to discrimination, Section 504 requires administrators, teachers, school psychologists, and other school personnel to identify students with disabilities and afford these students educational opportunities equivalent to those received by students without disabilities. Thus, students with disabilities should be allowed to participate in the same academic and nonacademic activities as their nondisabled peers (Smith & Patton, 1998).

Section 504 extends these protections only in programs or services that receive federal financial assistance. The Department of Justice defines a program receiving federal financial assistance as a program that receives "any grants, loans, contracts or any other arrangement by which the [school] provides or otherwise makes available assistance in the form of (a) funds, (b) services of federal personnel, or (c) real and personal property or any interest in or use of such property" (Section 504 Regulations, 28 C.F.R. § 41.3[e]).

In addition to elementary, secondary, and postsecondary schools that receive direct federal financial assistance, therefore, schools or programs that receive indirect federal financial aid (e.g., private colleges where students receive federal education grants) are also covered under the statute. Section 504 does not apply to schools that receive no direct or indirect federal financial assistance.

Who Is Protected?

The original definition of persons protected under Section 504 was extremely narrow. The law protected individuals with the ability to benefit from rehabilitative services. Congress recognized that this definition was not appropriate for major civil rights legislation, and in the Rehabilitation Act Amendments of 1974 developed a definition to clarify who was protected under Section 504. This definition is as follows:

> any person who (i) has a physical or mental impairment which substantially limits one or more of such person's major life activities, (ii) has a record of such an impairment, or (iii) is regarded as having such an impairment.
>
> (Section 504 Regulations, 34 C.F.R. § 104.3[j]

Section 504 only protects individuals who have disabilities as defined in the law. These eligibility criteria, however, are quite broad and inclusive. In fact, the broad scope of Section 504 was confirmed when Congress passed the Americans with Disabilities Act (hereafter ADA) Amendments Act of 2008 (Rozalski, Katsiyannis, Ryan, Collins, & Stewart, 2010; Zirkel, 2011). The following language from the ADA Amendments revealed congressional intent to ensure that the definition of disability was interpreted in an expansive manner. The intent was that the act's definition "shall be construed in favor of broad coverage of individuals under this Act, to the maximum extent permitted by the terms of this Act" (ADA Amendments Act of 2008). Let's examine the components of this definition.

Part 1 of the Definition: A Person Who Has a Physical or Mental Disability

The definition of a handicapping condition in Section 504 has three parts. Part 1 defines a person as disabled if that person has a physical or mental impairment that substantially limits one or more major life activities. This part has three components. The impairment must (a) be physical or mental, (b) affect a major life activity, and (c) be substantial. In *E. E. Black Ltd. v. Marshall* (1980), a federal district court commenting on the definition stated that the term *impairment* meant "any condition which weakens, diminishes, restricts, or otherwise damages an individual's health or physical or mental activity" (p. 1098).

Physical Impairment

Regulations written for Section 504 in 1989 define physical and mental impairments as:

> (A) any physiological disorder or condition, cosmetic disfigurement, or anatomical loss affecting one or more of the following body systems: neurological; musculoskeletal; special

sense organs, respiratory, including speech organs; cardiovascular; reproductive, digestive, genito-urinary; hemic and lymphatic; skin and endocrine.

(Section 504 Regulations, 34 C.F.R. § 104.3[j][2][i])

The scope of physical impairment has been recognized as including those disabilities that substantially impair physical performance. Physical conditions that have been recognized by courts as constituting a disability under Section 504 include arthritis, asthma, deafness, blindness, diabetes, Crohn's disease, multiple sclerosis, paralysis, cerebral palsy, epilepsy, cardiac problems, Ménière's disease, chronic fatigue syndrome, kidney disease, Tourette's syndrome, and hyperthyroidism. Physical characteristics or conditions, temporary or permanent, such as left-handedness, height, weight, strength capabilities, strabismus, and pregnancy, have generally not been considered to be under the purview of Section 504.

Mental Impairment   The scope of mental impairments includes mental illness, intellectual disabilities, and learning disabilities. The regulations for Section 504 define a mental impairment as:

> (B) any mental or psychological disorder, such as mental retardation, organic brain syndrome, emotional or mental illness, and specific learning disabilities.

(Section 504 Regulations, 34 C.F.R. § 104.3[j][2][i])

In considering whether certain individuals with psychological conditions (e.g., depression) are protected under Section 504, courts and the OCR have tended to answer in the affirmative if the conditions are recognized by medical authorities as constituting a mental impairment (Richards, 2010).

Mental impairments, however, do not extend to undesirable personality traits. In an employment-related Section 504 case, *Daley v. Koch* (1986), an applicant for a position of police officer was not hired when a police department psychologist determined that the applicant exhibited personality traits of poor judgment, irresponsible behavior, and poor impulse control. The court held that because the applicant had not been diagnosed as having a psychological illness or disorder, he did not have a disability under Section 504.

In the Rehabilitation Act Amendments of 1992, Congress added exclusions to Section 504. The term *impairments* specifically excluded individuals on the basis of homosexuality, bisexuality, transvestitism, transsexualism, pedophilia, exhibitionism, voyeurism, gender identity disorders, sexual behavior disorders, compulsive gambling, kleptomania, pyromania, or psychoactive substance abuse disorder resulting from illegal use of drugs (Section 504, 29 U.S.C. § 706[8][E]–[F]).

The Americans with Disabilities Act (1990) amended the definition of persons with disabilities in the Rehabilitation Act of 1973. Essentially, the definition was narrowed to exclude persons currently engaging in the illegal use or possession of drugs or alcohol. Individuals undergoing drug or alcohol rehabilitation and those who are not engaged in the illegal use of drugs or alcohol may be considered disabled under Section 504 if they are otherwise qualified.

Substantial Limitation of a Major Life Activity   The definition of a disability in Section 504 also requires that the mental or physical impairment must substantially limit one or more major life activities. That is, just because a student has a disability under Section 504 does not mean that the student qualifies for protection under the law, unless that disability substantially limits a major life activity. This requirement was added by Congress to ensure that only persons with significant physical and mental impairments were protected under Section 504.

Because Section 504 does not define the term "substantially," the question of what constitutes a substantial limitation of a major life activity has been the source of some confusion. It is clear, however, that when determining if a student is eligible for protection under Section 504, school district personnel must decide if an impairment substantially limits a major life activity for each student on an *individual* basis (*Letter to McKethan*, 1994). Congress provided the following guidance in 2008: "A person is considered an individual with a disability ... when [one or more of] the individual's important life activities are restricted as to the conditions, manner, or duration under which they can be performed in comparison to most people" (Senate Report No. 101-116, at 23).

The term *major life activity* means "functions such as caring for one's self, performing manual tasks, walking, seeing, hearing, breathing, learning, and working" (Section 504 Regulations, 34 C.F.R. § 104.3[j][2][ii]). The ADA Amendments of 2008 added to this list the following major life activities: eating, sleeping, standing, lifting, bending, speaking, breathing, learning, reading, concentrating, thinking, communicating, and the operation of a major bodily function (e.g., bladder, neurological, respiratory). These lists are not intended to be exhaustive; therefore, major life activities are not limited to the lists provided by Congress. From an educational perspective, a relevant life activity is learning. If a physical or mental impairment interferes with a student's ability to learn, the student is protected under Section 504. Smith and Patton (1998) pointed out, however, that learning in and of itself does not have to be affected for children to be eligible for protection under Section 504. Additionally, an impairment that substantially limits one major life activity, even if it does not affect other major life activities, is sufficient to be considered a disability under Section 504.

Smith (2002) asserted that "substantially limits" means that an individual is unable to perform a major life activity that the average person in the general population can perform. Additionally, it may mean that an individual is significantly restricted in the manner or duration in which he or she can perform the major life activity when compared to the manner or duration under which the average person can perform the activity. Additionally, the ADA Amendments of 2008 required that whether an impairment substantially limits a major life activity has to be determined with regard to the ameliorative effects of mitigating measures (Rozalski, et al., 2010). With respect to schools, this means that officials cannot determine that a disability does not substantially limit a major life activity just because there is a mitigating measure such as medication, assistive technology, or mobility aids.

Smith (2002) suggested that school personnel examine the following three factors to determine if a limitation is substantial. First, what is the nature and severity of the impairment? Here school personnel would determine if the impairment (a) is mild or severe, (b) results in failure or a student not achieving near expected levels, and (c) affects a major life activity, and if so, how? Second, what is the duration or expected duration of the impairment? Here school personnel would determine if the impairment (a) will be of such short duration that it will not cause a significant problem, and (b) will stop affecting the student even if there is no intervention. Third, what permanent or long-lasting effect results from the impairment? School personnel would determine if the impairment (a) will be short or long in duration, (b) will have a significant effect without intervention even if the impairment is of short duration, and (c) will negatively affect a student's academic, social, emotional, and behavioral status if the impairment is long in duration.

Students who have temporary disabilities may also be protected under Section 504. Neither the statute nor the regulations expressly require that a disability be permanent to be covered under the law (Norlin, 2014). According to OCR, a temporary impairment may constitute a disability and be protected under Section 504 if it is severe enough that it substantially limits one or more major life activities for an extended period of time (OCR, 2009). Although school personnel can only determine if a temporary disability qualifies a student for protection under Section 504, OCR decisions have held that a student with a broken leg who was confined to a wheelchair (*Sevier County {TN} School District*, 1995), a student with a broken dominant arm (*Georgetown Independent School District*, 1992), and illnesses, such as diabetes (*Coppell {TX} Independent School District*, 1996) could qualify as disabled under the law.

Additionally, a student with a disability that is episodic or in remission may also be covered under Section 504 if the disability would substantially limit a major life activity when active (ADA Amendments, 42 U.S.C. § 12102(4)(D)). Moreover, the ADA Amendments included individuals with episodic impairments that ebb and flow in severity (e.g., allergies, migraine headaches) if the disability would substantially limit a major life activity when active (42 U.S.C. 12102(4)(D)). Additionally, impairments that are in remission may also be protected under Section 504 against discrimination. Students with impairments that are episodic or in remission probably would not need a Section 504 plan because they may not be in need of accommodations.

Any student with a disability who is eligible for special education services under the IDEA will be covered under Section 504. Readers should note that the U.S. Court of Appeals for the 10th Circuit in *Ellenberg v. New Mexico* (2009) did not totally accept the notion of double coverage. According to the court, even though a student was eligible under the IDEA, that did not automatically establish that the student had a substantial limitation on his ability to learn. The court did note, however, that in the majority of cases if a student is eligible under the IDEA, that will usually mean there will be a substantial limitation of a major life activity.

Students with disabilities who are not eligible for the IDEA may also be covered under Section 504, as long as the disability substantially limits a major life activity. Examples include students with attention deficit disorder (*Joint Policy Memorandum*, 1991); attention deficit hyperactivity disorder (*Joint Policy Memorandum*, 1991); multiple chemical sensitivities (*Walpole Public Schools*, 1997); drug or alcohol addiction, if not currently engaging in illegal drug abuse (*Letter to Zirkel*, 1995); and contagious diseases (*School Board of Nassau County v. Arline*, 1987). Appendix A to the Section 504 regulations also lists the following examples of potentially covered diseases and conditions: orthopedic, visual, speech, and hearing impairments; cerebral palsy; epilepsy; muscular dystrophy; multiple sclerosis; cancer; heart disease; and diabetes. A student who is socially maladjusted may also have a disability under Section 504 if it substantially limits a major life activity. In an OCR letter of finding in *Irvine Unified School District* (1992), a student was found to be ineligible under the IDEA because although he was socially maladjusted, he was not emotionally disturbed. According to OCR the student could be eligible under Section 504 if it was determined that he or she had a mental impairment that substantially limited a major life activity.

Parts 2 and 3 of the Definition: A Person Who Has a Record of Such an Impairment or Who Is Regarded as Having Such an Impairment   Part 2

of the definition protects persons who have a record of impairment. Under this part of the definition, a student who once had a disability but no longer does may not be discriminated against because of the past disability. This part of the definition also protects students who have been incorrectly classified as disabled (Zirkel, 2014). According to Norlin (2014) an individual qualifying under this prong was either correctly or incorrectly classified as eligible under Part 1 of the definition and is discriminated against because of this belief.

Part 3 protects persons who are regarded as being disabled. Persons may be protected under Section 504 even if they do not actually have a disability but are regarded as having one. The purpose of this rule is to protect persons who may have only minor disabilities or no disabilities at all from being discriminated against because of the stereotypical beliefs or the negative reactions of others (Norlin, 2014).

The OCR defined being regarded as having a disability as meaning that the person:

> (1) has a physical or mental impairment that does not substantially limit major life activities but is treated by the [school] as constituting such a limitation; (2) has a physical or mental impairment that substantially limits major life activities only as a result of the attitudes of others towards such impairment; or (3) has none of the impairments [protected under 504] ... but is treated by a [school] as having such impairment.

(Section 504 Regulations, 34 C.F.R. § 104.3[j][2][iv])

These two parts of the definition are frequently misunderstood. Moreover, these parts of the definition generally only apply in the areas of employment and, occasionally, postsecondary education. In fact, they rarely apply in elementary and secondary education. According to the OCR, many school officials believe that if someone (e.g., a student's doctor or parent) regards a student as having a disability or if a student has a record of a disability, he or she is automatically entitled to protection under Section 504. This is an incorrect assumption. These parts of the definition are insufficient to trigger Section 504 protections in and of themselves. It is only when a student is discriminated against based on the perception that he or she has a disability (i.e., "regarded as") or because he or she had a disability (i.e., "has a record of") that a student is entitled to the protections of Section 504. For example, a school could discriminate against a student believed to have a communicable disease, even though the student does not have a communicable disease, by not allowing that student to eat lunch with the rest of the student body. This would violate the second part of the definition (i.e., "regarded as"). A school could also discriminate against a student who once exhibited serious behavior problems but no longer had such problems by not allowing the student to go on a field trip because of his or her history. This would violate the third part of the definition (i.e., "has a record of"). In both examples, a school taking these actions would be discriminating against the student, and therefore violating the student's rights under Section 504.

The second and third parts of the definition, however, cannot serve as the basis of a free appropriate public education (FAPE) under Section 504. This is because the student who is regarded as having a disability or who has a record of a disability "is not, in fact mentally or physically [disabled], [therefore] there can be no need for special education or related aids and services" (*OCR Memorandum*, 1992). That is, only students with a current mental or physical disability are entitled to receive an FAPE. Students who are discriminated against in schools because they are regarded as having a disability or have a record of having a disability, however, may bring a claim of discrimination if a school district discriminates against them because of these perceptions.

Clearly, the definition of disability under Section 504 is broader than that under the IDEA (Norlin, 2014). Whereas the IDEA requires that students have disabilities covered by the law and, as a result of their disability, require special education and related services, Section 504 does not have such specific requirements for protection. Students must have a disability that limits a major life activity (e.g., walking, seeing, hearing, learning).

Otherwise Qualified   Additionally, Section 504 protects only otherwise qualified individuals with disabilities from discrimination based solely on their disability. Individuals who are not otherwise qualified, therefore, are not protected. In the final regulations, the OCR used the term "qualified handicapped person" rather than the statutory language "otherwise qualified handicapped person." This was done because the OCR believed that the statute, if read literally, might be interpreted as meaning that "otherwise qualified handicapped persons" included persons who were qualified except for their handicap. The actual meaning, according to the OCR, includes all persons who were qualified in spite of their handicap.

Elementary and Secondary Schools   With respect to elementary and secondary schools, students are qualified if they are

> (i) of an age during which nonhandicapped persons are provided such services, (ii) of any age during which it is mandatory under state law to provide such services to handicapped persons, or (iii) [persons] to whom the state is required to provide a free appropriate public education [students served under the IDEA].
>
> (Section 504 Regulations, 34 C.F.R. § 104.3[k][2])

A state is not required to provide services to students who do not meet the school's age requirements. All students of school age, however, are by definition qualified.

The otherwise qualified provision also applies to a school's extracurricular activities. Smith (2002) gives three examples of how the otherwise qualified provision of Section 504 would apply to students with disabilities who try out for such activities. First, he gives an example of a student in a wheelchair who wants to try out for marching band. If the student was able to play an instrument but the school did not let the student try out for the band, that would constitute discrimination. If, however, the student could not play an instrument and the school did not let the student try out for the band, that would not constitute discrimination because the student was not otherwise qualified. In Smith's second example, a student with attention deficit hyperactivity disorder (ADHD) wanted to try out for the basketball team. If the coach let the student try out and he made the team, but the coach would not let him play on game days because the coach believed the student would present a problem, that would constitute discrimination. If, however, the student was cut from the team along with other students who were not sufficiently skilled, that would not be discrimination because the student was not otherwise qualified. In the final example, a high school student with a severe disability wanted to join the Spanish club. If the only requirement for being in the Spanish club was that a student attend high school, then that student would be otherwise qualified, and not allowing him to join would be discriminatory. However, if the requirement for joining the Spanish club was that the student had enrolled in and successfully passed a course in Spanish and the student had not taken Spanish, not allowing him to join the club would not be discriminatory because he was not otherwise qualified.

Postsecondary and Vocational Schools　With respect to postsecondary and vocational schools, students with disabilities must meet the academic and technical standards requisite to admission or to participation in the educational program (Section 504 Regulations, 34 C.F.R. § 104.3[K][3]). In postsecondary education and employment, the statutory language "no otherwise qualified individual with a disability … shall, solely by reason of his or her disability … ." becomes particularly important. A student who is otherwise qualified is one who can meet program requirements, academic and technical, if provided with reasonable accommodations (auxiliary aids or services). The term "otherwise qualified" is intertwined with the concept of reasonable accommodations. Tucker and Goldstein (1992) asserted the relationship between "reasonable accommodation" and "otherwise qualified" is as follows: "An individual with a disability is protected from discrimination under Section 504 only if he or she is able to perform in the … program at issue under existing conditions or with the provision of reasonable accommodations" (p. 5:1). *Reasonable accommodations* refer to the modifications of educational programs and facilities to make them accessible to persons with disabilities. If reasonable accommodations cannot be fashioned to permit the person with disabilities to participate in the program in spite of the disability, that person is not otherwise qualified (Dagley & Evans, 1995). The provision of reasonable accommodations will be examined in a later section of this chapter.

Technically Eligible Students　Richards (2010) referred to students with disabilities who are protected from discrimination under Section 504 but who do not require services from a school as "technically eligible." Such students have a mental or physical impairment that substantially limits one or more major life activities but does not need a Section 504 plan or services while at school. Richards noted that two types of technically eligible students are students whose impairment is in remission and need no services and students who control mitigating measures that result in the student not needing services from a school. In a Dear Colleague Letter (DCL) in 2012 (U.S. Department of Education, 2012), OCR provided the following example of a mitigating type of student protected by Section 504:

> For example, suppose a student who is diagnosed with severe asthma that is a disability because it substantially limits the major life activity of breathing and the function of respiratory system. However, based on the evaluation, the student doesn't need special education or related service as a result of the disability. This student participates fully in her school's physical education program and extracurricular activities; she does not need help in administering

her medicine; and she does not require any modifications to the school's policies, practices, or procedures. The school district is not obligated to provide the student with any additional services. The student is still a student with a disability, however, and therefore remains protected by the general nondiscrimination provisions of Section 504.... P. 7

Summary of Section 504 Coverage   The definition of a disability in Section 504 is broad; it covers many types of disabilities as long as they affect a major life activity. The law protects all students in a school who meet the broad definition of disability in Section 504 (i.e., physical or mental impairment that substantially limits a major life activity), including students who are not eligible under the IDEA. Thus, students who have disabilities who may not be eligible under the IDEA, such as students with ADHD, Tourette's syndrome, asthma, diabetes, arthritis, allergies, and AIDS, may also be covered. Technologically dependent children may qualify and students with alcohol or drug problems, if not currently engaging in the illegal use of drugs, would meet the definition of impairment. Students without disabilities who are treated as if they have disabilities are also protected. Students whose main problem is poor impulse control, antisocial behavior, or poor judgment will not be covered if they do not have a physical or mental impairment that substantially limits their learning or another major life activity. Students with disabilities who are eligible under the IDEA are also protected under Section 504; thus, these students are doubly covered. Figure 5.1 illustrates the coverage of Section 504.

The Structure of Section 504

Section 504 is codified at 29 U.S.C. §§ 706(8), 794, and 794a. The federal regulations for Section 504 are divided into seven subchapters, which are listed in Table 5.1.

FIGURE 5.1 ■
Coverage of Section 504

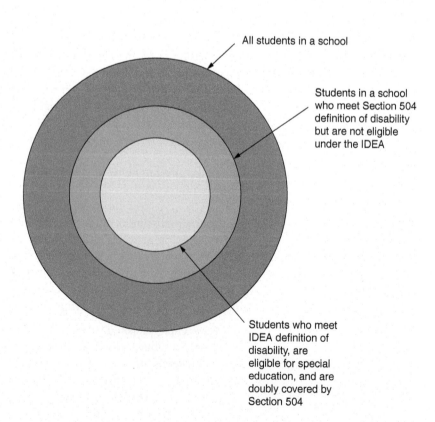

All students in a school

Students in a school who meet Section 504 definition of disability but are not eligible under the IDEA

Students who meet IDEA definition of disability, are eligible for special education, and are doubly covered by Section 504

TABLE 5.1 ■ Subchapters of Regulations for Section 504

Subchapter	Purpose	Contents
1—Subpart A	General provisions	States purposes, definitions
2—Subpart B	Employment practices	Prohibits discrimination in employment practices
3—Subpart C	Program accessibility	Describes accessibility and usability of facilities
4—Subpart D	Preschool, elementary, and secondary education	Prohibits discrimination in preschool, elementary, and secondary programs receiving federal financial assistance
5—Subpart E	Postsecondary education	Prohibits discrimination in postsecondary programs receiving federal financial assistance
6—Subpart F	Health, welfare, and social services	Prohibits discrimination in health, welfare, and social services receiving federal financial assistance
7—Subpart G	Procedures	Describes procedures for ensuring compliance with Section 504

MAJOR PRINCIPLES OF SECTION 504

Congress made a commitment to citizens with disabilities that "to the maximum extent possible, [persons with disabilities] shall be fully integrated into American life" (*Senate Report*, 1978). With respect to education, the regulations for Section 504 detailed criteria for schools to follow. The rules and regulations of Section 504 are not as complex and detailed as those contained in the IDEA (Norlin, 2014). Section 504 regulations, however, are specific with respect to postsecondary education.

Protection from Discrimination

All students with disabilities are protected from discrimination in elementary, secondary, and postsecondary schools. Discrimination refers to exclusion or unequal treatment of students with disabilities on the basis of their disability. For example, it is discriminatory for schools to provide academic or nonacademic programs or services for students without disabilities and not provide such services to children with disabilities. Similarly, Section 504 requires that individuals with disabilities have an equal opportunity to benefit from a school's academic or nonacademic programs or services, as do their nondisabled peers. This obligation, which is sometimes referred to as the comparability requirement, applies to every program in a school district (Norlin, 2014). Neither may school districts provide students with disabilities a program, aid, benefit, or service that is not as effective as those provided to students without disabilities. This requirement has been called the commensurate opportunity standard (Norlin, 2014). Providing different or separate programs, aids, benefits, or services to students with disabilities should only be done when necessary, and when provided, the programs, aids, benefits, or services should be equivalent to those provided to students without disabilities. According to Norlin (2014) when the OCR is investigating complaints regarding a school district's use of separate programs, aids, benefits, or services, school district officials will be required to justify the separate programs.

The concept of equivalency does not mean that services and benefits must be identical. Nor does it mean that the benefits or services must produce identical results. The benefits and services, however, must allow a student with disabilities an equal opportunity to benefit. As such, Section 504 requires that to ensure equal opportunity, adjustments to regular programs (i.e., reasonable accommodations) or the provision of different, and sometimes separate, services may at times be necessary.

Protection from discrimination includes the requirement that schools ensure that (a) buildings and structures are physically accessible, (b) programs are accessible, and (c) students with disabilities are educated in comparable facilities.

Physical Accessibility   School academic and nonacademic programs, structures, and activities must be physically accessible to students with disabilities. Section 504 prohibits the exclusion of students with disabilities from programs because a school's facilities are inaccessible or unusable. Regulations to Section 504 require that:

> No qualified handicapped person shall, because a (school district's) facilities are inaccessible to or unusable by handicapped persons, be denied the benefits of, be excluded from participation in, or otherwise be subjected to discrimination under any program or activity.

(Section 504 Regulations, 34 C.F.R. § 102.21)

For example, if a school has a chemistry classroom on the second floor and the second floor is not accessible to students with wheelchairs, it would be discriminatory to deny a student in a wheelchair the opportunity to take chemistry because the chemistry classroom was not accessible to that student. It would be the school's responsibility to (a) move the chemistry classroom to an accessible location or (b) make the chemistry classroom on the second floor accessible to the student.

Regulations require that "when viewed in its entirety," the program must be readily accessible and usable (Section 504 Regulations, 34 C.F.R. § 104.22). This means that school districts are not required to make all of their schools, or every part of a school, accessible to and usable by students with disabilities if a school's programs as a whole are accessible. However, a school district may not make only one school or a part of a school accessible when the result would be segregation of students with disabilities into one setting. For example, if a school district had a large high school campus with a number of buildings, only some of which were wheelchair accessible, the district would not have to make structural changes to all nonaccessible buildings. Administrators could reassign classes to the accessible buildings to accommodate students with disabilities. A district with only one wheelchair-accessible school, thereby requiring that all students needing wheelchairs attend only that school, would be in violation of Section 504 because students using wheelchairs would be segregated. School districts must meet the accessibility requirements of Section 504 even if they do not have students with mobility impairments.

The requirement of accessibility applies to all facilities within a school, such as classrooms, playgrounds, gyms, water fountains, swimming pools, parking lots, and restrooms. Schools can meet the physical accessibility requirements in various ways, including nonstructural alterations such as redesign of equipment, delivering services at alternate accessible sites, or assigning aides. Structural alterations are required only when there is no other feasible way to make facilities accessible. When school district personnel determine which of these means will be chosen to meet the program accessibility requirements, they are required to give priority consideration to methods that will allow the services to be provided in the most appropriate integrated setting. Districts must also inform persons with disabilities of where they can obtain information regarding accessible facilities.

In school facilities that were built prior to 1977, programs and activities must be made accessible to and usable by persons with disabilities. Facilities constructed after 1977 must be in compliance with the American National Institute's accessibility standards. Schools constructed after January 1991 must meet the Uniform Federal Accessibility Standards (1984). No specific guidelines exist for playgrounds, but the OCR has held that to meet the physical accessibility standards of Section 504, playgrounds must (a) allow student access and be firm, stable, and slip resistant; (b) allow a range of activities that are accessible through the use of ramps and transfer systems; and (c) include a surface beneath the equipment that is firm, stable, slip resistant, and resilient (Norlin, 2014).

Program Accessibility

It is not enough that programs be physically accessible for students with disabilities if the student is unable to benefit from the program. Therefore, the program must also be accessible. This means that at times it may be necessary to make modifications or accommodations to programs so that students may benefit from them.

Reasonable Accommodations

A program receiving federal financial assistance is required to provide reasonable accommodations to otherwise qualified individuals with disabilities. An educational institution or place of employment, therefore, must make modifications to the existing environment to eliminate barriers for individuals with disabilities. Section 504 regulations, however, only define reasonable accommodation as it applies to employment. Reasonable accommodation as applied specifically to preschool, elementary and secondary schools, and postsecondary institutions is not addressed. This led to disagreement and confusion regarding the reasonable accommodation standard. Dagley and Evans (1995) argued that even though the regulations suggest that reasonable accommodations are only required in the employment context, the judiciary has used the standard in making decisions regarding school district and postsecondary institutions' responsibilities under Section 504. This standard requires school officials to examine the individual needs of students with disabilities and make a professional judgment about what can and cannot be done to accommodate their needs (Dagley & Evans, 1995).

In *Alexander v. Choate* (1985), the Supreme Court held that Section 504 does not require that programs make substantial modifications, only reasonable ones. Modifications are substantial, and not required, if they impose an undue hardship on the program. Relevant factors in determining if modifications are reasonable include size, type, and budget of the program, as well as the nature and cost of the accommodation. Determining what constitutes a reasonable accommodation, as opposed to substantial accommodation, is difficult and subjective. What is reasonable varies given the specifics of a particular situation. The courts have offered some guidance, not so much by ruling what is reasonable but by ruling what is not reasonable.

Court Decisions Regarding Reasonable Accommodations

The U.S. Supreme Court, in *Southeastern Community College v. Davis* (1979), held that reasonable accommodations are those that do not impose excessive financial and administrative burdens or require a fundamental alteration in the program. Courts and OCR guidelines have held that Section 504 does not require that schools create new and special programs but that they make reasonable modifications to eliminate barriers in existing ones. A federal district court, in *Pinkerton v. Moye* (1981), held that a school district did not have to establish a self-contained program for students with learning disabilities because that would have required a substantial modification to the district's programs. In *William S. v. Gill* (1983), the court ruled that a school district was not required to send a student to a private residential school if the costs at the private school far exceeded the costs at the public school. The school district was not obligated under Section 504 to send the student to the private school, since it represented a service not available to students without disabilities. Some courts, in determining whether a change in a program would require a substantial modification, have asked whether the modification violates the basic integrity of the program. If it does, the change would not be reasonable.

Reasonable Accommodations in Schools

The U.S. Department of Education's regulations to Section 504 suggest reasonable accommodations that might be made by postsecondary institutions to assist students with disabilities in obtaining an education (Section 504 Regulations, 34 C.F.R. § 104.44[a]). Although the regulations do not specifically address elementary or secondary schools, they offer guidance for the modification of school programs to accommodate students at all levels.

Academic adjustments are a category of accommodations. Accommodations needed to ensure that academic requirements do not discriminate on the basis of disability may include changes in the length of time needed to complete a degree, substitution of courses required to complete a degree, and adaptations in how courses are taught. Further, schools may not impose rules on students with disabilities, such as prohibiting tape recorders, that have the effect of limiting the students' ability to benefit from or participate in classes or programs. Academic adjustments that might be made include modifying methods of instruction, modifying materials, and altering environmental conditions.

Regulations also address the modification of examinations. Course examinations and evaluations should reflect students' achievement rather than their disability. Modifications, therefore, should be made to an examination if a student's disability will impair the student's performance on the test. Modifications to ensure that examinations do not discriminate might include giving tests orally, allowing the student to dictate answers, shortening the length of the test, allowing more time to take the test, altering the test format (e.g., multiple choice, essays), printing the test with enlarged text, and reducing the reading level of the test.

Comparable Facilities

When a school operates a facility for students with disabilities, the facilities and services must be comparable to regular education facilities and services. This mandate goes beyond the accessibility requirement. The OCR does not intend to encourage the creation or maintenance of separate facilities, but clearly states that when separate facilities are used for students with disabilities, they must be comparable in attributes such as size, space, ventilation, furnishings, lighting, equipment, and temperature. This requirement is violated when schools provide separate facilities such as portable units and classrooms specifically for students with disabilities that are inferior to those provided for students without disabilities. This does not mean, however, that the facilities must be identical. Additionally, the placement of students with disabilities in portable units that were designated solely for use by students with disabilities would be a violation of Section 504. If, however, the portable units were used equally by all students in both general and special education, there would be no violation of Section 504.

Discrimination Versus Legitimate Considerations Regarding Disabilities

Protection from discrimination does not mean that the disabling condition cannot be considered by school administrators. In this respect, the definition of discrimination in Section 504 differs from the definition of discrimination in Titles VI (race) and VII (sex). This is because disabilities may affect an individual's ability to perform in a program or job by impairing functioning, whereas race and gender never tell anything about an individual's ability to perform (Tucker & Goldstein, 1992). A school administrator, therefore, may consider a disability if it is a relevant factor. What is not permissible under Section 504 is discrimination against a an individual with a disability based solely on an illegitimate or unjustifiable consideration of the disability. For example, if school administrators deny a student with disabilities the right to participate in an academic or nonacademic program (e.g., extracurricular activities, recess, meals, field trips, transportation, groups, or clubs) because of an erroneous conclusion that the disability would prevent the student from participating or because they failed to provide for reasonable modifications to allow participation, they may be guilty of discrimination. Additionally, schools will be seen as discriminating against individuals with disabilities if they (a) deny opportunity to participate in or benefit from any program or service available to individuals without a disability, (b) fail to provide aids and services that are provided to students without disabilities, or (c) provide different aids or services from those provided to students without disabilities, unless those services are required to allow equal opportunity.

Avoiding Discrimination

Regulations to Section 504 (Section 504 Regulations, 34 C.F.R. § 104.22) list actions that schools may take to avoid discriminating against students with disabilities. Such actions may include (a) altering structure, (b) redesigning equipment, (c) reassigning classes, (d) assigning paraprofessionals, (e) conducting interventions in the general education classroom, and (f) modifying classroom methods, materials, and procedures. (For a detailed list of potential modifications, see Zirkel, 2014.) Because the harassment and bullying of students with disabilities may constitute discrimination under Section 504, it is important if such actions occur that school officials appropriately respond to all such incidences. Appropriate responses may include investigating incidents, imposing discipline, providing training, and communicating with parents.

An example of discrimination against students with disabilities based solely on the disability occurred in *Rice v. Jefferson County Board of Education* (1989). In this case, the Jefferson County Board of Education charged students with disabilities larger fees to attend afterschool programs than they charged students without disabilities. The board justified the increased charges by maintaining that the school district had to provide care for the students with disabilities and that the additional costs of this care had to be passed on to these students. The court held that the board's action was discrimination in violation of Section 504, because the district failed to show that students with disabilities' attendance at programs created substantial additional costs for the district.

Discrimination in Postsecondary Education

Colleges, universities, and vocational and technical schools may not exclude a qualified individual with a disability from any aspect of the educational program or activities conducted by the school. According to Zirkel (2014), Section 504 claims most likely to arise in postsecondary education are in the areas of admissions and access to nonacademic programs or activities.

With respect to admission in postsecondary education, regulations to Section 504 protect qualified students with disabilities from being denied admission or being discriminated against solely because of their disability. To protect individuals from discrimination, a postsecondary school cannot inquire if an applicant has a disability. An important distinction between the responsibilities of elementary and secondary schools and those of postsecondary schools is that elementary and secondary schools have an affirmative duty to find students with disabilities, while in postsecondary schools, students must self-identify. After admission, however, the institution may make confidential inquiries about the disability to determine accommodations that may be required. Postsecondary institutions cannot limit the number of individuals with disabilities they accept.

In addition, postsecondary institutions cannot administer admission tests that may reflect adversely on students with disabilities, unless the tests have been validated as predictors of success and alternative tests are not available. Admissions tests must be selected and administered to students with disabilities to reflect actual aptitude and achievement rather than reflecting the impaired skills.

Discrimination and Access to Nonacademic Programs and Services

Another aspect of Section 504 involves access to nonacademic programs and services. Postsecondary institutions that provide housing to students without disabilities must provide comparable housing for students with disabilities. The housing must also be accessible. The regulations also require that the cost of housing for students with and without disabilities must be the same.

In physical education, athletics, intramural activities, and clubs, the postsecondary institution must provide qualified students with disabilities an equal opportunity to participate. If separate or different facilities or teams are required, they must be in the most integrated setting appropriate and only if no qualified students with disabilities are denied participation in the integrated activities.

Counseling, vocational, and placement services must be provided to students with disabilities to the same extent as those provided to students without disabilities. Additionally, qualified students with disabilities must not be counseled to more restrictive career options than are students without disabilities.

Often postsecondary institutions provide assistance to fraternities, sororities, or other organizations. If they do so, they must ensure that these organizations do not discriminate against or permit discrimination based on a disability. Furthermore, postsecondary institutions that provide financial assistance must not provide less assistance to students with disabilities than they provide to persons without disabilities. Neither can they limit the eligibility of students with disabilities.

Extracurricular Activities   On January 25, 2013, the OCR in the U.S. Department of Education issued a DCL that addressed the obligations of school districts under Section 504 of the Rehabilitation Act regarding the participation of students with disabilities in extracurricular activities. The DCL is available on the OCR website (www2.ed.gov/about/offices/list/ocr/letters/colleague-201301-504.html). The purpose of the DCL was to help school personnel understand their obligations in providing equal opportunity to students with disabilities in extracurricular athletics. In the DCL, the OCR cautioned school district personnel from operating their programs and activities on the basis of generalizations, assumptions, prejudices, or stereotypes about disability generally, or on the basis of a particular disability. When school district personnel offer extracurricular athletics in their schools, they must do so in a manner that affords qualified students with disabilities an equal opportunity to participate. This means that school personnel must make reasonable modifications and provide aids and services that are required so that students with disabilities have an equal opportunity to participate. The only exception to this requirement is when making certain modifications would fundamentally alter a particular athletic program or give a student an unfair advantage. Because participation in competitive athletic programs requires a level of skill or abilities on the part of the participants, equal opportunity to participate *does not* mean that every student with a disability is guaranteed an opportunity to participate in the competitive sport or is guaranteed a place on the team when other students have to try out to make the team; rather, it means school district personnel must afford qualified students with disabilities an equal opportunity to participate in the athletic activity or program.

Free Appropriate Public Education

Students with disabilities in elementary and secondary school are entitled to a free appropriate public education (FAPE) under Section 504 regardless of the nature or severity of their disabilities. This applies to all students with disabilities in a school's jurisdiction. A FAPE is required to protect persons with disabilities from discrimination (Section 504 Regulations, 34 C.F.R. §§ 100.6–100.10). School districts often have more difficulty meeting their FAPE obligations under Section 504 than they do meeting the physical accessibility and comparable facilities requirements.

 Enhansced eText Video Example 5.2: These **videos** show how Ehlena Fry challenged her school district for not complying with the ADA and eventually wound up in the U.S. Supreme Court: www.youtube.com/watch?v=t3xBxMJsTbA

Regulations implementing Section 504 define a free education as educational and related services that are provided at no cost to a student with a disability, excluding fees charged to all students. Even when a school district places a student in another school, even if the school is not in the district's boundaries, the home school district retains financial responsibility for the student. If students are placed in programs where they will be away from home, the school is also responsible for room, board, and nonmedical care (e.g., custodial and supervisory care).

Regulations further define an appropriate education as:

The provision of regular or special education and related aids and services that are designed to meet individual educational needs of handicapped persons as adequately as the needs of nonhandicapped persons are met and that are based on adherence to procedural safeguards.

(Section 504 Regulations, 34 C.F.R. 104.33[b][1])

An appropriate education must be individualized. It may consist of education in general education classes with supplementary aids and services or special education and related services in a separate classroom. Special education may consist of specially designed instruction in a classroom, at home, or in a residential setting, and may be accompanied by related services (e.g., psychological counseling, speech therapy) that are necessary for a student's education. A number of federal courts have held that the standard of FAPE under Section 504 is similar to the standard of FAPE under the IDEA (*Mark H. v. Lemahieu*, 2008; *W. B. v. Matula*, 1995).

Section 504 also requires that related services be provided to students with disabilities in the general education classroom as well as to students in a special classroom when necessary. Related services in the classroom are required under Section 504 if they are necessary to provide an education comparable to that offered to students without disabilities.

The definition of appropriate education under Section 504 is one of equivalency. That is, the educational services designed to meet the needs of students with disabilities must do so as adequately as services designed to meet the needs of students without disabilities. To ensure this equivalency, Section 504 requires that the student's teachers must be trained in instructing the student with the particular disability and that appropriate materials and equipment must be available. The equivalency requirement also applies to nonacademic activities. Regulations require that nonacademic and extracurricular activities be provided in a way that affords students with disabilities an equal opportunity for participation. Nonacademic activities include counseling (personal, academic, and vocational), transportation, health services, special interest groups, clubs, and physical, recreational, and athletic activities.

To meet the FAPE requirement, the educational program of a student with disabilities must be developed by a group of knowledgeable persons based on evaluation data. Moreover, school districts should document the provision of a FAPE. When students are covered only by Section 504 and do not receive dual coverage under the IDEA, school officials still must develop an appropriate educational program.

For students with disabilities who are eligible for services under the IDEA, and thus also are covered by Section 504, the FAPE standards must conform to the standards of the IDEA. For students with disabilities who are eligible under Section 504 but not under the IDEA, the standard for a FAPE involves the school making reasonable accommodations in order to provide a FAPE (*Southeastern Community College v. Davis*, 1979). OCR, however, seems to place a higher standard on school districts to meet the FAPE standard of Section 504 based on a student's educational needs (Zirkel, 2014). Zirkel (1996) asserted that the applicable FAPE standard may be higher than that of reasonable accommodations. This higher standard is based on the statutory language requiring that commensurate opportunity or educational equivalency for a FAPE be provided to students with disabilities under Section 504.

According to OCR (1988), a FAPE comprises many different elements. There are nondiscriminatory evaluation requirements, placement requirements, and periodic reevaluation of students served under Section 504. Schools must also adhere to procedural safeguards when developing and implementing a Section 504 plan. Additional information on school district responsibilities when developing a FAPE will be discussed later in the chapter.

Evaluation and Placement Procedures

The purpose of the Section 504 evaluation and placement requirements is to prevent misclassification and misplacement. Students with disabilities who are believed to need special education or related services must be evaluated prior to placement. According to Zirkel (2014), the matter of evaluation has been the subject of more OCR investigations than any other requirement of Section 504.

When determining placement for a student, the school must convene a group of persons knowledgeable about the student, the meaning of the evaluation data, and the placement options. Furthermore, the team must draw on information from a variety of sources. The group must establish procedures to ensure that all information gathered in the evaluation process is documented and considered. The team must be aware of different options for placement. Moreover, team decisions must be based on a student's individual needs. If a school seeks a significant change of placement, a reevaluation must be completed prior to the placement change. Even in cases in which a significant change of placement is not sought, schools must conduct periodic reevaluations of all students with disabilities.

Procedural Safeguards

Schools must establish a system of due process procedures to be afforded to parents or guardians prior to taking any action regarding the identification, evaluation, or educational placement of a student with a disability who is believed to need educational services. The OCR recommends, but does not require, compliance with the procedural safeguards of the IDEA as a way to ensure that the procedural safeguards of Section 504 are met.

Notice must precede any identification, evaluation, or placement action taken by the school. Parents must also be notified of their right to examine educational records. If there is a disagreement concerning an evaluation or placement action, parents or guardians may request a due process hearing. Schools may also request due process hearings. Hearing officers must be impartial and have no personal or professional conflicts of interest or connections with either school or student.

In the due process hearing, the parents have the opportunity to participate, present evidence, produce outside expert testimony, and be represented by counsel. Parents may have the student present at the hearing and open the hearing to the public if they choose to do so. Following the hearing, the hearing officer reviews all relevant facts and renders a decision. The decision of the officer is binding on all parties but may be appealed to federal court.

The procedural rights of parents are listed in Figure 5.2.

FIGURE 5.2 ■ Parental Rights Under Section 504

- Right to be notified of procedural rights under Section 504
- Right to be notified when their child is referred, evaluated, and placed
- Right to notification when eligibility is determined
- Right to an evaluation that uses information from multiple sources and is conducted by knowledgeable persons
- Right of the student to have access to equivalent academic and nonacademic services
- Right of the student to receive an appropriate education in the least restrictive setting, which includes accommodations, modifications, and related services
- Right to file a grievance with the school district
- Right to an evaluation prior to making a significant programming or placement change
- Right to be informed of proposed actions affecting the program
- Right to examine all relevant records and request changes
- Right to receive information in the parents' native language or primary mode of communication
- Right to periodic reevaluations
- Right to an impartial hearing when a disagreement occurs
- Right to be represented by counsel in the hearing
- Right to appeal the hearing officer's decision

SCHOOL DISTRICT RESPONSIBILITIES UNDER SECTION 504

School districts and schools have two major responsibilities under Section 504: (a) fulfilling general procedural responsibilities and (b) meeting educational obligations to students with disabilities.

Administrative Responsibilities

School districts' procedural responsibilities include (a) appointment of a Section 504 coordinator, (b) public notification of the school's responsibilities under Section 504, (c) establishment of grievance procedures, (d) self-evaluation, (e) staff training, and (f) child find.

Appointing a Section 504 Coordinator
School districts with 15 or more employees must appoint a Section 504 coordinator. The coordinator keeps the school district in compliance with the mandates of Section 504. Because this individual has many duties, it is important that the school district ensure his or her thorough training. Although the special education director is frequently the Section 504 coordinator, Zirkel (1996) suggests that someone other than the special education director—preferably a general education administrator—be appointed to fill this position. This choice is suggested because assigning the special education director could serve to reinforce the erroneous belief of many general educators that Section 504 is a special education law when, in fact, it is primarily a general education law.

Notifying the Public of a School District's Responsibilities Under Section 504
The coordinator must keep the public and internal staff notified that the district does not discriminate on the basis of disability in employment, educational services, or treatment. It is advisable that the coordinator head a multidisciplinary team whose responsibilities include the identification, evaluation, and placement of students with disabilities.

Ensuring That Procedural Safeguards Are Afforded to Students and Their Parents
School districts must establish and implement a system of procedural safeguards. During the evaluation process, notification should be given when eligibility is determined, when an accommodation plan is developed, and before there is any significant modification of the student's program.

Establishing Grievance Procedures
School districts are required to set up grievance procedures and notify parents and guardians of those procedures. The Section 504 coordinator is responsible for establishing grievance procedures, which must include appropriate procedural safeguards. There is no procedure set forth in Section 504 detailing the requirements of grievance procedures. The mechanics of the procedure, therefore, are left to the agency.

Zirkel (2014) suggested that a Section 504 grievance procedure include the following steps: First, have an informal discussion between parents and the Section 504 coordinator to attempt to resolve the dispute. Second, if the complaint is not satisfactorily resolved, parents should file a written grievance with the coordinator, who will then conduct an investigation and issue a written report. Third, if this action does not resolve the problem, the decision should be appealed to the school board. Finally, if a complaint to the school board does not resolve the problem, a complaint should be filed with the OCR.

Conducting a Self-Evaluation
The coordinator should conduct periodic self-evaluations of the school district to ensure that all Section 504 mandates are followed. If the self-evaluation finds discrimination, the school district must take steps to correct the situation. If

such remedial action is necessary, the OCR has suggested that the agency seek the assistance of organizations representing individuals with disabilities prior to undertaking the corrective procedures. The school district should also keep records of the self-evaluation process. The U.S. Department of Justice has published a technical assistance guide to conducting self-evaluations; it is available from the Coordination and Review Section, Civil Rights Division, U.S. Department of Justice, Washington, D.C.

Training Staff Regarding Their Responsibilities Under Section 504   Because of the lack of attention given to the requirements of Section 504, many general education teachers are unaware of the law's existence, let alone its requirements (Smith, 2002). An extremely important task of the Section 504 coordinator, therefore, is the training of staff in the meaning and requirements of the law. Zirkel (2014) includes the failure to conduct staff inservices on his "hit list" of Section 504 practices that school districts should avoid at all costs. It goes without saying that if teachers and other school staff are unaware of Section 504, they may inadvertently violate the law.

Developing a System   Section 504 requires that schools annually take steps to identify and locate children with disabilities who are not receiving an appropriate education and to publicize parental and student rights under the law. These duties, referred to as *child find*, require that school district officials locate and identify eligible students who reside in the school district. Thus, it is the responsibility of the school to identify and evaluate students who may qualify for special services under Section 504. This responsibility includes students transferring from other school districts, students in private schools, and homeless children. A school district may conduct screenings of students to comply with the child find requirements (Norlin, 2014). School districts have a great deal of leeway in determining how they will conduct screenings (*Letter to Veir*, 1993). When the screening process has identified a child as having a possible disability, the school district should conduct an expeditious and thorough evaluation of that student.

Educational Obligations

School districts' and schools' educational obligations to students with disabilities under Section 504 include (a) identification, (b) evaluation, (c) programming, (d) placement, and (e) reevaluation.

Identification   As previously discussed, a student with a possible disability may be identified in the child find process. A school has an affirmative duty to conduct a child find at least annually. In this effort, the school must notify students with disabilities and their parents of the school's obligation to provide a FAPE to students with disabilities (Section 504 Regulations 34 C.F.R. § 104.32). School personnel cannot just wait for eligible students with disabilities to present themselves and request services under Section 504 (Richards, 2010).

Most students who may be eligible for services under Section 504, however, are identified through a referral process. Teachers, parents, school administrators, or other school personnel may make referrals, although typically students are referred by teachers. Neither Section 504 nor its regulations specify a particular referral procedure; nonetheless, school districts should develop such a procedure and ensure that it is understood and correctly used by all school personnel. When parents refer their child for special education services, school personnel must either evaluate the student or refuse to evaluate and provide the parents with a notice of their procedural safeguards (*Bryan County {GA} School District*, 2009).

School district officials need to know and define what will "trigger" a referral for a Section 504 evaluation (Goldstein, 1994). Figure 5.3 lists suggestions and problems that should trigger a Section 504 referral. School districts and individual schools should have a clear procedure for referring students under Section 504.

FIGURE 5.3 ■
Considerations for Referring a Student for Services Under Section 504

- A student has an impairment that substantially limits a major life activity
- A student has a serious academic problem
- A student has a serious behavior problem
- A student transfers from another school district with a Section 504 plan
- A student was referred to special education but the decision was not to evaluate
- A student was referred to special education but the decision was that he or she was not eligible
- A student is being considered for grade retention
- A student is not benefitting from instruction
- A student returns to school following a serious illness or injury
- A student is evaluated as having an impairment from an outside source
- A student is referred by his or her parent
- A student has a chronic health condition
- A student is a potential dropout
- A student exits a special education program
- A student was found not eligible for Section 504 services due to mitigating measures
- Administrators, teachers, or staff express concerns about a student possibly having an impairment
- A school's response to intervention (RTI) program has not been effective in addressing a student's needs

It is crucial that school district personnel and teachers understand that students may be eligible for services under Section 504 even if they do not qualify for special education under the IDEA. In fact, the OCR has held that a blanket school district refusal to evaluate students who do not qualify under the IDEA is a violation of Section 504. It is advisable, therefore, that students with disabilities who have been referred for special education services under the IDEA should be referred for services under Section 504.

Evaluation   Following a referral, school personnel must decide if an evaluation for services under Section 504 is warranted. Prior to conducting an initial evaluation, a school must obtain parental consent (*Letter to Zirkel*, 1995) and provide parents with a notice of their procedural rights. The evaluation must be completed and an eligibility decision made before a student can receive services under Section 504. Schools must convene a multidisciplinary team to interpret evaluation data and make programming and placement decisions. The team is to be composed of persons knowledgeable about the child, the evaluation, and the placement options. The multidisciplinary team that conducts evaluations and makes programming and placement decisions under the IDEA may also be used for evaluation and placement under Section 504; however, unlike the IDEA, neither Section 504 nor the Section 504 regulations dictate the positions of the people who compose the team.

The two primary purposes of the evaluation are to determine (a) if a student is eligible for services under Section 504, which involves deciding if a student has a physical or mental impairment and if that impairment results in a substantial limitation to a major life activity, and (b) what educational programming will be required to ensure that the student receives a FAPE.

Regulations to Section 504 regarding evaluations require that

1. Tests and all evaluation materials have been validated for the specific purpose for which they are used and are administered by trained personnel in conformity with instructions provided by their producer;
2. Tests and other evaluation materials include those tailored to assess specific areas of educational need and not merely those which are designed to provide a single intelligence quotient; and

3. Tests are selected and administered so as best to ensure that, when a test is administered to a student with impaired sensory, manual, or speaking skills, the test results accurately reflect the student's aptitude or achievement level or whatever other factor the test purports to measure, rather than reflecting the student's impaired [abilities] except where those skills are the factors that the test purports to measure.

(Section 504 Regulations, 34 C.F.R. § 104.35[b])

Additionally, the evaluation that a school conducts must meet the following three criteria: First, the evaluation team must use a variety of assessment procedures and instruments to assess a student and draw upon information from this variety of sources. Second, schools should establish procedures to ensure that all information is documented and fully considered (Smith & Patton, 1998; Zirkel, 2003). Smith and Patton (1998) and Zirkel (2003) suggested that Section 504 coordinators develop evaluation forms that document the team's evaluation, data collection process, and decisions. Information on such forms should include (a) general referral information, (b) the rationale for conducting the evaluation, (c) eligibility criteria and determination, (d) placement decisions, (e) names of team members, (f) dates of recommended actions, and (g) projected review or reevaluation date. Third, schools must ensure that the evaluation is made by a team of persons, including persons knowledgeable about the student, the meaning of the evaluation data, and the placement options (Section 504 Regulations, 34 C.F.R. § 104.35). Readers should note that Section 504, unlike the IDEA, does not identify the specific individuals who must be on the Section 504 team, although the student's teacher should be included.

Two issues that may present difficulties for school districts when deciding if they should conduct evaluations are (a) parent referrals and (b) medical diagnosis. First, when a parent refers a student for evaluation under Section 504 and school personnel do not believe that the student will qualify, are they required to conduct an evaluation? The answer is no; if school personnel believe that a student who has been referred under Section 504 will not qualify, they are not required to evaluate him or her (Katsiyannis, Landrum, & Reid, 2002). Section 504 requires that in such situations the school district must inform the parents that they have the right to dispute the school's decision in an impartial hearing. It is advisable, therefore, that if a district denies a parent referral, it can demonstrate there was no evidence to indicate the child had a disability (Norlin, 2014). Readers should note that a school district's duty to evaluate a student continues even in situations in which the parents have withdrawn the student from the school (*West Seneca School District*, 2009).

Second, a medical diagnosis is not required as part of an evaluation (Zirkel, 2003). That is, school personnel should not decide whether or not a student is qualified as a student with a disability based on a medical diagnosis; nor should they require that parents provide a diagnosis from a physician or psychologist prior to determining a student's eligibility (Zirkel, 2003; Norlin, 2014). If, however, a Section 504 team decides that a medical diagnosis is needed, the district must ensure that it is not charged to the parents (*Letter to Williams*, 1994). Further, Norlin (2014) suggested that when parents refer their child for services under Section 504 and they have a medical diagnosis that a child has a disability (e.g., ADHD), the district should conduct an evaluation, even though the school district is only required to do so if it believes the child has a disability. Similarly, if parents have an independent evaluation that indicates that a child has a disability and makes a referral based on that independent evaluation, the district would be well advised to conduct an evaluation.

When a student has medical problems, school personnel have knowledge of the condition, and problems arise in a school setting, this should trigger a school district evaluation for Section 504 coverage. For example, in a 2009 OCR case, *Metro Nashville Public Schools* (2009), school district personnel had specific information related to a student's asthma condition provided by his physician and his need for medication every four hours. Because of his condition, the student was frequently absent from school and had repeated hospitalizations. He also had academic problems and behavioral issues while at school. According to the OCR an evaluation to determine if the student was eligible under Section 504 should have been conducted. In another OCR case, *Chesterfield Public Schools* (2009), the parents of a student with academic and behavior problems at school obtained a psychological evaluation of their child. The evaluation, which identified significant academic deficits and recommended services and further assessment, was presented to school personnel but the school did not act. The OCR determined that because the parents had provided the school with the psychological assessment, this should have triggered an evaluation to determine if the student was eligible under Section 504. In another OCR case from 2011, *Lordes Public Charter School* (2011), a school district did not have a staff or health plan to address a student's diabetes, so the student was placed on homebound instruction. The OCR determined that this was a significant change of placement and should have triggered a Section 504 evaluation by the school before placing the student on homebound instruction.

A request for evaluation by a student's parents or classroom teachers should trigger a school district evaluation (Norlin, 2014). Moreover, when parents have had a medical or psychiatric diagnosis indicating that their child had a physical or mental impairment and referred their child for a Section 504 evaluation, rulings by the OCR have held that when school district personnel have not evaluated the child, they have not met their obligations under Section 504 (*Anaheim {CA} Union High School District*, 1995; *Oak Harbor {WA} School District*, 2005; *Triton {MA} Regional Union School District*, 1994). However, students who have received a medical diagnosis are not automatically eligible for services under Section 504 services. The medical diagnosis should be considered when conducting an evaluation of a student. If the team determines that there is a physical or mental impairment, this impairment must substantially limit a major life activity.

Readers should note that unlike the IDEA, Section 504 does not give parents the right to obtain an independent educational evaluation at public expense if they disagree with the school district's evaluation. However, the OCR has ordered reimbursement of parents for the cost incurred in obtaining an evaluation when school districts have failed to evaluate a student (Norlin, 2014). Moreover, if a parent does provide the school district with an independent evaluation, school district personnel should include the results of the evaluation in their decision-making process.

If an evaluation will be conducted, it must be completed in a timely manner (*Garden City {NY} Union Free School District*, 1990). In fact, delays in completing student evaluations from 61 to 185 days were found to be in violation of Section 504 (*Philadelphia {PA} School District*, 1992). Similarly, a seven-month delay between referral and evaluation and a nine-month delay between evaluation and placement were violations of Section 504 (*Dade County {FL} School District*, 1993). However, there are no specific timelines for conducting an evaluation. School personnel need to conduct an evaluation as soon as feasible after the decision to evaluate has been made.

Richards (2010) diagnosed the most frequent eligibility errors that school districts make in conducting, or not conducting, evaluations for services under Section 504. According to Richards, one common error occurs when school district personnel focus on the symptoms and ignore the cause when determining eligibility. That is, an eligibility decision should be made based on the presence of a disability or impairment (e.g., social maladjustment, ADHD) rather than just symptoms (e.g., poor judgment, quick temper). An area in which the OCR has been particularly concerned is when school districts identify students with limited English proficiency (LEP) as having a disability under either the IDEA or Section 504 when they do not understand or speak English but do not have a language impairment (Richards, 2010). Although LEP may substantially limit a student's learning (i.e., a major life activity), it is not a physical or mental impairment; rather, students with LEP should be served in a school's bilingual or English as a second language program, which is not disability related. A similar problem occurs when a Section 504 committee concentrates on the educational problems that a student has (e.g., poor grades) and focuses on resolving those problems through Section 504 while ignoring the impairment that may give rise to those problems.

Another school district error that Richards identifies occurs when a school's Section 504 committee equates the presence of a disability with eligibility under Section 504. As previously discussed, it is important that committee members understand that the presence of a mental or physical impairment is not enough in and of itself to establish eligibility. The impairment must also lead to a substantial limitation in a major life activity (e.g., learning, breathing). According to Richards, another eligibility error that school districts make is determining a student to be eligible for services under Section 504 because his or her parents have refused or revoked consent for special education placement. Although students who are leaving special education should be referred and evaluated if it looks like they may be eligible under Section 504, Richards asserted that when parents reject FAPE under the IDEA, it is tantamount to rejecting FAPE under Section 504. Thus, schools in such situations would have no obligation to provide services to serve a student under Section 504 (Richards, 2010).

Educational Programming   Based on the evaluation data, the team should design the services that a student will receive. A school provides a FAPE through regular education or special education programming or related aids and services. In the past, the OCR has found that school districts have failed to meet their FAPE obligations under Section 504 when they have (a) failed to provide the complete range of education and related services needed by a student or (b) identified the complete range of education and related services a student needed but failed to provide them. Section 504 requires that school districts provide a FAPE to all eligible students, and there are sanctions when school districts fail to meet these obligations.

If an evaluation finds that a student has a disability under Section 504, a multidisciplinary team should develop an individualized education program that provides a FAPE for that student. This plan can involve general education and related services or special education and related services. Furthermore, it is advisable that school personnel document this program in a formalized intervention plan (Fossey, Hosie, Soniat, & Zirkel, 1995; Katsiyannis et al., 2002; Smith & Patton, 1998). This Section 504 plan, sometimes called an individualized accommodation plan, should document (a) the nature of the student's disability and the major life activity it limits, (b) the basis for determining the disability, (c) the educational impact of the disability, (d) necessary accommodations, and (e) placement. Figure 5.4 is an example of a Section 504 plan. School districts may require the use of Section 504 plans, which Zirkel (2011) pointed out are an administrative convenience for the school district and parents although neither regulations to the law nor any court decisions have addressed the need to develop written Section 504 plans.

Section 504 regulations indicate that the development of an individualized education program (IEP) is one way to ensure that this requirement is met (Section 504 Regulations, 34 C.F.R. § 104.33[b][2]). The IDEA requires IEPs for students in special education programs; however, using IEPs for students who are not IDEA eligible is not advisable. This is because it may result in confusion to parents and educators about whether the student is covered under IDEA or Section 504 (Huefner & Herr, 2012). Additionally, the IDEA's many requirements for IEPs are not necessary in Section 504 plans (Norlin, 2014).

The Section 504 plan should include accommodations and modifications to a student's educational program. The plan details the appropriate education that a student will receive

FIGURE 5.4 ▪ Sample Format for a Section 504

Section 504 Education Plan

I. Personal Information

Student's name: DOB: Age: Grade:

Address: Date of conference:

Date of implementation of Section 504 plan:

Parents or Guardians:

II. Referral Information

Date of referral: Source of referral:

Reasons for referral:

III. Section 504 Team

Coordinator: Teacher(s):

Principal:

Parents or Guardians:

Others:

IV. Evaluation Information

Dates of evaluation:

Results:

Impairment:

Major life activity affected:

  V. Educational Services

VI. Accommodations

VII. Related and Supplementary Services and Aids

VIII. Placement

IX. Monitoring and Evaluation Procedures

X. Date of Review of Section 504 Plan

and is the result of a multidisciplinary team planning process. Figure 5.5 contains a list of potential classroom accommodations.

Once a committee finalizes a Section 504 plan, school personnel are obligated to implement the plan as written. It is important, therefore, that the Section 504 team be thoughtful and deliberate in developing the plan and ensure that all staff and teachers understand and implement their responsibilities under the plan. Teams should avoid what Richards (2010) called the "all-you-can-eat-buffet" approach to developing accommodations in the plan (p. 47). According to Richards, too often teams use checklists of accommodations and

FIGURE 5.5 ■
Examples of Reasonable Accommodations in Classrooms

Classroom Modifications
- Adjust placement of student (e.g., preferential seating).
- Alter physical setup of classroom.
- Reduce distractions (e.g., study carrel).
- Provide increased lighting.
- Schedule classes in accessible areas.

Academic Adjustments
- Vary instructional strategies and materials.
- Allow more time to complete assignments.
- Adjust length of assignments.
- Modify pace of instruction.
- Use peer tutors.
- Provide outline of lectures.
- Use visual aids.
- Use advance organizers.
- Highlight texts and worksheets.
- Tape lectures.
- Adjust reading levels of materials.
- Use specialized curricular materials.
- Provide study guides.
- Give tests orally or on tape.
- Allow more time to complete tests.
- Allow students to dictate answers.
- Alter the test format.
- Use enlarged type.
- Reduce the reading level of the test.

Auxiliary Aids and Devices
- Provide interpreters.
- Provide readers.
- Use audiovisual aids.
- Tape tests.
- Provide assistive technology devices and services, such as laptop computers, Braille readers, text enlargement devices, or alternative input devices.

choose so many accommodations that accurate implementation of the plan is doubtful and classroom teachers may incorrectly believe they can pick which accommodations they wish to implement. Richards advises that school district personnel remember that the purpose of Section 504 is to level the educational playing field and only choose the accommodations that are necessary or they may forget to implement some of the accommodations (*Houston Independent School District v. Bobby R., 2000*). This can be done by ensuring that the needs as determined in the evaluation are addressed with an appropriate accommodation; where the evaluation does not show a need, there is no need to develop an accommodation.

Richards also pointed out that a frequent complaint from parents is that the Section 504 plan was not implemented as developed. When this occurs, a likely result is distrust of the school personnel by a student's parents and possible legal action. An example of such a situation occurred in *Corunna (MI) Public Schools* (2005). The OCR received a complaint from a parent of a student who had a Section 504 plan that called for the student's parents to receive a weekly report from all his teachers regarding his classroom behavior. Additionally, the plan called for consistent redirections, limits, and consequences. The plan had no effect on the student's classroom behavior. Additionally, the parents received two partially completed weekly reports and no others. The OCR determined that by failing to complete the weekly reports, the school had denied the student a FAPE. In interviews of the teachers, the personnel from OCR found that because there was no discussion of the plan following the meeting, members of the committee were confused as to what their responsibilities were regarding the behavior plan and the weekly reports. The OCR investigators found that the Section 504 plan requirements were ineffectively communicated to teachers who were not at the meeting.

In a similar situation, *Fayette County (KY) School District* (2003), the OCR ruled in favor of a school district. A student's parents filed a complaint with the OCR alleging their child's teachers were unaware of the contents of his Section 504 plan. The school, however, had evidence that showed that all the child's teachers had initialed the Section 504 plan agreeing to implement the accommodations, and then all the teachers were sent emails at the beginning of the school year reminding them of their duties under the plan. A serious problem may occur when a teacher knows of the responsibilities under a Section 504 plan but fails to perform those duties.

Richards (2010) suggested that in order to ensure implementation, a Section 504 committee would need strong and visible support of the principal of a school. Richards also noted that failure to implement a Section 504 plan is a violation of federal law and local policy; therefore, when a teacher balks at performing his or her duty under the plan, a principal needs to take appropriate action. Because employee contracts typically include provisions requiring that an employee will obey district policy, state law, and federal law, the appropriate action that a principal should take in such a situation is to take some action regarding a teacher's employment (e.g., official reprimand). Figure 5.6 is a form that may be used to alert and remind a student's teachers of their responsibilities under a Section 504 plan.

Placement   The Section 504 team must also decide where students can receive their educational services. Placement options may include regular classrooms, regular classrooms with related services, or special education and related services. Special education may be provided in regular classrooms, special classrooms, at home, or in private or public institutions, and may be accompanied by related services. If the school district cannot provide the

FIGURE 5.6 ■ Section 504 Plan Information Form

Student: _____   Date: _____

Teacher: _____   Subject: _____

Principal: _____   504 Coordinator: _____

Interventions:

This is the Section 504 plan for <u>student's name</u>. The plan requires that you implement the following interventions. Your signature signifies that you understand and will implement these interventions.

Parents/Guardians: _____   Teacher: _____

Principal: _____   504 Coordinator: _____

appropriate placement, it must assume the cost of alternative placements. The placement must allow for contact with students without disabilities to the maximum extent appropriate. This applies to both academic and nonacademic settings.

Least Restrictive Environment   Regulations to Section 504 require that students with disabilities be educated along with students without disabilities to the maximum extent appropriate to the needs of the student. Additionally, the general education classroom is the preferred placement unless it is demonstrated that an education with supplementary aids and services in the general education classroom cannot be achieved satisfactorily and that the needs of the student would be better served by placement in another setting. OCR guidelines and rulings have specified that districts must document the reasons why more restrictive placements are needed when the student is removed from the general education classroom (or a less restrictive setting).

In making placement decisions to move students with disabilities to more restrictive settings, schools may take into account the effect of a student's behavior on students without disabilities if the effect is deleterious. In an analysis of final regulations, the OCR stated that "where a handicapped child is so disruptive in a regular classroom that the education of other students is significantly impaired, the needs of the handicapped child cannot be met in that environment. Therefore, regular placement would not be appropriate to his or her needs and would not be required" (Section 504 Regulations, Appendix A, p. 384).

Neighborhood Schools   Section 504 also requires that when a student with disabilities is placed in a setting other than the general education classroom, the school must take into account the proximity of the alternative setting to the student's home. However, schools are not required to place students in schools closest to their homes. If a school does not offer an appropriate program or facilities, a student may be transferred to another school. The home school will still retain responsibility for the student and must provide transportation.

Schools must also ensure that in nonacademic and extracurricular services and activities, students with disabilities participate with students without disabilities to the maximum extent appropriate to their needs. This requirement is especially important when students' needs require that they are educated primarily in a segregated setting.

Reevaluation   Unlike the IDEA, there is no requirement in Section 504 that students be reevaluated every three years. Rather, Section 504 requires that students be reevaluated periodically or before a significant change in placement is made. If a school proposes a significant change in placement, the student must be reevaluated in a manner similar to the initial evaluation. In 1997, the OCR defined a significant change of placement as a substantial and fundamental change in a student's educational program (*Harlowtown Public Schools*, 1997). Norlin (2014) asserted that, generally, if a student placement is changed so that he or she receives the same programming and services in a similar environment, that will not be a significant change in placement, thus triggering a reevaluation. Examples of significant changes that will trigger an evaluation include a placement change such as moving a student from a full-time general education placement to a full-time special education class (*Fairbanks {AK} North Star Borough School District*, 1994) and changes in educational programming (*Montebello {CA} Unified School District*, 1993). Additionally, transitions from elementary school to middle school to high school are considered changes in placement, which trigger the reevaluation requirement of Section 504 (*Mobile County {AL} School District*, 1992). Graduation may also be a significant change in placement, although graduation may only trigger the procedural safeguards and not reevaluation requirements (Norlin, 2014).

Regulations also require that reevaluations should be conducted periodically. No timeline for reevaluations is provided; however, regulations specify that conducting reevaluations in accordance with the more detailed requirements of the IDEA constitutes compliance with Section 504 requirements. Figure 5.7 is a flowchart for a Section 504 team to follow from referral to planning and implementing a student's Section 504 plan.

FIGURE 5.7 ■ **Section 504 Flowchart**

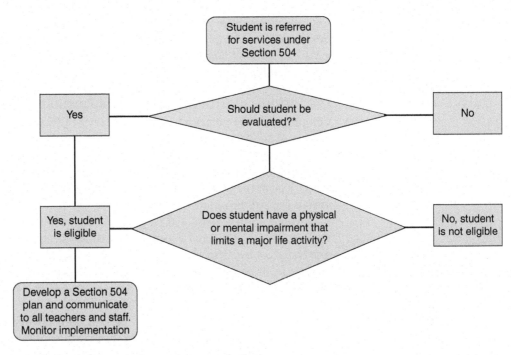

* Parent consent is required to conduct an evaluation

ENFORCEMENT OF SECTION 504

The primary vehicles by which parents can bring actions against a school district are through (a) filing a grievance with the school district's grievance coordinator, (b) requesting a due process hearing, (c) filing a complaint to the OCR of the U.S. Department of Education, or (d) filing a suit in federal court.

Podemski, Marsh, Smith, and Price (1995) suggested that schools attempt to avoid complaints and hearings by (a) focusing on the child by making good-faith efforts to provide appropriate programs; (b) involving the parents to the greatest extent possible; (c) conducting a thorough and individualized evaluation; (d) documenting all school and parent contacts, including phone calls, letters, and face-to-face correspondence, and sending important documents by registered mail; and (e) using mediation to resolve disagreements. Huefner and Herr (2012) argued that the best way for school districts to avoid legal liability under Section 504 is to take seriously the mandate not to discriminate against students with disabilities. If a parent filed a complaint with the OCR, Zirkel (2014) advised that a school attempt to reach a settlement with the complainant. This is referred to as *early complaint resolution* (ECR).

Filing a Grievance

Grievances can be filed with a school district's Section 504 coordinator if a parent, student, community member, or staff member believes that discrimination based on a disability has occurred. School districts must have a formal mechanism by which students, parents, and employees can file a grievance. Furthermore, the public must be notified regarding the grievance procedures. School districts may not use internal grievance procedures as a substitute for impartial due process hearings (*Leon County School District*, 2007).

Filing a Complaint with the Office of Civil Rights

Any person may file a grievance with his or her regional OCR office against a school district. All complaints filed with the OCR are investigated as long as they have merit (OCR

Complaint Resolution Manual, 1995). If a complaint has merit, the OCR will investigate the complaint. Complaints must be filed within 180 days from the date that the alleged violation occurred (*Stafford County Public Schools*, 2005). The OCR investigation process is depicted in Figure 5.8.

The Predetermination Settlement Process

The first step in the OCR investigation process is the predetermination settlement (PDS) process. The OCR initiated the PDS process in an attempt to reduce its massive complaint load (Martin, 1993). Through this process the school can avoid an on-site investigation and essentially close the matter without admitting to a violation by agreeing to actions that resolve the complainant's issues to the satisfaction of the OCR. If the complainant disagrees with the school district's actions, these actions can still be approved by the OCR.

According to Martin (1993), the advantage of the PDS process is that it saves an enormous amount of time and expense for both the school district and the OCR. The primary disadvantages are, first, that if the allegations are unfounded, there is no opportunity to dispute them, and, second, that the school must develop a reporting and monitoring timeline to assist the OCR in determining if the school district is fulfilling its commitment.

On-Site Investigation

If the PDS process is not successful, the OCR will then go to the on-site investigation option. In the investigative process, the OCR will request pertinent documentation and conduct staff interviews. These investigations are time consuming and uncomfortable for school district staff. Following the investigation, the OCR will issue a verbal finding of violation or a finding of no violation. If the finding is no violation, the matter is closed. If a violation is found to exist, however, the focus shifts to correction of the violation. Martin (1993) warns school districts that at this stage of the process, the OCR is not interested

FIGURE 5.8 ■
The OCR Investigation Process

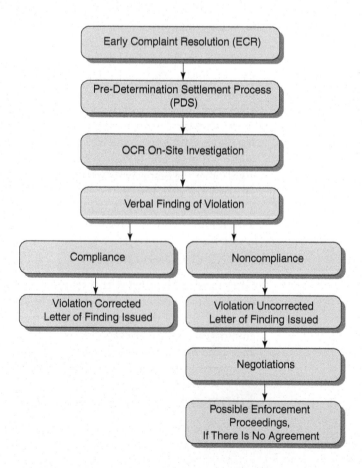

in discussing its legal findings or school district objections. Its focus is on the school district correcting the problem. If the district voluntarily complies to correct the complaint, and does so to the OCR's satisfaction, the OCR will issue a letter of finding (LOF) violation corrected. If, however, the school does not comply to the OCR's satisfaction, an LOF violation uncorrected will be issued. Following the issuance of this letter, the OCR and the district attempt to negotiate appropriate corrective action. If there is no agreement, the OCR can initiate enforcement proceedings to terminate federal funds to the school district. Terminations are unlikely to occur, however, and would only be imposed in the most egregious of cases. Any administrative decision, such as a decision to terminate, is subject to judicial review.

Filing for a Due Process Hearing

Parents may also request a Section 504 hearing to challenge a school district's actions. Individual states have policies regarding how Section 504 hearings will be handled. In many states, when a student is covered under Section 504 and the IDEA, both issues will be handled in an IDEA due process hearing. If an issue involves a Section 504 issue only, it will be resolved in a separate Section 504 hearing. Huefner (2000) reported that some states train hearing officers to preside over Section 504 cases and train separate hearing officers to preside over IDEA cases, whereas in other states IDEA hearing officers are also trained to hear Section 504 disputes.

Although Section 504 offers little direction with respect to conducting impartial hearings, the OCR has offered guidance in various letters and findings. Parents must be permitted to participate in the hearing, be represented by an attorney, and be able to review the decision (*Talbott County Public Schools*, 2008; *Polk County School District*, 2012). According to the OCR, due process hearings under Section 504 do not have to allow cross-examination of witnesses, nor do they require court reporters (*Houston Independent School District*, 1996). Whereas there are no specific timelines for completing hearings, the OCR indicates that it is reasonable and fair to look to the timelines in the IDEA case law and administrative rulings for guidance (*Letter to Anonymous*, 1991).

Filing a Suit in Federal Court

Often parents who file IDEA claims in courts also file claims under Section 504. In such situations, a court will first rule on the IDEA issue and then the Section 504 issue. If the issues are separate, a court will rule on the Section 504 issue. If a Section 504 lawsuit seeks relief under the IDEA, typically the claim must be first heard in a due process hearing. Courts have heard separate Section 504 cases if students were not also covered by the IDEA. In these situations, state law will determine if the parents can go directly to court or if they must exhaust administrative procedures (i.e., due process). In 2017, the U.S. Supreme Court issued a ruling in *Fry v. Napoleon Community School* (hereinafter *Fry*), that settled the issue regarding the necessity of exhausting administrative procedures in Section 504 cases. I next examine this important case.

Fry v. Napoleon Community Schools (2017)

Ehlena Fry, referred to as E.F. in the Supreme Court's decision, was an orphan in Calcutta, Indiana, when she was adopted by Stacy and Brent Fry. Ehlena had spina bifida, which severely limited her mobility and independence. When Ehlena was five years old, the Frys purchased a service dog for her. The service dog, a golden doodle named Wonder, was trained to help Ehlena with daily life activities. When Ehlena began elementary school, school officials in the Napoleon Community School District refused to allow her to bring Wonder to school with her because they provided Ehlena with a human aide who could do all the things the service dog could do; therefore, the use of the service dog was not necessary. The

Frys pulled Ehlena from the school, educated her at home, and eventually enrolled her in a different elementary school, where Ehlena and Wonder were welcomed.

In December 2016, the Frys filed a lawsuit in federal district alleging that the Napoleon School District's refusal to allow Wonder in the elementary school violated both Section 504 of the Rehabilitation Act and the Americans with Disabilities Act. The federal district court dismissed the case, holding that because the parents were seeking relief that was available under the IDEA, they had to exhaust their administrative remedies (e.g., due process hearing) under that law before they could seek remedies under other laws, such as Section 504. The U.S. Circuit Court of Appeals for the Sixth Circuit affirmed the district court's ruling, so the Frys filed with the U.S. Supreme Court, which agreed to hear the case. The Frys contended that the lower courts erred because they were only required to pursue and exhaust administrative remedies if they were seeking relief under the IDEA, which they contended they were not.

Writing for the 8-to-0 majority[2], Justice Elena Kagan reversed and remanded the lower court's decision ruling that when the Frys, or any family, file a lawsuit alleging discrimination under the ADA or Section 504, they do not need to first go through the administrative proceedings required by the IDEA unless the focus of the lawsuit is an allegation that a child did not receive a FAPE under the IDEA. Thus, when students with disabilities allege that a school has discriminated against them because of their disability, they are not required to use the IDEA's administrative proceedings simply because the alleged discrimination happened at school. It is only when a plaintiff is alleging that he or she has been denied a FAPE that the plaintiff must begin with the IDEA proceedings.

An important issue in such cases is, how are courts supposed to decide when a plaintiff is seeking relief for the denial of a FAPE, and when is he or she is not seeking relief for the denial of FAPE? According to Justice Kagan's opinion, it is important to look at the gravamen or essential nature of the plaintiff's complaint. If the gravamen or essential nature of the complaint seeks relief for a school district's failure to provide a FAPE, exhaustion through the administrative procedures of the IDEA are required. If, however, the gravamen or essential nature of the complaint is about discrimination, exhaustion is not required.

The High Court provided a three-part test that courts could use in making this determination. Justice Kagan explained the first two parts of the test as follows:

> First, could the plaintiff have brought essentially the same claim if the alleged conduct had occurred at a public facility that was not a school—say, a public theater or library? And second, could an adult at the school—say, an employee or visitor—have pressed essentially the same grievance? When the answer to those questions is yes, a complaint that does not expressly allege the denial of a FAPE is also unlikely to be truly about that subject; after all, in those other situations there is no FAPE obligation and yet the same basic suit could go forward. But when the answer is no, then the complaint probably does concern a FAPE, even if it does not explicitly say so; for the FAPE requirement is all that explains why only a child in the school setting (not an adult in that setting or a child in some other) has a viable claim (*Fry*, 2017, pp. 15-16).

The Frys' complaint alleged only disability-based discrimination, thus infringing on Ehlena's right to equal access in violation of Section 504 and the ADA, and did not address the adequacy of the school district's special education services, which would have violated Ehlena's FAPE and required the Frys to exhaust the administrative procedures. Using the two-part test, Justice Kagan wrote that:

> Consider, as suggested above, that the Frys could have filed essentially the same complaint if a public library or theater had refused admittance to Wonder. Or similarly, consider that an adult visitor to the school could have leveled much the same charges if prevented from entering with his service dog. In each case, the plaintiff would challenge a public facility's policy of precluding service dogs (just as a blind person might challenge a policy of barring

---

[2] Because Justice Scalia's replacement was not yet on the U.S. Supreme Court, only 8 justices ruled on this case.

guide dogs) as violating Title II's and §504's equal access requirements. The suit would have nothing to do with the provision of educational services. From all that we know now, that is exactly the kind of action the Frys have brought (*Fry*, 2017, p. 20).

The third part of the Supreme Court's test requires that a court examine the procedural history of the complaint and if that history includes using IDEA's complaint resolution mechanisms. In such a situation, the plaintiff's initial choice to use the IDEA procedures may indicate that he or she is seeking relief for the denial of FAPE. Because this issue was not addressed by neither the Frys nor the Napoleon School District's brief to the Supreme Court, the circuit courts' decision in *Fry* was vacated and the case was remanded back to the circuit courts for further proceedings consistent with the Supreme Court's opinion.

Remedies Under Section 504

Although no private right of action is specifically mentioned in Section 504, case law holds that such a right exists. In fact, some courts have held that a claimant under Section 504 has the right to a jury trial (*William S. and Kathleen S. v. Upper St. Clair School District*, 2004). According to Norlin (2014), it has been long settled in the courts that for a student with a disability to bring an action for a violation of his or her rights under Section 504, he or she must prove that (a) the student is an individual with a disability, (b) the student is otherwise qualified for a public elementary or secondary education (i.e., is of school age) or otherwise subjected to discrimination, and (c) the student has been excluded from a program or activity or denied the benefit of a program or activity solely by reason of his or her disability. Interestingly enough, an emerging trend in litigation is the use of Section 504 in cases seeking monetary damages for violations of the IDEA (Richards, 2014). According to Weatherly (2014), this may be due to the availability of monetary damages under Section 504 where no monetary damages are available under the IDEA.

Remedies that are available to individuals with disabilities who bring actions under Section 504 include injunctions (e.g., court orders to stop a certain practice, court orders to require specified changes in a student's program), attorney's fees, compensatory damages, reimbursement for costs incurred (e.g., tuition), and possibly monetary awards for damages. According to the U.S. Court of Appeals for the Eighth Circuit, monetary awards are only available in cases in which school districts act in bad faith or make gross errors in judgment (*Hoekstra v. Independent School District No. 283*, 1996). The U.S. Court of Appeals for the Sixth Circuit, however, ruled that punitive damages were not available under Section 504 (*Moreno v. Consolidated Rail Corporation*, 1996). Because Title II of the ADA, which applies to public schools, specifies the same remedies as Section 504, the Sixth Circuit decision implies that punitive damages are not available under either the ADA or Section 504.

In a number of decisions, the U.S. Court of Appeals for the various circuits have held that when there is a Section 504 issue, monetary damages are not available for mere violations of Section 504; rather, the conduct of school personnel must rise to the level of intentional discrimination, deliberate indifference, bad faith, or gross misjudgment in order to go to trial to seek monetary damages (Richards, 2014). In fact, the U.S. Court of Appeals for the Eighth Circuit, in *Todd v. Elkins School District No. 10* (1998), wrote that "liability may be imposed only when the decision by the professional is such a departure from accepted professional judgment, practice, or standards as to demonstrate that the person responsible actually did not base the decision on such a judgment" (p. 32).

Retaliation Claims Under Section 504

Section 504 prohibits anyone from attempting to thwart the exercise of rights granted under Section 504 (Norlin, 2014). This means that any action taken by a person to intimidate or retaliate against someone for exercising his or her Section 504 rights may be at legal liability. This protection against retaliation applies not only to students with disabilities, but also to parents, teachers, and paraprofessionals who are attempting to secure a student's rights or who are advocating for students with disabilities. The OCR has investigated many claims of retaliation. When investigating such claims, the OCR requires that persons filing the claims show that (a) they engaged in a protected activity, (b) they suffered an adverse action at the same time as they engaged in the protected activity or shortly thereafter, (c) the school district was aware of their protected activity, and (d) there is evidence of a causal connection between the protected activity and the adverse action. This is a difficult standard, and most OCR claims and court cases have ended when the OCR or the court did not find evidence to prove retaliation (Weatherly, 2014). Nonetheless, there have been findings in which the burden was met and a school district was found to have retaliated against a person who advocated for students with disabilities or otherwise acted to ensure that the students' rights under Section 504 were protected (e.g., *Settlegoode v. Portland Public Schools*, 2004; *Pollack v. Regional School Unit 75*, 2014).

COMPARISON OF THE IDEA AND SECTION 504

The IDEA and Section 504 form much of the legal foundation of special education. The IDEA, with its detailed rules and procedures, is often considered the more relevant of the two laws to educators. In fact, Section 504 has been viewed by many as the less detailed version of the IDEA (Champagne, 1995). Although there is a great deal of overlap between the two laws, there are also distinct differences. Table 5.2 compares and contrasts the two laws.

TABLE 5.2 ■ Comparison of the Individuals with Disabilities Education Act (IDEA) and Section 504

Component	IDEA	Section 504
Purpose of law	• Provides federal funding to states to assist in education of students with disabilities • Substantive requirements attached to funding	• Civil rights law • Protects persons with disabilities from discrimination in programs or services that receive federal financial assistance • Requires reasonable accommodations to ensure nondiscrimination
Who is protected?	• Categorical approach • Thirteen disability categories • Disability must adversely impact educational performance	• Functional approach • Students (a) having a mental or physical impairment that affects a major life activity, (b) with a record of such an impairment, or (c) who are regarded as having such an impairment • Protects students in general and special education
Free appropriate public education (FAPE)	• Special education and related services that are provided at public expense, meet state requirements, and are provided in conformity with the individualized education program (IEP) • Requires an IEP • Substantive standard is educational benefit	• General or special education and related aids and services • Written education plan • Substantive standard is equivalency
Least restrictive environment (LRE)	• Student must be educated with peers without disabilities to the maximum extent appropriate • Removal from integrated settings only when supplementary aids and services are not successful • Districts must have a continuum of placement available	• School must ensure that students are educated with their peers without disabilities

TABLE 5.2 ▓ (continued)

Component	IDEA	Section 504
Evaluation and placement	• Protection in evaluation procedures • Requires consent prior to initial evaluation and placement • Evaluation and placement decisions have to be made by a multidisciplinary team • Requires evaluation of progress toward IEP goals annually and reevaluation at least every three years	• Does not require consent; requires notice only • Requires periodic reevaluation • Reevaluation is required before a significant change in placement
Procedural safeguards	• Comprehensive and detailed notice requirements • Provides for independent evaluations • No grievance procedure • Impartial due process hearing	• General notice requirements • Grievance procedure • Impartial due process hearing
Funding	• Provides for federal funding to assist in the education of students with disabilities	• No federal funding
Enforcement	• U.S. Office of Special Education Programs (OSEP) (can cut off IDEA funds) • Compliance monitoring by state educational agency (SEA)	• Complaint may be filed with the Office of Civil Rights (OCR) (can cut off all federal funding) • Complaints can be filed with state's department of education

SUMMARY

Section 504 of the Rehabilitation Act of 1973 is a civil rights statute requiring that no otherwise qualified person with disabilities be excluded from participation in, be denied the benefits of, or be subjected to discrimination in any program receiving federal financial assistance. Although there are no funds available through Section 504, it is illegal for schools receiving federal funds to discriminate based on a student's disability.

Section 504 defines disabilities broadly. Students are protected under the statute if they have a physical or mental impairment that substantially limits a major life function, have a record of such an impairment, or are regarded as having such an impairment. The disability does not have to adversely affect educational performance, as is the case with the IDEA, and the student does not have to be in special education. Section 504 protects students with disabilities in both general and special education. All students protected under the IDEA are also protected under Section 504. The reverse, however, is not true.

In addition to offering protection from discrimination, Section 504 provides that schools must make reasonable accommodations—modifications to programs and services—if necessary to ensure that discrimination does not occur. Public schools are required to provide appropriate educational services to children protected by Section 504. The provision of general education and related services or special education and related services must be designed to meet the individual needs of students with disabilities as effectively as the education provided to students without disabilities meets their needs. To provide an appropriate education, schools are required to follow a process to ensure equivalency. Schools are required to educate students with disabilities along with students without disabilities to the maximum extent appropriate.

With respect to educational matters, the Office of Civil Rights of the U.S. Department of Education enforces Section 504. When a discrimination complaint is filed, the OCR will investigate. The OCR can enforce compliance by terminating all federal funding. Individuals can bring suit against a school district for violating students' rights under Section 504. Potential remedies that are available to persons who prevail in their lawsuits include injunctive relief, compensatory damages, tuition reimbursement, attorney's fees, and monetary damages.

Enhanced eText Application Exercise 5.1: *Fry, as next friends of E.F. v. Napoleon Community Schools et al.*

FOR FURTHER INFORMATION

Norlin, J. W. (2014). *What do I do when ... The answer book on Section 504* (4th ed.). Palm Beach Garden, FL: LRP Publications.

Richards, D. M. (2010). *The top section 504 errors: Expert guidance to avoid common compliance mistakes.* Palm Beach Garden, FL: LRP Publications.

Smith, T. E. C. (2002). *The Section 504 trainer's manual: A step-by-step guide for inservice and staff development.* Horsham, PA: LRP Publications. (This is a useful manual for conducting staff development activities. It contains a script and transparencies.)

Smith, T. E. C., & Patton, J. R. (1998). *Section 504 and public schools: A practical guide for determining eligibility, developing accommodation plans, and documenting compliance.* Austin, TX: ProEd.

Zirkel, P. A. (2014). *Section 504, the ADA and the schools* (3rd ed.). Palm Beach Garden, FL: LRP Publications. (This book offers complete and thorough coverage of Section 504 and the Americans with Disabilities Act. It begins with the statutes and regulations, both in annotated and unannotated form. The annotated regulations include a comprehensive compilation of court decisions and administrative rulings on Section 504, ADA, and the schools. Sample forms and letters to help school districts comply with Section 504 and the ADA are included.)

REFERENCES

Alexander v. Choate, 469 U.S. 287 (1985).

Americans with Disabilities Act Amendments, P.L. 110-235 § 2(b)(2)(5), 122 Stat. 3553 (2008).

Americans with Disabilities Act of 1990, 42 U.S.C. 12101 *et seq.*

Anaheim (CA) Union High School District, 20 IDELR 185 (OCR 1995).

Bryan County {GA} School District, 53 IDELR 131 (OCR 2009).

Champagne, J. F. (1995). Preface. In P. A. Zirkel (Ed.), *Section 504, the ADA and the schools.* Palm Beach Garden, FL: LRP Publications.

Cherry v. Matthews, 419 F. Supp. 922 (D.D.C. 1976).

Chesterfield (SC) Public Schools, 54 IDELR 299 (OCR 2009).

Civil Rights Act of 1964, 42 U.S.C. § 200d.

Congressional Record. (1977, April 26). Remarks of Sen. Hubert H. Humphrey, principal Senate author of Section 504, pp. 12, 216.

Coppell (TX) Independent School District, 24 IDELR 643 (OCR 1996).

Corunna (MI) Public Schools, 44 IDELR 16 (OCR 2005).

Dade County (FL) School District, 20 IDELR 267 (OCR 1993).

Dagley, D. L., & Evans, C. W. (1995). The reasonable accommodation standard for Section 504—eligible students. *Education Law Reporter, 97,* 1–13.

Daley v. Koch, 639 F. Supp. 289 (D.D.C. 1986).

Education Amendments of 1972, 20 U.S.C. § 1681 *et seq.*

E. E. Black v. Marshall, 497 F. Supp. 1088 (D. Haw. 1980).

Ellenberg v. New Mexico Institute, 52 IDELR 181 (10th Cir. 2009)

Fairbanks (AK) North Star Borough School District, 21 IDELR 856 (OCR 1994).

Fayette County (KY) School District 40 IDELR 130 (OCR 2003)

Fossey, R., Hosie, T., Soniat, K., & Zirkel, P. A. (1995). Section 504 and "front line" educators: An expanded obligation to serve children with disabilities. *Preventing School Failure, 39*(2), 10–14.

Garden City (NY) Union Free School District, EHLR 353; 327 (OCR 1990).

Georgetown (TX) Independent School District, 19 IDELR 643 (OCR 1992).

Gerry, M. H., & Benton, J. M. (1982). Section 504: The larger umbrella. In J. Ballard, B. A. Ramirez, & F. J. Weintraub (Eds.), *Special education in America: Its legal and governmental foundations* (pp. 41–49). Reston, VA: Council for Exceptional Children.

Goldstein, B. A. (1994, May). Legal and practical considerations in implementing Section 504 for students. Paper presented at the National Institute on Legal Issues of Educating Individuals with Disabilities, San Francisco, CA.

Fry v. Napoleon Community School District, 137 S.Ct. 743 (2017). Available for download at www.supremecourt.gov/opinions/16pdf/15-497_p8k0.pdf

Harlowtown Public Schools, 26 IDELR 1156 (OCR 1997).

Hoekstra v. Independent School District No. 283, 25 IDELR 882 (8th Cir. 1996).

Houston (TX) Independent School District, 25 IDELR 205 (OCR 1996).

Houston Independent School District v. Bobby R., 31 IDELR 185 (5th Cir. 2000)

Huefner, D. S. (2000). *Getting comfortable with special education law: A framework for working with children with disabilities.* Norwood, MA: Christopher-Gordon Publishers.

Huefner, D. S., & Herr, C. M. (2012). *Navigating special education law and policy.* Verona, WI: Attainment Publishing.

Irvine (CA) Unified School District, 353 IDELR 192 (OCR 1989).

Joint Policy Memorandum (OSERS, 1991). Policy Memorandum, 18 IDELR 116

Katsiyannis, A., Landrum, T., & Reid, R. (2002). Section 504. *Beyond Behavior, 11*(2), 9–15.

Letter to Anonymous, 18 IDELR 230 (OCR 1991).

Letter to McKethan, 23 IDELR 504 (OCR 1994).

Letter to Veir, 20 IDELR 864 (OCR 1993).

Letter to Williams, 21 IDELR 73 (OCR/OSEP 1994).

Letter to Zirkel, 22 IDELR 667 (OCR 1995).

Leon County (FL) School District, 50 IDELR 172 (OCR 2007).

Lordes Public Charter School, 57 IDELR 53 (OCR 2011).

Mark H. v. Lemahieu, 49 IDELR 91 (9th Cir. 2008).

Martin, J. (1993, April). Section 504 of the Rehabilitation Act of 1973. Paper presented at the international conference of the Council for Exceptional Children, San Antonio, TX.

Mesa (AZ) Unified School District No. 4, EHLR 312:103 (OCR 1988).

Metro Nashville (TN) Public Schools, 110 LRL 49252 (OCR 2009).

Mobile (AL) County School District, 19 IDELR 519 (OCR 1992).

Montebello (CA) Unified School District, 20 IDELR 388 (OCR 1993).

Moreno v. Consolidated Rail Corporation, 25 IDELR 7 (6th Cir. 1996).

Norlin, J (2014). *What do I do when ... The answer book on Section 504*. Palm Beach Garden, FL: LRP Publications.

Oak Harbor (WA) School District No. 201, 45 IDELR 228 (OCR 2005).

Office of Civil Rights (1988). *Free appropriate public education for students with handicaps: Requirements under Section 504 of the Rehabilitation Act of 1973*. Washington, DC: Office for Civil Rights.

Office of Civil Rights (March 2009). *Protecting students with disabilities: Frequently asked questions and Section 504 and the education of students with disabilities*. Washington DC: Author.

Office of Civil Rights Complaint Resolution Manual. (1995). In P. A. Zirkel, *Section 504, the ADA and the schools*. Horsham, PA: LRP Publications.

Office of Civil Rights Memorandum Re: Definition of a disability, 19 IDELR 894 (OCR 1992).

Office of Civil Rights Senior Staff Memorandum, 17 EHLR 1233 (OCR 1990).

Philadelphia (PA) School District, 18 IDELR 931 (OCR 1992).

Pinkerton v. Moye, 509 F. Supp. 107 (W.D. Va. 1981).

Podemski, R. S., Marsh, G. E., Smith, T. E. C., & Price, B. J. (1995). *Comprehensive administration of special education* (2nd ed.). Upper Saddle River, NJ: Merrill/Pearson Education.

Polk County School District, 2012

Pollack v. Regional School Unit 75, 63 IDELR 72 (D. Me. 2014).

Rehabilitation Act of 1973, Section 504 Regulations, 34 C.F.R. § 104.1 *et seq.*

Rehabilitation, Comprehensive Services, and Developmental Disabilities Act of 1978, Pub. L. No. 95-062.

Rice v. Jefferson County Board of Education, 15 EHLR 441.632 (1989).

Richards, D. M. (2010). *The top section 504 errors: Expert guidance to avoid common compliance mistakes*. Palm Beach Garden, FL: LRP Publications.

Rozalski, M. E., Katsiyannis, A., Ryan, J., Collins, T., & Stewart, A. (2010). Americans with Disabilities Act Amendments of 2008. *Journal of Disability Policy Studies, 21*, 22–28.

Schoenfeld, B. N. (1980). Section 504 of the Rehabilitation Act. *University of Cincinnati Law Review, 50*, 580–604.

School Board of Nassau County v. Arline, 480 U.S. 273 (1987).

Section 504 of the Rehabilitation Act of 1973, 29 U.S.C. § 794 *et seq.*

Section 504 Regulations, 28 C.F.R. § 41.3(e).

Senate Report No. 890, 95th Cong., 2nd Sess. 39 (1978).

Senate Report No. 101-116, at 23.

Settlegoode v. Portland Public Schools, 371 F.3d 503 (9th Cir. 2004)

Sevier County (TN) School District, 23 IDELR 1151 (OCR 1995).

Smith, T. E. C. (2001). Section 504, the ADA, and public schools: What educators need to know. *Remedial and Special Education, 22*, 336–343.

Smith, T. E. C. (2002). *The Section 504 trainer's manual: A step-by-step guide for inservice and staff development*. Palm Beach Garden, FL: LRP Publications.

Smith, T. E. C., & Patton, J. R. (1998). *Section 504 and public schools: A practical guide for determining eligibility, developing accommodation plans, and documenting compliance*. Austin, TX: ProEd.

Southeastern Community College v. Davis, 442 U.S. 397 (1979).

Stafford County (VA) Public Schools, 44 IDELR 14 (OCR 2005).

Talbott County (MD) Public Schools, 52 IDELR 205 (OCR 2008).

Todd v. Elkins School District No. 10, 28 IDELR 29 (8th Cir. 1998).

Triton (MA) Regional Union 68 School District, 21 IDELR 1077 (OCR 1994).

Tucker, B. P., & Goldstein, B. A. (1992). *Legal rights of persons with disabilities: An analysis of federal law*. Palm Beach Garden, FL: LRP Publications.

Uniform Federal Accessibility Standards (1984), 49 31528.

U.S. Department of Education, Office for Civil Rights, Dear Colleague Letter (2010, October 26), available at www2.ed.gov/about/offices/list/ocr/letters/colleague-201010.pdf.

U.S. Department of Education, Office for Civil Rights, Dear Colleague Letter (2012, January 19), available at www2.ed.gov/about/offices/list/ocr/docs/dcl-504faq-201109.html.

U.S. Department of Education, Office for Civil Rights, Dear Colleague Letter (2013, January 25), available at www2.ed.gov/about/offices/list/ocr/letters/colleague-201301-504.html.

W. B. v. Matula, 23 IDELR 411 (3d Cir. 1995).

Walpole Public Schools, 26 IDELR 976 (S.E. Mass. 1997).

Weatherly, J. (2014, November). The year in review (Part 2): Top special education decisions continued. Presentation at the Tri-State Special Education Law Conference. Omaha, NE.

West Seneca (NY) School District, 53 IDELR 237 (OCR 2009).

William S. v. Gill, 572 F. Supp. 509 (E.D. Ill. 1983).

William S. and Kathleen S. v. Upper St. Clair School District, 42 IDELR 35 (W.D. Pa. 2004).

Zirkel, P. A. (1996). The substandard for FAPE: Does Section 504 require less than the IDEA? *Education Law Reporter, 106*, 471–477.

Zirkel, P. A. (2003). Conducting legally defensible Section 504/ADA eligibility determinations. *Education Law Reporter, 176*, 1–11.

Zirkel, P. A. (2011). Does Section 504 require a Section 504 plan for each eligible non-IDEA student? *Journal of Law and Education, 40*, 407–416.

Zirkel, P. A. (2014). *Section 504, the ADA, and the schools* (3rd ed.). Palm Beach Garden, FL: LRP Publications.

Chapter 6

The Americans with Disabilities Act

> I now lift my pen to sign the Americans with Disabilities Act and say: Let the shameful walls of exclusion finally come tumbling down.
>
> PRESIDENT GEORGE HERBERT WALKER BUSH, REMARKS ON SIGNING THE AMERICANS WITH DISABILITIES ACT OF 1990, JULY 26, 1990, *WEEKLY COMPILATION OF PRESIDENTIAL DOCUMENTS* (VOL. 26, N. 30, P. 1165)

Learner Objectives

At the end of the chapter, students will be able to:

6.1 Describe the origins of the Americans with Disabilities Act.

6.2 Describe the purpose of the Americans with Disabilities Act.

6.3 Describe the structure of the Americans with Disabilities Act.

6.4 Describe eligibility of persons with disabilities under the Americans with Disabilities Act.

6.5 Describe the titles of the Americans with Disabilities Act.

6.6 Describe the purpose of the Americans with Disabilities Act Amendments of 2008.

6.7 Describe school district responsibilities under the Americans with Disabilities Act.

In 1990, President George H. W. Bush signed P.L. 101-336, the Americans with Disabilities Act (ADA), into law. This was the largest signing ceremony in White House history.

Enhanced eText **Video Example 6.1:** To view a short **video** of the signing ceremony in which President George H. W. Bush signed the ADA into law, go to: www.youtube.com/watch?v=evbyv-d9JWk

The ADA mandates protections for persons with disabilities against discrimination in a wide range of activities in both the public and private sector. The law focuses primarily on employment and public services. The impact of the ADA on special education services for students with disabilities in school districts is primarily limited to reinforcing and extending the requirements of Section 504 of the Rehabilitation Act of 1973 (Zirkel, 2014). Recall that Section 504 prohibits recipients of federal funds from discriminating against persons with disabilities in programs; under the ADA this prohibition against discrimination is extended to private employers and commercial entities that serve the public. In effect, the ADA extends the reach of Section 504 (Huefner & Herr, 2012).

The ADA also affects public education as an employer of persons with disabilities. Furthermore, public education is affected in the areas of public access and in the preparation of students with disabilities to take advantage of the law's provisions. Court decisions regarding the ADA and students with disabilities have been inconclusive regarding schools' responsibilities under the law (Zirkel, 2014). The courts, however, have tended to rule that the ADA is to be interpreted consistent with Section 504. Therefore, case law under

Section 504 may be used by courts for guidance in interpreting similar provisions of the ADA (Osborne, 1995). The U.S. Department of Justice maintains a webpage, www.ada.gov, which provides historical and updated information on the law.

The ADA's effect on the provision of a free appropriate public education (FAPE) provided to students, especially when a school is in compliance with the IDEA and Section 504, will be minimal (Wenkart, 1993). Moreover, no student-specific rights are granted in the ADA beyond those of Section 504. Wenkart (1993) conjectured that because nothing in the legislative history suggests an intention to enlarge the substantive rights of children with disabilities, the ADA may not add to rights already existing.

One of the few courts to address the relationship between the IDEA and the ADA, the U.S. Court of Appeals for the Tenth Circuit, ruled in *Urban v. Jefferson County School District R-1* (1994) that the placement rights of a student with disabilities are no greater under the ADA than under the IDEA. Congress believed substantive rights of students with disabilities to be adequately protected under the IDEA and Section 504. This does not mean, however, that public education is unaffected by the ADA. Areas of public education that are affected include employment, general nondiscrimination (which parallels the requirements of Section 504), communications, and program accessibility. Additionally, an important area of difference between Section 504, the IDEA, and the ADA is that the ADA applies to private schools.

Administrators and teachers need to be aware of how the courts will apply the ADA to the school setting. Furthermore, Zirkel (2014) contended that it would be a mistake for school officials to think they will be in compliance with the ADA because they adhere to the requirements of Section 504. School officials, therefore, should be aware of their responsibilities under both Section 504 and the ADA.

Finally, it is important that administrators, counselors, and teachers working with students with disabilities are aware of the content of the ADA because of the law's implications for the lives of the students they serve. When students with disabilities leave school and enter the workforce, they will need to engage in self-advocacy. A duty of educators, aptly stated by Marczely (1993), is to inform students with disabilities and their parents of the "power and promise the ADA gives them, and the ways in which that power and promise can be productively used" (p. 207).

The purpose of this chapter is to briefly review the provisions of the ADA; the development, purpose, and structure of the ADA; and the school district's responsibilities under the law. Additionally, the chapter will examine rulings on the ADA by the U.S. Supreme Court and the legislative response to these rulings, in the ADA Amendments of 2008 (Americans with Disabilities Act Amendments of 2008).

THE DEVELOPMENT OF THE ADA

Section 504 was the first federal effort to protect persons with disabilities from discrimination. Section 504 applied to the federal government, government contractors, and recipients of federal funds. Employers and public accommodations operated by the private sector and by state and local governments, however, were unaffected by the law. As a result, many persons with disabilities continued to suffer from discrimination in employment, education, housing, access to public services, and transportation. To rectify these continued inequities, President Ronald Reagan created the National Council on Disabilities, whose task was to recommend to Congress remedies for halting discrimination against persons with disabilities (Miles, Russo, & Gordon, 1992). After three years of study, the council made recommendations to Congress that were to form the basis of the ADA. According to Miles et al. (1992), the bill, introduced in 1988, stalled in Congress because of congressional inaction, even though it enjoyed the strong support of President George H. W. Bush and advocacy groups for persons with disabilities. In July 1990, both houses of Congress passed the bill that had recently arrived from the House-Senate

Conference Committee. On July 26, 1990, President Bush signed the ADA into law on the White House lawn. The signing was witnessed by more than 3,000 persons with disabilities, reportedly one of the largest ceremonies in White House history.

THE PURPOSE AND STRUCTURE OF THE ADA

In the introduction to the ADA, Congress reported that 43 million Americans had physical or mental disabilities. Congress found that discrimination against persons with disabilities existed in employment, housing, public accommodations, education, transportation, communication, recreation, institutionalization, health services, voting, and access to public services (ADA, 42 U.S.C. § 12101). Such discrimination denied persons with disabilities the opportunity to compete on an equal basis and disadvantaged them socially, vocationally, economically, and educationally. Unfortunately, Congress also found that persons with disabilities who had experienced discrimination had little or no recourse to redress such discrimination. Stating that America's proper goals in this regard were to assure persons with disabilities equality of opportunity, full participation, independent living, and economic self-sufficiency, Congress passed the ADA. Figure 6.1 lists examples of discriminatory practices that are prohibited by the ADA.

Purpose of the ADA

The primary purposes of the law are:

1. To provide a clear and comprehensive national mandate for the elimination of discrimination against individuals with disabilities;
2. To provide clear, strong, consistent, enforceable standards addressing discrimination against individuals with disabilities;
3. To ensure that the federal government plays a central role in enforcing the standards established in the Act on behalf of individuals with disabilities; and
4. To invoke the sweep of Congressional authority, including the power to enforce the 14th Amendment and to regulate commerce, in order to address the major areas of discrimination faced day to day by people with disabilities.

(ADA, 42 U.S.C. § 12101)

The ADA extends the civil rights and antidiscrimination protections of Section 504 from the federal government, its contractors, and recipients of federal funds to employers, state and local governments or any instrumentality of the government, and any privately-owned business or facility open to the public. The primary goal of the law, therefore, is that persons with disabilities will enjoy equal opportunity to fully participate in the life of the community

FIGURE 6.1 ■
Discriminatory Practices

- Practices that deny a person with a disability the ability to participate in or cause a person to be denied the benefits from goods, services, facilities, or accommodations.
- Practices that provide an unequal benefit in goods, services, facilities, or accommodations on the basis of a disability.
- Practices that provide goods, services, facilities, or accommodations that, even though equal, are different or separate from those provided to persons without disabilities.
- Practices used in eligibility determinations for the use of goods, services, facilities, or accommodations that effectively exclude persons with disabilities through screening procedures.
- Practices that tend to segregate. Goods, services, and facilities shall be provided in settings in which persons with and without disabilities are integrated.

and have an equal opportunity to live independently and enjoy economic self-sufficiency through the removal of the barriers that exclude them from the mainstream of American life (Turnbull, Turnbull, Stowe, & Huerta, 2006).

Who Is Protected?

The ADA follows Section 504 in defining those individuals protected by the law. The Section 504 definition of persons with disabilities therefore applies to the ADA. In the ADA, a person with a disability is defined as having:

> (i) a physical or mental impairment that substantially limits one or more of the major life activities of such individual;
>
> (ii) a record of such an impairment; or
>
> (iii) being regarded as having such an impairment.
>
> (ADA, 42 U.S.C. § 12102[2])

Physical and Mental Impairments

The first part of the definition describes a disability broadly. ADA regulations mirror the language in Section 504 in listing physical or mental impairments. Protected disabilities include any disorder affecting body systems, including neurological (including traumatic brain injury), physiological, musculoskeletal, sense, respiratory, cardiovascular, digestive, or psychological systems. Regulations to the ADA require that whether or not a person has a disability, an assessment should be conducted without regard to the availability of mitigating modifications or assistive devices (ADA Regulations, 28 C.F.R. § 38, Appendix A). For example, a person with epilepsy is covered under the first part of the definition even if the effects of the impairment are controlled by medication. The ADA includes persons with HIV (whether symptomatic or asymptomatic) and tuberculosis. If, however, a person with an infectious disease presents a "direct threat" (i.e., significant risk) of contagion or infection, he or she may be excluded from goods, services, facilities, privileges, advantages, and accommodations or denied a job if the threat cannot be eliminated by reasonable accommodations or modifications. The determination of a direct threat is made on an individual basis and relies on current medical or objective evidence to determine the nature, duration, and severity of the risk; the probability that injury will occur; and whether reasonable accommodations will alleviate the risk (ADA Regulations, 28 C.F.R. § 36.208).

For an individual to be covered under the ADA, the physical or mental disability must substantially limit one or more major life activities. These activities include caring for oneself, performing manual tasks, walking, seeing, hearing, speaking, breathing, learning, and working (ADA Regulations, 28 C.F.R. § 38, Appendix A). Persons are thus considered disabled under the first part of the definition when their "important life activities are restricted as to the conditions, manner, and duration under which they can be performed in comparison to most people" (ADA Regulations, 28 C.F.R. § 38, Appendix A).

Exclusions from Protection

Physical or mental disabilities do not include simple physical characteristics, nor do they include environmental, cultural, economic, or other disadvantages (e.g., prison record, being poor). Neither are the following conditions included as disabilities: (a) age (although medical conditions resulting from old age are disabilities); (b) temporary, nonchronic impairments such as broken limbs; (c) pregnancy; and (d) obesity (except in rare circumstances). Environmental illnesses (e.g., multiple chemical sensitivity, allergy to smoke) are not considered disabilities under the ADA unless the impairment actually limits one or more major life activities.

The ADA specifically excludes certain individuals from its definition of a person with a disability. Because courts had interpreted Section 504 as covering transsexuals and compulsive gamblers, Congress specifically excluded these individuals from coverage under the

ADA. Additionally, Congress acted to ensure that the ADA definition of disability would not include homosexuality, bisexuality, transvestitism, transsexualism, pedophilia, exhibitionism, voyeurism, gender identity disorders not resulting from physical impairments, and other sexual behavior disorders (ADA, 42 U.S.C. § 12211[a][b]). The law also specifically excludes persons with compulsive gambling disorders, kleptomania, or pyromania (ADA, 42 U.S.C. § 12211[b][2]).

Persons engaging in the illegal use of drugs and any disorders resulting from current illegal drug use are also excluded from protection under the ADA. Persons who have successfully completed or are participating in a supervised drug rehabilitation program and are no longer using illegal drugs are protected by the ADA. Persons who are discriminated against because they are erroneously believed to be engaged in illegal drug use are also protected. Furthermore, drug testing of employees is allowed under the law. The ADA effectively amends Section 504 to allow school districts to discipline students with disabilities for the use or possession of illegal drugs or alcohol in the same manner that students without disabilities would be disciplined (*OCR Staff Memorandum*, 1991).

Having a Record of a Disability or Being Regarded as Being Disabled

The second and third parts of the definition essentially protect individuals when a negative or discriminatory action is committed against them based on a record of a disability or because they are regarded as being disabled. Persons covered by these two parts are those who have been subject to discrimination because they had a history of being disabled and are treated in a discriminatory way because people still believe them to be disabled. Persons who are regarded as being disabled are subject to discrimination if a covered entity mistakenly believes that the person has a disability (*Murphy v. United Parcel Service*, 1999). It is this discriminatory treatment, which is based on false assumptions, that entitles these persons to protection. Examples of persons having a record of a disability include persons with histories of cancer, heart disease, or mental or emotional illness. Examples of persons regarded as having a disability include persons misclassified as having an impairment and those discriminated against because of the fears and stereotypes of others.

The U.S. Supreme Court and the ADA

Katsiyannis and Yell (2002) and Rozalski, Katsiyannis, Ryan, Collins, and Stewart (2010) reviewed a series of U.S. Supreme Court cases that addressed the issue of when a person with a disability is covered by the ADA. These cases, three of which have been referred to as the Sutton trilogy, were seen as sharply narrowing the scope of the ADA protections by restricting the numbers of persons with disabilities who were protected by the law (Rozalski et al., 2010). The first case, *Sutton v. United Air Lines* (1999), involved two sisters who applied to be commercial airline pilots at United Airlines. United Airlines required that pilots had to meet a minimum of 20/100 uncorrected visual acuity to be employed by the carrier; unfortunately, the Sutton sisters had uncorrected visual acuity of 20/200. United Airlines therefore rejected their applications. The Suttons sued in federal court. The case went to the U.S. Supreme Court, which ruled that a disability exists only when an impairment substantially limits a major life activity, not when it might, could, or would be substantially limiting if corrective measures were not taken. The Sutton sisters did not meet the high court's interpretation of the definition of disability in Section 504 because mitigating measures (i.e., corrective lenses) allowed them to fully correct their visual impairments.

Murphy v. United Parcel Service, Inc. (1999) involved an employee, Vaughn Murphy, who was hired by United Parcel Service (UPS) to drive commercial vehicles. Before he could drive for the company, Murphy had to pass the Department of Transportation health certification requirements. One of these requirements was that a driver must not have high blood pressure, which could interfere with the driver's ability to operate a commercial vehicle safely. Murphy, however, was hired despite having high blood pressure. When the error was discovered, Murphy was fired. A suit was filed under the ADA. Eventually, the U.S. Court of Appeals for the Tenth Circuit ruled that the employee's hypertension was not a disability because he functioned normally in everyday activities and as a result did not qualify for protection under the ADA. The case was appealed to the U.S. Supreme Court. The high court upheld the lower court's decision, concluding that Murphy was not substantially limited in the major life activity of working but rather was unable to perform only a particular job. The Supreme Court ruled that the fact that Murphy was only unable to perform this particular job, being a truck driver, was insufficient to prove that he was regarded as substantially limited in the major life activity of working. Because he was not disabled under the ADA, he was not protected under the law. Further, the Supreme Court reasoned that employees who can function normally when their impairments are treated do not qualify for protection under the ADA. To be covered under the ADA, a person must be presently substantially limited in his or her ability to work.

In a similar case, *Albertsons, Inc. v. Kirkingburg* (1999), a truck driver, Hallie Kirkingburg, was falsely certified as passing the Department of Transportation's vision standards for commercial truck drivers. His vision was correctly assessed in 1992, and subsequently, he was fired for failing to meet the basic vision standards. He eventually applied for and received a waiver allowing him to drive, but the company refused to rehire him. The employee sued under the ADA. The district court dismissed the ADA claim. However, the Ninth Circuit reversed this decision. The circuit court found that Kirkingburg had established a disability under the ADA by demonstrating that the manner in which he sees was significantly different from the manner in which most people see.

On appeal, the Supreme Court reversed the decision of the lower court, concluding that the extent of the limitation on a major life activity caused by the vision impairment was not substantial. The Court also observed that the appellate court erred in determining Kirkingburg's eligibility under the ADA. The high court found that even though the ADA's standard is that the physical or mental impairment must substantially limit a major life activity, the circuit court had endorsed a new standard, a "significant difference" standard, which the circuit court believed was sufficient to meet ADA eligibility criteria. The Supreme Court disagreed, holding that different is not the appropriate standard. The ADA only protects persons with disabilities that are substantial.

In *Toyota Motor Manufacturing, Ky., Inc. v. Williams* (2002), Ella Williams, a person with carpel tunnel syndrome and related impairments, sued Toyota for failing to provide her with reasonable accommodations as required by the ADA. She had been working in the engine fabrication assembly line, which aggravated her carpel tunnel syndrome. She was reassigned to positions that did not aggravate her problems. She took numerous medical leaves and filed a workers' compensation claim. This claim was settled; however, she sued, claiming that Toyota had not provided the accommodations. The suit was also settled. She was placed on a Quality Control Inspection Team, and her tasks on the team were modified so she only had to do visual inspections with only a few or no manual tasks. However, she eventually was assigned a task that required her to apply oil to the exterior of cars. Because of the pain to her shoulders and arms, she began missing work and was eventually terminated. She sued Toyota in U.S. district court. The district court ruled that Williams did not have a disability covered by the ADA because no major life activities were substantially limited. She appealed to the U.S. Court of Appeals, which reversed the lower court's ruling regarding the ADA claim. The U.S. Supreme Court decided to hear the case to determine the proper standard for assessing whether a person is substantially limited in performing manual tasks. The high court reversed the appellate court. In the majority opinion, Justice Sandra Day O'Connor wrote that to qualify as disabled under the ADA a person must prove that he or she has a physical or mental impairment and that the impairment prevents or severely restricts the performance of a major life activity. Moreover, O'Connor wrote that a major life activity must be of central importance to daily life. In other words, it is not enough to submit evidence of a disability; the individual must provide evidence that the limitation is substantial. The Court found that these conditions were not satisfied in Williams's case and that the appellate court had erred in the ruling.

In these ADA cases the U.S. Supreme Court held that (a) mitigating factors should be considered in determining if an impairment substantially limits a major life activity and (b) the terms "substantially limits" and "major life activity" should be strictly interpreted, thus creating a demanding standard for qualifying under the ADA.

The ADA Amendments of 2008

When Congress revisited the ADA in 2008 it specifically rejected the U.S. Supreme Court's interpretation of the law because such an interpretation made it difficult to obtain protection under the ADA. Congress believed that the high court had improperly eliminated protections for persons for whom the ADA was intended to protect and had incorrectly narrowed the scope of the law. Congress did this in four ways. First, the ADA amendments broadened the definition of disability. In fact, specific language was included in the law that required that the ADA be construed in favor of broad coverage of individuals to the maximum extent permitted by the law. The definition of disability was also extended to impairments that are either episodic or in remission as long as the impairment would substantially limit a major life activity when it was active. Second, the amendments expanded the definition of major life activity. A nonexhaustive list of major life activities was added to the law. These activities included, but were not limited to, caring for oneself, performing manual tasks, seeing, hearing, eating, sleeping, walking, standing, lifting, bending, speaking, breathing, learning, reading, concentrating, thinking, communicating, and working. The operation of major life activities such as functions of the immune system, normal cell growth, digestion, and neurological, brain, respiratory, circulatory, and reproductive functions were added to the list of major life activities. Third, mitigating factors may not be considered when determining whether a person has a disability under the ADA. Some examples of mitigating factors now included in the ADA are medication, medical supplies, equipment, low-vision devices, prosthetics, hearing aids and cochlear implants, mobility devices, oxygen therapy equipment, use of assistive technology, reasonable accommodations or auxiliary aids or services, and learned behavioral or adaptive neurological modifications. The only mitigating factor that can be considered is ordinary eyeglasses or contact lenses, so that individuals with bad, but correctible, visual acuity are not protected under the ADA. Whether or not an impairment substantially limits a major life activity must be determined without taking mitigating factors into account. Fourth, the ADA amendments lowered the standard for persons to be "regarded as" having a disability. Before the amendments were passed to prove an ADA claim under this section of the definition, courts required that an individual establish that an employer regarded him or her as substantially limited in a major life activity. The ADA amendments require that a person only needs to establish that he or she was subjected to discrimination because of a perceived mental or physical impairment, regardless of whether it is perceived to limit a major life activity. The language of the ADA Amendments of 2008 can be found on the U.S. Equal Opportunity Commission website: www.eeoc.gov/laws/statutes/adaaa.cfm.

In *Virginia Beach City Public Schools* (2009) the Office of Civil Rights (OCR) found that the Virginia Beach school district had failed to use the revised definition of disability in the ADA Amendments when a school-based team only considered the impact of a student's disability on learning and relied on the use of mitigating measures in making their eligibility decision.

Many portions of the ADA remained unchanged in the amendments. For example, to prove discrimination under the law, an employee was required to prove that he or she (a) was qualified to perform the essential functions of the position with or without accommodations and (b) was subjected to discrimination because of his or her disability, and that (c) there existed a causal connection between the disability and the discrimination. To prove failure to provide reasonable accommodations, the employee still had to prove that (a) the employer had notice of the disability and the need for a reasonable accommodation, (b) with reasonable accommodations the employee could have performed the essential functions of the position, and (c) the employer refused to make the reasonable accommodations.

On September 25, 2008, President George W. Bush signed the ADA Amendments into law. The amendments took effect on January 1, 2009.

Structure of the ADA

The ADA is codified at 42 U.S.C. §§ 12101–12213. The law consists of five titles or subchapters. These titles are listed in Figure 6.2. The sine qua non of the ADA is the protection of persons with disabilities from discrimination based on their disabilities. The ADA language that prohibits discrimination varies slightly in Titles I, II, and III. Differences between the titles also exist in definitions and enforcement.

Titles of the ADA   The ADA consists of five titles, which will be reviewed briefly in this section. The responsibilities of public schools under Title II and private schools under Title III will be emphasized.

Title I: Employment   Title I of the ADA addresses employment. Employers, employment agencies, labor organizations, and labor-management commit-

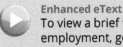

Enhanced eText **Video Example 6.2:** To view a brief **video** on the ADA and employment, go to: www.youtube.com/watch?v=QeHw7tCebrE

tees are referred to in the law as "covered entities." These entities may not discriminate against any qualified individuals with disabilities, including employees or applicants for employment. Neither the U.S. government nor private membership clubs are covered entities. After July 1994, all employers with 15 or more employees were covered by Title I. Public school and private school employees are included under this title as long as the school employs 50 or more persons. Religious schools may give preference to applicants of the particular religion and may require that employees conform to its religious tenets (ADA Regulations, 29 C.F.R. § 1630.16[A]).

Title I defines a qualified individual with a disability as "an individual with a disability who, with or without reasonable accommodation, can perform the essential functions of the employment position that such individual holds or desires" (ADA, 42 U.S.C. § 12111[8]). To be protected by the ADA in employment, a person must have a disability and be qualified; that is, the person must be able to perform the duties of the job with or without the provision of reasonable accommodations. The qualified individual with disabilities must satisfy the requisite skill, experience, education, and other job-related requirements of the employment position. In essence, he or she must be able to perform the essential elements of the job. The Equal Employment Opportunity Commission (1992) suggested that employers follow two steps in determining if an individual with disabilities is qualified under the ADA. First, the employer should determine if the individual meets the necessary prerequisites of the job (e.g., education, work experience, training, skills, licenses, certificates, and other job-related requirements). If the individual with disabilities meets the necessary job requirements, the employer may go to the second step of the determination, which is assessing if the individual can perform the essential functions of the job with or without reasonable accommodations.

FIGURE 6.2 ■
The Americans with Disabilities Act

Title I—Employment

Title II—Public Services

    Subtitle A—General Prohibitions

    Subtitle B—Public Transportation

Title III—Public Accommodations and Services Operated by Private Entities

Title IV—Telecommunications

Title V—Miscellaneous Provisions

Reasonable Accommodations   A reasonable accommodation is a modification to the job or the work environment that will remove barriers and enable the individual with a disability to perform the job. Reasonable accommodations include:

A. making existing facilities used by employees readily accessible to and usable by individuals with disabilities; and

B. job restructuring, part-time or modified work schedules, reassignment to a vacant position, acquisition or modification of equipment or devices, appropriate adjustment or modifications of examination, training materials or policies, the provision of qualified readers or interpreters, and other similar accommodations for persons with disabilities.

(ADA, 42 U.S.C. §12111[9] *et seq.*)

When determining a reasonable accommodation, the employer should

1. Analyze the particular job involved and determine its purpose and essential functions;
2. Consult with the individual with a disability to ascertain the precise job-related limitations imposed by the individual's disability and how those limitations could be overcome with a reasonable accommodation;
3. In consultation with the individual to be accommodated, identify potential accommodations and assess the effectiveness each would have in enabling the individual to perform the essential functions of the position;
4. Consider the preference of the individual to be accommodated that is the most appropriate for both the employee and the employer.

(ADA Regulations, 29 C.F.R. § 1630.9)

The ADA differentiates between reasonable and unreasonable accommodations. Accommodations that impose "undue hardship" on the employer (i.e., require significant difficulty or significant expense) are not required. Only those accommodations that are reasonable are required. Factors to be considered in determining if an accommodation would impose an undue hardship include (a) the nature and cost of the accommodation; (b) the number of persons employed; (c) the effect on expenses and resources; (d) the overall financial resources of the covered entity; (e) the number, type, and location of the employer's facilities; and (f) the type of operation of the employer.

Prohibition Against Discrimination   Title I protects persons with disabilities from discrimination in "job application procedures, the hiring, advancement, or discharge of employees, employee compensation, job training, and other terms, conditions, or privileges of employment" (ADA, 42 U.S.C. §12112[a]). Discrimination, according to the ADA, involves limiting or classifying applicants or employees in a way that adversely affects the employment status of that person, participating in contractual arrangements that indirectly discriminate against disabled persons, or following administrative procedures that have the effect of discriminating against persons with disabilities. Employers can also discriminate by not making reasonable accommodations for a qualified person with disabilities unless these accommodations would result in undue hardship. Neither may employees discriminate against associates of the persons with disabilities (e.g., relatives).

Title I is not an affirmative action mandate. That is, employers need not hire employees with disabilities to redress past discrimination. If two equally qualified people apply for a job or a promotion, one with a disability and one without, the employer may hire or promote the applicant without disabilities, as long as the employer's decision is not related to the applicant's disability. Employers have no obligations regarding Title I, however, when an applicant or employee is currently using illegal drugs.

Enforcement of Title I   The ADA adopts the enforcement procedures in Title VII of the Civil Rights Act (ADA, 42 U.S.C. § 2000[e] *et seq.*). Powers of enforcement are given to the

Equal Employment Opportunity Commission (EEOC), U.S. attorney general, and persons with disabilities who are subjected to discrimination. Clearly, the ADA allows both administrative and individual enforcement of its provisions. Individuals, however, must exhaust administrative remedies before taking judicial action.

In the area of education and the ADA, the U.S. Supreme Court in *Fry v. Napoleon Community Schools* (2017) reversed and remanded the lower court's decision ruling that when the Frys, or any family, file a lawsuit alleging discrimination under the ADA or Section 504, they do not need to first go through the administrative proceedings required by the IDEA unless the focus of the lawsuit is an allegation that a child did not receive a FAPE under the IDEA. Thus, when students with disabilities allege that a school has discriminated against them because of their disability, they are not required to use the IDEA's administrative proceedings simply because the alleged discrimination happened at school. It is only when a plaintiff is alleging that he or she has been denied a FAPE that the plaintiff must begin with the IDEA proceedings. (For coverage of *Fry v. Napoleon Community Schools*, see Chapter 5 on Section 504.)

Disability discrimination claims must be filed within 180 days of the alleged discrimination. The EEOC will investigate the claim and attempt to reach a settlement between the parties. If these attempts are not successful, the individual has the right to go to court. The remedies available under the ADA are injunctive relief (i.e., court orders to stop discrimination), reinstatement, and compensatory damages (e.g., back pay). Moreover, if an employer is found guilty of intentional discrimination "with malice or reckless indifference," a plaintiff may receive compensatory and punitive damages. The ADA contains damage caps on punitive damages that prevailing plaintiffs can collect. In cases where the employer has made good-faith efforts to reasonably accommodate an individual but has not succeeded in doing so, damages will not be awarded (ADA Regulations, 28 C.F.R. § 36.504 *et seq.*). When plaintiffs seek damages, they may ask for a trial by jury. The court in which the complaint is heard may, at its discretion, award attorney's fees.

Title II: Public Services   Title II contains two subtitles: Subtitle A prohibits discrimination by state and local governments, and Subtitle B covers discrimination in public transportation. Title II protects all qualified persons with disabilities from discrimination by public entities. Public entities are any state or local government or any department or instrumentality of the state or local government. According to the Department of Justice, an entity is considered public if it (a) operates using public funds; (b) has employees who are considered government employees; (c) receives significant assistance from the government in terms of property or equipment; or (d) is governed by an independent or elected board. Public schools fall under the purview of Title II.

To be protected under Title II, the individual with disabilities must be qualified. That is, the individual—with or without reasonable modifications to rules, policies, or practices; the removal of architectural, communication, or transportation barriers; or the provision of auxiliary aids and services—meets the essential eligibility requirements for the receipt of services or the participation in programs or activities provided by a public entity (ADA, 42 U.S.C. § 12131[2]).

Prohibition Against Discrimination   Discrimination on the basis of disability is prohibited. Specifically, Title II prohibits discrimination in employment, like Title I, and in accessibility, like Title III. Title II requires that a qualified person with disabilities cannot be excluded from participation in or be denied the benefits of the services, programs, or activities of a public entity or be subjected to discrimination by a public entity. Public schools and colleges, although not specifically mentioned in Title II, are public entities, so reasonable modifications will be required in employee hiring as well as in student programs.

The statutory language and regulations concerning discrimination are similar to those contained in Section 504 and provide similar protections. The ADA, unlike Section 504, contains no separate coverage for public schools, nor does it contain specific student requirements that schools must follow.

Subtitle B, concerning transportation, is a detailed compilation of accommodations that are required to make transportation accessible for persons with disabilities. Public school transportation is expressly omitted from Title II. Subtitle B is made up of two parts. Part 1 covers public transportation provided by bus or rail, excluding commuter services, or other means of conveyance with the exception of air travel. Part 1 covers new vehicles, used vehicles, remanufactured vehicles, paratransit services, new and altered facilities used to provide public transportation, and light or rapid rail systems. Part 2 concerns public transportation by intercity and commuter rail services covering accessible cars, new cars, used cars, remanufactured cars, new stations for use in intercity transportation, existing stations, and altered stations. The provisions of both parts require that intercity and commuter rail services be made readily accessible to and usable by individuals with disabilities.

Public entities must conduct self-evaluations to determine if they are in compliance with Title II. Additionally, covered entities must have information regarding adherence to Title II. Entities with 50 or more employees must keep a record of the self-evaluation available to the public for three years following the self-evaluation. Furthermore, they must have an ADA coordinator and establish a complaint procedure. Finally, when they make structural changes to comply with the ADA, they must develop transition plans regarding the changes to be made.

Enforcement of Title II   Enforcement of Title II mirrors enforcement of Section 504, which incorporates similar remedies and procedures. The Department of Justice oversees compliance with Title II. Individuals may file a complaint with the appropriate agency within 180 days of the alleged discrimination or bring a private lawsuit to recover actual damages. Punitive damages, however, are not available against the government or a governmental agency. Under Title II the exhaustion of administrative remedies is not required before going to a court for relief.

Title III: Public Accommodations Operated by a Private Entity   The purpose of Title III of the ADA is to prohibit discrimination by private entities that own public accommodations by providing persons with disabilities an equal opportunity to receive the benefits of goods and services in the most integrated settings. All privately-owned businesses, facilities open to the public, and commercial facilities (even if not open to the public) are subject to Title III. If a business is a place of public accommodation fitting into one of 12 categories, it is covered. The examples provided of public accommodations in the ADA are illustrative, not exhaustive (ADA, 42 U.S.C. §12181[7]). Figure 6.3 lists these categories.

Private schools from "nursery to postgraduate school" are specifically covered under Title III (ADA, 42 U.S.C. § 12181[7]). Title III also applies to private entities that offer

FIGURE 6.3 ■ Public Accommodations

- Places of lodging
- Bars and restaurants
- Places of exhibition or entertainment (e.g., concert halls, movie theaters)
- Places of public gathering (e.g., conference centers, lecture halls)
- Stores and shopping centers
- Service establishments, including barbershops, laundromats, hospitals, professional offices, and others
- Terminals and depots
- Cultural institutions (e.g., museums, galleries)
- Places of recreation (e.g., amusement parks, zoos)
- Places of education (nurseries and all schools from preschool to university)
- Places where social services are offered (e.g., day-care centers, homeless shelters, food banks)
- Places for exercise or recreation (e.g., golf courses, health clubs, gymnasiums)

examinations or courses related to applications, licensing, certification, or credentialing for secondary or postsecondary education, professional, or trade purposes (ADA Regulations, 28 C.F.R. § 36.102[a]).

Commercial facilities are covered under Title III. Commercial facilities are defined as facilities "that are intended for nonresidential use and whose operations will affect commerce" (ADA, 42 U.S.C. § 12181[2] *et seq.*). Commerce is any means of travel, trade, transportation, or communication between states or between the United States and a foreign country.

Private residences, private clubs, religious entities, and public entities are exempt from the Title III mandates. Public schools are exempt; however, private schools are not (Zirkel, 1993). Private religious schools are also exempt under Title III.

Prohibition Against Discrimination

Title III forbids discrimination against persons with disabilities on the basis of their disabilities. Two types of discrimination are addressed: overtly discriminatory practices on the basis of disability, and practices and structures that effectively discriminate against persons with disabilities whether or not there was intention to discriminate.

Title III also prohibits discrimination in privately operated public transportation services. These entities need not be primarily engaged in the transportation of people. Examples include shuttle services, student transportation systems, and transportation provided within a recreational facility (e.g., amusement park). Discrimination involves the imposition of eligibility criteria that serve to screen out persons with disabilities from using the transportation systems, failure to make reasonable modifications to ensure nondiscrimination, and failure to remove barriers to accessibility.

Requirements of Title III

Businesses open to the public (i.e., public accommodations) must comply with the requirements regarding the provision of goods and services, the prohibition against discrimination, the construction of new buildings, and the alteration of existing buildings. Commercial facilities are required to comply with the new construction and building alteration requirements only.

Public accommodations must modify their operations if they are discriminatory unless they can show that to do so would fundamentally alter the nature of the business. Businesses open to the public must also take steps to ensure effective communications with persons whose disabilities affect hearing, vision, or speech. Auxiliary aids and services, such as interpreters and readers, may be used. Businesses, however, are not required to provide personal devices (e.g., hearing aids, eyeglasses) or personal services (e.g., assistance in eating) to individuals.

Architectural Accessibility

Private entities operating public accommodations must remove architectural and structural barriers in existing facilities where the removal is "readily achievable" (i.e., easily accomplished and not unduly expensive or difficult). This obligation, however, does not extend to employee work areas within the public accommodations. If the removal of the barrier is not readily achievable, an obligation still exists to make goods and services available through alternative methods. Examples of alternatives to barrier removal include providing curb service or home delivery, retrieving merchandise from inaccessible shelves, and relocating activities to accessible locations. Figure 6.4 is a partial list of ways to remove architectural barriers. The list is not intended to be exhaustive.

The ADA provides no test for determining if the removal of these (or any other) barriers is readily achievable. The Department of Justice, and presumably the courts, will consider all claims that barrier removal is not readily achievable on a case-by-case basis. Factors in these determinations include the financial resources of the accommodation.

New Construction and Building Alterations

Public accommodations and commercial facilities are required to comply with ADA regulations regarding new construction and

- Installing ramps
- Making curb cuts in sidewalks and entrances
- Repositioning shelves
- Rearranging tables, chairs, and other furniture
- Repositioning telephones
- Adding raised markings on elevator control buttons
- Installing flashing alarm lights
- Widening doors and doorways
- Eliminating a turnstile or providing an accessible path
- Installing accessible door hardware
- Installing grab bars in toilet stalls
- Rearranging toilet partitions to increase maneuvering space
- Insulating lavatory pipes under sinks to prevent burns
- Installing a full-length bathroom mirror
- Repositioning the paper towel dispenser in the bathroom
- Creating designated accessible parking spaces
- Removing high-pile, low-density carpeting
- Installing vehicle hand controls

building alterations. All new construction must be accessible; however, alterations to existing facilities must only be made to the extent that they are readily achievable. The ADA contains detailed specifications on making new construction accessible.

Enforcement of Title III   Under Title III, persons who believe they have been subjected to discrimination may file a complaint with the Department of Justice. An individual may seek a court order to prohibit discrimination. Courts may award injunctive relief. Punitive damages, however, are not available (ADA, 42 U.S.C. § 12188[b][4]). In the area of transportation, claims may be filed with the Department of Transportation or with a court.

Title IV: Telecommunications   Title IV of the ADA involves the provision of telecommunication services for persons with hearing and speech impairments. Many individuals with these disabilities are unable to communicate by telephone, thereby cutting them off from an extremely important mode of communication. Title IV amends the Communications Act of 1934 (Communications Act, 47 U.S.C. § 151 *et seq.*) to require that phone companies (i.e., "common carriers") provide telecommunication services to allow persons with hearing and speech disabilities to communicate with persons without disabilities. To meet the ADA mandates, common carriers are required to establish systems of telephone relay services that connect telecommunication devices for the deaf to telephones. Title IV also requires that television public service announcements be close-captioned. Television broadcasters, however, are not required to close-caption television programs. The Federal Communications Commission assumed enforcement authority of Title IV.

Title V: Miscellaneous   The final title of the ADA contains a number of miscellaneous provisions. The following are some of the more important ones:

1. States are not immune from actions under the ADA (ADA, 42 U.S.C. § 12202). This provision of the law allows states to be sued under the ADA. Generally, if a law does not specifically allow states to be sued under the law, states will be considered immune from lawsuits under the doctrine of sovereign immunity. (See Chapter 14 for elaborations on sovereign immunity.)

2. Courts and administrative agencies may award attorney's fees to prevailing parties. Courts can also award expert witness fees (ADA, 42 U.S.C. § 12205). The award of attorney's fees includes fees assessed against the plaintiff if the lawsuit is frivolous, unreasonable, or groundless.

3. Retaliation and coercion against persons with disabilities seeking to enforce their rights under the ADA are prohibited. It is also illegal to coerce, intimidate, or threaten anyone attempting to help persons with disabilities exercise their rights under the ADA (ADA, 42 U.S.C. § 12203).

4. The ADA does not invalidate or limit the remedies, rights, and procedures of any federal, state, or local law in which protection for persons with disabilities is equal to or greater than the ADA (ADA, 42 U.S.C. § 12201).

5. The ADA does not apply a lesser standard than Section 504 of the Rehabilitation Act of 1973 (ADA, 42 U.S.C. § 12201[a]).

6. Where appropriate, parties are encouraged to seek to resolve disputes through some alternative method of dispute resolution rather than through litigation (ADA, 42 U.S.C. § 12212). This provision is, however, completely voluntary.

7. An Access Board was convened to issue minimum guidelines for Titles II and III of the ADA. The board issued a volume of guidelines more than 130 pages long (see 36 C.F.R. § 1191 *et seq.*). These guidelines are intended to ensure that facilities are made accessible to persons with disabilities.

SCHOOL DISTRICT RESPONSIBILITIES

Nothing in the ADA enlarges the right of students with disabilities to an appropriate education under either the IDEA or Section 504 (Wenkart, 1993). In fact, the ADA contains no specific student requirements such as

Enhanced eText **Video Example 6.3:**
This short **video** shows how Ehlena Fry challenged her school district for not complying with the ADA and eventually wound up in the U.S. Supreme Court:
www.youtube.com/watch?v=PIfyHn2_ImE

the FAPE requirement of the IDEA and Section 504 or transition plans under the IDEA (Zirkel, 1993). The ADA, however, will affect public education in other areas. In fact, schools may be liable for suits for remedies, possibly including monetary damages, when they violate the ADA (*Hoekstra v. Independent School District No. 283*, 1996). It is therefore important that school officials be aware of what constitutes compliance and noncompliance with the law. Figure 6.5 lists school district compliance requirements.

ADA Compliance Coordinator

School districts that employ 50 or more persons must have an ADA coordinator, and information should be made available on how to reach that person. The duties of the coordinator include coordinating ADA compliance activities, informing and involving the community,

FIGURE 6.5 ■ School District Compliance Responsibilities

1) Appoint an ADA compliance coordinator (if more than 50 employees).
2) Conduct a self-evaluation that covers nondiscrimination provisions, employment, accessibility, and communication.
3) Develop transition plans to bring the school into compliance with the ADA.
4) Maintain a file of self-evaluation, available for public inspection, for 3 years following completion of the evaluation.
5) Provide notice regarding services, programs, or activities of the school.
6) Know which students are protected under the ADA or Section 504.
7) Recognize that the ADA covers employees with disabilities.
8) Ensure that new construction is readily accessible and usable by persons with disabilities.

coordinating the school district's self-evaluation and transition plan, establishing a grievance plan, and investigating grievances (ADA Regulations, 28 C.F.R. § 35.107 *et seq.*). The ADA coordinator should also be responsible for informing interested persons regarding the services, programs, and activities offered by the school district. The coordinator should conduct staff inservice training to make employees aware of ADA requirements (ADA, 42 U.S.C. § 84.7[b]).

Self-Evaluation

The ADA requires that school districts conduct a self-evaluation. If a school has already completed a Section 504 self-evaluation, then the ADA self-evaluation will apply only to those policies and practices not included in the previous self-evaluation (28 C.F.R. § 35.105[d]). Provisions to ensure nondiscrimination, communication, employment, accessibility of programs and facilities, and staff training should be evaluated. Interested persons or organizations should be allowed to participate in the self-evaluation by submitting comments (ADA Regulations, 28 C.F.R. § 35.105 *et seq.*). The self-evaluation must be maintained for public inspection for three years. The description of the self-evaluation should include the names of interested persons consulted, a description of problems identified, and modifications to correct these problem areas.

Transition Plan

If areas of noncompliance with the ADA are identified, the school district must act to correct those deficiencies. If structural changes will be required to achieve program accessibility, a transition plan must be developed to guide completion of the necessary changes. This plan should identify accessibility problems and describe in detail methods to alleviate the problems.

The transition plan of the ADA is not to be confused with the transition plan required by the IDEA in the individualized education programs (IEPs) of students 16 years of age or older. The ADA does not require transition plans for students with disabilities.

Prohibition Against Discrimination

The ADA's Title I requirements prohibiting discrimination against qualified persons with disabilities in employment applies to schools. School districts must also comply with the nondiscriminatory provisions of Title II. Additionally, private schools are covered by Title III of the ADA, which requires that (a) programs, services, and activities should be provided in the most integrated setting feasible; (b) no written policies or procedures may exclude or discriminate; (c) school district contractors must not discriminate; (d) the use of criteria that screen out or have the effect of screening out eligible persons with disabilities are prohibited; and (e) modifications of policies, practices, and procedures that may discriminate must be made unless these changes will fundamentally alter the nature of the service, program, or activity.

SUMMARY

In 1990, the Americans with Disabilities Act became law. The purpose of the law was to prohibit discrimination against persons with disabilities based on their disability. The ADA is similar to Section 504 of the Rehabilitation Act of 1973, but is larger in scope. Where Section 504 prohibits discrimination against persons with disabilities in programs receiving federal financial assistance, the ADA extends these protections to the private sector. The ADA prohibits discriminatory practices in employment, housing, and transportation. The ADA also legislates accommodations to facilities so that they are free of barriers and accessible to persons with disabilities.

The ADA's effect on the provision of a free appropriate public education provided to students, especially when a school is in compliance with the IDEA and Section 504, will be minimal. The ADA grants no additional student-specific rights beyond those contained in Section 504 and the IDEA. This does not mean, however, that public education is unaffected by the ADA. Areas of public education that are affected include employment, general nondiscrimination (which parallels the requirements of Section 504), communications, and program accessibility. Additionally, administrators, counselors, and teachers working with students with disabilities need to become aware of the content of the ADA because of the law's implications for the lives of the students they serve. When students with disabilities leave school and enter the workforce, they will need to engage in self-advocacy. A duty of educators is the responsibility to inform students with disabilities and their parents of their rights contained in the ADA.

Enhanced eText **Application Exercise 6.1:** *Olmstead v. L.C., 1999.*

FOR FURTHER INFORMATION

Equal Employment Opportunity Commission. (1992). *A technical assistance manual on the employment (Title I) provisions of the Americans with Disabilities Act.* Washington, DC: Author (available from the EEOC, 189 L Street NW, Washington, DC 20507).

Coupe, B. W., Ness, A. D., & Sheetz, R. A. (1992). The Department of Justice's final regulations implementing Title III of the Americans with Disabilities Act. *Education Law Reporter, 71,* 353–359.

Marczely, B. (1993). The Americans with Disabilities Act: Confronting the shortcomings of Section 504 in public education. *Education Law Reporter, 78,* 199–207.

Rozalski, M. E, Katsiyannis, A., Ryan, J. B., Collins, T., & Stewart, A. (2010). Americans with Disabilities Act Amendments of 2008. *Journal of Disability Policy Studies, 21,* 22–28.

REFERENCES

Albertsons, Inc. v. Kirkingburg, 527 U.S. 555 (1999).

Americans with Disabilities Act, 42 U.S.C. § 12101 *et seq.*

Americans with Disabilities Act Amendments, Pub. L. 110-235 § 2(b)(2)(5), 122 Stat. 3553 (2008).

Americans with Disabilities Act Regulations, 28 C.F.R. §§ Part 36–38.

Communications Act, 47 U.S.C. § 611 *et seq.*

Equal Employment Opportunity Commission. (1992). *A technical assistance manual on the employment (Title I) provisions of the Americans with Disabilities Act.* Washington, DC: Author.

Fry v. Napoleon Community School District, 137 S.Ct. 743 (2017). Available for download at www.supremecourt.gov/opinions/16pdf/15-497_p8k0.pdf.

Hoekstra v. Independent School District No. 283, 25 IDELR 882 (8th Cir. 1996).

Huefner, D. S., & Herr, C. (2012). *Navigating special education law and policy.* Verona, WI: Attainment Publishing.

Katsiyannis, A., & Yell, M. L. (2002). Americans with Disabilities Act and the Supreme Court: Implications for practice. *Preventing School Failure, 47,* 39–41.

Marczely, B. (1993). The Americans with Disabilities Act: Confronting the shortcomings of Section 504 in public education. *Education Law Reporter, 78,* 199–207.

Miles, A. S., Russo, C. J., & Gordon, W. M. (1992). The reasonable accommodations provisions of the Americans with Disabilities Act. *Education Law Reporter, 69,* 1–8.

Murphy v. United Parcel Service, Inc., 527 U.S. 516 (1999).

OCR Staff Memorandum, 17 EHLR 609 (1991).

Osborne, A. G. (1995). Court interpretations of the Americans with Disabilities Act and their effects on school districts. *Education Law Reporter, 95,* 489–498.

Rehabilitation Act of 1973, Section 504, 29 U.S.C. § 794.

Rozalski, M. E., Katsiyannis, A., Ryan, J. B., Collins, T., & Stewart, A. (2010). Americans with Disabilities Act Amendments of 2008. *Journal of Disability Policy Studies, 21,* 22–28.

Sutton v. United Air Lines, Inc., 527 U.S. 471, 482 (1999), superseded by statute, P.L. 110-325, 122 Stat. 3553 (2008).

Toyota Motor Manufacturing, Ky., Inc. v. Williams, 534 U.S. 184, 197 (2002), superseded by statute, Pub. L. 110-325, 122 Stat. 3553 (2008).

Turnbull, H. R., Turnbull, A. P., Stowe, M. J., & Huerta, N. E. (2006). *Free appropriate public education: The law and children with disabilities* (7th ed.). Denver: Love Publishing.

Urban v. Jefferson County School District R-1, 21 IDELR 985 (D. Colo. 1994).

Virginia Beach (VA) City Public Schools, 54 IDELR 202 (OCR 2009).

Wenkart, R. D. (1993). The Americans with Disabilities Act and its impact on public education. *Education Law Reporter, 82,* 291–302.

Zirkel, P. A. (1993). The ADA and its impact on the schools. *Proceedings of the 14th National Institute on Legal Issues in Educating Individuals with Disabilities.* Horsham, PA: LRP Publications.

Zirkel, P. A. (2014). *Section 504, the ADA and the schools* (3rd ed.). Horsham, PA: LRP Publications.

Chapter 7

The Every Student Succeeds Act of 2015

Mitchell L. Yell, Ph.D.,
University of South Carolina

Mickey Losinski, Ph.D.
Kansas State University

> We want to make sure that through this piece of legislation, that our hard work, our focus, our discipline, our passion, and our commitment that every (student will be given educational opportunities) … Not just because it's good for the students themselves, not just because it's good for the communities involved, not only because it's good for our economy, but because it really goes to the essence of what we are about as Americans.
>
> PRESIDENT BARACK OBAMA BEFORE SIGNING THE EVERY STUDENT SUCCEEDS ACT,
>
> DECEMBER 10, 2015

Learner Objectives

At the end of the chapter, students will be able to:

7.1 Describe the development of the Elementary and Secondary Education Act.

7.2 Describe the purpose and goals of the Elementary and Secondary Education Act.

7.3 Describe the structure of the Elementary and Secondary Education Act.

7.4 Describe the Every Student Succeeds Act.

7.5 Describe the major principles of the Every Student Succeeds Act.

7.6 Describe the changes to ESEA that came from the Every Student Succeeds Act.

Our system of government is a federal system. The government of the United States is composed of a union of states united under a single central (i.e., federal) government. In this system, the federal government protects the people's rights and liberties, and it acts to achieve certain ends while simultaneously sharing authority and power with the states. The U.S. Constitution sets forth the nature of this arrangement in the 10th Amendment. The national government, therefore, has specific powers granted to it in the Constitution. Those powers not granted to the national government are within the province of the states.

The U.S. Constitution does not contain any provisions regarding education. Thus, the federal government has no authority to create a national education system, nor can it order states or local school districts to use specific curricula or adopt particular policies. Instead, the laws of the 50 states govern education.

The federal government's role in education has largely existed in the area of funding. The federal government's funding of education has never exceeded approximately 10% of the total amount of money spent on education. Therefore, 90% of all money expended on education is spent by states and local school districts. Nevertheless, federal involvement has been an important factor in the progress and growth of education.

Thus, the federal government's involvement has been indirect. The earliest method of indirect federal involvement in education was through federal land grants, where the federal government provided land to the states for the purpose of creating and aiding the development of public schools. In the Morrill Act of 1862, Congress also provided grants of land to each state to be used for colleges. In the land grants, the federal government had no direct control of education in the public schools or colleges.

In more recent times, the federal government has continued the indirect assistance to education through categorical grants. The purpose of the categorical grants is to provide supplementary assistance to the state systems of education and to shape educational policy in the states. States have the option of accepting or rejecting the categorical grants offered by the federal government. If states accept the categorical grants, they must abide by the federal guidelines for using these funds. Examples of categorical grants include the National Defense Education Act of 1958, the Higher Education Facilities Act of 1963, the Vocational Education Act of 1963, the Elementary and Secondary Education Act of 1965, and the Education for All Handicapped Children Act of 1975 (now the Individuals with Disabilities Education Act). The role of the federal government in guiding educational policy, therefore, has increased greatly through the categorical grants (Alexander & Alexander, 2012). Perhaps the most significant of these early laws was the Elementary and Secondary Education Act (ESEA) of 1965. This law has been reauthorized a number of times. The most important of these reauthorizations were the Improving America's Schools Act (IASA) of 1994, the No Child Left Behind Act (NCLB) of 2002, and most recently, the Every Student Succeeds Act (ESSA) of 2015.

This chapter examines this important law and its effect on the education of students in U.S. public schools. First, we review the historical developments that led to the passage of the ESEA and subsequent changes in the law. Second, we consider the major requirements and changes of NCLB. Third, we examine the major principles of the reauthorization and amending of ESEA in the ESSA of 2015.

The similarity of the acronyms ESEA and ESSA can be confusing, although both refer to the same law. The Elementary and Secondary Education Act or ESEA was the original name of the law and the Every Student Succeeds Act or ESSA is the most recent reauthorization. When we address the history of the law, we will refer to as ESEA. For the rest of the chapter, except when referring to the reauthorization of ESEA, we will use the acronym for the most recent reauthorization, ESSA.

Readers should also note that to gain a thorough understanding of the ESSA, it is important to understand how each individual state's Department of Education addresses and applies the requirements of the law, because states meet the requirements of the ESSA in their own unique way.

THE HISTORY OF FEDERAL INVOLVEMENT IN EDUCATION: FROM ASSISTANCE TO ACCOUNTABILITY AND BACK AGAIN

The Elementary and Secondary Education Act of 1965

The ESEA of 1965 was passed as part of President Lyndon Johnson's war on poverty. According to President Johnson, full educational opportunity should be "our first national goal" because "from the very beginning of our nation we have felt a fierce commitment to the ideal of education for everyone" (The LBJ Library, 2012). Although the legislation was controversial, it passed the U.S. House of Representatives on a 263 to 153 vote and the U.S. Senate on a 73 to 18 vote. In a ceremony at a one-room schoolhouse on his ranch in Texas, with his schoolmates and his former elementary teacher as guests, President Johnson signed the bill into law on April 7, 1965. During his remarks at the signing ceremony, President Johnson noted "education is the only valid passport from poverty" and that "as president of the United States I believe deeply that no law I have signed or will ever sign means more to the future of America" (The LBJ Library, 2012).

The ESEA was the first and most extensive piece of federal legislation ever enacted in education. The ESEA initiated several programs that focused on providing federal aid to assist states with the provision of educational programs for poor children. In the ESEA, federal funding was offered to states to improve educational opportunities for disadvantaged children.

The first part of the ESEA, Title I, was the largest section of the law. This part of the law authorized grants to states that agreed to adhere to the requirements set forth in the law. The states were to distribute funds to school districts. The districts, in turn, would distribute money to Title I schools, which were schools with large populations of disadvantaged or low-income students as determined by such measures as number of students on free and reduced-price lunch.

Title I funds could go to both schoolwide programs, which were programs that benefited an entire school population when more than 40% of the students were from low-income families, and targeted assistance programs, which were specialized programs for children who were failing or at risk of failing. In 2004, 90% of all public school districts and 60% of all public schools in the United States received Title I funds (Wright et al., 2004), and could spend their funds on schoolwide or targeted assistance programs.

The federal government developed a number of formulas to determine which schools would be Title I schools. These formulas involved collected data such as the number of students who were eligible to receive free or reduced-price lunch or the percentage of students within a school's attendance zone whose school was eligible to receive Title I funds. Schools could use these funds to supplement existing services paid for by local funds. Although the amount of federal money provided to the states has fluctuated in the years following passage of the ESEA, the federal government's commitment to assisting states to ensure that equal educational opportunities are provided to economically disadvantaged students has continued. In fact, since the passage of the ESEA, the federal government has spent more than $400 billion to help states educate children and youth from disadvantaged backgrounds.

A Nation at Risk

During the administration of President Ronald Reagan, Secretary of Education William Bennett assembled the National Commission on Excellence in Education (NCEE). In 1983, the NCEE issued its report entitled *A Nation at Risk.* The uncompromising report, which was extremely critical of the nation's education system, ignited a firestorm of controversy (Wright, Wright, & Heath, 2004). According to the report, our nation was at risk because the U.S. educational system was producing mediocre results and our students were falling further behind their foreign counterparts. In an often-quoted statement, the authors of the NCEE wrote that "Our nation is at risk…. The educational foundations of our country are presently being eroded by a rising tide of mediocrity that threatens our very future as a Nation and as a people…. If an unfriendly foreign power had attempted to impose on America the mediocre educational performance that exists today, we might well have viewed it as an act of war" (p. 1).

The report called for a commitment to the following: (a) placing education at the top of the nation's agenda; (b) strengthening high school graduation requirements; (c) adopting higher, measurable standards of academic performance; (d) increasing time devoted to learning; and (e) raising standards for teachers. Since the publication of *A Nation at Risk*, the federal government intensified its efforts to hold schools accountable for achieving educational results. The document was an important factor in the origin of the current educational reform efforts.

The National Education Summit and America 2000

In 1989, President George H. W. Bush convened the 50 governors as part of the first National Education Summit. The governors reached consensus regarding the state of education in the United States and the need for a national strategy to address the problems with public school education. As a result of this summit, eight educational goals were developed that were to be achieved by the year 2000. Six of these educational goals became part of President Bush's education legislation, America 2000.

According to President Bush's goals, by the year 2000

- Every child must have started school ready to learn.
- The U.S. must have increased the high school graduation rate to no less than 90%.
- In critical subjects—at the 4th, 8th, and 12th grades—students' performance would be assessed.
- U.S. students would be first in the world in math and science achievement.
- Every American adult would be a skilled, literate worker and citizen.
- Every school would offer the kind of disciplined environment that made it possible for students to learn.

President Bill Clinton made many of these goals the centerpiece of his Goals 2000: Educate America Act.

The Improving America's Schools Act of 1994

The federal role in education continued to increase with the passage of the IASA of 1994, a reauthorization and revision of the ESEA. The law focused on implementing standards-based education throughout the nation. In essence, the IASA created a new framework for the federal role in elementary and secondary education, a framework in which the federal government not only provided aid to schools serving economically disadvantaged students but extended federal support to the states' implementation of local and state standards-based reform. The IASA focused on states developing challenging academic standards, creating and aligning assessments for all students, holding schools accountable for results, and increasing aid to high-poverty schools (Cohen, 2002). In fact, many of the requirements introduced in the IASA were revised by and retained in NCLB (e.g., content standards, assessments, adequate yearly progress). Although state education officials were able to develop their own systems for addressing the mandates of the IASAs, they were required to meet the obligations created by the law in order to receive federal funds.

The National Education Standards and Improvement Council was created in the IASA. The purpose of the Council was to identify specific areas in which detailed educational standards should be developed. Additionally, the council had the authority to approve or reject the voluntary academic standards that were developed by states. Because of opposition in Congress, the council eventually was disbanded.

The National Assessment of Educational Progress

The National Assessment of Educational Progress (NAEP) is known as the nation's report card. It is a nationally representative and continuous assessment of American students' knowledge and skills. The NAEP is an extensive data collection system that includes achievement tests in a number of areas, including reading and math (Reckase, 2002). The nation's report card does not provide individual student or school scores. Instead, it provides information about subject matter achievement, characteristics of the student population, instructional experiences, and characteristics of the school environment for populations of students. Readers may access information on the NAEP at the following website: http://nces.ed.gov/nationsreportcard/.

In 2013, the NAEP results indicated that 64% of America's eighth-grade students and 65% of America's fourth-grade students scored at the basic or below basic level in reading. Students scoring at basic or below basic levels are not considered proficient readers. In mathematics, 64% of America's eighth-grade students and 58% of America's fourth-grade students scored at the basic level or below basic level. The overall reading scores on the NAEP have been relatively flat for many years; however, mathematics scores have shown some improvement. Wright and his colleagues noted that these scores remained largely unchanged despite massive increases in federal funding for education and decreases in class size (Wright et al., 2004). In fact, according to an investigation of the nation's educational system 20 years after the publication of *A Nation at Risk,* the Koret Task Force on K–12 Education (2003) reported that even though federal funding had risen over 50% since 1983, education outcomes had not improved, and the achievement gap between children from disadvantaged backgrounds and those from middle-class backgrounds or above had not narrowed. These reports of low achievement in general and specifically in reading, despite large infusions of federal education funding to the states, led to a movement to include stronger accountability mechanisms to ensure that public schools show measurable improvement in student achievement.

The No Child Left Behind Act of 2001

When President George W. Bush took office, he announced that passing No Child Left Behind (NCLB) was the number one priority of his administration's domestic agenda. No Child Left Behind reauthorized the ESEA and also built on the foundation laid in the IASA by including significant changes to the federal government's role in education. The most significant change was to require that all public schools bring every student up to state standards in reading and math within a certain period of time, thus closing the achievement gap based on race, ethnicity, and language (Cohen, 2002). An overwhelming bipartisan majority in both the House and the Senate passed the NCLB legislation (the final version of NLCB passed by a vote of 381 to 41 in the House and 87 to 10 in the Senate). The passage of NCLB increased federal spending on education by almost 25%, and the law also significantly increased federal requirements and mandates on the states.

No Child Left Behind required a major shift in the ways that teachers, administrators, and state Department of Education personnel thought about public schooling. It was a controversial law that placed educators under growing pressure to increase the achievement of all students and to narrow the test score gap between groups of students (Anthes, 2002; Education Commission of the States, 2002; Learning First Alliance, 2002). Moreover, educators were held responsible for bringing about these changes. Administrators and teachers also needed to understand and use effective scientifically-based instructional strategies and be able to evaluate students' instructional progress to make more effective instructional decisions. Clearly, NCLB put more pressure on the public education system to increase student achievement for all students than had any of the previous reauthorizations of the ESEA (Anthes, 2002; Yell & Dragsow, 2005).

The American Reinvestment and Recovery Act of 2009

The American Reinvestment and Recovery Act (ARRA) of 2009, which was commonly referred to as the Stimulus Act, was passed by the 111th Congress and signed into law by President Barack Obama on February 17, 2009. The law provided $10 billion of additional funding under Title I of the ESEA to assist school districts with high concentrations of students from families that lived in poverty. The law also provided funds for Title I school improvement grants. The primary purpose of the additional Title I funds was to improve the achievement of students living in poverty. Four specific goals of the law were to (a) help student progress toward rigorous college and career standards, (b) establish pre-kindergarten to college and career data systems that tracked progress and fostered continuous improvement, (c) improve teacher effectiveness, and (d) provide intensive support and effective interventions for the lowest performing schools (U.S. Department of Education, 2009).

Race to the Top

No Child Left Behind was due to be reauthorized in 2007. Nothing was accomplished in Congress, however, because of the lack of bipartisan cooperation. President Obama, therefore, announced that grants to states would be available through the Race to the Top initiative. Additionally, the U.S. Department of Education provided over $4 billion in competitive grants to the states to spur innovations and reform in education. The funding was made available through the ARRA.

The reforms were centered around the following four areas: (a) adopting standards and assessments that prepare students to succeed in college and the workplace and to compete in a global economy; (b) building data systems that measure student growth and success and inform teachers and principals about how they can improve instruction; (c) recruiting, developing, rewarding, and retaining effective teachers and principals, especially where they are needed most; and (d) turning around the lowest achieving schools. The Race to the Top grant applications were submitted to the U.S. Department of Education. States that were awarded funding submitted their own unique ambitious plans for reforming education in their LEAs. During the time that Race to the Top grant funds were available, 21 states and the District of Columbia received funding (Perez & Torres, 2017).

Waivers   During the time when the reauthorization of NCLB was languishing in Congress, officials in President Barack Obama's U.S. Department of Education granted waivers from some of the requirements of NCLB to states that submitted plans to the U.S. Department of Education. The purpose of these waivers was to grant states' relief from aspects of NCLB that were viewed by some as being outdated and unrealistic (Perez & Torres, 2017). Over 40 states took advantage of these waivers. The waivers were no longer honored after August 1, 2016.

Common Core   Today's students are preparing to enter a world in which colleges and businesses are demanding that students have sophisticated knowledge, skills, and abilities; therefore, it is crucial that students are prepared properly in elementary and high school. In 2009 the National Governors Association (NGA) and the Council of Chief State School Officers (CCSSO) came together in a state-led effort to establish a shared set of clear educational standards to ensure that students received a high-quality education that prepared them for college and careers. The NGA and CCSO developed these standards, called Common Core. The Common Core standards provided a way for teachers to monitor student progress and ensure that students were learning the critical skills and understanding necessary for success in college or a career. Readers may access information on these standards and their development on the following website: www.corestandards.org.

The Every Student Succeeds Act of 2015

On October 10, 2015, President Barack Obama signed the reauthorization of the ESEA, changing the name from NCLB to the Every Student Succeeds Act (ESSA). Whereas President Obama and many members of Congress viewed the intentions behind NCLB as laudable, the accountability provisions were seen in many quarters as being inflexible, overly punitive, and obstacles to progress. Specifically, NCLB was seen by many as encouraging states to set low achievement standards and failing to recognize or reward growth in student achievement. Moreover, the NCLB did little to elevate the teaching profession or recognize excellence in teaching.

With the ESSA reauthorization, many of the provisions of the NCLB were retained such as (a) academic content and achievement standards, (b) academic assessments of students in reading and math, (c) disaggregating testing data by an entire school and by subgroup, and (d) funding. Many provisions of NCLB, however, were also eliminated (e.g., adequate yearly progress or AYP).

Largely the ESSA involved a change in the level of the federal government's involvement in education. In this respect, the ESSA represented a significant shift away from NCLB. With the passage and signing of the ESSA, states were given much wider latitude in setting academic goals and holding schools and districts accountable for student achievement. For example, state education officials now assumed responsibility for determining when and how to intervene with low-performing schools. The U.S. Department of Education would play a very limited role in states' management of their educational system. Nonetheless, the law maintained the civil rights legacy underlying the ESEA of 1965 (Education Week, 2017).

SUMMARY OF THE FEDERAL ROLE IN EDUCATION

Although education is primarily a local and state responsibility, the federal government has been involved in providing funding to states. States and school districts provide approximately 90% of the funding, and they develop curricula and determine attendance, enrollment, and graduation requirements. Thus, the federal contribution to education is about 10%. Despite the low level of funding, the federal government's role in education has been an important one because it provides funds to assist states in critical areas such as the education of economically disadvantaged children.

Moreover, the federal role had evolved from one in which the government primarily provided federal assistance to the states to one in which the federal government was holding states accountable for improving the learning outcomes and achievement of all students. This movement from assistance to accountability can be seen in the evolution of the ESEA through NCLB. With the passage of the ESSA, however, the federal role in education clearly was diminished.

Since the publication of *A Nation at Risk* in 1983, the federal government has increased efforts to hold schools accountable for achieving educational results. These efforts, which required an increase in the role of the federal government in education, led to the passage of NCLB. In fact, NCLB represented an unprecedented increase in the role that the federal government played in education The ESSA was the most recent reauthorization of the ESEA of 1965. In the ESSA, Congress sought to reduce the role of the federal government in education, although funding to the states under the law was actually increased.

THE REAUTHORIZATION OF THE ESEA IN NCLB

On January 8, 2002, President George W. Bush signed the NCLB Act into law. In a departure from the usual practice of signing bills in the Rose Garden of the White House, NCLB was signed at a ceremony at Hamilton High School in Hamilton, Ohio, the home of Representative John Boehner, Chairman of the House Education Committee. President Bush and U.S. Secretary of Education Rod Paige then embarked on a daylong tour to participate in ceremonies to celebrate the signing of the law in the home states of Republican Senator Judd

Gregg of New Hampshire, Democrat Senator Ted Kennedy of Massachusetts, and Democrat Representative George Miller of California. These two senators and two congressmen led the bipartisan congressional efforts to pass this legislation.

No Child Left Behind represented a significant explanation of the federal government's rule in education. Because this law had such an important effect on public schools and also because ESSA represented a reaction to NCLB, it is important to understand NCLB. Moreover, many of the changes in ESSA were enacted in response to what many in Congress perceived as federal government overreach in education. Thus, in this section, we will address the requirements of this important law.

The Purpose of NCLB

The primary purpose of NCLB was to ensure that public school students achieved important learning goals while being educated by highly qualified teachers in safe schools (Yell & Drasgow, 2008). To fulfill this purpose, NCLB required that states and school districts ensure that all students reached 100% proficiency in reading and mathematics by the 2013–2014 school year and improve the performance of low performing schools. The law attempted to do this by requiring states to identify the most important academic content for students to learn and then assess students to determine if they were learning this content. Moreover, NCLB required that specific subgroups of students be identified and that statewide test results be reported separately for these subgroups.

The major requirements of the NCLB included: (a) establishing statewide standards and assessments, (b) requiring school districts to be accountable of student learning by meeting standards of adequate yearly progress and applying rewards and sanctions, (c) basing reading and mathematics on scientifically based research, and (d) ensuring that teachers were highly qualified in content areas.

The Goals of NCLB

The primary goals of NCLB were to ensure the following:

- All students would achieve important state identified academic learning standards as measured by statewide assessments.
- All teachers would be highly qualified.
- All students would be educated in school that were safe, drug free, and conducive to learning.
- All students would graduate from high school.

Schools would be held accountable for making demonstrable improvements to meet these goals. To assist states in meeting these goals, Congress and President Obama significantly increased federal funding to the states.

THE MAJOR PRINCIPLES OF NCLB

No Child Left Behind consisted of four overarching principles (a) requiring that states develop or adopt statewide academic learning standards and statewide assessments based on these standards, (b) requiring that states implement systems for holding schools accountable for improving students' performance through a goal based system, called adequate yearly progress, and a system of increasingly severe sanctions if these goals were not met, (c) requiring that instruction in reading and mathematics have a foundation in scientifically based research, and (d) requiring that public school students be taught by highly qualified teachers. We next review these principles.

Statewide Standards

The President and Congress believed that many schools operated without a clear set of expectations of what students should achieve in important academic subjects. In NCLB, therefore, states were required to: (a) establish their own standards of what students should know and be able to do and (b) provide guidelines to schools, parents, and communities that tell them what achievement is expected of all students. Although the idea of state standards was not new to NCLB, the law specifically required that states develop academic standards for all students in reading/language arts, math, and science. Additionally, states were free to develop standards in areas other than those required by NCLB. For example, a state could develop standards in social studies, although social studies standards were not required by NCLB.

The purpose of the state-defined standards was to provide guidelines to schools, parents, and teachers that told them what achievement would be expected of all students. To reach the goal of having every child proficient on state-defined standards by the target date, NCLB required every state to develop academic content standards for all public schools.

States were also to develop student achievement standards. These standards were to be explicit definitions of what students must know and be able to do to demonstrate proficiency on the content standards (O'Neill, 2004). The achievement standards therefore must have been aligned to the content standards. No Child Left Behind gave states a great deal of flexibility in determining these standards. States' achievement standards were required to include at least two levels of high achievement that indicated how well students were mastering the content standards. No Child Left Behind required that these high levels be designated "proficient" and "advanced." States were also required to have had a third level that designated students who have not attained proficiency on the content standards. This level was to be designated "basic." Additionally, education officials in each state would decide what scores on the statewide assessment separate the levels of achievement.

Statewide Assessments

No Child Left Behind required states to implement a statewide assessment system that was aligned to the state standards in reading/language arts, math, and science. The purpose of statewide testing was to measure how successfully students were learning what was expected of them and how they were progressing toward meeting these important academic standards. These tests had to be valid and reliable and have adequate technical data. Moreover, the state tests needed to enable stakeholders (e.g., teachers, administrators, parents, policy makers, and the general public) to understand and compare the performances of schools against the standards for proficiency as set by the states. Additionally, the tests were to produce individual student reports.

All public schools were required to participate in the statewide assessment by testing 95% of their students. This includes testing at least 95% of students in each of the following subgroups: (a) students from low-income families, (b) students with disabilities, (c) students with limited-English-proficiency, and (d) students from diverse racial and ethnic groups. The purpose of testing and reporting on the test scores by subgroups of students, called *disaggregating scores,* was to ensure that schools were responsible for improving the achievement of all students. States, therefore, were required to report the assessment results within the state and for each school for all students, for students in each subgroup, and also by migrant status and gender. The only exception to the disaggregation rule was when a subgroup was too small to yield statistically reliable information or when reporting such data would reveal personally identifiable information.

The results of these assessments were then reported to parents in annual report cards. States needed to include interpretive, descriptive, and diagnostic reports on the performance of all students. The purpose of this information was to provide parents with data about where their school stood academically, thus allowing them to know if their child's school and school district were succeeding in meeting state standards. These assessments, therefore, were also used to hold schools accountable for the achievement of all students.

Statewide Assessments and Students with Disabilities

According to NCLB, students with disabilities were an important part of a school's student body. These students spent the majority of their time in the general education classrooms and received most of their instruction from general education teachers. Moreover, the Individuals with Disabilities Education Act (IDEA) required that students with disabilities should have access to, be involved with, and progress in the general education curriculum. Congress and the President believed to ensure that instruction and achievement for students with disabilities was improved, all students with disabilities had to be assessed and the results of these assessments had to be included in the data used to determine if a school and school district made AYP. Congress and the President also believed that if students with disabilities were excluded from schools' accountability systems, these students would be ignored and not receive the academic attention that they deserved. By including students with disabilities in NCLB's assessment system, Congress made certain that schools would be held accountable for the educational performance of these students.

Students with disabilities were to be held to the standards for the grade in which each student was enrolled, although in some situations, accommodations were needed to get a true picture of a student's achievement (Elliott & Thurlow, 2003; Thurlow, Elliott, & Ysseldyke, 2001). No Child Left Behind, therefore, required that school districts provided students with disabilities access to appropriate accommodations if necessary to take the assessments.

To receive these accommodations or modifications, students with disabilities had to be eligible for special education services under the IDEA or services under Section 504 of the Rehabilitation Act. Members of each student's individualized education program (IEP) team or Section 504 planning team would determine how the student would participate in the statewide assessment. Under NCLB, the team could determine that a student would take: (a) the regular assessment given to all students, (b) the regular assessment with state-approved accommodations, or (c) an alternate assessment. Readers should note that the IEP team or Section 504 team could decide *how* the student would participate, not *whether* the student would participate.

If the team decided that a student would take the regular assessment with accommodations, the team could only require accommodations that were approved by the state. Additionally, these accommodations were supposed to be consistent with accommodations that were provided during instruction. States had to provide training and guidance to IEP and Section 504 teams on the appropriate use of testing accommodations.

Alternate Assessments

If the IEP team decided that a student would take an alternate assessment, the next step was to select from at least two types of alternate assessments. One was aligned with the state's academic content standards, and the other was aligned with a state's alternate achievement standards. Only students with the most significant cognitive disabilities could take an alternate assessment based on alternate achievement standards. Neither NCLB nor its implementing regulations, however, defined a significant cognitive disability. A definition was deliberately not provided so that states would have flexibility in determining which students could take an alternate assessment. All students who took an alternate assessment were scored as either proficient or not proficient.

In either case, when the IEP was developed, the team had to decide whether the student would take an alternate assessment and then include a statement on his or her IEP explaining why the regular assessment was not appropriate and how the student would be assessed using the alternate assessment. Additionally, the parents had to be informed of the consequences, if any, of taking the regular assessment with accommodations or taking the alternate assessment based on either the grade-level standards or alternate achievement standards. For example, to graduate with a regular high school diploma, some states did not allow students who take the regular assessment with accommodations or the alternate assessment.

Accountability

To receive federal funding under NCLB, states were required to submit accountability plans to the U.S. Department of Education. These plans defined the state's procedures for reporting school performance and its system for holding schools and school districts accountable for increasing student achievement. In accordance with the terms of NCLB, states had to have developed academic standards and tests to assess students' knowledge and skills in reading and mathematics in grades 3 through 8. Furthermore, states had to set state proficiency standards as goals that schools and school districts needed to attain within certain periods of time.

Adequate Yearly Progress

States were then to develop a definition, called adequate yearly progress (AYP), to use each year to determine if schools and school districts were meeting the state standards. In the accountability plans submitted to the U.S. Department of Education, each state would define its AYP criteria for increasing student achievement to meet the 100% proficiency goal in reading/language arts and math by the 2013–2014 school year. In addition to all students in a school, schools were also required to report AYP data for the following subgroups: students who were economically disadvantaged, students from diverse racial and ethnic groups, students with disabilities, and students with limited English proficiency. To ensure that all students, and the students from each of the subgroups, were making progress toward reaching the 100% proficiency goal by the target date, the state was to set specific targets for all students each year in reading/language arts and math. These specific targets were the AYP criteria.

AYP and Students with Disabilities

In NCLB, the statewide assessment scores of all students with disabilities were required to be reported both as a subgroup and as part of the larger student body. Congress's purpose in including students with disabilities with all students and then as a subgroup was to ensure that schools would be held accountable for the achievement of students with disabilities. Thus, schools and school districts would pay close attention to their instruction of these students and their educational progress.

Students who were assessed using an alternate assessment were also included in AYP. However, the federal government capped the number of students who passed the alternative assessment and can be counted as scoring proficient for purposes of determining AYP. This cap was set at 1% of the total school population at each grade level tested. This did not mean that there was a cap on the number of students with disabilities who could take an alternate assessment. Rather, it meant that a school or school district could only include students who scored proficient on the alternate assessment as proficient in the AYP calculation if the percentage of students comprised 1% or less of the total student population at their grade level. For example, in the fourth grade at Springdale School District, 1% of the students at that grade level took the alternate assessment and scored "proficient." Springdale School District could then count the students who scored proficient on the alternate assessment as proficient for AYP calculations. In the fifth grade, a total of 2% of the students at that grade level scored proficient on the alternate assessment. Because the amount exceeded the cap of 1%, however, all of the students above that cap had to be included in the AYP calculations as failing to demonstrate proficiency. This was despite the fact that the students were proficient on the alternate examination. Additionally, the 1% counted at the school district and at the state educational agency level but did not count at the individual school level. Therefore, a school that was small or had a higher percentage of students with significant cognitive disabilities was not penalized for purposes of AYP because the numerical cap did not apply.

Although there was variation by state, the 1% cap across the total student population accounted for approximately 9% of all students with disabilities. The U.S. Department of Education calculated this percentage based on incidence levels of students whom officials believed had significant cognitive disabilities.

Sanctions for Failing to Meet AYP

No Child Left Behind included a system of increasingly serious sanctions for low-performing schools who failed to meet AYP. In all cases, if a school failed to meet AYP, it would receive assistance to improve. The state would designate a school that had not achieved AYP for two consecutive years as "identified for improvement." When a school was first identified for improvement, the state provided technical assistance to enable the school to address the specific problems that led to its designation. The school, in conjunction with parents and outside experts, developed a two-year improvement plan. Although neither the law nor regulations specified whom those outside experts should be, they often were faculty from institutions of higher education and private consultants who had expertise in research-based strategies in the areas in which the school needed help. The school personnel, state officials, outside personnel, and parents would then develop a technical assistance plan for the school. This improvement plan must have involved the school's core academic subjects with the greatest likelihood of raising student achievement so that students would meet the proficiency standards.

Additionally, if a school failed to make AYP for two consecutive years, school officials were required to offer the parents of students in the school the option of transferring to another public school within the district. The rationale behind public school choice was that providing parents a variety of options when their children attend a school that needs improvement will help to ensure that quality educational opportunities are available to all students. When exercising the public school choice option, students could transfer to a public charter school or a public school within the district that has not been identified for improvement, corrective action, restructuring, or with the status of a persistently dangerous school. If a student with disabilities exercised the choice option, the new school became responsible for providing the student with a free appropriate public education.

If a school failed to make AYP for a third consecutive year, the school district was still obligated to provide technical assistance to the school and to offer school choice but the school was now also required to offer supplemental educational services, which could include private tutoring, to low-income (i.e., Title I) students. For students with disabilities, the supplemental services had to include a: (a) statement of specific achievable goals, (b) description of how a student's progress will be measured, and (c) timetable for improving achievement that was consistent with a student's IEP. If a school failed AYP for four consecutive years, the school was designated as needing corrective action, which could include replacing school staff, decreasing management authority at the school level, appointing an outside expert to advise school officials, extending the school day or school year, or restructuring the school.

Scientifically-Based Instruction

One of the major principles of NCLB required that states and school districts use scientifically based instructional programming to improve student achievement. In fact, the U.S. Department of Education called instructional programs that are based on scientific research a major pillar of NCLB (U.S. Department of Education, 2002). Too often, schools have used programs and practices based on fads, fancy, and personal bias, which have proven to be ineffective (Carnine, 2000). Unfortunately, when ineffective procedures are used, it is at the expense of students. No Child Left Behind emphasized using educational programs and practices that have been demonstrated to be effective by rigorous scientific research. The law emphasized scientifically based research because it is not subject to fads and fashions, and makes teaching more effective, productive, and efficient (O'Neill, 2004).

No Child Left Behind required the use of scientifically based research in all aspects of education (e.g., assessment, teaching, programs, instructional approaches, classroom management, monitoring student progress, professional development, technical assistance). The overarching goal of NCLB was to require schools, school districts, and states to rely on science when they make decisions regarding the most effective ways to improve student achievement.

The more than 700 pages of NCLB included more than 110 references to scientifically based research. O'Neill (2004) asserted that Congress's purpose in including so many references to scientific research in the law was to warn schools, school districts, and states that they must no longer rely on untested practices with no proof of effectiveness because reliance on such practices leads to widespread ineffectiveness and academic failure. Schools needed to rely on scientifically-based interventions to increase the academic performance of U.S. students.

Rod Paige, former secretary of the U.S. Department of Education, noted that the intent of NCLB was to require that rigorous standards be applied to educational research and that research-based instruction is used in classroom settings (Paige, 2002). Furthermore, he asserted that states would pay attention to this research and ensure that teachers use evidence-supported methods in classrooms. No Child Left Behind demanded the use of methods that really work: "no fads, not feel-good fluff, but instruction that is based upon sound scientific research" (Paige, 2002, p. 1). No Child Left Behind targeted federal funds to support programs and teaching methods that have actually improved student achievement.

What constituted sound scientific research? According to NCLB, scientifically-based research involved the application of rigorous, systematic, and objective procedures to obtain reliable and valid knowledge relevant to educational activities and programs. Moreover, it included research employing systematic empirical methods that drew on observation or experiments involving rigorous data analyses. The National Research Council (2002) reported that for a research design to be scientific, it must allow for direct, experimental investigation of important educational questions. No Child Left Behind defined scientifically based research as "research that applies rigorous, systematic, and objective procedures to obtain relevant knowledge" (NCLB, 20 USC § 1208[6]). This includes research that (a) uses systematic, empirical methods that draw on observation or experiment, (b) involves rigorous data analyses that are adequate to state hypotheses and justify the conclusions, (c) relies on measurement or observational methods that provide valid data for evaluators and observers and across multiple measures and observations, and (d) has been accepted by a peer-reviewed journal or approved by a panel of independent experts through a comparably rigorous, objective, and scientific review.

Highly Qualified Teachers

The quality and skill of teachers were understood to be extremely important factors in student achievement (Whitehurst, 2003). Congress recognized the importance of having well-prepared teachers in public school classrooms when it included provisions in the NCLB requiring that all new teachers hired in programs supported by Title I funds had to be highly qualified teachers beginning with the 2002–2003 school year. Additionally, the law required that by the end of the 2005–2006 school year, all teachers in public schools had to be highly qualified. No Child Left Behind also required that states ensure that paraprofessionals who work in the nation's public school classrooms were qualified.

To ensure that only highly qualified teachers taught in public school classrooms, each state was required to develop a plan to ensure that all of the state's public school teachers were highly qualified to teach the core academic subjects in which they provided instruction by the end of the 2005–2006 school year. The NCLB regulations defined core academic subjects as English, reading/language arts, mathematics, science, foreign languages, civics, government, economics, art, history, and geography. If a teacher taught in more than one of these core subjects, he or she had to be highly qualified in all of the subject areas taught. Additionally, NCLB required states to hold school districts accountable if they did not meet the highly qualified teacher requirements of the law. Schools had to provide notices to parents if their child's class was taught for 4 or more consecutive weeks by a teacher who did not meet the highly qualified requirements. Moreover, if a school district did not make adequate progress toward its state's measurable goal for increasing the number of highly qualified teachers in the district for two consecutive years, the school district had to develop an improvement plan to address the problem.

No Child Left Behind specified three basic requirements that public school teachers had to meet to be considered highly qualified. First, teachers needed a minimum of a bachelor's degree from a college or university. Second, teachers must have had a full state teacher certification or licensure for the area in which they taught. Third, teachers were required to demonstrate subject matter competency in the core academic subjects in which they taught. Teachers could demonstrate subject matter competency by passing a state-administered test in each of the core subjects they teach. The structure and content of the tests were determined by the individual states.

Special Education Teachers   The Individuals with Disabilities Education Improvement Act of 2004 required that special education teachers had to meet the same highly qualified standards as did general education teachers. This was true for both special education teachers who were new to the profession as well as for experienced special education teachers. Special education teachers also had to meet the same three general requirements to satisfy the highly qualified standards of NCLB: (a) a bachelor's degree, (b) a full state certification as a special education teacher or passed the state special education teacher licensing examination and held a state license to teach as a special education teacher (including certification obtained through state-approved alternative routes to certification), and (c) pass a state-administered test of subject knowledge and teaching skill to demonstrate competency in the core academic subjects.

For elementary special education teachers, this usually meant competency in areas of the basic elementary school curriculum (e.g., reading/language arts, writing, mathematics). Special education teachers in middle and high school who provided instruction in core academic subjects must have met the requirements of NCLB for being highly qualified in every core academic subject they teach. Teachers were thus required to take a state-administered test of content knowledge. This applied whether a special education teacher provided core academic instruction in a regular classroom, resource room, or another setting.

Reading First

In NCLB, Congress and the President recognized that "teaching young children to read is the most critical educational priority facing this country" (U.S. Department of Education, 2002, p. 1). No Child Left Behind, therefore, included an ambitious national initiative designed to help all children become successful readers by grade 3. The initiative was called Reading First, which President George W. Bush called the academic cornerstone of NCLB.

Three unique aspects of Reading First were that it (a) focuses on reading instruction that was supported by scientifically based reading research, (b) provided a large amount of money that states could receive to provide training to teachers and to implement professional development activities, and (c) emphasized early identification of children at risk for reading failure so that effective early instruction can be provided. To ensure that all children in the United States learned to read well by the end of third grade, Congress and the President emphasize the importance of using scientifically based reading research.

SUMMARY OF NCLB

The passage of NCLB represented an unprecedented escalation of the role of the federal government in education along with a substantial increase in funding to the states (Yell & Drasgow, 2008). No Child Left Behind attempted to improve the academic achievement of America's public school students by requiring states to (a) develop achievement standards that represented important learning goals, (b) develop or adopt statewide test to assess public school students on these important goals, (c) report school district results on these tests, (d) disaggregate students into subgroups for the purpose of reporting, and (e) require that states develop an accountability measure called adequate yearly progress to assess schools' progress. Rewards and sanctions provided an essential aspect of NCLB (Perez & Torres, 2017).

THE REAUTHORIZATION OF THE ESEA IN THE ESSA

Many educators and members in Congress believed that NCLB inapprioriately expanded the role of the federal government into educational matters traditionally left to the states and mandated accountability standards that could not be achieved. In reaction to these perceived problems, Congress enacted, and President Barack Obama signed, the ESSA in 2015. The law scaled back the federal government's footprint in education.

In 2014 Sen. Lamar Alexander (R–Tennessee), the Chairman of the Senate's Health, Education, Labor, and Pensions Committee (HELP), and Sen. Patty Murray, (D–Washington), the ranking member of the HELP Committee, wrote a bipartisan bill to reauthorize ESEA that was intended to repeal much of NCLB, pass the Republican-controlled Congress, and be signed by President Obama. At the same time, Rep. John Kline (R–Minnesota), Chairman of the House Committee on Education and the Workforce, developed another reauthorization bill. The House and Senate conferees then had to negotiate a single bill to send to President Obama. In early September 2015, most of the differences were ironed out. When Speaker of the House John Boehner retired from his position, the negotiated bill seemed to be in trouble, but the new Speaker of the House, Paul Ryan, was supportive of the reauthorized law. In December, the House and then the Senate passed the bill with significant bipartisan support. The ESSA was sent to President Obama, who signed the bill into law on December 10, 2015.

The Elementary and Secondary Education Act made significant changes in the federal government's role in education and in the ways that U.S. schools educated children. The intent of the ESSA was to preserve the standards-based reform intent of NCLB (e.g., high standards, accountability for results, standardized testing, and transparency) while doing away with many of its unpopular, unworkable, and overly stringent requirements and sanctions. The law also constrained the powers of the U.S. Secretary of Education in regards to issues such as state standards, assessments, and accountability while giving enhanced authority to the states. In this section, we will review the purpose, goals, and structure of the ESEA as amended by the ESSA.

The Purpose of the ESSA

The primary purpose of the ESSA was to ensure that students in all public schools achieved important learning goals while being educated in safe classrooms. Furthermore, as with NCLB, ESSA required schools to close academic gaps between economically advantaged students and students who were from different economic, racial, and ethnic backgrounds as well as students with disabilities. Moreover, states were still required to work with their lowest performing schools.

To measure progress, ESSA required that states administer assessments to all public school students, including those in charter schools. The ESSA, however, eliminated the adequate yearly progress standards, which progressively increased the percentage of students in a district that had to meet a proficiency standard. If a school district did not meet these proficiency levels, NCLB mandated that certain requirements be met and corrective actions applied, but in the ESSA, states were responsible for creating their own accountability systems that established long-term goals for all students. Thus, the ESSA reduced many of the more unpopular pieces of the NCLB (e.g., highly qualified teachers, AYP) while retaining much of the aid to schools.

The Goals of the ESSA

The primary goals of ESSA were:

- Upholding essential protections for America's underprivileged and high-need students.
- Demanding all students be educated towards high academic standards with college and career goals.

- Guaranteeing that necessary information was provided to stakeholders (e.g., educators, families, students) via yearly statewide assessments measuring students' progress toward the academic standards.
- Supporting and cultivating local innovations that included evidence-based interventions developed by local stakeholders.
- Supporting and increasing investments in access to high-quality <u>preschool</u>.
- Upholding expectations for accountability
- Allowing states to administer corrective actions to cultivate change in the lowest-performing schools.

Moreover, ESSA required states to test students in grades 3 through 8 and once in high school in reading and mathematics to ensure that these goals are met, and it holds schools, school districts, and states accountable for making demonstrable improvements toward meeting these goals. In an effort to assist states in achieving these goals, Congress significantly increased federal spending on education and gave states greater flexibility to use federal funds in ways that would be of the greatest benefit to individual school districts (Hess & Eden, 2017).

THE MAJOR PRINCIPLES OF THE ESSA

In the passage of the ESSA, Congress reorganized and eliminated many of the requirements of NCLB. Whereas NCLB represented a significant increase in the role of the federal government in education, which was traditionally the province of the states, the ESSA represented a rollback of the federal government's role in education. In the following section, we provide details about how the NCLB was amended with the ESSA reauthorization of 2015.

Statewide Standards

The Every Student Succeeds Act left much of the requirements regarding state standards unchanged. States were still required to develop or adopt challenging academic content standards. These standards still had to include at least three levels of proficiency (i.e., basic, proficient, and advanced) and at a minimum address reading/language arts, mathematics, and science. Because many states had already developed such standards under NCLB, this represented little change from the previous reauthorization. In an effort to remove the federal government from education, the Secretary of Education in the U.S. Department of Education was prohibited from requiring or even encouraging states to develop any particular standards (Education Week, 2017).

An important change in ESSA was the requirement that the standards in reading/language arts, math, and science had to be aligned with the higher education requirements of the state. In other words, state standards in high school were to relate directly to those standards developed for the colleges and universities within that state. This change was made to ensure that students graduating from public high schools were entering post-secondary education with the tools necessary to succeed.

Statewide Assessments

As with the state standards, much of NCLB's assessment requirements remain intact in the ESSA. The statewide assessments must be the same assessments used to measure the achievement of all public school students in a state, must be aligned with a state's academic standards, and must measure a student's proficiency on those academic standards (Gamm, 2017). The statewide assessment must be accessible to all students, including English Language Learners (ELL) and students with disabilities. Assessments may also be administered via a computer. Moreover, school districts must test 95% of their students on the statewide assessment.

As was the case with NCLB, the statewide assessments must be administered in reading and mathematics every year from grades 3 through 8 and at least once in grades 9 through 12. A statewide assessment in science must be administered at least once in grades 3 through 5, grades 6 through 9, and grades 10 through 12. Also, an English language proficiency assessment must be administered annually to ELLs.

There are also a few changes in the ESSA requirements on statewide testing. First, local education agencies (LEAs) now have the authority to be able to substitute a nationally recognized high school assessment for the state assessment, as long as that assessment has been approved by the state. In such cases, the nationally recognized exam must meet the same stipulations of technical adequacy including reliability and validity as the state assessment. Additionally, the assessment must be comparable to that being given by the state. Second, states are allowed to use innovative assessments within a pilot program, including competency-based assessments. Third, states are given leeway to administer the statewide tests via a single summative test or by using multiple assessments during an academic year as long as the tests yield a single summative score. Fourth, whenever possible, assessments should be designed in accordance with the principles of universal design for learning (UDL). Fifth, states must notify all parents in public schools that they may choose to have their children opt out of the mandated statewide assessment. However, if parents choose to have their children opt out of the assessments, all these children would be counted against the mandated 95% student participation rate.

The requirement that public schools participate in the statewide assessment by testing 95% of their students is unchanged from NCLB. This also includes testing and reporting at least 95% of students by gender and in each of the following subgroups: (a) students from low-income families, (b) students with disabilities, (c) students who are English language learners, (d) students from diverse racial and ethnic groups, (e) students with migrant status, and (f) students with homeless status. The purpose of disaggregating scores by subgroup is to ensure that schools are held responsible for improving the achievement of all students. The only exception to the disaggregation rule is when a subgroup is too small to yield statistically reliable information and when reporting such data may reveal personally identifiable information.

Assessment Accommodations   Students with disabilities who are eligible for services under the Individuals with Disabilities Education Act (IDEA) or Section 504 of the Rehabilitation act may have accommodations provided when they take the statewide assessment for the grade in which they are enrolled, as long as the accommodations are consistent with a state's guidelines regarding the use of such accommodations and do not invalidate the test. It is up to a student's individualized education program (IEP) planning team to determine if a student in special education takes the statewide assessment without accommodations, takes the assessment with state-approved accommodations, or takes an alternate assessment.

Alternate Assessments   Many of the provisions of the NCLB regarding alternative assessments remain, including the requirement that they be based on alternate achievement standards, along with some changes. States may adopt alternate academic achievement standards for students with the most significant cognitive disabilities so long as those standards (a) are aligned with the state content standards, (b) encourage access to the general education curriculum, (c) are included in the student's individual education program, (d) are consistent with professional conclusions regarding the standards achievable by the student, and (e) are aligned with post-secondary education or employment. States may not allow more than 1% of public school students in the state to take the alternate assessments in each subject (approximately 10% of students with disabilities). States may submit a request to waive the 1% cap for one year. The ESSA retains the prohibition against state-created tests based on modified academic achievement standards.

Additionally, parents of the 1% of children taking the alternate assessment must be clearly informed that their child will be assessed on alternate standards and that by doing so, the student's progress towards the requirements of a regular high school diploma may be affected. Further, consistent with the IDEA, parents must be informed that participating in the alternate assessments promotes progress towards the general education curriculum, that the alternative assessment has taken universal design for learning into consideration, and that staff are familiar and trained with assessing the student through the alternate assessment.

Under the ESSA, students with the most severe cognitive disabilities shall not be denied the ability to achieve a regular high school diploma simply because they took an alternate assessment so long as they meet all requirements for the diploma. The ESSA also allows students who take the alternate assessment to be included in a school's graduation rate so long as they graduate with a regular or state-designed alternate diploma. The ESSA restricts states from counting a GED or certificate of completion as a regular high school diploma for students with the most significant disabilities.

Accountability for Results

Perhaps the most significant changes from NCLB were in the accountability mechanisms in the ESSA. States were required to develop accountability plans, which were to be peer-reviewed by the U.S. Department of Education. In the accountability plans, states had to include: (a) academic achievement standards with the three levels of achievement; (b) long-term goals, including measures to assess interim progress toward the goals; (c) indicators to measure all public school students and subgroups on the annual statewide assessments, which included academic proficiency, graduation rates for high schools, student growth, an additional academic metric for elementary and non-high school secondary schools, and school success on a nonacademic measure (e.g., school climate, student engagement); and (d) a measure of the English language proficiency of its ELL students. High schools could also administer a nationally recognized test (e.g., SAT, ACT) rather than the statewide assessment. The purpose of the accountability systems was to ensure that public schools in the state could be differentiated based on the indicators so that low performing students and schools could be identified. In ESSA, the primary accountability measure of NCLB, the AYP mandate, was eliminated along with the sanctions to be applied to schools failing to achieve AYP.

Identification and Remediation of Low-Performing Schools

With the AYP mandates eliminated, the method used to determine low-performing schools also changed. States are now mandated to, at least every three years, develop a method for ranking schools in order to target schools for comprehensive support and improvement (CSI). These schools would include: (a) the 5% of schools deemed the lowest-performing, (b) those schools failing to graduate more than 66% of students, and (c) those schools that consistently have one subgroup that is under-performing. Schools designated as those meeting CSI criteria will be notified by the state that they fall into this category, and the LEA will partner with local stakeholders to develop an improvement plan.

Comprehensive Support and Improvement Plans

Comprehensive support and improvement plans (CSI) are not unlike those "identified for improvement" plans mandated under the NCLB, though without many of the penalties. First, the CSI plans must be informed by all assessment indicators and long-term goals, but not rely simply on state assessments in reading/language arts and mathematics. Once identified, the schools will undergo a needs assessment to determine what domains require improvement and identify disparities in resources across the LEA that may impact the school. Next, the interventions that are used to remedy the school's underperformance shall be evidence-based interventions, a semantic deviation from the NCLB language of scientifically-based instruction. Finally, once the CSI plan is approved by the state education agency (SEA), it shall be periodically monitored.

School districts may, but are not required to, provide students in a school designated as a CSI school the option to transfer to another public school served by the district. Thus, ESSA also allows parents to exercise a school choice option unless doing so is counter to state law. Priority in school choice will be given to those students who are designated as most in need (e.g., low-achieving, low-income). Students who transfer in this manner will also be allowed to stay at the new school until they have completed the highest grade in that school regardless of the improvement of the former school. School districts are permitted to use 5% of its funds under the ESSA to provide for transportation of students exercising school choice.

Targeted Support and Improvement   Each year states must notify schools in which all students or any subgroup of students are consistently underperforming that the school district will receive targeted support and improvement. The targeted support and improvement plans are similar to the CSI plans. These plans shall be informed by all indicators and include: (a) evidence-based interventions, (b) approval and monitoring by the local education agency, and (c) results in additional action if an unsuccessful plan has been enacted.

Continued Support for School and Local Education Agencies   The ESSA stripped many of NCLB's sanctions for school improvement timelines and accountability and supplanted them with more proactive and positive ones. For example, the SEA will establish exit criteria for one of the aforementioned tiered improvement plans. States will determine the length of time (not to exceed four years) schools have to meet the goals of the CSI plans. In instances where schools do not meet the timelines, the SEA may implement additional interventions, and may look into addressing school operations. Schools identified as those needing targeted support and improvement that do not meet the timelines would then be designated as CSI schools and be subject to the stipulations of such a designation.

Evidence-Based Interventions

The term "scientifically-based research" appeared more than 100 times in NCLB. The ESSA uses the term "evidence-based" and gives state officials the responsibility of determining the quality of evidence (Sparks, 2017). Under the ESSA, interventions may be considered evidence-based if the intervention shows statistically significant effects on improving student outcomes or other outcomes. There are three tiers of evidence: (a) strong evidence from at least one well-designed experimental study, (b) moderate evidence from at least one well-designed quasi-experimental study, or (c) promising evidence from at least one well-designed correlational study that controls for selection bias. According to the ESSA all three tiers—strong, moderate, and promising—constitute evidence that can be used by state officials to determine if an intervention or program is evidence based. If none of these levels of evidence are available regarding a specific intervention, the ESSA includes a fourth tier of evidence. According to this tier, if the rationale of an intervention is based on high-quality research or a positive evaluation that the intervention is likely to improve student outcomes, state officials may also use that level of evidence. Sparks (2017) asserted that the U.S. Department of Education will need to invest heavily in training and technical assistance to boost state personnel's capacity to understand and use the tiers of evidence to identify best practices.

Highly Qualified Teacher Requirements

The ESSA made important changes to NCLB's requirements regarding the certification of teachers. The most significant of these changes was that the ESSA removed the requirement that teachers in Title I schools had to meet the highly qualified requirements of NCLB. Under the ESSA, teachers in schools that receive Title I funds only need to have been certified by the state in which they teach.

The ESSA seeks to ensure that teachers have the needed pedagogical and content knowledge that will be verified through methods determined by the state. These methods may include "teacher performance assessments, in the academic subjects that the teachers teach to help students meet challenging State academic standards" (20 U.S.C. § 2101 (c)(4)(B)(i)(II)).

The ESSA also amended the IDEA to describe the qualifications of special educators (20 U.S.C. § 1412(a)(14)(C)). The law now mandates that any special educator that teaches in elementary, middle, or high schools must (a) have obtained a full state certification as a special education teacher or passed the state examination for teacher licensing, (b) not had certification waived on a temporary or provisional basis, and (c) hold at least a bachelor's degree. In addition, schools must report the teacher's qualifications and state plans must address inequities in the service of low-income and minority children by out-of-field or inexperienced teachers. With regard to paraprofessionals, the requirements under the ESSA remain consistent with those in the NCLB.

Additional Provisions of ESSA

The ESSA also included a number of provisions of interest to administrators and teachers of students with disabilities. Some of these provisions include the following:

- States are required to develop plans to address how the state will reduce bullying, harassment, restraint and seclusion, and suspensions and expulsions in schools.
- The ESSA will create a comprehension center on intervening with students who are at risk of not attaining full literacy skills. The purpose of the center will be to promote best practices in screening, assessing, and intervening with these students, and to promote effective professional development procedures.
- The Jacob K. Javitz law, which funds research into gifted education, is refunded, and states will be required to use teacher development funding to supported the education of gifted and talented students.
- The ESSA eliminates the Reading First initiative and created a more poorly funded program in literacy development that leaves decision-making on using the funds to local officials.
- The ESSA created a competititive grant program that states could use to attract, retain, and reward exeptional science, technology, enginerring, and math (STEM) programs.
- The ESSA includes a preschool development grant program that focuses on coordinating and augmenting access to early childhood education.
- The ESSA encourages LEAs to use funds in important areas such as developing evidence based multi-tiered systems of supports and postive behavioral interventions and supports.

SUMMARY OF ESSA

In the ESSA, Congress and President Barack Obama reduced the role of the federal government in education and increased the rules of state and local education officials in the education of public school students. The changes in the ESSA will directly affect education in U.S. public schools. Because of the accountability requirements of ESSA, it is important that district administrators, principals, and teachers know what the law requires of them. Specific requirements of how school districts can meet the mandates of the ESSA will be determined by officials in state departments of education. Adhering to the requirements of the law may be a daunting task; nevertheless, school districts need to ensure that all district administrators, teachers, and staff are well trained in their responsibilities under the ESSA. Moreover, preservice teachers require intensive training to prepare them to enter schools knowing and able to use evidence-based instructional strategies and methods to teach and collect meaningful data to monitor students' progress.

Enhanced eText **Application Exercise 7.1.** *Brown v. Board of Education,* 347 U.S. 483 (1954).

FOR FURTHER INFORMATION ON THE ESSA

Education Week (2017). *Inside the Every Student Succeeds Act: The new federal k-12 law.* Bethesda, MD: Education Week. Available at www.edweek.org/ew/marketplace/inside-essa-the-new-federal-k-12-law.html.

Gann, S. (2017). ESSA and IDEA: Assessment and accountability rules made simple.

Hess, F.M., & Eden, M. (2017). *The Every Student Succeeds Act: What it means for schools, systems, and states.* Cambridge, MA: Harvard Education Press.

FOR FURTHER INFORMATION ON EVIDENCE-BASED PRACTICES

Coalition for Evidence-Based Policy. (2002). *Identifying and implementing educational practices supported by rigorous evidence: A user friendly guide.* Washington, DC: Author. Available in PDF format at https://www2.ed.gov/rschstat/research/pubs/rigorousevid/rigorousevid.pdf.

Graham, S. (Ed.). (2005). Special issue: Criteria for evidence-based practice in special education. *Exceptional Children, 71,* 130–207.

National Reading Panel. (2000). *Teaching children to read: An evidence-based assessment of the scientific research literature on reading and its implication for reading instruction.* Washington, DC: National Institute on Child Development and Human Development.

National Research Council. (2002). *Strategic education research partnerships.* Washington, DC: National Academy Press.

U.S. Department of Education, Institute of Education Sciences. (2003). *Identifying and implementing educational practices supported by rigorous evidence: A user friendly guide.* Washington, DC: Author. Available at www2.ed.gov/rschstat/research/pubs/rigorousevid/rigorousevid.pdf.

REFERENCES

Alexander, K., & Alexander, M. D. (2012). *American public school* (8th ed.). Belmont, CA: Wadsworth/Cengage Publishing.

American Federation of Teachers. (1999). *Taking responsibility for ending social promotion: A guide for educators and state and local leaders.* Washington, DC: Author.

Anthes, K. (2002, April). *Two states progress on preparing for NCLB.* Atlanta, GA: State Action for Education Leadership Project.

Carnine, D. (2000). *Why education experts resist effective practices: And what it would take to make education more like medicine.* Washington, DC: Thomas B. Fordham Foundation.

Coalition for Evidence-Based Policy. (2002). *Bringing evidence-based policy to education: A recommended strategy for the U.S. Department of Education.* Washington, DC: Author. Available in PDF format at www.excelgov.org/usermedia/images/uploads/PDFs/CoalitionFinRpt.pdf.

Cohen, M. (2002, February). Assessment and accountability: Lessons from the past, challenges for the future. Paper presented at a conference sponsored by the Thomas B. Fordham Foundation, *No Child Left Behind: What Will It Take?* Available in PDF format at www.edexcellence.net/foundation/topic/topic.cfm?topic_id=5.

Commission on Excellence in Education. (1983). *A nation at risk: An imperative for educational reform.* Washington, DC: Author. Available at www.ed.gov/pubs/NatAtRisk/index.html.

Education Commission of the States. (2002). *No state left behind: The challenges and opportunities of ESEA 2001.* Denver, CO: Author. Available in PDF format at www.ecs.org/clearinghouse/32/37/3237.doc.

Education Week (2017). *Inside the Every Student Succeeds Act: The new federal k-12 law.* Bethesda, MD: Education Week. Available at www.edweek.org/ew/marketplace/inside-essa-the-new-federal-k-12-law.html.

Elementary and Secondary Education Act (ESEA) of 1965, 20 U.S.C. § 16301 *et seq.*

Elliott, J. L., & Thurlow, M. L. (2003). *Improving test performance of students with disabilities … on district and state assessments.* Thousand Oaks, CA: Corwin Press.

Every Student Succeeds Act, 20 U.S.C. § 6301 *et seq.*

Fletcher, J., & Lyon, R. (1998). Reading: A research-based approach. In W. Evers (Ed.), *What's gone wrong in America's classrooms.* Palo Alto, CA: Hoover Institution Press, Stanford University.

Gann, S. (2017). ESSA and IDEA: Assessment and accountability rules made simple.

Hess, F.M., & Eden, M. (2017). *The Every Student Succeeds Act: What it means for schools, systems, and states.* Cambridge, MA: Harvard Education Press.

Improving America's School Act (IASA) of 1994, 20 U.S.C. §16301 *et seq.*

Institute for Education Sciences, What Works Clearinghouse. (2017). *Standards Handbook* (version 4.0). Retrieved from https://ies.ed.gov/ncee/wwc/Docs/ReferenceResources/wwc_standards_handbook_v4_draft.pdf.

Koret Task Force on K–12 Education. (2003). Are we still at risk? Available at www.educationnext.org/20032/10html.

Lane, K. L., Gresham, F. M., & O'Shaunessey, T. E. (2002). *Interventions for children with or at risk for emotional and behavioral disorders.* Boston: Allyn & Bacon.

Learning First Alliance. (2002). *Major changes to ESEA in the No Child Left Behind Act.* Washington, DC: Author. Available at www.learningfirst.org.

Letter to Rainforth, 17 EHLR 222 (OSEP 1990).

Lyon, G. R. (2003, October 6). Speech at Family Service Guidance Center. Available at CJOnline/*Topeka Capital Journal,* www.cjonline.com/stories/041803/kan_educator.shtml.

National Reading Panel. (2000). *Teaching children to read: An evidence-based assessment of the scientific research literature on reading and its implication for reading instruction.* Washington, DC: National Institute on Child Development and Human Development.

National Research Council. (2002). *Strategic education research partnerships.* Washington, DC: National Academy Press.

No Child Left Behind, 20 U.S.C. §16301 *et seq.*

O'Neill, P. T. (2004). *No Child Left Behind compliance manual.* New York: Brownstone Publications.

Paige, R. (2002, November). Statement of Secretary Paige regarding Title I regulations. Retrieved August 2002 from www.ed.gov/news/speeches/2002/11/11262002.html?exp=0.

Perez, P.C. & Torres, M.S (2017). The evolution of NCLB to ESSA. In J.R. Decker, M.M. Lewis, E. Shaver, A.E. Blankenship-Knox, & Paige, M.A. (Eds.), *The principal's legal handbook* (6th ed.) (pp. D1-D18).

Reckase, M. (2002, February). Using NAEP to confirm state test results: An analysis of issues. Paper presented at a conference sponsored by the Thomas B. Fordham Foundation, *No Child Left Behind: What Will It Take?* Available in PDF format at www.edexcellence.net/foundation/topic/topic.cfm?topic_id=5.

Thurlow, M. L., Elliott, J. L., & Ysseldyke, J. E. (2001). *Testing students with disabilities: Practical strategies for complying with district and state requirements.* Thousand Oaks, CA: Corwin Press.

Torgeson, J. (2000). Individual differences in response to early intervention in reading: The lingering problem of treatment resistance. *Learning Disabilities Research and Practice, 15,* 55–64.

U.S. Department of Education. (2002). *No Child Left Behind: A desktop reference.* Washington, DC: Education Publications. Available in PDF format at www.ed.gov/admins/lead/account/nclbreference/index.html.

U.S. Department of Education. (2004). The facts about Reading First. Washington, DC: Author. Available in PDF format at www.ed.gov/nclb/methods/reading/readingfirst.html.

U.S. Department of Education (2009). American Reinvestment and Recovery Act of 2009: Title I, Part A funds for grants to local educational agencies. Available at www2.ed.gov/policy/gen/leg/recovery/factsheet/title-i.html.

Vaughn, S., & Schumm, J. S. (1996). Classroom interactions and inclusion. In D. L. Speech & B. Keogh (Eds.), *Research on classroom ecologies.* Mahwah, NJ: Lawrence Erlbaum.

Whitehurst, G. (2003). The Institute of Education Sciences: New wine, new bottles. Presentation at the Annual Conference of the American Educational Research Association. Available online at www.ed.gov/print/rschstat/research/pubs/ies.html.

Wright, P. D., Wright, P. D., & Heath, S. W. (2004). *No Child Left Behind.* Hartfield, VA: Harbor House Law Press.

Yell, M. L., & Dragsow, E. (2005). *No Child Left Behind: A guide for professionals.* Upper Saddle River, NJ: Merrill/Pearson.

Chapter 8

Free Appropriate Public Education

"To meet its substantive obligation under the IDEA, a school must offer an IEP reasonably calculated to enable a child to make progress appropriate in light of the child's circumstances."

CHIEF JUSTICE JOHN ROBERTS, *ENDREW F. V. DOUGLAS COUNTY SCHOOL DISTRICT* (2017, P. 15)

Learner Objectives

At the end of the chapter, students will be able to

8.1 Describe the free appropriate public education (FAPE) mandate of the Individuals with Disabilities Education Act.

8.2 Describe the components of a FAPE.

8.3 Describe the U.S. Supreme Court's decision in *Board of Education v. Rowley* (1982).

8.4 Describe the U.S. Supreme Court's decision in *Endrew F. v. Douglas County Board of Education* (2017).

8.5 Describe peer-reviewed research and how it affects a student's FAPE.

8.6 Describe the related services requirement associated with FAPE.

8.7 Describe methodology decisions and FAPE.

8.8 Describe placement decisions and FAPE.

8.9 Describe how a student's graduation affects FAPE.

8.10 Describe how a failure to implement a student's IEP may be a denial of FAPE.

Before the passage of the Education for All Handicapped Children Act in 1975 (EAHCA; now the Individuals with Disabilities Education Act, or IDEA), many students with disabilities were excluded from public schools. In fact, in the early 1970s Congress estimated that public schools in the United States were educating only an estimated 20% of all children with disabilities (Office of Special Education Programs [OSEP], 2000). Additionally, more than 3 million students with disabilities who were in public schools did not receive an education that was appropriate to their needs (Yell & Bateman 2017). As Chief Justice Rehnquist wrote, these students were often "left to fend for themselves in classrooms designed for education of their non-handicapped peers" (*Board of Education of the Hendrick Hudson School District v. Rowley,* 1982, p. 191).

To correct these problems and to ensure that all eligible students with disabilities received an appropriate public education, Congress passed the EAHCA. The law offered federal financial assistance to states to help them develop and improve educational programming for students who qualified for special education. To qualify for assistance, states were required to submit state plans that assured all students with disabilities the right to a *free appropriate public education* (FAPE).

In the years since the passage of the EAHCA, the question of what a FAPE comprises for students with disabilities has generated much controversy and litigation. Although the *free* education and the *public* education parts of a FAPE have rarely been disputed, what constitutes an *appropriate* education for any given child has frequently been the subject of debate and litigation (Yell & Crockett, 2011). This chapter will examine the FAPE mandate, including the components of a FAPE and important litigation that has addressed this mandate.

THE FAPE MANDATE OF THE IDEA

Students who are determined to be eligible for special education services under the IDEA are entitled to receive special education and related services that consist of specially designed instruction and services that meet their unique educational needs. Moreover, these services are provided at public expense. The law defines a FAPE as special education and related services that

A. are provided at public expense, under public supervision and direction, and without charge,
B. meet standards of the State educational agency,
C. include an appropriate preschool, elementary, or secondary school education in the state involved, and
D. are provided in conformity with the individualized education program.

(IDEA, 20 U.S.C. § 1401[a][18])

Thus, when individualized education program (IEP) teams develop and implement a special education program for a student with disabilities, it must be based on a full and individualized assessment of a student, which leads to specially designed instruction that meets the unique needs of the student. A FAPE, therefore, is determined on a case-by-case basis for each individual student in special education. The IEP is essentially the blueprint of a student's FAPE. (For elaboration on the IEP process and document, see Chapter 10)

When the EAHCA was first written, the congressional authors understood that they could not define a FAPE for each student by detailing the specific substantive educational requirements in the law, so instead they defined a FAPE primarily in terms of the procedures necessary to ensure that parents and school personnel would collaborate to develop an individual student's program of special education and related services. The legal definition of a FAPE, therefore, was primarily procedural rather than substantive.

The procedures detailed in the IDEA include such requirements as (a) providing notice to parents when their child's education program is discussed so the parents can participate in the discussions in a meaningful way, (b) inviting parents to participate in meetings to develop their child's educational program, (c) securing parental consent prior to initiating evaluations of their child or placing their child in a special education program, (d) allowing parents the opportunity to examine their child's educational records, and (e) permitting parents to obtain an independent educational evaluation at public expense if the parents disagree with the school's evaluation, including dispute resolution procedures that would allow a child's parents to request mediation, an impartial due process hearing, and to file a suit in federal or state court to resolve the issue. (See Chapter 12 for an elaboration of procedural safeguards.) The purpose of these procedural safeguards is to ensure that students' parents are involved throughout the special education process.

COMPONENTS OF A FAPE

Free appropriate public education consists of several components. Moreover, all of these components are required in an individual student's program of special education.

Free Education

Free education means that a school district may not charge the parents of students with disabilities for any of the special education services or related services that are included in his or her program. Neither may school districts refuse to provide special education services because of the cost of those services. In fact, school district officials may face legal problems if they create the perception among members of IEP teams that there are financial restrictions that they must follow when developing special education programs. IEP team members may consider cost when making decisions about a student's special education program, but such considerations are "only relevant when choosing between several options, all of which offer an appropriate education. When only one (option) is appropriate, then there is no choice" (*Clevenger v. Oak Ridge School Board*, 1984, p. 514). For example, if IEP team members had to choose between two residential options for a student in special education, and both options were appropriate, the team could choose the less expensive of the two placements. If only one option would provide a FAPE, even if it were more expensive, the team members would have to choose that option. In other words, decisions regarding FAPE are not made on the basis of the costs of a service; they must be based solely on what is appropriate for a student (Bateman, 2017).

The free component of a FAPE, however, pertains only to the parents or guardians of a student and does not relieve other governmental agencies, insurers, or third-party payers from valid obligations to pay for services. For example, Title XIX of the Social Security Act, which established Medicare, was amended in 1988 to allow payment for covered services for eligible children and youth with disabilities, even if the services were incorporated into their special education programs (Social Security Act, 42 U.S.C. § 1396).

It should be noted that the OSEP has determined that schools are not precluded from charging "maintenance" or "incidental" fees to the parents of students with disabilities for items such as art or lab supplies or field trips. The IDEA allows such fees to be charged to the parents of students with disabilities to the same extent that the same fees are charged to parents of children without disabilities (*OSEP Policy Letter*, 1992). In situations in which school-owned assistive technology devices, such as computers, are provided to a student as part of his or her FAPE and through the student's negligence or abuse the device is damaged or lost, students may be charged if such charges are allowed under state law. Schools may not charge students for normal wear and use of such devices (*Letter to Culbreath*, 1997).

The obligation to provide special education services at no cost to a student's parents includes the evaluation conducted to determine the student's FAPE. Thus, the school district must either provide or pay for a student's evaluation. In cases in which school district officials refer a student to a private evaluator or facility to conduct an evaluation, the school district has an obligation to ensure that the evaluation is completed at no cost to the parents (see *N. B. v. Hellgate Elementary School District*, 2008).

Public Education

A public education includes a preschool, elementary, or secondary education that meets state standards. When school district personnel determine that a student needs to attend a private school or facility in order to receive a FAPE, the local educational agency (LEA) or state educational agency (SEA) is still responsible for providing a FAPE, in addition to paying the costs of placement (IDEA Regulations, 34 C.F.R. § 300.145–300.147).

When parents choose to place their children in a private school or facility the children no longer have the right to receive a FAPE, as long as the school district made a FAPE available to the students. In such situations, the school district is not required to fund the student's education. Interestingly enough, when parents unilaterally remove their child from the public school system to a private school they may be considered to be knowingly and voluntarily waiving their child's right to a FAPE (IDEA Regulations, 34 C.F.R. § 300.317[a]). However, if a student's parents unilaterally remove their child to a private school setting because their child is not receiving a FAPE, and this is proved to be true, the parents' removal does not constitute a waiver and they could potentially collect tuition reimbursement from the public school district.

Appropriate Education

One of the most frequently disputed areas in special education involves the issue of what constitutes an appropriate education for an individual student. To ensure that each student covered by the IDEA receives an individualized FAPE, Congress requires that an IEP be developed for all students in special education. The IEP is the core of a student's FAPE and is the primary evidence of program appropriateness (Bateman, 2017). The special education and related services a student receives are delineated in, and must be provided in conformity with, the student's IEP.

The school district in which a student resides is responsible for developing his or her IEP in collaboration with the student's parents. Thus, the IEP is both a collaborative process between the parents and the school in which the educational program is developed and a written document, which contains the essential components of a student's educational program (Tatgenhorst, Norlin, & Gorn, 2014). The written document, developed by a team of educators and a student's parents, describes a student's educational needs and details the special education and related services that will be provided to the student (Bateman & Linden, 2012). The IEP also describes a student's goals and how his or her progress will be measured. The IDEA mandates the process and procedures for developing the IEP. The IEP is so important that a school's failure to develop and implement an IEP properly would likely render a student's entire special education program invalid in the eyes of the courts (Bateman, 2017).

The law includes specific requirements regarding the IEP process. For example, participants in the meeting must include, at a minimum, a representative of the public agency, the student's teacher, and the student's parents. Other individuals may be included at the request of the parents or school district. It is the task of this team to formulate the student's special education program. The IEP must include the following eight components: (a) a statement of the student's present level of academic achievement and functional performance (PLAAFP); (b) measurable annual goals, and sometimes short-term objectives; (c) a statement of how a student's progress toward the annual goals will be measured; (d) a statement of the specific special education, related services, and supplementary services based on peer-reviewed research; (e) the date the special education services will begin and the anticipated frequency, duration, and location of these services; (f) a statement of any individual accommodations that are needed to measure a student's progress on state- and district-wide assessments; (g) appropriate objective procedures for monitoring student progress; and (h) a statement of how a student's parents will be informed of his or her progress.

The IEP does not guarantee that a student will achieve the educational goals listed in the document, nor does it hold teachers or administrators liable if a student does not meet specified goals. The IEP, however, does commit the school to providing the special education and related services listed in the IEP and to making good-faith efforts to achieve the goals.

State Standards

A component of the FAPE mandate requires that an appropriate education meet the standards of the state educational agency. This is because providing an education to its citizens is the responsibility of the state rather than the federal government. The IDEA requires that states submit special education plans that assure qualified students with disabilities the right to a FAPE. These plans must meet the requirements set forth by the federal government in the IDEA. States, however, are free to impose more demanding standards than those contained in the federal law. When a state standard is more demanding, that standard must be applied

(Yell, Shriner, Thomas, & Katsiyannis, 2017). For example, most states mandate that teachers must meet certain requirements to be licensed or certified to teach special education. Additionally, some states require that transition services be provided at an earlier age than the federal law requires (e.g., South Carolina requires that transition services begin at age 13, rather than age 16 as does the IDEA).

Some states have more demanding FAPE standards than does the federal government in the IDEA. In fact, a state may adopt a maximizing standard. Interestingly, Arkansas, Iowa, and New Jersey had higher FAPE standards than the federal government, but the state legislatures amended the state statutes to bring them into line with the federal standards.

Special Education

The IDEA defines special education as specially designed instruction, provided at no cost to a student's parents, that is intended to meet the unique educational needs of a student (IDEA, 20 U.S.C. § 1401[29]). The regulations to the IDEA also include, if needed to provide a FAPE, education in a variety of settings outside the typical school environment (e.g., institutions; IDEA Regulations, 34 C.F.R. § 300.39[a][1]), as well as physical education (defined in IDEA Regulations, 34 C.F.R. § 300.39[b][2]) and vocational education (defined in IDEA Regulations, 34 C.F.R. § 300.39[b][5]). According to Tatgenhorst et al. (2014) because the FAPE is premised on meeting the unique educational needs of each student, the IDEA does not further define what types of curricula, methods, materials, procedures, and resources make up a special education. Rather, Tatgenhorst and his colleagues asserted that special education can best be thought of in terms of what it is not—special education is not regular education, because regular education programs are "designed and implemented without regard to the individual circumstances of any one particular student" (Tatgenhorst, et al., 2014p. 3:13). Special education, on the other hand, is uniquely designed with only an individual student in mind; that is, special education is "specifically designed instruction" that addresses the unique needs of a student (IDEA Regulations, 34 C.F.R. § 300.39[b][3]). Tatgenhorst et al. (2014) and Crockett and Yell (2017) argued that unique needs to which special education must address include academic needs, social needs, behavioral needs, emotional needs, health needs, and vocational needs.

Parent Participation

Parent participation in the development of a student's FAPE is absolutely essential for two basic reasons. First, state and federal special education law requires parent involvement (Yell & Crockett, 2011). Congress recognized that the receipt of special education services by children with disabilities depended in part on their parents' abilities to advocate on their behalf when it passed the EAHCA in 1975. Thus, Congress created a set of procedural safeguards to ensure that children would receive a FAPE (Yell, Shriner, Thomas, & Katsiyannis, 2018). In fact, parent participation is so crucial in developing a FAPE that school personnel actions that result in parents not being involved in the development of their child's special education program are grounds for an impartial due process hearing officer or court to rule that the student has been denied a FAPE (Bateman, 2017). For example, in *Drobnicki by Drobnicki v. Poway Unified School District* (2009), the U.S. Court of Appeals for the Ninth Circuit ruled that school district personnel's lack of efforts to include a student's parents in an IEP meeting amounted to a denial of a FAPE. According to the court's opinion, the school district did not meet its affirmative duty to schedule the IEP meeting at a mutually agreeable time and place, thus depriving the parents of the opportunity to participate in the IEP meeting, which resulted in the student not receiving a FAPE. Similarly, in *Doug C. v. Hawaii Department of Education* (2013), the U.S. Court of Appeals for the Ninth Circuit ruled that the failure of the Hawaii Department of Education to reschedule a student's IEP meeting when the parent had requested that they do so amounted to a denial of a FAPE to the student.

On May 21, 2007, the U.S. Supreme Court issued a ruling in the case *Winkelman v. Parma City School District* that emphasized the importance of parent involvement. The case addressed the right of the parents of Joseph Winkelman to represent him in an IDEA case, even though they were not attorneys. According to Wright and Wright (2007), the importance of this decision goes far beyond the issue of whether parents can represent their child in special education cases. A unanimous Supreme Court ruled that the IDEA grants parents independent, enforceable rights, which are not limited to procedural and reimbursement-related matters. Moreover, in the majority opinion, Justice Kennedy wrote that parental rights also include the entitlement to a FAPE for their child. In essence, the high court expanded the definition of a FAPE by ruling that the IDEA mandates that (a) parents must be meaningfully involved in the development of their child's IEP, (b) parents have enforceable rights under the law, and (c) parental participation in the special education process is crucial to ensuring that children with disabilities receive a FAPE (Yell & Crockett, 2011). Justice Kennedy also wrote: "We conclude IDEA grants independent, enforceable rights. These rights, which are not limited to certain procedural and reimbursement-related matters, encompass the entitlement to a free appropriate public education for the parents' child" (p. 2005). Clearly, a crucial component of a FAPE is that school districts must ensure that parents are involved in their children's special education identification, assessment, programming, and placement.

Second, researchers have shown that when parents of students with disabilities actively participate in their children's special education programs, students show greater achievement and fewer problem behaviors (Salend, 2006). According to a 2004 report by the Southeastern Educational Development Laboratory, "the evidence is consistent, positive, and convincing: families have a major influence on their children's achievement in school and through life. When schools, families, and community groups work together to support learning, children tend to do better in school, stay in school longer, and like school more" (Henderson & Mapp, 2002, p. 1). Iovannone, Dunlap, Huber, and Kincaid (2003) noted that parent involvement is a best practice in special education, and that "families are essential partners in educational planning and delivery of supports and services" (p. 161). (For further information see the OSEP Center for Parent Information and Resources at www.parentcenterhub.org/).

LITIGATION AND FAPE

The lack of a substantive definition of a FAPE in the IDEA has led to frequent disagreements between parents and schools regarding what constitutes an appropriate education for a particular student. State and federal courts, therefore, have often been required to define FAPE (Osborne, 1992). This litigation is instructive. By understanding FAPE litigation, schools can help ensure that they develop and implement appropriate special education programs for students with disabilities.

The FAPE litigation has evolved over the 44 years since the passage of the IDEA (then titled the EAHCA). Early court decisions set the standard of a FAPE as more than simply providing students access to education but less than the best possible educational program (Osborne, 1992). In *Springdale School District v. Grace* (1981), for example, the U.S. Court of Appeals for the Eighth Circuit held that FAPE did not require the state to provide the best education but instead required an appropriate education. The U.S. Court of Appeals for the Sixth Circuit, in *Age v. Bullitt County Public Schools* (1982), ruled that the existence of a better program did not make the school's proposed program inappropriate.

In 1982, the U.S. Supreme Court considered the meaning of a FAPE. The case, *Board of Education of the Hendrick Hudson School District v. Rowley* (hereafter *Rowley*), was the first special education case heard by the Supreme Court.

Board of Education of the Hendrick Hudson School District v. Rowley, *1982*

Amy Rowley, a student at the Furnace Woods School in the Hendrick Hudson Central School District, was deaf and entitled to a FAPE under the IDEA. The year before Amy's attendance at Furnace Woods Elementary School, a meeting was held between her parents and school officials to determine future placement and special education services. The IEP team decided to place Amy in the regular kindergarten class to determine what supplemental services she might need. Some of her teachers learned sign language, and a teletype machine was placed in the school office so that Amy could communicate with her parents, who were also deaf.

Originally the principal at Furnace Words had agreed to Amy's parents' request to provide a sign language interpreter; however, officials at the district office told the principal to exhaust all other options before assigning a sign language interpreter (Smith, 1996). When Amy began school and no interpreter was in her classroom, her parents were understandably upset. They contacted the principal, who agreed to place a sign language interpreter in Amy's class for a four-week trial period. After two weeks of the four-week trial had passed, the interpreter was pulled from Amy's class because of her negative reaction to him. Amy successfully completed her kindergarten year.

Amy's IEP was developed prior to her entry into first grade. Amy's IEP called for her to be educated in a general education classroom and to continue the use of her hearing aid. Amy also received instruction from a tutor for an hour daily and speech therapy for three hours a week. Amy's parents filed a complaint with the U.S. Department of Health, Education, and Welfare (HEW) alleging noncompliance with Section 504 of the Rehabilitation Act. The complaint was dismissed when the HEW officials determined that the school district had complied with Section 504. Amy's parents then requested a due process hearing.

In the ruling, the hearing officer agreed with the school district that the interpreter was not required by the IDEA. The Rowleys appealed the decision to the New York Commissioner of Education. The Commissioner upheld the hearing officer's decision. Amy's parents then sued in federal district court, claiming that the district's refusal to provide a sign language interpreter had denied Amy a FAPE.

Although Amy was doing better than the average child, the court ruled that Amy was not learning as much as she could without her handicap. Because of the disparity between Amy's actual achievement and her potential achievement, the district court ruled that Amy had been denied a FAPE. The district court held that the school district's special education had denied "an opportunity to achieve [her] full potential commensurate with the opportunity provided to other children" (*Rowley,* 1982, p. 534). Moreover, because FAPE requirements were unclear, the court stated that the responsibility for determining a FAPE had been left to the federal courts. The school district appealed the decision to the U.S. Court of Appeals for the Second Circuit. The appellate court affirmed the lower court's ruling. Interestingly enough, after the school district lost the appeal, the Hendrick Hudson School District provided her with a sign language interpreter. Amy, who was now in third grade, did quite well and reported enjoying school for the first time (Rowley, 2008).

The school district then appealed the decision to the U.S. Supreme Court. The high court granted certiorari to the case. The high court considered two questions: (a) What is a FAPE, and (b) what is the role of state and federal courts in reviewing special education decisions?

In his majority opinion, Supreme Court Chief Justice Rehnquist wrote that a FAPE consisted of educational instruction designed to meet the unique needs of a student with disabilities, supported by such services as needed to permit the student to *benefit* from instruction. The Court noted that the IDEA required that these educational services be provided at public expense, meet state standards, and comport with the student's IEP. If the special education program allowed a child to benefit from educational services and was provided in conformity with the IEP and other requirements of the IDEA, the student was receiving a FAPE. Justice Rehnquist also wrote that any substantive standard prescribing the level of education to be accorded students with disabilities was conspicuously missing from the language of the IDEA.

According to the Supreme Court, Congress's "intent ... was more to open the door of public education to handicapped children on appropriate terms than to guarantee any particular level of education once inside" (*Rowley*, 1982, p. 192). The Court disagreed with the lower courts' rulings that the goal of the IDEA was to provide each student with disabilities with an equal educational opportunity. Chief Justice Rehnquist also wrote that

> the educational opportunities provided by our public school systems undoubtedly differ from student to student, depending upon a myriad of factors that might affect a particular student's ability to assimilate information presented in the classroom. The requirement that states provide "equal" educational opportunities would thus seem to present an entirely unworkable standard requiring impossible measurements and comparisons. Similarly, furnishing handicapped children with only such services as are available to non-handicapped children would in all probability fall short of the statutory requirement of free appropriate public education. (*Rowley*, 1982, pp. 198–199)

The Supreme Court rejected the argument that school districts were required to provide the best possible education to students with disabilities (Wenkart, 2000).

The Supreme Court also ruled that the special education services provided to a student had to be "sufficient to confer some educational benefit upon the handicapped child" (p. 200). Therefore, the purpose of FAPE was to provide students with disabilities a "basic floor of opportunity" consisting of access to specialized instruction and related services individually designed to confer "educational benefit."

The *Rowley* Standard

The Supreme Court developed the so-called *Rowley* two-part test to be used by courts in determining if a school had provided a FAPE as required by the IDEA. The two-part test was as follows: "First, has the [school] complied with the procedures of the Act? And second, is the individualized education program developed through the Act's procedures reasonably calculated to enable the child to receive educational benefits?" (*Rowley*, pp. 206–207). If these criteria are met, a school has complied with FAPE requirements. The first part of the test was procedural and the second part of the test was substantive. With respect to the second part of the test, which required a court to assess a student's IEP and the educational benefit, the High Court noted that this determination would be more difficult than the procedural part of the test. In the majority opinion Chief Justice Rehnquist wrote that

> The determination of when handicapped children are receiving sufficient educational benefits to satisfy the requirements of the Act presents a more difficult problem. It is clear that the benefits obtainable by children at one end of the spectrum will differ dramatically from those obtainable by children at the other end, with infinite variations in between. We do not attempt today to establish any one test for determining the adequacy of educational benefits conferred upon all children covered by the Act. (*Rowley*, 1982, p. 180)

The Supreme Court applied the two-part test to the *Rowley* case and held that the school district had complied with the procedures of the IDEA, and Amy had received an appropriate education because she was performing better than many of the children in her class and was advancing easily from grade to grade. In a footnote to the majority opinion, Chief Justice Rehnquist wrote that the decision was a narrow one and that it should not be read too broadly and be interpreted to mean that every student with a disability who was advancing from grade to grade in a regular school was automatically receiving a FAPE. In fact, Chief Justice Rehnquist wrote, "We do not hold today that every handicapped child who is advancing from grade to grade in a regular public school system is automatically receiving a free appropriate public education" (*Rowley*, 1982, p. 207). Rather, the FAPE standard can only be arrived at through a multifactorial evaluation conducted on a case-by-case basis. The High Court also noted that in this case the sign language interpreter was not required to provide a FAPE to Amy Rowley. The decisions of the district and circuit court were thus reversed.

The Supreme Court also addressed how courts should examine whether schools had provided a FAPE to a student. Regarding this role, Rehnquist wrote that

> courts must be careful to avoid imposing their view of preferable educational methods upon the states. The primary responsibility for formulating the education to be accorded a handicapped child, and for choosing the educational method most suitable to the child's needs, was left by the Act to state and local education agencies in cooperation with the parents or guardian of the child. (*Rowley,* 1982, p. 207)

When hearing officers or judges rule on whether a school has provided a FAPE, they should (a) determine if the procedural requirements of the IDEA have been met, and (b) examine the IEP to determine if the special education program is reasonably calculated to enable a student to receive educational benefit. In making this determination, courts should not substitute their judgments for the judgments of educators, because courts lack the "specialized knowledge and experience necessary to resolve persistent and difficult questions of educational policy" (*San Antonio ISD v. Rodriguez,* 1973, p. 42).

The Supreme Court also ruled that students with disabilities do not have a right to the best possible education or an education that allows them to achieve their maximum potential. Rather, they are entitled to an education that is reasonably calculated to confer educational benefit. In a 1993 decision in *Doe v. Board of Education of Tullahoma City Schools,* the U.S. Court of Appeals for the Third Circuit used an interesting metaphor to drive this point home. According to the court, the IDEA does not require school districts to provide the educational equivalent of a Cadillac to every eligible student with disabilities, but school districts are required to provide the educational equivalent of a serviceable Chevrolet to every student.

Post-*Rowley* Litigation   The first principle of the *Rowley* test stressed the importance of schools adhering to the procedural requirements of the IDEA when determining if a school had provided a FAPE. Thus, a court could determine that a school district had denied a student a FAPE if the district did not adhere to the procedural safeguards of the IDEA. The second principle of the *Rowley* test was substantive. The principle required that courts examine a student's IEP to determine whether the IEP developed by the school was reasonably calculated to enable a student to receive educational benefits.

Procedural Violations of FAPE   If a school fails to adhere to the required procedural mechanisms, and the failure results in harm to the student, the school can be found to be denying a FAPE on procedural grounds (Yell, Katsiyannis, Ennis & Losinski, 2013). A number of post-*Rowley* decisions have ruled that schools have denied a FAPE based on procedural violation. Reasons for school district losses were as follows: (a) failing to include the classroom teacher in developing a student's IEP (*Deal v. Hamilton County Board of Education,* 2004), (b) delaying conducting a student's evaluation and developing his IEP for 6 months (*Tice v. Botetourt County School Board,* 1990), (c) changing a student's placement prior to developing an IEP (*Spielberg v. Henrico County Public Schools,* 1988), and (d) failing to notify a student's parents of their rights under the IDEA (*Hall v. Vance County Board of Education,* 1985).

Procedural violations, however, do not automatically require a finding of a denial of a FAPE. In fact, in some post-*Rowley* rulings, courts have held that technical violations of the IDEA may not violate the FAPE requirement of the IDEA if they result in no harm to the student's education. For example, the U.S. Court of Appeals for the Eleventh Circuit held that because the parents had participated fully in the IEP process, a school's technical violation in failing to notify parents of their rights did not warrant relief (*Doe v. Alabama Department of Education,* 1990). The U.S. Court of Appeals for the Sixth Circuit ruled that the failure of school officials to include a student's present level of educational performance and appropriate criteria for determining achievement of objectives did not invalidate the IEP when the parents were aware of this information (*Doe v. Defendant 1*, 1990). The school's procedural violations of inadequately notifying the parents of refusal to reimburse private tuition and failure to perform the 3-year evaluation in a timely manner were harmless errors because the parents had actual notice and their child's progress had not been harmed.

The Individuals with Disabilities Education Improvement Act (IDEIA) of 2004 included a provision requiring that in special education due process proceedings, impartial hearing officers must rule primarily on substantive grounds. They can base their rulings on procedural violations only when such violations have (a) impeded a student's right to a free appropriate public education, (b) impeded the parent's participation in the decision-making process, or (c) deprived a student of educational benefits (IDEA, 20 U.S.C. § 1415 [F][3][E][ii][I-III]). The crucial factor in a hearing officer's ruling is the degree of harm the procedural violation caused to the student's special education program. Thus, if school personnel have made procedural violations that have not caused significant difficulties in the delivery of special education programs and the student has still received a FAPE, a hearing officer is not supposed to consider these procedural issues to be a violation of the IDEA.

Substantive Violations of FAPE   The second principle of the *Rowley* test—whether a student's IEP is reasonably calculated to enable a student to receive educational benefits—has been a more difficult question for hearing officers and judges (Yell, Katsiyannis, Ennis, Losinski, & Christle, 2016). To answer this question hearing officers or judges have to determine what constitutes educational benefit for an individual student. Post-*Rowley* cases that have reached the level of the U.S. Court of Appeals for the various circuits have led to different interpretations of what degree of educational benefit is sufficient for a school to meet the second prong of the *Rowley* standard and thus to provide a FAPE.

Two circuit courts have required that school districts provide special education programs that conferred *meaningful* educational benefit, and that a minimal or trivial benefit was not sufficient to provide a FAPE (Yell & Bateman, 2017). These two circuits were the Third and Sixth.

The Higher Educational Benefit Standard

In a 1988 decision, *Polk v. Central Susquehanna Intermediate Unit 16* (1988), the U.S. Court of Appeals for the Third Circuit interpreted the *Rowley* decision and the degree of educational benefit that a school district must provide to confer a FAPE. In the discussion of Rowley, the Third Circuit court noted that Amy Rowley did very well in her general education class. Because of this, the Supreme Court was able to avoid the substantive second principle of the *Rowley* test and concentrate on the procedural principle. Clearly, the justices believed that Amy must have been receiving an appropriate education if she was one of the top students in her class and had been advanced to the next grade. In the case before the Third Circuit court, however, the court had to address how much benefit was required to meet the "meaningful" standard in educating the plaintiff, Christopher Polk.

Christopher Polk, a 14-year-old boy with severe mental and physical disabilities, required physical therapy services. The school's IEP, however, provided only consultative services of a physical therapist. Christopher's parents sued under the IDEA (then the EAHCA), claiming that the school had failed to provide an appropriate education. A federal district court held for the school district, finding that the *Rowley* standard held that the conferral of any degree of educational benefit, no matter how small, could qualify as an appropriate education. The appellate court reversed the district court, declaring that

> Congress did not write a blank check, neither did it anticipate that states would engage in the idle gesture of providing special education designed to confer only trivial benefit.... Congress intended to afford children with special needs an education that would confer meaningful benefit.

(*Polk*, p. 184)

The court also held that what constitutes a meaningful education can only be determined in the light of a student's potential. In *Ridgewood Board of Education v. N.E.* (1999), the Third Circuit again used the higher standard of meaningful benefit when it vacated a decision by a lower court holding that when school districts provide special education services conferring merely more than trivial educational benefit, that degree of benefit "is not enough to satisfy the FAPE standard" (*Ridgewood*, 1999, p. 247). The Third Circuit court noted that a student's IEP must provide "significant learning and meaningful benefit…(and) the benefit must be gauged in relation to a child's potential" (*Ridgewood*, 1999, p. 247).

The United States Courts of Appeals for the Sixth Circuit adopted the Third Circuit court's higher education benefit standard in *Deal v. Hamilton County School Board* (2004) holding that a "mere finding that an IEP had provided more than trivial advancement is insufficient" (*Deal,* 2004, p. 862). The Sixth Circuit court also observed that (a) in evaluating whether educational benefit is meaningful, the degree of benefit must be gauged in relation to a student's potential; and (b) that courts should adhere to "Congress's desire not to set unduly low expectations for disabled children" (*Deal,* 2004, p. 864).

These two circuit courts adopted a higher standard for educational benefit. A number of the other circuit courts of appeals, however, adopted a lower educational benefit standard when ruling on FAPE cases. This standard adopted by these courts has come to be known as the trivial or de minimis[1] standard.

The Lower Educational Benefit Standard

The U.S. Courts of Appeals for the Second, Fourth, Seventh, Eighth, Tenth, and Eleventh Circuits interpreted the second part of the *Rowley* educational benefit test as requiring only that school districts provide special education services that confer an educational benefit that is slightly more than trivial or de minimis. The most notable and recent of these rulings was by the U.S. Court of Appeals for the Eleventh Circuit *Endrew F. v. Douglas County School System* (2015).

Endrew F. was diagnosed with autism at age two and attention deficit hyperactivity disorder a year later. Endrew, who was called Drew by his parents and teachers, attended the Douglas County Schools in Colorado from preschool through fourth grade. During these years, he was in special education and had an IEP. By the end of fourth grade, Drew's parents had become dissatisfied with his special education program. His behavior had worsened and his parents believed that Drew's academic and functional progress had stalled. They noted that Drew's IEP goals had essentially been carried over from year to year, which indicated that he was not progressing. Drew's parents pulled him from public school and placed him at Firefly Autism House, a private school specializing in the education of students with autism.

The administrators and teachers in the private school, developed a behavior intervention plan for Drew as well as providing intensive academic instruction. Drew's behavior and academic performance improved. A few months after enrolling Drew in Firefly, his parents met with the IEP team at Douglas County schools. A new IEP was proposed for Drew, however, his parents rejected it because they believed it was no better than the previous IEPs. At the beginning of Drew's fifth grade year, Drew's parents decided they would prefer to enroll him in the public school, therefore they asked for an IEP meeting with personnel at his home school. They also requested that Drew's IEP include some of the same procedures that had been so successful at Firefly Autism House. When the school district presented Drew's parents with a proposed fifth grade IEP, which the parents believed was inappropriate because it was essentially the same as his fourth grade IEP, they pulled Drew from the Douglas County Schools and placed him back in the Firefly Autism House. They also filed a due process complaint seeking reimbursement for tuition at the Firefly Autism House. His parents contended that the proposed IEP was not reasonably

---

[1]*De minimis* is a Latin term meaning too trivial or minor to merit consideration.

calculated to enable Drew to receive educational benefit. The administrative law judge (ALJ) found that the school's IEP did provide a FAPE, therefore tuition reimbursement was denied.

The parents appealed to Federal district court, which affirmed the ALJ's decision. The district court found that changes to Drew's IEPs were sufficient to show that Drew made at least minimal progress, which was all that the Rowley standard required. The parents appealed to the U.S. Court of Appeals for the Tenth Circuit. The Circuit court noted that the school district's program conferred FAPE because Drew's IEP was calculated to provide educational benefit that was "merely more than de minimis" (*Endrew*, 2017, p. 9).

Drew's parents contended that the hearing officer and district court failed to recognize that the school district had made serious procedural and substantive errors resulting in the denial of FAPE (Yell & Bateman, 2017). The procedural errors were that the school district failed to (a) provide Drew's parents with reports on his progress as required by the IDEA, and (b) properly assess Drew's problem behavior and put into action an appropriate plan to address those behavior problems. In answering these two allegations, the circuit court noted the importance of progress monitoring and did not endorse the school district's efforts; nevertheless, the court held that these procedural errors did not constitute a denial of FAPE. The substantive errors committed by the school district, according to Drew's parents, were first that the district's IEPs were materially the same and he had made no progress toward his goals and objectives. Second, the parents alleged that the district failed to address Drew's severe problem behaviors. In the ruling, the circuit court noted that the case was a close call but found that Drew's IEPs had conferred some educational benefit because Drew had progressed somewhat on past IEPs. Thus, the parents were denied tuition reimbursement. Drew's parents appealed to the U.S. Supreme Court. At this point Drew's parents were no longer concerned about tuition reimbursement; rather, they wanted the High Court to clarify the meaning of a FAPE (Schimke, 2017).

Endrew F. v. Douglas County School District, *2017*

The question the High Court was asked to rule on was the following: What is the level of educational benefit school districts must confer on children with disabilities to provide them with a free appropriate public education guaranteed by the Individuals with Disabilities Education Act? On September 29, 2016, the Supreme Court announced it would hear the case and oral arguments were made before the Court on January 11, 2017. On March 22, 2017, the Supreme Court issued its ruling in this *Endrew F. v. Douglas County School District* (hereinafter *Endrew*).

Chief Justice John Roberts wrote the majority opinion in which the Supreme Court issued a unanimous[2] ruling vacating the Tenth Circuit Court's decision in the *Endrew* case and remanded the case back to the Tenth Circuit Court to apply the new standard created by the Supreme Court. The Court's new standard was "to meet its substantive obligation under the IDEA, a school must offer an IEP reasonably calculated to enable a child to make progress appropriate in light of the child's circumstances" (*Endrew*, 2017, p. 15). According to the Court, the new standard was "markedly more demanding than the 'merely more than de minimis' test applied by the tenth circuit" (*Endrew*, 2017, p. 14). In the decision, Justice Roberts wrote:

> When all is said and done, a student offered an educational program providing 'merely more than de minimis' progress from year to year can hardly been said to have been offered an education at all. For children with disabilities, receiving instruction that aims so low would be tantamount to 'sitting idly...awaiting the time they were old enough to drop out'. The IDEA demands more.

(*Endrew*, 2017, p. 14).

---

[2] Only 8 justices had heard this case because Justice Scalia's replacement was not on the court.

Although Justice Roberts wrote that the "IDEA cannot and does not promise any particular outcome," (*Endrew*, 2017, p. 10), he further noted that "a substantive standard not focused on student progress would do little to remedy the pervasive and tragic academic stagnation that prompted Congress to act" in 1975 (*Endrew*, 2017, p. 11).

Yell and Bateman (2017) identified five takeaways from the *Endrew* decision. First, the Supreme Court rejected the de minimis or trivial standard for determining educational benefit and replaced it with an educational benefit standard that requires that IEP teams offer an IEP reasonably calculated to enable a student to make appropriate progress in light of the child's circumstances. This standard is higher than the educational benefit standard in *Rowley*. According to *Rowley*, an IEP must be reasonably calculated to "confer some educational benefit" (*Rowley*, 1982, p. 200). The Supreme Court in *Endrew*, however, seemed to dismiss the some benefit language in *Rowley*, when Chief Justice Roberts wrote, "We find little significance in the Court's language (in *Rowley*) concerning the requirement that States provide instruction calculated to confer some educational benefit." (*Endrew*, 2017, p. 10). The new *Endrew* standard requires that a student's IEP enable him or her to make progress.

Second, the Supreme Court rejected the higher maximizing type standard that Drew's parents had sought, Rather the justices focused on the idea that children with disabilities should receive an education that shows progress in light of their unique disabilities and circumstances. In effect the justices chose a middle path between de minimis benefit, a very low level of educational benefit, and maximizing benefit, which would be the highest level of educational benefit.

Third, the Supreme Court in the *Endrew* decision did not replace or overturn the *Rowley* decision. Instead, the *Endrew* decision clarified *Rowley* by adding their new standard to the two-part *Rowley* test. In fact Yell and Bateman (2017) referred to the new FAPE standard as the two-part *Rowley/Endrew* test: Part 1—Has the school district complied with the procedures of the IDEA? and Part 2—Is the IEP reasonably calculated to enable a child to make progress appropriate in light of a student's circumstances?

Fourth, the Supreme Court settled the split among the U. S. Circuit Courts of Appeal with respect to the educational benefit question by rejecting the lower or de minimis educational benefit standard and embracing the higher educational benefit standard. Thus, the *Endrew* decision requires that a new approach be taken in FAPE cases, especially in the circuits that had adopted the low educational benefit standard.

Fifth, Yell and Batemen noted that the full implications of the *Endrew* decision would not become clear until hearing officers and judges apply the new *Rowley/Endrew* two-part test to the facts presented in future FAPE litigation. On August 2, 2017, the United States Circuit Court reacted to their previous decision in *Endrew* by vacating their prior opinion, and remanding to the United States District Court for the District of Colorado for further proceedings consistent with the Supreme Court's decision.

Weatherly and Yell (2017) noted that school district officials, special education administrators, and leaders in public school districts should take a number of actions to ensure that their special education teachers comply with the *Rowley* and *Endrew* decisions. First, all IEP team members should receive training in important areas such as the procedural requirements in the special education process. Foremost among these requirements is the mandate to ensure that a student's parents are meaningfully involved in the development of the IEP. In fact, according to Justice Roberts's majority opinion an IEP must be drafted in compliance with a detailed set of procedures that "emphasize collaboration among parents and educators and require careful consideration of the child's individual circumstances" (*Endrew*, 2017, p. 2). Moreover, Justice Roberts also wrote that "judicial deference to school authorities will depend on their having provided parents in the IEP process with the opportunity to "fully air their … opinion on the requisite degree of progress" (*Endrew*, 2017, p. 16). Clearly, the justices on the High Court recognized the importance of parental involvement in the special education process.

Weatherly and Yell (2017) also addressed the importance of the substantive requirements of the IDEA especially with respect to the development of students' IEPs. When teams create a student's special education program in the IEP process, it is important that the student's (a) present levels of academic achievement and functional performance are based upon current and relevant assessments, (b) annual goals are challenging, ambitious, and measurable, and (c) progress toward his or her annual goals is monitored through collected progress monitoring data. Furthermore, it is crucial that when progress monitoring data show that a student's annual goal or goals may not be met, that school personnel in conjunction with a student's parents determine why, and the student's teachers make the needed instructional changes and continue to collect data.

Because of the individualized nature of a student's special education program, it is appropriate that the Court did not provide a precise definition for judges or hearing officers to follow when determining whether a student's special education program provides meaningful or trivial benefit. This is because what constitutes a meaningful education for a specific student can only be determined on a case-by-case basis. There can be no clear formula that will apply to all students. It is clear, however, that courts and hearing officers when making decisions about a FAPE will look to the school's IEP to determine if a student's special education program has conferred progress appropriate in light of a student's circumstances. In fact, as Justice Roberts noted "the essential function of an IEP is to set out a plan for pursuing academic and function advancement" (*Endrew*, 2017, p. 11).

The Endrew *Decision on Remand*

The Supreme Court vacated the decision of the U.S. Circuit Court of Appeals for the Tenth Circuit and remanded the case to the circuit court for further proceedings consistent with the High Court's new educational benefit standard. On August 2, 2017, the tenth circuit court vacated their prior opinion and remanded the case to the U.S. District Court for Colorado to hold further proceedings consistent with the Supreme Court's opinion.

Judge Lewis Babcock of the U.S. District Court for Colorado issued his ruling on February 12, 2018 reversing his previous decision and holding that the Douglas County School District had failed to provide Endrew with a FAPE. Judge Babcock noted that Drew's most recent IEP was not substantively different from the IEP that had failed to allow him to progress. Moreover, the judge found that the IEP team had not provided Drew with programming to address his problem behavior, which failed to enable Drew to progress toward his academic and functional goals. The judge also ordered the school district to reimburse Endrew's parents for tuition in Firefly Autism House, transportation costs, and attorneys' fees and court costs (*Endrew F. v. Douglas County School District*, 2018).

The U.S Department of Education and the Endrew *Decision*

On December 7, 2017, the Office of Special Education and Rehabilitative Services (OSERS) in the U.S. Department of Education issued a question and answer document on the U.S. Supreme Court's unanimous ruling in *Endrew* (U.S. Department of Education, 2017). The question and answer document can be found at https://www2.ed.gov/policy/speced/guid/idea/memosdcltrs/qa-endrewcase-12-07-2017.pdf.

The intent of officials at OSERS in issuing this document was to provide parents, educators, and other stakeholders with a synopsis of this important ruling and describe how the decision in the *Endrew* case should inform school district's efforts to improve academic and functional outcomes for students with disabilities. The document includes 20 questions and OSERS responses to these questions. The document is divided into the following three sections:

Section 1: An overview of the Supreme Court's ruling in *Endrew*

Section 2: Clarification of FAPE requirement of the IDEA

Section 3: Considerations for implementation of the *Endrew* ruling.

In the document, officials in OSERS examined the importance of the new higher educational benefit standard developed by the Supreme Court and reiterated that to meet this higher standard, IEP teams must develop special education programs that "provide meaningful opportunities for appropriate academic and functional advancement and to enable the child to make progress" (U.S. Department of Education, 2017, p. 6). According to OSERS, IEP teams can accomplish this by focusing on the individualized needs of a student and conducting a thorough and meaningful assessments of all of a student's needs, and then focusing on (a) a student's academic and functional needs, (b) the views of the student's parents, (c) a student's disability, and (d) a student's potential for growth, when developing his or her IEP. Moreover, to ensure that a student's IEP is reasonably calculated to enable a student to make academic and functional progress, the student's IEP must include ambitious and challenging goals and objectives, and be revisited if he or she is not making the expected progress. Monitoring a student's progress is particularly important because, according to OSERS, the Supreme Court's decision in *Endrew* "clarified that the standard for determining whether an IEP is sufficient to provide FAPE is whether the child is offered an IEP reasonably calculated to enable the child to make progress that is appropriate in light of the child's circumstances" (U.S. Department of Education, 2017, p. 7). Officials at OSERS wrote that a student's "parents and other IEP team members should collaborate and partner to track progress appropriate to the child's circumstances" (U.S. Department of Education, 2017, p. 8) and also noted that LEAs and SEAs should provide support and guidance to school personnel to ensure that they develop IEPs that meet the new *Endrew* standard for conferring a FAPE.

METHODOLOGY AND FAPE

When is a particular methodology necessary to provide a FAPE? Moreover, who chooses what methodology schools will use when they educate children and youth with disabilities? This question seemingly was answered in the *Rowley* decision when the Supreme Court asserted that methodological decisions were best addressed by educational authorities.

The methodology issue has been examined by several courts. In these cases, the courts have examined the question of the school's choice of teaching methodologies in regard to FAPE. The plaintiffs in three cases—*Boughham v. Town of Yarmouth* (1993; hereafter *Boughham*), *Lachman v. Illinois State Board of Education* (1988; hereafter *Lachman*), and *Peterson v. Hastings Public Schools* (1993; hereafter *Peterson*)—brought actions against school districts, alleging a denial of a FAPE because the school districts had chosen particular educational methodologies the parents opposed. The school districts prevailed in all three cases.

The court in the *Lachman* decision stated that parents have no power under the IDEA to compel schools to choose a particular methodology over another. Similarly, the court in *Peterson* held that in a methodology case the court would still only review the second principle of the *Rowley* test. The court stated that if the IEP developed by the school is reasonably calculated to provide educational benefits to the student, the courts can require no more. Finally, the *Boughham* court, in holding for the school district, cited the Supreme Court's admonition in *Rowley* that courts should not get involved in making decisions about educational theory and methodology and should take care to avoid imposing their view of preferential educational methods.

In *Wall v. Mattituck-Cutchogue School District* (1996), the parents of an elementary student with learning disabilities brought an action against a school district in New York. The parents wanted their child to be taught reading using the Orton-Gillingham instructional procedure. The student, who was educated in a public school's self-contained special education classroom, was unilaterally placed in a private school that used the reading procedure. At a hearing, the parents did not challenge the appropriateness of the IEP; rather, they contested the school district's failure to offer the Orton-Gillingham program. The hearing officer found that the school district's program was appropriate. The parents appealed to the federal district court. The court, finding that the student had made progress in the school district's program, affirmed the ruling for the school district.

In a federal district court in California, in the case *Adams v. Hansen* (1985; hereafter *Adams*), the court found that the plaintiff, a student with dyslexia, had shown little progress in a public school program. The court found that the child had progressed four months in total reading achievement and eight months in math achievement in two years of public school instruction. Consequently, the student's mother had placed him in a private school. Finding that the student did not make sufficient academic progress in his two years in public school, but did so in the private school, the court ruled that the mother was entitled to reimbursement from the school district for tuition and travel expenses.

According to Huefner (1991), the court could have ended its analysis at this point. However, it went on to consider the educational methodology offered in the private school as opposed to the public school's educational methods. The court was impressed by testimony that the student had a "specific language disability [involving] all three learning modalities—auditory, visual, and sensory-motor" (*Adams,* p. 863)—but no relative strengths and weakness in the three modalities. Because of this "lack of relative strength," the court stated that the student needed an intensive "structured sequential simultaneous multi-sensory approach" (p. 864) that could not be provided in the public school. The *Adams* case, which was not appealed, seemingly went beyond the scope of judicial review as set forth in *Rowley*.

The cases reviewed seem to offer little encouragement to plaintiffs seeking to have the courts require schools to use favored educational procedures or methodologies. As held by the Supreme Court in *Rowley,* "once a court determines that the requirements of the [IDEA] have been met, questions of methodology are thus left for resolution by the states" (p. 207). The *Adams* case, however, indicates that courts may find it difficult to ignore comparisons between a public school's methodology and one used in a private school if only the latter results in significant progress. Interestingly enough a series of cases involving the parents of young children with autism and a program developed by Ivar Lovaas based on the principles of applied behavior analysis seemed to confirmed this. These cases involved school districts that had been confronted by parental demands to provide Lovaas treatment for children, often in their homes, or to reimburse parents for the expenses they incur as a result of securing the therapy. Some of the rulings in these cases in which parents using the Lovaas system prevailed, seemed to run counter to the *Rowley* admonition that methodology is best left to the educational authorities. On closer examination of these cases, however, Yell and Drasgow (2000) found that it was because the Lovaas programs were appropriate and the schools' programming was inappropriate, primarily because the school districts had no data to show the effectiveness of its program whereas the parents had data to support the efficacy of the Lovaas programming. The schools' programming was found to be inappropriate for additional reasons, including (a) lack of intensity of the programming, (b) inappropriate focus of the programs, and (c) lack of individualization (Yell & Drasgow, 2000).

Huefner (1991) contended that in situations in which parents were challenging a school district's special education programming, if a student was making meaningful progress in the public school's program, the courts would uphold the methodology even if it had been less effective than the alternative methodology. The *Endrew* decision would increases the likelihood that if special educations collect data on student progress and do show appropriate progress, a school district will prevail.

The case law on the methodology issue is clear: As long as the school offers an appropriate program, the choice of educational methodology is up to the school district. To prevail in such situations, school districts need to provide a FAPE that confers progress that is appropriate in light of a student's circumstances and must have formative evaluation data to show that a student is making progress in the school's programming.

PEER-REVIEWED RESEARCH AND FAPE

According to the IDEA, a student's IEP must contain: "A statement of the special education and related services and supplementary aids and services, based on peer-reviewed research to the extent practicable—that will be provided to the child" (IDEA, 20 U.S.C. § 1414[d][1] [A][i][IV]). When Congress reauthorized the IDEA in 2004 the writers of the bill believed that a pervasive problem in special education was an insufficient focus on applying replicable research on proven methods of teaching and learning in students' programs (Etscheidt & Curran, 2010). To ameliorate this problem, Congress added the PRR requirement to the IDEA.

When the regulations to the IDEA were released in 2006, the U.S. Department of Education did not define the term peer-reviewed research. The Department did explain that the term was a part of the definition of scientifically based research that was included in the reauthorization of the Elementary and Secondary Education Act, the No Child Left Behind (NCLB) Act of 2002. According to NCLB peer-reviewed research is "research that has been accepted by a peer-reviewed journal or approved by a panel of independent experts through a comparably rigorous, objective, and scientific review" (Elementary and Secondary Education Act, 20 U.S.C.§ 1208[6][B]). Additionally, in the commentary accompanying the 2006 regulations to the IDEA, officials at the U.S. Department of Education noted that peer-reviewed research (**PRR**) generally refers "to research that is reviewed by qualified and independent reviewers to ensure that the quality of the information meets the standards of the field before the research is published" (71 Fed. Reg. 46,664).

According to Etscheidt and Curran (2010), the purpose of the PRR requirement was to ensure that IEP teams selected educational strategies, programs, and procedures that reflected sound practices, which have been validated empirically whenever possible. IEP teams, therefore, should have strong evidence of the effectiveness of instructional programs and other services before they are included in students' IEPs (Etscheidt & Curran, 2010). Moreover, IEP team members should be prepared to discuss PRR at IEP meetings (Yell & Rozalski, 2013).

The PRR requirement also applies to the (a) selection and provision of special education methodology, (b) selection and provision of related services, and (c) selection and provision of supplementary aids, services, and supports provided in general education settings. IEP teams also consider PRR in nonacademic areas, such as behavioral interventions (71 Fed. Reg. 46,683 (2006)), professional development activities (71 Fed. Reg. 46,627 (2006)), and individualized family service plans (IFSPs) under part C of the IDEA (20 U.S.C. § 1436(d)(4)).

Officials in the Office of Special Education Programs (OSEP) in the U.S. Department of Education asserted that PRR generally referred to research that is reviewed by qualified reviewers to ensure that the quality of the information meets the standards of the field before the research is published. Furthermore, OSEP officials noted that determining whether particular services are peer-reviewed might require that teachers review the literature or other information on the use of evidence-based practices (*Letter to Kane*, 2010). However, according to an opinion issued by the U.S. Department of Education the IDEA's reference to PRR does not refer to evidence-based practices or emerging best practices, "which are generally terms of art that may or may not be based on peer reviewed research" (71 Fed. Reg. 46,665 (2006)). The U.S. Department of Education also clarified the relationship between PRR and the FAPE of the IDEA in comments to the 2006 regulations. According to the commentary,

[special education] services and supports should be based on peer-reviewed research to the extent that it is possible, given the availability of peer-reviewed research... States, school districts, and school personnel must, therefore, select and use methods that research has shown to be effective, to the extent that methods based on peer-reviewed research are available. This does not mean that the service with the greatest body of research is the service necessarily required for a child to receive FAPE. Likewise, there is nothing in the Act to suggest that the failure of a public agency to provide services based on peer-reviewed research would automatically result in a denial of FAPE. The final decision about the special education and related services, and supplementary aids and services that are to be provided to a child must be made by the child's IEP Team based on the child's individual needs ... if no such research exists, the service may still be provided, if the IEP team determines that such services are appropriate. (*Federal Register*, Vol. 71, No. 156, pp. 46,663–46,665)

Three court cases that have addressed the PRR requirement are *Waukee Community School District* (2007), *Rocklin Unified School District* (2007), and *Ridley School District v. M.R. and J.R.* (2012). *Waukee Community School District* (2007) began with a hearing officer's decision out of Iowa, which involved an eight-year-old girl with autism. A school district had used punitive behavioral interventions with the child, such as physical restraint and time out. The girl's parents filed for a due process hearing, contending that the use of time out and restraint procedures violated their child's IEP and the requirement in the IDEA that positive behavior supports be used in behavioral programs. The attorney for the school district argued that the behavioral interventions were supported by PRR and their use was a matter of professional judgment. The Hearing Officer, Susan Etscheidt, ruled that the procedures used by the child's teacher were not implemented in a manner consistent with PRR or appropriate educational practices. She also noted that the interventions were not adequately monitored and were not consistent with the positive behavioral supports mandate of the IDEA. The IEP team was ordered to reconvene to develop a new IEP and a new positive behavior support plan and to confer with an outside consultant with expertise in autism or challenging behaviors. The school district appealed to the federal district court and in *Waukee Community School District & Heartland Area Education Agency* (2008), the district court judge held that the preponderance of the evidence supported the hearing officer's finding that the interventions as implemented were not supported by research and thus violated the FAPE requirement of the IDEA.

In *Rocklin Unified School District* (2007), the parents of a six-year-old boy with autism requested a due process hearing asserting that the Rocklin School District developed an IEP for their son that did not provide a FAPE. Specifically, the parents argued that PRR supported the use of applied behavior analysis (ABA) and did not support the use of the eclectic methodologies, which the school district used in their son's special education program. Both the attorney for the parents and the attorney for the school district had expert witnesses testify at the hearing regarding PRR for students with autism. The hearing officer noted that both the parents and the school district had provided PRR to support the effectiveness of their approaches. The hearing officer asserted that:

> If the component parts of a plan are peer-reviewed, then it follows that the sum of those parts should be considered as peer-reviewed as well, particularly in the light of the moral, legal, and ethical constraints that prevent the truest form of scientific study from being conducted. The ultimate test is not the degree to which a methodology has been peer-reviewed, but rather, whether the methodology chosen was believed by the IEP team to be appropriate to meet the individual needs of the child.

(*Rocklin*, 2008, p. 234)

The parents appealed the decision to a federal district court in California, which affirmed the decision of the administrative law judge (ALJ) that the school district had not violated the FAPE provision of the IDEA (*Joshua A. v. Rocklin Unified School District*, 2009). With respect to the PRR, the district court reasoned that:

> It does not appear that Congress intended that the service with the greatest body of research be used in order to provide FAPE. Likewise there is nothing in the Act to suggest that the failure of a public agency to provide services based on (PRR) would automatically result in a denial of FAPE.

(*Rocklin*, p. 234)

In this case, the court concluded that the school district had not violated the FAPE requirement because the eclectic program had provided Joshua A. with a FAPE. The decision was appealed to the U.S. Court of Appeals for the Ninth Circuit (*Joshua A. v. Rocklin Unified School District*, 2009). The appellate court upheld the decision of the district court noting that the school district's eclectic program was (a) based on peer-reviewed research to the extent practicable and (b) was reasonably calculated to provide educational benefit.

The case *Ridley School District v. M.R. and J.R.* (2012) involved a young girl, E.R., with learning disabilities and health problems. In November 2007, E.R. was evaluated by the Ridley School District and was found to have learning disabilities in reading decoding and comprehension, math computation, reasoning skills, and written language. In March an IEP meeting was held in which the school district proposed that a phonics-based program, called *Project Read*, be used to teach E.R. reading. The special educator provided a report of *Project Read* from the Florida Center for Reading Research in which the Center concluded that the research studies of *Project Read* were promising and the curriculum was aligned with current research in reading. Toward the end of the school year, E.R. began attending a resource room 1 hour a day for assistance in reading and math. In a summer meeting of the IEP team it was decided that during the summer the teachers and support staff would receive training in the use of *Project Read* and provide 1 hour per day of reading instruction and 1 hour per day of math instruction in the resource room. The parents reviewed *Project Read* and determined it was not appropriate for E.R.

In the summer between the first and second grade E.R.'s parents removed her from the Grace Park Elementary School in the Ridley School District and placed her in a private school, Benchmark School, which specialized in educating students with learning disabilities. The parents, who believed that the Ridley School District was offering an education that did not provide a FAPE, subsequently filed a due process complaint against the Ridley School District.

The hearing officer found that the proposed IEPs were inadequate because they lacked appropriate specially designed instruction in the form of a research-based, peer-reviewed reading program. Because the Ridley School District had failed to provide E.R. a FAPE, the due process hearing officer awarded E.R.'s parents compensatory education and reimbursement for tuition and transportation. The school district filed an appeal with the federal district court. The district court reversed the ruling of the hearing officer, finding for the school district. The district court, disagreeing with the hearing officer, found that *Project Read* was research-based and peer-reviewed. The parents appealed to the U.S. Court of Appeals for the Third Circuit, which upheld the ruling of the district court.

The appellate court included an important discussion of the IDEA requirement that IEPs be based on peer-reviewed research. The court stated that it did not need to decide whether the lack of peer-researched curriculum by itself would lead to the denial of a FAPE because the court found that *Project Read* was based on peer-reviewed research. The court made the following two points regarding this requirement:

> First, although schools should strive to base a student's specially designed instruction on peer-reviewed research to the maximum extent possible, the student's IEP team retains flexibility to devise an appropriate program, in light of available research. Second, under the IDEA, courts must accord significant deference to the choices made by school officials as to what constitutes an appropriate program for each student.
>
> (*Ridley*, 2012, p. 33)

The court further wrote that:

> The IDEA does not require an IEP to provide the optimal level of services, we likewise hold that the IDEA does not require a school district to choose the program supported by the optimal level of peer-reviewed research. Rather, the peer-reviewed specially designed instructions in an IEP must be "reasonably calculated to enable the child to receive meaningful educational benefits in light of the child's intellectual potential."
>
> (*Ridley*, 2012, p. 34)

The appellate court did not create a test that lower courts and hearing officers could use to determine what would constitute an adequately peer-reviewed special education program. The court noted that judges and hearing officers should only "assess the appropriateness of an IEP on a case-by-case basis, taking into account the available research" (p. 37). The court further asserted that if a school failed to implement a program based on peer-reviewed research, even though such research was available, that fact would weigh heavily against the school district.

It is significant that the U.S. Court of Appeals seriously considered the peer-reviewed research requirement of the IDEA (Yell & Rozalski, 2013). The court noted that PRR supported *Project Read*. In 2012, Bateman and Linden asserted, "the clear language of the statute requires that the services in the IEP must be based on peer-reviewed research" (p. 54) and because the research on teaching reading is so clear it is likely that the courts will become more receptive to considering its importance in disputes. The following statement in the appellate court's decision regarding PRR shows that prescient nature of Bateman and Linden's assertion. In the opinion, the court wrote that

> we will not set forth any bright-line rule as to what constitutes an adequately peer-reviewed special education program; hearing officers and reviewing courts must continue to assess the appropriateness of an IEP on a case-by-case basis, taking into account the available research. We recognize that there may be cases in which the specially designed instruction proposed by a school district is so at odds with current research that it constitutes a denial of a FAPE.

(*Ridley*, 2012, p. 13)

These three decisions are important rulings that give a glimpse into how future hearing officers and judges may decide PRR cases. As these cases show, the PRR requirement of the IDEA is an important consideration that IEP teams need to address when developing special education programs. Nonetheless, these decisions, and the aforementioned guidance from the U.S. Department of Education, indicate that thus far courts have not used the PRR requirement to raise the standard of school districts' responsibility to provide a FAPE for IDEA-eligible students with disabilities. The standard remains the charge to provide an education that confers meaningful educational benefit to a student in special education (Etscheidt & Curran, 2010; Yell & Rozalski, 2013; Zirkel, 2008). As the *Ridley* court noted, it remains to be seen what will happen when courts are faced with school districts that provide educational programs that are at odds with current research. When IEP teams use procedures based on PRR and implement these procedures with fidelity, the special education programs they develop and implement will be much more likely to confer meaningful education benefit, and thus meet the substantive requirements of a FAPE (Yell & Rozalski, 2013). (For a description of what constitutes a peer reviewed article go to http://guides.lib.jjay.cuny.edu/content.php?pid=209679&sid=1746812)

RELATED SERVICES AND FAPE

The provision of a FAPE sometimes requires that students with disabilities be provided with related services in addition to their special education services. Related services are defined in the IDEA as "supportive services … as may be required to assist a child with a disability to benefit from special education" (IDEA Regulations, 34 C.F.R. § 300.16[a]). When related services are provided to a student with a disability, they must be included in the IEP, and they must be provided at no cost. Courts have ordered school districts to reimburse parents for the unilateral provision of related services when it has been determined that the service was necessary for educational benefit but was not provided by the school (*Fort Bend Independent School District v. Z.A.*, 2014; *P.K. ex. rel. S.K. v. New York City Department of Education*, 2011).

Regulations to the IDEA define related services as:

Transportation and such developmental, corrective, and other supportive services as are required to assist a child with a disability to benefit from special education. Related services include speech-language pathology and audiology services; interpreting services; psychological services; physical and occupational therapy; recreation, including therapeutic recreation; early identification and assessment of disabilities in children; counseling services, including rehabilitation counseling; orientation and mobility services; and medical services for diagnostic or evaluation purposes. Related services also include school health services and school nurse services, social work services in schools, and parent counseling and training.

(34 CFR § 300.34[a])

Additionally, related services that are more fully detailed in the regulations include (a) audiology, which includes identification of a student with hearing loss, determination of the extent of hearing loss, and the provision of rehabilitative services, counseling, and guidance of students, parents, and teachers regarding hearing loss; (b) counseling services, which include services provided by qualified social workers, psychologists, and guidance counselors; (c) parent counseling and training, which includes assisting parents in understanding the special needs of their child, providing parents with information about child development, and helping parents to acquire the necessary skills that will allow them to support the implementation of their child's IEP or individualized family services plan (IFSP); and (d) psychological services, which include administering assessments, interpreting assessments, counseling with other staff members in planning programs to meet the special education needs of students, planning and managing a program of psychological services, and assisting in developing positive behavioral intervention strategies.

Additionally, "the term related services does not include a medical device that is surgically implanted, the optimization of that device's functioning (e.g., mapping), maintenance of that device, or the replacement of that device" (34 CFR § 300.34[b][1]). The law does not, however, limit the rights of students with surgically implanted devices, such as cochlear implants or insulin pumps, to receive related services that the IEP team determines are needed to benefit from the special education services. In the 2006 regulations to the IDEA, the U.S. Department of Education noted that the maintenance and monitoring of surgically implanted devices, if it requires the expertise of a licensed physician, is not a related service; however, maintenance and checking to make sure a device is operational is a covered related service (Analysis of Comments and Changes, 2006).

The list of related services included in IDEA and its regulations is illustrative, not exhaustive. Except for medical services provided by a licensed physician and medical devices, there are no restrictions on IEP teams when they determine what related services a student needs to benefit from his or her special education. For example, transportation may be a related service under the IDEA when it enables a student to access the special education designated in a student's IEP (Sughrue, 2017). Additionally, when eligible students with disabilities have identified mental health needs, a means for addressing these needs is via related services such as counseling, psychotherapy, or even residential services (Yell, Smith, Katsiyannis, & Losinski, 2017).

Although the IDEA does not directly address the use of service animals, it is quite likely that use of service animals could be a related service. Service animals, usually dogs, have been trained to provide assistance to persons with disabilities. Some examples of such services include (a) assisting students who are visually impaired to navigate, (b) alerting students who are deaf or hard of hearing of to the presence of sounds, (c) providing physical support and stability to students with mobility impairments, and (d) preventing students with cognitive impairments or autism from wandering into potentially dangerous situations. Most litigation involving service animals, including a Supreme Court decision in *Fry v. Napoleon Community Schools* (2017), have involved Section 504 of the Rehabilitation Act or the Americans with Disabilities Act (ADA). (For further information on the Supreme Court's decision in

Fry v. Napoleon see Chapter 5 on Section 504 and Chapter 6 on the ADA). Although most decisions have not involved the related services provision of the IDEA, when the service animal is necessary to enable a student to benefit from his or her education, the service animal may be a related service. Moreover, if schools have rules and procedures that prohibit animals in schools, it is likely that these policies could violate Section 504 and the ADA, even in situations in which service animals are not required related services. It is not likely, in situations in which a student needs a service animal as a related service, that a school would not be responsible for providing, training, or caring for the service animal.

The team that develops a student's IEP is the proper forum to determine which related services are required in order to provide a FAPE (*Letter to Rainforth,* 1990). The IEP team, in addition to determining the types of related services to be provided, must determine the amount or frequency of the services provided and specify this in a student's IEP. The commitment of needed resources must be clear to the parents and other IEP team members (IDEA Regulations, Notice of Interpretation on IEPs, Question 51).

This is true for the type of related services and the amount of the services that are to be provided. Related services frequently complement the special education services a student receives, but related services can never be provided without an accompanying special education service (Pitasky, 2000). Some related services, such as speech therapy, may also qualify as a special education service. Nonetheless, related services cannot be included in a student's IEP if no special education is being provided to the student (Tatgenhorst et al., 2014).

Providing complex health services as related services to medically fragile students with disabilities has been a controversial issue. Difficulties have arisen when school districts attempted to distinguish school health services from medical services in providing the related services. School health services are "provided by a qualified school nurse or other qualified person" and are required under the IDEA (IDEA Regulations, 34 C.F.R. § 300.16). According to Lear (1995), the definition of school health services is extremely broad and may run the gamut from activities requiring almost no training (e.g., dispensing oral medication), to those requiring increased levels of training (e.g., catheterization), to those requiring extensive training and a substantial amount of time (e.g., tracheotomy care and chest physiotherapy).

When health care services must be provided by a physician, they are not allowed under the IDEA because they are excluded medical services. Medical services covered under the IDEA are only those services provided by a licensed physician for diagnostic or evaluation purposes; all other medical services provided by a licensed physician are excluded. A school health service, or the services of the school nurse, may be required if (a) the service is necessary to assist a child with disabilities in benefiting from special education, (b) the service must be performed during school hours, and (c) the service can be provided by a person other than a licensed physician, such as a school nurse or some other properly trained school employee (*Letter to Greer,* 1992).

Lower courts, such as in *Timothy W. v. Rochester (NH) School District* (1989), have ruled on the necessity for school districts to provide a FAPE to all qualified students with disabilities unconditionally and without exception. According to the IDEA regulations of 2006, school districts are responsible for providing services necessary to maintain the health and safety of a student while he or she is in school, with services pertaining to breathing, nutrition, and other bodily functions (e.g., nursing services, suctioning a tracheotomy, urinary catheterization), if these services can be provided by an individual with appropriate training rather than a licensed physician (Analysis of Comments and Changes, 2006). Additionally, school district personnel may obtain an independent medical reevaluation of the student to gather information about the student's condition (*Shelby S. v. Conroe Independent School District,* 2006).

When parents unilaterally provide related services to their child, they may seek reimbursement. The parents seeking reimbursement, however, must demonstrate that the services were needed for their child to receive a FAPE and that a school district failed to provide the services (Sughrue, 2017). In *Max M. v. Illinois State Board of Education* (1986), the parents sued a school district to receive reimbursement for psychotherapy that they provided for their son. The district court determined that because the school district had failed to provide their son with psychotherapy, despite the fact that the school district's consultant had advised that psychotherapy be provided, that the district had failed to provide a FAPE and was thus responsible for reimbursement.

The U.S. Supreme Court and Related Services

In 1984, the U.S. Supreme Court issued a ruling in a case involving related services. The case, *Irving Independent School District v. Tatro* (1984), was to assume a great deal of importance because it was the first high court ruling regarding related services. Amber Tatro, an eight-year-old born with spina bifida, a condition that resulted in orthopedic and speech impairments and a neurogenic bladder, was in need of a procedure called *clean intermittent catheterization* (CIC) to be performed every three to four hours to prevent kidney damage. The evidence presented in the case indicated that a layperson could perform this medically accepted procedure with less than an hour's training. Although the school district found that Amber qualified for special education services under the IDEA, the district would not provide CIC services. Amber's parents unsuccessfully pursued a due process ruling to have the school train personnel to provide CIC services. In an action brought by the Tatros in federal district court, the court ruled in favor of the school district, holding that CIC was not required by the IDEA. The court held that CIC was a medical service that was excluded from the related services mandate. The Tatros filed an appeal with the U.S. Court of Appeals for the Fifth Circuit. The appellate court reversed the district court's ruling in holding that CIC was a supportive service, not a medical service, and thus had to be provided by the school. The Irving Independent School District then filed a petition of certiorari with the U.S. Supreme Court.

The Supreme Court decided to hear the case. The high court concluded that the requested CIC service was a supportive service within the legal parameters of IDEA because the CIC service was necessary for Amber to attend school. Without the provision of the CIC service, therefore, Amber could not benefit from her special education program. Further, the Court ruled that the CIC service was not subject to exclusion as a medical service. The Court agreed with the Department of Education's definition of school health services and medical services and found it to be a reasonable interpretation of congressional intent. The Department of Education had defined *related services* to include school health services provided by a qualified school nurse or other qualified person.

To assist lower courts and schools in determining whether a particular service was covered, the Court established three criteria: (a) the student must be IDEA eligible, (b) the service must be necessary to assist the child to benefit from special education, and (c) the service must be performed by a nurse or other qualified person (services performed by a physician are excluded).

In *Tatro,* the Supreme Court adopted a "bright-line test" for lower courts to follow when making related services decisions (Katsiyannis & Yell, 2000). A bright-line test is clearly stated and easy to follow (Thomas & Hawke, 1999). The bright-line test that *Tatro* established was whether a physician provided the services. If the related services had to be provided by a physician, the school district was not responsible for providing the services. However, if a non-physician could provide the services, even if they were medical in nature, the school district was responsible for providing the services.

Despite the high court's ruling in *Tatro,* the controversy regarding school health services and medical services continued. In fact, a number of courts departed from the bright-line standard of *Tatro* and ruled that when numerous and complex health services were required for a particular student, they became medical in nature and were therefore not required under the IDEA. Thomas and Hawke (1999) referred to the standard developed by these courts as the "medical-services standard." That is, the administrative and medical complexity as well as the feasibility and cost of complex health services rendered them medical in nature. Appellate courts in other jurisdictions adopted the Supreme Court's bright-line test.

Because of the split in the circuit courts and the ongoing controversy on issues involving complex health services, it was inevitable that the Supreme Court would take a case on this issue. On March 3, 1999, the high court handed down a ruling in the case of *Cedar Rapids Community School District v. Garret F.* (1999; hereafter *Garret F.*). The case involved more complex and riskier procedures than those presented in *Tatro,* and the financial stakes were considerably higher. Garret Frey was paralyzed from a motorcycle accident when he was four years old. He was ventilator dependent and could only breathe with an electric ventilator or with someone pumping an air bag attached to his tracheotomy tube. Garret also required tracheotomy supervision and suctioning, repositioning in his wheelchair, assistance with food and drink, ventilator checks, catheterization, and observations and assessments to determine if he was in respiratory distress or if he was experiencing autonomic hyperreflexia (i.e., increases in blood pressure and heart rate in response to anxiety or a full bladder). For Garrett's first few years of school his parents provided for his nursing care during the school day. They used funds from their insurance and proceeds from a settlement with the motorcycle company to hire a licensed practical nurse to care for Garret's needs. When Garret entered middle school, his parents requested that the school district assume financial responsibility for the physical care during the school day. School district officials refused to provide the services because they believed that the school district was not legally obligated to provide continuous nursing care. Garret's parents requested a due process hearing.

After hearing extensive testimony, Larry Bartlett, the administrative law judge (ALJ), issued a ruling that relied on the bright-line standard, in which he ordered the school district to pay for the services. The ALJ found that although Garret was the only ventilator-dependent student in the district, most of the requested health services were already provided to other students. Whereas Garret needed a greater amount of complicated health care services than other students in special education, they were no more medical than the care in *Tatro.* Furthermore, the ALJ found that the distinction between health care services and medical services in the IDEA was that the former are provided by a qualified school nurse or other qualified person whereas the latter refers to services performed by a licensed physician. The ALJ, therefore, followed the bright-line standard. The school district appealed, and lost, in the district court and the U.S. Circuit Court of Appeals for the Eighth Circuit. The school district then appealed to the Supreme Court. The High Court agreed with the lower courts that the requested services were related services because Garret could not attend school without them and that the services were not excluded as medical services. Therefore, the High Court upheld the bright-line test established in *Tatro.* The Court acknowledged that the district may have legitimate concerns about the financial burden of providing the services Garret needs, but noted that its proposed cost-based standard as the sole test for determining the required services fell outside the Court's authority. Such a test would also challenge the IDEA's zero-reject principle, as Congress intended to open the doors of public education to all qualified children.

By reaffirming the bright-line test established in *Tatro,* the Supreme Court affirmed school districts' responsibility to provide any and all necessary health services to qualified students with disabilities irrespective of the intensity level or complexity. As long as the needed related service does not have to be provided by a physician, the service is considered a related service under the IDEA. This ruling also reaffirmed the intent of Congress to ensure access to an appropriate education to all eligible students with disabilities and preserve the zero-reject principle. The Court reasoned that this case was about whether meaningful access to the public schools would be assured, not the level of services that a school must finance once access is attained.

The primary principle that the U.S. Supreme Court adopted in these two important cases was that when related services are needed to provide eligible students with disabilities with access to an appropriate education, such services must be provided at school district expense. Thus, a student's IEP team must consider what related services a student needs to benefit from their special education and when such relate services are necessary, they should be included in his or her IEP. According to the U.S. Supreme Court, the only limit to related services are those services that must be provided by a licensed medical doctor.

EXTENDED SCHOOL YEAR AND FAPE

The IDEA does not specifically address the provision of special education programs that extend beyond the traditional school year of approximately 180 school days. The regulations written in 1999 define an *extended school year* (ESY) as special education and related services provided to a student with a disability beyond the normal school year FAPE (IDEA Regulations, 34 C.F.R. § 300.309). The regulations also require that a school district must ensure that ESY services are available as necessary if an IEP team determines, on an individual basis, that these services are needed to provide a FAPE. Furthermore, the regulations prohibit school districts from limiting ESY services to particular categories of disability or unilaterally limiting the type, amount, or duration of these services.

The requirement that school districts provide ESY services when necessary to provide a FAPE originated with the courts. In a number of cases, parents and advocates contended that extended breaks in educational programming could result in severe regression of skills and subsequent failure to recoup lost skills within a reasonable period of time. When self-sufficiency skills are lost, ESY services may be needed to provide a FAPE. ESY services are required only when the lack of such a program will result in denial of a FAPE. ESY is not, therefore, required for all students with disabilities. When found to be necessary, these services must be provided at no cost to the families. Additionally, ESY services must be offered, when necessary, even if the school district does not ordinarily provide summer school programming or other educational services outside the regular school year (Gorn, 2000). The determination of whether a student with disabilities must be provided with ESY programming must be made on an individual basis.

The courts have clearly stated that if ESY services are required to ensure the provision of a FAPE, they must be provided (*Alamo Heights Independent School District {ISD} v. State Board of Education*, 1986; *Cordrey v. Euckert*, 1990). SEA and local educational agency (LEA) policies that provide only the traditional number of school days have consistently been struck down by the courts (e.g., *Alamo Heights ISD v. Board of Education*, 1986; *Armstrong v. Kline*, 1979; *Bales v. Clark*, 1981; *Battle v. Commonwealth of Pennsylvania*, 1980; *Cordrey v. Euckert*, 1990; *Crawford v. Pittman*, 1983; *Georgia ARC v. McDaniel*, 1984; *Johnson v. Independent School District No. 4*, 1990; *Yaris v. Special School District of St. Louis County*, 1986). These policies have been overturned because the inflexibility of the traditional school year prohibits consideration of the rights of students to an individualized education or because the ESY services were determined to be necessary for students to receive a FAPE.

Many courts have based their decisions on the regression/recoupment problem (Boomer & Garrison-Harrell, 1995; Osborne, 1995; Tucker & Goldstein, 1992). In these cases, the students had regressed to such a degree on important skills during an extended break in educational programming that it took an inordinate amount of time to recoup the lost skills. Therefore, the students require an ESY program to avoid regression. Courts have held that regression may be in a number of areas, including academics, emotional or behavioral status, physical skills, self-help skills, or communication (*Cremeans v. Fairland Local School District*, 1993; *Holmes v. Sobol*, 1991; *Johnson v. Lancaster-Lebanon Intermediate Unit 13*, 1991). Very young children (i.e., birth to 3 years of age), covered under Part C, must also receive ESY services if needed to provide a FAPE. Additionally, in some situations in which a student with a severe disability regresses in skills quickly when there is a break in services,

ESY services have been awarded not only for summer break, but for shorter breaks during the school year as well (Pitasky, 2000).

In the ESY cases, school districts have not been ordered to provide these services because students would benefit from them but because they would be harmed by an interruption of special education services. It is important, however, that school districts be flexible in making ESY decisions and not rely solely on regression/recoupment considerations (Tatgenhorst et al., 2014). That is, criteria for determining extended school year should take into account individual factors and particular circumstances that may merit inclusion in an ESY program in addition to regression/recoupment.

In *Johnson v. Independent School District No. 4* (1990), the U.S. Court of Appeals for the Tenth Circuit gave some direction to school districts in making ESY determinations. According to the court, factors involved in determining if ESY is necessary to provide a FAPE may include the degree of impairment, the ability of parents to provide educational structure in the home, the availability of resources, a determination of whether the program is extraordinary or necessary, the student's skill level, and areas of the curriculum in which the child needs continuous attention. The court also noted that in using the regression/recoupment analysis, schools "should proceed by applying not only retrospective data, such as past regression and rate of recoupment, but also include predictive data, based on the opinion of professionals in consultation with the child's parents" (p. 1028).

Students who are determined to have disabilities under Section 504 but not under the IDEA must also be provided ESY services if such services are a necessary element to a FAPE. A number of the Office of Civil Rights (OCR) in the U.S. Department of Education have issued rulings that have indicated that ESY programming can be required under Section 504 (*Baltimore {MD} City Public Schools*, 1986; *Clark City {NV} School District,* 1989).

Katsiyannis (1991) recommended that SEAs and schools develop ESY policies. He suggested that school districts implement ESY policies that (a) clearly define the ESY program and objectives, (b) develop eligibility criteria, (c) generate a systematic referral process, and (d) construct a detailed plan for monitoring and data collection. He also suggests that LEAs provide inservice training on ESY programming for all administrators and teachers.

PLACEMENT AND FAPE

One of the critical determinations in providing a FAPE to students with disabilities is placement, which refers to the setting in which a FAPE will be delivered. Placement, however, refers to more than just the setting. It also includes factors such as (a) facilities, (b) equipment, (c) location, and (d) personnel required to deliver the special education and related services specified in an IEP (*Weil v. Board of Elementary and Secondary Education,* 1991). The placement decision must be made by a group of knowledgeable persons, typically the IEP team. School districts must ensure that parents take part in all placement decisions. Parents must be involved in the entire decision-making process. Additionally, parents must be provided with all the necessary information needed to help them make an informed decision. School officials, therefore, cannot make a placement decision unilaterally (Lake, 2007). Prior to deciding on a student's placement, the student must have been evaluated and his or her IEP developed.

Determining Placement

To choose the setting in which a student will be placed, IEP team members must draw on a variety of informational sources, including aptitude and achievement tests, teacher recommendations, physical condition, social or cultural background, and adaptive behavior, to provide the information needed to make the determination (IDEA Regulations, 34 C.F.R. § 300.533[a][1]). Additionally, the information that the team uses should be documented

(IDEA Regulations, 34 C.F.R. § 300.533[a][2]). According to the OSEP, no single factor should dominate decision making regarding placement; rather, all factors are to be considered equally (*OSEP Policy Letter*, 1994).

One such factor is parental preference regarding their child's placement. Although parental preference is an important consideration in the decision, according to the Office of Special Education and Related Services (OSERS), it is not the most important factor (*Letter to Burton,* 1991).

Placement Factors

When an IEP team makes a placement decision, it must consider three important factors. First, the IEP team must make the placement decision based on a student's IEP (IDEA Regulations, 34 C.F.R. § 300.552[a][2]). Placement decisions can only be made after the IEP has been developed and in accordance with its terms (Appendix A to 34 C.F.R., Part 300, Question 14). Thus, a student's placement cannot be determined prior to writing his or her IEP. Only after the IEP has been written can the team determine where a particular student's needs can best be met (Lake, 2007; Tatgenhorst et al., 2014). In fact, in *Spielberg v. Henrico County Public Schools* (1988), a decision to place a student prior to developing the IEP was held to be a violation of the IDEA. Placing a student in a particular setting prior to determining the student's program, therefore, would be putting placement ahead of his or her individual educational needs. According to Lake (2007), such a decision would be a serious mistake that could lead to a denial of a FAPE. The IEP is often developed and the placement determined in the same team meeting; therefore, the IEP and placement decision are actually two separate components of the special education decision-making process.

Second, a student's educational placement must be determined at least annually (IDEA Regulations, 34 C.F.R. § 300.552[a][1]). This means that the IEP, including the student's placement, should be reviewed at least once a year. Either the parents or school personnel may request a placement review more frequently than annually if necessary.

Third, the placement must be made in conformity with the least restrictive environment (LRE) requirement of the IDEA (IDEA Regulations, 34 C.F.R. § 300.533[a][4]). According to the LRE requirement, a student must be educated to the maximum extent appropriate with students without disabilities. Removal of the student from the general education environment occurs only when education in general education classes with the use of supplementary aids and services cannot be achieved satisfactorily (IDEA Regulations, 34 C.F.R. § 300.550). To ensure that the LRE mandate is met, school districts are required to ensure the availability of a continuum of alternative placements from which to choose the LRE (IDEA Regulations, 34 C.F.R. § 300.551).

The FAPE and LRE requirements of the IDEA are interrelated. LRE refers to the relative restrictiveness of the setting in which a student with disabilities is educated. The preferred environment is as close to the general education environment as is appropriate. Depending on what special education services an IEP team determines to be required for students to receive a FAPE, however, the LRE may be a more restrictive setting than the general education classroom. For example, a team could decide that a special school is the least restrictive and appropriate placement for a student. (See Chapter 12 for elaborations on the LRE requirements.)

In addition, the placement should be as close to home as possible. Unless otherwise indicated in the IEP, students should be placed in schools they would be attending if they did not have a disability. This is not an absolute right so much as it is a preference. If placements in home schools will not provide a FAPE, schools may place students in more distant schools (*Hudson v. Bloomfield Hills School District,* 1995).

Schools cannot unilaterally change students' placements. Placement decisions must be based on an existing IEP, so any change of placement must be supported either by that IEP or by a new IEP. If the school determines that a change in placement is necessary, the parents must be notified (IDEA Regulations, 34 C.F.R. § 300.504[a][1]) and be included in the decision-making process.

GRADUATION AND FAPE

A student is no longer eligible for a FAPE under the IDEA when (a) he or she reaches the maximum age to receive services under the IDEA (usually 21 years old), or (b) he or she graduates from high school with a regular diploma, whichever comes first (Pitasky, 2000). When students are no longer eligible for a FAPE, the school district's obligation to them ends. When students graduate with a graduation certificate, a certificate of attendance, or a special education diploma, rather than a regular diploma, they remain eligible to receive special education services (IDEA Regulations, 34 C.F.R. § 300.122[a][3][i][ii]) and are entitled to receive a FAPE until they age out of IDEA eligibility.

Before a student in special education can properly graduate, the student's IEP team should meet to determine if the student is ready to graduate. Several factors must be determined. First, the student must have achieved his or her IEP goals. It should be noted that if a student has met the school's regular high school graduation criteria, the school can graduate the student even if he or she hasn't met the IEP goals. However, if a student has met his or her IEP goals but not the graduation requirements, a school district would not be required to award the student a diploma. If a student has graduated but has not achieved the IEP goals, however, the student may claim that he or she did not receive a FAPE and is entitled to receive compensatory educational services. Second, the parent must receive a written notice because graduation is a change in placement and the procedural safeguards of the IDEA apply. Third, although the IEP team is not required to conduct an evaluation of the student prior to his or her graduation with a regular diploma and termination from IDEA services, the IDEIA 2004 requires that the IEP team provide the student with a summary of his or her academic achievement and functional performance. This summary must include recommendations on how to assist the student to meet his or her postsecondary goals (IDEA 20 U.S.C. § 1414[c] [5]). According to Richards and Martin (2005), the rationale for this section is to provide practical recommendations to help a student with future employment, additional training, or postsecondary schooling.

Readers should note that graduation requirements are determined solely by the state and the school district. Nevertheless, the IEP plays an important role in a student's graduation. For example, the IEP team could use the state's and school district's graduation requirements as a basis for planning transition services or writing annual "goals" (Gorn, 2000). Additionally, if graduation is contingent on a student completing an exit examination, the IEP team's role is to make decisions about the necessity of having the student use accommodations when testing. Although it may be unlikely, if a student has graduated with a regular diploma but could still benefit from special education services and has not aged out, the school district could continue to provide the student with special education services. In such a situation, the IEP team would still have the responsibility of determining a FAPE for the student.

IEP IMPLEMENTATION AND FAPE

According to Bateman (2017) when school districts fail to implement important parts of an IEP, this error can lead to a denial of FAPE. This is true even in cases where there no procedural or substantive errors committed by an IEP team. Although IDEA does not address IEP implementation, a few courts have examined school districts' failure to implement. The most important cases being the following out of the U.S. Courts of Appeals for the Fifth Circuit, *Houston Independent School District v. Bobby R.* (2000), and the U.S. Court of Appeals for the Ninth Circuit, *Van Duyn v. Baker School District 5J* (2007). These cases show a growing trend towards requiring that school districts' failure to implement a substantive or material aspect of a student's IEP before a court will rule that a school district has violated the FAPE requirement of the IDEA (King, 2009). According to Zirkel (2017), these courts established two primary standards to assess whether or not a school district's failure to implement an IEP would result in a denial of FAPE: The materiality-benefit standard and the materiality-alone standard.

In *Houston Independent School District v. Bobby R.* (2000; hereinafter *Bobby R.*), the U.S. Court of Appeals for the Fifth Circuit ruled that a school district's admitted failure to fully implement a student's IEP did not deprive the student of a FAPE because "the significant provisions of (the student's) IEP were followed, and, as a result, (the student) received an educational benefit" (*Bobby R.,* 2000, p. 349). The case involved the parents of a sixth-grade student with a learning disability and speech impairment. The school district's IEP had developed an IEP that included speech therapy, a phonics program, and various accommodations to help him succeed in school. Because the school admittedly did not implement many of the provisions of the IEP, the parents sought administrative review and eventually filed a lawsuit alleging that the failure to implement their child's IEP constituted a denial of FAPE. A hearing officer ruled in favor of the student's parents but the U.S. District Court overturned the administrative decision. The parents appealed to the circuit court, which ruled in favor of the school district, holding that the school district had met the two-part *Rowley* test. Because the parents had not alleged a procedural violation, therefore, the court ruled on the second substantive part of the *Rowley* test: Was the IEP reasonably calculated to provide educational benefit. In the opinion, the Court found that the student had benefitted because he had made some progress on standardized tests and concluded that:

> To prevail on a claim under the IDEA a party challenging the implementation of an IEP must show more than a de minimis failure to implement all elements of that IEP, and, instead, must demonstrate that the school board or other authorities failed to implement substantial or significant provision of the IEP (*Bobby R.*, 2000, p. 253).

Unfortunately, the court did not discuss what provisions in the student's IEP were significant, although in a footnote to the decision the court did find that a factor that could be considered significant in such cases could be made by determining if a student had benefited despite the implementation failure. By using this logic, and examining the student's increasing test scores, the circuit court determined that because the student had received educational benefit the school district had not violated FAPE. Zirkel (2017) referred to the *Bobby R.* standard as the materiality plus benefit standard. In other words, when hearing officers or judges use the *Bobby R.* standard when assessing IEP implementation failures they will examine (a) the significance or materiality of the IEP provisions that were not implemented and (b) whether a student had received educational benefit.

Although some circuit courts have used the *Bobby R.* standard with some changes (e.g., *Neosho School District v. Clark,* 2003; *Melissa S. v. School District of Pittsburgh,* 2006), a few district courts have criticized the ruling. For example, according to a district court in *Manalansan v. Board of Education of Baltimore City* (2001), expressed its criticism by noting that the IDEA

> creates substantive rights that can be enforced even if a child has been lucky enough to make progress despite a school districts failure to comply with federal law. In other words, when it is clear that the statute has been violated, a school should not be released from liability because a child has made some educational progress (*Manalansan*, 2001, p. 14).

In 2007, the U.S. Courts of Appeals for the Ninth Circuit in *Van Duyn v. Baker School District 5J* (2007) ruled in a case in which a student's parents alleged that the school district denied their child a FAPE when the district failed to implement his IEP. Christopher Van Duyn's parents and school personnel developed an IEP for Christopher a few months before he entered middle school. The IEP was very specific in terms of the services and amount of time in which services were to be provide. After the school year began, Christopher's parents brought an administrative action alleging that many portions of his school's IEP were not being implemented. The case eventually ended up in the circuit court.

In a 2-to-1 decision, the circuit court adopted the first part of the *Bobby R.* test, which required that a court determine whether a school district had failed to implement a significant or material portion of an IEP. The *Van Duyn* court, however, did not use the second part of the *Bobby R.* standard, which required proof of denial of educational benefit in order to determine that a failure to implement would lead to a denial of FAPE. Zirkel (2017) referred to the standard developed by the *Van Duyn* court as the materiality alone standard because the fifth circuit court rejected the *Bobby R.* educational benefit standard.

According to the court's 2-to-1 majority opinion

> We hold that a *material* failure to implement an IEP violates the IDEA. A material failure occurs when there is more than a minor discrepancy between the services a school provides to a disabled child and the services required by the child's IEP… We clarify that the materiality standard does not require that the child suffer demonstrable educational harm in order to prevail. (*Van Duyn*, 2007, p. 822).

The court applied this standard to Christopher's IEP and found that the school district had violated the materiality standard by failing to implement the amount of math instruction called for in the IEP (the IEP required 8 to 10 hours per week but the district only provided 5 hours per week). Thus, the court ruled that the Baker School District had violated Christopher's right to a FAPE.

When hearing officers or judges use the Fifth Circuit's *Van Duyn* standard in assessing IEP implementation failures, therefore, they will examine the significance or materiality of the IEP provisions that were not implemented but will not consider whether or not a student benefited. In fact, the Ninth Circuit Court in *Van Duyn* specifically rejected the Fifth Circuit's *Bobby R.* standard when they noted that "we would disagree with *Bobby R.* if it meant to suggest that an educational benefit in one IEP area can offset an implementation failure in another" (*Van Duyn*, 2007, p. 823 n. 3).

In the *Van Duyn* decision, the dissenting judge rejected the notion that courts should assess whether or not an IEP component was material. According to dissenting Judge Ferguson

> Judges are not in a position to determine which parts of an agreed-upon IEP are or are not material. The IEP Team, consisting of experts, teachers, parents, and the student, is the entity equipped to determine the needs of a special education student, and the IEP represents this determination. Although judicial review of the content of an IEP is appropriate when the student or the student's parents challenge the sufficiency of the IEP … such review is not appropriate where, as here, all parties have agreed that the content of the IEP provides FAPE. (*Van Duyn*, 2007, p. 827).

This approach, which has been referred to as the per se standard (King, 2009, Zirkel, 2017, Zirkel & Bauer, 2016), finds an automatic denial of FAPE on a proven failure to fully implement a student's IEP (Zirkel, 1970). Although the per se view currently has no binding case law authority, Zirkel (2017) asserted that states' complaint investigation process and OCR use the per se standard when a failure to implement an IEP is alleged.

IS THERE A NEW FAPE STANDARD?

When the EAHCA was passed in 1975, Congress intended that the law open the doors of public education for students with disabilities. Thus, the emphasis of the original law was on access to educational programs rather than any level of educational opportunity (Eyer, 1998; Yell & Drasgow, 2000). The law has been dramatically successful in opening the doors of public education to students with disabilities in public education. However, when the IDEA was authorized in 1997 and again in 2004, Congress believed that the promise of the IDEA had not been fulfilled for too many children with disabilities (House of Representatives Report, 1997). The underlying theme of IDEA 1997 and IDEIA 2004, therefore, was to improve the effectiveness of special education by requiring demonstrable improvements in the educational achievement of students with disabilities. Indeed, a quality education for each student with disabilities became the new goal of the IDEA in 1997 (Eyer, 1998) and in 2004. As Eyer (1998) wrote,

> The IDEA can no longer be fairly perceived as a statute which merely affords children access to education. Today, the IDEA is designed to improve the effectiveness of special education and increase the benefits afforded to children with disabilities to the extent such benefits are necessary to achieve measurable progress. (p. 16)

The IDEA requires that schools further the educational achievement of students with disabilities by developing an IEP that provides a special education program designed to confer measurable and meaningful educational progress in the least restrictive environment. Moreover, school districts are also required to provide instruction that is grounded in scientifically based research. In fact, school districts may be vulnerable to special education lawsuits if they don't offer programs that are based on peer-reviewed research (Tatgenhorst et al., 2014).

Additionally, IDEIA 2004 instructed hearing officers to make their decisions on substantive grounds based on a determination of whether a student received a FAPE (IDEA, 20 USC § 1415[f][3][E][i]). This section of the law certainly does not lessen the importance of following the procedural requirements of the IDEA; however, it does require that hearing officers attend first and foremost to the educational benefits received by the student. In cases in which a procedural violation is alleged, a hearing officer may only rule that the student did not receive a FAPE because the procedural violation (a) impeded the student's right to a FAPE, (b) impeded the parent's opportunity to participate in the IEP process, or (c) caused a deprivation of educational benefits (IDEA 20 USC § 1415[f][3][E][ii]). Clearly, IDEIA 2004 continues the trend to improve the effectiveness of special education and improve results for students with disabilities that Eyer noted in IDEA 1997 (Eyer, 1998).

The reauthorization of the IDEA in 2004 reemphasized the importance of developing and delivering special education programs that confer educational benefit. To ensure that students actually benefit, IEP teams must ensure that programs are (a) based on student needs, (b) meaningful and contain measurable annual goals, (c) grounded in scientifically based practices, and (d) measured on an ongoing basis to ensure that students make progress. Furthermore, if the data show that a student is not progressing, the IEP team must make changes to a student's program and continue to collect data to monitor progress.

Both the IDEA reauthorizations of 1997 and 2004 seemed to elevate the standards of FAPE (Blau, 2007; Eyer, 1998; Huefner, 2008; Johnson, 2003; Yell et al., 2007). For example, in IDEA 1997 Congress added the requirement that a student's IEP goals be measurable and that these goals must facilitate the student's progress in the general curriculum. (The National Center on Accessible Educational Materials at http://aim.cast.org/ has information to help students with disabilities access the general education). Additionally, a student's IEP must include a method for measuring his or her progress toward the goals and a means for reporting this progress to the student's parents. In the IDEIA of 2004, Congress emphasized that "improving educational results for children with disabilities is an essential element of our national policy of ensuring equality of opportunity, full participation, independent living, and economic self-sufficiency for individuals with disabilities" (IDEA, 20 U.S.C. § 1400[c][1]). The IDEIA also required that special education services be based on peer-reviewed research. According to Etscheidt and Curran (2010), the peer-reviewed research may affect the substantive FAPE standards of the IDEA. Although, it does not appear that courts have elevated the FAPE standard because of the peer-reviewed research (Zirkel, 2008), nonetheless, as Huefner (2008) asserted, this requirement suggested that members of IEP teams must be familiar with research and be able to defend their selection of services. Moreover, these services must allow a student to advance appropriately toward attaining his or her annual goals. Furthermore, if a student is not making progress, the IEP team must address this problem. As Huefner (2008) noted following the reauthorization of the IDEA in 2004:

> The purpose of IDEA is no longer to provide a "basic floor of opportunity." The expectation of academic and functional progress calls for more than a floor. Although IDEA does not expect, let alone guarantee any certain standard of achievement, it expects meaningful or substantive progress both toward general curriculum goals and the student's unique educational goals (such as social/behavioral, physical, functional, and developmental goals) resulting from the disability.
>
> (p. 378)

Huefner's position proved to be prescient with respect to the Supreme Court's decision in *Endrew*. In *Endrew*, the High Court announced a new FAPE standard for determining educational benefit. Thus, there is a new and higher benchmark for implementation of a student's IEP, which now must be designed to confer more than just some educational benefit (Yell & Bateman, 2017; Weatherly & Yell, 2017). IEPs must now be developed for a student to make progress appropriate in light of the student's circumstances.

LESSONS FROM LITIGATION AND LEGISLATION

Principles from the body of FAPE case law and the IDEA can provide useful guidance to school districts to assist them in developing appropriate programs for students with disabilities.

Principle 1: Involve parents as full partners in the IEP process. A FAPE depends on ensuring that parents are meaningfully involved in their children's special education identification, assessment, programming, and placement. The IDEA grants parents an enforceable right to pursue a FAPE for their child with a disability, and as members of the IEP team, parents are considered equal partners with school personnel in determining the components of their child's appropriate education.

Principle 2: Provide administrators, teachers, and staff training on their responsibilities under the IDEA. A FAPE depends on having school-based personnel who understand and can meet their responsibilities under the IDEA. Administrators or teachers who don't understand their responsibilities and thus violate students' rights can cause special education disputes, which in turn could lead to hearings and court cases. The new requirements of the IDEA will also mean that teachers need to become fluent in research-based practices and progress monitoring systems. Because general education has not met a student's unique educational needs and he or she is provided special education services, it is incumbent on administrators and special education teachers to develop legally sound programs that provide meaningful educational benefit (Yell, Shriner, & Katsiyannis, 2006).

Principle 3: Develop educationally meaningful and legally sound IEPs. The IEP is the centerpiece, the heart and soul of the IDEA (Bateman & Linden, 2012). It is the procedure by which a student's FAPE is developed and delivered. To ensure that a student's IEP confers meaningful educational benefit, it is necessary that school-based personnel (a) conduct relevant assessments that provide complete information on a student's unique educational needs; (b) develop ambitious measurable annual goals, based on these assessments, which guide a student's special education program; (c) determine the research-based special education and related services that will be provided to the student; (d) provide any related services necessary for a student to benefit from his or her education; and (e) monitor student progress by collecting and reacting to meaningful data.

School personnel can ensure that programs deliver a FAPE by using educational practices that show evidence of producing meaningful outcomes and then implementing these programs with integrity. Because special education programs must be calculated to enable a student to make educational progress, if special educators don't use effective instructional strategies and monitor student progress, this standard is not likely to be realized. School personnel can thus ensure that special education programs confer educational progress by collecting data to determine if their interventions are working and their students are making progress toward meeting their measurable annual goals. Adjusting instruction in response to student progress data will make it more likely that students will make progress that leads to increased academic achievement and functional performance.

Principle 4: Provide access to the general education curriculum. An important component of a FAPE is providing special education students access to the general curriculum. Students' IEPs should not include the general curriculum; rather the PLAAFP statement in a student's IEP must describe how the student's disability affects involvement in the general curriculum, and the annual goals and special education services must include instructional methods that facilitate access to the general curriculum by meeting the student's individual academic and functional needs.

Principle 5: Place students in the least restrictive appropriate environment. Special educators should begin with the assumption that all students with disabilities should be educated with nondisabled students in the general educational setting. The LRE mandate has two components: (a) students with disabilities must be educated along with students without disabilities to the maximum extent appropriate, and (b) students with disabilities should be removed from integrated settings only when the nature or severity of the disability is such that an appropriate education with the use of supplementary aids and services cannot be achieved satisfactorily in the general education setting. The congressional authors of the IDEA recognized that at times an integrated setting will not provide an appropriate education and thus a more restrictive setting may be necessary. The crucial issue, therefore, in determining placement is what placement is appropriate for the student.

Principle 6: Fully implement the IEP as written. When parents and school personnel collaboratively develop a student's IEP, which is his or her FAPE, that IEP should be implemented as written. This means that all staff involved in executing a student's IEP, including general education teachers and related services personnel, must understand and carry out their responsibilities as agreed upon. As Zirkel (2017) noted, the IEP is a commitment. School district personnel must ensure that this commitment to students and their parents is fulfilled.

These guidelines, extrapolated from court rulings, will help to ensure that students in special education receive a FAPE by helping teams of parents and educators to be vigilant in meeting students' individual needs and diligent in using data and peer-reviewed research to guide instruction. School personnel can ensure that programs deliver a FAPE by using educational practices that show evidence of producing meaningful progress. Students' IEP teams must develop and implement measurable and research-based IEPs, and special education teachers must collect meaningful data to monitor their students' progress toward meeting their annual goals and then adjust instruction in response to student performance. If this occurs, it will make it more likely that students in special education will make educational progress.

SUMMARY

A free appropriate public education consists of special education and related services, provided at public expense, that meet the standards of the state educational agency and are provided in conformity with the IEP. In *Board of Education v. Rowley* (1982), the U.S. Supreme Court first addressed the issue of FAPE. Thirty-five years after the *Rowley* decision,

the U.S. Supreme Court in *Endrew F. v. Douglas County School District* (2017) issued its second ruling on FAPE. In this decision, the High Court specifically addressed the question of what level of educational benefit is required for a school district to provide a FAPE. A unanimous Court ruled that "to meet its substantive obligation under the IDEA, a school must offer an IEP reasonably calculated to enable a child to make progress appropriate in light of the child's circumstances" (*Endrew*, 2017, p. 15).

The U.S. Supreme Court, in *Rowley* (1982) and *Endrew* (2017), also ruled that a FAPE does not require schools to maximize the potential of students with disabilities. Rather, a FAPE is a specially designed program that meets the individual needs of students and is reasonably calculated to enable a student to progress. The Supreme Court in these two decisions provided lower courts with a two-part test for determining a school's compliance with the FAPE mandate. First, the court must determine whether the school has complied with the procedures of the IDEA. Second, the court will examine the IEP to ascertain if the IEP was reasonably calculated to enable a student to progress in light of his or her circumstances. If these requirements are met, a school has complied with FAPE requirements. According to the *Rowley and Endrew* decisions, courts are to give deference to educational determinations made by school officials. Educational procedures and methodology, therefore, are the responsibility of the schools. It is the responsibility of the courts to determine compliance with the IDEA.

A student's FAPE is realized through the development of an IEP. In determining the special education and related services to be provided to students, a knowledgeable group of persons, which must include a representative of the school, the student's teacher, and the parents of the child, formulate the IEP. The IEP delineates the special education and related services to be provided by the school. Once the IEP has been developed, decisions concerning students' placements are made. Placement decisions must be in conformity with the LRE rules of the IDEA, which require placement in general education settings when appropriate.

The U.S. Supreme Court's rulings in *Rowley* and *Endrew* have provided guidance for courts to determine whether students in special education are provided with a FAPE. Originally passed to open the doors of public education to students with disabilities, the IDEA now requires accountability, research-based instruction, ambitious and challenging goals, and progress monitoring of students with disabilities. Clearly, this emphasis on accountability for student outcomes requires changes in the ways that teams of parents and educators develop IEPs.

Enhanced eText Application Exercise 8.1. *Endrew F. v. Douglas County School District RE-1, 137 S.Ct. 988 (2017).*

FOR FURTHER INFORMATION

Smith, R.C. (1996). *A case about Amy*. Philadelphia, PA: Temple University Press.

Tatgenhorst, A., Norlin, J. W., & Gorn, S. (2014). *What do I do when … The answer book on special education law* (6th ed.). Palm Beach Gardens, FL: LRP Publications.

U.S. Department of Education, Office of Special Education Programs' (OSEP's) IDEA website (2017). Available at https://sites.ed.gov/idea/.

U.S. Department of Education, Office of Special Education and Rehabilitative Services (2017). *Questions and answers (Q&A) on U.S. Supreme Court Decision Endrew F. v. Douglas County School District Re-1*. Available at https://www2.ed.gov/policy/speced/guid/idea/memosdcltrs/qa-endrewcase-12-07-2017.pdf.

Yell, M.L. & Bateman, D.F. (2017). *Endrew F. v. Douglas County School District (2017): FAPE and the Supreme Court. Teaching Exceptional Children, 50,* 1-9.

REFERENCES

Adams v. Hansen, 632 F. Supp. 858 (N.D. Cal. 1985).

Age v. Bullitt County Public Schools, 701 F.2d 233 (1st Cir. 1982).

Alamo Heights Independent School District v. State Board of Education, 790 F.2d 1153 (5th Cir. 1986).

Analysis of Comments and Changes to 2006 IDEA Part B Regulations, 71 Fed. Reg. 46,571 (2006).

Armstrong v. Kline, 476 F. Supp. 583 (E.D. Pa. 1979), *aff'd in part and remanded sub nom.*

Aron, L. (2005). Too much or not enough: How have the courts defined a free appropriate education after *Rowley? Suffolk University Law Review, 39,* 1–18.

B.B. v. State of Hawaii Department of Education, 46 IDELR 213 (D. Haw. 2006).

Bales v. Clark, 523 F. Supp. 1366 (E.D. Va. 1981).

Baltimore (MD) City Public Schools, EHLR 311:42 (OCR 1986).

Bateman, B. D. (2017). Individualized education programs. In J. M. Kauffman and D. P. Hallahan (Eds.), *Handbook of Special Education, 2nd ed.,* (pp. 91–124). Philadelphia, PA: Taylor & Francis/Routledge.

Bateman, B. D., & Linden, M. (2012). *Better IEPs: How to develop legally correct and educationally useful programs* (5th ed.). Verona, WI: IEP Resources/Attainment.

Battle v. Commonwealth of Pennsylvania, 629 F.2d 269 (3d Cir. 1980), *cert. den. Scanlon v. Battle,* 452 U.S. 968 (1980), further decision, 513 F. Supp. 425 (E.D. Pa. 1980); 629 F.2d 269 (3d Cir. 1980).

Blau, A. (2007). The IDEA and the right to an "appropriate" education. *Brigham Young University Education and Law Journal, 1,* 1–24.

Board of Education v. Diamond, 808 F.2d 987 (3d Cir. 1986).

Board of Education of the Hendrick Hudson School District v. Rowley, 458 U.S. 176 (1982).

Boomer, L. W., & Garrison-Harrell, L. (1995). Legal issues concerning children with autism and pervasive developmental disorder. *Behavioral Disorder, 21,* 53–61.

Boughham v. Town of Yarmouth, 20 IDELR 12 (1993).

Burlington School Committee v. Massachusetts Department of Education, 556 IDELR 389 (U.S. 1985).

Carter v. Florence County School District Four, 950 F.2d 156 (4th Cir. 1991).

Cedar Rapids Community School District v. Garret F., 526 U.S. 66 (1999).

Central Susquehanna Intermediate Unit 16, 2 ECLPR 109 (SEA Pa. 1995).

Chester County Intermediate Unit 23, 23 IDELR 723 (SEA Pa. 1995).

Clark City (NV) School District, 16 EHLR 311 (OCR 1989).

Clevenger v. Oak Ridge School Board, 744 F.2d 514 (6th Cir. 1984).

Cordrey v. Euckert, 917 F.2d 1460 (6th Cir. 1990).

Crawford v. Pittman, 708 F.2d 1028 (5th Cir. 1983).

Cremeans v. Fairland Local School District, 633 N.E. 2d 570 (Ohio App. 1993).

Crockett, J. B., & Yell, M. L. (2008). Without data all we have are assumptions: Revisiting the meaning of a free appropriate public education. *Journal of Law and Education, 37*(3), 381–392.

Crockett, J. B., & Yell, M. L. (2017). IEPs, least restrictive environment, and placement. In E.A. Shaver and J.R. Decker (Eds.). *A guide to special education law* (p. 65-97). Cleveland, OH: Education Law Association.

Cypress-Fairbanks Independent School District v. Michael F., 118 F.3d 245 (5th Cir. 1997).

Daniel, P. T. K. (2008). "Some benefit" or "maximum benefit": Does the No Child Left Behind Act render greater educational entitlement to students with disabilities? *Journal of Law and Education, 37*(3), 347–366.

Daniel, P. T. K., & Meinhart, J. (2007). Valuing the education of students with disabilities: Has government legislation caused a reinterpretation of free appropriate public education? *Education Law Reporter, 222,* 512–524.

Deal v. Hamilton County Board of Education, 392 F.3d. 840 (6th Cir. 2004).

Delaware County Intermediate Unit #25 v. Martin and Melinda K., 831 F. Supp. 1206 (E.D. Pa. 1993).

Doe v. Alabama Department of Education, 915 F.2d 651 (11th Cir. 1990).

Doe v. Board of Education of Tullahoma City Schools, 9 F.3d 455 (6th Cir. 1993).

Doe v. Defendant 1, 898 F.2d 1186 (6th Cir. 1990).

Doe v. Lawson, 579 F. Supp. 1314 (D. Mass. 1984), *aff'd.* 745 F.2d 43 (1st Cir. 1984).

Doe v. Smith, EHLR 559:391 (N.D. Tenn. 1988).

Drobnicki by Drobnicki v. Poway Unified School District, 53 IDELR 210 (9th Cir. 2009).

Doug C. v. Hawaii Department of Education 61 IDELR 91 (9th Cir. 2013).

Dzugas-Smith v. Southold Union Fee School District 59 IDELR 8 (E.D. N.Y. 2012).

E.W. v. Rocklin Unified School District, 46 IDELR 192 (E.D. Cal. 2006).

Endrew F. v. Douglas County School District RE-1, 137 S.Ct. 988 (2017). Retrieved March 22, 2017 from www.supremecourt.gov/opinions/16pdf/ 15-827_0pm1.pdf

Endrew F., by and through his parents and next friends, Joseph and Jennifer F. v. Douglas County School District RE-1, Available at http://blogs.edweek.org/ edweek/speced/Endrew%20Order.pdf

Etscheidt, S., & Curran, C. M. (2010). Reauthorization of the Individuals with Disabilities Education Improvement Act (IDEA, 2004): The peer-reviewed research requirement. *Journal of Disability Policy Studies, 21,* 29–39.

Eyer, T. L. (1998). Greater expectations: How the 1997 IDEA amendments raise the basic floor of opportunity for children with disabilities. *Education Law Report, 126,* 1–19.

Fairfax County Public Schools, 22 IDELR 80 (SEA Va. 1995).

Florence County School District Four v. Carter, 114 S. Ct. 361 (1993).

Fort Bend Independent School District v. Z.A., 62 IDELR 231 (S.D. TX. 2014).

Frederick County Public Schools, 2 ECLPR 145 (SEA Md. 1995).

G.D. v. Westmoreland, 17 IDELR 751 (1st Cir. 1991).

Georgia ARC v. McDaniel, 511 F. Supp. 1263 (N.D. Ga. 1981), *aff'd.* 716 F.2d 1565 (11th Cir. 1983), 740 F.2d 902 (11th Cir. 1984).

Gorn, S. (2000). *What do I do when … The answer book on assessing, testing, and graduating students with disabilities.* Horsham, PA: LRP Publications.

H. B. v. Las Virgenes, 48 IDELR 31 (9th Cir. 2007).

Hall v. Vance County Board of Education, 774 F.2d 629 (4th Cir. 1985).

Henderson, A. T., & Mapp, K. L. (2002). *A new wave of evidence: The impact of school, family, and community connections on student achievement.* Austin, TX: Southwest Educational Development Laboratory, National Center for Family & Community Connections with Schools. Available at www.sedl.org/connections/resources/evidence.pdf. Retrieved May 24, 2008.

Holmes v. Sobol, 18 IDELR 53 (W.D. N.Y. 1991).

House of Representatives Report on P.L. 105-17 (1997). Available at http://wais.access.gpo.gov.

Houston Independent School District v. Bobby R., 200 F.3d 342 (5th Cir. 2000).

Hudson v. Bloomfield Hills School District, 23 IDELR 612 (E.D. Mich. 1995).

Hudson v. Wilson, 558 EHLR 186 (W.D. Va. 1986).

Huefner, D. S. (1991). Judicial review of the special educational program requirements under the Education for All Handicapped Children Act: Where have we been and where should we be going? *Harvard Journal of Law and Public Policy, 14,* 483–516.

Huefner, D. S. (2008). Updating the FAPE standard under IDEA. *Journal of Law and Education, 37,* 367–380.

In re Child with Disabilities, 23 IDELR 471 (SEA Conn. 1995).

Independent School District No. 318, 24 IDELR 1096 (SEA Minn. 1996).

Individuals with Disabilities Education Act, 20 U.S.C. § 1400 *et seq.*

Individuals with Disabilities Education Act Regulations, 34 C.F.R. § 300.533 *et seq.*

Iovannone, R., Dunlap, G., Huber, H., & Kincaid, D. (2003). Effective educational practices for students with autism spectrum disorders. *Focus on Autism and Other Developmental Disabilities, 18,* 150–165.

Irving Independent School District v. Tatro, 468 U.S. 883 (1984).

J.C. v. Central Regional School District, 23 IDELR 1181 (3d Cir. 1996).

Johnson, S. F. (2003). Reexamining *Rowley:* A new focus in special education law. *Brigham Young University Education and Law Journal, 2,* 561–587.

Johnson v. Independent School District No. 4, 921 F.2d 1022 (10th Cir. 1990).

Johnson v. Lancaster-Lebanon Intermediate Unit 13, 757 F. Supp. 606 (E.D. Pa. 1991).

Joshua A. v. Rocklin Unified School District, 52IDELR 1 (9th Cir. 2009).

K.K. v. Alta Loma School District, 60 IDELR 159 (C.D. Cal. 2013).

Karl v. Board of Education, 736 F.2d 873 (2d Cir. 1984).

Katsiyannis, A. (1991). Extended school year policies: An established necessity. *Remedial and Special Education*, 12, 24–28.

Katsiyannis, A., & Yell, M. L. (2000). The Supreme Court and school health services: *Cedar Rapids v. Garret F. Exceptional Children*, 66, 317–326.

L.F. v. Houston Independent School District, 58 IDELR 63 (5th Cir 2012).

Lachman v. Illinois State Board of Education, 852 F.2d 290 (7th Cir. 1988).

Lake, S. E. (2007). *Slippery slope: The IEP missteps every team must know—and how to avoid them.* Horsham, PA: LRP Publications.

Lear, R. (1995). The extent of public schools' responsibility to provide health-related services. In *Proceedings of the 16th Annual Institute on Legal Issues of Educating Students with Disabilities.* Alexandria, VA: LRP Conference Division.

Letter to Burton, 17 EHLR 1182 (OSERS, 1991).

Letter to Culbreath, 25 IDELR 1212 (OSEP 1997).

Letter to Greer, 19 IDELR 348 (OSEP 1992).

Letter to Kane (OSEP 2010).

Letter to Rainforth, 17 LRP 1295 (OSEP 1990).

Malkentzos v. DeBuono, 923 F. Supp. 505 (S.D. N.Y. 1996).

Mandlawitz, M. (1996). Lovaas, TEACCH, and the public system: The court as referee. In *Proceedings of the 17th National Institute on Legal Issues of Educating Individuals with Disabilities.* Alexandria, VA: LRP Publications Conference Division.

Manual R. v. Ambach, 635 F. Supp. 791 (E.D. N.Y. 1986).

Max M. v. Illinois State Board of Education, 684 F. Supp. 514 (N.D. Ill. 1986).

Melissa S. v. School District of Pittsburgh, 183 F. App'x 184 (3d Cir. 2006).

N. B. v. Hellgate Elementary School District, 50 IDELR 241 (9th Cir. 2008).

Neosho R-V School District v. Clark, 315 F.3d 1022 (8th Cir. 2003)

Tatgenhorst, A., Norlin, J.W., & Gorn, S. (2014). *What do I do when … The answer book on special education law* (6th ed.). Palm Beach Gardens, FL: LRP Publications.

Office of Special Education Programs. (2000). IDEA 25th anniversary website. Available at www.ed.gov/offices/OSERS/IDEA25th.html.

Osborne, A. G. (1992). Legal standards for an appropriate education in the post-*Rowley* era. *Exceptional Children*, 58, 488–494.

Osborne, A. G. (1995). When must a school district provide an extended school year program to students with disabilities? *Education Law Reporter*, 99, 1–9.

OSEP Policy Letter, 20 IDELR 1155 (OSEP 1992).

OSEP Policy Letter, 21 IDELR 674 (OSEP 1994).

Peterson v. Hastings Public Schools, 831 F. Supp. 742 (D. Neb. 1993).

Pitasky, V. M. (2000). *The complete OSEP handbook.* Horsham, PA: LRP Publications.

P.K. ex. Rel. S.K. v. New York City Department of Education, 819 F. Supp 2nd 90 (E.D.N.Y. 2011).

Polk v. Central Susquehanna Intermediate Unit 16, 853 F.2d 171 (3d Cir. 1988).

Richards, D. M., & Martin, J. L. (2005). *The IDEA amendments: What you need to know.* Horsham, PA: LRP Publications.

Ridley School District v. M.R. and J.R., 680 F.3d 260 (3d Cir. 2012).

Rocklin Unified School District, 48 IDELR 234 (SEA Cal. 2007).

Rowley, A.J., (2008). Rowley revisited: A personal narrative. *Journal of Law and Education*, 37 (3), 312–326.

Salend, S. J. (2006). Explaining your inclusion program to families. *Teaching Exceptional Children*, 38(4), 6–11.

San Antonio ISD v. Rodriguez, 411 U.S. 1 (1973).

Schimke, A. (2018). Inside one Colorado family's long legal journey to affirm their son's right to a meaningful education. Downloaded on February 24, 2018 from https://www.chalkbeat.org/posts/co/2017/11/15/inside-one-colorado-familys-long-legal-journey-to-affirm-their-sons-right-to-a-meaningful-education/.

Seals v. Loftis, 614 F. Supp. 302 (E.D. Tenn. 1985).

Section 504 Regulations, 34 C.F.R. § 104.33(a).

Shelby S. v. Conroe Independent School District, 45 IDELR 269 (5th Cir. 2006).

Sherman v. Pitt County Board of Education, 93 EDC 1617 (SEA N.C. 1995).

Smith, R.C. (1996). *A case about Amy.* Philadelphia, PA: Temple University Press.

Social Security Act, 42 U.S.C. § 1396.

Spielberg v. Henrico County Public Schools, EHLR 558:202 (E.D. Va. 1988).

Springdale School District v. Grace, 494 F. Supp. 266 (W.D. Ark. 1980), aff'd, 656 F.2d 300, vacated, 73 L.Ed. 2d 1380, 102 S.Ct. 3504 (1982), on remand, 693 F.2d 41 (8th Cir. 1982), cert. den. 461 U.S. 927 (1983).

Sughrue, J.A. (2017). Related services under the IDEA. In E.A. Shaver & J.R. Decker (Eds.). A Guide to Special Education Law (pp 99-118). Cleveland, Ohio: Education Law Association.

Tatgenhorst, A., Norlin, J. W., & Gorn, S. (2014). *What do I do when … The answer book on special education law* (6th ed.). Palm Beach Gardens, FL: LRP Publications.

Thomas, S. B., & Hawke, C. (1999). Health-care standards for students with disabilities: Emerging standards and implications. *Journal of Special Education*, 32, 226–237.

Thompson R2-J School District v. Luke, 48 IDELR 63 (U.S. Dist. Court, Colo., 2007).

Tice v. Botetourt County School Board, 908 F.2d 1200 (4th Cir. 1990).

Timothy W. v. Rochester (NH) School District, 875b F.2d 954 (1st Cir. 1989).

Tucker, B. P., & Goldstein, B. A. (1992). *Legal rights of persons with disabilities: An analysis of public law.* Horsham, PA: LRP Publications. (Looseleaf service updated annually. The most recent update was February 2010.)

Tuscaloosa County Board of Education, 21 IDELR 826 (SEA Ala. 1994).

Union City School District v. Smith, 15 F.3d 1519 (9th Cir. 1994).

U.S. Department of Education, Office of Special Education and Rehabilitative Services (2017). *Questions and answers (Q&A) on U.S. Supreme Court Decision Endrew F. v. Douglas County School District Re-1.* Retrieved from https://www2.ed.gov/policy/speced/guid/idea/memosdcltrs/qa-endrewcase-12-07-2017.pdf on December, 7, 2017.

Walsh, J. (2011, November). *Preventing the predetermination claim.* Paper presented at the Tri-State Regional Special Education Law Conference, Omaha, NE.

Wall v. Mattituck-Cutchogue School District, 24 IDELR 1162 (E.D. N.Y. 1996).

Waukee Community School District, 48 IDELR 26 (SEA Iowa 2007).

Waukee Community School District & Heartland Area Education Agency, 51 IDELR 15 (S.D. Iowa 2008).

Weatherly, J. J. (2013, November). *Avoiding special education litigation.* Paper presented at the Tri-State Special Education Law Conference, Omaha, NE.

Weatherly, J.J. & Yell, M.L. (2017). *Endrew F. v. Douglas County School District* (2017): Recommendations for Administrators and Implications for Developing IEPs [Webinar]. Retrieved from www. pubs.cec.sped.org/webscotus20172/.

Weil v. Board of Elementary and Secondary Education, 931 F.2d 1069 (5th Cir. 1991).

Wenkart, R. D. (2000). *Appropriate education for students with disabilities: How courts determine compliance with the IDEA.* Horsham, PA: LRP publications.

Winkelman v. Parma City School District, 550 U.S. 516 (2007).

Wright, P., & Wright, P. W. (2007). Supreme Court rules: parents have independent, enforceable rights. Wrightslaw. Available at www. wrightslaw.com/law/art/winkelman.pwanalysis.htm. Retrieved on March 1, 2010.

Yaris v. Special School District of St. Louis County, 1984, 661 F. Supp. 996 (E.D. Mo. 1986).

Yell, M.L. & Bateman, D.F. (2017). *Endrew F. v. Douglas County School District* (2017): FAPE and the Supreme Court. *Teaching Exceptional Children, 50*, 1-9.

Yell, M. L. & Crockett, J. (2011). Free appropriate public education (FAPE). In J. M. Kauffman and D. P. Hallahan (Eds.), *Handbook of special education* (pp. 77–90). Philadelphia, PA: Taylor & Francis/ Routledge.

Yell, M. L., & Drasgow, E. (2000). Litigating a free appropriate public education: The Lovaas hearings and cases. *Journal of Special Education, 33,* 206–215.

Yell, M. L., Drasgow, E., Bradley, R., & Justesen, T. (2004). Critical legal issues in special education. In A. McCray Sorrells, H. J. Reith, & P. T. Sindelar (Eds.), *Issues in special education* (pp. 16–37). Boston: Allyn & Bacon.

Yell, M. L., Katsiyannis, A., & Hazelkorn, M. (2007). Reflections on the 25th anniversary of the Supreme Court's decision in *Board of Education v. Rowley. Focus on Exceptional Children, 39*(9), 1–12.

Yell, M. L. & Rozalski, M. E. (2013). The peer-reviewed research requirement of the IDEA: An examination of law and policy. In B. G.

Cook, M. Tankersley, & T. J. Landrum (Eds.), *Evidence-based practices* (pp. 1–26). London: Emerald.

Yell, M. L., Shriner, J. G., & Katsiyannis, A. (2006). Individuals with Disabilities Education Improvement Act of 2004 and IDEA Regulations of 2006: Implications for educators, administrators, and teacher trainers. *Focus on Exceptional Children, 39*(1), 1–21.

Yell, M. L., Shriner, J.G., Thomas, S. S., & Katsiyannis, A. (2018). Special education law for leaders and administrators of special education. In J. Crockett, M. L. Boscardin, & B. Billingsley (Eds.), *Handbook of Leadership and Administration for Special Education* (2nd ed.). Philadelphia, PA: Routledge.

Yell, M.L., Smith, C., Katiyannis, A., & Losinski, M. (2017). Mental health services, free appropriate public education, and students with disabilities: Legal considerations in identifying, evaluating, and providing services. *Journal of Positive Behavior Interventions*, DOI: 10.1177/1098300717722358.

Zirkel, P. A. (2008). Have the amendments to the Individuals with Disabilities Education Act razed *Rowley* and raised the substantive standard for "free appropriate public education"? *Journal of the National Association of Administrative Law Judiciary, 28*, 396–418.

Zirkel, P.A. (2017). Failure to implement the IEP: The third dimension of FAPE under the IDEA. *Journal of Disability Policy Studies,*

Zirkel, P. A., & Bauer, E. T. (2016). The third dimension of FAPE under the IDEA: IEP implementation. *Journal of the National Association of Administrative Law Judiciary, 36*, 409–427.

To hear the oral arguments made before the U.S. Supreme Court in *Board of Education of the Hendrick Hudson School District v. Rowley* (1982) go to the following website: www.oyez.org/cases/1981/80-1002

To hear the oral arguments made before the U.S. Supreme Court in *Endrew F. v. Douglas County School District* go to the following website: www.oyez.org/cases/2016/15-827

To hear the oral arguments made before the U.S. Supreme Court in *Irving Independent School District v. Taro* (1984) go to the following website: www.oyez.org/cases/1983/83-558

To hear the oral arguments made before the U.S. Supreme Court in *Cedar Rapids Community School District v. Garret F* (1984) go to the following website: www.oyez.org/cases/1998/96-1793

Chapter 9

Identification, Assessment, and Evaluation

The IEP must be appropriate in light of a child's circumstances...A focus on the individual child is at the core of the IDEA. The instruction offered must be "specially designed" to meet a child's "unique needs" through an "individualized education program"...An IEP is not a form document. It is constructed only after careful consideration of the child's level of achievement, disability, and potential for growth.

CHIEF JUSTICE JOHN ROBERTS, *ENDREW F. V. DOUGLAS COUNTY SCHOOL DISTRICT* (2017, P. 12)

Learner Objectives

At the end of the chapter, students will be able to

9.1 Describe the purposes of a special education assessment.

9.2 Describe the assessment process in special education.

9.3 Describe the child find requirement of the IDEA.

9.4 Describe the procedural and substantive requirements of an initial special education evaluation.

9.5 Describe the protection in evaluation procedures of the IDEA.

9.6 Describe the importance of the assessment to a student's free appropriate public education.

Assessment is the process of collecting data for the purpose of making decisions about students (Salvia, Ysseldyke, & Witmer, 2017). The assessment is the initial step in providing special education services to a student with disabilities and because it is the key to detecting a student's disability or disabilities, it sets the parameters for a student's special education programs if a student is determined to be eligible for special education (Tatgenhorst, Norlin, & Gorn, 2014). It is, therefore, an integral part of the learning and teaching process in special education (Yell, Shriner, Thomas, & Katsiyannis, 2018; Reschly, 2000). Indeed, according to the U.S. District Court in Kirby v. Cabell (2006)

> This deficiency goes to the heart of the IEP; the child's level of academic achievement and functional performance is the foundation on which the IEP must be built. Without a clear identification of [the student's] present levels, the IEP cannot set measurable goals, evaluate the child's progress and determine which educational and related services are needed. (p. 166)

The Individuals with Disabilities Education Act (IDEA) requires that before a student is placed in a special education program, he or she must be assessed[1] or evaluated to determine

---

[1]The terms *assessment* and *evaluation* are used interchangeably in the IDEA and regulations.

(a) whether the student has an IDEA disability, (b) if the student requires special education and related services because of his or her disability, and (c) the nature and extent of the student's academic and functional needs that will be addressed in the individualized education program (IEP).

The purpose of the assessment is twofold: (a) to determine a student's eligibility for special education services and (b) to determine the student's educational needs for planning a student's IEP (Yell, Shriner, Thomas, & Katsiyannis, 2018). With respect to the provision of a free appropriate public education (FAPE), the second purpose is very important because the assessment forms the basis of a student's annual goals and special education services. According to Yell and Drasgow (2001), the assessment/evaluation process answers the who, what, how, and where questions in special education. That is, the primary purposes of this process are to determine (a) *who* should receive special education services (i.e., classification and eligibility decisions), (b) *what* instructional services will be monitored (i.e., program planning decisions), (c) *how* a student's progress will be monitored (program evaluation decisions), and (d) *where* the student's special education services can be most effectively delivered (i.e., placement decisions).

The assessment of a student is a critically important part of the process that leads to the development of a FAPE for a student. It is important because the goals of a student's educational program, the special education services he or she will receive, and the monitoring of a student's progress are based on the assessment or evaluation data. As Huefner (2000) noted, "It is difficult to overstate the importance of a full [assessment] of the child prior to the development of the IEP. An accurate evaluation of the child's strengths, weaknesses, and current levels of performance is the basis of all that will follow" (p. 156).

The assessment process must be individualized, which means that the procedures and methods of the evaluation must address a student's unique needs, rather than being a general assessment that can be used interchangeably with all students. Deficiencies in a school's evaluation process and procedures are a serious matter, especially if the school has reason to suspect the student may have a disability. Such deficiencies can lead to the deprivation of a FAPE and possible hearings or even court actions (Yell, Shriner, Thomas, & Katsiyannis, 2018). The assessment is the keystone upon which a student's IEP, and therefore FAPE, is based (Yell, Shriner, Thomas, & Katsiyannis, 2018). The purpose of this chapter is to examine federal statutes, regulations, cases, and administrative guidelines involving the identification, assessment, and evaluation of students with disabilities for determination of eligibility for and placement in special education. The issue of including students with disabilities in accountability efforts will also be addressed.

DEFINITION OF ASSESSMENT

According to Salvia, Ysseldyke, and Witmer (2017), the assessment information that is collected may include test data, work samples, and the results of observations, interviews, and screenings. Assessment in special education involves decisions in several areas, including prereferral classroom decisions, entitlement decisions, programming decisions, and accountability/outcome decisions (Salvia, Ysseldyke, & Witmer, 2017).

Prereferral Decisions

Classroom teachers sometimes attempt prereferral classroom interventions prior to formally referring a student for special education. This can be done on a formal basis (e.g., suggestions by a teacher assistance team). Teachers may use assessment tools to assist them in making decisions regarding prereferral interventions. Prereferral interventions are used in the general education classroom to attempt to ameliorate the problem prior to referral to special education. Informal prereferral assessments may include classroom tests, daily observations, and interviews.

Multi-Tiered Systems of Support (MTSS) and response to intervention (RTI) systems are being used in many public school districts in the United States, usually as a system to allow for early detection and intervention for struggling learners while they are in general education. Both MTSS and RTI systems are generally a multi-tiered instructional framework that is implemented schoolwide and addresses the needs of all students in a school, including struggling students and students with disabilities, and integrates assessment and intervention in a multi-level instructional and behavioral system to maximize student achievement and reduce problem behaviors (U.S. Department of Education, 2011). In the multi-tiered instructional framework school personnel (a) identify students who are at risk for poor learning outcomes, (b) monitor student progress, (c) provide evidence-based interventions, and (d) adjust the intensity and nature of these interventions depending on a student's responsiveness to instruction. The U.S. Department of Education does not subscribe to any particular RTI model; however, officials in the department recognize four core characteristics that underlie all RTI models:

1. Students receive high quality research-based instruction in their general education setting
2. Continuous monitoring of student performance
3. All students are screened for academic and behavior problems
4. Multiple levels (tiers) of instruction that are progressively more intense, based on the student's response to instruction

(U.S. Department of Education 2011, p. 2)

In a sense, MTSS and RTI systems are used as prereferral systems because when students are unable to achieve even though they have been moved through the most intensive tier of the system, they are usually referred to special education. In fact, school districts should monitor students' progress in an MTSS or RTI system and when it is apparent that a student may require specialized instruction, the student should be referred for special education evaluation (Tatgenhorst et al., 2014). When such systems are properly developed and implemented, they can serve as a support to the district's child find system and may allow for more accurate referrals by ensuring that students who truly need special education services are referred for a special education evaluation (Tatgenhorst et al., 2014).

In 2011, the Director of the Office of Special Education Programs (OSEP) in the U.S. Department of Education, Melody Musgrove, became so concerned that school districts were using RTI systems to delay or deny eligibility evaluation under the IDEA that she wrote an open letter to all state directors of special education in the United States. The letter described the child find requirements of the IDEA and ended with a request that state education agencies (SEAs) and local education agencies (LEAs) examine their RTI policies to ensure that they were being used appropriately and not being used to delay or deny timely initial evaluations of students suspected of having a disability. The letter is available at www2.ed.gov/policy/speced/guid/idea/memosdcltrs/osep11-07rtimemo.pdf. In *Letter to Ferrera* (2012), officials at OSEP noted that it is appropriate for school district personnel to consider RTI before referring a student; school district personnel should not use RTI as a reason for failing to respond to parents' request for a special education evaluation of their child.

Entitlement Decisions

The second category of assessment decision involves so-called entitlement decisions. Entitlement decisions are those identification and classification decisions, based on individualized assessment, that are used to identify students as having disabilities and to determine if they require special education and related services. Salvia, Ysseldyke, and Witmer (2017) include screening, referral, and eligibility decisions under entitlement decisions.

Screening is the process of collecting data to determine whether more intensive assessment is necessary. Screenings are typically done with all students in a particular school or school district. Students scoring below a certain cutoff point on the screening instruments are considered for further assessment. When screenings are conducted in this manner and not conducted selectively with individual students, they are not subject to the rules and regulations of the IDEA (IDEA Regulations, 34 C.F.R. § 300.500[3][b]) or Section 504. If they are conducted with an individual or a small group of individuals to determine interventions or placements, however, they do require parental consent (*Letter to Holmes*, 1992).

Referral decisions usually involve a determination by a teacher or parent that a student may need special education. According to the IDEA, either a parent of a child with a disability, personnel from the state educational agency, another state agency, or the school district may initiate the referral request. Usually a teacher who completes a referral form brings a student to the attention of a school's multidisciplinary team (MDT). The referral is a formal request made to the MDT to evaluate a student for the presence of a disability. Although school districts may have procedures regarding referrals, referrals are not subject to the federal special education laws. Following a student referral, the MDT determines if the student requires further assessment to determine eligibility for special education. The final type of entitlement decision, therefore, is the determination of eligibility. Evaluations for eligibility are subject to the rules and regulations of the IDEA.

Just because a student is referred for a special education evaluation, either by a parent, teacher, or through a prereferral or MTSS/RTI process, the student is not automatically evaluated for special education services. These processes identify those students who are suspected of having a disability and needing special education services. Students who are suspected may then be evaluated for special education services.

The initial evaluation involves an evaluation of an individual student's unique needs and requires that a student's parents give written consent to the school district to conduct the evaluation. Child find activities such as screening do not require formal written consent from students' parents because they are conducted with all or many students as opposed to an individual student. In *Letter to Gallo* (2013) personnel from OSEP wrote that whether school districts are required to obtain consent from parents before collecting evaluation data depends on the purpose of the data collection. This particular letter involved a question about the collection of functional behavioral assessment (FBA) data within a school district's RTI model. According to OSEP parental consent would be required if the FBA were being conducted as part of an initial evaluation or reevaluation.

Programming Decisions

Bateman (2017) compared a student's assessment/evaluation to the foundation upon which a student's special education program is built. She also noted that the special education program must stand solidly and squarely on a foundation of current, accurate evaluations of the student's level of performance in academic and functional areas. The result of the special education assessment decisions, which are reflected in a student's IEP in the present levels of academic achievement and functional performance (PLAAFP), are the foundations of a student's IEP. Thus, the assessment results are used in (a) planning individualized instruction, (b) writing goals, (c) determining special education services to be provided, and (d) monitoring student progress.

In a U.S. district court decision out of West Virginia, *Kirby v. Cabell County Board of Education*, 2006, the judge found that a school district had not provided a student with a FAPE largely because the evaluation did not provide sufficient information on a student's academic problems. According to the court the present levels of academic achievement and functional performance were the foundation of a student's IEP.

Unfortunately, far too often, evaluations of students for special education services focus exclusively on eligibility using standardized tests and ignore the informal tests, curriculum-based assessments, and direct observations that will lead directly to a student's educational programs. (For elaboration on IEPs, see Chapter 10.) When this is the case, the assessment gives little direction to the IEP team in planning a student's specialized instruction.

Accountability/Outcome Decisions

The final area of assessment decisions in special education, according to Salvia, Ysseldyke and Witmer (2017), involves accountability/outcome decisions. Accountability/outcome decisions involve the collection of assessment data to monitor students' progress as well as to evaluate specific programs and the schoolwide, statewide, or national performance of students. In a sense, the special education assessment process is an ongoing process involving both formative and summative evaluations. With respect to formative assessment, special education teachers are required to do frequent and systematic assessments of a student's progress throughout a student's special education program and to report a student's progress to his or her parents. The assessment completed at the beginning of the year thus becomes a baseline by which the special education teacher can evaluate a student's progress during the year. With respect to summative assessment, the IEP team must conduct a reevaluation if it is determined that the educational needs of a student warrant a reevaluation (IDEA Regulations, 34 C.F.R. § 303[a]). Regulations to the IDEA prohibit a reevaluation from being conducted more than once a year, unless a student's parents or teachers and school district personnel agree otherwise (IDEA Regulations, 34 C.F.R. § 303[a]). Additionally, the IDEA requires that a reevaluation be conducted every 3 years. The purpose of these summative evaluations is to determine (a) whether a student continues to have a disability, (b) a student's educational needs, (c) a student's present levels of performance, (d) whether a student continues to need special education services, and (e) whether any modifications are needed to a student's IEP (IDEA Regulations, 34 C.F.R. § 305[a][1-1v]).

THE ASSESSMENT/EVALUATION PROCESS

When a parent, personnel from a state educational agency or other state agency, or personnel from a school believe a student may have a disability, the student is usually referred to a school's MDT. According to the IDEA regulations, the team members are a group of qualified professionals including a student's parents, general education teachers, and someone qualified to conduct individualized assessments of students (IDEA Regulations, 34 C.F.R. § 300.306 & 34 C.F.R. § 300.308[b]). This team, which is often composed of an administrator, special education teacher, general education teacher, and a school psychologist, is responsible for deciding if the student should receive a complete evaluation. If the answer is yes, then the team must seek written parental consent to conduct the assessment. If the parents give consent, then the team must conduct a full and individualized assessment of the child and coordinate the collection of educationally relevant information. Based on the assessment data, the team then decides if the student has an IDEA disability and requires special education and related services.

If the MDT decides that the student is eligible for special education services, the team must determine the student's specific individual needs. Additionally, according to the U.S. Supreme Court's decision in *Endrew F. v. Douglas County School District* (2017) these decisions must be based on a student's academic and functional needs as determined in the full individualized assessment. Moreover, the IEP team must also consider additional factors such as the student's disability, potential for growth, and the views of his or her parents. In this respect, the assessment serves as an indicator of the student's needs as well as a baseline by which the team can measure student progress in the program. Without such a baseline, the MDT and the IEP team cannot show if a child made educational progress.

If the MDT determines that a student is eligible for special education services under the IDEA, an IEP team is formed to plan the student's academic and functional program. Of course, this process culminates in the development of an IEP for the student. The IEP, which is a written document that serves as a blueprint for a student's educational program as determined by the IEP team, constitutes a student's FAPE. The IEP begins with the present levels of performance statement, which describes a student's academic and functional needs as determined in the assessment. This statement leads directly to the goals and special education services. All areas of need identified in the assessment must be included in the present levels of performance. Then all need statements in the present levels of performance lead to a goal, a service, or both. The U.S. Department of Education described the relationship between the present levels statement and the rest of the IEP as follows:

> There should be a direct relationship between the present levels of performance and the other components of the IEP. Thus, if the statement describes a problem with the child's reading level and points to a deficiency in reading skills, the problem should be addressed under both goals and special education and related services provided to the child.

(IDEA Regulations, 34 C.F.R. § 300 app. C, q. 36, 1997).

Because the entire IEP is based on the assessment, it must be thorough and individualized to produce an IEP that results in a FAPE. Hearing officers and courts have ruled against school districts that failed to conduct thorough evaluations. For example, in *Council Rock School District v. M.W.* (2012), a federal district court held that the Council Rock School District failed to evaluate the emerging behavior problems of a student. The student's teachers had expressed concerns regarding the student's problem behaviors; unfortunately, neither the assessment nor the student's resulting IEP addressed the behavioral issues. Because the district failed to address these behaviors, the judge found that the school district had failed to provide a FAPE.

According to Yell, Shriner, Thomas, and Katsiyannis (2018), to ensure that a thorough assessment is conducted for each student, the IDEA mandates procedural and substantive requirements schools must follow when conducting the assessment. *Procedural requirements* include such things as involving the student's parents in the assessment and conducting the assessment in a timely manner. *Substantive requirements* refer to the manner in which the assessment is conducted. These requirements compel school personnel to assess a student in such a manner that an educational program can be developed that confers meaningful benefit to the student. The procedural and substantive requirements of the assessment form the framework that guides the MDT in assessing a student and, in turn, guides the development of the student's IEP. The procedural and substantive requirements for conducting the assessment are covered in the next section.

Procedural Requirements

To ensure that the MDT conducts an appropriate assessment, the IDEA includes rigorous procedural requirements that must be followed during the assessment process. Strict adherence to these procedural requirements is extremely important because major procedural errors by an MDT may render an IEP inappropriate in the eyes of a hearing officer or judge (Bateman, 2017; Bateman & Linden, 2012; Yell, Shriner, Thomas, & Katsiyannis, 2018). When procedural violations are detected in the assessment process, hearing officers and judges scrutinize the effects of the violations. If the violations interfere with the development of the IEP, and a student did not receive an appropriate education as a result, the IEP and the student's program of special education will be ruled invalid. Thus, school districts must meet their procedural responsibilities when conducting the assessment. The law's procedural requirements are listed in Table 9.1. To view a brief video and the changes to evaluation and reevaluation requirements in the IDEA go to www2.ed.gov/policy/speced/guid/idea/memosdcltrs/osep11-07rtimemo.pdf.

TABLE 9.1 ■ Procedural Requirements for Conducting an Assessment

Key Points	Explanation
Consent	• The school must obtain consent for the initial assessment and for any reevaluations conducted. • The school may use mediation or due process procedures to secure permission to evaluate, if parents refuse consent.
Parent participation	• The school must include parents in the initial assessment. • The student's parents may participate in the reevaluation process.
Assessment tools	• The school is required to use a variety of assessment tools to gather relevant, academic, and functional information about the student, including information provided by the parents. • The assessment team must use technically sound instruments that assess students in all areas of the suspected disability, including cognitive, behavioral, physical, and developmental factors. • The team may not use a single procedure as the sole criterion for determining eligibility or planning educational programs. • The tests must be nondiscriminatory. • Tests must be administered in the student's native language or mode of communication, unless it is not feasible to do so.
Standardized tests	• The tests must have been validated for the specific purpose for which they are intended. • The tests must be administered by trained personnel. • The tests must be administered in accordance with the instructions provided by the producer of the test.
Assessment process	• The student must be assessed in all areas of the suspected disability. • The assessment must be sufficiently comprehensive to identify all of the student's educational needs, regardless of disability. • The assessment must provide information that directly assists the team in determining the educational needs of the student.
Statewide assessments	• The students in special education programs must participate in statewide and districtwide assessments of achievement. • Testing accommodations and alternative assessments, if needed, must be provided to students with disabilities.
IEP team	• The IEP team must include someone qualified to interpret the instructional implications of the assessment results.
Reevaluation	• The assessment data must be reviewed every 3 years. • The team determines that no additional data are needed to assess continued eligibility. The school does not have to conduct a new assessment, unless the parents request it.

Substantive Requirements

A thorough and individualized assessment that (a) addresses all areas of a student's needs, (b) was conducted by knowledgeable persons, and (c) results in the development of an IEP that confers meaningful educational benefit to a student will meet the substantive requirements of the law. The following four elements are necessary to ensure that an assessment meets the IDEA's substantive requirement (Yell & Dragsow, 2001). These elements are also depicted in Table 9.2.

First, the assessment must be a *full and individualized examination* of a student's needs. This means that the assessment must provide an in-depth look at every potential area of deficiency. Bateman (2017) asserted that best practice requires individualization of the assessment. Individualization involves matching assessment carefully and precisely to (a) the referral concerns, (b) the nature of the problem, (c) the characteristics of the student, and (d) the student's learning and behavior patterns. Additionally, the assessment must be matched to parental concerns. According to the U.S. Supreme Court in *Endrew F. v. Douglas County School District* (2017), the IEP is based on the present levels of a student's performance, which must allow a judgement regarding a student's "potential for growth" (*Endrew*, 2017, p. 16).

Assessing all students in a similar manner by using a standard battery of tests is the antithesis of this requirement (Reschly, 2000). Properly conducted assessments, therefore, not

TABLE 9.2 ■ IDEA Substantive Requirements for an Assessment

Key Points	Explanation
Full and individualized assessment	• The school must conduct a full and individualized assessment to determine whether a student has a disability under the IDEA and to determine the student's educational needs. • The assessment should assist the IEP team in planning a student's program of special education, related services, and supplementary aids and services.
Team decision making	• The assessment team must include professionals with expertise in the student's disability area and the student's parents. • The team makes the decisions about the process and results of the assessment. • The parents of a child with disabilities being evaluated must be allowed to participate in the process.
Link between assessment and intervention	• The results of the assessment must lead directly to intervention. • The areas of need identified in the assessment must be addressed in the student's IEP through the goals, special education services, or both.
Data collection	• The IEP must include data collection methods that can be used to determine if a student is making progress toward meeting his or her goals. • The student's progress toward his or her goals must be assessed, and the results of the assessment must be reported to parents at least as often as students in general education receive report cards.

only should consist of standardized tests (e.g., standardized achievement test, standardized intelligence measure), but should also include interviews, direct observations, curriculum-based measures, curriculum-based assessments, and other similar measures. If the assessment is incomplete, the IEP, and thus the student's special education program, will not provide an appropriate education.

Second, a *team of knowledgeable persons* must make decisions regarding the process and results of the assessment. This means that a team of school personnel, parents, and other professionals will use the assessment data to assist them in determining eligibility and make classification decisions based on their well-informed judgments. Furthermore, people who make these educational decisions should have expertise in the specific areas being assessed. For example, if the team needs a functional behavioral assessment, at least one team member should have expertise in this area. If a school district's personnel do not have the necessary knowledge, experience, and expertise to conduct a functional assessment, the district must ensure its personnel are trained or hire outside consultants to conduct the assessment. In sum, assessment information should inform the decision-making process but not determine it. Teams should not rely on formulas or quantitative guidelines alone to make their decision. The IDEA requires the exercise of professional judgment when making eligibility and instructional planning decisions, and total reliance on formulas is not legal (Bateman & Linden, 2012).

Third, the *assessment information must lead to intervention.* If the assessment reveals an area of educational need, the first task of a student's IEP team is to review and use the assessment data to determine the student's educational needs. These needs are then written into the IEP in statements in the present levels of academic achievement and functional performance (PLAAFP) section. These statements describe the student's performance in areas that are adversely affected by his or her disability. The purpose of the PLAAFP statements is to identify these areas of need, academic and nonacademic, so that an appropriate educational program can be devised.

The IDEA requires that the performance statements in the IEP lead directly to education planning. Each PLAAFP, therefore, must lead to a measurable annual goal and a special education service or, in some cases, only a special education or related service (e.g., counseling). Academic or nonacademic needs that are described in the assessment phase must be addressed in the student's educational program. Failure to directly link assessment and intervention is a primary reason that school districts lose in due process hearings when their IEPs are challenged (Bateman, 2017; Yell, Shriner, Thomas, & Katsiyannis, 2018).

Fourth, the IEP team must *collect meaningful data to monitor student progress.* The assessment is the baseline by which we develop our instructional or behavioral programs. The IDEA requires monitoring a student's progress during instruction (i.e., formative evaluation) so that we can modify a student's program if necessary. The IDEA also requires that monitoring data be reported to a student's parents. The assessment process is not just about following procedures; it is about developing special education programs that are reasonably calculated to enable students to make educational progress.

Teachers must continuously collect meaningful data to document student progress toward IEP goals and thus to document the program's efficacy. This means that the data must be collected over the course of instruction so that student progress is continually monitored. Appropriate data will provide objective evidence of student performance, which can be used to guide instructional decisions. Schools can meet the FAPE standards by collecting meaningful data and by demonstrating that these data were used to guide their instructional decisions.

PROTECTION IN EVALUATION PROCEDURES

Regulations that implement the IDEA require schools to evaluate students when a disability is suspected. The regulatory language of the IDEA on conducting evaluations is comprehensive and detailed. It is the responsibility of the schools to locate and evaluate students with special needs in accordance with these regulations. It is therefore important that schools be aware of the procedural requirements of both laws.

Child Find

All states must ensure that all students with disabilities, from birth to age 21, residing in the state who are in need of special education and related services or are suspected of having disabilities, regardless of the severity of the disability, and being in need of special education are identified, located, and evaluated (IDEA Regulations, 34 C.F.R. § 300.111[a]). These requirements, located in Part B of the IDEA, include children with disabilities who are attending private schools, migrant children, homeschooled, and homeless children. This is called the *child find system.* Part C includes similar child find requirements.

School districts have an affirmative obligation to conduct a child find for children residing in their jurisdictions (*San Francisco Unified School District*, 2011). In other words, school district personnel cannot sit back and wait for children with possible disabilities to be referred. They must have proactive programs to seek out and identify children with disabilities (*M.J.C. v. Special School District No. 1*, 2012). Moreover, school districts retain responsibility for an affirmative child find even in situations in which they contract with another agency to conduct the activities (*Oregon City School*, 2012).

A child find program may include (a) public awareness programs, (b) mailings to parents, (c) television and radio advertisements, and (d) coordinated activities with local service agencies, such as hospitals and clinics, to identify children and youth with disabilities (Zirkel, 2015). A child is not automatically eligible for special services under the IDEA because he or she has been identified during child find. Children who are located through this process must be evaluated to determine eligibility within a reasonable period of time (Zirkel, 2015).

If district officials fail to meet their child find obligations, they may deprive children of a FAPE. This is a serious violation of the IDEA, which could result in a district having to pay compensatory education, or tuition reimbursement, from the time that the district should have suspected the child had a disability (*Lakin v. Birmingham*, 2003; Shaver, 2017; Tatgenhorst et al., 2014). This can become an especially difficult problem when school district personnel are aware of a student with an academic or behavioral problem but fail to refer the student for a special education evaluation (*E.S. v. Konocti Unified School District*, 2010).

According to the ruling in *Montgomery County Board of Education* (2008), school districts may attempt prereferral interventions before referring a child for an evaluation under the IDEA. However, if such interventions result in a delay in evaluating a child for special education, this may also be a violation of the IDEA (*El Paso Independent School District v. Richard R.*, 2008). Similarly, the federal district court in *El Paso Independent School District v. Richard R.* (2008) found that the El Paso School District had failed to meet its child find requirements under the IDEA when it did not identify or assess a student who had a disability. Additionally, the court found that when a parent requests an evaluation, this overrides a school district policy requiring school personnel to first consider general education interventions before conducting an evaluation. School officials must take care to ensure that prereferral intervention procedures do not violate the child find requirement of the IDEA (Walker & Daves, 2010). In an unusual case, *Compton Unified School District v. Addison* (2010), a school district argued that they did not violate child find when the district simply ignored a high school student's academic and emotional problems! According to the U.S. Court of Appeals for the Ninth Circuit, by ignoring the student's possible disability, the school district did indeed violate the child find obligations of the IDEA.

Monitoring student progress can play an important part in a school's child find system. For example, in *Daniel P. v. Downingtown Area School District* (2011), a school district was found not to have committed a child find violation because it closely monitored the progress of a student with disabilities in the district's RTI program. Similarly, in *Ridley School District v. M.R.* (2011), it was found that a school district did not violate child find when a student's progress was closely monitored and that school personnel had no reason to believe that the student might need specialized instruction.

Parental Consent

In a reasonable amount of time prior to conducting an evaluation, the school must notify the parents in writing of its intent to conduct an evaluation and obtain their consent to proceed. The notice must be understandable to the general public and must contain an explanation of the parents' due process rights as well as descriptions of what the school is proposing and the evaluation procedures to be used. If the parents refuse to consent to the evaluation or fail to respond to a request to evaluate a child, the school may use hearing procedures to get permission to conduct the evaluation. The school district, however, is not required to request a hearing (IDEA Regulations, 34 C.F.R. § 300.302[a][3][i-ii]). Similarly, if the school refuses a parental request to conduct an evaluation, the parents may also challenge the refusal through the IDEA's hearing procedures.

Following parental consent for preplacement evaluation, the IDEA does not require that consent be obtained for subsequent evaluations, even when the school uses additional assessment procedures following the initial evaluation (*Carroll v. Capalbo*, 1983; *Letter to Tinsley*, 1990). This is because parental consent is for the entire evaluation process, not for individual parts (*Letter to Graham*, 1989). The exception to this is when a school district is conducting a reevaluation of a student, school personnel are required to obtain parental consent (IDEA Regulations, 34 C.F.R. § 300.300[c][1][i]). According to the Office of Special Education Programs (OSEP) in the U.S. Department of Education, parental consent is not needed for assessments when those assessments are administered on a schoolwide or districtwide basis (*Letter to Christiansen*, 2007).

Prereferral Evaluation

Prereferral evaluations have become an important component in the referral process (Salvia, Ysseldyke, & Witmer, 2017). Prereferral interventions are conducted in the general education classroom to attempt to ameliorate or remediate the problem prior to referral to special education. These interventions are typically based on informal prereferral evaluations such as classroom tests, daily observations, and interviews. Because of the informal nature of prereferral assessments and interventions, they are not considered evaluation and are not subject to the strictures of the IDEA (IDEA Regulations, 34 C.F.R. § 300.302). Similarly, MTSS and RTI systems when used in schools with the entire student body do not require that schools obtain parental permission, even when students have disabilities and the purpose of the evaluation is to identify a student for purposes of providing a special education. It is only when individual students with disabilities are targeted for evaluation that parental permission for evaluation is required. Many school districts across the country have adopted or are developing MTSS and RTI systems. Such systems may in effect become a prereferral intervention; however, it is important that in such situations that the MTSS or RTI procedure does not result in a delay of referral of a potentially eligible student to special education (Bateman & Linden, 2012; U.S. Department of Education, 2011; Walker & Daves, 2010; Yell & Walker, 2010).

Preplacement Evaluation

The preplacement evaluation is the initial evaluation of a student for special education. A school's MDT determines the need for an evaluation based on referral or screening information that indicates that a student may have a disability. Following consideration of the referral or screening results, the MDT may choose to conduct an evaluation. If the MDT has reason to believe that a child may have a disability and need special education services, the team must proceed with an evaluation as soon as the MDT obtains parental permission. After a student is identified during the screening or referral process as possibly having a disability, the MDT must conduct the evaluation in a timely manner (*Kelly Inquiry*, 1981). IDEA 2004 established a timeframe of 60 days to complete an evaluation after receiving parental consent. This timeframe does not apply, however, if a parent fails to produce the child for the evaluation. Additionally, many states have chosen their own time limits for conducting an evaluation. Typically, such time limits will be between 30 and 45 days. Delays in preplacement evaluations may result in due process hearings, court actions, and the possible imposition of remedies such as tuition reimbursement, attorney's fees, or compensatory education (*Bartow {GA} County School District*, 1995; *Chicago Board of Education*, 1984; *Foster v. District of Columbia Board of Education*, 1982; *Letter to Williams*, 1993).

The MDT may choose not to conduct an evaluation if there is no reasonable basis to suspect that a disability exists (*Letter to Williams*, 1993; Tatgenhorst et al., 2014). The IDEA does not require an evaluation of every child for whom an evaluation is requested (Lake, 2014). If a school declines a parental request to evaluate a student, the district must notify the parents in writing of the refusal. The notification must include the reasons for the refusal and inform the parents of their due process options (*OSEP Policy Letter*, 1994). Although refusing a parental request to evaluate is an option, a school district invites court action and possible remedies for violation of the IDEA if it is later determined that a student did have a disability requiring services under either law. Parents may use the dispute resolution procedures of the IDEA if the school district refuses to conduct an evaluation. On the other hand, if a parent refuses the school district's request to evaluate the child, the district may pursue a due process hearing to obtain permission to conduct an evaluation. School districts, however, are not required to pursue a due process hearing (Lake, 2014).

Comprehensiveness of the Evaluation

The IDEA requires that prior to the initiation of special education placement or services, a full, comprehensive, and individualized evaluation of the child's educational needs must be conducted. Thus, the evaluation is the first step in providing special education and related services to a student with disabilities. The purpose of the evaluation is twofold: (1) to determine whether a child has a disability covered under the IDEA and if he or she needs special education, and (2) to determine the content of the child's special education program.

The evaluation must include all suspected areas of need, including, when appropriate, health, vision, hearing, social and emotional status, general intelligence, academic performance, communicative status, and motor abilities (IDEA Regulations 34 C.F.R. § 300.532[f]). The evaluator should also collect (a) relevant functional and developmental information, (b) information from a student's parents, (c) information relating to allowing a student to access and progress in general education, and (d) classroom-based assessments and observations from teachers and related service providers (IDEA Regulations, 34 C.F.R. § 300.305). Additionally, school district personnel must conduct an assistive technology evaluation if needed (*Letter to Fisher*, 1995).

Qualifications of Evaluators

The evaluation is conducted by members of the MDT, which must include at least one teacher or specialist in the area of the child's suspected disability. When a learning disability is suspected, the team must also include the student's general education teacher or a person qualified to teach students with learning disabilities, as well as a person qualified to conduct an individual diagnostic examination of the student, such as a school psychologist. The team's evaluators must be qualified in assessing and evaluating children with disabilities. Additionally, the OSEP has stated that evaluators must meet the qualification criteria established by the producer of the evaluation instrument (*OSEP Policy Letter*, 1995a). Interestingly, the U.S. Court of Appeals for the Ninth Circuit found in *Seattle School District v. B.S.* (1996) that a school district had failed to properly consider an independent evaluation obtained by a student's parents because the school team did not have a member with knowledge in the student's suspected disability.

Parental participation in the evaluation process is allowed, although it is not required (*OSEP Policy Letter*, 1993a). Parents may inquire about the qualifications of the examiner; therefore, the OSEP has recommended that school districts have written criteria for evaluators (*OSEP Policy Letter*, 1995a).

Evaluation Materials and Procedures

The IDEA details the specific requirements of the evaluation procedures and materials in a legally correct preplacement evaluation (IDEA Regulations, 34 C.F.R. § 300.532). An important decision that the MDT must make is which tests and instruments will be used to assess students. A variety of assessment tools and procedures must be used to gather relevant functional, developmental, behavioral, and academic information about the child being evaluated. Moreover, the instruments used must be technically sound. Figure 9.1 lists the requirements of the IDEA regarding the selection of evaluation materials and procedures to follow in conducting the evaluation.

The evaluation materials must be provided and administered in the child's native language or other mode of communication unless it is not feasible to do so. This requirement is especially important when evaluating a student with limited English proficiency. According to the IDEA, a student's native language is the language normally used by the student's parents (IDEA Regulations 34 C.F.R. § 300.12). The reasoning behind this regulation is that the tests used must reflect a student's actual ability rather than his or her fluency in English. If a student is bilingual and shows age-appropriate English proficiency, however, the school district may test the student in English even though English may not be the student's native language. English may also be used in testing even when it is not the language used by the student's parents (*Greenfield Public School,* 1994; IDEA Regulations, 34 C.F.R. § 300.12, Note [1]).

FIGURE 9.1 ■ IDEA Evaluation Material and Procedures Requirements

1. Test and other evaluation materials must be
   - provided and administered in the student's native language or mode of communication unless not feasible to do so.
   - validated for the specific purpose for which they are used.
   - administered by trained personnel in conformity with instructions.
2. The evaluation must be tailored to assess specific areas of educational need.
3. The evaluation must be designed to reflect the student's aptitude or achievement level rather than reflecting the student's disabilities, unless intended to do so.
4. No single procedure is used as the sole criterion to determine FAPE.
5. Decisions are made by a multidisciplinary team, including one person knowledgeable in the area of suspected disability.
6. The student is assessed in all areas of suspected disability.

The term *mode of communication* refers to the means of communication normally used by individuals who are deaf, blind, or have no written language, and may include Braille, sign language, oral communication, or technologically enhanced communication (IDEA Regulations, 34 C.F.R. § 300.12, Note [2]).

Tests used for preplacement evaluation must be validated for the specific purpose for which they are being used. A valid test is one that measures what it purports to measure (Salvia, Ysseldyke, & Witmer, 2017). The IDEA, however, does not set forth rules or regulations regarding the determination of test validity. Presumably, tests validated by their publishers will fulfill this criterion.

Additionally, the evaluation must be designed to assess specific areas of educational need rather than merely providing a single intelligence score. Assessment instruments must be selected and administered to ensure that they accurately reflect the student's aptitude or achievement levels, rather than the student's impaired skills (unless they purport to measure the impaired skills). Finally, no single procedure can be used as the sole criterion for placement or determining the appropriate program. The selection of the evaluation materials is left to the school district or state as long as the aforementioned criteria are met. The evaluation must include all existing evaluation data, classroom observations, and information provided by the child's parents. Figure 9.2 lists the IDEA's requirement for the written report.

Special Rules for Eligibility Determination

When making the eligibility decision, the IDEA does not allow a student to be determined to have a disability if the determining factor is lack of appropriate instruction in reading, including instruction in the essential components of reading instruction: phonemic

FIGURE 9.2 ■ Written Report for Specific Learning Disability

1. The MDT shall prepare a written report of the evaluation results consisting of
   - whether the student has a specific learning disability
   - what the basis for making the determination is
   - what relevant behavior was noted during the observation
   - whether educationally relevant medical findings apply
   - whether there is a severe discrepancy between achievement and ability that is not correctable without special education
   - whether environmental, cultural, or economic disadvantage affects the child's ability to learn
2. Team members shall certify in writing whether the report reflects their conclusions. If it does not, the dissenting member must submit a separate statement

awareness, phonics, vocabulary, fluency, and reading comprehension. Neither can the determining factor be lack of instruction in math or limited English proficiency.

The IDEA prohibits states from requiring that local school districts take into consideration a severe discrepancy between achievement and ability when determining eligibility. Furthermore, states must permit school districts to use "a process that determines if the child responds to scientific, research-based interventions" (IDEA Regulations, 34 C.F.R. § 300.307{a}{2}). In the literature, this has been referred to as a *response-to-intervention* model. School districts may choose to continue to use a severe discrepancy model, a response-to-intervention model, or other research-based procedures for identifying students with learning disabilities. To view a brief report by OSEP on identifying students with learning disabilities go to http://idea.ed.gov/explore/view/p/%2Croot%2Cdynamic%2CTopicalBrief%2C23%2C. In a case out of the U.S. Courts of Appeal for the Ninth Circuit, *Michael P. v. Department of Education, State of Hawaii* (2011), the court held that the Hawaii Department of Education violated the IDEA by having a policy that did not permit school districts to use RTI. (For elaborations on response to intervention, see Chapter 14.) The criteria for identifying a learning disability also require an observation of a student in the general education classroom, and the preparation of a written report of the evaluation results is required (IDEA Regulations, 34 C.F.R. § 300.311).

Nondiscriminatory Evaluation

The IDEA requires schools to select and administer tests that are not racially or culturally discriminatory. This requirement, however, is not specific and does not provide guidance to a school district in determining if an assessment measure is discriminatory or whether local norming to adjust for economic deprivation or discrimination is required (*OSEP Policy Letter*, 1992).

An area of particular concern in special education is the overrepresentation of minority students. Much of this concern has focused on the selection of discriminatory evaluation materials and procedures, especially the use of tests that result in a global score indicating an intelligence quotient (IQ). The primary concern has been that IQ tests, when used for making placement decisions, may result in the overreferral of minority students or students from economically disadvantaged backgrounds.

Larry P. v. Riles, 1979   In *Larry P. v. Riles* (1979; hereafter *Larry P.*), a federal district court in California banned the use of standardized IQ instruments to evaluate African American students for placement in classes for students with educable mental retardation (EMR). The court ruled that such tests contained racial and cultural bias and discriminated against students from racial minorities. The decision was affirmed by the U.S. Court of Appeals for the Ninth Circuit. In 1986, the *Larry P.* ban was expanded to include IQ testing of African American students for all special education placements.

Parents in Action on Special Education (PASE) v. Hannon, 1980   Shortly after the first *Larry P.* decision, a federal district court, in *Parents in Action on Special Education v. Hannon* (1980), arrived at a different conclusion regarding standardized IQ tests. According to the court, the Wechsler Intelligence Scale for Children (WISC), the WISC-R, and the Stanford-Binet IQ tests were not racially or culturally discriminatory. The court further held that they could be used in the special education placements of African American children. The court also found that the school district had not used the IQ tests as the sole basis for special education placement, thereby complying with the IDEA.

Crawford v. Honig, 1994   The *Larry P.* ban on IQ testing for purposes of placing African American students in special education classes was vacated in 1994 by the U.S. Court of Appeals for the Ninth Circuit in *Crawford v. Honig*. The action was brought by African American students who sought to have standardized IQ tests administered in special education evaluations so that they could qualify for special education for students with learning disabilities. A federal district court consolidated the case with *Larry P.* and vacated the 1986 modification, which had prohibited IQ tests in all special education placements. The court, however, left the original ban against using IQ tests to place African American students in EMR classes in effect. The *Larry P.* plaintiffs, the superintendent of public instruction, and the California State Board of Education appealed the decision to vacate the modification to the Ninth Circuit court. The appellate court affirmed the lower court's ruling, stating that the 1986 modification inappropriately expanded the scope of the original injunction because the modification was not supported by factual findings. The appellate court decision did not address the underlying facts of *Larry P.*, only the propriety of extending the original ban on IQ tests. In fact, the court indicated that the discriminatory nature of IQ tests was a disputed issue of fact to be addressed in future *Larry P.* proceedings.

Nevertheless, the decision of the appellate court seemed to indicate that the IDEA does not prohibit the use of IQ tests per se in special education evaluations. This holding affirmed a position taken by the Office of Special Education and Rehabilitative Services (OSERS) a year earlier, that the appropriate use of IQ tests is not prohibited (*Letter to Warrington*, 1993). According to Gorn (1996), IQ tests can be a valuable part of the evaluation process as long as they are valid, are not racially or culturally discriminatory, and are not used as the sole criterion for placement.

INTERPRETING EVALUATION DATA

When the evaluation is completed, the MDT must draw on the results of all the instruments used, as well as other information provided in the decision-making process. The law requires that professional judgment be relied on; sole reliance on formulas or quantitative guidelines is not permitted (Bateman & Linden, 2012).

Drawing on the information gathered during the evaluation process, the MDT first determines a student's eligibility—that is, whether a student has a disability covered under the IDEA. Second, the MDT determines whether, because of the disability, a student requires special education and related services. Regulatory guidelines for interpreting evaluation data are reported in Figure 9.3.

School districts have been cited for determining students were not eligible for services under IDEA but then failing to assess them for eligibility under Section 504. This problem has occurred frequently with students having attention deficit disorder (ADD) or attention deficit hyperactivity disorder (ADHD) who were ineligible for services under the IDEA (*Anaheim School District*, 1993; *Calcasieu Parish {LA} Public School District*, 1992; *LaHonda-Pescadero {CA} Unified School District*, 1993; *Petaluma City {CA} Elementary School District*, 1995).

The MDT's decision must be documented in written form. The IDEA further requires that team members certify that the final team decision reflects their conclusions. If team members disagree with the team decision, they may attach a separate report detailing their

FIGURE 9.3 ■
Interpreting Evaluation Data

When interpreting evaluation data, the MDT must

- draw on information from a variety of sources, including aptitude and achievement tests, teacher recommendations, physical condition, social or cultural background, and adaptive behavior.
- ensure that information is documented and carefully considered.
- ensure that decisions are made by a team, including a person knowledgeable about the student, the meaning of the evaluation data, and the placement options.
- ensure that the placement decision is made in accordance with least restrictive environment requirements.

views. Finally, the IDEA does not address whether the decision must be by majority vote, although it does not have to be unanimous. In a policy letter, the OSEP stated that the school district was required to comply with the decision made by the MDT as a whole (*Letter to Greer,* 1992). The OSEP did not further elaborate on what "as a whole" meant, nor has it defined how many people, at a minimum, are required on the MDT.

Medical Diagnosis and Eligibility Determination

Multidisciplinary teams may use a medical diagnosis as part of the eligibility determination, when appropriate. It is clear, however, that a medical diagnosis cannot be used as the sole basis for eligibility determination (Joint Policy Memorandum, 1991). Furthermore, a medical diagnosis may not be required as part of an evaluation, although if an MDT believes a medical diagnosis is necessary, it must be provided at public expense (*Letter to Parker,* 1992; *Response to Veir,* 1993). Although schools do not have to consult a physician when determining eligibility and services for a student with ADD or ADHD, the MDT must have someone on the committee with specific knowledge of how to identify and treat these disorders (*Letter to Shrag,* 1992) when a student has a medical diagnosis of disability that is not synonymous with an IDEA determination of a disability (Tatgenhorst et al., 2014). A medical diagnosis of disability, therefore, is not enough to determine the existence of a disability (see *Marshall Joint School District No. 2 v. C.D.,* 2010). The MDT establishes whether or not a student has a disability and needs special education, although they certainly may consider the results of an examination by a medical professional.

REEVALUATION

The educational needs of students with disabilities change over time. The IDEA therefore requires that students in special education be reevaluated every three years, unless the parent and school district personnel agree that a reevaluation is not needed. Parents, however, may request a reevaluation at any time. A reevaluation is a comprehensive evaluation conducted on a student already in special education. The reevaluation is usually similar to the original preplacement evaluation, and it must meet the same procedural requirements under the IDEA as did the original evaluation (e.g., the school district must obtain parental consent). The reevaluation, however, does not have to be identical to the preplacement evaluation; it can consist of different assessment procedures so long as they address the student's current educational needs (*Letter to Shaver,* 1990). In the reevaluation, the school district examines the student to determine whether he or she continues to have a disability and the educational needs of the student.

Regulatory language is unclear with respect to when it may be necessary to reevaluate more frequently than every three years. A ruling in *Corona-Norco Unified School District* (1995) found that more frequent evaluations may be warranted when there is a substantial change in the student's academic performance or disability. Reevaluations must also be conducted prior to any significant change in placement under Section 504, although the IDEA does not have a similar requirement. A federal district court has used the Section 504 regulation (Section 504 Regulations, 34 C.F.R. § 104.35[a]) as authority for requiring a reevaluation under the IDEA when a school district made a significant change in placement (*Brimmer v. Traverse City Area Public Schools,* 1994). A reevaluation is also required when a school is contemplating the long-term suspension or expulsion of a student with disabilities. (For elaborations on suspension and expulsion, see Chapter 13.)

If a full and complete reevaluation is not needed to collect additional information, the reevaluation should focus on collecting information about how to teach the student in the most appropriate manner. If an IEP team determines that additional data are not needed, the team must notify the student's parents of the determination, the reasons for it, and the parents' right to request a full evaluation.

Informed parental consent is required for a school to conduct a reevaluation. Until the IDEA Amendments of 1997, parental consent for a reevaluation was not required. This requirement does not apply, however, if the school district can demonstrate that reasonable steps were taken to obtain consent but the parents failed to respond. When a parent requests a reevaluation, the student must be reevaluated unless the district challenges the parents' request in a due process hearing.

The IDEA does not require a complete reevaluation when a student graduates from a regular high school or ages out of IDEA eligibility. Instead, the student's IEP team must provide a student with a written summary of his or her academic achievement and functional performance, which should include recommendations on how to assist the student to meet his or her academic and functional goals.

INDEPENDENT EDUCATIONAL EVALUATIONS

If a student's parents disagree with a school district's evaluation, the parents have the right to request that the school district pay for an independent educational evaluation (IEE), An IEE is an evaluation conducted by a qualified examiner who is not employed by the school district responsible for the education of the student in question (IDEA Regulations, 34 C.F.R. § 300.502[a][3]). A student's parents have the right to request one IEE at any time the school district conducts an evaluation if the parents disagree with the results of the school district's evaluation. Following such a request a school district must (a) file a due process complaint to request a hearing to show that its evaluation is appropriate, or (b) ensure that an IEE is provided at public expense (IDEA Regulations, 34 C.F.R.§ 300.502[b][2]). School districts have to choose one of these options without unnecessary delay. In *Regional School Unit #61* (2011) and *Baldwin County Board of Education* (1994), SEAs in Maine and Alabama cannot simply ignore a parent's request for an IEE. Of course, parents can always obtain an IEE at their own expense (*Phillip v. Jefferson Board of Education*, 2013).

When a student's parents' request an IEE, the school district must provide information about where the IEE may be obtained. When a parent requests an IEE, school district officials must either (a) provide the IEE at public expense or (b) file a due process complaint to request a hearing in which they attempt to prove that their evaluation was appropriate. Moreover, these actions must be taken without unnecessary delay; that is, school district personnel must comply with the parent's request or initiate a due process hearing as soon as possible after receiving the request for an IEE. The federal district court in *Pajaro Valley Unified School District* (2007) found that a school district had violated the IEE requirement of the IDEA when officials took almost 3 months before acting on the parents' IEE request.

If district officials go to a hearing and their evaluation is found to be appropriate, the parents still have a right to obtain an IEE, but not at public expense. If, however, the parents deny a school district an opportunity to conduct an evaluation of their child, they may forfeit their right to obtain an IEE at public expense (*Muscogee County Board of Education*, 2008). Parents may also request an IEE if a school does not evaluate for assistive technology devices or services (*Letter to Fisher*, 1995). According to the U.S. Court of Appeal for the Third Circuit in *M.Z. v. Bethlehem Area School District* (2013) when a hearing officer determines that a school district failed to conduct an appropriate reevaluation there is only one remedy open to the hearing officer: to order an IEE at school district expense.

Although the school district is under no obligation to accept the results of the IEE, it must consider the IEE as part of its decision-making process. Results of an IEE may also be presented as evidence at a hearing. School district responsibilities regarding the IEE are listed in Figure 9.4. Tatgenhorst and his colleagues (2014) suggested that school district personnel should document their consideration of a parent's IEE. They further suggested that the districts should document (a) the manner in which the IEE was made available to an IEP team,

FIGURE 9.4 ■
**Independent
Educational Evaluation
Requirements**

1. Schools must, on request, provide parents information on where to obtain an IEE.
2. If parents disagree with the school's evaluation, they have the right to an IEE at public expense.
3. If school personnel believe their evaluation is appropriate, they may initiate a hearing. If a hearing officer finds the evaluation appropriate, parents are still entitled to an IEE, but not at public expense.
4. The results of the IEE, even if paid for by the parents, must be considered in the special education decision-making process.
5. The results of the IEE, even if paid for by the parents, may be presented as evidence at a hearing.
6. A hearing officer may request an IEE as part of a due process hearing. This IEE must be performed at public expense.

(b) the meeting at which the IEE was discussed, and (c) if the district personnel disagree with the findings and recommendations of the IEE, the reasons for the disagreement.

Apparently, the school district may choose whether it will fund the IEE in advance, pay the examiner directly, or reimburse the parent (Tatgenhorst et al., 2014). This issue is not addressed in the IDEA, however, if the refusal to fund the IEE in advance denies the parent the right to seek an IEE, the parent may seek relief (*Edna Independent School District,* 1994). In situations where the school district refuses to fund the IEE, the parent must prevail at a due process hearing to secure the public funding.

Parents should notify the school district when they disagree with the school's evaluation and plan to request an IEE at public expense. The school district must respond within a reasonable amount of time and either agree to fund the IEE or request a hearing to show that its evaluation was appropriate. Often school districts will challenge an IEE when they believe their evaluation was appropriate or when the IEE obtained by parents did not dispute the district's evaluation (Freedman, 1996 (Yell, et al., 2017). If parents have obtained the IEE to provide additional information or more meaningful information, they will not have a claim for public funding (*Millcreek Township School District,* 1995), nor will public funding be ordered if the findings of the independent evaluator are consistent with the district's findings (*Brandywine School District,* 1995). The criterion for public funding, therefore, involves the appropriateness of the district's evaluation. IEEs are typically funded when the district has been negligent in conducting the evaluation, when the evaluation was inadequate, when all sources of information were not considered, or when major procedural safeguards were not followed (*Carbondale Elementary School District 95,* 1996; *Douglas School District,* 1993; *Livingston Parish {LA} School Board,* 1993).

If the parents already have secured an IEE and requested payment, the district might contend in a hearing that the IEE was inappropriate, deficient, or conducted by an unqualified examiner. In a policy letter, the OSEP stated that a district may disqualify an independent evaluator chosen by a parent and may refuse to pay if the evaluator does not meet the district's criteria (*OSEP Policy Letter,* 1995b).

A school district may establish a fee structure for the IEE that the parents cannot exceed (*OSEP Policy Letter,* 1995b). The purpose of the maximum fee set by the school district is to eliminate unreasonable and excessive fees. School district limitations on the parents' choice of an independent examiner, the location of the IEE, and the fees for the evaluation will be upheld as long as they are reasonable (Tatgenhorst, et al., 2014). The school district, however, must allow the parents the opportunity to demonstrate that unique circumstances justify an IEE that does not fall within the district's fee structure (*OSEP Policy Letter,* 1993b).

When parents initiate an IEE, the results of the evaluation must be considered by the school district in decisions regarding the education of the evaluated student. The district is not, however, obligated to accept or act on the recommendations made in the IEE. Although the IDEA does not detail what *consider* means in this context, the U.S. Court of Appeals for the Second Circuit, in *T. S. v. Board of Education of the Town of Ridgefield and State of Connecticut*

FIGURE 9.5 ▦ Advice Regarding IEEs

- School district officials must inform parents of their right to receive an IEE, where they may obtain an IEE, and the conditions for obtaining the IEE at public expense.
- If parents disagree with the school district's evaluation and request an IEE, the school district must either:
  a) Request a due process hearing to show its evaluation was appropriate
  b) Ensure that an IEE is provided at public expense
- School district officials should establish the allowable IEE costs at prevailing community rates and communicate this to parents and inform parents that if they believe a more expensive IEE is warranted, they must inform the school district.
- School district officials must inform parents that they may choose their own private evaluator, but that the school district rates still apply.
- When the results of an IEE are presented at an IEP meeting, all team members must discuss and seriously consider these results.
- If the IEE team believes the recommendations in the IEE are incorrect, they must discuss these concerns at the meeting.
- The IEP team must consider all information sources and attempt to incorporate the recommendations from the IEE as appropriate.

Department of Education (1993), used the definition "to reflect on or think about with some degree of caution" (p. 89). The parents in this case argued that the school's MDT had not considered the IEE when only two members of the team had read the IEE prior to the meeting. The court rejected the argument, finding that nothing in the IDEA suggested that all team members had to read the IEE to consider it. The circuit court's decision indicated that it is important that a school district document consideration of the IEE. According to Tatgenhorst et al., (2014), school districts should (a) document how the IEE was made available to the MDT or IEP team; (b) record the findings of the IEE and the team's review and discussion of the report; and (c) put any reasons for disagreement with the IEE in writing. The OSEP has held that a school does not need to document the results of the rejected IEE in the IEP (*OSEP Policy Letter*, 1993c), but that the school should review the IEE and discuss its results in all programming and placement decisions (*OSEP Policy Letter*, 1995b).

Freedman (1996) stressed the importance of actively listening to and addressing parents' concerns when confronting parental requests for an IEE. Preventive actions and cooperative participation on the part of school district personnel are crucial. Figure 9.5 contains advice to school district officials regarding IEEs.

ACCOUNTABILITY EFFORTS AND STUDENTS WITH DISABILITIES

The early 1980s witnessed a series of reports that alerted the public to a crisis in American education and led to calls for improving the educational system. The publication of *A Nation at Risk* (National Commission on Excellence in Education, 1983) was especially influential in leading to calls for educational reform. The widespread criticism of the public school system and the perceived need to reform education led to efforts to increase accountability in our educational system. One result of this movement was the No Child Left Behind Act (NCLB) of 2001 (a reauthorization of the Elementary and Secondary Education Act). Three tools adopted to increase accountability in education were (a) development of standards and outcomes for U.S. students, (b) the use of student assessments through the adoption of statewide testing, and (c) the use of minimum competency tests. Although many of the requirements of NCLB were eliminated with the passage of the Every Student Succeeds Act (ESSA) of 2015, the tools retained much of their importance.

Including Students with Disabilities in Accountability Efforts

No Child Left Behind led to a burst of activity in the area of developing standards and assessments for students and this activity has continued with the passage of Every Student Succeeds Act. Standards are statements of criteria against which comparisons can be made. The purpose of educational standards is to guide instruction regarding what students should know and be able to do. In addition to developing standards and assessments in reading and mathematics, many states developed standards and outcomes in other academic content areas, as well as in health and physical education, the arts, and vocational education (Shriner, Ysseldyke, & Thurlow, 1994). An area of concern in the development of standards is how to include and address the needs of students with disabilities. Various options for including students with disabilities include setting separate standards, maintaining a single set of standards but allowing a range of performance relative to them, allowing standards to be demonstrated using alternative measures (e.g., portfolios), excluding students with disabilities from assessment, and using the IEP as a document and process in linking the student's program to the local, state, or national standards (Shriner et al., 1994). If the last option is used, the IEP team will be charged with preparing IEPs that are aligned to these standards.

The IDEA Amendments of 1997 required that students with disabilities participate in state- and district-wide assessments of student progress, with or without accommodations, whichever is appropriate for individual students. Furthermore, NCLB and ESSA required that school districts disaggregate assessment data by subgroups, including students with disabilities. States had to report to the public on the assessment of students with disabilities with the same frequency and detail as they report on the assessment of students without disabilities. States also had to report the number of students with disabilities participating in statewide regular assessments and, eventually, the numbers participating in alternative assessments. The data on the performance of students with disabilities had to be disaggregated when the report was filed to the federal government.

The IEP meeting is the proper forum for considering whether students with disabilities can appropriately participate in regular assessments or whether they need modifications in the administration of the state tests. According to Ysseldyke, Thurlow, McGrew, and Vanderwood (1994), the IEP should list any accommodations of the test or testing situation. Possible testing accommodations include altering the manner in which the assessment is presented (e.g., use of magnifying equipment, signing of directions), the manner of student response (e.g., using a computer for responding, giving responses orally), accommodations in setting (e.g., testing alone in a study carrel, testing with a small group), and time (e.g., more frequent breaks during testing, extending the testing session over several days). If an IEP team decides that a student will not participate in a particular state- or district-wide assessment of achievement, the IEP must include a statement of why the assessment is not appropriate and how the student will be assessed.

LESSONS FROM LITIGATION AND LEGISLATION

The assessment/evaluation of a student is extremely important in the special education process. It is the means by which students are identified for special education services and it becomes the foundation of a student's IEP. In the following section I extrapolate principles from the litigation and legislation for conducting educationally appropriate and legally sound initial special education assessments.

Principle 1: Ensure that administrators, special education teachers, general education teachers, and evaluation personnel understand the importance of the identification/assessment/evaluation process. The importance of the assessment process cannot be overemphasized because it forms the basis of a student's FAPE. Educators should know and understand both federal and state requirements regarding the identification/assessment/evaluation process. From the initial identification in the child find process, to referral, assessment, IEP development, and progress monitoring, the assessment is critical in the special education programming for students. Thus, it is crucial that all involved personnel understand their responsibilities under the law and carry them out in an appropriate manner. When the identification/assessment/evaluation process is not done properly, the likely result is that a student will not receive a FAPE.

Principle 2: Don't use a schoolwide MTSS or RTI program or prereferral interventions to delay or deny special education evaluation. Response to intervention systems are widely used in America's public schools. However, school officials must be careful that such systems are used to delay or deny possible special education evaluation. This is especially important when parents refer their child for evaluation. If school personnel agree that the student may have a disability, they must conduct an evaluation. It is also important that when students do not succeed in the first tier of a schoolwide RTI system that their progress be closely monitored.

Principle 3: Involve a student's parents in the assessment process. When a student has been identified as possibly having a disability and may be eligible for special education services, his or her parents should be notified and informed about the proposed evaluation. The school district must obtain the parents' written consent before conducting the proposed initial evaluation. Additionally, a student's parents should be invited to participate in the identification, assessment, and evaluation process. Parents can provide valuable input into the assessment process. The parents should also be notified of their right to obtain an IEE at public expense if they disagree with the school district's evaluation.

Principle 4: Use a variety of assessment instruments to allow the team to determine eligibility. To determine eligibility all assessment instruments must be reliable and valid and must provide information about all of a student's unique educational and behavioral needs. Moreover, instruments should be chosen to ensure a full and individualized evaluation of all of a student's academic and behavioral needs related to his or her suspected disability. Do not use assessment instruments that discriminate on the basis of race, ethnicity, or native language. To determine eligibility students must (a) have an IDEA-related disability and (b) require special education and related services because of their disability. Moreover, a person or persons with special expertise in the student's suspected disability should be included on the MDT and IEP teams (e.g., if a student exhibits problem behavior, a person with expertise in behavioral issues should be on the team).

Principle 5: Conduct relevant and meaningful assessments that will help the IEP team plan students' special education programs. As Bateman (2017) aptly wrote, "the IEP must stand solidly and squarely on a foundation of current, accurate evaluations of the student's level of performance in academic and functional areas" (p. 93). Because the assessment is the basis of a student's special education program, including annual goals and special education services, as well as the basis for monitoring a student's progress in his or her program, it is the foundation of a student's FAPE. A relevant and meaningful assessment is the path to meaningful special education programming. Do not use only formal and standardized tests as a means of determining a student's unique needs upon which to develop a student's IEP. Assessment procedures and strategies such as curriculum-based measurement, curriculum-based assessment, direct observations, interviews, work samples, functional behavioral assessments, and criterion-referenced tests will provide valuable information for instructional and behavioral planning and programming.

SUMMARY

Before a student can be placed in special education or related services, the student must be identified as having a disability and needing special education services to meet his or her individual needs. The evaluation is important in identifying a student as eligible for special education and crucial in the development of the student's FAPE.

Parents' written consent is required prior to conducting an initial evaluation. After permission is received, the evaluation must be conducted in a timely manner. The MDT must then make eligibility decisions based upon the evaluation data. If the parents refuse consent and the MDT believes the child needs special educational services, the school district may pursue a due process hearing to obtain permission to conduct the evaluation.

The evaluation must be individualized and conducted in all areas related to the suspected disability. The MDT's charge is to use the results of the evaluation to determine if the student is eligible for services under the IDEA or Section 504 and to further determine if, because of the disability, the student needs special education and related services to meet his or her needs.

The IDEA Amendments of 1997 required that students with disabilities participate in state- and district-wide assessments. Furthermore, states are required to report on the assessments of students with disabilities under NCLB. IEP teams must determine if students in special education can participate in such assessments or if they require modifications in administration of these assessments. The IEP must also list any testing modifications needed. If the team determines that a student cannot participate in regular assessments, the IEP must include a statement of why the student cannot participate and how the student will be assessed.

Enhanced eText **Application Exercise 9.1.** *Kirby v. Cabell County Board of Education* (2006).

FOR FURTHER INFORMATION

Bateman, B. D., & Linden, M. A. (2012). *Better IEPs: How to develop legally correct and educationally useful programs* (5th ed.). Verona, WI: Attainment.

Shriner, J. G., Ysseldyke, J. E., & Thurlow, M. L. (1994). Standards for all American students. *Focus on Exceptional Children, 26*(5), 1–19.

REFERENCES

Anaheim School District, 20 IDELR 185 (OCR 1993).

Baldwin County Board of Education, 21 IDELR 311 (SEA Ala. 1994).

Bartlett, L. D., Weisenstein, G. R., & Etscheidt, S. (2002). *Successful inclusion for educational leaders.* Upper Saddle River, NJ: Merrill/Pearson.

Bartow (GA) County School District, 22 IDELR 508 (OCR 1995).

Bateman, B. D. (2017). *Individual education programs for children with disabilities.* In J. M. Kauffman & D. P. Hallahan (Eds.), *The handbook of special education* (2nd ed., pp. 91–112). New York: Routledge.

Bateman, B. D., & Linden, M. A. (2012). *Better IEPs: How to develop legally correct and educationally useful programs* (5th ed). Verona, WI: Attainment.

Brandywine School District, 22 IDELR 517 (SEA Del. 1995).

Brimmer v. Traverse City Area Public Schools, 22 IDELR 5 (W.D. Mich. 1994).

Calcasieu Parish (LA) Public School District, 20 IDELR 762 (OCR 1992).

Carbondale Elementary School District 95, 23 IDELR 766 (SEA Ill. 1996).

Carroll v. Capalbo, 563 F. Supp. 1053 (D.R.I. 1983).

Chicago Board of Education, EHLR 257:568 (OCR 1984).

Compton Unified School District v. Addison, 54 IDELR 71 (9th Cir. 2010).

Corona-Norco Unified School District, 22 IDELR 469 (Cal. 1995).

Council Rock School District v. M.W. 112 LRP 38641 (M.D. Pa. 2012).

Crawford v. Honig, 37 F.3d 485 (9th Cir. 1994).

Daniel P. v. Downingtown Area School District, 57 IDELR 224 (E.D. Pa. 2011).

Douglas School District, 20 IDELR 458 (SEA S.D. 1993).

E.S. v. Konocti Unified School District, 55 IDELR 226 (N.D. Cal. 2010).

Edna Independent School District, 21 IDELR 419 (SEA Tex. 1994).

El Paso Independent School District v. Richard R., 50 IDELR 256 (W.D. Tex. 2008).

Eyer, T. (1998). Greater expectations: How the 1997 IDEA Amendments raise the basic floor of opportunity for children with disabilities. *Education Law Reporter, 126*, 1–19.

Foster v. District of Columbia Board of Education, EHLR 553:520 (D.D.C. 1982).

Freedman, M. K. (1996). Independent educational evaluations: Love 'em or hate 'em, but do 'em right. In *Proceedings of the 16th Annual Conference on Special Education Law.* Horsham, PA: LRP Publications.

Gorn, S. (1996). *What do I do when . . . The answer book on special education law.* Horsham, PA: LRP Publications.

Greenfield Public School, 21 IDELR 345 (SEA Mass. 1994).

Huefner, D. S. (2000). *Getting comfortable with special education law: A framework for working with children with disabilities*. Norwood, MA: Christopher-Gordon Publications.

Individuals with Disabilities Education Act (IDEA), 20 U.S.C. § 1400 *et seq.*

Individuals with Disabilities Education Act Regulations, 34 C.F.R. § 300.1 *et seq.*

Joint Policy Memorandum, 18 IDELR 116 (OSERS 1991).

Kauffman, J. M. (2001). *Characteristics of emotional and behavioral disorders of children and youth* (7th ed.). Upper Saddle River, NJ: Merrill/Pearson.

Kelly Inquiry, 211 EHLR (EHA 1981).

Kirby v. Cabell County Board of Education, 46 IDELR 156 (S.D. W. Va. 2006).

LaHonda-Pescadero (CA) Unified School District, 20 IDELR 833 (OCR 1993).

Lake, S. E. (2014). *What do I do when . . . The answer book on special education practice and procedure* (2nd ed.). Horsham, PA: LRP Publications.

Lakin v. Birmingham, 39 IDELD 152 (6th Cir. 2003).

Larry P. v. Riles, 495 F. Supp. 926 (N.D. Cal. 1979), *aff'd in part, rev'd in part*, 793 F.2d 969 (9th Cir. 1986).

Letter to Ackenhalt, 22 IDELR 252 (OCR 1994).

Letter of Christianson, 48 IDELR 161 (OSEP 2007).

Letter to Ferrera, 60 IDELR 46 (OSEP 2012).

Letter to Gallo, 61 IDELR 173 (OSEP 2013).

Letter to Fisher, 23 IDELR 565 (OSEP 1995).

Letter to Graham, 213 EHLR 212 (EHA 1989).

Letter to Greer, 19 IDELR 348 (OSEP 1992).

Letter to Holmes, 19 IDELR 350 (OSEP 1992).

Letter to Parker, 19 IDELR 963 (OSEP 1992).

Letter to Shaver, 17 EHLR 356 (OSERS 1990).

Letter to Shrag, 18 IDELR 1303 (OSEP 1992).

Letter to Tinsley, 16 EHLR (OSEP 1990).

Letter to Warrington, 20 IDELR 593 (OSERS 1993).

Letter to Williams, 20 IDELR 1210 (OSEP 1993).

Livingston Parish (LA) School Board, 20 IDELR 1470 (OCR 1993).

M.J.C. v. Special School District No. I, 58 IDELR 288 (D. Minn. 2012).

M.Z. v. Bethlehem Area School District, 60 IDELR 273 (3d Cir. 2013).

Marshall Joint School District No. 2 v. C.D., 54 IDELR 307 (5th Cir. 2010).

Michael P. v. Department of Education, State of Hawaii, 57 IDELR 123 (9th Cir. 2011).

Millcreek Township School District, 22 IDELR 1011 (SEA Pa. 1995).

Montgomery County Board of Education, 51 IDELR 259 (SEA Ala. 2008).

Muscogee County Board of Education, 6 ECLPR 55 (SEA Ga. 2008).

National Commission on Excellence in Education. (1983). *A nation at risk: The imperative for educational reform*. Washington, DC: U.S. Government Printing Office.

Oregon City Schools, 112 LRP 41264 (OCR 2012).

OSEP Policy Letter, 18 IDELR 741 (OSEP 1992).

OSEP Policy Letter, 20 IDELR 1219 (OSEP 1993a).

OSEP Policy Letter, 20 IDELR 1222 (OSEP 1993b).

OSEP Policy Letter, 20 IDELR 1460 (OSEP 1993c).

OSEP Policy Letter, 21 IDELR 998 (OSEP 1994).

OSEP Policy Letter, 22 IDELR 563 (OSEP 1995a).

OSEP Policy Letter, 22 IDELR 637 (OSEP 1995b).

Pajaro Valley Unified School District v. J.S., 47 IDELR 12 (N.D. Cal. 2007).

Parents in Action on Special Education v. Hannon, 506 F. Supp. 831 (N.D. Ill. 1980).

Petaluma City (CA) Elementary School District, 23 IDELR 245 (OCR 1995).

Phillip v. Jefferson Board of Education, 60 IDELR 30 (11th Cir. 2013).

Regional School Unit #61, 111 LRP 48320 (SEA Me. 2011).

Reschly, D. J. (2000). Assessment and eligibility determination in the Individuals with Disabilities Education Act of 1997. In C. Telzrow & M. Tankersley (Eds.), *IDEA Amendments of 1997: Practice guidelines for school-based teams* (pp. 65–104). Bethesda, MD: National Association of School Psychologists.

Response to Veir, 20 IDELR 864 (OCR 1993).

Ridley School District v. M.R., 61 IDELR 159 (E.D. Pa. 2011).

Salvia, J., Ysseldyke, J. E., & Witmer (2017). *Assessment in special and inclusive education* (13th ed.). Boston: Cengage Learning.

San Francisco Unified School District, 57 IDELR 87 (SEA Cal. 2011).

Seattle School District v. B.S., 82 F.3d 1493 (9th Cir. 1996).

Section 504 of the Rehabilitation Act of 1973, 29 U.S.C. § 794 *et seq.*

Section 504 Regulations, 34 C.F.R. § 104.1 *et seq.*

Shriner, J. G., Ysseldyke, J. E., & Thurlow, M. L. (1994). Standards for all American students. *Focus on Exceptional Children*, 26(5), 1–19.

Stateline.org. (2010). Available at www.stateline.org/live/ViewPage.action?siteNodeId=136&languageId=1&co/ntentId=33244.

T. S. v. Board of Education of the Town of Ridgefield and State of Connecticut Department of Education, 10 F.3d 87 (2d Cir. 1993).

Tatgenhorst, A., Norlin, J., Gorn, S. (2014). *What do I do when . . . The answer book on special education law*. Palm Beach Gardens, FL: LRP Publications.

U.S. Department of Education, Office of Special Education Programs (2011). A response to intervention process cannot be used to delay/deny an evaluation for special education under the Individuals with Disabilities Education Act (IDEA).

Walker, D., & Daves, D. (2010). Response to intervention and the courts: Litigation-based guidance. *Journal of Disability Studies*, 21, 40–46.

Yell, M.L. & Bateman, D.F. (2017). *Endrew F. v. Douglas County School District* (2017): FAPE and the Supreme Court. *Teaching Exceptional Children*, 50, 1–9.

Yell, M. L., & Crockett, J. (2011). Free appropriate public education (FAPE). In J. M. Kauffman and D. P. Hallahan (Eds.), *Handbook of special education* (pp. 77–90). Philadelphia, PA: Taylor & Francis/Routledge.

Yell, M. L., & Drasgow, E. (2000). Litigating a free appropriate public education: The Lovaas hearings and cases. *Journal of Special Education*, 33, 206–215.

Yell, M. L., Shriner, J. G., Thomas, S. S., Katsiyannis, A. (2018). Special education law for leaders and administrators of special education. In J. Crockett, M. L. Boscardin, & B. Billingsley (Eds.), *Handbook of Leadership and Administration for Special Education* (2nd ed.). Philadelphia, PA: Routledge.

Yell, M. L., & Walker, D. (2010). The legal basis of response to intervention: Analysis and implications. *Exceptionality, 18,* 124–137.

Ysseldyke, J. E., Thurlow, M. L., McGrew, K., & Vanderwood, M. (1994). *Making decisions about the inclusion of students with disabilities in large-scale assessments* (Synthesis Report 13). Minneapolis: University of Minnesota and National Center on Educational Outcomes.

Zirkel, P.A. (2015). Special education law: Illustrative basics and nuances of key IDEA components. *Teacher Education and Special Education, 38* (4), 263–275.

Chapter 10

The Individualized Education Program

An IEP must aim to enable the child to make progress: the essential function of an IEP is to set out a plan for pursuing academic and functional advancement.

CHIEF JUSTICE JOHN ROBERTS, *Endrew F. v. Douglas County School System* (2017, P. 11)

Learner Objectives

At the end of the chapter, students will be able to

10.1 Describe the individualized education program mandates of the Individuals with Disabilities Education Act and the regulations implementing the law.

10.2 Describe the purposes of the individualized education program.

10.3 Describe the procedures for developing a student's individualized education program.

10.4 Describe the required participants on a student's individualized education program planning team.

10.5 Describe the required components of a student's individualized education program.

10.6 Describe the procedural and substantive requirements of a student's individualized education program.

10.7 Describe the decisions in major cases that have addressed the individualized education program mandate of the IDEA.

10.8 Describe the effect of the U.S. Supreme Court's rulings in *Board of Education v. Rowley* (1982) and *Endrew F. v. Douglas County School District* (2017) on IEP development.

The individualized education program (IEP) is the "modus operandi" of the Individuals with Disabilities Education Act (IDEA) (*Burlington School Committee v. Massachusetts Department of Education*, 1985, p. 361); it is the means by which a student's free appropriate public education (FAPE) is developed and delivered (Bateman, 2017). All aspects of the student's special education program are directed by the IEP and monitored throughout the IEP process (Smith, 1990). The goals of a student's program, the educational placement, the special education and related services, and the evaluation and measurement criteria that are developed in the IEP process are contained in the document. Because the IEP process develops and formalizes a FAPE for a student with disabilities, the IEP is so important that the failure to properly develop and implement it may render a student's entire special education program invalid in the eyes of the courts (Bateman, 2017; Bateman & Linden, 2012; Huefner & Herr, 2012; Katsiyannis, Yell, & Bradley, 2001). In fact, the IEP is at the center of most IDEA disputes because it is the "primary evidence of the appropriateness of a student's special education program—its development, implementation, and efficacy" (Bateman, 2017).

Schools must follow both the procedural and substantive requirements of the IEP to ensure that a student receives an appropriate education. Procedural requirements compel schools to follow the law when developing an IEP and include such things as (a) providing notice to parents, (b) adhering to state-mandated timelines, (c) involving the student's parents in educational decision making, (d) conducting complete and individualized evaluations, (e) ensuring that all the necessary IEP team members attend the IEP meetings, (f) including the appropriate content in the IEP, and (g) ensuring that the IEP is implemented as written (Yell, Katsiyannis, Ennis, & Losinski, 2013). Substantive requirements compel schools to provide an education that enables a student to make progress appropriate in light of his or her circumstance (Yell & Bateman, 2017). To ensure that IEPs are reasonably calculated to enable students to make progress, educators should (a) thoroughly assess a student's academic and functional needs; (b) develop ambitious and challenging goals based on those needs; (c) provide evidence-based special education and related services; and (e) monitor a student's progress toward his or her goals and make instructional changes when necessary (Yell, Shriner, Thomas, & Katsiyannis, 2017). The procedural and substantive requirements of the IEP form the framework that guides the development and implementation of a student's individualized special education program. According to the U.S. Supreme Court in *Endrew F. v. Douglas County School District* (2017), "An IEP must aim to enable a child to make progress; the essential function of an IEP is to set out a plan for pursuing academic and functional advancement" (*Endrew*, 2017, p. 11).

The Center for Parent Resources and Information, funded by the Office of Special Education Programs (OSEP) in the U.S Department of Education, maintains a website called "All About IEPs" at www.parentcenterhub.org/repository/iep/. The website contains answers to frequently asked questions about IEPs. Additionally, OSEP maintains a website that contains useful resources on IEPs (https://sites.ed.gov/idea/). A link on the website connects to the Building the Legacy website, which contains related statutes, regulations, and training materials on Part B and Part C of the IDEA.

Since their inception in 1975, IEPs have been fraught with problems (Bateman, 2017; Lake, 2007; Yell, Meadows, et al., 2013). For example, Smith (1990) identified several problems with IEP development, including lack of adequate teacher training in developing IEPs, poorly developed team processes, mechanistic compliance with the paperwork requirements, and excessive demands on teacher time that are still true today (Bateman, 2017). Additional problems with the IEP requirements are minimal coordination with general education (Bateman & Linden, 2012), the failure to link assessment data to instructional goals (Bateman & Linden, 2012; Yell, Meadows, et al., 2013), the failure to develop measurable goals and objectives to evaluate student achievement (Bateman, 2017; Bateman & Herr, 2003; Yell, Katsiyannis, Ennis, Losinski, & Christle, 2016), and not allowing a student's parents to make meaningful contributions to the IEP process (Bateman & Linden, 2012; Lake, 2002; Yell, Katsiyannis, et al., 2013). Furthermore, the IEP process has been replete with such legal errors as failing to (a) report current levels of educational performance; (b) ensure parents' meaningful participation in the IEP process, (c) include appropriate goals, objectives, and evaluation procedures; (c) ensure that key personnel are at IEP meetings; (d) use appropriate procedures to excuse IEP team members, (e) include a student's parents in determining IEP services or placement (i.e., predetermination); and (e) ensure a continuum of alternative placements (Bateman, 2017; Bateman & Linden, 2012; Lombardo, 1999; Lake, 2007; Norlin, 2009; Yell, Katsiyannis, et al., 2013). Lake (2002) also noted that failing to address transition programming or positive behavior supports when required is a critical error that is often made by IEP teams. Another major problem occurs when school districts do not provide or fully implement the services in the IEP (Bateman & Linden, 2012; Lake, 2002; Zirkel, 2017).

The challenges facing schools are further compounded by the recent changes in legislation. The federal government amended and reauthorized the IDEA in 1997 and again in 2004 in ways that have had, and will continue to have, an impact on the ways schools develop IEPs. The changes in these two authorizations emphasize accountability and the use of peer-reviewed research in special education and hold schools to a higher level of responsibility for developing and implementing valid and beneficial IEPs.

Bateman and Linden (1996) asserted that:

> Sadly, most IEPs are horrendously burdensome to teachers and nearly useless to parents and children. Far from being creative, flexible, data-based, and individualized applications of the best of educational interventions to a child with unique needs, the typical IEP is empty, devoid of specific services to be provided. It says what the IEP team hopes to accomplish, but little if anything about the special education interventions and the related services or classroom modifications that will enable (the student) to reach those goals. . . . Many if not most goals and objectives couldn't be measured if one tried, and all too often no effort is made to actually assess the child's progress toward the goal.

(p. 63)

Despite their assessment of the problems with IEPs in schools today, Bateman and Linden (2012) noted that "a well-designed IEP can change a child's schooling experience from one of repeated failure, loss of self esteem, and limited options to one of achievement, directions, and productivity" (p. 9). If IEPs are to become such a tool, special educators must understand how to develop an IEP that is educationally meaningful and legally correct.

This chapter will examine the IEP mandate of the IDEA, including (a) the purposes of the IEP; (b) the IEP development process, including the IEP team and content requirements; (c) the placement process; (d) substantive issues when developing IEPs; (e) litigation that has addressed the IEP mandate of the IDEA; and (f) procedures for developing legally correct IEPs.

PURPOSES OF THE IEP

The responsibility to make a FAPE available to serve every student in special education rests with the public school district and ultimately with the state (Bateman, 2017). The development of an IEP, however, is a collaborative effort between school personnel and parents to ensure that a student's special education program will meet his or her individual needs and confer meaningful educational benefit. In fact, the most basic of all IDEA requirements related to the IEP is that the parents are full and equal partners with the school-based personnel in IEP development (Bateman, 2017). The IEP serves other important purposes too, including communication and collaboration, management, accountability, compliance and monitoring, and evaluation.

Communication and Collaboration

The IEP is developed during an IEP meeting or meetings. The IEP meeting serves as a communication vehicle between parents and school personnel, who are equal participants in IEP planning. This process is an opportunity for collaboration in planning the student's education. In fact, collaboration is a key principle of the IDEA. Together, parents and school personnel determine a student's needs and the services the school will provide to meet those needs. Additionally, they decide what the anticipated outcomes will be. The IEP meeting can also be a forum for resolving differences that may arise regarding a student's educational needs. If differences cannot be resolved at the IEP meeting, procedural safeguards are available to either party. (See Chapter 12 for elaborations on procedural safeguards.)

Management

The IEP is a management tool in two major ways. First, the IDEA sets forth procedures (i.e., the IEP process) that govern how a school will determine the special education and related services that will provide a FAPE. Second, the IEP document lists the resources the IEP team determines are necessary for the student to receive an appropriate education. The IEP is a written commitment that the school will provide a student the special education and related services designed to meet the student's unique needs. In this sense, the IEP is like a contract because it obligates the school district to provide a FAPE by delivering specified special education and related services listed in the IEP.

Accountability

The IEP is a legally constituted mechanism that commits the school to provide the student with an appropriate special education program. Schools are accountable for implementing the IEP, including the special education services, related services, and supplementary aids and services, as it was developed. Additionally, the school is also accountable for revising and rewriting the IEP when necessary. The IEP is not, however, a performance contract that imposes liability on a teacher, the IEP team members, or school officials if a student does not meet the IEP goals. That is, the IEP is not a guarantee that the student will accomplish all goals and objectives within the stated time period. The IEP does, however, commit the school district to providing the special education and related services and to making good-faith efforts to carry out its provisions. If parents believe that good-faith efforts are not being made to properly implement the IEP, they may ask for revisions in the program or invoke due process procedures.

Compliance and Monitoring

The IEP may be used by state or federal governmental agencies to monitor the special education services provided by schools. Moreover, the courts may use an IEP to assess a school's compliance with the FAPE mandate of the IDEA. The IEP may be inspected to ensure that a student is receiving an appropriate special education and that the school is meeting all of the legal requirements as agreed to by school personnel and parents in the IEP process. As the officials in the U.S. Department of Education noted in the regulations to the IDEA:

> The (school district) must ensure that all services set forth in the child's IEP are provided, consistent with the child's needs as identified in the IEP. The (school district) may provide each of these services directly, through its own staff resources; indirectly by contracting with another public or private agency; or through other arrangements . . . the services must be provided at no cost to the parents, and the (school district) remains responsible for ensuring that the IEP services are provided in a manner that appropriately meets the student's needs as specified in the IEP.

(Appendix A to 34 C.F.R. Part 300, Question 31, 1999 regulations)

Evaluation

Finally, the IEP is an evaluation tool. The annual goals in the document are measured using the criteria listed in the IEP to determine the extent of the student's progress. To evaluate student progress toward meeting goals, the IEP must contain goals that are measurable, and the appropriate school personnel must ensure that the goals will be measured. Furthermore, the IEP must describe how a student's annual goals will be measured and include a schedule for reporting on a student's progress toward his or her goals. A U.S. federal district judge in *Escambia County Board of Education v. Benton* (2005) memorably confirmed the evaluation purpose of the IDEA when he wrote that:

> Without meaningful measurable objectives and goals, Benton's educators and parent were engaged in a futile endeavor to pin the tail on a moving donkey while blindfolded in a dark room. . . . The mushy, ambiguous, unquantifiable goals often listed in Benton's IEPs are at odds with the IDEA. . . . Vague and unmeasurable objectives are the handmaiden of stagnation, as a program cannot possibly confer an educational benefit to Benton if his teachers and parents do not know where they are trying to take Benton and how they will know when he has arrived.

(p. 1264)

THE IEP MANDATE

The IEP is created in a planning process in which school personnel and parents work together to develop a program of special education and related services that will result in meaningful educational benefit for the student for whom it is developed. Because the IEP is the foundation of a student's FAPE it must be individualized; that is, the IEP must be developed to meet the unique needs of a student. Schools cannot use standard IEPs, nor can IEPs be based on available services. Neither can IEPs be designed by disabling condition or any other categorical programming.

The IEP is a written statement for a student with a disability that is developed, reviewed, and revised in accordance with the requirements of the IDEA (IDEA Regulations 34 C.F.R. §§ 300.320 to 300.324). It is a written document that describes a student's needs and provides a blueprint of the services the district will provide to meet those needs (Bateman & Linden, 2012; Yell, Katsiyannis, et al., 2013). An IEP must be developed for each student in special education. Furthermore, it must be in effect before special education and related services are provided to an eligible student. To summarize, the IEP is both a process in which an IEP team develops an appropriate program and a written document delineating the special education and related services to be provided to an eligible student. Although the process has no required format for holding an IEP meeting and no required form for the IEP, the IDEA spells out extensive mandatory procedural requirements schools must follow when developing IEPs. The purpose of these procedures is to help ensure that teams of individuals collaborate to create an individualized and meaningful IEP that provides a FAPE.

IEP DEVELOPMENT: PROCEDURAL REQUIREMENTS

Strict adherence to IEP procedural requirements, including notice, consent, and participation in meetings, is extremely important, since major procedural errors on the part of a school district may render an IEP inappropriate (Bateman & Linden, 2012; Yell, Katsiyannis, et al., 2013). When procedural violations occur in the IEP process, the IDEA directs due process hearing officers to primarily consider the substantive aspects of a student's education (IDEA Regulations 34 C.F.R. §. 300.513[a] [2][i-iii]). Thus, when a school district commits a procedural violation, courts and hearing officers will scrutinize the effects of the violation to see if it interfered with the student's FAPE, impeded the parents' participation, or deprived a student of educational benefit. If the violations interfere with the student's education in these ways, the IEP will most likely be ruled invalid. According to a decision in *Michael D.M. v. Pemi-Baker Regional School District* (2004):

Enhanced eText **Video Example 10.1**
This short video describes the information that must be included in an IEP.
www.youtube.com/watch?v=Bli0xanOVcs

> Before an IEP is set aside, there must be some rational basis to believe that procedural inadequacies compromised the pupil's right to an appropriate education, seriously hampered the parents' opportunity to participate in the formulation process, or caused a deprivation of education benefits.
>
> (p. 1133)

The IEP Planning Process

When parents, teachers, or other school personnel believe that a student may need special education services, they can refer the student to a school's multidisciplinary team (MDT). If the team determines that the referred student may be a student with disabilities and decides

FIGURE 10.1 ■ **The IEP Process**

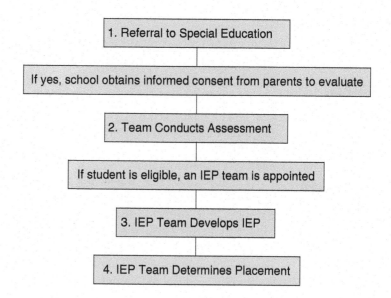

that a special education evaluation is needed, it is the team's task to obtain informed consent for the evaluation and, if granted, to conduct the evaluation. If the student is determined to be eligible under the IDEA, then an IEP team is convened and an IEP is developed.

School personnel generally initiate the referral process; however, if parents of a student with disabilities believe that their child's educational progress is not satisfactory or believe that their child may have a disability, they may request the meeting. If school personnel initiate the referral process, the parents of the referred student must be notified. Because the IDEA provides no specific requirements regarding the referral process, states and local school districts are free to develop their own referral procedures.

Following referral, if the MDT believes that the student may have a disability under the IDEA, the team contacts the student's parents to obtain informed consent to conduct an evaluation. If parents consent to the evaluation, the school assesses the student to determine the possible presence of a disability that adversely affects educational performance. The IDEA also requires that eligibility determination be made within 60 days of consent for evaluation or within the timeframe set by a state. A flowchart of this process is depicted in Figure 10.1.

If the MDT finds a student is eligible for special education and related services, the next step is to convene the IEP team and develop the student's program of special education and related services. When developing a student's IEP, the team must consider (a) the strengths of the student, (b) the concerns of the student's parents for improving the education of their child, (c) the results of the most recent evaluation of the student, and (d) the academic, developmental, and functional needs of the student. In the 2017 U.S. Supreme Court decision in *Endrew F. v. Douglas County School District*, IEP teams were also to consider a child's "potential for growth" when developing his or her IEP (*Endrew*, 2017, p. 12).

The school must convene an IEP team within 30 calendar days to develop the IEP. The purpose of the time limit is to ensure that there will not be a significant delay between when a student is evaluated and determined eligible and when the student begins to receive services.

When developing the IEP, the participants discuss and develop a student's special education program. Regulations to the IDEA delineate the procedural requirements, including the required participants in the meeting and the actual content of the IEP, that must be followed in conducting the meeting and developing the IEP. During the meeting, participants review the results of the evaluation, the student's current records (including the current IEP if one exists), and other relevant information. The purpose of the meeting is to develop the student's educational program and document it in the IEP.

The actual format, procedures, and forms used in IEP meetings are not dictated by federal law but are the responsibility of the states and schools. Although many states have developed electronic IEP forms for school districts' use, school districts are usually free to develop their own forms and procedures. Federal statutes and regulations, however, mandate procedures that must be followed by schools in the IEP process.

A 1996 letter to OSEP queried the agency about a common practice in IEP meetings of bringing a completed IEP to the meeting and presenting it to the parents. This is not permissible (*Letter to Helmuth,* 1990). What is allowed, however, is bringing a draft IEP to the meeting as long as the parents understand it is a draft only and the document does not interfere with the discussion of all aspects of the IEP before making final decisions about a student's educational program (Yell, Conroy, Katsiyannis, & Conroy, 2014). As a judge in *Doyle v. Arlington County School Board* (1992) explained, "school officials must come to the IEP table with an open mind. But this does not mean they should come to the IEP table with a blank mind" (p. 1262).

The parents' signatures are not required on the IEP form; however, parental consent is required for the initial special education placement.[1] If parents have been told that a signature on the IEP constitutes consent for special education placement, the IEP can be used in this manner. Consent means that parents have been informed of all relevant aspects of the IEP, that they understand and agree in writing to the provision of a special education, and that they understand that the granting of consent is voluntary and can be revoked at any time. If the IEP is used to signify consent to placement in special education, language regarding the provision of consent should be included on the document. Furthermore, having the participants in the process sign the IEP is a way to document attendance.

The IDEA imposes no specific time limits within which the IEP must be implemented following its development, although the Office of Special Education Programs (OSEP) has indicated that generally no delay is permissible between the time the IEP is written and the provision of special education begins (*OSEP Policy Letter,* 1991b). Regulations specify only that the IEP must be implemented as soon as possible after the IEP meeting. A delay in implementation is permitted in two situations only: when the IEP meeting takes place during the summer or a vacation and when circumstances, such as arranging transportation, require a short delay. In most situations, however, the school should provide services immediately following IEP finalization.

In *D.D. v. New York City Board of Education* (2006), the U.S. Court of Appeals for the Second Circuit addressed this issue as follows:

> Plaintiff's right to a free appropriate public education requires that their IEPs be implemented as soon possible. "As soon as possible" is, by design, a flexible requirement. It permits some delay between when the IEP is developed and when the IEP is implemented. It does not impose a rigid, outside time frame for implementation. Moreover, the requirement necessitates a specific inquiry into the causes for delay. Factors to be considered include, but are not limited to: (1) the length of the delay, (2) the reasons for the delay, and (3) the steps taken to overcome whatever obstacles have delayed prompt implementation of the IEP. Nonetheless, just because the as-soon-as-possible-requirement is flexible does not mean it lacks a breaking point.

(p. 188)

A delay in implementing a student's IEP may result in the denial of a FAPE if a hearing officer or court determines that a student is denied a significant portion of the services in the IEP. Such was the situation in *Wilson v. District of Columbia* (2011) when, because of a delay

---

[1]OCR found that a school district was not at fault for failing to implement an intial IEP when the parents refused to sign a consent form, which OCR held was necessary for an initial placement in special education (Davenport [IA] Community School District, 1993).

in implementing an IEP, a student was not transported to an extended school year program for 3 out of 4 weeks.

The IDEA's regulations require that the IEP be in place at the beginning of the school year (IDEA Regulations, 34 C.F.R. § 300.323[a]). When a school district fails to have a final IEP in place by the beginning of the school year, the district will have committed a procedural violation. As previously mentioned, if such a procedural violation was committed, a hearing officer or court would assess the violation to determine if the violation resulted in loss of educational opportunity for the student, thus violating the FAPE requirement of the IDEA. To ensure that this requirement is met, school personnel may hold the IEP meeting at the end of the preceding school year or during the summer months (*Myles S. v. Montgomery County Board of Education,* 1993).

In two cases, *M.M. v. School District of Greenville County* (2002) and *C.H. v. Cape Henlopen School District* (2010), a student's final IEP was not in place by the beginning of the school year, however, both courts determined that this was due to the student's parents refusing to cooperate with school district personnel. Because of this lack of cooperation, neither court held the school districts responsible for the delay.

In the 2004 amendments to the Individuals with Disabilities Education Improvement Act (hereafter IDEIA 2004), Congress included five provisions intended to streamline the IEP planning process, especially during reviews and revisions. First, a member of the IEP team was not required to attend the IEP meeting or other meetings if the student's parents and the school personnel agreed in writing that the person's attendance was not necessary because his or her area of curriculum or related services was not being modified or discussed at a meeting. This provision gives IEP team members an opportunity to be excused from all or part of an IEP meeting, thus releasing certain members, most likely general education teachers or related service providers, from having to spend their time in meetings that do not directly concern them.

Second, a member of the IEP team may be excused from the IEP meeting if he or she submits a request in writing to the parents and the IEP team and both the parents and the IEP team agree to excuse his or her attendance. Such excusals can only be made when a student's parents provide written consent. This means that the parents fully understand and agree to the excusal and that they also have been told that their granting of consent is voluntary and can be revoked at any time. Additionally, a member of the IEP team may be excused from a team meeting if the meeting does not involve a discussion of the member's area of curriculum of related service. Moreover, this does not mean that if a particular member of the IEP team is not available for an IEP meeting, that member is excused (*Vestavia Hills County Board of Education,* 2008). In this state level hearing, a school district was ruled to have violated the IDEA by holding an eligibility meeting by failing to ensure that all the mandatory IEP team members were present. A student's special education teacher and speech therapist were not present at the meeting and the general education teacher arrived to the meeting 30 minutes late. Because the parents did not excuse the team members, their absence deprived the student's parents of critical information regarding their son's performance. According to OSEP (2011) a school district that routinely excuses IEP team members from attending an IEP team meeting will not be in compliance with the requirements of the IDEA (*Letter to Rangel-Diaz,* 2011). The bottom line regarding excusal of IEP team members is that school district personnel should rarely use these types of excusals and certainly never abuse them (Lake, 2007).

Third, the IDEA allows the IEP team to complete its work by means other than face-to-face meetings. Meetings can be held via conference calls, videoconferencing, or other means. Additionally, placement meetings, mediation meetings, resolution sessions, and the administrative aspects of due process hearings may be held using alternative means if the parents and school personnel agree this is acceptable.

Fourth, the IDEA encourages school districts to consolidate IEP meetings and reevaluation meetings whenever possible. Finally, IDEA 2004 allows the IEP team to make changes to the IEP by amending it rather than redrafting the entire document. These provisions were added in 2004 to make the IEP planning process more flexible and convenient for parents and school personnel.

A provision in the IDEA also addresses what a school district's response should be when parents refuse to give their consent to special education placement or services. If parents of a student who has been determined to be eligible for special education services do not give their consent, the school may *not* provide service or use a due process hearing procedure to allow provision of services. In such a situation, the school district will not be considered to be in violation of the requirement to make a FAPE available to the student because it did not provide special education and related services, even though the student may have needed them.

Finally, the IDEA includes provisions regarding students with IEPs who transfer into a school district from another school district or from another state. The school district that receives a transfer student with an IEP must provide the student with a FAPE. This means that the receiving school district must (a) provide the special education services that were in the student's previous IEP, (b) consult with the student's parents, (c) conduct an evaluation, and (d) develop a new IEP, if appropriate.

The IEP Team

The IDEA delineates the persons who are to compose the IEP team as well as persons who are permitted, but not required, to attend (IDEA Regulations 34 C.F.R. § 300.321[a] [1-6]). Bateman and Linden (2012) pointed out that teaming is not a pointless procedural requirement; rather it is a system built into the IDEA to ensure that the needs of a student with disabilities are understood and that the IEP is based on these unique needs. Figure 10.2 lists the required and discretionary participants of the IEP team. The school district is responsible for having the required participants at the IEP meeting. IEPs have been invalidated by the courts and due process hearing officers when the required participants were not involved in the process and their absence affected the document's development (*Doug C. v. State Department of Hawaii*, 2013; *Girard School District*, 1992; *In re Child with Disabilities*, 1990; *New York City School District Board of Education*, 1992; *OSEP Policy Letter*, 1992; *W. G. v. Board of Trustees of Target Range School District No. 23*, 1992). In *Board of Education of the City School District of the City of New York* (1996) a student's teacher was so late to the

FIGURE 10.2 ▓ IEP Team Members

Required Participants

- The student's parents or guardian
- A special education teacher (at least one)
- A general education teacher (at least one)
- A representative of educational agency(ies) (a) qualified to provide or supervise the provision of special education; (b) knowledgeable about the general education curriculum; and (c) knowledgeable about the availability of resources in the school
- A person who can interpret the instructional implications of the evaluation results (may be one of the preceding team members)
- The child, when appropriate (required for a transition IEP)

Discretionary Participants

- Related services providers
- A person with expertise in assistive technology
- For a transition IEP, a representative of the agency that is likely to provide or pay for the transition services
- Other persons, at the discretion of the parents or the school. These individuals must have knowledge or special expertise about a student or his or her disability.
- Part C provider if a child is eligible for Part C

IEP meeting that the parents had already left. The school district team then continued the meeting and finalized the IEP, even though the student's parents were no longer present. A due process hearing officer held that the IEP was not valid because the IEP team did not include the student's parents when many important decisions were made. Additionally, when a student's general education teacher left an IEP meeting before a student's placement was discussed, a state review officer held that this procedural violation (i.e., leaving the meeting early) infringed on the parents' rights, and therefore the IEP violated the student's right to a FAPE (*Board of Education of Wappingers Central School District*, 2004).

Generally, the number of participants in the IEP meeting should be small because the meeting will tend to be more open and allow for more active parent involvement. Moreover, smaller team meetings may be less costly, easier to arrange and conduct, and more productive. Bateman and Linden (2012) noted that the authority to (a) determine the needs of a student with a disability, (b) establish and measure the student's goals, and (c) identify needed special education services rests solely with the IEP team and no one else, neither a student's parents nor school district staff or officials, may veto or refuse to deliver any services included in the IEP. Let's look next at the required participants.

The Student's Parents or Guardians   The most basic of all the requirements of the IDEA is that parents are full and equal participants with the school district personnel in the development of their child's IEP (Yell, Katsiyannis, Ennis, & Losinski, 2013). Equal partnership includes the right to active participation in all discussions and meaningful input into decisions regarding their child's special education program. To this end, parents are an integral part of the IEP process. This includes meaningful participation in all special education decision making, including IEP development and placement decisions. Bateman (2017) asserted that when parental participation is abridged or denied, a denial of FAPE would most likely be found. In fact, the U.S. Court of Appeals has held that interference with parental participation in IEP development undermines the very essence of the IDEA (*Amanda J. v. Clark County School District*, 2001). In a number of cases IEPs that were developed without parental input have been invalidated and the school district was found to have denied FAPE, thus violating the IDEA (*Doug C. v. Hawaii Department of Education*, 2013; *New York City School District Board of Education*, 1992; *Shapiro v. Paradise Valley Unified School District No. 69*, 2003).

The school is required to follow specific procedures to ensure that parents attend and fully participate in the IEP meeting (IDEA Regulations, 34 C.F.R. § 300.322[a]). Figure 10.3 contains the requirements to ensure parental participation. This includes giving parents a notice of the IEP meeting so they have an opportunity to attend and holding the meeting at a mutually agreeable time and location. If school district personnel make inadequate efforts to schedule an IEP meeting at a time and place acceptable to the parents and school district personnel, that failure may be a denial of FAPE (Bateman, 2017). The notice may be either written or oral and must include information about the time, purpose, and location of the meeting and the participants, by positions, who will be at the meeting. The OSEP considers a notice given 10 days in advance of the meeting to be adequate. The bottom line is that schools must make good-faith efforts to ensure that parents can be involved in the IEP planning process. If a parent cannot attend the meeting, the school may use alternative methods, such as conference calls, to hold the meeting. In such situations, it is important that the IEP team keep detailed records of telephone calls, e-mails, letters, and other correspondence.

When a student's parents are divorced, the school only has to invite the custodial parent. In such a situation, however, the IDEA's requirements would also be satisfied if the noncustodial parent attends. Unless parental rights have been terminated, a noncustodial parent has the right to attend all IEP-related meetings. If a parent's rights have been terminated, then the parent with custody of the child would have to give his or her permission for the noncustodial parent to attend IEP planning meetings.

FIGURE 10.3 ▨
**Parental Participation in
the IEP Meeting**

The educational agency shall take steps to ensure parental participation by:

- Notifying parents of the meeting early enough to ensure participation
- Scheduling the meeting at a mutually agreeable time and place
- Including the following content in the notice:
  - The purpose, time, and location of the meeting and who will be in attendance
  - For a transition IEP, an invitation to the student and the name of the additional agencies invited
- Using alternative methods if neither parent can attend (e.g., individual or conference telephone calls)
- Giving the parents a copy of the IEP if they request it

If allowed by a state, school districts may recognize foster parents who are a child's primary caregivers as parents for IDEA purposes if the biological parents do not have authority to make legal decisions for their child. According to Bateman and Linden (2012), any errors in deciding who the parent is or which parent to include in the IEP process should be made on the side of inclusion rather than exclusion.

When school district personnel are unable to convince a student's parents to attend an IEP meeting, they may hold an IEP meeting and develop an IEP, but only when they have made a number of efforts to contact and convince the parents to attend and these efforts have been thoroughly documented. When parents remove themselves from the IEP process or if they delay the meeting via numerous cancellations, a hearing officer or court will likely rule in favor of the school district if the parents allege a denial of FAPE (Bateman, 2017; *Doe v. Hampden-Wilbraham Regional School District*, 2010; *K.E. v. Independent School District No 15*, 2011; *Horen v. Board of Education of the City of Toledo Public School District*, 2013; *L.I. v. State of Hawaii Department of Education*, 2011).

A Representative of the Local Educational Agency

The IEP team must include a representative of the school or school district. This individual must be (a) qualified to provide or supervise the provision of the special education and to ensure that the educational services specified in the IEP will be provided, (b) knowledgeable regarding school district resources and have the authority to commit them, and (c) knowledgeable about the general education curriculum (IDEA Regulations, 34 C.F.R. § 321 (a)(4)(i-iii)). This person cannot be the student's teacher or represent the student's teacher (*OSEP Policy Letter*, 1992). The school principal, the special education administrator, or any member of the school staff designated by the principal or administrator may fill the position as long as they meet the requirements of the IDEA (e.g., be able to provide or supervise the provision of special education services) and have the authority to commit school district resources. For example, guidance counselors may be used as local educational agency (LEA) representatives if they meet the three criteria (*Letter to Cormany*, 2000). Furthermore, the representative must actually participate in the IEP meeting and not just appear briefly to sign documents (*Letter to Davila*, 1992).

Because OSEP has consistently held that school officials, such as school board members, may not change decisions made by the IEP teams, it is the duty of the representative of the school or school district to ensure that the IEP is not vetoed by other administrators who are not part of the team (*OSEP Policy Letter*, 1991b, 1991c). In fact, Bateman (2017) asserted that it would be a clear violation of the IDEA for school officials to set up a system whereby administrators or school district officials made final decisions regarding services and programs determined at an IEP meeting that they did not attend. According to Bateman and Linden (2012), a failure to include a properly authorized district representative on a team would be a procedural error that would violate the IDEA; however, such an error *would not* excuse the district's failure to implement a student's IEP. However, in *Bray v. Hobert City School Corporation* (1993) a federal district court decided that a school district's failure to include someone with the authority to commit school district's resources on an IEP team was a substantive denial of FAPE.

The Student's Special Education Teacher   Until the passage of the IDEA Amendments of 1997, the IEP did not specify if the teacher on the core IEP team should be a student's general education or special education teacher. In the 1997 amendments, both were added as required participants of the IEP team. The participation of the student's special education teacher or provider is required to ensure that the person who will implement the IEP will be involved in its development. If a special education teacher involved in educating the student is not a member of the IEP team, the IEP may not be valid (*Board of Education of the Arlington Central School District*, 2004; *Board of Education of the West Seneca Central School District*, 2004; *Brimmer v. Traverse City*, 1994; *R.B. v. Napa Valley Unified School District*, 2007; *S.B. v. Pomona Unified School District*, 2008). The special education teacher on the IEP team "should be the person who is or who will be, implementing the IEP" (Commentary on the IDEA regulations, Fed. Reg., 46,761, 2006). The U.S. Court of Appeals for the Fifth Circuit, in *S.H. v. Plano Independent School District* (2012), held that a school district's IEP team was not properly constituted because the special education teacher on the team had never taught the student and was not the planned teacher.

Many school districts appoint case managers to coordinate the IEP process, and some states require the appointment of a case or IEP manager, although case managers are not mandated by the IDEA. The manager's role usually is to coordinate the evaluation process, collect and synthesize all reports and relevant information, communicate with parents, and participate in and conduct the IEP meeting. The case manager is often the student's special education teacher.

The Student's General Education Teacher   The IDEA Amendments of 1997 added a student's general education teacher to the core IEP team if the student is participating, or may participate, in general education. Congress, finding that general education teachers often played a central role in the education of students with disabilities, required that to the extent appropriate, the general education teacher should participate in the development of the IEP, including the determination of appropriate behavioral interventions and strategies and supplementary aids and services, program modifications, and support for school personnel. Congress, however, did not intend that the general education teacher participate in all aspects of the IEP team's work (Senate Report, 1997).

When a student (e.g., a middle school or high school student) has multiple teachers, only one teacher is required to attend the IEP meeting. The school, however, may allow the other teachers to attend. Administrators may not take the place of teachers in IEP meetings (*OSEP Policy Letter*, 1992). In *Hensley v. Colville School District* (2009), a court found no procedural violation of the IDEA occurred even though the general education teacher on the team had never taught the student, but would be responsible for implementing his IEP in the future. Similarly, in *R.B. v. Napa Valley Unified School District* (2007), the U.S. Circuit Court of Appeals for the Ninth Circuit held that the teacher does not have to be the current teacher, but could have taught the student previously.

The primary purpose of having a general education teacher on the team is to ensure input from someone who understands the general curricula. Additionally, general education teachers need to know what supplementary services will be provided for students in their classrooms. If there is no general education teacher on the IEP team, the school district is vulnerable to charges of predetermination, which could lead to a denial of FAPE and violation of the IDEA (Bateman, 2017; *Deal v. Hamilton County Board of Education*, 2004; *M.L. v. Federal Way School District*, 2004).

A Person Who Can Interpret the Instructional Implications of the Evaluation Results   In the IDEA Amendments of 1997, an individual who can interpret the instructional implications of the evaluation data was added to the core IEP team.

One of the previously mentioned team members or an additional member can fill this role. Often school psychologists fill this role. The individual was added to the team to ensure that the IEP process begins with all members understanding the student's individual needs as determined in the evaluation and how the evaluation results affect the student's instructional needs. According to Bateman (2017) few cases have dealt with this requirement, probably because parents are unaware how important the relationship is between the evaluation data and the subsequent special education programming.

The Student, When Appropriate   The school must inform parents that the student may attend the meeting. The student, however, should only be present when appropriate. Additionally, if parents decide that their child's attendance will be helpful, the child must be allowed to attend. Whenever possible, the school and parents should discuss the appropriateness of having the student attend prior to making a decision. In cases where transition services are discussed, the student must be invited. Beginning at age 16, and earlier in some states (e.g., South Carolina), students become an integral part of the IEP process because of transition requirements. Thus, they should attend the IEP meeting (IDEA Regulations, 34 C.F.R. § 300.321[b][1]). If a student is unable to attend the meeting, the school district is required to ensure that the student's preferences and interests are considered (*Gibson v. Forest Hills*, 2013).

Related Services Personnel   When it is determined that the student will require related services, it is appropriate that related services personnel (e.g., counselor, social worker, school nurse, physical therapist) attend the IEP meeting and be involved in writing the IEP. The IDEA does not require that related services personnel attend the meeting; however, if related services personnel do not attend the IEP meeting, they should provide a written recommendation to the IEP committee regarding the nature, frequency, and amount of related services to be provided to the student. In 2004, Congress added school nursing services to the list of potential related services required under the IDEA. Whenever a student has a health-related need, a registered school nurse should be a member of the IEP team to help the team define and make decisions about the student's education-related health needs. Related services personnel are the most common example of "other individuals" (Mehfoud, 2013).

Transition Services Personnel   When a student turns 16 years old, transition services must be included in his or her IEP (e.g., some states require that transition services be included in the IEPs of students who are younger than 16). A previous IEP requirement to provide transition planning in the IEPs of 14-year-old students was removed when the IDEA was reauthorized in 2004. When transition services are to be considered at the IEP meeting, the school must invite the student and a representative of the agency likely to provide or pay for the transition services. If the student does not attend, the school must take steps to ensure that the student's interests and preferences are considered in designing the transition plan.

Additionally, the IEP team must invite a representative of the agency that will be participating in transition services. If the agency does not send a representative, the school must take steps to ensure that the agency participates in the planning process.

According to Prince, Plotner, and Yell (2014), the transition members of a student's IEP team may not be regular participants on the team. They may be individuals from outside the school (e.g., business owners, managers, representatives from vocational schools) who can provide information about post-school services and assist in providing those services. When this information is available before the student graduates, the IEP team can modify the IEP in accordance with the information provided by transition team members (Etscheidt, 2008; Prince et al., 2014).

Other Individuals at the Discretion of the Parents or School   Either the school or the parents may invite other persons to the meeting. Weber (2002) contended that confidentiality rules might prevent the attendance of persons who are not employed by the school district unless the parents give consent in writing. This rule would not apply to attorneys working for the school district or to related services personnel. The U.S. Department of Education, however, discourages the involvement of attorneys (Pitasky, 2002). In IDEA 2004, Congress specifically prohibited attorneys from collecting fees in IDEA cases for any time in which they attended IEP-related meetings, unless a hearing officer or judge required such meetings.

When the school does invite additional persons, it must inform the parents. Parents are not similarly required to inform the school districts of additional persons they will bring to the IEP meeting. It would be appropriate, however, for the school to inquire if the parents intend to bring other participants. Parents may also request the presence of school personnel at the IEP (Martin, 1996).

Lombardo (1999) suggested that school districts should seriously consider appointing "experts" to IEP teams. By doing this, especially when the school district does not have staff with meaningful expertise in a particular area, the district shows it is serious about developing a meaningful intervention program. In such situations, it is also advisable that the school district get the experts to develop meaningful staff development activities.

Parents may bring anyone who is familiar with education laws or the student's needs, including, for example, independent professionals (e.g., psychologists, therapists). The school district is required to consider recommendations offered by the additional participants, but it is not required to accept the recommendations.

Content of the IEP

The IDEA requires that, at a minimum, eight components be present in the IEP. States and local agencies, however, may require additional elements. Failure to include all of these elements in IEPs is a frequent source of litigation (Tatgenhorst, Norlin, & Gorn, 2014). In fact, IEPs have been invalidated by the courts when the required elements were not written into the IEP and their absence affected the student's FAPE (*Big Beaver Falls Area School District v. Jackson*, 1993; *Board of Education of the Casadaga Valley Central School District*, 1994; *Burlington School District*, 1994; *In re Child with Disabilities*, 1993; *New Haven Board of Education*, 1993; *OSEP Policy Letter*, 1991a; *School Administrative Unit #66*, 1993; *Utica County Schools*, 2013). It is crucial, therefore, that these elements be discussed at the IEP meeting and included in the document. Figure 10.4 lists the eight elements required in the IEP (IDEA Regulations, 34 C.F.R. § 300.346). Figure 10.5 is a flowchart depicting the development of an IEP.

The IDEA also requires that the IEP team address participation and involvement in the general education curriculum. According to Congress, the addition of this language is not intended to result in an increase in the size of the IEP document (e.g., a greater number of goals and objectives); rather, the new focus is intended to place attention on the accommodations and adjustments needed for the student with disabilities to successfully participate in the general education curriculum (Senate Report, 1997). Congress wrote the new focus into the 1997 amendments because the IDEA presumes "that children with disabilities are to be educated in regular classes" (Senate Report, 1997, p. 21).

The content requirements of the IEP essentially answers four questions that determine a student's special education program: (a) What are a student's unique educational needs that must be addressed in developing the student's IEP? (b) What goals will enable a student to achieve meaningful educational benefit? (c) What services will be provided to address a student's educational needs and enable the student to achieve the goals? (d) How will we monitor a student's progress to determine if his or her program is effective?

Present Levels of Academic Achievement and Functional Performance   The first component of an IEP is a statement of the student's present levels of academic achievement and functional performance (PLAAFP). This statement, which

FIGURE 10.4 ■
Content of the IEP

The IEP for each IDEA-eligible student must include:

1. A statement of a student's present levels of academic achievement and functional performance

2. A statement of a student's measurable annual goals, including academic and functional goals; short-term instructional objectives for students who take alternate assessments

3. A statement of how the student's progress toward meeting the annual goals will be measured and when periodic reports on the student's progress toward the goals will be provided to the parents

4. A statement of the special education, related services, and supplementary aids and services, based on peer-reviewed research, to be provided to the student and a statement of the program modifications or supports for school personnel

5. An explanation of the extent, if any, to which the student will not participate with students without disabilities in general education

6. A statement of any accommodations necessary to measure the academic and functional performance of the student on state- or district-wide assessment of student achievement or a statement of why a student cannot participate in the regular assessment and how the alternate assessment was selected

7. The projected date for beginning the services and modifications and the anticipated frequency, location, and duration of those services

8. A statement of appropriate measurable postsecondary goals based on age-appropriate transition assessment services and the transition services needed to assist the student in reaching those goals (Transition services must be included in the IEPs of students who are 16 years old.)

until the passage of IDEA 2004 was present levels of educational performance, must include information about how the student's disability affects his or her involvement and progress in the general education curriculum. For preschool children, this statement should specify how the disability affects the child's participation in appropriate activities. The purpose of the statement is to describe the problems that interfere with the student's education so that annual goals can be developed (Bateman, 2017). The PLAAFP statement is the starting point from which teams develop the IEP and measure its success. In fact, according to the Supreme Court in *Endrew* (2017) a student's IEP is "constructed only after careful consideration of the child's present level of achievement, disability, and potential for growth" (*Endrew,* 2017, p. 12).

The PLAAFP statement should contain information on the student's academic performance; test scores and an explanation of those scores; physical, health, and sensory status; emotional development; social development; and prevocational and vocational skills. In IDEA 2004, the new term for present levels emphasizes that in addition to academic achievement, IEP teams must also address other areas of student need, which may include nonacademic or functional areas such as behavioral problems, communication, difficulties, daily life activities, and mobility. The IEP should also specify how a student's problems affect his or her performance in the general education curriculum. Labels (e.g., learning disabled, emotionally disturbed) are not appropriate substitutions for descriptions of educational performance.

Moreover, there must be a direct relationship between a student's present levels of performance and the annual goals and services that will be provided to meet those goals (U.S. Department of Education, 2006; *Simi Valley Unified School District*, 2005). Thus, the statement of current educational performance becomes a baseline from which the student's needs may be considered (Bateman, 2017; Yell, Meadows, Drasgow, & Shriner, 2013).

The statement of needs should be written in objective terms using data from the multidisciplinary team's evaluation. When test scores are included in this section, an explanation of the results should be provided. The results of these scores should be understandable to all parties involved. Areas of educational performance in which the student has deficiencies should have corresponding goals and objectives, and any program or service must also relate to the current needs.

FIGURE 10.5 ■
Flowchart of the IEP Development Process

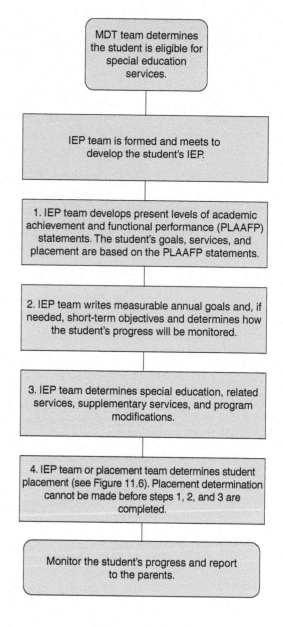

The importance of present level statements was described well in the opinion of the hearing officer in *Board of Education of the Rhinebeck Central School District* (2003), where he wrote that:

> both the 2000–2001 IEP and 2001–2002 IEP were deficient in that they lacked *adequate objective data* [italics added] by which to measure the student's present levels of performance in reading and language arts. The lack of objective data resulted in an inadequate basis upon which to measure his progress in those areas and to develop meaningful, measurable goals.
>
> (p. 148)

Similarly, a U.S. District Court, in *Kirby v. Cabell County Board of Education* (2006), noted that a school district's IEP was invalid and failed to provide a FAPE because the IEP did not include any present levels statements. According to the court:

> This deficiency goes to the heart of the IEP; the child's level of academic achievement and functional performance is the foundation upon which the IEP must be built. Without a

clear identification of (a student's) present levels, the IEP (team) cannot set measurable goals, evaluate the child's progress, and determine which educational and related services are needed.

(p. 694).

Measurable Annual Goals   The IEP team determines annual goals for students in special education. The IDEA Amendments of 1997 required that these annual goals be "measurable." The goals are written to reflect what a student needs to become involved in and to make progress in the general education curriculum and in other educational areas related to the disability. These goals focus on remediation of academic or nonacademic problems and are based on the student's current level of educational performance. At least one goal should be written for each identified area of need. Failure to write measurable goals for each need area can render an IEP inappropriate (Bateman, 2007; *Board of Education of the St. Louis Central School District*, 1993; *Burlington School District*, 1994; *Liberty Union High School District*, 2017; *New Haven Board of Education*, 1993). Moreover, goals must be measurable and specific (*Escambia County Public Schools v. Benton*, 2005; *Kirby v. Cabell County Board of Education*, 2006; *Liberty Union High School District*, 2017). Goals that are vague and not measurable (e.g., "will demonstrate improvement," "will improve") will not meet the requirements of the law (Bateman, 2007; *Board of Education of the Carmel School District*, 2005).

Annual goals are projections the team makes regarding the progress of the student in one school year. In writing the annual goals, IEP teams should consider the student's past achievement, current level of performance, practicality of goals, priority needs, and amount of instructional time devoted to reaching the goal (Bateman & Linden, 2012) and potential for growth (Yell & Bateman, 2017). Whereas goals should be written for a level that the student has a reasonable chance of reaching, courts have indicated that when goals are so unambitious that achieving them will not result in meaningful improvements in performance, such goals may render the IEP inappropriate (*Adams v. Hansen*, 1985; *Carter v. Florence County School District Four*, 1991). In fact, a U.S. District Court found that the IEP goals in reading and math for Shannon Carter were so unambitious that they "ensured her program's inadequacy from inception" (*Carter*, 1991, p. 456), thus denying her a FAPE. According to the court, "much more progress was necessary in order to provide Shannon with an appropriate education" (*Carter*, 1991, p. 453). The 2017 Supreme Court's decision in *Endrew* (2017) also noted the importance of students working to achieve "challenging" goals (*Endrew*, 2017, p. 14).

In the reauthorization in 2004, Congress removed benchmarks and short-term objectives (STOs) from the IEP, unless a student takes an alternate achievement test based on alternate achievement standards. Even though federal law no longer requires STOs, state law may still mandate that STOs be included in students' IEPs. Many officials in Congress believed that (a) STOs were not necessary when an IEP contained measurable goals, (b) STOs were nonfunctional, and (c) STOs merely resulted in additional paperwork for teachers, with no corresponding benefit. Instead, Congress stressed the requirement that special education teachers monitor their students' educational progress during the school year and use that data to alter the program if necessary. An IEP, therefore, must include information about how the student's progress toward each goal will be measured and when and how a student's progress will be reported to parents. In the report to the parents, the teacher must include information regarding how the goals are measured and whether the student is likely to achieve stated goals if his or her current rate of progress continues. Clearly, Congress intended that revisions to the IEP would be made if progress toward goals were inadequate (Bateman, 2007; Huefner & Herr, 2012).

The purpose of measurable annual goals and objectives is to help determine whether a student is making educational progress and if the special education program is providing meaningful educational benefit. Goals and objectives, correctly written, enable teachers and parents to monitor a student's progress in a special education program and make educational adjustments when necessary (Bateman, 2007; Deno, 1992). In fact, Congress viewed the requirement of "measurable" annual goals as crucial to the success of the IEP (Senate Report, 1997).

It seems that one of the biggest challenges that IEP teams face is writing measurable annual goals (Bateman, 2007; Bateman & Herr, 2003; Bateman & Linden, 2012; Lake, 2007). The purpose of annual goals is to develop an individualized metric to measure a student's program (Lake, 2002). A decision in the hearing of *Rio Rancho Public Schools* (2003) emphasized the importance of writing measurable goals. In the opinion, the hearing officer wrote that:

> The purpose of measurable annual goals and objectives is to enable a child's teacher(s), parents, and others involved and implementing that child's IEP, to gauge, at intermediate times during the school year, how well the child is progressing toward achievement of the annual goal. . . . This information allows the IEP team to determine whether a child is making adequate progress, and, if not, to revise the IEP accordingly.

(p. 140)

The reauthorization of the IDEA in 1997 and 2004 placed an emphasis on developing measurable annual goals and then actually measuring them. The reauthorized IDEA requires that IEPs include a description of (a) how a student's goals will be measured and (b) when reports on how the student is progressing toward all the annual goals will be provided to his or her parents. The progress reports must be given to the students concurrent with the issuance of report cards. In other words, IEP teams must now ensure that a student's goals are measurable, say how they will measure the goals, and then actually measure them. Moreover, if a student is not progressing on a pace to meet his or her goals, the teacher must make instructional changes to the student's program and continue to monitor progress.

Following the passage of IDEA 1997, Huefner (2000) predicted that hearing officers and courts would begin to carefully scrutinize a student's IEP and goals to see if he or she had actually made progress toward the goals. She further asserted that for IEP teams, this meant that if a student is not progressing at the expected rate, the team should be prepared to explain why the gap exists or to revise the IEP. Similarly, Lake (2002) wrote that failing to change instructional procedures in the face of lack of student progress could lead to a ruling that a school had denied FAPE. Moreover, when Chief Justice John Roberts wrote the opinion for the Supreme Court in *Endrew*, he noted that the purpose of the IEP is to set out a plan that will enable a student to make academic and functional progress. Clearly, the IDEA and now the U.S. Supreme Court decision places even greater emphasis on the importance of IEP teams monitoring student progress on a frequent and ongoing basis and changing a student's educational program if he or she is not progressing toward the annual goals.

Because IEP teams have had such difficulty in developing measureable annual goals, it is important that both preservice and inservice training address this crucial requirement. An excellent book that fully describes the process of writing measurable goals is *From Gobbledygook to Clearly Written Annual IEP Goals* (Bateman, 2007). In her book, Dr. Bateman not only describes how to write measurable goals but also leads readers through the process of taking goals that are not measurable, which she called gobbledygooks, and rewriting them so they are measurable. In 1962, Mager wrote one of the first books on developing measurable goals and objectives in which he noted that three elements are necessary for a goal or objective to be measurable: (a) an observable target behavior (i.e., the visible behavior the learner will be engaging in), (b) the conditions (i.e., the conditions in which we will measure student behavior), and (c) the criterion (i.e., how we will recognize success). Table 10.1 depicts these components.

Special Education, Related Services, and Supplementary Aids and Services
The third requirement is a statement of the specific educational services to be provided by the school. This includes special education, related services, and supplementary aids and services required to assist a student in attaining the IEP goals and objectives. The statement of services must be unambiguous so that the school's commitment of resources is

TABLE 10.1 ■ The Three Components of a Measurable Annual Goal

Component	Characteristics	Examples
Target behavior	Observable, measurable, and repeatable	To write, to read aloud, to initiate, to count (No invisible behaviors open to interpretation, such as to understand, to enjoy, to improve)
Conditions under which we measure the target behavior	The materials the teacher uses to measure or the environment in which the measurement occurs	Materials (e.g., given a worksheet of basic facts, given a story starter and 3 minutes to write) Environment (e.g., when playing with children at recess)
The criterion for acceptable performance	What the student has to accomplish to reach the goal—the criterion for mastery	Accuracy, speed, fluency (e.g., read 48 words per minute with less than 2 errors; write 24 correct word sequences)

clear to parents and other members of the team. The U.S. Court of Appeals for the Ninth Circuit recently ruled in *M.C. v. Antelope Valley Union High School District* (2017) that a school district violated the IDEA's procedural requirements by failing to accurately detail the special education service.

Statements of related services address the services and equipment provided to help students benefit from special education; that is, the services provided to students should enable them (a) to advance appropriately toward attaining annual goals; (b) to be involved in and progress in the general education curriculum and to participate in extracurricular and other nonacademic activities; and (c) to be educated with other children with and without disabilities. This requirement commits the school district to providing these services at no charge to parents. The team must determine the special education and related services needs of a student based on the student's needs, not on the availability of services. In addition to enumerating the types of services, the IEP should also include the amount, frequency, and duration of services. If the required services are not available in the district but are determined by the IEP team to be necessary, they must be provided through contracts or arrangements with other agencies.

In IDEA 2004, Congress added a requirement that a student's special education services be based on peer-reviewed research (PRR) when possible. This language was included to align the IDEA with the No Child Left Behind Act's requirement regarding the importance of basing instruction on research-validated practices. The PRR requirement applies to the (a) selection and provision of special education methodology, (b) selection and provision of related services, which are services that are required to assist a student to benefit from special education, and (c) selection and provision of supplementary aids, services, and supports provided in regular education settings (Yell & Rozalski, 2013).

In commentary to the 2006 regulations to the IDEA, the U.S. Department of Education declined to provide a definition of peer-reviewed research but did note that the term generally referred "to research that is reviewed by qualified and independent reviewers to ensure that the quality of the information meets the standards of the field before the research is published" (71 Fed. Reg. 46,664).

According to Etscheidt and Curran (2010), the intent in including the PRR requirement was to ensure that the selection of educational approaches by IEP teams reflects sound practices that have been validated empirically whenever possible. When the services in a student's IEP are based on PRR, therefore, there should be reliable evidence that the program or service works. IEP teams, therefore, should have strong evidence of the effectiveness of instructional programs and other services before they are included in students' IEPs (Etscheidt & Curran, 2010). The PRR requirement applies to the (a) selection and provision of special education methodology, (b) selection and provision of related services, which are services that are required to assist a student to benefit from special education, and (c) selection and provision of supplementary aids, services, and supports provided in regular education settings.

In commentary to the IDEA regulations by officials in the U.S. Department of Education this requirement was explained as follows:

> services and supports should be based on peer-reviewed research to the extent that it is possible, given the availability of peer-reviewed research. . . .States, school districts, and school personnel must, therefore, select and use methods that research has shown to be effective, to the extent that methods based on peer-reviewed research are available. This does not mean that the service with the greatest body of research is the service necessarily required for a child to receive FAPE. Likewise, there is nothing in the Act to suggest that the failure of a public agency to provide services based on peer-reviewed research would automatically result in a denial of FAPE. The final decision about the special education and related services, and supplementary aids and services that are to be provided to a child must be made by the child's IEP Team based on the child's individual needs . . . if no such research exists, the service may still be provided, if the IEP team determines that such services are appropriate.

> (*Fed. Reg.*, Vol. 71, No. 156, pp. 46,663–46,665)

Litigation on the PRR requirement has supported this view (Yell & Rozalski, 2013). In a decision out of the U.S. Court of Appeals for the Third Circuit, *Ridley School District v. M.R. and J.R.* (2012), the court supported a school district's choice of a reading curriculum used in the program of a student with a learning disability. The court found that both the parent's choice of a reading program and the school district's choice had research supporting its use, and because the IDEA did not require that the program with the greatest amount of PRR be used, the choice of methods was up to the IEP team. Interestingly, the court did recognize that there might be situations in which a school district develops a program that denies a student his or her right to a FAPE because the school's program is at odds with the current research.

The supplementary aids and services that are provided as part of a student's special education program must also be included in the IEP. It is not necessary, however, to include components of a student's educational program that are not part of the special education and related services required by the student. In fact, Bateman and Linden (2012) contended that nonmandatory educational services should not be included in the IEP, because adding particular nonmandated services to the IEP may create an obligation on the part of the school district to provide the services while the IEP is in effect. Moreover, in a report on the IDEA Amendments of 1997, the Senate Committee on Labor and Human Resources noted that while teaching and related services methodologies are appropriate subjects to discuss in an IEP meeting, they should not be written into the IEP (Senate Report, 1997).

The Extent to Which Students Will Not Participate in the General Education Classroom

The IEP must also delineate the amount of time the student will not participate in general education classes with students without disabilities. Students with disabilities must be allowed to interact with their peers to the maximum extent appropriate in both academic and nonacademic settings. When choosing the setting for a student's special education, the IEP team must place the student in the least restrictive environment (LRE) that is appropriate. A statement in the IEP regarding the extent of integration with students without disabilities is required to document the team's LRE decision (Yell et al., 2004). A mere conclusory statement that the multidisciplinary team has determined a particular setting to be the LRE would not pass legal scrutiny. According to the court in *Thorndock v. Boise Independent School District* (1988), a statement is required that describes a student's ability or inability to participate in a general education program and essentially provides justification for the team's decision.

If modifications in the general education classroom are necessary to ensure that the student participates in general education, the modifications must be incorporated into the IEP (*OSEP Policy Letter*, 1993). This applies to any general education programs in which a student participates.

Students' Participation in the Administration of State- or District-Wide Assessments of Student Achievement   The IDEA also requires that all students with disabilities be included in state- and district-wide assessments of student progress. Because students with disabilities may need individual accommodations to participate in these assessments, the IEP must include a statement detailing all such accommodations. If the IEP team determines that a student cannot be accurately assessed, even with modifications, using the regular assessment, the IEP must state why the assessment is not appropriate and list alternative assessments that will be used in place of the state- or district-wide assessments. Readers should check with their state Department of Education regarding which accommodations are appropriate and what constitutes an alternate assessment. In other words, students with disabilities are to take the regular statewide assessment unless the IEP specifies how they will take the test or specifies that the student will take an alternate assessment and then justifies why this is necessary. Thus, the IEP does not determine if a student will take a statewide assessment, but rather how he or she will take it.

The Projected Date of Initiation and Anticipated Duration of the IEP

The IEP must be initiated as soon as possible after it is written. The only exceptions are if the IEP is written during a vacation period, over the summer, or when circumstance requires a short delay (such as working out transportation arrangements). When a student moves from another district, the delay should not be more than a week. A student must not be placed in a special education program prior to the initiation date in the IEP.

Transition Services   If a student is 16 years old, the IEP must contain a statement of needed transition services. Transition services are those services that help a student to prepare for life after school. This requirement was added to the IDEA in 1990. Several states require that transition services be included in the IEPs of students who are younger than 16 (e.g., South Carolina requires transition services in a student's IEP when he or she turns 13). Transition services are:

> a coordinated set of activities for a student, designed within an outcome-oriented process, which promotes movement from school to post-school activities, including post-secondary education, vocational training, integrated employment (including supported employment), continuing and adult education, adult services, independent living, or community participation. The coordinated set of activities shall be based upon the individual student's needs, taking into account the student's preferences and interests, and shall include instruction, community experiences, the development of employment and other post-school adult living objectives, and, when appropriate, acquisition of daily living skills and functional vocational evaluation.

(IDEA, 20 U.S.C. § 1401[a][19])

Congress was concerned that many high-school-age students in special education drop out of school or leave the school setting unprepared for adult life and responsibility (Norlin, 2010). Norlin (2010) noted that Congress added these requirements to the IEP to ensure that the IEP team would carefully consider where each student is heading after he or she leaves school and to determine what services will assist a student in reaching his or her post-school goals. The most crucial component of transition services, like special education services in general, is individualization.

The purpose of including transition services in the IEP, therefore, is to (a) infuse a longer-range perspective into the IEP process; (b) assist each student to make a meaningful transition from the school setting to a post-school setting, which could include further education, employment, or independent living; and (c) help students better reach their potential as adults (Prince et al., 2014). Most often the transition services focus on the transition from school to work. An IEP that includes transition services must address the areas listed in the IDEA's definition (i.e., instruction, community services, and employment and other adult-living objectives). If any of these required services are not included in a student's transition plan, the IEP must include an explanatory note detailing the reasons for exclusion.

According to Lake (2002), four of the most frequent transition mistakes made by schools are failing to (a) address transition in the IEP of a student who is 16 or older, (b) include the required or proper transition participants at the IEP meeting, (c) inform the parents about the role of transition planning, and (d) develop a transition plan that includes a coordinated set of activities to help the student meet his or her post-school goals. Lake (2007) asserted that failing to comply with the aforementioned procedural requirements may result in a substantial deprivation of a student's right to a FAPE.

Courts have not looked kindly on school districts that failed to include transition requirements when they were needed, or when school districts developed minimal and largely meaningless transition plans. For example, a federal district court found that a minimal approach to the IEP team's responsibility to include transition plans did not meet the legal requirements of the IDEA. In *Yankton School District v. Schramm* (1995), the extent of the plaintiff's transition plan required that the student would need public and private transportation along with the provision of assistive devices when appropriate. In all of the transition areas of the plaintiff's IEP, the team had just written "not applicable." Clearly, the school district did not understand its responsibilities under the IDEA.

In IDEA 2004, Congress altered the transition requirements in IEPs by requiring that IEP teams include appropriate measurable postsecondary goals that are based on appropriate transition assessments. Furthermore, these goals must be related to training, further education, employment, and when appropriate, independent living skills. The law also includes a provision designed to facilitate the transition to a student's post-school life. IEP teams are no longer required to conduct an evaluation prior to graduation from high school with a regular diploma or by aging out of IDEA eligibility; now the IEP team is required to prepare recommendations and a summary of the student's academic achievement and functional performance, which includes recommendations on how to assist the student to meet his or her postsecondary goals. The student gives this summary to representatives of the postsecondary school he or she will attend or to future employers. OSEP's website "Building the Legacy: IDEA 2004" contains a section of OSEP prepared materials on secondary transitions (http://idea.ed.gov/explore/view/p/%2Croot%2Cdynamic%2CTopicalArea%2C14%2C).

Reporting Requirements and Measurement Criteria to Determine Progress Toward the Annual Goals

The IEP must include a statement of how a student's progress toward the annual goals will be measured. This requirement is a response to the movement toward greater accountability in education. The measurement criteria and procedures must be appropriate for evaluating progress toward the particular goal. The purpose of this provision is to inform parents and educators of how a student's progress toward his or her annual goals will be measured. According to Etscheidt (2006), progress monitoring is essential to evaluating the appropriateness of a student's special education program.

Additionally, the IEP must include a statement that addresses how a student's parents will be regularly informed about their child's progress toward the annual goals. Parents of students with disabilities must be informed about their child's progress as regularly as are parents of children without disabilities (e.g., through regular report cards). Congress suggested providing an IEP report card along with a student's general education report card (Senate Report, 1997). Furthermore, Congress noted that such a report card could list the IEP goals and rank each goal on a continuum of progress.

There is probably less substantive compliance with this component of the IEP than any other (Yell et al., 2012). Appropriate evaluation of a student's progress toward meeting IEP goals and objectives is essential. Without such evaluation, the goals and objectives are meaningless because it will be impossible to determine success or failure. If the goals and objectives of the IEP cannot be measured or evaluated, the IEP will not appropriately address the student's needs. The Idaho State Supreme Court, in *Thorndock v. Boise Independent School District* (1988), held that because a student's IEP goals and objectives lacked objective measurement criteria, the IEP was inappropriate. Similarly, in *Board of Education of the Casadaga Valley Central School District* (1994), the IEP of a student was invalidated because it failed to set forth objective criteria and evaluation procedures. The importance of progress monitoring was described as follows in the decision in *Escambia County Public School System* (2005): "Periodic review of progress on the goals and objectives provides the disabled student's teacher with supportive data needed to make a determination of the success of the intervention ..." (p. 248).

An important consideration that IEP teams must make is the nature of the data that will be collected and analyzed. Anecdotal data and other subjective procedures are not appropriate for monitoring progress, and should not be the basis of a progress monitoring system (Yell & Drasgow, 2000). Rather, the most appropriate progress monitoring systems are those in which objective numerical data are collected, graphed, analyzed, and used to make instructional decisions. Two examples of such systems are curriculum-based measurement (Deno, 1985; Yell, Meadows, et al., 2013) and applied behavior analysis (Alberto & Troutman, 2012). Standardized tests are not required in measuring a student's progress toward his or her goals (*Pierce v. Mason City School District Board of Education*, 2007); rather, a better practice for reporting progress is to formatively assess a student's performance on the goal activity itself (Bateman, 2017; Yell et al., 2012).

A federal district court in Virginia addressed the importance of data collection in *County School Board of Henrico County, Virginia v. R.T.* (2006). The parents of a young child with autism, R.T., sued the Henrico School District for tuition reimbursement. The boy's parents had placed R.T. in a private school because he failed to make progress in the school district's program. The boy's teacher and other school district personnel countered that R.T. had made progress in the school's program. The court, however, did not find the testimony credible because the evidence of R.T.'s progress was based only on anecdotal information. The teacher's testimony was also given little credence because she was not seen collecting data during the school day. The court wrote, "[the teacher's] assessment of R.T. is entitled to little weight because it is based on anecdotal, rather than systematic, data collection."

According to Etscheidt's (2006) review of administrative and judicial decisions, hearing officers and courts may be unwilling to accept assertions that a student has progressed in his or her special education program absent proof of progress in the form of data. Moreover, Etscheidt listed the following areas of concern with respect to progress monitoring: (a) The IEP team fails to develop a plan for monitoring a student's progress, (b) the IEP teams fails to implement the progress monitoring plan, (c) the IEP team uses inappropriate tools for monitoring progress, and (d) the progress monitoring data are not collected frequently enough to meet the requirements of the IEP or to provide meaningful data to the IEP team. Etscheidt further suggested that IEP teams develop plans for monitoring students' progress that specify the who, where, and when of progress monitoring. She also noted that it is important to monitor progress toward both academic and behavioral goals. In 2017, the U.S. Supreme Court in *Endrew* announced a new standard of educational benefit that was necessary for a student to receive a FAPE. According to the High Court, "to meet its substantive obligation under the IDEA, a school must offer an IEP reasonably calculated to enable a child to make progress appropriate in light of the child's circumstances" (*Endrew*, 2017, p. 11). The Court also noted that "the IEP must aim to child to make progress. After all, the essential function of an IEP is to set out a plan for pursuing academic and functional advancement" (*Endrew*, 2017, p. 11). In the majority opinion, Chief Justice Roberts also wrote that in cases in which hearing officers and judges are examining a student's IEP, the "reviewing court may fairly expect (school) authorities to be able to offer a cogent and responsive explanation that shows the IEP is reasonably calculated to enable the child to make progress appropriate in light of his circumstances" (*Endrew*, 2017, p. 16).

Special Considerations in IEP Development   The IDEA includes a section that requires that five special considerations be included in an IEP, if necessary. First, in the situation of a student whose behaviors impede his or her learning or the learning of others, regardless of the student's disability category, the IEP team should consider the use of positive behavioral interventions, strategies, and supports to address the behavior problems proactively (IDEA, 20 U.S.C. § 1414[d][3][B][i]). Thus, when a student with disabilities engages in misbehavior or classroom disruptions, or violates a school's code of conduct, this may indicate that the student's IEP needs to include appropriate behavioral interventions and supports (U.S. Department of Education, 2016). This is especially important when the misbehavior is apparent or can be anticipated based on a student's PLAAFP statements or past behavior. In situations in which a student exhibits behavioral challenges, positive behavioral programming may be necessary to ensure the student receives a FAPE (U.S. Department of Education, 2016). Necessary programming in a student's IEP to address the behavioral problems could include those supports needed to allow students to be educated in a general education classroom setting or whatever setting may be determined to be a student's LRE. Such behavioral programming could include meetings with a behavioral coach, social skills instruction, counseling, and training for general education teachers

Second, when an IEP is developed for a student with limited English proficiency, the student's language needs that relate to the IEP must be considered. Third, in developing an IEP for a student who is blind or visually impaired, the IEP must provide for instruction in Braille and the use of Braille unless the team determines that instruction in Braille is not appropriate. Fourth, when a student is deaf or hearing impaired, the IEP team must consider the student's language and communication needs, opportunities for direct communications with peers and professionals in the student's language and communication mode, academic level, and full range of needs, including opportunities for direct instruction in the student's language and communication mode. Finally, the IEP team should consider whether the student requires assistive technology devices and services.

Placement Decisions   A student's placement must be made at least annually and be made by a group of persons, including the student's parents, as long as these persons are knowledgeable about the student, the meaning of the evaluation data, and the various placement options. The placement decision, which is not technically part of the IEP process, is usually made by a student's IEP team; this practice is permissible, although not strictly required (Bateman, 2017). A student's placement must follow development of the IEP and be based on the IEP (Bateman, 2017; Yell, et al., 2013). In fact, the practice of placing a student prior to developing his or her IEP, which has been referred to as shoehorning, is a clear violation of the IDEA (Tatgenhorst et al., 2014). Tatgenhorst and his colleagues (2014) also noted that placement options should not be improperly dictated by either official or unofficial policy.

Making preplacement decisions or final placement determinations outside the proper forum is a serious mistake and can lead to a denial of a FAPE (Lake, 2002). For example, predetermination refers to the practice of making decisions regarding a student's placement or programming without actually involving parents in the decision-making process. When a hearing officer or court finds that a school district has engaged in predetermination it is very likely that the school district has denied FAPE, thus violating the IDEA.

When making placement decisions, the team must also determine the LRE in which a student can receive an appropriate education. According to the IDEA, students with disabilities should be educated with students who are not disabled to the maximum extent appropriate. It is only when education in the regular educational environment, with the use of supplementary aids and services, cannot be achieved satisfactorily that a student with disabilities may be placed in a more restrictive setting such as a special school or special class. The determination of the LRE for a student is a complex issue that we will further explore in Chapter 12.

IEP DEVELOPMENT: SUBSTANTIVE REQUIREMENTS

The U.S. Supreme Court in *Board of Education of the Hendrick Hudson Central School District v. Rowley* (1982; hereafter *Rowley*) and *Endrew F. v. Douglas County School District* (2017) addressed the critical importance of the IEP. In part one of the test developed in *Rowley* to guide lower courts in determining compliance with the FAPE mandate of the IDEA, the High Court directed the courts to determine if the procedures of the IDEA were followed. In the second part of the test, which was revised in 2017 in the *Endrew* ruling, courts were directed to determine whether the IEP was "reasonably calculated to enable the {student with disabilities} to make progress appropriate in light of his or her circumstances. (See Chapter 8 for elaborations of the *Rowley* and *Endrew* tests). When hearing officers and judges are called on to determine whether a school district has offered a FAPE to a student, the hearing officers and judges, acting on the directives from the *Rowley* and *Endrew* decisions, will examine the content of the student's IEP.

Parental Participation

One of the most important of the IDEA mandates is that parents must be equal partners in the IEP process. Parental participation is so crucial to the IEP process that the IDEA contains specific guidelines that schools must follow to ensure equal parental participation. In fact, the U.S. Department of Education and Congress

 Enhanced eText Video Example 10.2 This short video shows you who is involved in an IEP meeting and lets you watch an IEP meeting in progress. www.youtube.com/watch?v=ok0irMNfKmY&list=PLe5kwkmYRwFi3vHOfJia0v3A4XxfAy-X1&index=2

considered strengthening the role of parents in the special education process one of the most important goals of the IDEA Amendments of 1997 (Senate Report, 1997). In *Endrew*, the U.S. Supreme Court noted the importance of parental involvement in the IEP process and affirmed that school personnel and a student's parents must collaborate on the development of a student's IEP and that judicial deference will depend on school personnel providing a student's parents input on issues such as the requisite degree of progress that the student's IEP should pursue (Yell & Bateman, 2017).

The school must take steps to ensure that one or both parents are present at the IEP meeting or are afforded an opportunity to participate. The school must give parents or guardians sufficient notice of the IEP development meeting so that they have an opportunity to attend. The notice provided by the school must explain the purpose of the meeting, its time and location, and the persons to be in attendance. Participants in the meeting do not have to be identified by name; however, they must be identified by position (Norlin, 2009).

The meeting may be conducted without the parents in attendance if the school is unable to convince the parents to attend. The school must have a record of its attempts to arrange a meeting. Examples of the documentation of these attempts include items such as (a) detailed records of telephone calls made or attempted, and the results of those calls; (b) copies of correspondence and any responses received; and (c) detailed records of visits made to the parents' home or place of employment, and the results of those visits.

The IDEA does not specify how far in advance the school district must notify parents, but it does state that notification must be early enough to ensure that parents have the opportunity to attend the IEP meeting. Furthermore, school personnel have to work with parents to hold a meeting at a mutually agreeable time and place. The school does not have to honor every parental request to schedule the meeting, but the district must make good-faith efforts to mutually agree on scheduling. In determining the meeting time and place, however, school personnel are allowed to consider their own scheduling needs (*OSEP Policy Letter*, 1992). An IEP meeting can be held without parents in attendance if the school is unable to convince them that they should attend. In such cases, the school personnel must keep a record of their attempts to arrange the meeting. If parents refuse to participate, the school district still has a responsibility to provide a FAPE to eligible students (Norlin, 2009).

The school must also make efforts to ensure that parents understand the proceedings, including arranging for an interpreter for parents who are deaf or whose native language is not English. If requested, the school must give the parents a copy of the IEP. The IEP meeting may be videotaped or audiotaped at the discretion of either the parents or the school (*Letter to Breecher,* 1990). The party taping the proceedings may obtain the consent of the other party, but consent is not required. Recordings must be kept confidential.

When the parents cannot be located, surrogate parents must be appointed to represent the interests of the student. Surrogate parents have all the rights and responsibilities of the parent; they are entitled to participate in the IEP meeting, view the student's educational records, receive notice, provide consent, and invoke a due process hearing. If the parents can be located but are unwilling to attend, the educational agency is not empowered to appoint a surrogate parent (*Letter to Perryman,* 1987). In such situations, the school should hold the meeting and document attempts to involve the parents.

Although parental participation is extremely important in the development of the IEP, parents do not have an absolute veto over the final results (*Buser v. Corpus Christi Independent School District,* 1994). When the parents and school personnel cannot reach an agreement on an IEP, they should, when possible, agree to an interim special plan for serving the student until the disagreement is resolved (*Letter to Boney,* 1991). If no agreement is reached, the last IEP (if one exists) remains in effect until a final resolution. When the school and parents agree about basic IEP services but disagree about a related service, the IEP should be implemented in the areas of agreement. Additionally, the IEP should document the points of disagreement, and attempts to resolve the disagreement should be undertaken. If the disagreement concerns a fundamental issue, such as placement, the school should remind the parents of their right to call a due process hearing and attempt to develop an interim educational program. If agreements cannot be reached, the use of mediation or some informal means for resolving the disagreements prior to going to due process should be recommended. If a due process hearing is initiated, the school may not change the current educational placement unless the parents and school agree otherwise. For example, if the student is in a general education classroom and the parents cannot agree on a special education placement, even if they agree on the need for special education, the student must remain in the general education classroom unless the school and parents can agree on an interim placement. The same is true if the student is currently in a special education placement.

A completed IEP may not be presented to the parents in the IEP meeting. According to the OSEP, presenting a completed document to the parents for review would minimize the parents' contributions, even if the document was to be used only as a basis for discussion (*Letter to Helmuth,* 1990). IEP team members must avoid predetermination of a student's program or placement. Predetermination occurs when the school personnel on the IEP team unilaterally determine the student's program and placement prior to the actual IEP meeting, thus denying a student's parents meaningful involvement in the IEP process. When parents are denied meaningful participation in development of their child's IEP, it is very likely that a court will rule the school has violated the FAPE requirement of the IDEA. According to the U.S. Court of Appeals for the Ninth Circuit in a unpublished decision, *H.B. v. Las Virgenes Unified School District* (2007), "a school district violates IDEA procedures if it independently develops an IEP, without meaningful parental participation, and then simply presents the IEP to the parent for ratification ... [a school district] must maintain an open mind ..." (p. 34).

Schools may prepare a draft of an IEP, however, to present to the parents at the IEP meeting for discussion purposes. This draft may consist of evaluation findings, statements of present levels of academic achievement and functional performance, recommendations regarding goals and objectives, and the kinds of special education and related services recommended. At the beginning of a meeting in which the draft document is presented, it must be clarified that the document is only a working draft for review and discussion. IEP teams must avoid actions that could be interpreted as predetermination. One way this can be done, even when a draft IEP is brought to the meeting, is to consider parental input and be willing to incorporate suggestions by parents into a student's IEP.

REVIEWING AND REVISING THE IEP

The IEP must be reviewed—and, if necessary, revised—at least annually. The review must be conducted under the following circumstances: (a) the student has shown a lack of progress toward the annual goals, and in the general education curriculum where appropriate; (b) the results of a reevaluation need to be considered; (c) the parents have provided additional information about the child; (d) the student's needs are anticipated to change; and (e) other considerations as deemed appropriate. Whenever any member of a student's IEP team, including the student's parents, believes a student is not progressing, they may convene the IEP team to revise the IEP as appropriate to address the lack of progress (IDEA Regulation 34 C.F.R. § 300.324[b][1][i-ii][A]).

The timing of these meetings is to be left to the school's discretion. The parents or the school, however, may initiate the IEP reviews as often as either party deems necessary (Norlin, 2009). If either the school or parents decide that major components of the IEP (e.g., annual goals or special education services) need revision, a new IEP meeting must be called.

The IEP remains in effect until it is revised or until a new IEP is written. The IEP cannot be revised unless the parents are notified about the proposed change and the reasons for the change. When students move from one district to another, their previous IEP is to be implemented until the new district evaluates the student and writes a new IEP. If the current IEP is not forwarded by the student's former school district or is inappropriate, the new district should conduct an IEP meeting as soon as possible. If the IEP is appropriate and can be implemented as written, however, the new district can use it without developing a new IEP.

If a school district proposes to change any aspect of the student's special education program, or refuses to change aspects of the student's program, it must issue prior notification to the parent. The notice must include a full explanation of proposed actions, justification for the changes, reasons for the rejection of alternatives, parental appeal rights, and other procedural safeguards. As long as the school provides adequate notice and conducts meetings in accordance with procedures set forth in the IDEA, parental consent is not required for review and revision of the IEP. If parents reject revisions, they have the option of calling for a due process hearing. OSEP, in the U.S. Department of Education, revised their question and answer document on IEPs, evaluations, and reevaluations in 2010 (www2.ed.gov/policy/speced/guid/idea/iep-qa-2010.pdf).

Communicating the Requirements of the IEP and Implementing the IEP

The IDEA requires that the IEP must be implemented as developed. This requirement applies to a student's special and general education teachers and related service providers. The federal regulations implementing the IDEA require that school district officials ensure that every student's IEP is "accessible to each regular education teacher, special education teacher, related services provider, and any other service provider who is responsible for its implementation" (IDEA Regulations, 34 C.F.R. § 300.321[d][1]). Moreover, school district officials must also ensure that each "teacher and provider . . . is informed of his or her specific responsibilities related to implementing the child's IEP; and the specific accommodations, modifications, and supports that must be provided for the child in accordance with the IEP (IDEA Regulations, 34 C.F.R. § 300.323[d][2]).

According to Martin (1996), some administrators misread the Family Educational Rights and Privacy Act (FERPA) as prohibiting release of IEP information to teachers because it is confidential. This is an incorrect understanding of the requirements of FERPA. (Chapter 14 details the requirements of FERPA.) Teachers working with a student who has an IEP are entitled to review the information contained in the document. Schools have an affirmative duty to inform these teachers of any requirements in the IEP.

Failing to implement an IEP as written is a significant error that certainly may constitute a denial of a student's FAPE, thus violating the IDEA (Jacobs, 2013; Yell, Conroy, Katsiyannis, & Conroy, 2014). Failing to properly implement an IEP was the subject of a recent state educational agency decision, *District of Columbia Public Schools* (2012), and a ruling by the U.S. Court of Appeals for the Sixth Circuit, *Woods v. Northport Public School* (2012). In *District of Columbia Public Schools,* the school district was determined to have violated the IDEA when a student with learning disabilities was not provided with the 5 hours per week of speech and language services as required in the student's IEP. In *Woods v. Northport Public School,* a school district violated the IDEA because it did not provide the resource room as specified in the IEP, nor did the district hire an autism consultant to work with a student's teachers, which was also required in the IEP. The state education agency in Minnesota, in *Farmington Independent School District #192* (2007), also found that a school district violated the IDEA and state law by failing to implement accommodations in students' IEPs. Additionally, failing to show that a student's teachers received copies of the IEP that they were responsible for implementing and thus failing to understand their duties can be "fatal" to a school district's defense to a legal action that the district failed to implement the student's IEP (Martin, 2014, p. 1). For example, *In re student with a disability* (2011), the state educational agency of Montana ruled that a school district failed to implement a student's IEP when school district officials could not show evidence of implementation of the provisions of the IEP or show that it provided the IEP to the student's teachers. Developing a form in which all teachers and related service providers who are responsible for implementing an IEP sign, thereby acknowledging that they have viewed the IEP and understand their responsibilities would help to alleviate such difficulties.

If a teacher is not implementing an IEP as required, the school must take steps to correct the situation. In *Doe v. Withers* (1993), an IEP required general education teachers to modify testing by giving oral examinations to a student with learning disabilities. The student's social studies teacher deliberately chose not to modify tests, even though it was required by the IEP. The parents prevailed in a lawsuit against the teacher. The court assessed the teacher compensatory and punitive damages in the amount of $15,000. In *Sharon Watson v. Campbell Independent School District* (1997) a teacher's contract was not renewed when she failed to attend a student's IEP meetings, was uncooperative and confrontational when asked to attend the IEP meeting, and failed to implement the student's IEP (Walsh, 2013).

Placement in Private Schools

When a school district places a student in a private setting, the IEP remains the responsibility of the district. Prior to placement, the school district should hold an IEP meeting that includes a representative of the private agency. In subsequent meetings, the responsible school district may allow the private facility to conduct annual reviews, but the district retains responsibility for ensuring that the parents and a representative of the home school district participate and agree to any changes in the IEP (Weber, 2002). In situations where public schools provide special education services to students in private or parochial schools, the public school is responsible for the IEP. A representative of the private or parochial school attends the meeting.

In 2011, OSEP published a question and answer document on serving students with disabilities placed by the parents in public schools. This document, which is available online at http://idea.ed.gov/uploads/Private_School_Q_A_April_2011_1.pdf, provides thorough guidance regarding this important issue.

STANDARDS-BASED IEPS

The IDEA and the law's implementing regulations require IEPs to include information that allows a student to be involved in and progress in the general education curriculum. The following sections of the IEP include such information: (a) the PLAAFP statement on how a student's disability affects his or her involvement and progress in the general education curriculum (34 C.F.R.§ 300.320[a][1][i]), (b) the measurable annual goals should include goals that meet the student's needs and enable him or her to be involved in and make progress in the general education curriculum (34 C.F.R. § 300.320[a][2][i][A]), and (c) the statement of special education services should include services provided to a student to allow him or her to be involved in and make progress in the general education curriculum.

The IDEA's references to the general education curriculum and the importance of academic content standards in No Child Left Behind (NCLB) and now the Every Student Succeeds Act (ESSA), have come together in the notion of standards-based IEPs. According to the standards-based IEP approach, the task of the IEP team is to (a) determine how a student is currently performing academically, (b) compare that performance to what he or she may be expected to do on grade-level academic standards for the grade in which the student is enrolled, and (c) write goals and determine services that will help to close that gap (Ahearn, 2010; U.S. Department of Education, 2015; Stanberry, 2015; Yell, Shriner, Thomas, & Katsiyannis, 2017). In a sense, the difference between a traditional IEP and a standards-based IEP, is that in the latter a student's IEP team always keeps the general education curriculum and the state academic standard for that student's grade in mind when crafting the student's program of special education. Moreover, the intent of the IEP is to provide a program that will help to close the gap between what the student knows or can do and what her or she is expected to know or be able to do.

It is very important that educators understand what a standards-based IEP is not. A standards-based IEP is not a restatement of the state content standards nor is it an IEP in which a student's goals are taken from the state standards (Shriner, Carty, Goldstone, & Thurlow, 2017; Karvonen, 2009; Yell, Shriner, et al., 2017). Furthermore, the expectation that a student's IEP be aligned with a state standards does not mean that the IEP can only include appropriate grade-level standards and the related grade-level curriculum (Karvonen, 2009; Shriner, Plotner, & Rose, 2010; Yell, Shriner, et al., 2017).

In 2015, the Office of Special Education and Rehabilitative Services (OSERS) in the U.S. Department of Education issued a Dear Colleague Letter (DCL) that addressed IEPs and academic content standards. (The DCL is available at www2.ed.gov/policy/speced/guid/idea/memosdcltrs/guidance-on-fape-11-17-2015.pdf).

According to the DCL "an IEP for a child with a disability, regardless of the nature or severity of the disability, (should be) designed to give the child access to the general education curriculum" (U.S. Department of Education, 2015, p. 3). Officials at OSERS and stressed that IEP-grade level standards

> alignment must guide, but not replace, the individualized decision-making required in the IEP process. In fact, the IDEA's focus on the individual needs of each child with a disability is an essential consideration when IEP teams are writing annual goals that are aligned with State academic content standards (U.S Department of Education, 205, p. 4).

OSERS also recognized that students with the most significant cognitive disabilities will be measured against a state's alternate achievement standards. Moreover, in situations in which a student's present levels of academic achievement are significantly below the grade in which the student is enrolled, "in order to align the IEP with grade-level content standards, the IEP team should estimate the growth toward the State academic content standards... that the child is expected to achieve in the year covered by the IEP" (U.S. Department of Education, 2015, p. 5). For example, if a child with a learning disability is in sixth grade but is only reading at a second-grade level, the goals should be sufficiently ambitious so as to close the gap but would not require that by the end of the year the student would be reading grade-level materials. Additionally, the student's special education and related services, supplementary services, and program modifications would be designed to help the student make progress toward his or her grade-level standard.

In a question and answer document on the U.S. Supreme Court's ruling in *Endrew F. v. Douglas County School District* (U.S. Department of Education, 2017), OSERS again stressed that the alignment of a student's special education program and a state's academic content standards "must guide, and not replace, the individual decision-making required in the IEP process. This decision-making continues to require careful consideration of the child's present levels of achievement, disability, and potential for growth" (U.S. Department of Education, 2017, p. 7). Thus, as always, the key to IEP development is individualization.

SECTION 504 AND THE IEP

Section 504 of the Rehabilitation Act of 1973 (hereafter Section 504) does not require the preparation of an IEP for students protected under the law. Regulations to Section 504 allow a school district to use an IEP to fulfill the law's requirements, although this is only one method of meeting those requirements. Consequently, it is good practice to prepare a written individualized plan to document educational services the school district provides to a student under Section 504 (Fossey, Hosie, Soniat, & Zirkel, 1994; Norlin, 2009). Furthermore, Martin (1996) contended that when an IEP committee determines that a student is not eligible for services under the IDEA or that a student no longer requires services, the committee should automatically refer students for consideration for protection under Section 504. A student who does not qualify under the IDEA, or who no longer qualifies, might meet eligibility criteria for services under Section 504.

If a school district fails to implement the components written into a student's IEP, that may also violate Section 504 of the Rehabilitation Act. For example, in *Antioch (CA) Unified School District* (2010), the Office of Civil Rights (OCR) found that a school district's teachers would unilaterally change, reduce, or not provide accommodations written into students' IEPs in violation of Section 504.

LESSONS FROM LITIGATION AND LEGISLATION

In *Rowley* and *Endrew,* the U.S. Supreme Court directed hearing officers and lower courts to review schools' IEP processes and written documents when determining compliance with the FAPE mandate of the IDEA. In using the High Court's two-part *Rowley/Endrew* test, hearing officers and lower courts are first to examine the procedural aspects of the IEP process; second, they must examine the IEP itself to determine whether the IEP was reasonably calculated to enable a student to make progress appropriate in light of the student's circumstances.

The post-*Rowley* cases have indicated that procedural flaws may invalidate an IEP. Before a court will invalidate an IEP, however, the court must have reason to believe that the procedural error (a) compromised a student's right to an appropriate education, (b) resulted in excluding parents from the IEP process, or (c) caused the student to be deprived of educational rights.

Substantively, the U.S. Supreme Court in *Endrew* held that the IEP must be reasonably calculated to enable a student to progress appropriately in light of his or her circumstances. An IEP that produces only trivial educational advancement or merely halts educational regression will not pass legal muster (Crockett & Yell, 2008). To determine substantive compliance with the FAPE mandate, courts and hearing officers have examined the following factors: (a) the IEPs present levels of academic achievement and functional performance (e.g., *Rio Rancho Public Schools*, 2003), (b) the IEPs goals and objectives (e.g., *Philadelphia City School District*, 2006), (c) the special education services, related services, supplementary aids, and services (e.g., *Anchorage School District v. Parents of M.P.*, 2006), (d) the methods used to monitor student progress (e.g., *Escambia County Public School System*, 2005), (e) a student's actual progress (e.g., *Cranston School District v. Q.D.*, 2008), and (f) IEP implementation (e.g., *DB v. District of Columbia*, 2010).

The litigation regarding the appropriateness of IEPs indicates the importance of carefully adhering to the requirements set forth in the IEP. The case law puts a premium on involving parents in the IEP process and in developing an IEP that will result in educational benefit to the student. The following principles are offered to provide guidance to school district personnel in developing and implementing educationally meaningful and legally sound IEPs.

Principle 1: Ensure the procedural requirements of the IDEA are followed. When ruling on a FAPE case, hearing officers and judges will apply the two-part *Rowley/Endrew* test. The first part of the *Rowley* test is a procedural litmus test. When applying this test, hearing officer and judges will determine whether a school district adhere to the IDEA's procedures when developing a student's program of special education. If procedural errors are found, the hearing office or judge will then determine if the procedural error or errors deprived a student of educational benefit or the student's parents an opportunity to be involved in the special education process. If a procedural error or errors did deprive a student or his or her parents in such a way, a hearing office or judge would likely rule that the school district denied the student a FAPE. Thus, procedural errors, in and of themselves, may be a violation of the IDEA's FAPE mandate (Weatherly & Yell, 2017).

Principle 2: Involve a student's parents in the development of his or her IEP. The most basic of IEP requirements is that a student's parents be full, equal, and meaningful participants in the development of their child's IEP (Bateman, 2017; Yell et al., 2013). The critical role of a student's parents was emphasized by Congress in the findings and purposes provision of the IDEA: "Almost 30 years of research and experience has demonstrated that the education of children with disabilities can be made more effective by—strengthening the role and responsibility of parents and ensuring that families . . . have meaningful opportunities to participate in the education of their children at school and at home" (IDEA, 20 U.S.C. § 1400 [c][5][B][2006]). In fact, the U.S. Supreme Court in *Winkleman v. Parma City School District* (2007) asserted that that IDEA grants parents independent, enforceable rights. These rights, which are not limited to certain procedural and reimbursement-related matters, encompass the entitlement to a free appropriate public education for the parents' child" (p. 533). As Bateman (2017) aptly noted, few, if any, of IDEA's procedural rights are more vigorously protected by courts (p. 93). It is, therefore, of paramount importance that a student's parents be involved in the formation of a student's IEP. In fact, the U.S. Court of Appeals for the Ninth Circuit in *Amanda J. v. Clark County School District* (2001) held that "Procedural violations that interfere with parental participation in the IEP formulation process undermine the very essence of the IDEA" (p. 892).

School district officials must ensure that all IEP team members understand the importance of parental involvement. IEP members must schedule IEP meetings at a mutually agreed on time and place and be certain that a student's parents understand the objectives of the meeting. Parents should be encouraged to be actively involved in discussions and frequently asked for their thoughts and opinions. If an IEP team member is assigned to take notes he or she should not attempt to record all discussions but only record the major discussion points, and especially those in which a parent is involved.

It is permissible for IEP team members to discuss a student's program informally prior to a meeting and even to bring a draft IEP to the meeting. When a draft is brought, a student's parents must be told that it is a working document and only an initial draft.

Principle 3: Assemble an appropriate IEP team. The IDEA and implementing regulations are very clear as to what persons are to comprise a student's IEP team. When school districts fail to ensure the presence of the required IEP team members it is committing a procedural error that may thwart a school district's ability to provide a FAPE. Due process hearing officers and courts have invalidated IEPs when the required participants were not involved in the process and their absence affected the document's development. It is likely that hearing officers and courts will conclude that the IEP developed by an improperly constituted IEP team will likewise be defective and will not provide FAPE.

IEP members can be excused from a meeting when the member's area of curriculum or related service is not being discussed. In such situations, the parents must agree to the excusal in writing. It is important that the LEA representative in the meeting ensure that all required school members will attend the entire meeting.

Principle 4: Develop an IEP that will enable a student to make progress. According to Yell and his colleagues (2014) four questions lie at the heart of the IEP: (1) What are the student's unique educational needs that must be considered in developing the instructional program? (2) What measurable goals will enable the student to achieve meaningful educational benefit? (3) What services will be provided to the student to address each of his or her needs? (4) How will the team monitor the student's progress to determine if the instructional program is effective? These questions are addressed in the four major components of the IEP: the present levels of academic achievement and functional performance, the measurable annual goals and a description of how the goals will be measured, the statements of special education services, and the method chosen to monitor.

To ensure that the IEP provides an appropriate education, school personnel must (a) conduct thorough and relevant assessments; (b) base measurable annual goals on educational needs identified in current assessments; (c) ensure that the goals and objectives are meaningful, ambitious, and challenging, and (d) measure student progress toward meeting these goals frequently and systematically so that educators may adjust educational procedures if the procedures do not produce the desired outcomes within the timeframe indicated in the IEP. It is especially important that IEP teams continuously monitor and measure student progress and maintain specific date to demonstrate that progress has been made. "An IEP must aim to enable the child to make progress: the essential function of an IEP is to set out a plan for pursuing academic and functional advancement" (*Endrew*, 2017, p. 11).

Principle 5: Ensure that all teachers and related service providers understand their responsibilities as listed in a student's IEP. Students' general education teachers, special education teachers, related service providers, and LEA representatives must thoroughly understand their responsibilities in implementing their IEPs. As we have seen in an earlier section of this chapter, when important parts of an IEP are not implemented as intended or are not implemented at all, a school district may be held liable for violating the IDEA by failing to provide a FAPE. Moreover, there certainly may be ramifications to a teacher or related service provider whose errors led to the denial of FAPE.

To ensure that teachers and related service providers understand their responsibilities, Walsh (2013) suggested that a student's IEP be provided to each teacher and related service provider responsible for implementation, along with a copy of confidentiality requirements. Rather than giving teachers the entire IEP, which might not be read, it may be more useful to provide a brief form that details a specific teacher's responsibilities. Figure 10.6 is an example of a form to alert teachers to their responsibilities regarding a student's IEP. Note that such forms should be given to all of a student's teachers and related service providers.

Principle 6: Ensure that the IEP is implemented as written. According to Lake (2007) an IEP is similar to a contract because the school district promises, in writing, to provide specific educational services to a particular student in order to ensure that the student

FIGURE 10.6 ▉ IEP Responsibilities

IEP Responsibilities—Teachers

Name of Student: _____

Name of Teacher: _____

Date: _____

At [Student's name] IEP meeting, held on [date], the IEP team determined the following accommodations and program modifications would be implemented in all of [Student's name] general education classes. These classroom alterations are written into [Student's name]'s IEP, which is available for your review in [location of IEP]. [Student's name] special education teacher will contact you to discuss the IEP. You are responsible for ensuring that these required alterations to your classroom are implemented.

Accommodations:

Program Modifications:

Supplementary Aids and Services:

* This is confidential educational information from the student's IEP and release of this information without permission granted by the student' parents may be a violation of the Family Education Rights and Privacy Act (FERPA). This information can be shared without obtaining permission with persons who have an educational reason for accessing it (e.g., paraprofessional who works with the student, a substitute teacher).

Signature of Teacher: _____

Signature of LEA Representative: _____

receives a FAPE. Lake also pointed out that a student's IEP is not a guarantee of performance; it is a guarantee of resources and services. Thus, when an IEP is developed it is crucial that it be implemented as written and that all involved school district personnel make good-faith efforts to assist the student to reach the meaningful goals as developed by the IEP team. As Jacobs (2013) asserted, the IEP is a legally binding document, not a list of suggestions, and there are no acceptable excuses for failing to properly implement a student's IEP. Jacobs also stressed that in due process hearings in which parents have challenged an IEP, even though they were involved in its development, the school district will often win or lose based on the faithfulness of its implementation of the IEP. Martin (2014) asserted that administrators, special education and general teachers, and related service providers must understand that if they fail to carry out their responsibilities as written in an IEP, they are placing the school district, and possibly themselves, at legal risk. As the U.S. Court of Appeals for the Ninth Circuit in *M.C. v. Antelope Hills High School District* (2017) noted the "IEP is a contract. It is signed by the child's parents and the school's representatives, and thus embodies a binding commitment" (p. 11). An IEP is not a contract in the sense that it guarantees student success; rather it is like a contract in that the school commits to providing certain special education and related services and making good faith efforts to ensure student progress.

SUMMARY

The IEP is the keystone of the IDEA, and special education is embodied in the IEP. The IEP is developed at a meeting that includes, at a minimum, a representative of the school or school district, the student's special education and general education teachers, the parents, and the student, when appropriate. Other persons may be invited at the discretion of the parent or school. If the student is being evaluated for the first time, a member of the evaluation team or a person familiar with the evaluation must be on the IEP team.

The IEP is developed in accordance with state and federal mandates. The program must include (a) the student's present level of educational performance; (b) annual goals and benchmarks or short-term objectives; (c) special education and related services to be provided; (d) the extent to which the student will not participate in the general education program; (e) student participation in state- or district-wide assessments and modifications if needed; (f) projected date of initiation and anticipated duration of the IEP;

(g) transition services for students 16 years of age, or, when determined appropriate, 14 years of age or older; and (h) appropriate objective criteria and evaluation procedures for determining, on at least an annual basis, whether the IEP goals are being met.

The IDEA emphasizes the importance of involving a student's parents in the IEP process. The law delineates specific procedures that schools must follow to ensure meaningful parental participation. Schools must communicate the requirements of the IEP to a student's general and special education teachers. Courts have stressed the importance of following proper procedures in IEP development, writing meaningful goals and objectives, evaluating a student's progress toward the goals, and communicating the results of this progress. Moreover, the U.S. Supreme Court in *Endrew* (2017) ruled that a student's IEP must be reasonably calculated to enable him or her to make progress appropriate in light of his or her circumstances.

> Enhanced eText **Application Exercise 10.1.** *M.L. v. Federal Way School District* (2004).

FOR FURTHER INFORMATION

IEP Development

Bateman, B. D. (2007). *From gobbledygook to clearly written annual IEP goals.* Verona, WI: IEP Resources/Attainment.

Bateman, B. D. (2017). Individual education programs for children with disabilities. In J. M. Kauffman & D. P. Hallahan (Eds.), *Handbook of special education* (2nd ed.). (pp. 91–106). New York: Routledge.

Bateman, B. D., & Herr, C. M. (2003). *Writing measurable IEP goals and objectives.* Verona, WI: IEP Resources/Attainment.

Bateman, B. D., & Linden, M. (2012). *Better IEPs: How to develop legally correct and educationally useful programs* (5th ed.). Verona, WI: IEP Resources/Attainment.

Dragsow, E., Yell, M. L., & Robinson, T. R. (2001). Developing legally and educationally appropriate IEPs: Federal law and lessons learned from the Lovaas hearings and cases. *Remedial and Special Education, 22,* 359–373.

Lake, S. E. (2002). *IEP procedural errors: Lessons learned, mistakes to avoid.* Palm Beach Garden, FL: LRP Publications.

Lake, S. E. (2007). *Slippery slope! The IEP missteps every team must know— and how to avoid them.* Horsham, PA: LRP Publications.

Mager, R. F. (1997). *Preparing instructional objectives: A critical tool in the development of effective instruction* (3rd ed.). Atlanta, GA: The Center for Effective Performance. (This textbook was first published in 1962.)

Norlin, J. W. (2009). *What do I do when: The answer book on individualized education programs* (3rd ed.). Palm Beach Garden, FL: LRP Publications.

Yell, M.L., Katsiyannis, A., Ennis, R.P., & Losinski, M. (2013). Avoiding procedural errors in IEP development. *Teaching Exceptional Children, 46* (1), 56-64.

Yell, M.L., Katsiyannis, A., Ennis, R.P., Losinski, M., Christle, C. (2016). Avoiding substantive errors in IEP development. *Teaching Exceptional Children, 49* (1), 31-40.

Parental Participation

Turnbull, A. P., Turnbull, H. R., Taylor, R. A., Erwin, E. J., & Soodak, L. C. (2005). *Families, professionals and exceptionality: Positive outcomes through partnership and trust* (5th ed.). Upper Saddle River, NJ: Merrill/Pearson.

REFERENCES

Adams v. Hansen, 632 F. Supp. 858 (N.D. Cal. 1985).

Ahearn, E. (2006). Standards-based IEPs: Implementation in selected states. Alexandria, VA: Project Forum, National Association of State Directors of Special Edcation. Retrieved from www.projectforum.org/docs/Standards-BasedIEPs-ImplementationinSelectedStates.pdf

Alberto, P. A., & Troutman, A. C. (2012). *Applied behavior analysis for teachers* (9th ed.). Upper Saddle River, NJ: Merrill/Pearson.

Amanda J v. Clark County School District, 207 F.3d 877 (9th Cir. 2001).

Anchorage School District v. Parents of M.P., 45 IDELR 253 (9th Cir. 2006).

Antioch (CA) Unified School District, 110 LRP 49063 (OCR 2010).

Bateman, B. D. (2007). *From gobbledygook to clearly written annual IEP goals.* Verona, WI: Attainment/IEP Resources.

Bateman, B. D., & Herr, C. M. (2003). *Writing measurable IEP goals and objectives.* Verona, WI: Attainment/IEP Resources.

Bateman, B.D. (2011). Individualized Education programs for children with disabilities, in J.M. Kauffman & D.P. Hallahan (Eds.) *Handbook of special education* (pp. 91–90). Philadelphia, PA: Taylor & Francis/Routledge.

Bateman, B. D. & Linden, M. (1996). *Better IEPs: How to develop legally correct and educationally useful programs* (3rd ed.). Verona, WI: IEP Resources/Attainment.

Bateman, B. D., & Linden, M. (2012). *Better IEPs: How to develop legally correct and educationally useful program* (5th ed.). Verona, WI: IEP Resources/Attainment.

Big Beaver Falls Area School District v. Jackson, 624 A.2d 806 (Pa. Cmwlth 1993).

Board of Education of the Arlington Central School District, 42 IDELR 226 (SEA N.Y. 2004).

Board of Education of the Carmel School District, 43 IDELR 76 (SEA N.Y. 2005).

Board of Education of the Casadaga Valley Central School District, 20 IDELR 1023 (SEA 1994).

Board of Education of the City School District of the City of New York, 24 IDELR 199 (SEA, N.Y. 1996).

Board of Education of the Hendrick Hudson Central School District v. Rowley, 458 U.S. 176 (1982).

Board of Education of the Rhinebeck Central School District, 39 IDELR 148 (2003).

Board of Education of the St. Louis Central School District, 20 IDELR 938 (SEA 1993).

Board of Education of Wappingers Central School District, 42 IDELR 131 (SEA NY 2004).

Board of Education of the West Senaca Central School District, 104 LRP 256 (SEA NY 2004).

Board of Education of the Whitesboro Central School District, 21 IDELR 895 (SEA N.Y. 1994).

Bray v. Hobert City School Corporation, 19 IDELR 1101 (N.D. Ind. 1993).

Brimmer v. Traverse City, 872 F. Supp. 447 (W.D. Mich. 1994).

Burlington School District, 20 IDELR 1303 (SEA 1994).

Buser v. Corpus Christi Independent School District, 20 IDELR 981 (S.D. Tex. 1994).

C.H. v. Cape Henlopen School District, 54 IDELR 212 (3d Cir. 2010).

Carter v. Florence County School District Four, 950 F.2d 156 (4th Cir. 1991).

County School Board of Henrico County, Virginia v. R.T., 433 F. Supp. 2d 692 (E.D. Va. 2006).

Cranston School District v. Q.D., 51 IDELR 41 (D. R.I. 2008).

Crockett, J. B., & Yell, M. L. (2008). Without data all we have are assumptions: Revisiting the meaning of free appropriate public education. *Journal of Law and Education, 37,* 381–388.

DB v. District of Columbia, 720 F. Supp. 2d 83 (D.D.C. 2010).

D.D. v. New York City Board of Education, 46 IDELR 181 (2d Cir. 2006).

Davenport (IA) Community School District, 20 IDELR 1398 (OCR 1993).

Deal v. Hamilton County Board of Education, 392 F.3d 840 (6th Cir. 2004).

Deno, S. L. (1985). Curriculum-based measurement: The emerging alternative. *Exceptional Children, 52,* 219–232.

Deno, S. L. (1992). The nature and development of curriculum-measurement. *Preventing School Failure, 36,* 5–11.

District of Columbia Public Schools, 113 LRP 14159 (SEA D.C. 2012).

Doe v. Hampden-Wilbraham Regional School District, 54 IDELR 214 (D.C. Mass. 2010).

Doe v. Withers, 20 IDELR 442 (W. Va. Cir. Ct. 1993).

Doug C. v. State Department of Hawaii, 720 F.3d. 1038 (9th Cir. 2013).

Doyle v. Arlington County School Board, 806 F. Supp. 1253 (E.D. Va. 1992).

Endrew F. v. Douglas County School District, 580 U.S. __ (2017). Available online at https://www.supremecourt.gov/opinions/16pdf/15-827_0pm1.pdf

Escambia County Public School System v. Benton, 406 F. Supp. 2d 1248 (S.D Ala. 2005).

Etscheidt, S. K. (2006). Progress monitoring: Legal issues and recommendations for IEP teams. *Teaching Exceptional Children, 38*(3), 56–60.

Etscheidt, S. K. (2008). Issues in transition planning: Legal decisions. *Career Development and Transition for Exceptional Individuals, 29,* 28–47.

Etscheidt, S., & Curran, C. M. (2010). Peer-reviewed research and individualized education programs (IEPs): An examination of intent and impact. *Exceptionality, 18,* 138, 150.

Family Educational Rights and Privacy Act (FERPA), 20 U.S.C. § 1232 *et seq.*

Farmington Independent School District #192, 107 LRP 60675 (SEA Minn. 2007).

Fossey, R., Hosie, T., Soniat, K., & Zirkel, P. (1994). Section 504 and "front line" educators: An expanded obligation to serve children with disabilities. *Preventing School Failure, 39,* 10–14.

Gibson v. Forest Hills School District Board of Education, 61 IDELR 97 (S.D. Ohio 2013).

Girard School District, 18 IDELR 1048 (OCR 1992).

Hall v. Vance County Board of Education, 774 F.2d 629 (4th Cir. 1985).

H.B. v. Las Virgenes Unified School District, 48 IDELR 31 (9th Cir. 2007).

Hensley v. Colville School District, 51 IDELR 279 (Wash. Ct. App. 2009).

Honig v. Doe, 485 U.S. 305 (1988).

Horen v. Board of Education of the City of Toledo Public School District, 53 IDELR 79 (2012)

Huefner, D. S. (2000). The risks and opportunities of the UDEA requirements of IDEA 97. *Journal of Special Education, 33,* 195–204.

Huefner, D. S. & Herr, C. (2012). *Navigating special education law and policy.* Verona, WI: Attainment.

In re Child with Disabilities, 16 EHLR 538 (SEA Tenn. 1990).

In re Child with Disabilities, 20 IDELR 455 (1993).

In re student with a disability, 111 LRP 8947 (SEA Mont. 2011).

Individuals with Disabilities Education Act, 20 U.S.C. § 1401 *et seq.*

Individuals with Disabilities Education Act Regulations, 34 C.F.R. § 300.1 *et seq.*

Jacobs, M. (2013, March). The new seven deadly sins: Common legal errors that lead to litigation. Paper presented at the Spring Administrators Conference, Columbia, SC.

K.E. v. Independent School District No 15, F.3d 795 (8th Cir. 2011).

Karvonen, M. (2009). Developing standards-based IEPs. In M. Perie (Ed.) Considerations for alternative assessment based on modified achievement standards (AA-MAS): Understanding the eligible population and applying that knowledge to their instruction and assessment (pp. 51–89). New York: New York Comprehensive Center & New York Department of Education

Katsiyannis, A., Yell, M. L., & Bradley, R. (2001). Reflections on the 25th anniversary of the Individuals with Disabilities Education Act. *Remedial and Special Education, 22*, 324–334.

Kirby v. Cabell County Board of Education, 46 IDELR 156 (S.D. W.Va. 2006).

L.I. v. State of Hawaii Department of Education, 58 IDELR 8 (D. Haw. 2011).

Lake, S. E. (2002). *IEP procedural errors: Lessons learned, mistakes to avoid.* Horsham, PA: LRP Publications.

Lake, S. E. (2007). *Slippery slope: The IEP missteps every team must know— and how to avoid them.* Horsham, PA: LRP Publications.

Letter to Boney, 18 IDELR 537 (OSEP 1991).

Letter to Breecher, 17 EHLR 56 (OSEP 1990).

Letter to Cormany, 34 IDELR 9 (OSEP 2000).

Letter to Davilia, 18 IDELR 1036 (OSERS 1992).

Letter to Helmuth, 16 EHLR 503 (OSEP 1990).

Letter to Perryman, EHLR 211 438 (OSEP 1987).

Letter to Rangel-Diaz, 58 IDELR 78 (OSEP 2011).

Liberty Union High School District, 117 LRP 28201 (SEA CA 2017).

Lombardo, L. (1999). *IEPs and the IDEA: What you need to know.* Horsham, PA: LRP Publications.

Martin, J. L. (2014, November). *Strategies and legal issues in implementing IEPs in compliance with the IDEA.* Paper presented at the annual Tri-State Regional Special Education Law Conference: Omaha, NE.

Mager, R. F. (1962). *Preparing instructional objectives.* Palo Alto, CA: Fearon Publishers.

Martin, R. (1996). Litigation over the IEP. In *Proceedings of the 16th National Institute on Legal Issues in Educating Individuals with Disabilities.* Alexandria, VA: LRP Publications.

M.C. v. Antelope Valley Union High School District, (9th Cir. 2017). Available online at http://cdn.ca9.uscourts.gov/datastore/opinions/2017/03/27/14-56344.pdf

Mehfoud, K. S. (2013, November). Efficient and legal IEP meetings. Presentation at the Annual Tri-state Regional Special Education Law Conference. Omaha, NE.

Michael D.M. v. Pemi-Baker Regional School District 41 IDELR 267 (D.C. N.H. 2004).

M.L. v. Federal Way School District, 387 F.3d. 1101 (9th Cir. 2004).

M.M. v. School District of Greenville County, 37 IDELR 183 (4th Cir. 2002).

Myles S. v. Montgomery County Board of Education, 20 IDELR 237 (M.D. Ala. 1993).

New Haven Board of Education, 20 IDELR 42 (SEA 1993).

New York City School District Board of Education, 19 IDELR 169 (SEA N.Y. 1992).

Norlin, J. W. (2009). *What do I do when: The answer book on individualized education programs* (3rd ed.). Palm Beach Garden, FL: LRP Publications.

Norlin, J. W. (2010). *Postsecondary transition services: An IDEA compliance guide for IEP teams.* Palm Beach Garden, FL: LRP Publications.

Norlin, J. W. (2014). *What do I do when . . . The answer book on special education law* (5th ed.). Palm Beach Garden, FL: LRP Publications.

OSEP Policy Letter, 18 IDELR 530 (OSEP 1991a).

OSEP Policy Letter, 18 IDELR 627 (OSEP 1991b).

OSEP Policy Letter, 18 IDELR 969 (OSEP 1991c).

OSEP Policy Letter, 18 IDELR 1303 (OSEP 1992).

OSEP Policy Letter, 20 IDELR 541 (OSEP 1993).

Philadelphia City School District, 46 IDELR 206 (SEA Pa. 2006).

Pierce v. Mason City School District Board of Education, 48 IDELR 7 (S.D. Ohio 2007).

Pitasky, V. M. (2002). *What do I do when . . . The answer book on placement under the IDEA and Section 504.* Horsham, PA: LRP Publications.

Pocatello School District #25, 18 IDELR 83 (SEA Idaho 1991).

Prince, A. M. T., Plotner, A. J., & Yell, M. L. (2014). Legal update on postsecondary transition. *Journal of Disability Policy Studies, 25*, 41–47.

R.B. v. Napa Valley Unified School District, 48 IDELR 60 (9th Cir. 2007).

Ridley School District v. M.R. and J.R., 680 F.3d 260 (3d Cir. 2012).

Rio Rancho Public Schools, 40 IDELR 140 (SEA N.M. 2003).

S.B. v. Pomona Unified School District, 50 IDELR 72 (C.D. CA 2008).

School Administrative Unit #66, 20 IDELR 471 (1993).

Section 504 of the Rehabilitation Act Regulations, 34 C.F.R. § 104.33(b)(2).

Senate Report of the Individuals with Disabilities Act Amendments of 1997. Available online at http://wais.access.gpo.gov.

S.H. v. Plano Independent School District, 59 IDELR 183 (5th Cir. 2012).

Shapiro v. Paradise Valley Unified School District No. 69, 38 IDELR 91 (9th Cir. 2003).

Sharon Watson v. Campbell Independent School District, Dkt. No. 239-R1-897 (Commissioner Decision, Sept. 1997).

Shriner, J.G., Carty, S. Goldstone, L. & Thurlow, M.L. (2017). Teacher perspectives on the impact of standards and professional development on individualized education programs. *Journal of Special Education Leadership, 30* (2), 67–81.

Shriner, J. G., Plotner, A., & Rose, C. A. (2010). Development of Individual Education Programs for students with emotional or behavioral disorders: Coordination with transition plans. In D. Cheney (Ed.). *Transition of secondary students with emotional or behavioral disorders: Current approaches for positive outcomes,* 2nd ed.) (pp. 171–214), Champaign, IL: Research Press.

Simi Valley Unified School District, 44 IDELR 106 (SEA Cal. 2005).

Smith, S. W. (1990). Individualized education programs (IEPs) in special education—from intent to acquiescence. *Exceptional Children, 57*, 6–14.

Sanberry, K. (2015). *Standards-based IEPs: What you need to know.* Retrieved 03/11/2016 from https://www.understood.org/en/school-learning/special-services/ieps/standards-based-ieps-what-you-need-to-know.

Tatgenhorst, A., Norlin, J. W., & Gorn, S. (2014). *What do I do when: The answer book on special education law* (6th ed.). Palm Beach Garden, FL: LRP Publications.

Thorndock v. Boise Independent School District, 767 P.2d 1241 (1988).

U.S. Department of Education, 71, Federal Register 4666, 2006.

U.S. Department of Education, Office of Special Education and Rehabilitative Services, (2015) Dear colleague letter on IEPs and state academic content standards. Retrieved 03/11/2016 from www2.ed.gov/policy/speced/guid/idea/memosdcltrs/guidance-on-fape-11-17-2015.pdf.

U.S. Department of Education, Office of Special Education and Rehabilitative Services, (2016) Dear colleague letter on PBIS in IEPs.

Retrieved 03/11/2016 from https://www2.ed.gov/policy/gen/guid/school-discipline/files/dcl-on-pbis-in-ieps--08-01-2016.pdf.

U.S. Department of Education, Office of Special Education and Rehabilitative Services (2017). *Questions and answers (Q&A) on U.S. Supreme Court Decision Endrew F. v. Douglas County School District Re-1.* Retrieved from www2.ed.gov/policy/speced/guid/idea/memosdcltrs/qa-endrewcase-12-07-2017.pdf on December, 7, 2017.

Utica County Schools, 113 LRP 7453 (S.E. Mich. 01/29/2013).

Vestavia Hills County Board of Education, 51 IDELR 59 (SEA Ala. 2008).

W. G. v. Board of Trustees of Target Range School District No. 23, 960 F.2d 1479 (9th Cir. 1992).

Walsh, J. (2013, November). General education teachers and special education. Paper Presented to the Tri-State Regional Special Education Law Conference. Omaha, NE.

Weatherly, J., & Yell, M.L. (2017). *Endrew F. v. Douglas County School District* (2017). Webinar retrieved at http://pubs.cec.sped.org/webscotus20172/.

Weber, M. C. (2002). *Special education law and litigation treatise.* Palm Beach Garden, FL: LRP Publications.

Wilson v. District of Columbia, 56 IDELR 125 (D.D.C. 2011).

Winkleman v. Parma City School District, 550 U.S. 516 (2007).

Woods v. Northport Public Schools, 112 LRP 5878 (W.D. Mich. 2012).

Yankton School District v. Schramm, 900 F. Supp. 1182 (D.S.D. 1995).

Yell, M.L. & Bateman, D.F. (2017). *Endrew F. v. Douglas County School District* (2017): Free appropriate public education and the U.S. Supreme Court. *Teaching Exceptional Children, 50*, 1–9.

Yell, M. L., Conroy, T., Katsiyannis, A., & Conroy, T. (2013. Individualized education programs (IEPs) and special education

programming for students with disabilities in urban schools. *Fordham Urban Law Review, 41*, 669–684.

Yell, M. L., & Drasgow, E. (2000). Litigating a free appropriate public education: The Lovaas hearings and cases. *Journal of Special Education, 33*, 206–215.

Yell, M. L., Drasgow, E., Bradley, R., & Justesen, T. (2004). Critical legal issues in special education. In A. McCray Sorrells, H. J. Reith, & P. T. Sindelar (Eds.), *Issues in special education* (pp. 16–37). Boston: Allyn & Bacon.

Yell, M. L., Katsiyannis, A., Ennis, R. P., & Losinski, M. (2013). Avoiding procedural errors in IEP development. *Focus on Exceptional Children, 46*(1), 56–66.

Yell, M.L., Katsiyannis, A., Ennis, R. P., Losinski, M., & Christle, C. A. (2016). Avoiding substantive errors in IEP development. *Teaching Exceptional Children, 49* (1), 31–40.

Yell, M. L., Meadows, N., Drasgow, E., & Shriner, J. G. (2013). *Evidence-based practices in educating students with emotional and behavioral disorders* (2nd ed.). Upper Saddle River, NJ: Pearson/Merrill Education.

Yell, M. L. & Rozalski, M. E. (2013). The peer-reviewed research requirement of the IDEA: An examination of law and policy. In B. G. Cook, M. Tankersley, & T. J. Landrum (Eds.), *Evidence-based practices* (pp. 1–26). London: Emerald.

Yell, M. L., Shriner, J.G., Thomas, S. S., & Katsiyannis, A. (2017). Special education law for leaders and administrators of special education. In J. Crockett, M. L. Boscardin, & B. Billingsley (Eds.) *Special Education Leadership Handbook*. Philadelphia, PA: Routledge.

Chapter

11

Placing Students in the Least Restrictive Environment

We are concerned that children with handicapping conditions be educated in the most normal possible and least restrictive setting, for how else will they adapt to the world beyond the educational environment, and how else will the nonhandicapped adapt to them?

SENATOR ROBERT T. STAFFORD, *CONGRESSIONAL RECORD*, MAY 20, 1974

LEARNER OBJECTIVES

At the end of the chapter, students will be able to

11.1 Describe the least restrictive environment mandate of the IDEA.

11.2 Describe the differences among the concepts of least restrictive environment, mainstreaming, and inclusion.

11.3 Describe the continuum of alternative placement and how school district personnel are to use the continuum.

11.4 Describe relevant considerations that team members should address when determining a student's placement in the least restrictive environment.

11.5 Describe the decisions in major cases that have addressed the least restrictive environment mandate.

11.6 Describe the model for determining a student's least restrictive environment.

Justice Potter Stewart, writing for the U.S. Supreme Court in *Sheldon v. Tucker* (1960), stated that in a

> series of decisions this court has held, even though a governmental purpose be legitimate and substantial, that purpose cannot be pursued by means that broadly stifle fundamental personal liberties when the end can be more narrowly achieved. The breadth of legislative abridgment must be viewed in the light of less drastic means for achieving the same purpose.

(p. 482)

Although this decision did not involve the education of students with disabilities, the Court set forth the following principle that has had a profound effect on special education: that persons have a right to be free of unnecessary restrictions when the government undertakes actions that have consequences for those individuals, even though the actions are legitimate.

In 1954, the U.S. Supreme Court, in *Brown v. Board of Education,* declared that the practice of segregation could not be used in public education. Again, although the decision did not involve the education of students with disabilities, advocates argued that the principles in *Brown* were true for all persons, including those with disabilities. In *Hairston v. Drosick*

(1976) the principles developed in *Brown* were used by the Court in a case involving the education of a child with spina bifida. The judge in the case wrote:

> A child's chance in this society is through the educational process. A major goal of this educational process is the socialization process that takes place in the regular classroom, with the resulting capability to interact in a social way with one's peers. It is, therefore, imperative that every child receive an education with his or her peers insofar as it is at all possible.

(p. 184)

Unfortunately, these types of interactions were seldom the case with students who had disabilities. In the 1950s and 1960s when students with disabilities did receive an education in public schools, the programs in which they were educated often consisted of substandard services with limited or non-existent supplies; classes were held in poor facilities, delivered by inadequately trained teachers (Martin, 2013), and often took place in segregated settings in which students had little or no contact with their peers who did not have disabilities (Winzer, 1993). Two pioneers in special education, Dr. Maynard Reynolds and Dr. Evelyn Deno from the University of Minnesota, however, believed that students with disabilities should be educated alongside their nondisabled peers whenever appropriate (Yell & Christle, 2017). In two seminal articles published in 1962 by Reynolds and 1970 by Deno, these authors developed models to help ensure that students with disabilities were integrated systematically into normal classroom settings when appropriate. According to Reynolds, the normal school life of all students with disabilities should be preserved and that when special placements were needed to provide a suitable environment "it should be no more special than necessary" (p. 369). Reynolds also warned, however, that to delay or deny special education services to a student who needed such services would be inexcusable. Deno proposed what she termed a "cascade system of special education services" (p. 235), which was an organizational structure for making decisions about the placement and special education service delivery to students with disabilities. She depicted the cascade using a tapered design to indicate the difference in the number of children who would be served at each level, with the majority of students served in the regular classroom and the fewest students served in the homebound and hospital settings. Deno conceived the purpose of the cascade model, as making available whatever setting was required to provide appropriate learning experiences to students in as close to a normal setting as possible. These two influential articles were to provide the basis of what was to become the continuum of alternative placements model.

On May 20, 1974, Senator Robert Stafford of Vermont introduced an amendment to the Education of the Handicapped Act of 1974 intended to prevent the educational segregation of students with disabilities. The amendment required that school districts ensure that a student's placement be in the least restrictive appropriate educational setting (Stafford, 1978). This amendment was later incorporated into the Education for All Handicapped Children Act (EAHCA) in what has become known as the least restrictive environment (LRE) mandate.

The LRE mandate has been the subject of considerable controversy and debate. The controversy is not a recent occurrence. In fact, according to Martin (2013) in an early Congressional hearing regarding what was commonly referred to as "mainstreaming," Dr. Donald Bigelow, then the training program director in the Office of Education, testified about the importance of using funds appropriated for special education to promote mainstreaming. The chair of the subcommittee that was holding the hearing, Representative Hugh L. Carey from New York, however, worried about the possible misuse of funds and specifically about students with disabilities drowning in the mainstream.

The purpose of this chapter is to examine the issue of placing students with disabilities in least restrictive settings. In this chapter I: (a) review the legislative basis of the LRE mandate, (b) explain the major cases that have interpreted LRE, and (c) propose a model for determining the LRE for students with disabilities.

LRE, MAINSTREAMING, AND INCLUSION

The terms *least restrictive environment, inclusion,* and *mainstreaming* are often used interchangeably. They are not, however, synonymous concepts. According to Rozalski, Stewart, and Miller (2010), *inclusion,* or full inclusion, is a general philosophical stance that sometimes is adopted by schools as practice. It is simply the idea that all students with disabilities will spend the majority or all of their time in the general educational environment. Similarly, *mainstreaming* is a somewhat dated term that also refers to a philosophy of educating students with disabilities in settings with nondisabled students. *Least restrictive environment* refers to the mandate within the Individuals with Disabilities Education Act (IDEA) that students with disabilities should be educated to the maximum extent appropriate with their peers who do not have disabilities. The LRE mandate ensures that schools educate students with disabilities in integrated settings, alongside students without disabilities, to the maximum extent appropriate. Least restrictive environment is not a particular setting. Moreover, LRE does not mandate either inclusion or mainstreaming (Bateman & Linden, 2012). The Mountain Plains Regional Resource Center at Utah State University prepared this primer on LRE: http://files.eric.ed.gov/fulltext/ED498472.pdf.

Champagne (1993) defined restrictiveness as "a gauge of the degree of opportunity a person has for proximity to, and communication with, the ordinary flow of persons in our society" (p. 5). In special education, this means that a student with disabilities has the right to be educated with students in the general education environment. The general education environment is considered the least restrictive setting because it is the placement in which there is the greatest measure of opportunity for proximity and communication with the "ordinary flow" of students in schools.

From this perspective, the less a placement resembles the general education environment, the more restrictive it is considered (Tatgenhorst, Norlin, & Gorn, 2014). Specifically, a student with disabilities has the right to be educated in a setting that is not overly restrictive considering what is appropriate for that student. Appropriateness entails an education that will provide meaningful benefit for a student. When the educational program is appropriate, a student with disabilities should be placed in the general education environment, or as close to it as is feasible, so long as the appropriate program can be provided in that setting.

Although placement in the general education classroom may be the LRE for some students with disabilities, it is not required in all cases. The IDEA requires mainstreaming or inclusion when the general education classroom setting can provide an appropriate education. The U.S. Court of Appeals for the Fourth Circuit in *Carter v. Florence County School District Four* (1991) expressed this view:

> Under the IDEA, mainstreaming is a policy to be pursued so long as it is consistent with the Act's primary goal of providing disabled students with an appropriate education. Where necessary for educational reasons, mainstreaming assumes a subordinate role in formulating an educational program.

(p. 156)

The LRE Mandate

The IDEA requires that, when appropriate, students with disabilities be educated in settings with children without disabilities. The law provides that,

> to the maximum extent appropriate, children with disabilities, including children in public or private institutions or other care facilities, are educated with children who are not disabled, and that special classes, separate schooling, or other removal of children with disabilities from the regular educational environment occurs only when the nature or

severity of the disability is such that education in regular classes with the use of supplementary aids and services cannot be achieved satisfactorily.

(IDEA, 20 U.S.C. § 1412(a)(5)(A))

There are two parts to the LRE requirement of the IDEA. The first addresses the presumptive right of all students with disabilities to be educated with students without disabilities. Schools must make good-faith efforts to place and maintain students in less restrictive settings. This presumptive right, however, is rebuttable; that is, the principle sets forth a general rule of conduct (i.e., integration) but allows it to be rebutted when integration is not appropriate for a student (Turnbull, Stowe, & Huerta, 2007). The IDEA favors integration, but recognizes that for some students more restrictive or segregated settings may be appropriate. Clearly, the law anticipates that placements in more restrictive settings may sometimes be necessary to provide an appropriate education.

To ensure that schools make good-faith efforts to educate students in less restrictive settings, the LRE mandate also requires that before students with disabilities are placed in more restrictive settings, efforts must first be made to maintain a student in less restrictive settings with the use of supplementary aids and services. It is only when an appropriate education cannot be provided, even with supplementary aids and services, that students with disabilities may be placed in more restrictive settings. Supplementary aids and services may include assistive technology devices or services, behavioral interventions, teaching adaptations, personnel training, a teacher's aide, or resource rooms.

The IDEA further requires that state education agencies ensure that the LRE requirement extends to students in public schools, private schools, and other care facilities. States are required to ensure that teachers and administrators in all public schools are fully informed about the requirements of the LRE provision and are provided with the technical assistance and training necessary to assist them in this effort.

Enhanced eText **Video Example 11.1**
To view a brief **video** on LRE by Yservideos go to:
www.youtube.com/watch?v=I7HFRF8y288

Continuum of Alternative Placements

Senator Stafford (1978), an original sponsor of the IDEA, wrote that Congress included the LRE principle in the law in recognition that for some students an education in the general education classroom would not be appropriate. For these students, placements in more restrictive settings would be required to provide an appropriate education. The U.S. Supreme Court, in *Board of Education of the Hendrick Hudson School District v. Rowley* (1982), interpreted congressional intent similarly:

> Despite this preference for "mainstreaming" handicapped children—educating them with nonhandicapped children—Congress recognized that regular education simply would not be a suitable setting for the education of many handicapped children ... the act thus provides for the education of some handicapped children in separate classes or institutional settings.

(p. 192)

The Office of Special Education and Rehabilitation Services (OSERS) of the U.S. Department of Education also recognized "that some children with disabilities may require placement in settings other than the general education classroom in order to be provided with an education designed to address their unique needs" (*Letter to Goodling*, 1991, p. 214).

To ensure that students with disabilities are educated in the LRE that is most appropriate for their individual needs, the IDEA requires that school districts have a range or continuum of alternative placement options to meet their needs. The continuum represents an entire spectrum of placements where a student's special education program can be implemented. Regulations require that

A. Each [school district] shall ensure that a continuum of alternative placements is available to meet the needs of children with disabilities for special education and related services

B. The continuum required ... must:

    (1) Include the alternative placements ... (instruction in regular classes, special classes, special schools, home instruction, and instruction in hospitals and institutions); and

    (2) Make provision for supplementary services (such as resource room or itinerant instruction) to be provided in conjunction with regular class placement.

(IDEA Regulations, 34 C.F.R. § 300.115(a–b))

The purpose of the continuum is to allow school personnel to choose from a number of options in determining the LRE most appropriate for the student. OSERS has emphasized the importance of school districts' maintaining a continuum of placements "in order to be properly prepared to address the individual needs of all children with disabilities" (*Letter to Frost,* 1991, p. 594). If the local school district is unable to provide the appropriate placement, the state may bear the responsibility of ensuring the establishment and availability of a continuum of alternative placements (*Cordero v. Pennsylvania,* 1993). Figure 11.1 shows the continuum of placements (IDEA Regulations, 34 C.F.R. § 300.115(b)(1)).

A school district may not refuse to place a child in an LRE because it lacks the appropriate placement option (Tatgenhorst et al., 2014). Moreover, if gaps in the continuum exist within a school district, the district must fill them through whatever means are required (e.g., consortium-type arrangements). This does not mean that each school district must provide for a complete continuum within its own boundaries. When the educational needs of a student cannot be met in district programs, however, the district is obligated to provide a placement where the student's needs can be met. The regulations implementing the IDEA require that the various alternative placements in the continuum of placements are to be available to the extent necessary to implement the individualized education program (IEP). This may necessitate the district's sending the student to another school (public or private) that provides the needed placement. In such cases, the neighborhood school district retains financial responsibility for the student's education.

FIGURE 11.1 ■ **Continuum of Placements**

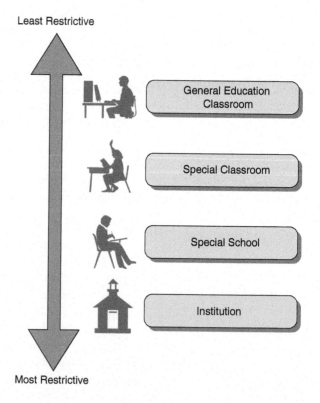

Least Restrictive

General Education Classroom

Special Classroom

Special School

Institution

Most Restrictive

The IEP team determines the placement along this continuum that is the least restrictive setting in which a student will receive an appropriate education. Restrictiveness is defined, for purposes of the continuum, by proximity to the general education classroom. Education in the general education classroom is the preferred option so long as it is consistent with an appropriate education. If a student cannot receive a meaningful education in the general education classroom, another placement, in which the student will receive a meaningful education, is required.

CONSIDERATIONS IN EDUCATIONAL PLACEMENTS

Determining a Student's Placement

A team of qualified individuals and a student's parents and other persons who are knowledgeable about a student, the meaning of the evaluation data, and the placement options is the group that determines a student's placement (IDEA Regulations, 34 C.F.R. § 300.116[a][1]). Although this team is often also a student's IEP team, it does not need to be (Bateman, 2017) as long as the IEP team is properly constituted (IDEA Regulations, Appendix A to Part 300, Notice of Interpretation, Question No. 37, 1999). The team is responsible for determining the placement along the continuum that is the least restrictive setting in which a student will receive an appropriate education. Moreover, the team must make the placement decision at least annually (IDEA Regulations, 34 C.F.R. § 300.116[b][1]).

According to Yell and Christle (2017), there are three major placement errors that IEP teams need to avoid. First, placement decisions should not be based solely on factors that are unrelated to a student's actual needs. Examples of such factors include determining a student's placement based on a student's category of disability, the severity of a student's disability, the availability of services, or administrative convenience. Second, a student's placement must not be predetermined. Predetermination of placement occurs when an IEP team decides on a student's placement prior to the actual IEP meeting (Yell, Katsiyannis, Ennis, & Losinski, 2013). This does not mean that the IEP team members cannot come to the meeting with opinions and even a draft IEP, but that a final placement decision cannot be made until the parents are present and are meaningfully involved in the decision. Thus, a student's IEP team must be open and willing to consider parental concerns and thoughts throughout the placement discussion. Third, an IEP team should not determine a student's placement prior to developing his or her IEP. The federal regulations to the IDEA require that a student's placement "must be based on the child's IEP" (IDEA Regulations, 34 C.F.R. § 300.116[b]). Tatgenhorst, et al. (2014) referred to the team determining a student's placement prior to writing his or her IEP as "Shoehorning."

Placement in the Neighborhood School

Unless the IEP requires otherwise, students with disabilities should be educated in the school they would attend if they were not in special education (IDEA Regulations, 34 C.F.R. § 300.116(b)(3)). Moreover, the IDEA requires that if special education students cannot be placed in the neighborhood school, they must be placed as close to home as possible (IDEA Regulations, 34 C.F.R. § 300.116(b)(3)). Placement in the neighborhood school, however, is not an absolute right. The IEP team determines what constitutes an appropriate education for a student. If an appropriate education cannot be provided in the neighborhood school, the IEP team may choose a placement in a school that will provide an appropriate education.

The goal of educating a student with disabilities in the neighborhood school must be balanced with the requirement that a student's education be appropriate and individualized (Huefner & Herr, 2012). Courts have repeatedly held that the IDEA does not guarantee special education services in a student's neighborhood school (*Barnett v. Fairfax County School*

Board, 1991; *Flour Bluff Independent School District v. Katherine M.,* 1996; *Hudson v. Bloomfield Hills School District,* 1995; *Lachman v. Illinois Board of Education,* 1988; *Murray v. Montrose County School District,* 1995; *Schuldt v. Mankato ISD,* 1991). Thus, the IDEA contains a preference in favor of education in the neighborhood school, but it is not an absolute right.

In *Schuldt v. Mankato ISD* (1991), the U.S. Court of Appeals for the Eighth Circuit ruled that a school district did not have to make the neighborhood school wheelchair-accessible for a student with spina bifida, since an elementary school only a few miles away was fully accessible. The court found that

> the school district satisfied its obligation under [IDEA] to provide [a student with disabilities] with a fully integrated public education by busing ... the child to a nearby school, and therefore, did not violate the Act by refusing to modify the neighborhood elementary school nearest to the child's home to make it accessible.

(p. 1357)

If the neighborhood school cannot provide a free appropriate public education (FAPE), the school is not required to place a student with disabilities in that school. Schools retain the right to determine how to use their resources in the most efficient manner. If district administrators choose to concentrate resources at particular schools for particular needs and disabilities, it is allowed by the IDEA.

In *Flour Bluff Independent School District v. Katherine M.* (1996), the U.S. Court of Appeals for the Fifth Circuit, ruled that the IDEA indicates a preference for placement in the neighborhood school but that this is not a mandate. Furthermore, the court indicated that proximity is only one factor of many that the IEP team must consider in determining placement.

In *Murray v. Montrose County School District* (1995), the U.S. Court of Appeals for the Tenth Circuit held that although the IDEA gives a preference to education in the neighborhood school, the IDEA does not guarantee it. Similarly, in *Urban v. Jefferson County School District R-1* (1994), the Tenth Circuit Court reaffirmed this principle and extended it to Section 504 and the Americans with Disabilities Act (ADA) as well as the IDEA.

Nonacademic Programming

Both the IDEA and Section 504 extend LRE requirements to nonacademic settings. Regulations implementing the IDEA extend the LRE requirements to areas such as extracurricular services, meals, recess periods, counseling services, athletics, transportation, health services, recreational activities, and special interest groups or clubs sponsored by the school (IDEA Regulations, 34 C.F.R. § 300.306(a)). Additionally, if a student requires a restrictive placement to receive an appropriate education, but will not have contact with students without disabilities in that placement, the LRE requirement extends to other settings and situations in which students with and without disabilities can be integrated. Recess periods, physical education classes, or student meal times might be used to provide for the necessary integrated experiences.

Section 504 also extends the LRE requirement to nonacademic settings, including extracurricular activities:

> In providing or arranging for the provision of nonacademic and extracurricular services and activities ... a [school] shall ensure that handicapped persons participate with nonhandicapped persons in such activities and services to the maximum extent appropriate to the needs of the handicapped person.

(Section 504 Regulations 34 C.F.R. § 104.34[b])

Nonacademic settings include activities such as counseling services, physical recreational athletics, transportation, health services, recreational activities, special interest groups, school-sponsored clubs, and employment by a school (Section 504 Regulations, 34 C.F.R. § 104.37(a)(2)).

The Interests of Peers Without Disabilities

The IDEA indicates that a legitimate consideration in determining the LRE for a student with disabilities is the needs of the student's peers. An analysis of the federal regulations in Section 504 contains language regarding the interests of a student's peers:

> where a [student with disabilities] is so disruptive in a regular classroom that the education of other students is significantly impaired, the needs of the [student with disabilities] cannot be met in that environment. Therefore regular placement would not be appropriate to his or her needs.
>
> (Section 504 Regulations, 34 C.F.R. § 104 Appendix A, Paragraph 24)

The IDEA includes identical language in a comment to the LRE regulations (IDEA Regulations, comment following 34 C.F.R. § 300.552):

> [I]f a child with a disability has behavioral problems that are so disruptive in a regular classroom that the education of other children is significantly impaired, the needs of the child with a disability generally cannot be met in that environment. However, before making such a determination, LEAs must ensure that consideration has been given to the full range of supplementary aids and services that could be provided to the child in the regular educational environment to accommodate the unique needs of the child with a disability.
>
> (Fed. Reg., Comments to 34 C.F.R. § 300.116 at 46,589)

The purpose of the comment is to provide guidance with respect to determining proper placement of the student with disabilities when the student is so disruptive that the education of other students is affected.

If the student has a health condition that poses an actual risk of contagion to other students, the student may be placed in a setting in which the risk is minimized. Such a placement would not violate the LRE mandate of either the IDEA or Section 504 (Zirkel, 2014).

JUDICIAL STANDARDS OF REVIEW

Few areas in special education law have been the subject of more debate and controversy than the LRE mandate. Disagreements between parents and schools over LRE have led to a considerable amount of litigation. A number of these cases have made their way to the U.S. Courts of Appeals, but thus far the U.S. Supreme Court has not accepted a case interpreting the LRE mandate. Because the High Court has not heard an LRE case, the LRE interpretations by the circuit courts are the highest authority available. These decisions are important because lower courts and hearing officers in a circuit court's jurisdiction will follow the guidance of the circuit court. Additionally, IEP teams should follow these rulings when making placement decisions.

The results of these cases have been mixed, with some decisions favoring inclusive placements and others restrictive placements. The decisions of the circuit courts with respect to the proper standard of review to be used in determining a district's compliance with the LRE mandate, however, show consistency. There are four primary tests or standards that circuit courts have developed. These tests have been developed in other circuits. The following sections will examine these cases and the methods they have adopted for determining a school district's compliance with the mainstreaming requirement.

The Roncker Test (Sixth and Eighth Circuits)

One of the earliest LRE decisions was *Roncker v. Walter* (1983; hereafter *Roncker*). The decision is controlling authority in the Sixth Circuit, which covers the states of Kentucky, Ohio, Michigan, and Tennessee.

The case involved Neill Roncker, a nine-year-old classified as having moderate intellectual disabilities. School personnel believed that the most appropriate placement for Neill was in a special school for children with disabilities. The parents objected, stating that their child would benefit from contact with his peers in a general education setting, and brought suit against the school district challenging the placement. The issue did not involve Neill's placement in a general education classroom; both sides agreed that he required special education. The Ronckers contended, however, that Neill could be provided the special education services in a setting that would allow greater integration and contact with students without disabilities.

The U.S. District Court for the Southern District of Ohio ruled in favor of the school district. The court stated that the mainstreaming requirement allowed schools' broad discretion in the placement of students with disabilities. The court, finding that Neill had not made significant progress while in an integrated setting, ruled that the school district had acted properly in determining Neill's placement.

The Ronckers appealed to the U.S. Court of Appeals for the Sixth District. The circuit court reversed the decision of the district court, stating that

> the act (PL 94-142) does not require mainstreaming in every case but its requirement that mainstreaming be provided to the maximum extent appropriate indicates a very strong congressional preference.

(p. 1063)

Although the court noted the importance of balancing the benefits of segregated special education services against the benefits of mainstreaming, the *Roncker* decision is best known for what has been referred to as the *Roncker* portability test (Huefner & Herr, 2012):

> In a case where the segregated facility is considered superior, the court should determine whether the services which make that placement superior could feasibly be provided in a nonsegregated setting. If they can, the placement in the segregated school would be inappropriate under the Act.

(*Roncker*, p. 1063)

Courts using this test must determine if the services that make the segregated setting more appropriate can be transported to the nonsegregated setting. If the services can be transported, those modifications are required by the LRE mandate. (See Figure 11.2 for the *Roncker* test.)

The U.S. Court of Appeals for the Eighth Circuit adopted the Sixth Circuit court's *Roncker* portability standard in *A. W. v. Northwest R-1 School District* (1987). The U.S. Court of Appeals for the Eight Circuit has appellate jurisdiction over the following states: Arkansas, Iowa, Minnesota, Missouri, Nebraska, North Dakota, and South Dakota. The case involved A.W., a young student with severe intellectual disabilities, who had been placed in a state school for students with disabilities. His parents wanted A.W. to receive his education at his home elementary school, House Springs Elementary School located in the Northwest R-1 School District in Missouri. The federal district court found that A.W. would benefit only minimally from education at House Springs Elementary School and concluded that the LRE requirements of the IDEA (then the Education for all Handicapped Children Act) did not require placement in the mainstream classroom. The parents, believing that the district court had misinterpreted the law's mainstreaming provisions, appealed the decision.

FIGURE 11.2 ■ The *Roncker* Portability Test

1) Can the educational services that make a segregated placement superior be feasibly provided in an unsegregated setting?

2) If so, the placement in the segregated setting is inappropriate.

The Eighth Circuit court recognized that the law revealed a strong congressional preference for mainstreaming but that Congress also recognized that the regular classroom might not be a suitable setting for the education of many students with disabilities. The district court had analyzed the school district's program using the two-part *Rowley* test and turned to the Sixth Circuit court's *Roncker* test to analyze the issue of mainstreaming. The Eighth Circuit court upheld the ruling of the district court and added, "We believe that the Sixth Circuit in *Roncker* correctly interpreted the Act's mainstreaming provision" (p. 160).

The Daniel *Test (Second, Third, Fifth, Tenth, and Eleventh Circuits)*

Perhaps the seminal case regarding the LRE mandate came from the U.S. Court of Appeals for the Fifth Circuit in *Daniel R.R. v. State Board of Education* (1989; hereafter *Daniel*). The Fifth Circuit is the controlling authority on LRE in the states Louisiana, Mississippi, and Texas.

The plaintiff in the case, Daniel, was a six-year-old child with Down syndrome enrolled in the El Paso, Texas, Independent School District. At his parents' request, Daniel was placed in a prekindergarten class for half of the school day and an early childhood special education class for the other half. Shortly after the beginning of the school year, Daniel's teacher informed the school placement committee that Daniel was not participating in class and was failing to master any of the skills taught, even with almost-constant attention and instruction from the teacher and aide. The committee met and decided that the prekindergarten class was inappropriate for Daniel. Daniel was removed from the prekindergarten class, attended only the early childhood special education class, and interacted with children from the prekindergarten class at recess and lunch. The parents exercised their right to a due process hearing. The hearing officer agreed with the school in concluding that Daniel could not participate in the prekindergarten class without almost-constant supervision from the teacher, that he was receiving little educational benefit, and that he was disrupting the class because his needs absorbed most of the teacher's time. The officer also noted that the teacher would have to modify the curriculum totally to meet Daniel's needs. The parents filed an action in the district court and, eventually, the circuit court.

The circuit court found that the imprecise nature of the IDEA's mandates was deliberate and that Congress had chosen to leave the selection of educational policy and methods in the hands of local school officials. However, Congress had created a statutory preference for mainstreaming while at the same time creating a tension between the appropriate education and mainstreaming provisions of the act. By creating this tension, Congress recognized that the general education environment would not be suitable for all students with disabilities and, at times, a special setting or school may be necessary to provide an appropriate education. Essentially, the *Daniel* court said that when the provisions of FAPE and mainstreaming are in conflict, the mainstreaming mandate becomes secondary to the appropriate education mandate.

The *Daniel* court declined to follow the Sixth Circuit's analysis in *Roncker*, stating that the *Roncker* test necessitated "too intrusive an inquiry into educational policy choices that Congress deliberately left to state and local school districts" (p. 1046). Congress, according to the court, had left the choice of educational methods and policies to the schools. The court's task, therefore, was to determine if the school had complied with the IDEA's requirements.

The court believed that the statutory language of the LRE mandate provided a more appropriate test for determining a school's compliance with the mainstreaming requirement than did the *Roncker* inquiry. Relying on this language, the court developed a two-part test for determining compliance with the LRE requirement. (See Figure 11.3, the *Daniel* two-part test.)

First, the court must ask whether education in the general education classroom, with the use of supplementary aids and services, could be satisfactorily achieved. To make this determination, the court must decide whether the school has taken steps to accommodate a

FIGURE 11.3 ■ The Daniel Two-Part Test

> 1) Can education in the general education classroom with supplementary aids and services be achieved satisfactorily?
> 2) If a student is placed in a more restrictive setting, is the student integrated to the maximum extent appropriate?

student with disabilities in the general education classroom. These attempts take the form of supplying supplementary aids and services and modifying the curriculum. In determining whether the school complied with this part of the test, the court must also decide if the student will receive benefit from the general education classroom and if the mainstreamed student will negatively affect the education of classroom peers. If the school has not attempted to mainstream the student to the maximum extent appropriate, the school will fail the first part of the test. The inquiry will thus end because the school district has violated the LRE mandate.

If the school passes the first part of the test, the court then moves to part two. Here the court asks whether the school has mainstreamed the student to the maximum extent appropriate; that is, by relying on the continuum of placements, the school must provide the student with as much exposure to students without disabilities as possible. The *Daniel* court suggested that students who are educated primarily in segregated settings should be placed in integrated settings outside the special education classroom when feasible (e.g., nonacademic classes, lunch, recess).

If the school meets both parts of the two-part test, then its obligation under the IDEA is fulfilled. After applying the two-part test in *Daniel*, the Fifth Circuit determined that Daniel's needs were so great and that he required so much of the teacher's time that it was affecting the education of the other students negatively. The court, finding that the school district had met the requirements of the two-part test, affirmed the decision of the district court that the school district had satisfied the LRE requirement of the IDEA.

In addition to the test, the *Daniel* court provided further direction for lower courts to follow in LRE cases in noting that the court's "task is not to second-guess state and local school officials; rather, it is the narrow one of determining whether state and local school officials have complied with the Act" (p. 1048).

The *Daniel* decision has proved to be a very persuasive decision and has subsequently been adopted in the U.S. Court of Appeals for the Second Circuit (*L.B. and J.B. ex rel. K.B. v. Nebo School District*, 2004), Third Circuit (*Oberti v. Board of Education of the Borough of Clementon School District*, 1993), Tenth Circuit (*P. v. Newington Board of Education*, 2008), and Eleventh Circuit in *Greer v. Rome City School District* (1991).

The Rachel H. Test (Ninth Circuit)

On January 24, 1994, the U.S. Court of Appeals for the Ninth Circuit affirmed a district court's decision in *Sacramento City Unified School District Board of Education v. Rachel H.** (1994; hereafter *Rachel H.*). This case is the legal authority for the Ninth Circuit, which covers Alaska, Arizona, California, Hawaii, Idaho, Montana, Nevada, Oregon, and Washington.

The case involved Rachel Holland, an 11-year-old girl with moderate intellectual disabilities. From 1985 to 1989, Rachel attended a number of special education programs in the Sacramento School District. In the fall of 1989, Rachel's parents requested that she be placed in a general education classroom during the entire school day. The district contended that Rachel's disability was too severe for her to benefit from being in a general education class and proposed that she be placed in special education for academic subjects, attending the general education class only for nonacademic activities (e.g., art, music, lunch, recess). The parents removed Rachel from the school and placed her in a private school. The parents also requested a due process hearing. The hearing officer held for the parents, stating that the school district had failed to make an adequate effort to educate Rachel in the general education classroom. The school appealed the decision to the district court. The court, relying on the decisions in the *Roncker, Daniel,* and *Greer* cases, considered four factors in making its decision. (See Figure 11.4 for the *Rachel H.* four-factor test.)

The first factor concerned the educational benefits available to Rachel in the general education classroom with supplementary aids and services as compared with the educational benefits of the special education classroom. The court found that the district, in presenting evidence, had failed to establish that the educational benefits of the special education classroom were better than or even equal to the benefits of the general education classroom.

The second factor the court considered was the nonacademic benefits of each classroom. The court decided that the Hollands' testimony, that Rachel was developing social and communication skills as well as self-esteem, was more credible than the district's testimony that Rachel was not learning from exposure to other children and that she was becoming isolated from her peers. The second factor, therefore, was decided in favor of the Hollands.

Third, the district court examined the impact of Rachel's presence on others in the general education classroom—specifically, whether Rachel's presence was a detriment to others because she was disruptive or distracting, and if she would take up so much of the teacher's time that the other students would suffer. Both parties agreed that Rachel followed directions and was not disruptive. Also, the court found that Rachel did not interfere with the teacher's ability to teach the other children. The court ruled that the third factor was in favor of placement in the general education class.

The final factor in the court's decision involved evaluating the cost of placement in the general education classroom. The court found that the school district had not offered persuasive evidence to support its claim that educating Rachel in the general education class would be far more expensive than educating her in the combined general education and special education placement. Thus, the cost factor did not provide an impediment to educating Rachel in general education. Weighing the four factors, the district court determined that the appropriate placement for Rachel was full-time attendance in the general education classroom with supplemental aids and services.

An appeal to the Ninth Circuit was heard on August 12, 1993, and the court delivered its opinion on January 24, 1994. The circuit court affirmed the decision of the district court. The higher court stated that the school district had the burden of demonstrating that its proposed placement provided mainstreaming to the maximum extent appropriate. The circuit court adopted the district court's four-factor test in determining that the school district had not met the burden of proof that Rachel could not be educated in the general education classroom. The court found the Hollands' position for inclusion to be more persuasive.

The school district filed a petition to have the U.S. Supreme Court review this case. The High Court denied the petition, however, and did not hear the case, so the ruling of the appellate court stands.

In *Clyde K. v. Puyallup School District* (1994), the U.S. Court of Appeals for the Ninth Circuit applied its four-factor test to a case involving inclusion and a student with behavioral disorders. The case was especially noteworthy because it answered questions heretofore un-examined at the appellate court level.

The dispute involved Ryan K., a 15-year-old with attention deficit hyperactivity disorder (ADHD) and Tourette's syndrome. Ryan was receiving special education in the general

FIGURE 11.4 ■ The *Rachel H.* Four-Factor Test

1) The educational benefits of the general education classroom with supplementary aids and services as compared with the educational benefits of the special classroom

2) The nonacademic benefits of interaction with students without disabilities

3) The effect of the student's presence on the teacher and on other students in the classroom

4) The cost of mainstreaming

education classroom with supplementary resource room help. His behavior, however, became increasingly disruptive. He used obscenities, was noncompliant, harassed female students with sexually explicit remarks, and physically assaulted classmates. Following two serious incidences of assaultive behavior, Ryan was suspended. When he returned, the school district had a paraprofessional observe his classroom behavior for 3 days. School officials met to review the IEP and concluded that Ryan's objectives could be met if he was placed in a segregated special education program called Students Temporarily Away from Regular Schools (STARS). His parents were notified of the proposed placement change. School personnel suggested that Ryan be placed in STARS while they and his parents developed a plan to reintegrate Ryan in the general education classroom. The parents initially agreed but subsequently changed their minds concerning the placement in STARS. They requested a new IEP and a due process hearing.

Ryan's parents brought their attorney to the IEP meeting to discuss Ryan's return to the general education classroom. The parents contended that the STARS program was overly restrictive and that the appropriate placement would be the general education classroom with a personal aide. During the course of discussions, the parents' attorney abruptly ended the meeting, stating that Ryan would be in the general education class the next day. According to the court, the attorney insisted that the parents leave despite pleas by school district personnel that they continue the meeting.

A due process hearing was convened. The hearing officer concluded that the school district had complied with the requirements of the IDEA. The parents appealed to the district court, which, after reviewing the record of the administrative hearing and hearing additional testimony, affirmed the decision of the hearing officer. The parents then appealed to the U.S. Court of Appeals for the Ninth Circuit.

In its ruling, the circuit court applied the four-factor test it had established in *Rachel H.* The first factor considers the academic benefits of the general education classroom. The court noted that Ryan was not receiving academic benefits from the general education classroom and that testing had actually indicated academic regression. The court also noted that the school district had made efforts to provide supplementary aids and services to accommodate Ryan in the general education classroom (e.g., staff training about Ryan's disabilities, special education support in a resource room, and the involvement of a behavioral specialist). Because of the severity of Ryan's behavioral problems, the court did not believe that the presence of a personal aide would have made a meaningful difference.

The nonacademic benefits of the general education class setting are the second factor in the *Rachel H.* test. The court stated that testimony indicated that Ryan was a social isolate and seemed to benefit little from modeling. The court believed, therefore, that the nonacademic benefits of the general education class setting were minimal.

The third factor—the negative effects the student's presence had on the teacher and peers—was considered the most important by the court. Noting that Ryan's aggressive behavior, sexually explicit remarks, and profanity had an overwhelming negative effect on the teachers and peers, the court stated that the school had a statutory duty to ensure that all students with disabilities receive an appropriate education. This duty, however, did not require that schools ignore the student's behavioral problems. According to the court, schools have an obligation to ensure that all students are educated in safe environments:

> Disruptive behavior that significantly impairs the education of other students strongly suggests a mainstream placement is no longer appropriate. While school officials have a statutory duty to ensure that disabled students receive an appropriate education, they are not required to sit on their hands when a disabled student's behavioral problems prevent him and those around him from learning.

(p. 1402)

The Ninth Circuit Court held that the STARS program was the LRE. The court also stated that the slow and tedious working of the court system made it a poor arena in which to resolve disputes regarding a student's education. The judgment of the district court was thus affirmed.

In an interesting and highly unusual move, the circuit court, in a footnote to the decision, criticized the attorney for the plaintiffs for "hardball tactics" and counterproductive dealings with the school district, which destroyed potential channels for constructive dialogue. The court noted that because of the litigation, Ryan spent 2 years in a self-contained placement that was originally intended to be a short-term interim placement, and that "Ryan's experience offers a poignant reminder that everyone's interests are better served when parents and school officials resolve their differences through cooperation and compromise rather than litigation" (p. 1402).

The DeVries *Test (Fourth Circuit)*

DeVries v. Fairfax County School Board (1989; hereafter *DeVries*) was the first major LRE case heard by the U.S. Court of Appeals for the Fourth Circuit. The Fourth Circuit court is the controlling authority in the states of Maryland, North Carolina, South Carolina, Virginia, and West Virginia.

Michael DeVries was a 17-year-old high school student with autism who attended the Fairfax Public School system. Michael's IEP team determined that the most appropriate program for Michael would be at a county vocational center at West Potomac High School, which was miles away from his home school, Annandale High School. Michael's parents disagreed and filed for a due process hearing. The case was eventually heard in the federal district court in Virginia. The district court held that the vocational center was the appropriate and least restrictive educational environment for Michael. The district court's ruling was appealed and on August 16, 1989, the U.S. Court of Appeals for the Fourth Circuit handed down its ruling affirming the decision of the district court.

The circuit court agreed with the district court that Michael could not be satisfactorily educated in regular classes even with the use of supplementary aids and services. Although the circuit court noted that Congress had expressed a strong preference for students with disabilities to be educated in the mainstream, it also stated that mainstream placement would not be appropriate for every student with a disability. The court then cited the Sixth Circuit court's decision in *Roncker* and held that in a situation in which the segregated facilities are considered superior, a court should consider whether the services that make the special setting superior could feasibly be provided in a nonsegregated setting. Thus, the Fourth Circuit seemingly applied some of the Sixth Circuit's *Roncker* test and *Daniel* test while also contributing its own three-part test. According to this test, mainstreaming is not required when (a) a student with a disability would not receive educational benefit from mainstreaming in a general education class; (b) any marginal benefit from mainstreaming would be significantly outweighed by benefits that could feasibly be obtained only in a separate instructional setting; or (c) the student is a disruptive force in the general education classroom (*DeVries*, p. 879).

Hartmann v. Loudoun County Board of Education (1997; hereafter *Hartmann*) was another LRE case heard by the U.S. Court of Appeals for the Fourth Circuit. Mark Hartmann was an 11-year-old child with autism. His family lived in Loudoun County, Virginia, where he attended Ashburn Elementary School. Based on Mark's previous IEP, school officials decided to place him in a general education classroom. To facilitate his educational progress, school officials hired a full-time aide, provided specialized training for his teacher and aide, provided three hours per week of instruction with a special education teacher (who also served as a consultant to Mark's teacher and aide), and provided five hours per week of speech therapy. Additionally, the entire staff at Ashburn Elementary received inservice training on autism and inclusion. The IEP team also included the supervisor of the Loudoun County program for children with autism to provide assistance in managing Mark's behavior. Finally, the IEP team received assistance from two consultants.

FIGURE 11.5 ■ The DeVries/Hartmann Three-Factor Test

Mainstreaming is not required when:

1) A student with a disability would not receive educational benefit from mainstreaming in a general education class.
2) Any marginal benefit from mainstreaming would be significantly outweighed by benefits that could feasibly be obtained only in a separate instructional setting.
3) The student is a disruptive force in the general education classroom.

Despite the measures taken, the IEP team determined that Mark was making no academic or behavioral progress in the general education setting. Moreover, his behavior problems were extremely disruptive in class. Because of his aggression toward others (e.g., kicking, biting, punching), five families asked to have their children transferred to another classroom. The IEP team proposed that Mark be moved to a program for children with autism in a regular elementary school. Mark would receive his academic instruction and speech therapy in the special class and attend a general education classroom for art, music, physical education, library, and recess. The parents disagreed with the IEP, asserting that it violated the mainstreaming provision of the IDEA. The school district initiated a due process hearing. The due process hearing officer upheld the school district's IEP, and the state review officer affirmed the decision. The Hartmanns then challenged the hearing officer's decision in federal district court. The district court reversed the due process decision, specifically rejecting the administrative findings and ruling that the school had not taken appropriate steps to include Mark in the general education classroom. The school district filed an appeal with the U.S. Court of Appeals for the Fourth Circuit. Finding that the IDEA's mainstreaming provision established a presumption, not an inflexible mandate, the circuit court reversed the district court's ruling.

The circuit court also admonished the district court for substituting its own judgment for that of Mark's teachers. According to the circuit court the district court had essentially substituted its own judgment regarding Mark's education program for the judgment of local school officials.

The court reaffirmed that mainstreaming is not required when (a) a student with a disability would not receive educational benefit from mainstreaming in a general education class; (b) any marginal benefit from mainstreaming would be significantly outweighed by benefits that could feasibly be obtained only in a separate instructional setting; or (c) the student is a disruptive force in the general education classroom (see Figure 11.5). Finally, according to the circuit court the LRE provision only created a presumption, and the presumption reflected congressional judgment that receipt of social benefits is a subordinate goal to receiving educational benefit.

Summary of Judicial Standards of Review

Although a number of LRE cases have been heard by the U.S. Courts of Appeals, there exist only four acknowledged tests for determining placement in the LRE. These tests, or judicial standards of review, are the *Roncker* test, the *Daniel* test, the *Rachel H.* test, and the *DeVries/Hartmann* test. Of these tests, the *Daniel* test has proved the most persuasive, subsequently being adopted by the U.S. Courts of Appeals for the Second, Third, Fifth, Tenth, and Eleventh Circuits. These standards are important because they provide lower courts in the circuits with guidance in ruling on similar cases. They are also instructive to school district personnel because they indicate the relevant factors that courts will examine in LRE cases. Table 11.1 lists the standards of review and the circuits and states in which they are the controlling authority.

The U.S. Court of Appeals for the First Circuit, which is the controlling authority in Maine, Massachusetts, New Hampshire, Puerto Rico, and Rhode Island, and Seventh Circuit,

TABLE 11.1 ■ Judicial Standards of Review in LRE Cases

Roncker *Test* (6th & 8th Circuits)	Daniel *Test* (2nd, 3rd, 5th, 10th, & 11th Circuits)	Rachel H. *Test* (9th Circuit)	DeVries *Test* (4th Circuit)
Arkansas	Alabama	Alaska	Maryland
Iowa	Connecticut	Arizona	North Carolina
Kentucky	Delaware	California	South Carolina
Michigan	Georgia	Hawaii	Virginia
Minnesota	Florida	Idaho	West Virginia
Missouri	Louisiana	Montana	
Nebraska	Mississippi	Nevada	
North Dakota	New Jersey	Oregon	
Ohio	New York	Washington	
South Dakota	Pennsylvania		
Tennessee	Texas		
	Vermont		

which is the controlling authority in Illinois, Indiana, and Wisconsin, have not adopted any of the formal LRE tests. In fact, in the case *Beth B. v. Van Clay* (2002; hereafter *Beth B.*) the U.S. Court of Appeals for the Seventh Circuit specifically abjured the adoption of any specific circuit court test. In the opinion, the judges wrote that because each student's educational situation was unique, they found it unnecessary to adopt a formal test to apply when deciding LRE cases. The IDEA, the judges noted, provided enough of a framework for their discussion of the situation in *Beth B.* The Seventh Circuit court has appellate jurisdiction in the states of Illinois, Indiana, and Wisconsin. In a later case decided by the Seventh Circuit court in 2007, *Board of Education of Township High School No. 211 v. Ross* (2007), the court again declined to adopt a specific LRE test but did note that in deciding LRE cases the court would ask whether education in a mainstream setting was appropriate and, if not, whether reasonable measures would have made the setting appropriate. Thus, without directly saying so, the Seventh Circuit seemed to use parts of the *Roncker* and *Daniel* tests in arriving at their decisions.

Although the application of the facts of particular cases to the LRE requirements of the IDEA may certainly result in different rulings, the essential applications of the LRE language in the law as seen in the circuit courts' standards of review are quite similar. It seems unlikely that the U.S. Supreme Court will soon hear an LRE case because of the uniformity among the various circuits.

FACTORS IN DETERMINING THE LRE

Clearly, several factors must be considered when determining placement. Ensuring that schools comply with the LRE mandate of IDEA is one of these factors. Additionally, it is important that IEP teams consider the standards established in the courts when determining placement. Figure 11.6 is a flowchart based on these judicial standards.

Individualization

The IEP team determines the least restrictive appropriate setting. The IDEA, its regulations, and comments to these regulations make it clear that the IEP team can only make this

FIGURE 11.6 ■
Determining the Least Restrictive Environment Flowchart

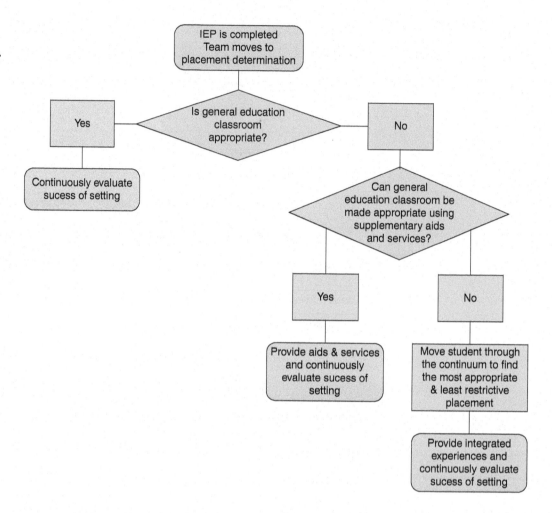

decision by examining students' needs and determining their goals based on this assessment. Federal regulations require that "the overriding rule ... is that placement decisions must be made on an individual basis" (IDEA Regulations, 34 C.F.R. § 300.552, comment). In 1991, OSERS interpreted the LRE mandate as requiring that "children with disabilities should be educated with nondisabled children to the maximum extent appropriate; however, the determination of whether to place a child with disabilities in an integrated setting must be made on a case-by-case basis" (*Letter to Stutler and McCoy, 1991,* p. 308).

Because of the individualized nature of the LRE placement, there are no simple rules to guide IEP teams in making placement decisions. The legislation and litigation do, however, provide guidance regarding the decision-making process. Clearly, certain actions are never "appropriate," such as developing blanket policies regarding LRE decisions. For example, schools must never refuse to place particular categories of students with disabilities in general education classes; neither should they refuse more restrictive placements when required.

The decisions in *Greer v. Rome City School District* (1991) and *Oberti v. Board of Education* (1993) are particularly instructive, as the courts delineated the inappropriate actions by the school districts that resulted in the districts' losses in these cases. Perhaps the most important reason for these losses was the courts' unwillingness to accept assertions of appropriateness of restrictive settings without some proof by school districts as to the inappropriateness of the general education classroom. In both *Greer* and *Oberti,* the school districts did not have data from direct experience to indicate that the general education class placement was not appropriate. For example, in *Oberti* the plaintiff was a student who exhibited significant behavior problems in the general education classroom. Although the school district's special education director testified that the school had attempted to keep the student in the general education classroom through various procedures, the IEP did not contain a behavioral plan. In *Greer*, the court ruled against the school district because (a) the IEP team failed to consider the full continuum of placements in determining the LRE; (b) the school made no attempt to assist the student to remain in the mainstream setting; and (c) the school district developed the IEP prior to the IEP meeting and did not clearly inform the Greers of the full range of services that may have been required to maintain their child in the general education classroom. Conversely, in the *A.W. v. Northwest, Clyde K., Daniel, DeVries, L.B. v. Nebo, Hartmann,* and *P. v. Newington* decisions, in which the school districts prevailed, school officials had attempted and documented a number of efforts to maintain the students in the general education classroom.

Benefits to the Student

The *Greer* court noted "several factors that a school district may consider in determining whether education in the regular classroom may be achieved satisfactorily" (p. 697). First, the school may compare the educational benefits of the general education classroom (with supplementary aids and services) with those received in the special education classroom. This comparison should include both academic and nonacademic (e.g., language, role-modeling) activities. If the school determines that the self-contained setting will provide "significantly" greater benefits and that in the general education classroom the student will fall behind peers in the self-contained class, the general education environment may not be appropriate.

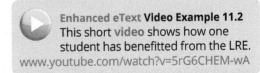

Enhanced eText **Video Example 11.2**
This short video shows how one student has benefitted from the LRE.
www.youtube.com/watch?v=5rG6CHEM-wA

Effect on Peers

School personnel may consider the effect the presence of a student with disabilities in a general education classroom would have on the education of other students in that classroom. A student who disrupts the education of others due to behavior problems or because of needing constant teacher attention may not be appropriately placed in a general education classroom. In weighing this factor, however, the school is cautioned by both the *Oberti* and *Greer* courts of their obligation to first consider the use of supplementary aids and services to accommodate a student.

The decision in *Clyde K.* further confirmed the legitimacy of considering the rights of other students in determining placement. In this case, a crucial factor in the school district's restrictive placement's being upheld was the use of supplementary aids and services. Similarly, school districts also prevailed in the removal of disruptive students in *MR v. Lincolnwood Board of Education* (1994) and *VanderMalle v. Ambach* (1987).

Appropriateness

The IDEA requires that schools provide a FAPE for all students with disabilities. The law also requires that to the maximum extent appropriate, students with disabilities should be educated with students without disabilities. When an appropriate education is not possible in the general education classroom, the FAPE and LRE provisions seem to be in conflict. This apparent conflict has provoked much controversy and confusion. The FAPE and LRE requirements do not actually conflict; however, both are important elements in the special education decision-making process.

Legislation and litigation regarding LRE and FAPE indicate that the school's primary obligation is to provide the student with disabilities with a FAPE. The LRE principle, although important, is secondary (Bateman & Linden, 2012; Champagne, 1993). The language of the law reinforces this by requiring that students with disabilities be educated in the

LRE to the maximum extent appropriate, and by further requiring that schools have a continuum of alternative placements. In determining placement, the IEP team balances FAPE with the preference for educating students with disabilities with their peers in the general education classroom. The team selects the most integrated setting that is compatible with the delivery of an appropriate education. That setting is the LRE. In practice, however, this requirement has proved to be difficult to apply (Champagne, 1993; Huefner & Herr, 2012).

Integration

The IDEA clearly requires the maximum amount of integration that is appropriate given a student's needs. The LRE mandate was a clear expression of congressional preference for educating students with disabilities in the general education classroom when appropriate. As Champagne (1993) asserted, the IDEA requires the maximum integration that will "work" for a student. An appropriate interpretation of the LRE cases is that students with disabilities belong in integrated settings and that schools must make good-faith efforts to make this possible.

The Use of Supplementary Aids and Services

A key to meeting the LRE mandate is a school's proper use of supplementary aids and services. School districts must make good-faith efforts to maintain students in a general education class placement, and the provision of various supplementary aids and services is a means by which schools can maintain students with disabilities in these settings. Supplementary aids and services may include assistive technology services or devices, prereferral interventions, consultation, behavior management plans, paraprofessionals, itinerant teachers, and resource rooms. According to the court in *Daniel*, schools are required to provide supplementary aids and services and to modify the general education classroom when they mainstream students with disabilities. If such efforts are not made, schools will be in violation of the IDEA. Furthermore, if the school has made these efforts, lower courts must examine whether the efforts are sufficient, because the IDEA

> does not permit [schools] to make mere token gestures to accommodate [students with disabilities], its requirement for modifying and supplementing regular education is broad.... Although broad, the requirement is not limitless.... [Schools] need not provide every conceivable aid or service to assist a child.... Furthermore, the [IDEA] does not require regular education instructors to devote all or most of their time to one [student with disabilities] or modify the curriculum beyond recognition.

(p. 1048)

The question of the limit of supplementary aids and services that must be attempted or considered by the school remains undecided. In the *Daniel* decision, the court determined that the school district had fulfilled its requirements under the law, whereas the court's rulings in the *Greer* and *Oberti* cases held that the school districts had not. In the *Oberti* case, the court believed that the school district had made negligible efforts to include the student, Rafael Oberti, in a general education classroom by mainstreaming him without a curriculum plan, behavior management plan, or special support to the teacher. The *Greer* court found that the school district failed to consider the full range of supplementary aids and services (including a resource room and itinerant instruction) that might have assisted the student, Christy Greer, in the mainstream placement. The court acknowledged that testimony by officials indicated that the school district had considered supplementary aids and services; however, this consideration was not reflected in the minutes of the IEP meeting nor in the IEP itself. Neither had the school district made efforts to modify the mainstream curriculum to accommodate Christy.

The courts' direction regarding the importance of school districts providing supplementary aids and services to place and maintain students in LREs is clear. Whether the school district needs to actually *attempt* a general education class placement with supplementary aids and services or is merely obligated to consider these services is, however, uncertain. However dicta in *Greer* and *Oberti* required that school districts must show that they have "considered" a range of supplementary aids and services. Certainly educators may need to show that such considerations were made prior to concluding that an education in the general education classroom was not appropriate. Clearly, when there is a reasonable likelihood that a student can receive an appropriate education in the general education classroom with the use of supplementary aids and services, then the general education placement must be attempted (Tatgenhorst et al., 2014). When the general education classroom is clearly inappropriate for a student, however, it is not required that a student be placed in the general education classroom to fail prior to being moved to a more appropriate, restrictive placement (*Poolaw v. Bishop,* 1995).

A MODEL FOR DETERMINING LRE

Notwithstanding the courts' guidance in making LRE decisions, placement teams find that determining the educational placement that constitutes the most appropriate and least restrictive setting for students with disabilities is tremendously difficult. Champagne (1993) asserted that school districts should adopt a sequential model in making placement decisions. The sequential model is an organized way of applying the LRE requirement to whatever facts a particular student's situation requires. Thus, the model preserves the "core statutory imperative" that placements are based on the student's educational needs. According to his model, an IEP team should go through the following steps.

Step 1: The team determines that a student is eligible for services.

Step 2: The team defines what constitutes appropriate educational services for the student.

Step 3: The team asks whether these appropriate educational services can be delivered in the general education classroom in its current form. If the answer is yes, then the general education setting becomes the student's primary placement. If it is no, go to Step 4.

Step 4: The team asks whether these appropriate educational services can be delivered in the general education classroom if the setting is modified through the addition of supplementary aids and services. If yes, then the general education setting with supplementary aids and services becomes the student's primary placement. If no, go to Step 5.

Step 5: If the team determines that the general setting, even with supplementary aids and services, is not appropriate, the team should determine placement by moving along the continuum of alternative placements one step at a time, from the least restrictive setting to more restrictive ones. At each step, ask whether the services called for in the IEP can be delivered in that setting. If yes, then the setting becomes the student's primary placement. If no, go to Step 6.

Step 6: The team asks whether the services called for in the IEP can be delivered in the slightly more restrictive settings if they are modified through the use of supplementary aids and services. If yes, that is the primary placement; if no, repeat Step 5 for a placement on the continuum that is slightly more restrictive, and then, if necessary, go to Step 6 for that setting. (In this manner, the placement team moves along the continuum of alternative placements, one step at a time, repeating Steps 5 and 6 until a yes answer is obtained.)

Step 7: In the context of the primary placement chosen, ask if there are additional opportunities for integration for some portion of the student's school day. If yes, design a split placement by including the student in the integrated setting for part of the school day and in the more restrictive setting for part of the school day.

LESSONS FROM LITIGATION AND LEGISLATION

The LRE mandate of the IDEA requires that to the maximum extent appropriate students with disabilities receive their education alongside their nondisabled peers in the regular classroom environment. It is only when education in the regular classroom with supplementary aids and services cannot be achieved satisfactorily that a student with disabilities can be moved to a more restrictive setting such as a special class or a special school. Information from legislation and principles extrapolated from the body of case law on LRE can provide guidance to school districts.

Principle 1: The primary objective when developing a student's special education program is appropriateness. To this end the first task of a student's IEP team is to develop an individualized program of special education services, related services, supplementary aids and services, and program modifications that confers meaningful educational benefit upon that student. To this end, a student's special education programs must be individualized and address his or her unique educational needs. The results of the program must be measured on a formative basis and reported to the student's parents. Moreover, considerations of a student's placement, which also must be individualized, are made following the determination of the student's program. After a team determines the content of the IEP, a team's attention can turn to the setting where this program can be implemented.

Principle 2: Place students in settings in which they have the most contact with their nondisabled peers. Following the determination of the content of a student's program, a student's IEP team or placement team determines the setting in which the program can be implemented. It is important that programming be determined prior to making a placement decision. Furthermore, because an important component of the IDEA is that students with disabilities should be educated in settings with their nondisabled peers to the maximum extent appropriate, a student's IEP team should determine what aids, supports, or program modifications that he or she may need to be involved in the general education classroom. It is advisable that school district personnel consider the general education classroom, with the provision of supplementary aids and services, to be the default setting for students with disabilities. IDEA appears unambiguous regarding LRE: The IEP team is to determine the setting with the greatest degree of integration in which an appropriate education can be delivered.

Principle 3: Use the continuum of placements to determine the least restrictive appropriate placement. When a student's IEP or placement team determines that an appropriate education cannot be delivered in the general education setting, even with the provision of supplementary aids and services, the team may move the student to the next most appropriate restrictive setting along the continuum of alternative placements. School district personnel should not substitute either a policy of full inclusion or automatic placement in a segregated setting for the continuum of placements. Nonetheless, when students with disabilities are educated in more restrictive settings, the IEP/placement team must seek opportunities in which the student may be educated in integrated settings with their nondisabled peers.

SUMMARY

The LRE mandate of the IDEA sets forth a clear congressional preference for integrating students with disabilities in general education classrooms. The LRE mandate has two specific components: First, students with disabilities must be educated along with students without disabilities to the maximum extent appropriate; second, students with disabilities should be removed from integrated settings only when the nature or severity of the disability is such that an appropriate education with the use of supplementary aids and services cannot be achieved satisfactorily in the general education setting. Recognizing that at times an integrated setting would not provide an appropriate education and thus a more restrictive setting may be necessary, IDEA regulations include a continuum of alternative placement options that vary in the degree of restrictiveness. The purpose of the continuum is to make appropriate educational placements available to students based on their individual needs. Standards for making determinations in LRE cases have been developed and adopted by many of the circuits in the U.S. Courts of Appeals.

Enhanced eText Application Exercise 11.1: *Daniel R. R. v. State Board of Education,* 874 F.2d 1036 (5th Cir. 1989).

FOR FURTHER INFORMATION

Champagne, J. F. (1993). Decisions in sequence: How to make placements in the least restrictive environment. *EdLaw Briefing Paper, 9 & 10,* 1–16.

Sharp, K. G., & Pitasky, V. M. (2007). *The current legal status of inclusion.* Palm Beach Garden, FL: LRP Publications.

REFERENCES

Americans with Disabilities Act of 1990, 42 U.S.C. 12101 *et seq.*

A.W. v. Northwest R-1 School District, 813 F.2d 158 (8th Cir. 1987).

Barnett v. Fairfax County School Board, 17 EHLR 350 (4th Cir. 1991).

Bateman, B., & Linden, M. A. (2012). *Better IEPs: An updated guide to understanding IEPs.* Verona, WI: Attainment.

Beth B. v. Van Clay, 282 F.3d. 493 (7th Cir. 2002).

Board of Education of Township High School No. 211 v. Ross, 486 F.3d 267 (7th Cir. 2007).

Board of Education of the Hendrick Hudson School District v. -Rowley, 458 U.S. 176 (1982).

Brown v. Board of Education, 347 U.S. 483 (1954).

Carter v. Florence County School District, 950 F.2d 156 (4th Cir. 1991).

Champagne, J. F. (1993). Decisions in sequence: How to make placements in the least restrictive environment. *EdLaw Briefing Paper, 9 & 10,* 1–16.

Clyde K. v. Puyallup School District, 35 F.3d 1396 (9th Cir. 1994).

Cordero v. Pennsylvania, 19 IDELR 623 (E.D. Pa. 1993).

Daniel R. R. v. State Board of Education, 874 F.2d 1036 (5th Cir. 1989).

Deno, E. (1970). Special education as developmental capital. *Exceptional Children, 37* (3), 229–237.

DeVries v. Fairfax County School Board, 882 F.2d 876 (4th Cir. 1989).

Education for All Handicapped Children Act of 1975, 20 U.S.C. § 1401 *et seq.*

Education of the Handicapped Amendments of 1974, Pub. L. No. 93-380, 88 Stat. 580.

Flour Bluff Independent School District v. Katherine M., 24 IDELR 673 (5th Cir. 1996).

Greer v. Rome City School District, 950 F.2d 688 (11th Cir. 1991).

Hairston v. Drosick, 423 F. Supp. 180 (S.D. W. Va. 1976).

Hartmann v. Loudoun County Board of Education (4th Cir. 1997). Available at www.law.emory.edu/4circuit/july97/962809.p.html.

Hudson v. Bloomfield Hills School District, 23 IDELR 612 (E.D. Mich. 1995).

Huefner, D. S., & Herr, C. (2012). *Navigating special education law and policy.* Verona, WI: Attainment.

Individuals with Disabilities Education Act of 1990, 20 U.S.C. § 1401 *et seq.*

Individuals with Disabilities Education Act Regulations, 34 C.F.R. § 300 *et seq.*

Kerham v. McKenzie, 862 F.2d 884 (D.C. Cir. 1988).

Lachman v. Illinois Board of Education, 852 F.2d 290 (7th Cir. 1988).

L.B. and J.B. ex rel. K.B. v. Nebo School District, 379 F.3d 966 (10th Cir. 2004).

Letter to Frost, 19 IDELR 594 (OSERS 1991).

Letter to Goodling, 18 IDELR 213 (OSERS 1991).

Letter to Stutler and McCoy, 18 IDELR 307 (OSERS 1991).

MR v. Lincolnwood Board of Education, 20 IDELR 1323 (N.D. Ill. 1994).

Martin, E. (2013). *Breakthrough: Federal Special Education Legislation: 1965–1981.* New York: Bardolf & Company.

Murray v. Montrose County School District, 22 IDELR 558 (10th Cir. 1995).

Oberti v. Board of Education of the Borough of Clementon School District, 995 F.2d 1204 (3d Cir. 1993).

P. v. Newington Board of Education, 546 F.3d 111 (2d Cir. 2008).

Poolaw v. Bishop, 23 IDELR 407 (9th Cir. 1995).

Reynolds, M.C. (1962). A framework for considering some issues in special education. *Exceptional Children, 28* (7), 367–370.

Roland M. v. Concord School Committee, 910 F.2d 983 (1st Cir. 1990).

Roncker v. Walter, 700 F.2d 1058 (6th Cir. 1983).

Rozalski, M., Steward, A., & Miller, J (2011). How to determine the least restrictive environment for students with disabilities. In J. M. Kauffman and D. P. Hallahan (Eds.), *Handbook of special education* (pp. 77–90). Philadelphia, PA: Taylor & Francis/Routledge.

Sacramento City Unified School District Board of Education v. -Holland, 786 F. Supp. 874 (E.D. Colo. 1992).

Sacramento City Unified School District Board of Education v. -Rachel H., 14 F.3d 1398 (9th Cir. 1994).

Schuldt v. Mankato ISD, 937 F.2d 1357 (8th Cir. 1991).

Section 504 Regulations, 34 C.F.R. § 104 *et seq.*

Sheldon v. Tucker, 364 U.S. 479 (1960).

Stafford, R. (1978). Education for the handicapped: A senator's perspective. *Vermont Law Review, 3*, 71–76.

Tatgenhorst, A., Norlin, J. W., & Gorn, S. (2014). *What do I do when … The answer book on special education law* (6th ed.). Palm Beach Garden, FL: LRP Publications.

Turnbull, H. R., Stowe, M., & Huerta, N. E. (2007). *Free appropriate public education: The law and children with disabilities* (6th ed.). Denver, CO: Love.

Urban v. Jefferson County School District R-1, 21 IDELR 985 (D. Colo. 1994).

VanderMalle v. Ambach, 667 F. Supp. 1015 (S.D.N.Y. 1987).

Winzer, M.A. (1993). *The history of special education: From isolation to integration*. Washington DC: Gallaudet University Press.

Yell, M.L. & Christle, C.A. (2017). The foundation of inclusion in federal legislation and litigation. In C.M. Curran & A.J. Petersen (Eds.) *The handbook of research on classroom diversity and inclusive education practice* (pp 27–74). Hershey, PA: IGI Global.

Zirkel, P. (2014). *Section 504, the ADA, and the schools* (3rd ed.). Horsham, PA: LRP Publications.

Chapter

12

Procedural Safeguards

The history of liberty has largely been the history of the observance of procedural safeguards.

JUSTICE FELIX FRANKFURTER, *McNabb v. U.S.* (1943, p. 347)

Learner Objectives

At the end of the chapter, students will be able to

12.1 Describe the procedural rights of parents.

12.2 Describe the notice and consent requirements of the IDEA.

12.3 Describe the dispute resolution of the IDEA.

12.4 Describe the purpose and conduct of a due process hearing.

12.5 Describe alternatives to the dispute resolution system of the IDEA.

12.6 Describe judicially awarded remedies for parents who prevail against school districts in due process hearings and court cases.

When the Education for All Handicapped Children Act was passed in 1975, Congress wanted to ensure that students with disabilities would be treated fairly and provided with an appropriate education. One way in which they accomplished this was to provide students, and their parents, with procedural protections to ensure that they would be meaningfully involved with school districts when educational programs were being planned and implemented. The procedural safeguards were designed to afford the parents or guardians of students with disabilities meaningful involvement in the educational programming and placement of their children (*Christopher P. v. Marcus*, 1990; *Polera v. Board of Education of the Newburgh Enlarged City School District*, 2002). The procedural protections in the IDEA were based on the due process clauses of the 5th and 14th Amendments to the U.S. Constitution, which hold that no state may deprive any person "of life, liberty, or property without due process of law." These amendments give persons, including students, two types of due process rights: procedural rights and substantive rights (Yell, Katsiyannis, Ennis, & Losinski, 2013).

In special education, procedural safeguards guide the method by which school officials make decisions regarding the education of students with disabilities, and substantive due process rights are those personal rights that school officials may not abridge (Valente & Valente, 2005). According to the U.S. Supreme Court, Congress established the elaborate system of safeguards to "guarantee parents both an opportunity for meaningful input into all decisions affecting their child's education and the right to seek review of any decisions they think inappropriate" (*Honig v. Doe*, 1988, p. 598). In the recent U.S. Supreme Court ruling in (*Endrew F. v. Douglas County School District*, 2017), the High Court emphasized the importance of the IDEA's procedural safeguards. Writing for the unanimous Supreme Court, Justice Roberts asserted that "an IEP must be drafted in compliance with a detailed set of procedures.... These procedures emphasize collaboration among parents and educators and require careful consideration of the child's individual circumstances" (*Endrew*, 2017, p. 2).

The procedural safeguards of the Individuals with Disabilities Education Act (IDEA) include (a) notice and consent requirements, (b) the right to examine relevant records, (c) procedures to protect the rights of a student when parents are unavailable, (d) the independent educational evaluation, (e) voluntary mediation, (f) the opportunity to present a complaint to the state education agency (SEA), and (g) the due process hearing. Additionally, parents may challenge the actions of a school district before an SEA and may eventually file suit in state or federal court. Substantive due process rights concern the content and implementation of a student's individualized education program (IEP). These rights are addressed in other chapters.

This chapter reviews the procedural rights included in the IDEA, beginning with a discussion of the procedural rights of parents and the general procedural requirements of the IDEA. In addition, it focuses on the different dispute resolution systems and alternative types of remedies that courts can award to parents who prevail in lawsuits against schools.

PROCEDURAL RIGHTS OF PARENTS

In 2009, the Office of Special Education Programs (OSEP) in the U.S. Department of Education issued a document entitled *Questions and Answers on Procedural Safeguards and Due Process Procedures for Parents and Children with Disabilities* (2009) that was issued after the 2006 regulations to the IDEA took effect.

Identification of Parents

Procedural safeguards must be extended to the parents of students with disabilities under the IDEA. Because of the importance that Congress attached to meaningful parental involvement, it is obvious that the identification of a student's parents is an important requirement under the law. The biological or adoptive parents who reside with a child are considered parents for purposes of the IDEA. Additionally, other adults may also be considered parents under the IDEA. Regulations to the IDEA define a parent as a biological or adoptive parent, a guardian, a person acting as a parent of the child (e.g., grandparent, stepparent) who lives with the child, a foster parent (unless prohibited by state law), or a surrogate parent who has been appointed following the procedures of the law (IDEA Regulations, 34 C.F.R. § 300.30(a)). Tatgenhorst, Norlin, and Gorn (2014) asserted that there are two routes to parental eligibility under the law: living with the child in a parental role or having legal responsibility for a child who resides elsewhere.

Because of the IDEA's encouragement of parental involvement, it seems likely that noncustodial parents should also be allowed to participate in the development of their child's special education program (Tatgenhorst et al., 2014). The IDEA, however, neither compels a school district to include a noncustodial parent in special education planning nor prohibits the inclusion of that parent. The decision to include noncustodial parents in the decision-making process is seemingly left to the school district. Tatgenhorst et al. (2014) suggested that the involvement of noncustodial parents in the special education process is best resolved by agreement between the parents.

The IDEA does not address situations in which parents of a student are divorced and live apart and one agrees with an IEP but the other disagrees. According to the OSEP in the U.S. Department of Education, when a student's parents are divorced, IDEA rights apply to both parents unless state law or court order specifies otherwise (*Letter to Biondi*, 1997).

According to the U.S. Court of Appeals for the Second Circuit in *Taylor v. Vermont Department of Education* (2002), states have the authority to determine who makes educational decisions on behalf of a child as long as the state does so in a manner consistent with federal statutes. In this case, the biological mother of a child with a disability challenged a school district's decision to exclude her from decisions regarding her child's IEP. The district court had held that decision because the child's mother had her rights curtailed by a Vermont divorce decree. In her appeal to the appellate court, the child's natural mother claimed that she was entitled to exercise parental rights under the IDEA and Family Educational Rights and Privacy Act (FERPA), and that state law cannot abrogate these federal rights. The appellate court held that the IDEA and FERPA allow a state to determine who makes decisions for a child with disabilities and, therefore, affirmed the lower court's decision dismissing the mother's claims.

In *Fuentes v. Board of Education of the City of New York* (2009), the U.S. Court of Appeals for the Second Circuit held that because the father of a child with a disability was a noncustodial parent, and the custody agreement between the parents did not expressly grant him educational decision-making authority, the father did not have the right to make decisions about his child's education. The father, therefore, did not have the legal right to challenge the provision of his child's special education under the IDEA.

Greismann (1997) asserted that in such situations school districts should conclude the IEP process and proceed with implementing the IEP. According to Greismann, "[IDEA] regulations do not require both parents to be in agreement and if one parent believes the IEP is appropriate, that arguably satisfies the parental consent provision of the [IDEA]" (p. 3). The parent in disagreement with the IEP, however, should be notified of his or her due process rights under the IDEA.

The role of foster parents is only briefly addressed in the regulations to the IDEA in the definition of a parent. According to the regulatory language a foster parent may be a parent for purposes of the rights and responsibilities under the IDEA unless state law, regulations, or contractual obligations with a state or local entity prohibit a foster parent from acting as a parent (IDEA Regulations, 34 C.F.R. § 300.30(a)). In fact, a state may allow a foster parent to act as a parent for purposes of the IDEA if (a) a foster parent is legally responsible for a foster child's welfare and (b) the natural parents' authority to make educational decisions has been relinquished (Tatgenhorst et al., 2014). The primary question concerns when a foster parent becomes a parent under federal or state law. If a foster parent becomes a parent under the law, a surrogate parent need not be appointed to represent the student. The crucial determinant may be whether the foster care placement is permanent. OSEP has not established guidelines as to the length of time that a foster care relationship must exist to be considered permanent, but it has asserted that a state policy that considered foster placements in excess of 6 months to be long term, and therefore permanent, had to be followed (*Hargan Inquiry*, 1990). There are no guidelines regarding the appointment of foster parents who do not meet the standards of permanent parents as surrogate parents for a child. Decisions regarding the designation of foster parents as "parents" under the IDEA should be made on a case-by-case basis.

Another situation that may create confusion as to who is the parent with respect to procedural safeguards occurs when a student with disabilities is living with a person other than his or her biological parents, such as a child's grandparent, stepparent, or other relative and that person does not have legal custody (Tatgenhorst et al., 2014). Again, the IDEA does not directly address this issue but rather leaves it to the states to decide. The U.S. Court of Appeals for the Seventh Circuit in *Family & Children's Center, Inc. v. School City of Mishawaka* (1994) ruled that a state may define the term "parent" more expansively than the federal government does in the IDEA, and allow a wider range of individuals to represent children and youth in IDEA claims.

When students reach the age of majority according to state law they become legally competent to act on their own behalf. According to the IDEA:

> A state may provide that, when a student with a disability reaches the age of majority under State law that applies to all students (except for a student with a disability who has been determined to be incompetent under State law)—all (IDEA) rights according to parents under Part B of (IDEA) transfer to the student.

(20 U.S.C § 614(d)(1)(A)(VIII)(cc))

A year before a student in special education reaches the age of majority under state law, the student's IEP must include a statement that the student has been informed of his or her rights under the IDEA that will transfer to the child on reaching the age of majority (IDEA Regulations, 34 C.F.R. § 300.520).

Thus, when a student reaches the age of majority, the parents' procedural safeguards immediately transfer to the student. A U.S. district court in Kansas dismissed a student's parent from a due process hearing because the student had reached the age of majority in Kansas and the parent lacked standing (i.e., did not have legal authority) to pursue an action under the IDEA (*Neville v. Dennis*, 2007). According to Tatgenhorst et al. (2014), however, a student's parents always retain the right to receive all notices sent by the school district.

Surrogate Parents

The IDEA requires that parents be central participants in the special education decision-making process. If the child does not have a parent, the parent cannot be found, the child is homeless, or the child is a ward of the state,* the IDEA requires that a surrogate parent be appointed. The surrogate parent is appointed to safeguard the educational rights of the child with disabilities by acting as an advocate for the child (Tatgenhorst et al., 2014). Because a surrogate parent is considered a "parent" under the IDEA, he or she has all the rights, responsibilities, and procedural safeguards of a natural parent under the IDEA (Tatgenhorst et al., 2014). The surrogate parent must have no conflicts of interest, must have the requisite knowledge and skills to ensure that the child is adequately represented, and may not be an employee of the school or be involved in the education or care of the child. If a child is a ward of the state, a court appoints the surrogate parent of the child. IDEIA 2004 extends the same surrogate parents' provisions to homeless children whose parents cannot be located. The appointment should take place within 30 days after it is determined that the child needs a surrogate.

The public agency responsible for the surrogate parent must have procedures for determining whether a student needs a surrogate parent and for assigning the surrogate parent. Regulations to the IDEA require that school districts determine the need for surrogate parents when the natural parents have not been located after making reasonable efforts. What constitutes a reasonable effort, however, is not clear. A federal district court found that a school district had made reasonable efforts to locate parents when it made repeated telephone calls and sent letters to the child's residence and the parents' last known address (*Jesu D. v. Lucas County Children Services Board,* 1985).

If the parents' whereabouts are known but they do not make themselves available, there is no need to appoint a surrogate parent, even if the child is in a foster placement (*Hargan Inquiry,* 1990). If the parents can be located but seem to have no interest in their child's educational program or refuse to participate in the special education process, the IDEA does not empower school districts to appoint surrogate parents (*Letter to Perryman,* 1987). Neither can a school district appoint a surrogate parent to represent the interests of the child nor obtain an injunction to prohibit parents from participating in the process, even if the parents act in bad faith or attempt to "sabotage" the process (*Board of Education of Northfield High School District 225 v. Roy H. and Lynn H.,* 1995). Under the IDEA, the appointment of surrogate parents does not terminate parental rights, nor do the surrogate parents act as replacements for parents in other matters.

GENERAL PROCEDURAL REQUIREMENTS

School districts must establish and maintain procedural safeguards in accordance with the IDEA and state law requirements (see Figure 12.1 for a list of the IDEA's procedural safeguards). The safeguard notice and subsequent notices must (a) provide a full explanation

---

*A child is a ward of the state when the state has assumed legal responsibility to make decisions regarding the child (Shrybman, 1982).

FIGURE 12.1 ▓
**Procedural Safeguards
of the IDEA**

The procedural safeguard notice to parents must fully explain the following safeguards:

1. The right to receive an independent educational evaluation
2. The right to receive prior written notice before a school poses or refuses to take a specific action
3. The right to access their child's educational records
4. The right and opportunity to present and resolve complaints (This includes [a] the time period in which to make a complaint, [b] the opportunity for the school to resolve the complaint, and [c] the availability of mediation.)
5. The placement of a child during the pendency of the due process hearing
6. The procedures for students who are placed in an interim alternative educational setting
7. The requirements for unilateral placement by parents of a child in private schools at public expense
8. The requirements for due process hearings, including information regarding the disclosure of evaluation results and recommendations
9. The requirements for state-level appeals (if applicable in the state)
10. The right to file a civil action, including the time period in which parents must file
11. The attorney's fees requirements

of the procedural safeguards, (b) be written in the native language of the parents (unless it is clearly not feasible to do so), (c) be written in an easily understandable manner, and (d) be available to parents of students with disabilities. Additionally, a copy of the procedural safeguards must be made available to parents of a child with a disability one time a year. An additional copy shall be given to a child's parents when (a) a child is initially referred or the parent requests an evaluation, (b) a parent first files a complaint for a due process hearing, or (c) a parent requests a copy. A school district may place the procedural safeguard notice on its website.

Notice Requirements

The IDEA requires that schools notify parents at various stages in the special education process regarding their substantive and procedural rights. Also, once during every school year school districts are required to provide parents with a copy of the procedural safeguard afforded them by the IDEA. School districts are also required to provide parents with the procedural safeguards (a) after the initial referral, (b) upon receiving a parental request for evaluation, (c) upon receipt that the parent has filed a complaint with the SEA and first due process complaint, (d) when a school district's disciplinary removal constitutes a change of placement, and (e) upon receiving a parental request (IDEA Regulations, 34 C.F.R. § 300.504(a)). School districts may also place a notice of procedural safeguards on their website.

The IDEA also requires that written notice be provided to parents prior to the school's proposing to initiate or change the identification, evaluation, educational placement, or provision of a **free appropriate public education (FAPE)** to the child, or prior to the school's refusing to make such changes (IDEA Regulations, 34 C.F.R. § 300.503(a)). The purpose of notifying parents is to provide them with information to protect their rights and the rights of their child, to allow them to make informed decisions, and to enable them to fully participate in the special education process (Tatgenhorst et al., 2014). Notice must be provided to parents after an appropriate decision has been reached concerning identification, evaluation, or placement. Furthermore, notice must be given in a reasonable amount of time prior to the implementation of the decision (*Letter to Helmuth,* 1990). Because a school district's failure to provide notification is a serious matter, school districts often use various methods to document that the required notices have been sent. Such efforts may include keeping records and copies of phone calls, e-mails, home visits, or letters sent or attempted. The IDEA, however, does not require that school districts have parents acknowledge the receipt of a notice in writing.

FIGURE 12.2 ▨
Content of Notice Requirements of the IDEA

1. A full explanation of all procedural safeguards and how parents may obtain a copy of the procedural safeguards
2. A description of the action proposed or refused by the school:
   i. An explanation of why the action is being taken
   ii. A description of any options considered
   iii. Reasons why the school proposed or refused to take an action
3. A description of each evaluation procedure the school used to make its decision
4. A description of any other factors that were relevant to the school's decision
5. A description of where parents may obtain assistance to understand their procedural rights
6. If the language or mode of communication is not written, the school shall ensure that:
   i. The notice is translated orally or by other means to the parents in their native language or mode of communication.
   ii. The parent understands the content of the notice.
   iii. There is written evidence that these requirements have been met.

The notice must be written so that it is understandable to the general public. Sending parents a copy of the pertinent statutes and regulations is not an appropriate form of notice (*Max M. v. Thompson,* 1984). Moreover, the notice must provide enough information for parents to understand what the school district is proposing or why a particular option was chosen. Additionally, the notification must be in a parent's native language unless it is clearly not feasible to do so. Figure 12.2 lists the IDEA's specific requirements regarding the content of the notice (IDEA Regulations, 34 C.F.R. § 300.503(b)). In *Adams County School District* (2010), the Colorado SEA held that a school district's failure to provide a parent prior written notice in her native language contributed to the parent's confusion and misunderstanding and resulted in the parent being denied a meaningful opportunity to participate in the IEP process.

Consent Requirements

According to Lake (2014), because parental consent is a key procedural safeguard, to be in compliance with the IDEA it is critical that school district personnel know when and how to obtain consent. The IDEA requires informed parental consent prior to taking any of the following actions: (a) evaluating a child to determine whether the child is eligible to receive special education and related services (initial evaluation only), (b) providing special education and related services to a child, (c) reevaluating a child, (d) allowing an IEP team member to be excused from attending an IEP meeting, (e) implementing an individualized family services plan (IFSP) in place of an IEP, and (f) accessing a child's private insurance information (IDEA Regulations, 34 C.F.R. § 300.300 *et seq.*). When a school obtains consent, it has a student's parents' permission to carry out the action proposed in the notice. Once a student is initially placed in a special education program, the IDEA does not require that parental consent be obtained for subsequent evaluations or for changes in the student's special education program. In these situations, however, the school must provide notice of intent to evaluate or change placement, and must follow the requirements for changing the IEP. Moreover, Shrybman (1982) recommended that school districts obtain consent in such situations even though it is not legally required. States may have more stringent consent requirements, but they must not have the effect of excluding a child from special education.

When obtaining consent, the school district personnel must ensure that the parents are fully informed, which means that the parents (a) have been informed about all information relevant to the activity for which consent is sought, in their native language or other form of communication; (b) understand and agree in writing to the proposed action for which their consent is sought; and (c) understand their granting of consent is voluntary and may

FIGURE 12.3 ■
**Consent Procedures
of the IDEA**

Parental consent must be obtained before conducting a/an:

✓ Preplacement evaluation
✓ Initial placement in special education
✓ Reevaluation (unless the LEA can demonstrate that it took measures to secure parental consent but was unsuccessful)

be revoked at any time (IDEA Regulations 34 C.F.R. § 300.9(a)–(c)). Figure 12.3 lists the IDEA's specific requirements regarding consent and the content of the consent notice (IDEA Regulations, 34 C.F.R. §§ 300.504–300.505).

The right of revocation is somewhat limited because the opportunity to revoke consent is only available while the activity for which consent was given is taking place. For example, if consent is given for an evaluation, the time in which consent can be revoked ends when the evaluation is completed (*Letter to Williams*, 1991). When given in a timely manner, a revocation of consent has the same effect as an initial refusal to consent.

IDEA requires that even after special education and related services are being provided to a student, if the student's parents revoke consent in writing, the school district must cease providing services. However, school district personnel must provide prior written notice to the parents before stopping the services.

IDEA 2004 addressed a situation that arises when parents refuse to grant consent for what school personnel believe are needed special education services. If school district personnel are considering whether to conduct an initial evaluation of a student but do not have parental permission or a response from the parents of the student, the school district may pursue the initial evaluation by applying for mediation and due process procedures. If, however, parental refusal to provide consent comes when the school district is providing special education services, the school district may not go to a hearing officer to order the parents to bring the child to the service center. In such situations, the school district will not be considered in violation of the FAPE requirement of the IEP because it did not provide a special education.

Moreover, when a parent revokes consent for services under the IDEA, the revocation applies to the total special education program, not just part of it. In other words, parents cannot revoke consent for only a part of a program and choose to retain another part of the program. In essence, special education services are a take-it-or-leave-it proposition; parents either consent to all of the services or revoke consent for the entire program (Tatgenhorst et al., 2014). After parents revoke consent, the student becomes a general education student. If parents later change their minds regarding the revocation of consent, the parents always have the option of requesting an initial evaluation. Interestingly enough, if a child's parents refuse to provide consent for an initial evaluation for special education eligibility, the school district may pursue permission to evaluate through the due process procedures of the IDEA. A school district, however, is not obligated to pursue an initial evaluation in this manner and the school district does not violate the child find requirements of the IDEA if officials choose not to pursue the initial evaluation (Office of Special Education and Rehabilitative Services, 2011). Tatgenhorst et al. (2014) asserted that it is in the long-term interest of students, more efficient, and less expensive for school district personnel to work with parents to try to change their viewpoint and obtain consent.

Opportunity to Examine Records

The IDEA contains specific requirements concerning parental access rights (IDEA Regulations, 34 §§ C.F.R. 300.610–300.627). The regulations require that the parents of a child with a disability shall be afforded an opportunity to inspect and review all educational records with respect to the identification, evaluation, and educational placement of the child, and the provision of FAPE to the child (IDEA Regulations, 34 C.F.R. § 300.501(a)). The IDEA does

FIGURE 12.4 ■
**Parents' Inspection
and Review Rights**

- Schools shall permit parents to inspect and review any educational records relating to their child.
- The school must comply with the request without unnecessary delay and before any meeting regarding the child's education (45 days or less).
- The school must respond to reasonable requests for explanations and interpretations of records.
- Parents can request that the school provide copies of the records if failure to provide these copies would prevent the parents from exercising their rights.
- Parents can have a representative inspect and review the records.
- Schools must assume that parents have the right to inspect records unless they have been advised that the parents do not have the right under the applicable state laws.
- Schools must keep a record of parties obtaining access to educational records, including name of the party, date, and purpose.
- Schools shall provide parents with a list of types and locations of educational records used by the school.
- Parents who believe that information in the records is inaccurate or misleading may request that the school amend the information. If the school refuses to amend the records, the parents must be informed of their right to request a hearing.

not define educational records but rather used the definition of educational records from the Family Educational Rights and Privacy Act (FERPA). FERPA defines educational records as those records that are (a) directly related to a student and (b) maintained by an educational agency or institution (FERPA Regulations, 34 C.F.R. § 99.3). According to a U.S. District Court in the Northern District of Illinois in *Jaccari J. v. Board of Education of the City of Chicago, District # 299* (2009), parents have the right to examine all records that relate to their children including records, files, documents, and other materials that contain information directly related to a student that are maintained by the school district. For more information on FERPA see Chapter 14.

Schools must permit parents to inspect and review all educational records collected, maintained, and used by the school concerning the student's special education. When parents ask to review educational records, they must be allowed to do so without unnecessary delay. Additionally, requests to inspect records must be granted prior to any meeting regarding the student's IEP or a due process hearing. The length of time between the parents' request to the school and the inspection or review of the records cannot exceed 45 days (IDEA Regulations, 34 C.F.R. § 300.613(a)). Figure 12.4 lists specific inspection and review rights granted to parents under the IDEA.

The IDEA's confidentiality of information requirements direct school district personnel to keep a record of all persons obtaining access to the student records. The records maintained must include the name of the party obtaining access, the date access was given, and the purpose for which the records were used (IDEA Regulations, 34 C.F.R. § 300.614). This requirement, however, does not extend to parental access.

Independent Educational Evaluation

The IDEA's procedural safeguards include the right of parents to obtain an independent educational evaluation (IEE) of their child (IDEA Regulations, 34 C.F.R. § 300.502 *et seq.*). Under certain circumstances, the school may be required to provide this evaluation at public expense. (For elaborations on IEEs, see Chapter 10.)

An IEE is an evaluation conducted by a qualified examiner who is not employed by the public agency responsible for the education of the child (IDEA Regulations, 34 C.F.R. § 300.502(a)(3)). If the parents disagree with the school's evaluation, they may request an IEE at public expense. If, however, school personnel believe the evaluation to be appropriate, they may request a due process hearing. If the hearing officer determines that the school's evaluation was appropriate, the parents retain the right to an IEE,

Enhanced eText **Video Example 12.1**
To view a brief **video** on asking
for an Independent Educational
Evaluation go to:
www.youtube.com/watch?v=1O9z7iaukOo

- The parents of a child with disabilities have the right to obtain one IEE of the child at public expense.
- On request, schools shall provide to parents information about where an IEE may be obtained.
- Parents have the right to an IEE at public expense if they disagree with the school's evaluation.
- The school may initiate a hearing to show that its evaluation was appropriate. If the final decision is in favor of the school, the parents still have the right to an IEE, but not at public expense.
- If parents obtain an IEE at private expense, the results of the evaluation must be considered by the school.
- If a hearing officer requests an IEE, the cost must be borne by the school.

but not at public expense. When parents obtain an evaluation at their own expense, school personnel must consider it in the special education decision-making process. The IEE may also be presented as evidence at an impartial due process hearing.

Parents have received reimbursement for IEEs when schools have violated procedural safeguards (*Akers v. Bolton*, 1981), when parents have taken unilateral actions that were later determined necessary (*Anderson v. Thompson*, 1981), and when the IEE was later used to determine placement (*Hoover Schrum, Ill. School District No. 157*, 1980). The U.S. Court of Appeals for the Fourth Circuit has held that only one IEE at public expense is required (*Hudson v. Wilson*, 1987). A due process hearing officer may also request that an IEE be performed at public expense. Specific requirements of school districts regarding IEEs are listed in Figure 12.5.

DISPUTE RESOLUTION

When Congress passed the Education for All Handicapped Children Act in 1975, it included elaborate procedural protections to ensure that schools would include parents in all educational decision making involved in providing a FAPE. However, if parents believed a school district has not followed the procedures of the IDEA or if they disagreed with actions involving the identification, evaluation, or placement of their child, the IDEA included dispute resolution mechanisms that parents may access. If students are eligible under the IDEA, the dispute resolution mechanisms include mediation, resolution sessions, and due process hearings, and each state has a complaint investigation and resolution process. Additionally, students covered by the IDEA may also use the dispute resolution systems under Section 504 (Zirkel & McGuire, 2010).

There are three routes that parents may pursue when they have disputes with their child's school district: Investigative, adjudicative (Zirkel, 2016), and voluntary mediation. The investigative route involves a child's parents filing a complaint with their state's educational agency. If state officials find merit to the complaint, they will conduct an investigation and issue and enforce their findings. The adjudicative route is a more legalistic procedure that begins with an optional mediation session, and may proceed to a resolution session, then to a due process hearing, and possibly state or federal court. The voluntary mediation system is available under both the state complaint systems and the hearing system. I will next review these dispute resolution processes, beginning with the state complaint.

State Complaint Procedures

States are required to develop compliant procedures when parents disagree with a school district regarding IDEA matters (IDEA Regulations § 300.151-300.153). The complaints must be filed within 1 year of the occurrence of the violation and can be filed on any issues involving identification, evaluation, placement, or programming. School districts may not file complaints with a state. An advantage that parents have in the state complaint is that there is minimal burden on them as complainants (Zirkle, 2017). According to Zirkle (2017), it costs parents nothing to file a state complaint, they are not required to go through the ordeal of a hearing and parents do not need to hire an attorney.

The procedures that are developed by a state must allow parents to go through a state-sponsored complaint process in which they can file a complaint against the school district that they contend has violated Part B of the IDEA (e.g., eligibility decisions, denial of FAPE). When parents file a complaint with an SEA, they must also notify the LEA that they are filing the complaint. The complaint must include the following information: (a) a statement that the LEA has violated a requirement of the IDEA, (b) the facts upon which the complaint is based, and (c) their signatures and contact information. If the violation concerned a specific child, the complaint must also include the name and address of the child, the name of the child's school, a description of the problem, and a proposed resolution of the problem.

If state officials determine that an investigation is needed, the state then has 60 days to conduct an on-site investigation of the complaint. Prior to conducting the investigation, however, state officials must allow the parents' filing the complaint to submit additional information and allow school district personal to respond to the complaint. The school district must be given a similar opportunity. School district personnel are also allowed to propose a solution to the complaint. Moreover, the parent filing the complaint and school district personnel may enter mediation to resolve the complaint. After state officials have reviewed all relevant information, they must determine if an investigation is needed. If the decision is that an investigation is required, the SEA must conduct an on-site investigation.

Following the investigation, state officials must make a written ruling on their decision. Moreover, the written decision must (a) address each allegation in the complaint, (b) detail the state's findings of fact and conclusions, and (c) provide the reasoning behind the decision (IDEA Regulations, 34 C.F.R. § 300.152[a]). The state must have procedures for effective implementation of the final decision, which include technical assistance activities, negotiations, and corrective actions to achieve compliance. The IDEA grants SEAs broad discretion in awarding remedies in cases of IDEA violations. In fact, Tatgenhorst et al. (2014) asserted that SEA may award any remedy for a violation that a court or hearing officer may award (see section later in this chapter on remedies).

If a student's parents who filed a state complaint are not satisfied with the resolution of the issue they may file for a due process hearing about the same issues (*Letter to Lieberman*, 1995). State complaints are not confidential, and if state officials choose to do so, state complaints can be made public. If a state posts written decisions on its website, it must ensure that special education confidentiality rules are not violated.

The state complaint process has the potential to provide parents with a less costly and more efficient mechanism for reducing disputes than does the due process hearing (*OSEP Memorandum 94-16*, 1994). Zirkle (2016) noted that the state complaint procedures have the following differences from the adjudicative hearing system: (a) complaints can be filed by any person or organization, except by a school district; (b) the process to file a complaint is very easy and attorneys are not required; and (c) the complaint system has a 60-day processing timeline, as opposed to 75 days for a due process hearing. Zirkle (2016) noted that there were also areas of similarity between the state complaint system and due process system. These similarities include the subject matter jurisdiction, requirements for a written complaint and written decision, remedial authority, and determination of procedural and substantive issues.

Mediation

Another dispute resolution procedure in the IDEA, which is neither investigative nor adjudicative, is the voluntary mediation system. The IDEA Amendments of 1997 added voluntary mediation requirements to the procedural safeguards (IDEA Regulations, 34 C.F.R. § 300.506 *et seq.*). Prior to the amendments, many states had already adopted some form of mediation. The federal standard, however, provided for greater uniformity among the states and furnished a model for the states that had not yet implemented mediation. The IDEA Regulations of 2006 retained and "strongly encouraged" mediation (IDEA Regulations 34 C.F.R. § 300.506(a)). State education agencies pay for the costs of mediation sessions, including the fee charged by the mediator. Moreover, states must maintain a list of qualified mediators and must track and report the number of mediations held and number of settlements reached through those mediations.

Mediation is a dispute-resolution and collaborative problem-solving process in which a trained impartial party facilitates a negotiation process between parties who have reached an impasse (Dobbs, Primm, & Primm, 1991; Goldberg & Huefner, 1995; Lake, 2014). The role of the mediator is to facilitate discussion, encourage open exchange of information, assist the involved parties in understanding each other's viewpoints, and help the parties to reach mutually agreeable solutions. The mediator has no authority to impose solutions on either party. In mediation sessions, the focus is on the negotiated resolution of the conflict rather than factual presentations, witnesses, or formal rules of evidence (Goldberg & Huefner, 1995; Lake, 2014). Mediation is an intervening step that may be used prior to conducting a formal due process hearing (Lake, 2014). According to the National Center for Dispute Resolution in Special Education (Consortium for Appropriate Dispute Resolution in Special Education; CADRE, 2010) best practices used by various states to conduct mediation include:

- Creating a system that affords respect to all participants and focuses on the educational needs of children
- Prohibiting the use of mediation as a ploy to camouflage inadequate services
- Ensuring that each side enters mediation understanding their rights and able to represent their interests
- Defining training needs for all parties involved and providing training workshops
- Involving school personnel and parents in training prior to the mediation session
- Privatizing the mediation office so it is not part of a school district, to ensure the perception that the process is independent
- Surveying parties involved in mediation over a period of time following the sessions to determine if agreements have been effectively implemented
- Ensuring that mediation fosters a fair, candid, and respectful dialogue during a dispute

When a mediation session is conducted, the mediator, a neutral third party, helps the parents and the school personnel arrive at their own solution to the disagreement.

Although a mediation session is structured, it is less formal and adversarial than due process hearings or court proceedings. Advantages of mediation include the following: (a) takes less time, (b) costs less, (c) allows for greater discussion of the issues, and (d) helps to maintain a workable relationship between schools and parents (Dobbs et al., 1991; Primm, 1990). Dobbs, Primm, and Primm (1993) reported that a questionnaire given to parents and school personnel following special education mediation sessions revealed that 90% of the parents and 99% of the teachers who had been involved in the mediation would recommend the process to others to help resolve disputes.

States are required to offer mediation as a voluntary option for parents and school districts to resolve disputes. The IDEA clearly specifies that mediation cannot be used to delay or deny parents' right to an impartial due process hearing. The IDEA does not require that parents enter mediation to resolve their disputes prior to filing for a due process hearing. If parents choose not to use mediation, school districts and SEAs may establish procedures to require parents to meet with a disinterested third party who would encourage and explain the benefits of mediation to them. Such meetings must be held at a time and place convenient to the parents.

Because states have been successful in using mediation systems that both allowed and disallowed attorneys at mediation sessions, Congress left to the states decisions regarding the attendance of attorneys at mediation. OSEP, however, discouraged the use of attorneys in mediation because it "may have the potential for creating an adversarial atmosphere that may not necessarily be in the best interests of the child" (*Letter to Chief State School Officers*, 2000). When a school district and parents go to mediation, both parties should be involved in selecting a mediator from the list maintained by the SEA. The mediator must be impartial, so employees of the involved school districts or persons with personal or professional conflicts of interest are not allowed to mediate. Furthermore, the mediator must be experienced, trained, and knowledgeable about the law. Mediators do not have to be attorneys. When mediation is used, the states will bear the costs.

Mediation resolutions are to be put into a legally binding written agreement. The agreement includes the discussions that occurred during mediation, which must be kept confidential. Furthermore, the agreement is signed by both parties and is enforceable in a state or federal court. The discussion from the mediation session, however, cannot be used as evidence in subsequent due process hearings or civil actions. Parties in the mediation process may be required to sign a confidentiality pledge prior to the commencement of mediation. In early 2014 acting under a directive from OSEP, officials at CADRE were asked to create a set of resources for parents regarding dispute resolution. These parent guides, which are available on the CADRE website (www.directionservice.org), include a guide on IDEA's special education mediation.

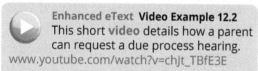

Enhanced eText **Video Example 12.2**
This short **video** details how a parent can request a due process hearing.
www.youtube.com/watch?v=chJt_TBfE3E

The Due Process System

The due process hearing system is adjudicative, because it is conducted very much like a trial. States may either have a one-tiered hearing system or a two-tiered hearing system. Most states have a one-tier system of due process hearings. In a one-tier state, the state educational agency or another state agency is responsible for conducting the hearing and the losing party may file an appeal with a state of federal court. In a two-tier system, the first level hearing is conducted by a local school district and the losing party may file an appeal with the state department of education. After this decision is issued, the losing party may appeal to state or federal court.

Resolution Session

Congress, in IDEA 2004, developed the resolution session as an intermediary step between the meditation session and the due process hearing. Within 15 days of receiving a parent's complaint, the school district is required to convene a meeting with the parents and relevant members of the IEP team, including the school representative, to discuss the complaint and attempt to resolve it. The school district is not allowed to bring an attorney to a resolution session unless the parents bring an attorney to the meeting. Additionally, the two sides can waive the resolution session if both sides agree to such an action. A single party, either parents or school officials, cannot unilaterally waive the resolution meeting (Lake, 2014). The IDEA does not require a resolution meeting when a local educational agency (LEA) is the party that files for a hearing. Neither does the law specify a particular format or procedure for conducting resolution meetings.

Essentially, the parents give the school district 30 days in which to resolve the issue. If no resolution is reached within 30 days of filing the complaint, the due process hearing may take place. If the complaint is settled, both parties will sign a legally binding agreement. Moreover, this settlement agreement is enforceable in any state or federal court that has jurisdiction. According to Richards and Martin (2005), by including a resolution session prior to a due process hearing, Congress attempted to add a prehearing forum to resolve parent complaints outside of the legal process.

The Due Process Hearing

The purpose of the due process hearing is to resolve disputes between the parents of children and youth with disabilities and school districts regarding the identification, evaluation, programming, placement, or provision of a FAPE to a student with disabilities under the IDEA (IDEA Regulations, 34 C.F.R. § 300.507).

In a due process hearing an impartial third party, the due process hearing officer, will hear both sides of a dispute, examine the issues, and settle the dispute (Anderson, Chitwood, & Hayden, 1990; Lake, 2014). Congress deliberately chose an adversarial system for resolving disputes, believing it was the best way to ensure that both parents and school officials would receive an equal opportunity to present their case (Goldberg & Huefner, 1995). Parents must file within 2 years of the date that they knew, or should have known, of the action that forms the basis of the complaint (IDEA Regulations, 34 C.F.R. § 300.511(c)). If the state has an explicit time limit, however, that time limit must be followed. The time limitation will not apply to a parent, however, if the school district had taken actions to prevent a parent's request for a hearing or if the district withheld important information from the parent (IDEA Regulations, 34 C.F.R. § 500.511(f)).

The due process hearing may also be used to seek resolution of procedural violations if the violations adversely affect a student's education (Lake, 2014). In addition to parents, students who have reached the age of majority can request hearings, as may schools (IDEA Regulations, 34 C.F.R. § 506(a)), when parents refuse to consent to an evaluation. When school districts request due process hearings it is often because of parents' refusal to consent to an evaluation or in response to a parental request for an independent educational evaluation (Tatgenhorst et al., 2014).

In a hearing both the parents and school districts have the following rights: (a) the right to be accompanied and advised by an attorney and by individuals with special expertise with respect to the problems of children with disabilities, (b) the right to present evidence and confront, cross-examine, and compel the attendance of witnesses, (c) the right to prohibit the introduction of any evidence at the hearing that has not been disclosed to the party at least 5 days before the hearing, (d) the right to obtain a written or electronic verbatim record of the hearing (at the option of the parents), and (e) the right to obtain a written or electronic finding of fact and decisions (at the option of the parents). Parents also have the right to have their child who is the subject of the hearing present. Parents may also open the hearing to the public. A case out of Kansas, *P.R. v. Shawnee Mission Unified School District No. 512* (2012), showed why it is important to take advantage of these rights. In this case, a U.S. district court denied the plaintiffs' motion to present additional evidence that was not presented at the due process hearing.

The IDEA leaves the choice of the agency that conducts due process hearings to individual states (IDEA Regulations, 34 C.F.R. § 506(b)). Many states assign the conduct of hearings to the SEA, an intermediate educational agency, or the local school district. The agency responsible for the hearing is required to inform the parents of any free or low-cost legal and other relevant services if requested to do so by the parents (IDEA Regulations, 34 C.F.R. § 506(c)). The hearing must be conducted at a time and place that is convenient to the parents (IDEA Regulations, 34 C.F.R. § 300.512(d)).

No less than 5 days before the hearing, both parties are required to disclose any evaluations or information that they intend to bring out at the hearing. If either party fails to file this information in time, the hearing officer may prevent the late party from introducing new evidence or raising new issues without the consent of the other party.

State laws or regulations direct the method by which due process hearings are requested. If the due process hearing is conducted by the school district, the request normally goes through the district. The nature of the disagreement and the names of the parties involved should be included in the request.

The U.S. Court of Appeals for the Ninth Circuit has ruled that due process hearings may be requested by parents even if their child has not been formally accepted into special education (*Hacienda La Puente Unified School District v. Honig*, 1992). Also, parents can request a due process hearing even if their child is not attending public school, but the reason that the child is not in the public school must be related to the public school's failure to provide a FAPE (*S-1 v. Turlington*, 1981).

The Impartial Hearing Officer

The integrity of the due process hearing is maintained by ensuring that the hearing officer is impartial. The officer must have no involvement with the child, the parent, the school system, or the state. That is, he or she must have no personal or professional interest that might conflict with his or her objectivity in the hearing.

Potential hearing officers are not considered employees of the public agency if the school pays the hearing office only for conducting the hearing and for no other reason. No guidelines for the training and evaluation of hearing officers are provided in the IDEA. In IDEA 2004, however, Congress added qualifications for hearing officers. Persons used as hearing officers must have competence in conducting hearings, knowledge of special education law, and knowledge of how to write legally appropriate decisions (IDEA Regulations, 34 C.F.R. § 300.551(c)).

School districts must maintain a list of persons who may serve as due process hearing officers. If parents request a copy of the list, it must be provided by the school district. Although parents are given no right to participate in the selection of the hearing officer, they can challenge the selection of the officer. Challenges to the impartiality of a hearing officer must be made during the due process hearing or subsequent administrative or judicial reviews (*Colin K. v. Schmidt*, 1983).

Zirkel and Scala (2010) found that 33 states use part-time hearing officers and 18 use full-time officers. Additionally, the authors reported that 45 states use hearing officers with a legal background primarily in the law and 6 states use hearing officers with a legal background primarily in special education. Interestingly, Zirkel and Scala also found that the District of Columbia, New York, California, New Jersey, and Pennsylvania accounted for 85% of all due process hearings conducted in the United States in 2008–2009.

The Role of the Hearing Officer

When a dispute concerning a student's special education reaches the due process hearing level, the authority to decide the issue passes from the parents and the school to the hearing officer (Shrybman, 1982). The primary duties of the hearing officer are to inform the parties of their rights during the hearing; allow all parties the opportunity to present their cases; conduct the hearing in a fair, orderly, and impartial manner; and render a decision in accordance with the law. According to the U.S. Supreme Court,

> the role of the [hearing officer] … is functionally comparable to that of a judge…. More importantly, the process of agency adjudication is currently structured so as to assure that the hearing examiner exercises his independent judgment on the evidence before him, free from pressures by the parties or other officials within the agency.

(*Butz v. Economou*, 1978, p. 513)

According to IDEA 2004, decisions of the hearing officer shall be made on substantive grounds. This means that the hearing officer must determine whether the student in question received a FAPE that provided meaningful educational benefit. A hearing officer can rule against a school on procedural grounds only if the procedural violation (a) impeded the student's right to receive a FAPE, (b) impeded the parents' opportunity to participate in educational decision making, or (c) caused a deprivation of educational benefits. In *A. G. v. District of Columbia* (2011) a hearing officer's decision was reversed and remanded because according to the court the hearing officer made a ruling on procedural formalities rather than relying on substantive grounds.

According to Tatgenhorst et al. (2014) due process hearing officers have authority to award most types of relief such as order for future conduct, tuition reimbursement, or award of compensatory education and can order school districts to implement an educational program, conduct an evaluation, or effect a placement. A hearing officer cannot award attorney's fees and neither does the hearing officer have any authority over outside agencies.

The hearing officer must render a decision no later than 45 days after the request for the hearing. A copy of the decision must be mailed to each of the parties. The decision of the hearing officer is final unless it is appealed. In a two-tiered state, the decision is appealed to the SEA. In a one-tier state, the complainant may go directly to the courts.

Hearing officers cannot be held liable for actions taken in their official capacity. The U.S. Supreme Court, in *Butz v. Economou* (1978), held that hearing officers, like judges, have immunity from damages when fulfilling their duties as hearing officers. The high court held that "persons … in performing their adjudicatory functions … are entitled to absolute immunity for their judicial acts. Those who complain of error in such proceedings must seek agency or judicial review" (p. 514).

Hearing officers may, however, be sued for damages resulting from actions taken in their individual capacities. If hearing officers take actions that they know, or should have known, are violations of the student's constitutional rights, or if they take actions with malicious intent to deprive a student of his or her rights, they may be held liable for damages (Shrybman, 1982). The Supreme Court has ruled that hearing officers cannot be held liable for monetary damages if there were reasonable grounds for their actions and if they acted in good faith (*Schever v. Rhodes,* 1974) or if they merely made mistakes in judgment (*Butz v. Economou,* 1978).

Either party in a hearing has the right to appeal the hearing officer's decision. In a two-tier state, the party files an appeal with the appropriate agency. Following review of the hearing officer's decision, the aggrieved party may file a civil action in state or federal court. In a one-tier state, the aggrieved party may file a civil action in state or federal court immediately following the decision in the due process hearing. An appeal of a hearing officer's decision must be filed within 90 days of the decision. If the decision is appealed to a state or federal court, the court must receive the records of the hearing and will hear additional evidence at the request of the party. The IDEA directs court officials to base their decisions on the preponderance of the evidence, and the court may grant relief to the prevailing parties.

The Stay-Put Provision

Unless the school and parents agree otherwise, when a request for a hearing is made, the IDEA's "stay-put" provision is invoked. According to this provision,

> During the pendency of any administrative or judicial proceeding regarding a complaint, unless the public agency and the parents of the child agree otherwise, the child involved in the complaint must remain in his or her present educational placement.

(IDEA Regulations, 34 C.F.R. § 300.513)

The U.S. Supreme Court, in *Honig v. Doe* (1988), stated that the stay-put provision prevents schools from unilaterally moving students from placement to placement. Essentially, the stay-put provision acts as an automatic preliminary injunction pending a resolution of a due process hearing or judicial action. The objective of the stay-put provision is to maintain stability and continuity for the student until the dispute is resolved (Tatgenhorst, Norlin, & Gorn, 2014), but it can be suspended during the pendency of a review by an agreement between the schools and the parents regarding placement.

A comment to the regulation states that although the student's placement may not be changed, the school may use its normal procedures for dealing with students who are endangering themselves or others (IDEA Regulations, 34 C.F.R. § 300.513, Note). There is, however, no "dangerous exception" that allows the school to suspend the stay-put rule (*Honig v. Doe,* 1988).

The IDEA abrogates the stay-put amendment when a student with a disability (a) brings a weapon to school or a school function; (b) uses, sells, or solicits the sale of illegal drugs; or (c) inflicts serious bodily injury upon another person while at school or a school function. In such situations, an administrator may immediately remove the student to an interim alternative setting for up to 45 *school* days. If a due process hearing is requested, the stay-put placement becomes the current setting, which is the interim alternative educational placement. During the pendency of the proceedings, therefore, the student remains in the interim alternative setting. (For elaborations on the discipline of students with disabilities, see Chapter 13.)

The U.S. Court of Appeals for the District of Columbia ruled that the stay-put provision applies during due process hearings, during state administrative reviews, and at the trial court level but does not apply to the appellate level (*Anderson v. District of Columbia,* 1989). According to the court, a school is not required to maintain the current educational placement if an appeal goes to the appellate court.

If students are not in special education and the hearing concerns their eligibility to receive special education services, they must remain in the general education placement until the dispute is resolved. Similarly, if students are in special education and the dispute concerns a change of placement, they must remain in the placement where they were when the request was made. If the dispute involves initial admission to public school, students must be placed in the public school program until the dispute is resolved.[†]

The Conduct of the Hearing   The purpose of the due process hearing is to provide a legally constituted forum in which the contending parties have an opportunity to present their cases to an impartial hearing officer. From the perspective of a hearing officer, the purpose of the hearing is to give the parties an opportunity to present the information necessary for an informed ruling to be made.

Although the conduct of hearings varies among hearing officers, usually hearings are conducted in a professional manner but with a more informal atmosphere than a trial court. There should be a structure to the hearing so that everyone clearly understands his or her role and participates fully. Shrybman (1982) warned that hearing officers must be in control of the proceedings and not allow any participants to abuse the process. Proceedings that erupt into acrimonious exchanges accomplish little.

Either party in a hearing has the right to a written record of the hearing. Parents may, at their option, require an electronic record of the hearing. In such situations, court reporters must be used. In addition to meeting the legal mandate, the verbatim record is essential for hearing officers in writing their decision and, if the decision is appealed, for review of the hearing decision. According to Shrybman (1982), if no verbatim record is available, the case must be reheard.

The hearing room should be arranged in a manner that is conducive to the orderly presentation of evidence and testimony (Shrybman, 1982). The arrangement should allow all participants to see and hear each other clearly. Often hearing rooms are set up like a trial court, with the hearing officer in a central position and the respective parties on the sides.

The hearing officer typically opens the hearing with a call to order and an introductory statement. This statement should include the introduction of the hearing officer and the case, a statement of legal authority for the hearing, an explanation of the purpose of the hearing and the role of the hearing officer, an acknowledgment of persons present, an explanation of the rights of the parties in the hearing, and instructions on appropriate decorum and the structure and procedures to be followed during the hearing (Ginn, Carruth, & McCarthy, 1988; Hamway, 1994; Shrybman, 1982).

Shrybman (1982) suggested a format to which hearings should adhere. The hearing should begin with preliminary matters such as questions, objections, or requests from participants. Following the preliminaries, representatives of each party should present a brief opening statement outlining their positions. During the opening statement, evidence is not presented. When opening statements have been completed, the evidence is presented. The formal rules of evidence that are used in courts do not apply to administrative hearings. Relevancy and reliability should be the rules for introducing evidence in the hearing (Guernsey & Klare, 1993). Because the school district is legally responsible for the student's placement and special education program and bears

---

[†] IDEA 2004 requires that if a student transfers into a school district within a state with an existing IEP, this is not to be treated as an initial admission and the school should continue to provide a FAPE by implementing the existing IEP until the team either adopts the previous IEP or completes the IEP planning process.

FIGURE 12.6 ■
**Possible Format for a
Due Process Hearing**

Introduction of the officer and the case
- Hearing officer makes opening statements:
    - statement of legal authority for the hearing
    - explanation of the purpose for the hearing
    - explanation of the hearing officer's role
- Persons present are introduced.
- Parties are informed of due process rights.
- Instructions of decorum, structure, and procedures of the hearing are made.
- Preliminary matters are addressed.

Presentations
- Public school representatives present.
- Parents present.
- Cross-examinations are conducted and additional evidence is presented.
- Closing statements are made.

Closing the hearing
- The hearing officer:
    - explains the issuance of the decision
    - explains appeal procedures
    - thanks participants and closes the hearing

the burden of proof as to the appropriateness of the education, the school system should present its case first. Shrybman (1982) asserted that "it is the responsibility of the public schools to provide a [child with disabilities] with a free appropriate public education so they must always stand ready to prove that their conduct on behalf of the student meets this fundamental legal requirement" (p. 325). During the presentation, the school will present documents and testimony to support its position. The parents or their counsel, if they have one, may cross-examine the school district's witnesses after their testimony. After the school's presentation, the parents present their case. The school's counsel may cross-examine the parents' witnesses at this time. After both sides have completed their initial presentations and offered their witnesses and evidence, they should have the opportunity to cross-examine witnesses again and present additional evidence. Finally, both parties conclude with a closing statement that summarizes their positions.

Following the presentations and concluding statements, the hearing officer should close the hearing. This may be done by briefly stating when the decision will be available, telling how transcripts can be obtained, explaining the appeal procedures, and adjourning the hearing. Figure 12.6 outlines this format for the due process hearing.

Appeals and Civil Actions   In states with a two-tiered process, the decision of the hearing officer can be appealed to the SEA. In an appeal, the agency reviews the entire hearing record, ensures that procedures were followed, seeks additional evidence if necessary, allows additional arguments at its discretion, and makes an independent decision. If additional evidence is heard at the state review, the protections available to parties in the original due process hearing are available at the review (e.g., disclosure of evidence 5 days prior to the hearing, the right to cross-examine witnesses).

The appeal is usually made to the office of special education of the state's Department of Education. The IDEA contains no timeline in which an appeal must be made, although individual states may address the issue. A written copy of the findings must be sent to both parties within 30 days of the date of the appeal to the state. Unless appealed, this decision is final and binding on all parties. Either party may appeal the SEA's decision and may file a civil action in a state or federal court (IDEA Regulations, 34 C.F.R. § 300.511). IDEA 2004 includes a time limit for filing civil actions. The party that brings the action, either the parent or school district, has 90 days from the date of the administrative decision to bring such an action. If the state has set a specific timeline, both parties must adhere to that schedule.

In a one-tier state, the civil action may be filed following the due process hearing. In a two-tier state, the civil action usually cannot be filed until all of the administrative options have been exhausted; that is, both the due process hearing and the SEA hearing must have been completed before an action may be filed in state or federal court. An exception to the exhaustion rule may exist if administrative hearings would be futile or inadequate (*Honig v. Doe,* 1988). Although the time-consuming nature of a hearing is not, by itself, a basis for overturning the exhaustion rule (*Cox v. Jenkins,* 1989), situations such as the agency's failure to properly implement administrative appeal measures may provide such a basis.

The court will usually not rehear the case, nor will it focus on the entire case. Rather, the court will review the record to determine the presence of serious error of law at the hearing level. Following a review of pertinent materials, courts can affirm the decision of the lower authority, modify the decision of the lower authority, reverse the decision of the lower authority, or remand all or part of the lower authority's decision. To remand means that the court will order the lower authority to conduct further proceedings in accordance with the court's instructions (Weber, 1992).

A party in a due process hearing may also file a civil action if the other party fails to follow the decision of the hearing officer. In this case, the purpose of the civil action is to have the decision enforced. Parents usually bring enforcement actions against schools. Schools, however, have little legal leverage to force parents to comply with a decision (Shrybman, 1982).

School District Responsibilities in the Hearing

Success in the due process hearing is critical to the ultimate outcome of the case. Schools further cite evidence that most decisions by due process hearing officers are upheld on review and that the vast majority of cases never go to court. It is critical to all parties, therefore, that the school districts make the best possible case at this level.

Schools must prepare seriously when approaching a due process hearing. The results of the initial hearing are critical because appeals will often be based solely on the transcripts of the initial hearing (Reusch, 1993). If schools do not succeed in making their case at this level, they probably will not succeed on appeal (Zirkel, 1994).

The Burden of Persuasion in an Administrative Hearing

Ultimately, if parents and school district officials cannot settle their differences, the IDEA provides for an impartial due process hearing. The IDEA does not, however, assign the burden of persuasion at such a due process hearing to any particular party. To prevail in any legal proceeding, including impartial due process hearings, after both sides have presented their evidence, the party with the burden of persuasion must have convinced the trier of fact, the due process hearing officer or judge, of the existence of certain facts (Conroy, Yell, & Katsiyannis, 2007). This is a very important issue because the party who is allocated the burden will lose if the hearing officer or judge is not persuaded by the evidence that the party presents.

In 2005, the U.S. Supreme Court answered the question of who should bear the burden of persuasion in special education administrative hearings in *Schaffer v. Weast.* Brian Schaffer was a student with learning disabilities (LD) and a speech–language impairment. His parents believed that the placement offered by the Montgomery County Public School System lacked the smaller classes and intensive services that Brian needed. His parents enrolled Brian in a private school and initiated a due process hearing seeking compensation from the Montgomery School District for their private school expenses. The administrative law judge (ALJ) who presided over the hearing determined that the evidence presented by the parties at the hearing was equally compelling; therefore, his ruling would depend on which party bore the burden of persuasion. After deciding that the burden of persuasion belonged to Brian's parents because they challenged the IEP, the ALJ found that the Schaffers had not met their burden and ruled in favor of the school district. Brian's parents appealed the ALJ's ruling to the U.S. district court in Maryland. The district court reversed the ALJ's decision, finding that the burden of persuasion should have been placed on the school district. The school district, therefore, should have had to prove the adequacy of the IEP. The district court remanded the case back to the ALJ.

The school district appealed to the Fourth Circuit Court of Appeals, but before the Fourth Circuit could hear the appeal, the ALJ ruled that, with the burden now on the school district, the district had failed to prove the adequacy of its IEP. The school district again appealed the ALJ's decision to the U.S. district court, and the district court again placed the burden of persuasion on the school district. The school district then appealed to the Fourth Circuit Court of Appeals for a second time. The Fourth Circuit, relying on what it called the normal rule, held that the district court erred in assigning the burden of proof to the school district and reversed the decision. According to the normal rule, when a statute, such as the IDEA, is silent about which party bears the burden of persuasion, the burden is normally placed on the party who initiated the proceeding and is seeking relief. Because Brian Schaffer's parents initiated the due process hearing, therefore, the burden of proof was placed on them. Brian's parents had argued that because the school district had greater resources and expertise they should bear the burden of persuasion. Brian Schaffer's parents appealed to the U.S. Supreme Court. The Supreme Court decided to hear the case and on November 14, 2005, in a 6–2 decision, it affirmed the Fourth Circuit's decision, which placed the burden of persuasion on the parents challenging the IEP.

In the majority decision Justice O'Connor explained that in a statutory cause of action, a court should first look at the law itself. If the law is silent regarding which party has the burden of persuasion, as is the IDEA, the Court begins with the default rule that the party bringing the case should bear the burden of persuasion. She also noted that the Court's ruling in *Schaffer v. Weast* should be construed narrowly to the case at hand:

> The burden of proof in an administrative hearing challenging an IEP is properly placed upon the party seeking relief. In this case, that party is Brian, as represented by his parents. But the rule applies with equal effect to school districts: If they seek to challenge an IEP, they will in turn bear the burden of persuasion before an ALJ.

(*Schaffer v. Weast*, 2005, p. 62)

Two justices, Breyer and Ginsburg, dissented to the decision, finding that although courts ordinarily allocate the burden of proof to the initiating party seeking relief, there were factors, such as policy considerations, convenience, and fairness, requiring that the burden of proof be assigned to the school district. Justice Ginsburg reasoned that because school districts must provide each student in special education with an IEP that meets his or her special needs, the district should have demonstrated the adequacy of the IEP. She further argued that school districts are far better equipped to demonstrate that they have fulfilled their obligation under the IDEA than the parents are to show that the schools have not met their obligations under the law. Justice Breyer argued in his dissent that the law is silent as to who bears the burden of persuasion in administrative hearings; therefore, Congress left it for the states to decide the issue. He also pointed to the IDEA's provisions that assign the establishment of procedures for the hearing to the state and its agencies. Because the ALJ in Brian Schaffer's case looked for a federal, rather than a state, burden of persuasion, Justice Breyer would have remanded the case back to the ALJ to determine how he would assign the burden of persuasion.

Since the U.S. Supreme Court decided *Schaffer* in 2005, the U.S. Department of Education, in its final regulations implementing the 2004 IDEA amendments (effective August 14, 2006), declined to assign the burden of persuasion in due process hearings. Relying on the *Schaffer* decision, the Department of Education's position was that because "the Supreme Court precedent is binding legal authority, further regulation in this area is unnecessary. In addition, we are not aware of significant questions regarding the burden of production that would require regulation" (71 Fed. Reg. 46,540, at 46,706).

ALTERNATIVES TO THE DUE PROCESS HEARING

Criticisms have been leveled at the system of dispute resolution, especially due process hearings, as being too expensive, time consuming, adversarial, and emotionally draining for all parties involved (Goldberg & Huefner, 1995; Zirkel, 1994; Zirkel & Scala, 2010). The hearings rarely solve problems and soothe anger; more often, they alienate and sustain antagonism and undermine cooperation (Beekman, 1993; Goldberg & Huefner, 1995). Parents also tend to view the due process system as unfair (Goldberg & Kuriloff, 1991). Finally, both sides have the right to be represented by attorneys (although it is not required), and the presence of attorneys may contribute to the adversarial nature of the proceedings (Shrybman, 1982). In a 1994 case from the U.S. Court of Appeals for the Ninth Circuit, the court upbraided an attorney for the use of "hardball tactics" in dealing with a school (*Clyde K. v. Puyallup School District*, 1994). The court also noted that the interests of schools, parents, and students would be more effectively served by compromise and cooperation rather than through adversarial positioning.

Zirkel (1994) asserted that the current system of special education due process hearings serves the best interests of neither the school nor the child. He suggested a five-part solution to the problems inherent in the hearing process. First, the due process hearing should be the final stage for most special education disputes. The hearing officer's decision should be binding on both parties. Judicial review would only be available for an occasional case that presents an important legal issue. This suggestion would require an amendment to the IDEA to delete the option of a second tier. The single tier would be at the state level to remove the possible influence of the school district's paying the hearing officer. The selection, training, and payment of hearing officers would become the responsibility of an independent state agency. Zirkel's second suggestion states that because the due process hearing would escalate in importance under the first suggestion, regulations would specify that hearing officers must have expertise in special education. Third, the conduct of due process hearings would be changed to a problem-solving model rather than an adversarial model. To reinforce the less adversarial model, the fourth suggestion is that attorney's fees would be limited to the judicial stage. School districts could not be represented by counsel at the hearing unless the parents chose to be represented by counsel. This suggestion would require amending the attorney's fees provision of the IDEA. Finally, hearings in routing cases should be limited to one full day. Zirkel believed that by using this model, the due process hearing would become a faster and less expensive problem-solving process.

There are a number of alternative procedures that parents and school districts may use to address problems under the IDEA. Some of these are formal and some are informal. The state of Minnesota has developed an innovative approach to resolving special education conflicts: the facilitated IEP meeting. In the facilitated IEP meeting, the IEP team, in addition to the school-based IEP team members and a student's parents, include an impartial facilitator. The role of the facilitator is to promote effective communication among team members and assist the team in developing a student's IEP. The facilitator attempts to keep the team focused on IEP development while addressing any conflicts that may arise. To be effective, the IEP facilitator must have expertise in IEP development and conflict resolution. CADRE maintains an introductory PDF titled "Facilitated IEP meetings: An emerging practice" on their website (www.directionservice.org/cadre/pdf/Facilitated%20IEP%20for%20CADRE%20 English.pdf). According to the Alliance and CADRE Consortium (2004), the role of the facilitator includes the following:

- Guiding the discussion of a student's IEP by keeping the focus on the student and his or her needs
- Assisting the IEP team with disagreements that arise during the IEP meeting
- Helping to maintain open communication among IEP team members

- Helping to keep team members on task and within an allotted time limit for the IEP meeting
- Maintaining impartiality in the meeting and not taking sides or placing blame
- Not imposing a decision on the IEP team

Recent data collected by CADRE showed that 29 states offer facilitated IEP meetings. An additional 12 states were developing or exploring the use of IEP facilitation (CADRE maintains a series of videos on the facilitated IEP process at www.directionservice.org/cadre/fieptrainingvideos.cfm).

There are other types of alternative dispute resolution systems. For example, the South Carolina Special Education Services uses an ombudsman. The ombudsman acts as a third party and takes an active role in facilitating a resolution. The goal of the ombudsman is to resolve a dispute before it reaches the level of a state complaint or due process hearing. Additional methods that states may adopt include third-party consultation and evaluation (Lake, 2014). This is an alternative dispute resolution system in which an outside expert in special education is brought in to examine an issue and offer an opinion. The conclusions are typically nonbinding unless both parties agree to accept them, in which case the parties may enter into a binding settlement agreement.

REMEDIES

When dispute resolutions are not successful, parents may file a suit in state or federal court. When a suit is filed, a court will usually defer to the facts as determined during the due process or administrative hearing, although the court may also hear additional evidence at the request of either party. The IDEA authorizes courts to provide relief (i.e., redress or assistance) to the prevailing party. According to the language of the IDEA,

> the court shall receive the records of the administrative proceedings, shall hear additional evidence at the request of a party, and basing its decision on the preponderance of the evidence, shall grant such relief as the court determines is appropriate.

(IDEA, 20 U.S.C. § 1415(e)(2))

The statute, however, does not clarify what exactly "appropriate relief" might entail. Determination of what constitutes appropriate relief has been left to the discretion of the courts. The types of relief provided by courts to redress violations of the law are referred to as *remedies* (Black, Nolan, & Nolan-Haley, 1990). Early interpretations of appropriate relief in special education cases were narrowly drawn; that is, relief was usually limited to ordering that a school refrain from a particular practice (e.g., expelling students with disabilities) or add a service to a student's educational program (e.g., provide extended-school-year services). Additionally, the courts often required the parties to arrive at a cooperative agreement regarding the matter (Dagley, 1995). In recent years, however, the courts have expanded the definition of appropriate relief. The following sections examine five types of remedies: attorney's fees, injunctive relief, tuition reimbursement, compensatory education, and punitive damages.

Attorney's Fees

When Congress passed the original Education for All Handicapped Children Act (EAHCA) in 1975, the law contained no provision for reimbursement of attorney's fees. Parties who prevailed in suits against school districts prior to 1984, therefore, had to seek reimbursement for attorneys through other means. Reimbursement of attorney's fees was usually sought through Section 505 of the Rehabilitation Act of 1973 or Section 1988 of the

Civil Rights Attorney's Fees Award Act, both of which allowed courts to grant reimbursement of attorney's fees to prevailing parties. In 1984, however, this practice was halted by the U.S. Supreme Court in *Smith v. Robinson* (1984; hereafter *Smith*).

Smith v. Robinson, 1984   In *Smith*, the parents of a child with cerebral palsy prevailed in their claim against a school district that had discontinued their child's special education program. The parents sued successfully for attorney's fees under Section 505 of the Rehabilitation Act in federal district court. On appeal, however, the attorney's fee award was overturned by the U.S. Court of Appeals. The appellate court ruled that attorney's fees were not available under the IDEA. The parents appealed to the U.S. Supreme Court. In a 5–4 ruling, the high court affirmed the ruling of the appeals court. In the majority opinion, Justice Blackmun stated that Congress had intended that the IDEA be the exclusive remedy for protecting the rights of students with disabilities. This law, therefore, was the only avenue by which special education actions could be pursued. Moreover, because the law contained no provisions for attorney's fees, none were available. In another special education decision handed down on the same day as *Smith*, *Irving Independent School District v. Tatro* (1984), the parents were denied attorney's fees even though they prevailed in their action.

Justice Brennan, in a dissenting opinion, asserted that the majority had misconstrued and frustrated congressional intent in the ruling. He stated that Congress would have to revisit the matter so that the parents of children who must sue for their rights under the law can be recompensed if they prevail. Congress did revisit the law and in 1986 passed the Handicapped Children's Protection Act (HCPA).

The Handicapped Children's Protection Act   The HCPA amended the IDEA to allow the provision of attorney's fees to parties prevailing in special education lawsuits (HCPA, 20 U.S.C. § 1415). The HCPA consisted of three major parts: (a) authorization of the courts to award reasonable attorney's fees to parents of a child with disabilities when they prevail in a lawsuit under the IDEA, (b) clarification of the effect of the IDEA on other laws, and (c) retroactive application of the HCPA (Yell & Espin, 1990). Thus, in the HCPA, Congress overturned the Supreme Court's decision in *Smith*.

The major purpose of the HCPA is to allow parents to recover attorney's fees in successful actions under the IDEA without having to use other laws to sue. The HCPA provided that

> In any action or proceeding brought under [the HCPA], the court, in its discretion, may award reasonable attorneys' fees as part of the costs to the parents or guardian of a [child with disabilities] who is the prevailing party.
>
> (IDEA, 20 U.S.C. § 1415(e)(4)(B), 1990)

The law made the attorney's fees provision retroactive to cases pending on or brought after the date of *Smith* but before the passage of the HCPA. The effect of this clause was to allow plaintiffs to sue for attorney's fees if they had been denied fees because of the *Smith* ruling.

Issues in the Award of Fees   Since the passage of the attorney's fees provision of the IDEA, numerous issues have arisen. Some of these issues will be briefly examined next.

Prevailing Party   The HCPA contains several stipulations regarding the reimbursement of attorney's fees. A major proviso in the law is that parents can collect attorney's fees only if they are the prevailing party. If parents did not prevail on a major point of their suit, therefore, they are not entitled to attorney's fees. Subsequent cases have held that for plaintiffs to prevail they must succeed on any significant issue in their action (*Angela L. v. Pasadena Independent School District No. 2*, 1990; *Burr v. Sobol*, 1990; *Mitten v. Muscogee County School District*, 1989). That is, for parties to prevail it is not necessary that they are successful in obtaining all relief or even the primary relief sought, but merely that they succeed on some significant issue (Blanck, Goldstein, & Myhill, 2013). Findings of bad faith or unjustified conduct on the part of school officials are not required in the awarding of fees (*Mitten v. Muscogee County School District*, 1989).

In many cases brought to trial, school districts have made good-faith efforts to provide services to students with disabilities, but parents and the schools have not been able to agree regarding the specific services required. In such cases, the determination of the prevailing party is decidedly more difficult for the courts (Dagley, 1994). In these instances, the courts have often turned to the U.S. Supreme Court's ruling in *Hensley v. Eckerhart* (1983; hereafter *Hensley*) for guidance. In *Hensley*, the Court defined a significant relief standard as relief on any significant issue that achieved some of the benefits the party sought in bringing the suit. Relief on a significant issue would result in that party's prevailing, and thus being awarded attorney's fees. In a later ruling by the high court in *Texas State Teachers Association v. Garland Independent School District* (1989), the *Hensley* standard was further clarified. According to the Court's decision, parties are considered to have prevailed when they succeed on a significant issue they raise. It is not necessary that the plaintiff prevail on the most significant issue or on the majority of issues raised. Furthermore, to be eligible for an award of attorney's fees, the plaintiff must be able to point to the resolution of the dispute that changes the legal relationship between the parties.

The HCPA addresses the calculation of fee awards as follows:

> For the purpose of [the HCPA], fees awarded shall be based on rates prevailing in the community in which the action or proceeding arose for the kind and quality of services furnished. No bonus or multiplier may be used in calculating the fees.

(IDEA, 20 U.S.C. § 1415(e)(4)(C), 1990)

Expert Witness Fees   In addition to the costs of litigating the case, attorney's fees may include costs of tests and evaluations, time spent in monitoring and enforcing a judgment, travel time, secretarial tasks, and the work of paraprofessionals (e.g., paralegals, law clerks). A decision from the U.S. Court of Appeals for the Eighth Circuit in *Neosho R-V School District v. Clark* (2003), however, denied expert witness fees to a prevailing party in an IDEA case. The court granted attorney's fees to the prevailing party but declined to award fees for an expert witness. The U.S. Court of Appeals for the Seventh Circuit also denied expert witness fees to a prevailing party in *T. D. v. LaGrange School District No. 102* (2003).

In 2006, the U.S. Supreme Court addressed the issue of expert witness fees. In *Arlington Central School District Board of Education v. Murphy*, the High Court ruled that fees for expert witnesses are not available under the IDEA. The case involved the parents of a child with a disability, Ted and Pearle Murphy, who sought tuition reimbursement for a private school placement. Previously the federal district court and the U.S. Court of Appeals for the Second Circuit had ruled in favor of the Murphys on the merits of the case. Following the decision in the appeals court, the Murphys sought to be reimbursed for the fees they had spent on an expert witness whom they had used during the proceedings. The district court awarded the Murphys over $8,000 in fees for the expert witness. The school district appealed the decision to the circuit court. When the appellate court affirmed the lower court's ruling, the school district appealed to the U.S. Supreme Court. In a 6–3 ruling, the Supreme Court reversed the lower court's award of expert witness fees to the Murphys. Writing for the majority, Justice Alito reasoned that because Congress had not specifically mentioned expert witness fees in the IDEA, such fees were not available. This was despite the following language from the conference committee report on the passage of the 1986 IDEA reauthorization: "The conferees intend that the term 'attorneys' fees as part of the costs' include reasonable expenses and fees of expert witnesses ..." (p. 5). To counter this language, in the conference committee report Justice Alito wrote "legislative history is simply not enough"—that the key is not what a majority of both houses intended, but what they put in the text of the law (p. 304). In his dissent, Justice Breyer wrote that there were two major reasons for including expert witness fees: (1) that it was what Congress intended and (2) that it furthers the purposes defined in the IDEA. To override the Supreme Court's ruling in this case, in June 2009 and then again in March 2011, the IDEA Fairness and Restoration Act was introduced in both the House of Representatives and in the Senate. The purpose of the act was to allow parents to recover expert witness costs for due process hearings and civil actions under the IDEA. This act was not passed into law.

Attorney's Fees Denied   The law prohibits the awarding of attorney's fees in cases where parents have rejected a properly made settlement offer if they ultimately obtained essentially the same relief as originally offered. The HCPA also permits courts to reduce attorney's fees if they find that the parents or attorneys have unreasonably protracted the final resolution of the matter or if the fees unreasonably exceed the prevailing community rates. This provision of the law, which has been termed the *vexatious litigant provision,* provides schools with protection against parents and attorneys who become overly adversarial to the point of working to protract proceedings and undermine efforts at settlement (Dagley, 1994).

Limits on the Attorney's Fees Provision

Language added to the IDEA in the amendments of 1997 served to limit the situations in which attorneys could seek reimbursement from school districts. Attorney's fees could be reduced in situations in which the attorney representing the parents failed to provide the LEA with information regarding the specific nature of the dispute. The language also required that parents notify school officials in a timely manner about the problem and any proposed solutions. Additionally, because Congress believed that the IEP process should be devoted to considering students' needs and planning for their education rather than being used as an adversarial forum, the IDEA specifically excluded the payment of attorney's fees for an attorney's participation in the IEP process. The only exception was when the IEP meeting is ordered in an administrative or court proceeding. Similarly, attorney's fees were not available for mediation sessions prior to the filing of a due process action.

The amendments also adopted the *Hensley* standard for determining the amount of any attorney's fees award. That is, in determining awards, courts are required to assess the degree to which the plaintiff prevailed on significant issues.

Buckhannon Board & Care Home Inc. v. West Virginia Department of Health and Human Resources, 2001

In 2001, the U.S. Supreme Court issued a ruling in *Buckhannon Board & Care Home Inc. v. West Virginia Department of Health and Human Resources.* Although this case did not involve special education, the ruling has had a significant effect on attorney's fees available under the IDEA. The case involved an agency, Buckhannon Board & Care Home, which operated assisted living facilities in West Virginia. The state would regularly conduct inspections of the facilities. Following one such inspection, the state ordered Buckhannon to close its facilities because they did not meet state requirements. Buckhannon sued the State of West Virginia, claiming that the state statute violated the Fair Housing Act of 1988 and the Americans with Disabilities Act. During the time in which the lawsuit was pending, the state legislature of West Virginia eliminated the requirement that had led to the closing of the Buckhannon facility. The district court dismissed the lawsuit, declaring that the issue was moot. Buckhannon then sued for attorney's fees based on a legal concept called the *catalyst theory.*

According to the catalyst theory, a plaintiff may be considered the prevailing party, and be awarded attorney's fees, if it obtained its desired outcome because its legal action brought a voluntary change in the defendant's behavior, conduct, or policies. In this case Buckhannon claimed that because of its lawsuit, the State of West Virginia dropped an illegal requirement from its laws. The case ultimately went to the U.S. Supreme Court. The High Court ruled that the party could only be a prevailing party for purposes of awarding attorney's fees if it achieved the desired result in court or through a court-ordered consent decree. Even if the party's lawsuit brought about the desired change, unless a court ordered the change, attorney's fees cannot be awarded. The Court, therefore, rejected the catalyst theory as a basis for attorney's fee awards. The Court's opinion did not specifically mention attorney's fee awards under the IDEA; nevertheless, several circuit courts have applied the demise of the catalyst theory to IDEA-related cases.

For example, in *J. C. v. Regional School District #10, Board of Education* (2002), the U.S. Court of Appeals for the Second Circuit extended the scope of the Supreme Court's ruling in *Buckhannon* to claims for attorney's fees awards under both the IDEA and Section 504. Specifically, the court reversed a ruling awarding attorney's fees to parents who had successfully convinced a school district to fund an IEE because a hearing officer had not ordered the evaluation. Even though the voluntary funding of the IEE had led to a termination of an expulsion hearing, which may have been the direct result of the parents' complaint, according to *Buckhannon*, no fees were available.

IDEA 2004 and Attorney's Fees   In an effort to discourage IDEA-related litigation, Congress acted to alter the attorney's fees provision. According to IDEA 2004, in any IDEA-related action, a court may award reasonable attorney's fees to a prevailing party who is the parent of a child in special education. A court may also award attorney's fees to a school district against the parents' attorney who files a complaint or a subsequent cause of action that is frivolous, unreasonable, or without foundation, or if the parents' attorney continued to litigate after the litigation became unreasonable or without foundation. Additionally, a court could award the SEA or the school district attorney's fees against the attorney of a parent, or against the parent, if the complaint or the cause of action was brought for an improper purpose such as harassment, causing unnecessary delay, or increasing the cost of litigation. Although this provision attracted quite a bit of attention, such awards may have already been allowed under Rule 11 of the Federal Rules of Civil Procedure.

Injunctive Relief

An injunction is a judicial remedy awarded for the purpose of requiring a party to refrain from or discontinue a certain action. An injunction is a preventive measure that guards against a similar action being committed in the future. Injunctions are not remedies for past injustices. For example, if parents believed that their child was not receiving an appropriate education and a court granted an injunction, typically the injunction might compel the school district to provide the education that the court deemed appropriate. Injunctive relief is available under the IDEA.

Two major types of injunctions are preliminary and permanent injunctions. Preliminary injunctions, which are temporary, are issued prior to a trial. To be granted a preliminary injunction, the plaintiffs (i.e., the party bringing the lawsuit) must convince the court that harm may result if the injunction is not issued. Plaintiffs must also show that there is a substantial likelihood that in a trial they would succeed in obtaining a permanent injunction, which is the second type of injunction. A permanent injunction is awarded when a court, after hearing the case, is convinced that such an injunction is required to prevent harm. The party seeking the injunction bears the burden of proof.

The U.S. Court of Appeals for the Eighth Circuit, in *Light v. Parkway School District* (1994), gave schools guidance in seeking an injunction for dangerous and disruptive student behavior. The circuit court developed a two-part test for obtaining an injunction. The court ruled that schools must first prove a child is substantially likely to cause injury. Second, the school must show that all reasonable steps have been undertaken to reduce the risk the student would cause injury.

When school officials attempt to obtain an injunction, they must convince the court that they will likely succeed on the merits of the case in trial (Mattison & Hakola, 1992).

Furthermore, the district must persuade the court that without the injunction the school or students will suffer harm, that the harm to the student removed from school by the injunction does not outweigh the harm caused to the school district, and that the injunction is in the public interest.

Tuition Reimbursement

Tuition reimbursement is typically an award to compensate parents for the costs of a unilateral placement of their child in a private school when the public school has failed to provide an appropriate education. Tuition reimbursement is not a monetary award in the traditional sense, but rather is viewed by the courts as the school district's reimbursing the parents for the education that should have been provided in the first place. The appropriate education the parents had to obtain, therefore, is provided at no cost to the parents.

The U.S. Supreme Court examined the question of tuition reimbursement under the IDEA in *Burlington School Committee of the Town of Burlington v. Department of Education of Massachusetts* (1985), *Florence County School District Four v. Carter* (1993), *Board of Education of the City School District of the City of New York v. Tom F.* (2007), and *Forest Grove School District v. T. A.* (2009). In the *Burlington* case, the High Court ruled on a unilateral change of placement made by the parents of a child with learning disabilities. In *Carter*, the Court considered a unilateral placement in a school that was not approved by the state. In both instances, prior to the Supreme Court's ruling, the lower courts were split as to whether tuition reimbursement was available and if it was only available when the parents placed their child in an approved school.

Burlington School Committee v. Department of Education, 1985

Burlington involved a school district's education of a third grader, Michael Panico, who had learning disabilities and emotional problems. Michael's father became dissatisfied with his son's lack of progress and obtained an independent evaluation of the boy. The evaluation indicated that Michael should be placed in a private school for students with learning disabilities. When the Burlington school district offered placement in a highly structured class within the district, Michael's father withdrew him from the school and placed him at a state-approved facility in Massachusetts. Following a hearing, the state board of appeals found that the public school placement was inappropriate. The hearing officer ordered the school board to fund the private school placement and to reimburse the parents for expenses they had incurred.

The school district filed a lawsuit in a federal district court. While the case was being heard, the school district agreed to fund the cost of the private school education, though it refused to reimburse the parents. The court, determining that the proposed public school placement was appropriate, ruled in favor of the school district.

Michael's father appealed the decision. The U.S. Court of Appeals for the First Circuit reversed the ruling of the lower court. The appeals court ruled that the IDEA did not bar reimbursement when the parents of a child with disabilities had to unilaterally change the child's placement, if the court found that the parents' action was appropriate. Reimbursement was not available, however, when the school district had proposed and could implement an appropriate placement. The school district filed an appeal with the U.S. Supreme Court. The school district argued that the parents had violated the stay-put rule, which required that students remain in their current placement during the review process.

In unanimously affirming the ruling of the appeals court, the High Court stated that parents who unilaterally place their children with disabilities in a private school setting are entitled to reimbursement for tuition and living expenses if a court finds that the school had proposed an inappropriate IEP. If the school's proposed placement, however, was found to be appropriate, the school would not have to reimburse the parents. Justice Rehnquist, writing for the majority, noted that the IDEA gave the courts broad discretion in granting relief.

The majority opinion also stated that to deny reimbursement, when appropriate, would be to deny the parent meaningful input in the development of an appropriate education and would lessen the importance of the procedural safeguards. Rehnquist asserted that the decision requiring reimbursement did not constitute a damage award, but rather "required the [school district] to belatedly pay expenses that it should have paid all along and would have been borne in the first instance had it developed a proper IEP" (*Burlington*, pp. 370–371).

The High Court also commented that if the school's placement was found to be appropriate, parents were not entitled to reimbursement. Parents who unilaterally change their child's placement, therefore, do so at their own risk.

In noting that the IDEA conferred broad discretion, the High Court was saying that courts, in ordering appropriate relief, have a great deal of leeway. As the *Burlington* decision indicates, this discretion clearly includes the power to award tuition reimbursement. Parents are not required to bear the costs of providing an appropriate education for their children with disabilities (Mattison & Hakola, 1992).

Chief Justice Rehnquist negated the possibility of school districts' using the stay-put provision as a defense against unilateral placements made by parents. Rehnquist noted that if the stay-put provision was read in such a way as to prohibit parents from making unilateral placements, parents would be forced to either (a) leave their child in what may be an inappropriate placement or (b) obtain an appropriate education only by sacrificing any claim for reimbursement. The majority opinion stated that "the [IDEA] was intended to give handicapped children both an appropriate education and a free one; it should not be interpreted to defeat one or the other of these objectives" (*Burlington*, p. 372).

The Supreme Court also recognized that related expenses, in addition to tuition, may also be awarded to parents. Subsequent decisions have held that such expenses may include the following: cost of transportation and costs incurred during transportation (*Taylor v. Board of Education*, 1986); lost earnings by parents for time expended related to protecting their child's rights and interest on tuition loans (*Board of Education of the County of Cabell v. Dienelt*, 1988); costs of residential placement (*Babb v. Knox County School System*, 1992); expenses for related services (*Rapid City School District v. Vahle*, 1990); reimbursement for psychotherapy (*Max M. v. Illinois State Board of Education*, 1986); and insurance reimbursement when the parents had financed the tuition with their insurance (*Shook v. Gaston County Board of Education*, 1989).

Following the *Burlington* decision, numerous issues regarding tuition reimbursement were litigated. A primary issue involved reimbursement for parents who unilaterally placed their child in an unapproved school, one that had not been approved by the SEA. Lower courts were split on this issue. The Supreme Court put this controversy to rest in *Carter*.

Florence County School District Four v. Carter, 1993   Shannon Carter was a high school student in Florence County School District Four in Florence, South Carolina. Educational evaluations, done privately and by the school district, indicated that she had a learning disability and attention deficit disorder (ADD). Her parents requested that Shannon be placed in a self-contained classroom in a neighboring school district. Because the Florence school district had no self-contained setting, it proposed that Shannon receive instruction from a special education teacher in a resource room. The parents refused the placement and requested a due process hearing. They continued to press for placement in a neighboring school district's self-contained classroom or placement at Trident Academy, a private school in Charleston, South Carolina. The hearing officer decided in favor of the school district. The Carters took Shannon out of the public school and placed her at Trident Academy. The Carters also appealed the hearing officer's decision to the state reviewing officer. The reviewing officer upheld the original decision. The Carters filed suit in the federal district court.

After hearing the evidence from court-appointed evaluators, the district court held that the school district's program was "wholly inadequate" and directed the school district to reimburse the Carters for expenses incurred at Trident Academy. The school district appealed the decision to the U.S. Court of Appeals for the Fourth Circuit. The circuit court ruled that even though Trident Academy was not on the state's list of approved special education schools, the school had to reimburse the Carters for tuition at Trident Academy. The school district appealed to the U.S. Supreme Court.

The Supreme Court requested that the solicitor general's office of the Department of Justice file a brief outlining the government's position. The Department of Justice filed a brief recommending that the Fourth Circuit Court's decision be upheld (Wright, 1994). Seventeen states filed amicus curiae (friend of the court) briefs supporting the school district. The High Court affirmed the circuit court's decision in ruling that the school district had to reimburse the parents for placement in the school, even though it was not on the SEA's approved list. The High Court stated that limiting parental reimbursement to state-approved schools would be contrary to the IDEA when the school district had not complied with the law. Furthermore, the Court determined that applying state standards to parental placements would be fundamentally unfair in situations where parents have to find a private school that offers an appropriate education.

In *Carter,* the Supreme Court held that parents could be reimbursed for the use of unapproved personnel and schools for services obtained when school districts failed in their duty to offer an appropriate education for students with disabilities under Part B of the IDEA. The U.S. Court of Appeals for the Second Circuit, in *Still v. Debuono* (1996), ruled that the principles announced in *Carter* were equally applicable to Part H, now Part C, of the IDEA. Although Part C imposes a requirement that early intervention services are provided by qualified personnel, privately obtained services provided by unapproved personnel are reimbursable.

Board of Education of the City School District of the City of New York v. Tom F., 2007

Tom Freston, the father of a son with a disability, sought tuition reimbursement for a private school placement. His son, Gilbert, had a learning disability. The New York City school district had proposed a placement for Gilbert that his father believed was inappropriate. He placed Gilbert in a private school and later filed for tuition reimbursement. After several administrative hearings, he won reimbursement for the private school. The school district appealed the hearing officer's ruling, but it was upheld at the state review level. The New York Board of Education then filed a suit in federal district court claiming that Tom Freston was not entitled to tuition reimbursement because Gilbert was never enrolled in the public school, and therefore the district did not have an opportunity to provide an appropriate education. The U.S. district court agreed with the New York Board of Education and reversed the decision. The court held that the IDEA did not allow reimbursement of private school tuition because Gilbert had never been enrolled in the public school. Tom Freston filed an appeal with the U.S. Court of Appeals for the Second Circuit. The appellate court reversed and remanded (sent back) the ruling of the district court, reasoning that the IDEA did not require that a student be enrolled in an inappropriate public school program before being eligible for tuition reimbursement for an appropriate private school placement.

The New York Board of Education filed an appeal with the U.S. Supreme Court. The High Court heard the case, but Justice Kennedy recused (removed) himself from the case. The decision was a nullity; therefore, the ruling of the appellate court stood. Because there was no national precedent from the case and other circuits were split on this question, in *Forest Grove v. T. A.* (2009) the U.S. Supreme Court took a similar case on whether parents must first put their child in a public school placement prior to seeking tuition reimbursement for a private school placement (Conroy, Yell, Katsiyannis, & Collins, 2010).

Forest Grove v. T. A., 2009

T. A. was a student who struggled in school since he had been in kindergarten. When he entered high school a school psychologist evaluated him. The school psychologist determined that T. A. was not eligible for special education services. T. A. completed his sophomore year, but his problems worsened. His parents hired a private psychologist who diagnosed T. A. with ADHD and disabilities relating to learning and memory. The psychologist recommended a structured, residential learning environment; therefore, his parents enrolled T. A. in private school, notified the school district of their placement, and requested a due process hearing regarding his eligibility for special education services. The school district again evaluated T. A. and concluded that he was not eligible for special education services because his ADHD did not have a sufficiently significant effect on his educational performance. Because the school district had determined that T. A. was not eligible for special education, it did not offer him an IEP.

After hearing testimony from numerous expert witnesses, the hearing officer found that T. A. was eligible for special education services but that the school district failed to identify him as eligible and failed to offer him a FAPE. Moreover, the hearing officer found that the private school placement was appropriate and that therefore the school district was responsible for reimbursing T. A.'s parents for his private school tuition. The school district appealed and the U.S. district court for the District of Oregon set aside the reimbursement award, ruling that the IDEA prevented reimbursement for students who had not previously received special education and related services.

The Ninth Circuit Court of Appeals reversed the district court's decision. The appeals court held that T. A.'s parents were eligible for private school tuition reimbursement, "appropriate" relief under the IDEA. The U.S. Supreme Court granted certiorari to hear the case to determine whether the IDEA established a bar to tuition reimbursement for students who have not previously received special education services under the authority of a public education agency. In a 6–3 decision, the Supreme Court held that the IDEA does not bar reimbursement in such situations. The High Court noted that the *Burlington* and *Carter* cases involved the adequacy of a proposed IEP, whereas in T. A.'s case, the school district failed to provide an IEP at all. The Court found the differences "insignificant." The Court considered failing to propose an IEP to be just as serious as failing to provide an adequate one; therefore, the same reasoning applied.

The Supreme Court found that the 1997 amendments to the IDEA did not alter the text of the IDEA, which it previously held in *Burlington*, gives courts broad authority to grant "appropriate" relief. To rule otherwise, the Court found, would be contrary to the IDEA's purpose of providing all children with disabilities with a FAPE and to the IDEA's "child find" obligation to identify, locate, and evaluate all children with disabilities. The majority also found that excusing school districts that refused to find children eligible for special education "would produce a rule bordering on irrational" (pp. 2494–2495).

The Court also rejected an argument made by the school district that allowing parents to enroll their children in private schools and then sue a school district for tuition reimbursement, even though their child hadn't been identified as having a disability under the IDEA, would put a tremendous financial burden on school districts. Moreover, parents would be encouraged to enroll their children in private school without cooperating with school districts. The Supreme Court also outlined the criteria for private school tuition reimbursement under the IDEA: A court or hearing officer must conclude that the school district failed to provide a FAPE and that the private school placement was proper under the IDEA. Additionally, a court must consider all relevant factors in determining the amount of reimbursement, including the notice provided by the parents and the school district's opportunity to evaluate the child (Yell, Ryan, Rozalski, & Karsiyannis, 2009). The Supreme Court, therefore, concluded that reimbursement for the cost of private school special education services might be awarded under the IDEA "regardless of whether the child previously received special education or related services through the public school" (p. 2496).

Compensatory Education

Compensatory educational services are designed to remedy the progress lost by students with disabilities because they were previously denied a FAPE (Blanck et al., 2013; Zirkel, 1991). The award of compensatory education is the award of additional educational services, above and beyond the educational services normally due a student under state law (Katsiyannis & Herbst, 2004). Typically, compensatory education extends a student's eligibility for educational services beyond age 21 as compensation for inappropriate educational services (Mattison & Hakola, 1992). According to Katsiyannis and Herbst (2004), when students currently attending school are awarded compensatory education, it may take the form of extended-day programs, extended-school-year services, summer school, tutoring, compensatory-related services (e.g., occupational or physical therapy), or future compensatory education (i.e., provision of educational services after the student turns 21). Following the *Burlington* decision, the issue of compensatory education received a great deal of attention in the courts. Even though the early decisions tended to rule that compensatory education was not available, most recent decisions have ruled that compensatory educational services are remedies available in the IDEA (Zirkel, 1994).

Compensatory Awards Under the IDEA

An example of judicial thinking regarding compensatory education was delivered by the U.S. Court of Appeals for the Eighth Circuit in *Meiner v. Missouri* (1986). The appeals court ruled in favor of an award of compensatory education, explaining that

> Like the retroactive reimbursement in *Burlington,* imposing liability for compensatory educational services on the defendants "merely requires [them] to belatedly pay expenses that [they] should have paid all along." Here, as in *Burlington,* recovery is necessary to the child's right to a free appropriate public education. We are confident that Congress did not intend the child's entitlement to a free education to turn upon her parent's ability to front its costs.
>
> (p. 753)

In a policy letter, the OSEP stated a similar position on compensatory education: "In certain instances, compensatory education may be the only means through which children who are forced to remain in an inappropriate placement, due to their parents' financial inability to pay for an appropriate placement, would receive FAPE" (*Letter to Murray,* 1992, p. 496). The OSEP further stated that hearing officers or SEAs could award compensatory education. Courts have also reached similar conclusions regarding a hearing officer's ability to award compensatory education (*Murphy v. Timberlane Regional School District,* 1993).

Compensatory education may be ordered if it is determined that a school district did not provide an appropriate education. Such a violation could involve programming or procedural violations (Mattison & Hakola, 1992). Additionally, compensatory education awards may take the form of either extending the student's eligibility beyond age 21 or providing summer programming (*Letter to Murray,* 1992). Zirkel (1995) asserted that compensatory education may also extend to educational services beyond the regular school day.

Zirkel (1995) referred to compensatory educational services as the "coin of the realm" (p. 483) in relief cases arising under the IDEA. This is because tuition reimbursement represents an up-front risk that many parents cannot afford; also, unlike attorney's fees awards, parents need not resort to litigation to receive an enforceable award of compensatory education. A due process hearing officer and the SEA may grant awards of compensatory educational services.

Punitive Damages

Punitive damage awards, which are monetary awards in excess of actual damages, are intended to serve as punishment and recompense for a legal wrong. Extensive litigation has examined whether courts can order the award of punitive damages in special education cases brought under the IDEA. The answer from the courts has been a resounding no; punitive damages are not available under the IDEA (*A. W. v. Jersey City Public Schools,* 2007; *Bradley v. Arkansas Department of Education,* 2002; *Chambers v. School District of Philadelphia Board of Education,*

2009; *Colin K. v. Schmidt*, 1983; *Diaz-Fonesca v. Commonwealth of Puerto Rico*, 2006; *Hall v. Knott County Board of Education*, 1991; *Heidemann v. Rother*, 1996; *Hoekstra v. Independent School District No. 283*, 1996; *Meiner v. Missouri*, 1986; *Sellars v. School Board of the City of Manassas*, 1998).

In *Anderson v. Thompson* (1981), the U.S. Court of Appeals for the Seventh Circuit held that punitive damages were unavailable under the IDEA. In this influential ruling, the court stated that although there was no basis for awarding damages in the law's legislative history, damages might be available in exceptional circumstances. Such circumstances might include the school district's acting in bad faith in failing to comply with the IDEA (*Anderson v. Thompson*, 1981) or intentional violation of a student's right to a FAPE (*Taylor v. Honig*, 1990).

Section 1983

Mattison and Hakola (1992) asserted that school districts and individuals could be held liable for punitive damages for violations of the IDEA through other laws, such as Section 1983 (Mattison & Hakola, 1992). They pointed to the HCPA, which became the attorney's fees provision of the IDEA. In overturning the U.S. Supreme Court's decision in *Smith*, Congress restored parents' right to sue school districts under other laws beyond the IDEA. According to the statutory language, "Nothing in this chapter shall be construed to restrict or limit the rights, procedures, and remedies available under the Constitution, Title V of the Rehabilitation Act of 1973, or other federal statutes" (IDEA, 20 U.S.C. § 1415(e)(3)(f), 1994). They believed that this language may indicate that Section 1983 of the Civil Rights Act (Civil Rights Act, 42 U.S.C. § 1983) could possibly be used by attorneys in special education lawsuits, even though this was not specifically mentioned in the IDEA (Mattison & Hakola, 1992). In fact, in their review of legislative history of the HCPA, Mattison and Hakola (1992) maintained that Congress clearly sought to restore plaintiffs' ability to use Section 1983 of the Civil Rights Act in special education lawsuits.

The primary significance of Section 1983 to plaintiffs in special education lawsuits is the availability of monetary damages under the law. Section 1983 was derived from the Civil Rights Act of 1871. The basic purpose of this law, which was referred to as the *Ku Klux Klan Act*, was to protect freed slaves from denial of their federal rights by state and local governments (Mattison & Hakola, 1992; Sorenson, 1992). This was accomplished by providing a legal action for damages and injunctive relief. In the last few decades, courts have extended the protections of Section 1983 to any person whose rights under the U.S. Constitution or federal statutes are violated by a governmental entity or official. Thus, persons can sue for violations of their federal rights. The relief that is available under Section 1983, specifically monetary damages, certainly makes it an attractive vehicle for parents seeking damages for an IDEA violation (Tatgenhorst et al., 2014).

However, courts have not clearly answered whether Section 1983 claims can be based on violations of the IDEA. Although some courts have recognized that Section 1983 is now available to plaintiffs as a result of the HCPA, the results of cases in which plaintiffs have used Section 1983 based on violations of the IDEA have been mixed. Some courts have concluded that plaintiffs can use Section 1983 to bring claims based on violations of the IDEA (*Goleta Union Elementary School District v. Ordway*, 2001; *Hiller v. Board of Education of the Brunswick Central School District*, 1988; *Mrs. R v. Tirrozi*, 1987; *Marie O. v. Edgar*, 1997), while others have ruled that a Section 1983 violation cannot be based solely on IDEA violations (*Barnett v. Fairfax County School Board*, 1991; *Diaz-Fonesca v. Commonwealth of Puerto Rico*, 2006; *Padilla v. School District No. 1 in the City and County of Denver, Colorado*, 2000; *Sellars v. School Board of the City of Manassas*, 1998). *Jackson v. Franklin County School Board* (1986) also recognized that a suit could be brought under both the IDEA and Section 1983, thereby leading to awards of monetary damages.

Doe v. Withers, 1983

In *Doe v. Withers* a jury assessed monetary damages against a teacher under Section 1983. In this case, a history teacher had refused to comply with the IEP requirement that tests be read orally to a student with learning disabilities. The teacher was aware of the requirement and deliberately ignored it. As a result of the teacher's action, the student failed the history course. The following semester, a substitute teacher replaced the history teacher. The substitute implemented oral reading of tests, and the student's grades improved dramatically. The parents brought an action under Section 1983 against the school district and the history teacher. A jury found in favor of the parents and awarded them damages against the history teacher in the amount of $5,000 in compensatory damages and $10,000 in punitive damages.

L. S. v. Mount Olive Board of Education, 2011

This case involved an 11th grade English teacher who co-taught her class with a special education teacher in the Mount Olive School District in New Jersey. The English teacher required that the students read *Catcher in the Rye* by J.D. Salinger. One of the assignments was to write a psychological evaluation of the protagonist, Holden Caulfield. To help the special education students in the class, the special education teacher decided to obtain a psychological evaluation that the students could use as a model for their assignment. He went to the school social worker to see if he could get such a report. The social worker provided the special education teacher with a psychiatric evaluation of an 11th grade student who attended the school, called S.S. by the court. The social worker also gave the teacher instructions to redact all information that identified the student before distributing it to the class. The special education teacher redacted the name and address of S.S. but failed to redact the student's age, religion, name of family members, physical conditions, past medical and psychiatric history, exams, and diagnosis. The special education teacher passed out the evaluation to the class. As the class read the report one of the students, who was a friend of S.S., asked, "Is this about S.S.?" The special education teacher denied that it was about S.S.

Coincidentally, S.S.'s parents were in the school that day meeting with the principal. As they were leaving the school, their son's friend saw them and handed them the psychiatric evaluation that she had received in the English class. The parents immediately told school personnel about the incident. The principal collected all the reports that had been handed out in class and destroyed them. The damage, however, had been done.

S.S.'s parents filed a complaint with the New Jersey Department of Education, alleging that the Mount Olive School District breached S.S.'s confidentiality. The department issued a report and found that Mount Olive district personnel were uninformed of the importance of maintaining the privacy of students with disabilities and the confidentiality of the records of those students. The parents also filed a suit in federal court against the Mount Olive School Board seeking remedies under various legal avenues, including Section 1983. The court dismissed all of the claims except those against the special education teacher and the school social worker, holding that they were liable under Section 1983 for violating the confidentiality of S.S.'s educational records. Although the final determination of this lawsuit is not available, it probably never will be because it is likely that the lawsuit was settled out of court.

W. B. v. Matula, 1995

In an indication that monetary damages may be available, the U.S. Court of Appeals for the Third Circuit ruled that a lawsuit seeking punitive damages under the IDEA, Section 504, and Section 1983 against a school district and several educators was permissible. *W. B. v. Matula* (1995) reversed a decision by a federal district court granting summary judgment (i.e., a preverdict rendered by a court in response to a motion by a plaintiff or defendant) for the school district of Mansfield Township, New Jersey, regarding a question of damages because of a failure on the part of a school district to properly evaluate and educate a student with a disability. The circuit court remanded the case to the district court for a trial on the damages claim.

The case involved a first-grade boy with behavioral problems and attention deficit hyperactivity disorder (ADHD). The student's parents wanted an evaluation, which the school district initially declined to conduct. When the district conducted an evaluation a year after first being requested to do so, it found that the student did have ADHD but did not qualify for special education. The school district did find the boy eligible for services under Section

504 but failed to provide the necessary services. An independent evaluation determined that the boy had Tourette's syndrome, severe obsessive-compulsive disorder, and ADHD. Several due process hearings were held and the district reclassified the student, implemented an IEP, and paid $14,000 to settle all the disputes with the parents. Following an administrative hearing in late 1994, the district was further ordered to pay for a private school placement for the student. The boy's parents sued in federal district court against nine school officials (including the school principal and two general education teachers).

The case eventually was appealed to the circuit court, which, in dicta, rejected the school district's argument that damages were unavailable in a Section 1983 action premised on an IDEA violation. According to the court, when the IDEA was amended in 1986, Congress specifically allowed IDEA violations to be redressed by Section 504 and Section 1983 actions. The Third Circuit court's decision was widely seen as a strong indication that lawsuits seeking monetary damages for violations of the IDEA and Section 504 were available. Rather than going back to trial on the damages action, the school district agreed to an out-of-court settlement. The district paid a total of $245,000, including a $125,000 cash payment to the family in addition to court costs and attorney's fees.

In *Whitehead v. School Board of Hillsborough County* (1996), a federal district court agreed with the Third Circuit that compensatory and punitive damages were available under Section 504. The court disagreed regarding the IDEA, however, stating that relief under the law was generally limited to reimbursement that compensates parents for the cost of services the school should have provided.

Franklin v. Gwinett County Public Schools, 1992

An important development occurred in the U.S. Supreme Court's ruling in *Franklin v. Gwinett County Public Schools* (1992; hereafter *Franklin*), even though the case did not involve special education. In *Franklin*, a high school student was repeatedly sexually abused and harassed by a teacher. The student brought suit against the school and the teacher under Title IX of the Education Amendments of 1972. Subsequently, the teacher resigned and charges against him were dropped. A federal district court then dismissed the suit against the school, ruling that Title IX did not allow an award of damages. The U.S. Court of Appeals for the Eleventh Circuit affirmed the district court's decision. On appeal, the U.S. Supreme Court reversed the lower courts' rulings, holding that monetary damages were available under Title IX, even though not specifically mentioned in the law. According to the Court majority opinion:

> The general rule, therefore, is that absent clear direction to the contrary by Congress, the federal courts have the power to award any appropriate relief in a cognizable cause of action brought pursuant to a federal statute.
>
> (p. 1035)

Most courts have not granted punitive damages under the IDEA, and the use of Section 1983 to sue for violations of the IDEA has been prohibited by the courts of appeals for the Third, Fourth, Eighth, and Tenth Circuits. On the other hand, the courts of appeals for the Second, Seventh, and Eighth Circuits follow the view that Section 1983 is an available remedy for violations of the IDEA (Tatgenhorst et al., 2014). Additionally, some courts have found punitive damages available for violations of Section 504 or the Americans with Disabilities Act (ADA) in cases involving bad faith or gross misjudgment. Courts are usually loath to open the public coffers to punitive damages unless Congress clearly makes such a remedy available under the law (Blanck et al., 2013). Congress did not make punitive damages an available remedy under the IDEA. At present, the generally accepted view is that punitive damages are not available under the IDEA, although the issue is not settled and a few courts have ruled that punitive damages are available using other legal vehicles. Because of the split in the circuit courts, monetary damages for IDEA violations under Section 1983 may be an issue that the U.S. Supreme Court will eventually decide.

LESSONS FROM LEGISLATION AND LITIGATION

The following recommendations are offered to help ensure that school districts are in compliance with the IDEA and developing and providing special education programs that confer meaningful education benefit.

Principle 1: Adhere to the procedural systems developed by school districts to ensure that IDEA's procedural requirements are met. States and school districts typically have knowledgeable people develop systems of procedural safeguards for administrators and teachers to use (e.g., notice and consent forms, flowcharts, procedural safeguard notices for parents) when identifying, evaluating, programming, and placing students with disabilities. It is important that school district personnel fulfill these procedural requirements.

Principle 2: Ensure that administrators and teachers understand their responsibilities under the IDEA. The IDEA is a complex and ever-changing law. School district officials must ensure that all personnel are prepared to fulfill their duties to students with disabilities and their parents (Yell, Conroy, Katsiyannis, & Conroy, 2013). School personnel should also have a thorough understanding of Section 504 and the family Educational Rights and Privacy Act. Ongoing professional development activities regarding special education laws should be provided to administrators, teachers, and staff to keep them abreast of important developments in legislation and litigation.

Principle 3: Ensure that parents are meaningfully involved in the development of their child's special education program. School district personnel must ensure parental involvement in identification, assessment, programming, and placement of their child. One method that school districts could use to ensure such involvement is to have a staff member assume the role of a parent contact who would be responsible for contacting parents and helping them prepare for meetings.

Principle 4: Ensure that all administrators, teachers, and related services understand their roles in individual children's IEPs. So, for example, if an IEP requires that a student will have tests read to him or her, all tests must be read to the student. It may be useful to appoint a person, such as the student's special education teacher, to ensure that all aspects of the IEP are implemented appropriately.

SUMMARY

In the IDEA, Congress created substantive and procedural rights for students with disabilities. The substantive rights include the FAPE, an education that results in meaningful benefit, guaranteed to each student in special education. The procedural rights, referred to in the IDEA as *procedural safeguards,* are meant to ensure that schools follow proper procedures in planning and delivering a FAPE to students with disabilities. The procedural safeguards require involvement of both parents and professionals in the special education decision-making process.

The procedural safeguards consist of seven components: notice requirements, consent requirements, the opportunity to examine records, procedures to protect the rights of the child when the parents are unavailable, the independent educational evaluation, voluntary mediation, and the due process hearing. The heart of the procedural safeguards is the due process

hearing. When there is a disagreement over identification, evaluation, placement, or any matters pertaining to a FAPE, parents may request a due process hearing. The purpose of the hearing is to resolve differences by presenting information to an impartial due process hearing officer. The task of the hearing officer is to make a final decision regarding the settlement of the disagreement. Either party can appeal the decision.

The due process hearing procedure has been the subject of much criticism. The process is time consuming, expensive, and emotionally difficult, and tends to create an adversarial relationship between the parents and the school. In an attempt to alleviate the adversarial nature of many disputes between parents and school districts, the IDEA Amendments of 1997 required states to offer parents voluntary mediation. IDEA 2004 inserted a resolution session between mediation and the due process hearing.

In special education, not only are parents involved in the process of designing an appropriate education for their child, but they may also serve as the stimulus for forcing school districts to comply with the laws. When parents or school districts go to court, they often seek to determine the responsibilities for the delivery of educational services. Typically the parents, believing that the school district's IEP will not offer an appropriate education, will seek to have different services provided. If a court finds that a school district has committed statutory or procedural violations under either the IDEA or Section 504, it may award some form of relief to redress these violations. Such awards are usually in the form of injunctive relief, tuition reimbursement, and attorney's fees. Increasingly, courts are awarding compensatory educational services. Most courts have generally not granted punitive damages under the IDEA, although a few have indicated that such damages may be available. Some courts have found punitive damages available for violations of IDEA and Section 504 in cases involving bad faith.

School districts need not act in bad faith, however, to be directed to provide relief. When intentional violations do occur, they may lead to courts' ordering larger awards to plaintiffs. Minor or inconsequential violations will not lead to relief; however, violations that result in the provision of an inappropriate education or result in parents not being involved in the special education process will lead to relief. The best defense to prevent such awards is in providing an appropriate and meaningful education and collecting data to show educational progress.

> **Enhanced eText Application Exercise 12.1.** *Burlington School Committee of the Town of Burlington v. Department of Education of Massachusetts*, 471 U.S. 359 (1985).

FOR FURTHER INFORMATION

Anderson, W., Chitwood, S., & Hayden, D. (1990). *Negotiating the special education maze: A guide for parents and teachers* (2nd ed.). Alexandria, VA: Woodbine House.

Dobbs, R. F., Primm, E. B., & Primm, B. (1991). Mediation: A common sense approach for resolving conflicts in special education. *Focus on Exceptional Children, 24,* 1–11.

Goldberg, S. S., & Huefner, D. S. (1995). Dispute resolution in special education: An introduction to litigative alternatives. *Education Law Reporter, 99,* 703–803.

Nation Center for Dispute Resolution in Special Education. Available at www.directionservice.org/cadre/index.cfm.

Shrybman, J. A. (1982). *Due process in special education,* Rockville, MD: Aspen.

U.S. Department of Education, Office of Special Education Programs (2013, July 23). Dispute resolution procedures under Part B of the Individuals with Disabilities Education Act, OSEP memo 13-08. Available at https://www2.ed.gov/policy/speced/guid/idea/memosdcltrs/acccombinedosersdisputeresolutionqafinalmemo-7-23-13.pdf.

Zirkel, P. A., & Scala, G. (2010). Due process hearing systems under the IDEA: A state-by-state survey. *Journal of Disability Policy Studies, 21,* 3–8.

REFERENCES

A. G. v. District of Columbia, 57 IDELR 9 (D.D. Cir. 2011).

A. W. v. Jersey City Public Schools, 486 F.3d 791, 47 IDELR 282 (3d Cir. 2007).

Adams County School District, 55 IDELR 219 (SEA Colo. 2010).

Akers v. Bolton, 531 F. Supp. 300 (D. Kan. 1981).

Anderson, W., Chitwood, S., & Hayden, D. (1990). *Negotiating the special education maze: A guide for parents and teachers* (2nd ed.). Alexandria, VA: Woodbine House.

Anderson v. District of Columbia, 877 F.2d 1018 (D.C. Cir. 1989).

Anderson v. Thompson, 658 F. Supp. 1205 (7th Cir. 1981).

Angela L. v. Pasadena Independent School District No. 2, 918 F.2d 1188 (5th Cir. 1990).

Arlington Central School District Board of Education v. Murphy, 548 U.S. 291 (2006).

Babb v. Knox County School System, 965 F.2d 104 (6th Cir. 1992).

Barnett v. Fairfax County School Board, 927 F.2d 146 (4th Cir. 1991).

Beekman, L. E. (1993). Making due process hearings more efficient and effective (aka how to run a hearing—and get away with it!). In *Proceedings of the 14th National Institute on Legal Issues of Educating Individuals with Disabilities.* Horsham, PA: LRP Publications.

Black, H. C., Nolan, J. R., & Nolan-Haley, J. M. (1990). *Black's law dictionary* (6th ed.). St. Paul, MN: West Publishing Company.

Blanck, P., Goldstein, B. A., & Myhill, W. N. (2013). *Legal rights of persons with disabilities: An analysis of federal law* (2nd ed.). Palm Beach Garden, FL: LRP Publications.

Board of Education of County of Cabell v. Dienelt, 843 F.2d 813 (4th Cir. 1988).

Board of Education of the City School District of the City of New York v. Tom F., 128 S.Ct. 17 (2007).

Board of Education of Northfield High School District 225 v. Roy H. and Lynn H., 21 IDELR 1171 (N.D. Ill, 1995).

Bradley v. Arkansas Department of Education, 37 IDELR 181 (8th Cir. 2002).

Buckhannon Board & Care Home Inc. v. West Virginia Department of Health and Human Resources, 35 IDELR 160 (U.S. 2001).

Burlington School Committee of the Town of Burlington v. Department of Education of Massachusetts, 471 U.S. 359 (1985).

Burr v. Sobol, 888 F.2d 258 (2d Cir. 1990).

Butz v. Economou, 438 U.S. 478 (1978).

City of Rancho Verdes v. Abrams, 544 U.S. 113 (2005).

Christopher. P. v. Marcus, 16 IDELR 1347 (2d Cir. 1990).

Chambers v. School District of Philadelphia Board of Education, 53 IDELR 139 (3d Cir. 2009).

Civil Rights Act, 42 U.S.C. § 2000 *et seq*. Section 1983, 42 U.S.C. § 1983 (Civil Rights Act of 1871).

Clyde K. v. Puyallup School District, 35 F.3d 1396 (9th Cir. 1994).

Colin K. v. Schmidt, 715 F.2d 1 (1st Cir. 1983).

Conroy. T., Yell, M. L., & Katsiyannis, A. (2007). *Schaffer v. Weast*: The Supreme Court on the burden of persuasion in due process hearings. *Remedial and Special Education, 29*, 108–117.

Conroy, T. E., Yell, M. L., Katsiyannis, A., & Collins, T. (2010). The U.S. Supreme Court and parental rights under the Individuals with Disabilities Education Act. *Focus on Exceptional Children, 43*, 1–16.

Consortium for Appropriate Dispute Resolution in Special Education (2010). *Encouraging the use of mediation and other collaborative strategies to resolve disagreements about special education and early intervention programs.* Retrieved from www.directionservice.org/cadre/index.cfm.

Cox v. Jenkins, 878 F.2d 414 (D.C. Cir. 1989).

Dagley, D. L. (1994). Prevailing under the HCPA. *Education Law Reporter, 90*, 547–560.

Dagley, D. L. (1995). Enforcing compliance with IDEA: Dispute resolution and appropriate relief. *Preventing School Failure, 39*(2), 27–32.

Diaz-Fonesca v. Commonwealth of Puerto Rico, 45 IDELR 268 (1st Cir. 2006).

District of Columbia Public Schools, 257 EHLR 208 (OCR 1981).

Dobbs, R. F., Primm, E. B., & Primm, B. (1991). Mediation: A common sense approach for resolving conflicts in special education. *Focus on Exceptional Children, 24*, 1–11.

Dobbs, R. F., Primm, E. B., & Primm, B. (1993). Mediation. In *Proceedings of the 14th National Institute on Legal Issues of Educating Individuals with Disabilities.* Horsham, PA: LRP Publications.

Doe v. Withers, 20 IDELR 442 (W. Va. Cir. Ct. 1993).

Education Department General Administration Regulations (EDGAR), 34 C.F.R. § 99.22.

Endrew F. v. Douglas County School District RE-1, 137 S.Ct. 988 (2017). Retrieved March 22, 2017 from www.supremecourt.gov/opinions/16pdf/15-827_0pm1.pdf

Family & Children's Center, Inc. v. School City of Mishawaka (1994).

Florence County School District Four v. Carter, 114 S.Ct. 361 (1993).

Forest Grove School District v. T. A., 129 S.Ct. 2484 (2009).

Franklin v. Gwinett County Public Schools, 112 S.Ct. 1028 (1992).

Fuentes v. Board of Education of the City of New York, 52 IDELR 152 (2d Cir. 2009).

Ginn, M., Carruth, E., & McCarthy, G. (1988). *South Carolina handbook for hearing officers.* Columbia: South Carolina Department of Education.

Goldberg, S. S., & Huefner, D. S. (1995). Dispute resolution in special education: An introduction to litigative alternatives. *Education Law Reporter, 99*, 703–803.

Goldberg, S. S., & Kuriloff, P. J. (1991). Evaluating the fairness of special education hearings. *Exceptional Children, 57*, 546–555.

Goleta Union Elementary School District v. Ordway, 38 IDELR 64 (C.D. Cal. 2001).

Greismann, Z. (1997, February 23). Question and answer. *The Special Educator, 12*(14), 3.

Guernsey, T. F., & Klare, K. (1993). *Special education law.* Durham, NC: Carolina Academic Press.

Hacienda La Puente Unified School District v. Honig, 976 F.2d 487 (9th Cir. 1992).

Hall v. Knott County Board of Education, 941 F.2d 402 (6th Cir. 1991).

Hamway, T. J. (1994). Presenting expert testimony in due process hearings: A guide to courtroom survival. In *Proceedings of the 15th National Institute on Legal Issues of Educating Individuals with Disabilities.* Horsham, PA: LRP Publications.

Handicapped Children's Protection Act of 1986, 20 U.S.C. § 1415.

Hargan Inquiry, 16 EHLR 738 (OSEP 1990).

Heidemann v. Rother, 84 F.3d 1021 (8th Cir. 1996).

Hensley v. Eckerhart, 461 U.S. 424 (1983).

Hiller v. Board of Education of the Brunswick Central School District, 687 F. Supp. 735 (N.D.N.Y. 1988).

Hoekstra v. Independent School District No. 283, 103 F.3d 624 (8th Cir. 1996).

Honig v. Doe, 479 U.S. 1084 (1988).

Hoover Schrum, Ill. School District No. 157, 257 EHLR 136 (OCR 1980).

Hudson v. Wilson, 828 F.2d 1059 (4th Cir. 1987).

Individuals with Disabilities Education Act (IDEA), 20 U.S.C. § 1400 *et seq.*

Individuals with Disabilities Education Act Amendments of 1997, Pub. L. No. 105-17, 105th Cong., 1st sess.

Individuals with Disabilities Education Act Regulations, 34 C.F.R. § 300.1 *et seq.*

Irving Independent School District v. Tatro, 468 U.S. 883 (1984).

J. C. v. Regional School District #10, Board of Education, 36 IDELR 31 (2d Cir. 2002).

Jaccari J. v. Board of Education of the City of Chicago, District # 299, 52 IDELR 177 (SEA Ill. 2009).

Jackson v. Franklin County School Board, 806 F.2d 623, 630 (5th Cir. 1986).

Jesu D. v. Lucas County Children Services Board, 1984–85, EHLR 556;484 (N.D. Ohio 1985).

Katsiyannis, A., & Herbst, M. (2004). Punitive damages in special education. *Journal of Disability Policy Studies, 15*, 9–11.

Lake, S. E. (2014). *What do I do when … The answer book on special education practice and procedure* (2nd ed.). Palm Beach Garden, FL: LRP Publications.

Letter to Biondi, 29 IDELR 972 (OSEP 1997).

Letter to Chief State School Officers, 33 IDELR 247 (OSEP 2000).

Letter to Helmuth, 16 EHLR 550 (OSEP 1990).

Letter to Lieberman, 23 IDELR 351 (OSEP 1995).

Letter to Murray, 19 IDELR 497 (OSEP 1992).

Letter to Perryman, EHLR 211:438 (OSEP 1987).

Letter to Williams, 18 IDELR 534 (OSEP 1991).

Light v. Parkway School District, 41 F.3d 1223 (8th Cir. 1994).

Marie O. v. Edgar, 27 IDELR 40 (7th Cir. 1997).

Mattison, D. A., & Hakola, S. R. (1992). *The availability of damages and equitable remedies under the IDEA, Section 504, and 42 U.S.C. Section 1983.* Horsham, PA: LRP Publications.

Max M. v. Illinois State Board of Education, 629 F. Supp. 1504 (N.D. Ill. 1986).

Max M. v. Thompson, 592 F. Supp. 1450 (N.D. Ill. 1984).

McNabb v. U.S., 318 U.S. 332 (1943).

Meiner v. Missouri, 673 F.2d 969 (8th Cir. 1986).

Mitten v. Muscogee County School District, 877 F.2d 932 (11th Cir. 1989).

Mrs. R v. Tirrozi, 559 IDELR 184 (2d Cir. 1987).

Murphy v. Timberlane Regional School District, 819 F. Supp. 1127 (D. N.H. 1993).

Nation Center for Dispute Resolution in Special Education. Available at www.directionservice.org/cadre/index.cfm.

Neosho R-V School District v. Clark, 315 F.3d 1022 (8th Cir. 2003).

Neville v. Dennis, 48 IDELR 241 (D. Kan. 2007).

Office of Special Education and Rehabilitative Services (2011). *Questions and answers on individualized education programs (IEPs), evaluations, and reevaluations,* Retrieved from http://idea.ed.gov/explore/view/p/,root,dynamic,QaCorner,3, on 3/33/2012.

OSEP Memorandum 94-16, 21 IDELR 85 (OSEP 1994).

P.R. v. Shawnee Mission Unified School District No. 512, 58 IDELR 283 (D. Kan. 2012).

Padilla v. School District No. 1 in the City and County of Denver, Colorado, 33 IDELR 217 (10th Cir. 2000).

Polera v. Board of Education of the Newburgh Enlarged City School District, 36 IDELR 231 (2d Cir. 2002).

Primm, E. B. (1990). Mediation: A comment under Part B; common sense for Part H. *Early Childhood Report, 1*(6), 4–6.

Questions and Answers on Procedural Safeguards and Due Process Procedures for Parents and Children with Disabilities (2009). Retrieved from http://idea.ed.gov/explore/view/p/,root,dynamic,QaCorner,6.

Rapid City School District v. Vahle, 733 F. Supp. 1364 (D. S.D. 1990).

Reusch, G. M. (1993). Special education disputes: Practical issues facing school board attorneys. In *Proceedings of the 14th National Institute on Legal Issues of Educating Individuals with Disabilities.* Horsham, PA: LRP Publications.

Richards, D. M., & Martin, J. L. (2005). The *IDEA amendments: What you need to know.* Horsham, PA: LRP Publications.

S-1 v. Turlington, 635 F.2d 342 (5th Cir. 1981).

Schaffer v. Weast, 546 U.S. 49 (2005).

Schever v. Rhodes, 416 U.S. 232 (1974).

Section 504 of the Rehabilitation Act of 1973 Regulations, 34 C.F.R. § 104.36 et seq.

Sellars v. School Board of the City of Manassas, 27 IDELR 1060 (4th Cir. 1998).

Shook v. Gaston County Board of Education, 882 F.2d 119 (4th Cir. 1989).

Shrybman, J. A. (1982). *Due process in special education.* Rockville, MD: Aspen.

Smith v. Robinson, 468 U.S. 992 (1984).

Sorenson, G. P. (1992). Special education discipline in the 1990s. *West's Educational Law Reporter, 62*(2) 387–398.

Still v. Debuono, 25 IDELR 32 (2d Cir. 1996).

T. D. v. LaGrange School District No. 102, 349 F.3d 469 (7th Cir. 2003).

Tatgenhorst, A., Norlin, J. W., & Gorn, S. (2014). *What do I do when ... The answer book on special education law* (6th ed.). Palm Beach Gardens, FL: LRP Publications.

Taylor v. Board of Education, 649 F. Supp. 1253 (N.D.N.Y. 1986).

Taylor v. Honig, 910 F.2d 627, 629 (9th Cir. 1990).

Taylor. v. Vermont Department of Education, 313 F.3d 768 (2d Cir. 2002).

Texas State Teachers Association v. Garland Independent School District, 489 U.S. 782 (1989).

Valente, W. D., & Valente, C. M. (2005). *Law in the schools* (6th ed.). Upper Saddle River, NJ: Pearson/Merrill.

W. B. v. Matula, 67 F.3d 484 (3d Cir. 1995).

Weber, M. (1992). *Special education law and litigation treatise.* Horsham, PA: LRP Publications.

Whitehead v. School Board of Hillsborough County, 932 F. Supp. 1393 (M.D. Fla. 1996).

Wright, P. W. (1994). Shannon Carter: The untold story. In *Proceedings of the 15th National Institute on Legal Issues of Educating Students with Disabilities.* Horsham, PA: LRP Publications.

Yell, M. L., Conroy, T., Katsiyannis, A., & Conroy, T (2013). Individualized education programs (IEPs) and special education programming for students with disabilities in urban schools. *Fordham Urban Law Review, 41,* 669–684.

Yell, M. L., & Espin, C. A. (1990). The Handicapped Children's Protection Act of 1986: Time to pay the piper? *Exceptional Children, 56,* 396–407.

Yell, M. L., Katsiyannis, A., Ennis, R. P., & Losinski, M. (2013). Avoiding procedural errors in IEP development. *Focus on Exceptional Children, 46*(1), 56–66.

Yell, M. L., Ryan, J. B., Rozalski, M. E., & Katsiyannis, A. (2009). The U.S. Supreme Court and special education: 2005 to 2009. *Teaching Exceptional Children, 41*(3), 68–75.

Zirkel, P. A. (1991). Compensatory educational services in special education cases. *Education Law Reporter, 67,* 881–887.

Zirkel, P. A. (1994). Over-due process revisions for the Individuals with Disabilities Education Act. *Montana Law Review, 55,* 403–414.

Zirkel, P. A. (1995). The remedy of compensatory education under the IDEA. *Education Law Reporter, 67,* 881–887.

Zirkel, P. A. (2016). A comparison of the IDEA's dispute resolution processes: Complaint resolution and impartial hearings. *West's Education Law Reporter, 326,* 1–8.

Zirkel, P. A., & McGuire, B. L. (2010). A roadmap to legal dispute resolution for students with disabilities. *Journal of Special Education Leadership, 23,* 100–112.

Zirkel, P. A., & Scala, G. (2010). Due process hearing systems under the IDEA: A state-by-state

Zirkel, P. A. (2017). The complaint procedures avenue of the IDEA: Has the road less travelled made all the difference. *Journal of Special Education Leadership, 30* (2), 88-97.

Chapter 13

Disciplining Students with Disabilities

(The Department of Education) encourages school environments that are safe, supportive, and conducive to teaching and learning, where educators actively prevent the need for short-term disciplinary removals by actively supporting and responding to behavior...the authority to implement disciplinary removals does not negate their obligation to consider the implications of the child's behavioral needs, and the effects of the use of suspension (and other short-term removals) when ensuring the provision of FAPE.

United States Department of Education, Office of Special Education Programs, (2016, p. 2)

Learner Objectives

At the end of the chapter, students will be able to

13.1 Describe the procedural due process rights of students.

13.2 Describe the substantive due process rights of students.

13.3 Describe how the IDEA affects the discipline of students with disabilities.

13.4 Describe how problem behavior should be addressed in a student's IEP.

13.5 Describe legal requirements regarding the use of functional

behavioral assessments and behavior intervention plans.

13.6 Describe legal requirements when suspending students with disabilities.

13.7 Describe the manifestation determination.

13.8 Describe permitted, controlled, and prohibited discipline procedures.

Discipline refers to procedures teachers use to maintain a classroom climate that is conducive to learning (Walker, Ramsey, & Gresham, 2004). Teachers generally think of discipline as techniques they can use to manage misbehavior (Curwin & Mendler, 1999). However, discipline involves more than just using procedures to control student misbehavior; it is also a means of teaching students about the effects of their behavior on others and to help them learn to control and manage their own behavior (Yell, Rozalski, & Drasgow, 2001). Indeed, discipline should help maintain an effective classroom environment and positively affect the learning of students in that classroom.

Discipline has long been an important concern of administrators, teachers, and parents. It is not surprising, therefore, that courts and legislators have addressed issues regarding the use of disciplinary procedures with students in public schools. In fact, the law has been an important force in the development of how we use discipline. Thus, it is important that teachers understand the legal requirements and constraints that guide school personnel when disciplining students.

The use of disciplinary procedures with students with disabilities has proved to be an especially controversial and confusing issue. Although the Individuals with Disabilities Education Act (IDEA) and the regulations implementing the laws are quite detailed, until 1997 the law did not address the discipline of students with disabilities. This lack of statutory and regulatory guidance resulted in uncertainty among school administrators and teachers regarding appropriate disciplinary procedures that could be used with students eligible for special education services.

During this time, however, many judicial decisions had addressed this issue, and these decisions led to the formation of a body of case law. Generally, the case law indicates that disciplinary actions against students with disabilities are subject to different rules and limitations than those applicable to students without disabilities (Tatgenhorst, Norlin, & Gorn, 2014). Osborne and Russo (2009) asserted that often school and district administrators lament that students with disabilities are immune from discipline but noted that nothing could be further from the truth! Because of the different rules, a dual standard of discipline exists between students with and those without disabilities, but this difference is primarily in the areas of proactively addressing problem behavior in a student's IEP and the procedural safeguards that must be followed when a student with disabilities is subject to disciplinary consequences. For administrators to contend that all students were treated equally in terms of discipline and, thus, that there is no dual disciplinary standard would not be convincing to a court, because students with disabilities do, in fact, have special protections against certain types of disciplinary procedures.

In the IDEA Amendments of 1997, the subject of disciplining students with disabilities was finally addressed in federal legislation. In the process of drafting these amendments, Congress heard testimony regarding the difficulties school administrators and teachers faced when having to discipline students with disabilities. To ameliorate these problems, Congress added a section to the IDEA that specifically addresses discipline issues. In doing so, Congress sought to strike a balance between school officials' duty to ensure that schools are safe and conducive to learning and their continuing obligation to ensure that students with disabilities receive a free appropriate public education (FAPE). In the Individuals with Disabilities Education Improvement Act (hereafter IDEA 2004), the 2004 reauthorization of the IDEA, Congress made a few changes to the disciplinary requirements. Essentially, the IDEA provides students with disabilities with a shield of procedural safeguards that are not available to students who are not disabled, and these safeguards have changed only slightly since the IDEA Amendments of 1997 (Yu, 2009).

The purpose of this chapter is to examine the discipline of students with disabilities. It begins with a discussion of the rights of school personnel to regulate the behavior of all students and then examines the obligations of school personnel in disciplinary matters. Next, the use of disciplinary procedures with students protected by the IDEA is reviewed. It is important to note that state law may also address many of these issues.

DISCIPLINE IN THE SCHOOLS

To operate efficiently and effectively, schools must have rules to regulate student conduct. If students violate reasonable school rules, they should be held accountable. Student accountability to rules usually implies that violators will be subject to disciplinary sanctions. Courts have recognized the importance of student management and have granted latitude to teachers to exercise this control through the use of discipline.

The courts' recognition of the importance of school authority over student behavior originates from the English common law concept of *in loco parentis* (i.e., in place of the parent). According to this concept, parents acquiesce in the control over their children when their children are placed in the charge of school personnel (Alexander & Alexander, 2012). The principal and the teacher have the authority not only to teach but to guide, correct, and discipline a student to accomplish educational objectives (Smith & Yell, 2013). *In loco parentis* does not mean that the teacher stands fully in the place of parents in controlling their child during the school day, but that school officials, acting in concert with appropriate laws and regulations, have a duty to maintain an orderly and effective learning environment through reasonable and prudent control of students. Although the concept does not have the importance it once did, it is nevertheless an active legal concept that helps to define the school-student relationship. With respect to the use of disciplinary procedures, the doctrine implies that teachers have the duty to see that school order is maintained by requiring students to obey reasonable rules and commands and to respect the rights of others.

All students, with and without disabilities, have rights in disciplinary matters based on the due process clause of the 5th and 14th Amendments to the U.S. Constitution (see Appendix B). In practice, however, the due process protections afforded students are limited by the state's interest in maintaining order and discipline in the schools. The courts, therefore, have had to strike a balance between student rights and the needs and interests of the schools.

The two general areas of due process rights afforded students are procedural and substantive. In terms of discipline, procedural due process involves the fairness of methods and procedures used by the schools; substantive due process refers to the protection of student rights from violation by school officials and involves the reasonableness of the disciplinary processes (Valente & Valente, 2005). School authorities are vested with broad authority for establishing rules and procedures to maintain order and discipline. Unless a student can show that he or she was deprived of a liberty or property interest, there is no student right to due process. According to a federal district court in Tennessee, "teachers should be free to impose minor forms of classroom discipline, such as admonishing students, requiring special assignments, restricting activities, and denying certain privileges, without being subjected to strictures of due process" (*Dickens v. Johnson County Board of Education*, 1987, p. 157).

PROCEDURAL DUE PROCESS: THE RIGHT TO FAIR PROCEDURES

School districts can meet these requirements by taking actions such as (a) developing reasonable and appropriate schoolwide discipline policies and procedures, (b) extending due process protections to students when using certain disciplinary procedures, and (c) ensuring that discipline sanctions are applied in a nondiscriminatory manner (Yell, 2011).

Developing Schoolwide Discipline Policies

Schools must develop rules that regulate student conduct. This is necessary to maintain discipline and to operate efficiently and effectively. Students should clearly know which behaviors are acceptable and which behaviors are prohibited. If students violate reasonable school rules by behaving in ways that are prohibited, they will be held accountable. Student accountability to rules implies that violators will be subject to disciplinary sanctions or consequences (Smith & Yell, 2013).

School officials understand that if students know what types of behavior are prohibited when they are in school and what the consequences of engaging in these prohibited behaviors will be it becomes more likely students will conduct themselves appropriately and not engage in the prohibited behaviors. Numerous courts have addressed the issue of schoolwide discipline policies and have tended to give great authority to teachers and school officials to write rules that govern student behavior when they are in school (Yell, Katsiyannis, Bradley, & Rozalski, 2000).

When schools develop policies that regulate student conduct, they must ensure that the rules and consequences are rational and reflect a school-related purpose. Rules should be clear enough to allow students to distinguish permissible from prohibited behavior. School rules that are too vague or general may result in the violation of students' rights because students will not have a clear understanding of them. In fact, if a court finds that a school rule is so vague that students may not understand what behavior is prohibited, it is likely the rule would be legally invalid. Thus, teachers and administrators must take care that their school rules are sufficiently clear and are communicated to students. Finally, rules must be school-related. School officials may not prohibit or punish conduct that is not related to their school's educational purposes.

Courts also have granted school officials the authority to impose reasonable consequences on students who break school rules. The most important requirement for schoolwide consequences for misconduct is that they are rational and fair. Consequences that are excessive and unsuitable to the particular circumstances may be legally invalid. School officials must use reasonable means to achieve compliance with a school's rules. Reasonableness refers to procedures that are rational and fair, not excessive or unsuitable to the educational setting. The disciplinary sanctions used in schools must not consist of penalties that are unnecessary or excessive for the achievement of proper school purposes (Hartwig & Reusch, 2000).

Many school officials assume that because of the IDEA's restrictions on suspensions and expulsions, regular school district discipline policies do not apply to students with disabilities. This is a mistaken assumption. Students with disabilities who attend public school are subject to a school district's regular discipline policies and procedures (Norlin, 2007). In a few situations, however, general discipline policies must be changed when applied to students in special education. These situations are when the school district's disciplinary policy (a) deprives a student of his or her special education and related services (i.e., long-term suspensions or expulsions without providing educational services), (b) triggers the procedural safeguards of the IDEA (e.g., changes a student's placement without a change in the individualized education program [IEP] or without notice), or (c) interferes with a student's IEP, behavior intervention plan (BIP), or Section 504 accommodation plan.

If a student's IEP team determines that (a) he or she will be subject to the school district's regular disciplinary policy, and (b) the policy does not violate the requirements of the IDEA, the team may use the student's IEP or BIP to affirm that the student will be subject to the district's regular discipline policies and procedures (Norlin, 2007). Including a copy of the school's discipline policy along with the IEP or BIP will accomplish this. If a student's parents agreed to the IEP or BIP, then they are simultaneously consenting to using the school's regular discipline policy. The Office of Special Education Programs (OSEP) in the U.S. Department of Education seemingly supported such a view in a comment to the 1999 IDEA regulations: "in appropriate circumstances the IEP team ... might include specific regular or alternative disciplinary measures that would result from particular infractions of school rules" (*OSEP questions and answers*, 1999, p. 12,589). If an IEP team decides that a student will be subject to an alternative discipline plan, this plan should be included in the student's IEP or BIP.

Extending Due Process Protections to Students

The importance of education to a student's future requires that disciplinary actions resulting in students being deprived of an education (e.g., suspension, expulsion) are subjected to the standards of due process. The purpose of due process procedures is to ensure that official decisions are made in a fair manner. Due process procedures in school settings do not require the full range of protections afforded to persons in formal court trials, such as representation by counsel and cross-examination of witnesses (Sorenson, 1993). The procedures do, however, include the basic protections such as notice, hearing, and impartiality.

The U.S. Supreme Court in *Goss v. Lopez* (1975; hereafter *Goss*) outlines the due process protections in schools, which must be afforded to all students. The case, which is a seminal case in the area of discipline, involved nine high school students who had been suspended from school without a hearing. At issue was whether the students had been denied due process of law under the 14th Amendment. The Supreme Court ruled that the students had the right to at least minimal due process protections in cases of suspension. The High Court stated that, "Having chosen to extend the right to an education ... [the state] may not withdraw the right on grounds of misconduct absent fundamentally fair procedures to determine whether the misconduct had occurred" (p. 574). The Court, noting the broad authority of the schools to prescribe and enforce standards of behavior, held that states are constrained to recognize a student's entitlement to a public education as a property interest that is protected by the 14th Amendment. Because education is protected, it may not be taken away without adhering to the due process procedures required by the amendment. The school had argued that a 10-day suspension was only a minor and temporary interference with the students' education; the High Court disagreed, stating that a 10-day suspension was not **de minimis** (i.e., trivial or minor) but was a "serious event in the life of the suspended child" (p. 576). The imposition of the 10-day suspension, therefore, must include "the fundamental requisite of due process of law ... the opportunity to be heard" (Grannis v. Ordean, 1914, p. 388).

The opportunity to be heard, when applied to the school setting, involves the right to notice and hearing. The right to notice and hearing requires that students are presented with the charges against them and have an opportunity to state their case (Tatgenhorst et al., 2014). The due process protections to be afforded to students will not shield them from properly imposed suspensions, but they will protect them from an unfair or mistaken exclusion. The Court in *Goss* recognized the necessity of order and discipline and the need for immediate and effective action, stating that suspension is a "necessary tool to maintain order ... [and] a valuable educational device" (p. 572). Although the prospect of imposing cumbersome hearing requirements on every suspension case was a concern, the justices believed that schools should not have the power to act unilaterally, free of notice and hearing requirements. The Court held that when students are suspended for 10 days or less, therefore, the school needs only to give them oral or written notice of the charges, an explanation of the reasons for the suspension, and an opportunity to present their side of the story.

The requirement does not imply a delay between the time notice is given and the time of a student's hearing. The disciplinarian could informally discuss the misconduct with students immediately after the behavior occurs and give them an opportunity to present their version of the facts. In such situations, notice and hearing would precede the disciplinary action. If, however, the behavior posed a danger to students or teachers or a threat to disrupt the academic process, a student could be immediately removed and the notice and hearing could follow as soon as possible. In this event, notice of disciplinary hearings should follow within 24 hours and the hearing should be held within 72 hours. The basic due process protections prescribed by the High Court in *Goss* applied solely to short suspensions of 10 days or less. Longer suspensions or expulsions, according to the Court, require more extensive and formal due process procedures. Figure 13.1 lists the due process protections that must be afforded to students in short- and long-term suspensions. In addition to these guidelines, it is permissible to immediately remove dangerous students from the school setting. Additionally, brief in-school sanctions do not require a due process hearing.

The due process protections outlined in *Goss* must be extended to *all* students who face suspensions, including students with disabilities. In fact, the IDEA does not create more rigorous procedural protections for students with disabilities than the minimal protections in *Goss* (Norlin, 2007). If suspensions of students with disabilities exceed 10 consecutive school days or amount to a change in placement, however, the procedural protections of the IDEA apply.

These due process protections will not shield students from properly imposed suspensions. Rather, the purpose of the protections is to protect students from an unfair or mistaken suspension. The protections that must be afforded to students who are suspended are limited by the school's interest in maintaining order and discipline.

FIGURE 13.1 ■ Due Process Protections for All Students

Short-Term Suspension (may be a formal or informal meeting)

- Written or oral notice of charges
- Opportunity to respond to charges

Long-Term Suspension and Expulsion (must be a formal meeting)

- Written notice specifying charges
- Notice of evidence, witnesses, and substance of testimony
- Hearing (advance notice of time, place, and procedures)
- Right to confront witnesses and present their own witnesses
- A written or taped record of the proceedings
- Right of appeal

Ensuring That Discipline Practices Are Nondiscriminatory

Recall from Chapter 6 that all students with mental or physical impairments that affect a major life function are protected from discrimination under Section 504 of the Rehabilitation Act of 1973 (hereafter Section 504). This includes students with disabilities who are not covered by the IDEA and students in special education who are covered. This means that Section 504 also protects all IDEA-eligible special education students.

Discrimination refers to unequal treatment of qualified students with disabilities based solely on the basis of the disability. School districts may violate Section 504 when disciplining students with disabilities in four primary ways: (a) disciplining students with disabilities by using procedures that are not used with nondisabled students who exhibit similar misbehavior; (b) disciplining students with disabilities by using procedures that are more harsh than those used with nondisabled students who exhibit similar misbehavior; (c) suspending (long-term), expelling, or changing the placement of a student with disabilities for misbehavior that is related to the student's disability; or (d) disciplining a student using procedures that are prohibited in the IEP or behavior intervention plan.

To ensure that discipline is not applied in a discriminatory manner, which would thus violate Section 504, school officials should adopt the following procedures: First, schools must use the same disciplinary procedures for students with and without disabilities. In such situations, it would reinforce this fact if IEP teams or Section 504 teams would include the school's regular disciplinary policy in a student's IEP or Section 504 accommodation plan. Second, schools must conduct manifestation determinations to assess the relationship between a student's disability and misconduct before using long-term suspensions, expulsions, or making changes of placements (see the section on manifestation determinations). If no relationship exists, a student may be suspended or expelled. Third, administrators must ensure that all school officials and the student's teachers understand the contents of the IEP, BIP, or Section 504 plans and follow the interventions and disciplinary procedures listed in these documents (Yell et al., 2001). Discipline plans that are written into IEPs or Section 504 plans preempt a school district's regular disciplinary code (Norlin, 2007).

SUBSTANTIVE DUE PROCESS: THE RIGHT TO REASONABLENESS

Courts have given schools great authority in promulgating rules governing student behavior. The power to establish rules and regulations, however, is not absolute, for when these regulations are developed, they must not violate constitutional principles. Generally, this requires that the regulation of student behavior be reasonable. To be reasonable, rules must have a rationale and a school-related purpose, and the school must employ reasonable means to achieve compliance with the rule. Schools may not prohibit or punish conduct that has no adverse effect on public education. Neither may they employ disciplinary penalties or restraints that are unnecessary or excessive for the achievement of proper school purposes (Hartwig & Reusch, 2000). Reasonableness essentially means that procedures must be rational and fair and not excessive or unsuitable for the educational setting.

Rules must be sufficiently clear and specific to allow students to distinguish permissible from prohibited behavior. School rules that are too vague or general may result in the violation of students' rights. Appropriate school rules are specific and definitive; they provide students with information regarding behavioral expectations.

A federal district court in Indiana addressed the issue of the reasonableness of a school's use of discipline in *Cole v. Greenfield-Central Community Schools* (1986). The plaintiff, Christopher Bruce Cole, an elementary student, exhibited management and adjustment problems and was diagnosed as emotionally disturbed under Indiana state law. The school had attempted, and documented, numerous positive and negative procedures in efforts to control and modify Christopher's behavior. Included in the disciplinary procedures were time-out, response cost, and corporal punishment. The plaintiff sued the school, contending that in using these procedures the school had violated his civil rights.

The court recognized that although Christopher had a disability covered by the IDEA, he was not immune from the school's disciplinary procedures. The court held that the validity of the plaintiff's claim, therefore, rested on the "reasonableness" of the disciplinary procedures used by the school in attempting to manage Christopher's behavior. To determine reasonableness, the court analyzed four elements: (a) Did the teacher have the authority under state and local laws to discipline the student? (b) Was the rule violated within the scope of the educational function? (c) Was the rule violator the one who was disciplined? (d) Was the discipline in proportion to the gravity of the offense? Finding that all four elements of reasonableness were satisfied, the court held for the school district.

THE IDEA AND DISCIPLINE

Administrators and teachers face a different set of rules and limitations in using disciplinary procedures with students with disabilities who are protected by the IDEA (Norlin, 2007; Tatgenhorst et al., 2014). This dual standard only exists, however, when disciplinary procedures may result in a change of placement. The determination of what constitutes a change of placement under the IDEA is critical. Under the IDEA, changes of placement cannot be made without following the procedural requirements of the law.

In the IDEA Amendments of 1997, Congress addressed several issues related to discipline. According to a congressional report (*Senate Report*, 1997), the goals of the disciplinary provisions of the IDEA were as follows:

1. All students, including students with disabilities, deserve safe, well-disciplined schools and orderly learning environments.

2. Teachers and school administrators should have the tools they need to assist them in preventing misconduct and discipline problems and to address those problems, if they arise.

3. There must be a balanced approach to the issue of discipline of students with disabilities that reflects the need for orderly and safe schools and the need to protect the right of students with disabilities to a FAPE.

4. Students have the right to an appropriately developed IEP with well-designed behavior intervention strategies.

Congress sought to expand the authority of school officials to protect the safety of all children by maintaining orderly, drug-free, and disciplined school environments, while ensuring that the essential rights and protections for students with disabilities were protected (Letter to Anonymous, 1999). In writing the discipline provisions, Congress sought to help school officials and IEP teams (a) respond appropriately when students with disabilities exhibit serious problem behavior and (b) appropriately address problem behavior in the IEP process (Yell et al., 2000). In 2000, Kenneth Warlick, then the director of OSEP, wrote a letter briefly summarizing some of the discipline provisions of the IDEA (*Letter to Osterhout, 2000*).

In the IDEA 2004, Congress sought to give school districts more authority when disciplining students with disabilities. Specifically, Congress made significant changes in four areas. First, the law now allows school personnel to consider any unique circumstances on a case-by-case basis when they consider changing the placement of a student who has violated a code of student conduct. According to Richards and Martin (2005), this language allows a school administrator to consider any unique circumstances when deciding to seek a long-term disciplinary removal. Furthermore, the authors assert that this language may be a response to school districts' zero-tolerance policies in which administrators are required to take specified actions in certain circumstances. Second, Congress altered this manifestation requirement. Third, Congress added a behavior that can lead to a 45-day removal. Finally, the stay-put rule was modified in disciplinary situations. These changes will be covered in later sections of this chapter.

It is important that school personnel are aware of the law and regulations and are able to effectively implement their provisions. Three major points underlie the disciplinary provisions of the IDEA. First, the law emphasizes the use of positive behavioral interventions, supports, and services for students with disabilities who exhibit problem behaviors. The purpose of positive programming is to teach appropriate behaviors that increase the likelihood of a student's success in school and in post-school life, rather than merely using punishment-based programming to eliminate inappropriate behavior. These procedures must be included in students' IEPs when appropriate. Second, school officials may discipline a student with disabilities in the same manner as they discipline students without disabilities, with a few exceptions. A school's regular disciplinary procedures can be used with students with IEPs as long as they (a) are used with nondisabled students *and* students with disabilities (i.e., the procedures are not discriminatory), (b) do not result in a unilateral change in a student's placement (i.e., suspension in excess of 10 cumulative school days that constitutes a pattern of exclusion, change of educational placement made by school personnel and not the IEP team, suspension for 10 consecutive days, and expulsions from school), and (c) do not result in the cessation of educational services.

Third, discipline should be addressed through the IEP process. Yell et al. (2000) predicted that school districts were most likely to violate the FAPE and disciplinary provisions of the IDEA by (a) failing to address problem behavior and discipline in the IEP process and (b) not following the behavioral plans and disciplinary procedures indicated in a student's IEP and in the IDEA (e.g., a principal unilaterally expels a student with disabilities rather than adhering to the discipline plan in the IEP). An advantage of addressing discipline through the IEP process is that if school personnel and parents can arrive at solutions to a student's discipline problems through this process (e.g., changing a student's placement to an alternative school rather than moving to expel him or her), there is no need to invoke the disciplinary provisions of the IDEA. Let's examine the major discipline additions to the IDEA since 1997.

In 2016, the Office of Special Education and Rehabilitative Service (OSERS) and Office of Special Education Programs (OSEP) issued a dear colleague letter that addressed the importance of schools and school districts implementing programs that encourage school environments that are safe, supportive, and conducive to teaching and learning (U.S. Department of Education, 2016). Such schoolwide programs can prevent the need for using short-term disciplinary removals because the programs effectively support and responding to behavior.

The OSERS/OSEP letter, however, also was a reminder to school personnel that the authority to implement disciplinary removals does not lessen their obligation to consider the implications of a student with disabilities behavioral needs, and the effects of suspensions and other short-term removals when ensuring the provision of FAPE.

Addressing Problem Behavior in the IEP Process

The IDEA requires that if a student with disabilities exhibits problem behaviors that impede his or her learning or the learning of others, then the student's IEP team shall consider the use of "positive behavioral interventions and supports, and other strategies to address that behavior" (IDEA, 34 C.F.R. § 300.324(a)(2)(1)). Comments to the federal regulations to the IDEA in 1999 indicated that if a student has a history of problem behavior, or if such behaviors can be readily anticipated, then the student's IEP must address that behavior (IDEA Regulations, 34 C.F.R. § 300, Appendix A, Question 39). This requirement applies to all students in special education, regardless of their disability category. The purpose of addressing problem behavior in the IEP is to teach appropriate behaviors while preventing the problem behaviors that may lead to disciplinary sanctions.

In 2016 the Office of Special Education and Rehabilitative Services (OSERS) and the Office of Special Education Programs (OSEP) in the U.S. Department of Education issued a Dear Colleague Letter in which officials asserted that recent data on short-term disciplinary removals from students' current placements suggested that may students with disabilities may not be receiving appropriate behavioral interventions and supports in the IEPs. The OSERS/OSEP letter, therefore, addressed how IEP teams should address student's problem behavior by including positive behavioral interventions and supports in a student's IEP (U.S. Department of Education, 2016). The document also strongly suggested that the use of short term disciplinary procedures should trigger a school's personnel to consider whether a student's IEP addressed his or her misbehavior. Officials from OSERS and OSEP noted that when a student with disabilities experienced behavioral challenges that resulted in suspensions or other exclusionary disciplinary measures, the IEP team may need to reevaluate the student's IEP to ensure that the IEP appropriately addresses his or her behavior so that the student receives FAPE.

Officials in OSERS and OSEP also identified circumstances that, when present, may indicate that a school district had failed to provide a FAPE to a student with disabilities who was experiencing behavioral challenges that impeded his or her learning or the learning of others. These circumstances included failing to (a) consider the inclusion of positive behavioral interventions and supports in response to the student's behavior, (b) schedule an IEP Team meeting to review the IEP to address behavioral concerns after a reasonable parental request, (c) discuss the parent's concerns about the student's behavior and its effects on the student's learning during an IEP meeting, or (d) implement the behavior supports in a student's IEP or where school personnel have implemented behavioral supports that are not included in the IEP that are not appropriate for the student. (The OSERS/OSEP DCL is available online at www2.ed.gov/policy/gen/guid/school-discipline/files/dcl-on-pbis-in-ieps--08-01-2016.pdf).

Neither the IDEA, the regulations, nor the DCL indicated what behaviors should be addressed in the IEP. The lack of specificity is consistent with the IDEA's philosophy of allowing IEP teams to make individualized decisions for each student (Norlin, 2007). It is up to the IEP team, therefore, to determine which behaviors are significant enough to require interventions formally written into the IEP. Drasgow, Yell, Bradley, and Shriner (1999) inferred from previous hearings and court cases that these problem behaviors may include (a) disruptive behaviors that distract teachers from teaching and students from learning, (b) noncompliance, (c) verbal and physical abuse, (d) property destruction, and (e) aggression toward students or staff.

These problem behaviors should be addressed in the following manner. First, when a student exhibits problem behavior, the IEP team must determine if the behavior impedes his or her learning or other students' learning. Second, if the team decides that the problem behavior does interfere with the student's learning, they must conduct an assessment of the behavior. Third, the IEP team must develop a plan based on the information gained from the assessment to reduce problem behaviors and increase socially acceptable behaviors. According to the 2016 DCL, a student's parent and teachers could decide to amend an IEP to address the misbehavior without convening the full IEP team to make such changes.

The results of the team's decisions must be included in the IEP. This means that the IEP of a student with serious problem behaviors must include the information from the assessment in the present levels of performance section of the IEP. Because educational needs must be addressed by developing appropriate special education programming, the IEP must also include (a) measurable goals and objectives and (b) special education and related services that address the problem behavior. Moreover, if the student's behavioral program involves modifications to the general education classroom, these modifications must be included in the IEP. When an IEP team addresses a student's problem behavior, the needs of the individual student are of paramount importance in determining the behavior strategies that are appropriate for inclusion in the child's IEP (OSEP questions and answers, 1999).

If an IEP team fails to address a student's problem behaviors in the IEP, then that failure may deprive the student of a FAPE (Drasgow et al., 1999; OSEP, 2016). This could result in legal actions against the offending school district. The importance of including positive programming that addresses significant problem behavior in students' IEPs was emphasized by Thomas Hehir, former director of the U.S. Department of Education's Office of Special Education Programs, who stated that "the key provision in [IDEA] is using positive behavioral interventions and supports" (*Letter to Anonymous*, 1999, p. 707) in the IEPs of students who exhibit significant problem behaviors. Failure to do so "would constitute a denial of the free appropriate public education [mandate of the IDEA]" (IDEA Regulations, Appendix B, Question 38).

The results of an IEP team's failure to address a student's behavior in a student's IEP occurred in the remanded *Endrew F.* decision from the U.S. Supreme Court. The U.S. Supreme Court's unanimous ruling in *Endrew F.* vacated the lower courts' rulings and sent the case back to the lower courts to reconsider the case in light of the High Court's FAPE standard. In February 2018, the judge from U.S. District Court of the District of Colorado reversed himself and ruled that the Douglas County School District had failed to provide Endrew with a FAPE. A major reason that the judge ruled against the school district is because the IEP team had failed to adequately address Endrew's behavior in his IEP. Specifically, the judge held that the "IEP offered to him by the District in this case was insufficient to create an educational plan that was reasonably calculated to enable (Endrew) to make progress, even in light of his unique circumstances, based on the continued pattern of unambitious goals and objectives of his prior IEPs" (*Endrew F.*, 2018, p. 15). Moreover, the judge held that Endrew's academic and functional progress "was clearly impacted by the District's lack of success in providing a program that would address (Endrew's) maladaptive behaviors" (*Endrew F.*, 2018, p. 16).

Functional Behavioral Assessment   The IDEA encourages, and sometimes demands, that IEP teams address problem behaviors by conducting functional behavioral assessments (FBAs) and by developing education programming based on the results of the assessment (Drasgow & Yell, 2002).

An FBA is a process that searches for an explanation of the purpose behind a problem behavior (OSEP questions and answers, 1999). Although the U.S. Department of Education has not defined an FBA, it is reasonable to assume Congress intended that the term be consistent with the meaning in the professional literature (Drasgow et al., 1999; Norlin, 2012). An FBA is a process to gather information about factors that reliably predict and maintain problem behavior in order to develop more effective intervention plans (Horner & Carr, 1997; O'Neill et al., 1997). In essence, an FBA is used to develop an understanding of the cause and purpose of problem behavior (Drasgow et al., 1999).

Conducting an FBA should be part of the process of addressing problem behavior. Moreover, the purpose of an FBA, or any special education assessment, is not merely to determine eligibility. Rather, its purpose is to determine the educational needs of students with disabilities and then to develop effective programming to meet those needs.

The IDEA does not detail the components of an FBA. Neither did the U.S. Department of Education include additional information on FBAs in the final regulations. This means that the composition of FBAs is left to states, school districts, and IEP teams. According to the OSEP, a definition was not offered in the IDEA regulations because IEP teams need to "be able to address the various situational, environmental, and behavioral circumstances raised in individual cases" (*OSEP questions and answers*, 1999).

The decision to conduct an FBA and develop a BIP, therefore, is left up to the professional judgment of the IEP team. In certain situations, though, an IEP team *must* conduct an FBA and write a BIP. These situations are when a team conducts a manifestation determination in conjunction with a disciplinary change of placement or when a student is placed in an interim alternative educational setting (IAES).

Functional Behavioral Assessments and Discipline

The IDEA requires that the IEP team must meet and conduct or revise an FBA and BIP within 10 business days from when a student is (a) first removed for more than 10 school days in a school year, (b) removed in a manner that constitutes a change in placement, or (c) placed in an IAES for a weapons or a drug offense. In such situations, the IEP team must convene to conduct an FBA and develop a BIP. Martin (1999) suggests, however, that IEP teams should conduct an FBA if a student is approaching 10 cumulative days of suspension rather than waiting until the 10-day limit has been reached. Additionally, an FBA must be conducted when a manifestation determination team has determined that a student's misconduct was related to his or her disability.

For subsequent removals of a student who already has an FBA and BIP, the IEP team members can individually review the BIP and its implementation. The review of the student's behavior may take place without a meeting unless one or more of the team members believe that the plan (or its implementation) needs modification (IDEA Regulations, 34 C.F.R. § 300.520(c)). The regulations did not intend that school personnel develop behavioral interventions within 10 days of removing a student from the current placement. Instead, the regulations are intended to require that public schools expeditiously conduct the FBA. Moreover, the regulations ensure that the IEP team develops appropriate behavioral interventions based on the assessment. Those interventions must then be implemented as quickly as possible.

School officials should also consult their state's laws and rules in regards to FBS and BIP requirements. This is because states may add to, but not subtract from, the FBA/BIP requirements of the IDEA (Zirkel, 2017). For example, the states of California, Minnesota, and New York have FBA/BIP requirements that go beyond the federal requirements,

The purpose of conducting an FBA is to develop educational programming that is related to the cause and purpose of the problem behaviors. According to Tatgenhorst et al. (2014), the IDEA clearly requires that IEP teams should consider and implement behavioral goals and interventions, often referred to as a BIP, for students with behavior problems well before the point when the student is facing a disciplinary removal.

Behavior Intervention Plans

The IEP team develops a BIP based on the FBA. The IDEA does not provide details about the composition of the plan beyond indicating that the plan has to be individualized to meet the needs of different students in different educational environments. The U.S. Department of Education also refused to define a BIP. Congress and the Department of Education apparently expected that the term *behavioral intervention plan* had a commonly understood meaning in special education (Norlin, 2007).

Behavior plans need to be individualized, proactive, and multidimensional. This means that IEP teams should implement multiple strategies aimed at preventing problem behavior before it becomes severe enough to warrant sanctions such as suspension or expulsion

(Drasgow et al., 1999; Norlin, 2007; Yell et al., 2000). In fact, behavioral plans that merely describe acts of prohibited misconduct and then specify consequences for misbehavior are almost certainly illegal because they are reactive and not proactive (Norlin, 2007).

The behavior change program should emphasize multiple strategies that include teaching prosocial behaviors. The key component of the plan is using positive behavioral interventions that do not rely on coercion or punishment for behavior change (Dunlap & Koegel, 1999). Whether or not a team develops a formal BIP or not, the IEP of a student with behavioral problems, regardless of that student's special education category, must include goals, services, and plans for addressing that student's behavioral needs (*M.M. and C.M. v. District 0001 Lancaster County School*, 2012).

When an IEP addresses behavior, the process for developing and writing the IEP is the same as would be for academics. First, the need for behavioral programming will be addressed in the present levels of educational performance. Second, measurable behavioral goals will be listed in the annual goal section along with the procedures that will be used to measure a student's progress toward the goals and the method for reporting a student's progress to his or her parents. Third, the behavioral programming will be addressed. Because the IDEA and regulations do not specify the required components of a BIP but yet it is considered an important part of a student's IEP, some hearing officers have evaluated BIPs using the same criteria they use to evaluate an IEP (Yu, 2009). For example, in *Lake Travis Independent School District v. M.L.* (2007), a hearing officer applied the Fifth Circuit's four-factor FAPE test to determine the appropriateness of a BIP. The four factors were as follows: (a) Is the BIP individualized based on a complete and individualized assessment? (b) Is the BIP administered in the least restrictive environment? (c) Does the BIPs provide services in a coordinated and collaborative manner? (d) Does the BIP demonstrate positive academic and nonacademic benefits?

The initial language regarding FBAs and BIPs first made its appearance in the IDEA as an IEP team's actions after a student with disabilities had been suspended. In that sense, the FBA/BIP requirements seem to be a reactive mechanism. It is important to note, however, that IEP teams have always needed to address problem behaviors that students with disabilities exhibit. Moreover, if these problems are serious and interfere with a student's ability to receive educational benefit, the IEP team must address the behaviors in the student's IEP through measurable annual goals, special education services, and progress monitoring procedures. Failing to develop IEPs that address the behavioral needs of students can result in the denial of a FAPE. An example of such a situation occurred in *Neosho R-V School District v. Clark* (2003), where the U.S. Court of Appeals for the Eighth Circuit found that a student's need for behavior interventions existed long before the school district made an effort to establish one. Similarly, in *Council Rock School District v. M.W.* (2012) and *Baldwin Park Unified School District* (2012), a U.S. district court and a state educational agency (SEA) found that school districts in Pennsylvania and California had denied FAPE by failing to address problem behavior in students' IEPs even though long-standing behavioral concerns had been identified by the students' teachers.

Despite the presence of positive behavioral intervention and support plans, Congress recognized that school officials still needed clarification of which disciplinary procedures could be used when students with disabilities exhibit serious misbehavior. Most discipline procedures used with students in public schools are permitted under the IDEA (e.g., time-out, in-school suspension). When the student misconduct is serious enough to warrant suspension or expulsion, however, the strictures of the IDEA must be followed.

Disciplinary Procedures

Most types of in-school disciplinary procedures that are used as part of a schoolwide discipline plan may be used with students in special education. In fact, when using in-school discipline with students, school officials are least likely to make mistakes that may lead to legal problems (Yu, 2009). The exceptions are disciplinary procedures that result in a student being suspended, removed to an interim placement, or expelled from school, which are much more likely to cause a change in a student's placement because he or she has been removed from the school setting (Yu, 2009).

Short-Term Disciplinary Removals

The IDEA authorizes school officials (i.e., building-level administrators) to unilaterally suspend students with disabilities, or place students in an alternative educational program on a short-term basis, to the same extent that such suspensions or removals are used with students without disabilities. According to the U.S. Department of Education, the reason that school officials may make such decisions unilaterally (i.e., acting by themselves) is because maintaining safety and order in the school may sometimes require that students with disabilities be removed from the school environment immediately (*Letter to Anonymous*, 1999). To react quickly to such situations, the building-level administrator can remove a student with disabilities from school without having to convene an IEP team, conduct a manifestation determination, or seek permission to do so from a student's parents. School officials, however, must afford a student his or her due process rights (i.e., oral or written notice of the charges, an explanation of the evidence that supports the charges, and an opportunity to present his or her side of the story).

The IDEA does not establish a specific limitation on the number of days in a school year that students with disabilities can be suspended from school. As a result of this lack of information in the statute and regulations, confusion exists regarding the number of days that students with disabilities can be suspended without violating the IDEA. Students with disabilities may be removed from school for up to 10 cumulative or consecutive school days as long as such suspensions are used with nondisabled students as well.

School officials must keep four critical points in mind when using short-term suspensions. First, 10 consecutive days is the upper limit on out-of-school suspensions. If a suspension exceeds this limit, it becomes a change of placement. In this situation, if school officials do not follow the IDEA's change-of-placement procedures (e.g., written notice to the student's parents, convening the IEP team), the suspension is a violation of the law (see section on change-of-placement procedures for an explanation of this area of the law).

Second, when the total number of days that a student has been suspended equals 10 or more cumulative days in a school year, educational services must be provided. At this point the IEP team has to meet for a number of reasons. The team must determine what services will be provided and where, conduct an FBA, and develop a BIP. If an FBA and BIP are already a part of the IEP, they must be reviewed. Third, the IEP team must address the change-of-placement issue. In other words, the team must examine the previous suspensions to see if they amounted to a unilateral change of placement. According to Yu (2009), the key to ensuring compliance with the IDEA when using short-term suspensions is to keep track of the number of school days that a student has been suspended from school.

Fourth, when multiple suspensions total more than 10 cumulative school days, even though each individual disciplinary removal has been less than 10 consecutive days, this may constitute a change of placement. Additionally, if the removal constitutes "a pattern of removals" (IDEA Regulations, 34 C.F.R. § 300.536(a)(2)), this will also be a change in placement.

Provided Educational Services

Educational services must be provided after the 10th cumulative day of removal. For example, if a student is suspended for 10 cumulative days in the fall semester and is then suspended for 3 more days in the spring term, educational services must be provided from the first day in which cumulative suspensions exceed 10 days or, in this case, the first day of suspension in the spring. School officials may implement additional short-term suspensions for separate incidents of misconduct, therefore, as long as they provide educational services to the suspended student. Although not directly addressed in the IDEA, if a student is suspended for less than 10 school days, a school district is not required to continue educational services as long as the school district does not provide services to nondisabled children suspended for less than 10 school days (71 Fed. Reg. 46,717, 2006).

School officials in consultation with the student's special education teacher should determine the content of the educational services, if the suspensions equal less than 10 cumulative days.

When suspensions exceed 10 cumulative days, the IEP team must determine educational services. The educational services provided to students must allow them to (a) progress in the general education curriculum, (b) receive special education and related services, and (c) advance toward achieving their IEP goals. Because of limits on the number of days in which a student with disabilities may be removed from the school setting, school officials should use out-of-school suspensions judiciously and in emergency situations. Moreover, school personnel should keep thorough records of the number of days in which students with disabilities are removed from schools for disciplinary reasons so they do not inadvertently violate IDEA provisions.

The frequency and number of short-term removals, if they are excessive, may be indicative of a defective IEP. Martin (1999) asserted that the greater the number of short-term disciplinary removals, the greater the likelihood that a hearing officer will find that the behavior portion of the IEP is inappropriate and a deprivation of the student's right to a FAPE. Indeed, if a student is approaching 10 cumulative days of suspension, the IEP team should be convened to review the student's behavioral plans, conduct an FBA, and develop or review the student's BIP. Martin (1999) also suggested that the IEP team should also conduct a manifestation determination prior to the 11th day of accumulated short-term removals.

When a Short-Term Disciplinary Removal Becomes a Change of Placement

A long-term suspension of more than 10 consecutive days is a change of placement under the IDEA. Because such a suspension is a change of placement, the school district must follow the IDEA's change-of-placement procedures. This means that a school district must provide the parents of the suspended student with written notice prior to initiating the change. The purpose of such a notice is to give the parents an opportunity to object if they disagree with the placement change. The written notice should include an explanation of the applicable procedural safeguards (OSEP questions and answers, 1999). If a student's parents object to the change of placement, the school district may not suspend the students beyond the 10 consecutive days. The only exception to this rule is when the team conducts a manifestation determination and decides the student's misconduct is not related to his or her disability (see a later section for elaborations on the manifestation determination).

A series of short-term suspensions may also become a change in placement. The question of when disciplinary removals amount to a change of placement, however, can only be determined by a student's IEP team. To determine if a series of short-term suspensions has become a change in placement, an IEP team must determine the circumstances surrounding the suspension, including (a) the length of each removal, (b) the total amount of time the student is removed, and (c) the proximity of the removals to one another (IDEA Regulations, 34 C.F.R. § 300.536(a)). Nevertheless, neither the IDEA nor the regulations provide clear guidance as to when repeated short-term suspensions of fewer than 10 school days amount to a change of placement. Ultimately, this question will be answered by due process hearing officers and judges. The decision to classify a series of suspensions as a change in placement can only be decided on a case-by-case basis. It is important, therefore, that when a series of short-term suspensions amounts to more than 10 cumulative school days, the IEP team must be convened to determine whether these suspensions may be a change in placement.

Removal of a student for fewer than 10 cumulative or 10 consecutive school days probably will not amount to a change in placement. Similarly, if a series of short-term suspensions of not more than 10 days each is used for separate incidences of misbehavior, it probably will not be a change of placement, as long as the suspensions do not create a pattern of exclusion. However, school officials must not assess repeated short-term suspensions as a means of avoiding the change-of-placement procedures required when using long-term suspensions. According to Norlin (2007), subterfuge of this nature, if detected, will invariably result in a finding that a school district violated the requirements of the IDEA.

Norlin (2007) reviewed decisions from the U.S. Department of Education's Office of Civil Rights (OCR) regarding when accumulated short-term suspensions become a change of placement. He listed eight decisions from 1990 to 1997 in which the OCR decided that multiple suspensions leading to between 13 and 31 days of removal were significant changes of placement and thus violated the law. However, the OCR also decided that a district's removal of a student on two separate occasions resulting in a total of 15 days of removal and another district's removal of a student on five separate occasions for a total of 38 days of removal did not result in a change of placement. It should be noted that the OCR decisions only address violations of Section 504 and not of the IDEA. Nonetheless, because the rules regarding disciplinary removals are similar under Section 504 and the IDEA, these decisions are useful indicators of when multiple suspensions may become a change of placement.

Finally, readers are cautioned that state law regarding suspensions of students with disabilities should be consulted because some states put a ceiling on the number of days that students with disabilities can be suspended during a school year. If state law allows fewer days of suspension than does the IDEA, then school officials must adhere to the state guidelines.

Change in Placement   The case law clearly indicates that schools may not unilaterally change the placement of a student with disabilities. If the school proposes a change in placement, and the student's parents contest the proposal, the stay-put provision comes into play and the student cannot be removed from the then-current educational placement. The only exception is when a student brings a weapon to school or uses, possesses, or sells illegal drugs. In such situations, school officials may immediately and unilaterally move a student to an interim alternative educational setting.

The determination of what constitutes a change of placement is important to understanding the limits of discipline under the IDEA. Minor changes in the student's educational program that do not involve a change in the general nature of the program do not constitute a change in placement. For example, in *Concerned Parents and Citizens for Continuing Education at Malcolm X v. The New York City Board of Education* (1980), a circuit court held that a change in the location of the program, in and of itself, did not constitute a change of placement.

A change in the educational program that substantially or significantly affects the delivery of education to a student constitutes a change in placement and is not permissible. *Honig v. Doe* (1988; hereafter *Honig*) established that any suspension of more than 10 days constitutes a change in placement. The 10-day rule became the federal norm in the IDEA. Indefinite suspensions or expulsions in excess of 10 days, therefore, constitute a change in placement. According to Yu (2009), when a student's IEP team has determined that disciplinary actions have resulted in a change of placement, it is important that school officials take the following actions. First, ensure that procedural safeguards are followed. Failure to notify the student's parents of their right to appeal a decision to suspend may result in a finding that the school district has violated the IDEA. Second, continue to provide educational services for suspensions beyond 10 school days. Third, if related services have been missed during a suspension time that lasts beyond 10 days, these services must be made up. Fourth, an IEP team meeting should be held prior to reaching 10 cumulative days to conduct a manifestation determination and revise the student's IEP.

Long-Term Disciplinary Removals   Long-term suspension and expulsion qualify as a change of placement. Courts have long held that expulsion is a unilateral change of placement that is inconsistent with the IDEA (*Doe v. Maher*, 1986; *Honig v. Doe*, 1988; *Kaelin v. Grubbs*, 1982; *Prince William County School Board v. Malone*, 1985; *S-1 v. Turlington*, 1981; *Stuart v. Nappi*, 1978). Because expelling a student with disabilities would result in a placement change, the procedural safeguards of the IDEA would automatically be triggered. In 1988, the U.S. Supreme Court handed down the most important decision regarding long-term suspension and expulsion in *Honig*.

Honig v. Doe (1988;) involved the proposed expulsion of two students with emotional disabilities from the San Francisco public school system. Both students, following separate behavior incidents, had been suspended from school and recommended for expulsion. In accordance with California law, the suspensions were continued indefinitely while the expulsion proceedings were being held. Attorneys for the students filed a joint lawsuit in federal district court. The district court issued an injunction that prevented the school district from suspending any student with disabilities for misbehavior causally related to the student's disability. The school district appealed. The U.S. Court of Appeals for the Ninth Circuit, in *Doe v. Maher* (1986), held that expulsion is a change in placement, triggering the procedural safeguards of the law. The California superintendent of public instruction, Bill Honig, filed a petition of certiorari with the U.S. Supreme Court. One of the issues raised on appeal concerned the stay-put provision. Honig contended that the circuit court's interpretation of the rule—that no student with a disability could be excluded from school during the pendency of the administrative review regardless of the danger presented by the student—was untenable. A literal reading of this provision, according to Honig, would require schools to return potentially violent and dangerous students to the classroom, a situation Congress could not have intended.

Ruling in *Honig*   On January 20, 1988, the U.S. Supreme Court issued a ruling in the case renamed *Honig v. Doe.* Justice Brennan, writing for the majority, rejected Honig's argument that Congress did not intend to deny schools the authority to remove dangerous and disruptive students from the school environment. Stating that Congress had intended to strip schools of their unilateral authority to exclude students with disabilities from school, the High Court declined to read a dangerousness exception into the law. The Court ruled that during the pendency of any review meetings, the student must remain in the then-current placement unless school officials and parents agree otherwise. Expulsion, the Court held, constituted a change in placement.

The Court noted that this decision regarding the stay-put provision did not leave educators "hamstrung." While the ruling would not allow a school to change a student's placement during proceedings, it did not preclude the use of a school's normal disciplinary procedures for dealing with students with disabilities (Yell, 2011; Yu, 2009). Such normal procedures included time-outs, the use of study carrels, detention, restriction of privileges, and suspension for up to 10 days. These procedures would allow the prompt removal of dangerous students. During the 10-day period, school officials could initiate an IEP meeting and "seek to persuade the child's parents to agree to an interim placement" (*Honig*, p. 605). If a student was truly "dangerous" and the parents refused to agree to a change, school officials, according to the High Court, could immediately seek the aid of the courts. When seeking the aid of the courts, the burden of proof would rest upon the school to demonstrate that going through the IDEA's procedural mechanisms (i.e., due process hearing) would be futile and that in the current placement the student was "substantially likely" to present a danger to others. The stay-put provision, therefore, does not preempt the authority of the courts from granting an injunction to temporarily remove the student from the school. In effect, the Court did read a dangerousness exemption into the stay-put rule; however, this determination could only be made by a judge and not by school officials.

School officials should explore alternatives to long-term suspensions or expulsions because of the likelihood of violating the IDEA. Furthermore, because of the IDEA's change-of-placement procedures, if a school district has zero-tolerance policies, it is important they not be applied rigidly with students who are protected under the law (Yu, 2009).

Removal for 45 School Days   School officials may unilaterally exclude a student with disabilities from school for up to 45 school days without regard to whether the misbehavior was a manifestation of the student's disability if the student (a) brings, possesses, or acquires a weapon at school, on school premises, or at a school function (e.g., school dances, class trips, extracurricular activities); (b) knowingly possesses, uses, or sells illegal drugs, or sells a controlled substance at school, on school premises, or at a school function; or (c) has inflicted serious bodily injury to another person while at school, on school premises, or at a school function. A weapon is defined as a device, instrument, material, or substance that is

Enhanced eText **Video Example 13.1**
This short **video** details suspensions, expulsions, and manifestation determinations.
https://www.youtube.com/watch?v=JOZb7rpAS_4

used for, or is readily capable of, causing death or serious bodily injury. (For a list of weapons covered under the IDEA, see the *Federal Criminal Code*, 18 U.S.C. § 930(g).) A *controlled substance* refers to a legally prescribed medication (e.g., Ritalin) that is illegally sold by a student. (For a list of controlled substances covered by the IDEA, see the *Controlled Substances Act*, 21 U.S.C. § 812[c]). *Serious bodily injury* refers to any physical injury that results in risk of death, physical pain, disfigurement, or loss or impairment of a bodily function. In the event of such exclusions, students must be placed in an appropriate IAES.

If school officials decide that a student with disabilities is dangerous to him- or herself or others even though the student has not committed a weapons or drug offense or injured another student or teacher, school officials may request that an impartial hearing officer remove the student to an interim setting for not more than 45 school days. In such situations school officials must demonstrate that maintaining the student in his or her current placement is substantially likely to result in an injury to the student or others. (See the section on *Honig* injunctions.)

The Manifestation Determination

The IDEA requires that within 10 school days of any decision to change the placement of a student with a disability because of a violation of a code of student conduct, the school, the parents, and relevant members of the IEP team (as determined by the parent and school administrator) shall review all relevant information in the student's file, including the student's IEP, any teacher observations, and any relevant information provided by the parents.

The manifestation determination is a hearing to ascertain if a student's misbehavior was caused by or was substantially related to the student's disability (Dagley, McGuire, & Evans, 1994; *OSEP Memorandum 95-16*, 1995; Senate Report, 1997; Tatgenhorst et al., 2014; Walsh, 2009). The reasoning behind the manifestation determination is that students should not be denied special education services because of misbehavior that could be anticipated as a result of their disabilities (Dagley et al., 1994; Yell, 2011). Specifically, the team determines if (a) the student's misconduct was caused by or had a direct and substantial relationship to the student's disability, or (b) the student's misconduct was the direct result of the school district's failure to implement the IEP (IDEA Regulations, 34 C.F.R. § 300.530(e)(1)).

This manifestation determination may not be made by administrators or school officials who lack the necessary expertise to make special education placement decisions, and the team's decision may not be made using normal school procedures for disciplining students without disabilities; that is, school boards, members of school boards, administrators acting unilaterally, or any one school representative may not make the manifestation determination (*OSEP Memorandum 95-16*, 1995).

If the determination is made that the disability was not related to the misbehavior and that the IEP is appropriate, the student can be disciplined as any other nondisabled student would be disciplined. For example, the student could be placed on a long-term suspension, expelled, or placed in an interim setting. Students must continue to receive educational services. That is, they must continue to work on their IEP goals and on the general curriculum, although in a different setting.

If the team determines that a relationship between behavior and disability exists or that a student's IEP was not implemented, the student may not be expelled, although school officials will still be able to initiate change-of-placement procedures. The standard specifies that if a relationship exists between a student's misbehavior and the school's failure to properly implement the IEP, the IEP team must conclude that the misbehavior was a manifestation of the student's disability. In such a situation, the student's IEP team must conduct an FBA and implement a BIP for the student, or review the BIP if one was already in place. Also, the student must be returned to the setting from which he or she was removed, unless the IEP team and the parents agree to a change in placement when they develop the new BIP.

Conducting the Manifestation Determination

Although numerous cases have referred to the manifestation determination, the courts have offered little guidance to schools regarding standards for making this determination. As Dagley et al. (1994) wrote "a careful reading of court cases implicating the relationship test creates the suspicion that no one really knows how to conduct the relationship test" (p. 326). In the IDEA Amendments of 1997, Congress provided guidance to IEP teams in conducting manifestation determinations. According to Yu (2009), one of the frequent errors made by school districts is not having the appropriate school personnel at the meeting. Generally, a student's IEP team, including a student's parents, conducts the review. It is important that the team include a person at the meeting who has specific information about the incident that led to the disciplinary action. Additionally, because the results of manifestation hearings are frequently challenged in due process hearings, the team members should carefully document the results of their deliberations and be able to explain the rationale supporting their decision (Walsh, 2009).

When conducting the test, the IEP team shall consider the behavior subject to the disciplinary action and relevant information, including evaluation and diagnostic results and the student's IEP and placement. Moreover, all decisions must be based on an individualized inquiry informed by up-to-date evaluation data. Team members responsible for collecting and interpreting the data should be qualified and knowledgeable regarding the student, the misbehavior, and the disability. Moreover, the data used to inform the decision-making process should be recent and collected from a variety of sources. Data collection procedures should include a review of records of past behavioral incidences, interviews, direct observation, behavior rating scales, and standardized instruments. Finally, the team must consider any other relevant information supplied by the student's parents.

If a student's parents disagree with the findings of the team they may request a due process hearing to appeal the decision. If there is an appeal an expedited hearing must be held. After the request has been made, the school district must arrange for the hearing to be held within 20 school days. Additionally, a resolution session must be held within 7 calendar days of the filing, unless the parties waive the resolution session or request mediation. After the due process hearing has been completed, the hearing officer must issue his or her decision within 10 school days. When the hearing is being conducted the student remains in the interim setting.

Assessing the Relationship

In conducting the manifestation determination, the team must look to the implementation of a student's IEP and the relationship between the misconduct and the student's disability. If the IEP is not being implemented as written, the determination is essentially over because such problems indicate the presence of a causal relationship between the misbehavior and the disability. The IEP team must also assess the relationship between misconduct and disability: Was the misconduct caused by the disability, or was there a direct and substantial relationship between the misconduct and the disability? A direct and substantial relationship is a rigorous standard to meet.

Courts have clearly indicated what will not constitute proper lines of inquiry in the manifestation determination. First, the determination must be independent of a student's disability classification. The court in *S-1 v. Turlington* (1981) noted that a causal relationship between misconduct and behavior can occur in any disability area, not just in students with behavioral disabilities; that is, the test should be conducted when suspending or expelling any student protected by the IDEA, regardless of the student's disability classification. Second, the manifestation determination is not an inquiry into whether a student knew the difference between right and wrong. According to the Fifth Circuit court in *Turlington,* determining whether students are capable of understanding rules or regulations or right from wrong is not tantamount to determining that the student's misconduct was or was not a manifestation of the disability.

Interim Alternative Educational Settings

The IDEA requires that a FAPE must be made available to all eligible students with disabilities, even those who have been suspended or expelled from school (IDEA Regulations, 34 C.F.R. § 300.530(d)(1)(i)). When a student is suspended in excess of 10 cumulative days in a school year, the school district must continue to provide educational services (71 Fed. Reg. 46,717, 2006). This means that on the 11th cumulative day of a student's removal from school, educational services must begin. These services are provided in an interim alternative educational setting (IAES).

The IDEA describes three specific circumstances when an IAES may be used for disciplinary purposes. First, an IAES may be used for a short-term disciplinary removal from school for 10 days or less. School officials may unilaterally impose a short-term suspension on a student with a disability for less than 10 consecutive days for violating school rules and for additional removals for not more than 10 consecutive days in a school year for separate incidences of misconduct, as long as these removals do not constitute a change in placement. After 10 days of removal in a school year, educational services must be provided to suspended children. An alternative to out-of-school suspension is placement in an IAES. There is not an absolute limit on the total number of short-term placements in an IAES, as long as a FAPE is provided and the proximity and pattern of removal does not constitute a change in placement (Telzrow & Naidu, 2000). Second, an IAES may be used in situations when a student with disabilities is removed from school for a longer term (e.g., long-term suspension, expulsion). Third, a hearing officer can order placement in an IAES.

When a student is placed in an IAES for a short-term disciplinary removal, school officials, in consultation with the student's special education teacher, can determine the content of his or her educational programming. In such short-term removals it is not required, therefore, that the IEP team determines the services. For a long-term removal in an IAES, however, the student's IEP team must determine the setting and services that will be offered. In both situations, the IAES must (a) allow the student to continue to participate in the general curriculum, although in a different setting; (b) provide the services necessary to allow the student to meet his or her goals from the IEP; and (c) include services designed to keep the misbehavior from recurring. Additionally, the school must continue to provide the special education services, supplementary aids and services, program modifications, and related services listed in the IEP, including the interventions to address the student's problem behavior. The IDEA regulations define the general curriculum as the same curriculum taken by students without disabilities. According to a U.S. district court in Maine in the case *Farrin v. Maine School Administrative District No. 59* (2001), an appropriate IAES will provide courses in the general curriculum that allow a student to advance from grade to grade and eventually allow a student to graduate. According to the U.S. Department of Education, to ensure that a student participates in general education it is not necessary that the school must replicate every aspect of a student's education that he or she received prior to being removed from school (e.g., some hands-on equipment in a chemistry class). The Department of Education referred to this as a "modified FAPE" (71 Fed. Reg. 46,716, 2006).

Although the use of homebound instruction or tutoring as an IAES is not specifically prohibited by the IDEA, homebound placements can be problematic (Katsiyannis & Maag, 1998). This is because (a) school districts must continue to provide the services listed in a student's IEP while he or she is in the IAES, and (b) the IDEA requires that students in special education be placed in the least restrictive environment. If a student receives related services such as counseling, physical therapy, or speech, these services must be part of the student's program in the IAES. Clearly, providing these services in a homebound setting would be difficult. In answers to a series of questions regarding discipline, the Office of Special Education and Rehabilitative Services (OSERS) noted that in most circumstances homebound instruction is inappropriate as a disciplinary measure; however, the final decision regarding placement must be determined on a case-by-case basis (*Department of Education answers questions*, 1997). Norlin (2007) noted that in hearings, it would be up to school district officials to justify homebound placements. If districts have in-school suspension programs or alternative schools, and instead opt for placing a student in a homebound setting, it may be difficult to justify to a hearing officer the use of the more restrictive homebound setting. Finally, in one state-level hearing, a school's use of a homebound placement was overturned when the hearing review officer ruled that the homebound placement was inappropriate because it failed to provide the services that previously were included in a student's IEP (*Board of Education of the Akron Central School District*, 1998).

Telzrow and Naidu (2000) suggested that for short-term IAES placements, schools should develop and use in-school suspension programs as their IAESs. Using such programs for an IAES means that students continue to work on their individualized goals and objectives and receive the special education, related services, and behavioral programming that are required by their IEPs. These authors also suggest that school districts consider the use of alternative programs or schools for long-term IAES placements, as long as these programs include the academic and behavioral programming and parental involvement as required in a student's IEP.

The Stay-Put Provision

When parents disagree with a change in placement proposed by a school district, the IDEA's stay-put provision prohibits the district from unilaterally changing placement. This provision requires that "during the pendency of any proceedings ... unless the [school] and the parents ... otherwise agree, the child shall remain in the then current placement of such child" (IDEA Regulations, 34 C.F.R. § 518(a)). The purpose of the stay-put provision is to continue students in their current placement (i.e., their placement before the dispute arose) until the dispute is resolved. The stay-put provision effectively operates to limit the actions of a school district (Yu, 2009). The court in *Zvi D. v. Ambach* (1982) asserted that the stay-put procedures operated as an automatic preliminary injunction because a request for a hearing automatically requires that schools maintain a student's placement. It is permissible to move a student during the pendency of a hearing only when the parents and school agree on an interim change of placement.

IDEA 2004 significantly altered the stay-put rule. First, school officials may move a student to an IAES for no more than 45 school days for the aforementioned infractions. If a parent objects to this placement change and requests a due process hearing, the stay-put rule would normally function to keep a student in the previous placement during the hearing. With the new language in IDEA 2004, the stay-put placement is the IAES; that is, a student will remain in that setting during the pendency of the hearing.

DISCIPLINING STUDENTS NOT YET ELIGIBLE FOR SPECIAL EDUCATION

The IDEA provides protections for students with disabilities who have not been determined to be eligible for services under the IDEA and who violated a code of student conduct. If a student's parents assert that their child is protected by the IDEA, the student will be protected by the law only if the school had knowledge that the child had an IDEA disability before the behavior incident that precipitated the disciplinary action.

For a school to be determined to have prior knowledge, school personnel must have known of or suspected that the student had a disability because (a) the parent expressed a concern in writing to school administrative or supervisory personnel, (b) the parent requested an evaluation for special education, or (c) the student's teacher expressed concern to supervisory personnel that the student had a disability and needed special education services. In such situations students may be protected under the IDEA even if they are not currently eligible. The only exception to this rule is if the student's parent refused to consent to an evaluation that the school sought. If the school had no prior knowledge of a possible disability, the school may discipline the student who exhibited the problem behavior. If a parent of a student who is being disciplined requests an evaluation for special education during the disciplinary period, the school must conduct the evaluation in an expedited manner. If a school district did have knowledge, then the student could still be suspended for up to 10 days, but school personnel must conduct an expedited evaluation. If an evaluation shows the existence of a disability and that student is eligible for special education, the disciplinary requirements of the IDEA must be followed. If the evaluation indicates no disability, then the student may be disciplined without adhering to the rules of the IDEA.

Federal regulations provide an exception to the knowledge rules. Even if one of the three elements were present, a school district will be determined to not have knowledge if district personnel had conducted an evaluation and determined that the student was not eligible for special education services, the student's parents refused to allow an evaluation, or the parent refused special education services under the IDEA (IDEA Regulations, 34 C.F.R. § 300.534(a)). If a school district has no knowledge, then a student may be disciplined as a student without disabilities. The parent, however, may request an expedited special education evaluation.

In a memorandum, the OSEP took the position that students not previously identified as eligible under the IDEA could not invoke the stay-put provision to avoid disciplinary sanctions such as expulsion (*OSEP Memorandum 95-16,* 1995). In situations in which a request for an evaluation or due process hearing was made following a disciplinary suspension or expulsion, school districts were not obligated to reinstate students to in-school status during the pendency of the evaluation or hearing. The stay-put setting in such situations would be the out-of-school placement.

Referral to Law Enforcement and Courts

School personnel may report to police a crime committed by a student with a disability who is protected by the IDEA. Moreover, law enforcement and judicial authorities can exercise their authority under the law when confronted with a crime committed by a student who is in special education. Furthermore, the school personnel can transmit copies of all the student's special education and disciplinary records to law enforcement.

Honig *Injunctions*

If the parents refuse to agree to a change of placement, however, and the school is convinced that the student is truly dangerous, school officials can request an injunction or temporary restraining order (TRO) from a hearing officer to remove the student from the school environment. A TRO issued to remove a dangerous student with disabilities from school has been frequently referred to as a *Honig* injunction. When an injunction is issued, schools may use the time when a student is not in school to determine if a change of placement is needed or to conduct a manifestation determination.

Obtaining an Injunction   In *Honig,* the Supreme Court stated that any action brought by a school district to obtain a TRO will carry a presumption in favor of a student's current educational placement. School officials can overcome this preference only by "showing that maintaining [the] child in his or her current placement is substantially likely to result in injury either to himself or herself, or to others" (p. 606). Prior to the IDEA Amendments of 1997, only courts could grant *Honig* injunctions, but now hearing officers can grant such injunctions. School officials must convince a hearing officer that unless a student is removed from the current placement, the student is dangerous and substantially likely to injure him- or herself or others. Additionally, school officials must prove that reasonable steps have been taken to minimize the risk of harm in the current setting; that the current IEP is appropriate; that the interim setting allows the student to participate in the general education curriculum, although in a different setting; and that the student can continue to work on IEP goals. Furthermore, the school must demonstrate these factors with substantial evidence, which the IDEA defines as being beyond a preponderance of the evidence (IDEA Amendments, 1997).

The substantial evidence requirement would seem to be a difficult threshold to meet. Nevertheless, in a number of post-*Honig* rulings, schools have been granted discipline-related TROs (e.g., *Binghamton City School District v. Borgna*, 1991; *Board of Education of Township High School District No. 211 v. Corral*, 1989; *Board of Education of Township No. 211 v. Linda Kurtz-Imig*, 1989; *Light v. Parkway School District*, 1994; *Prince William County School Board v. Willis*, 1989; *Texas City Independent School District v. Jorstad*, 1990).

THE LEGAL STATUS OF DISCIPLINARY PROCEDURES

In *Honig,* the U.S. Supreme Court ruled that typical disciplinary procedures—those that are often used for establishing school discipline, such as restriction of privileges, detention, and removal of students to study carrels—may be used with students with disabilities. Such disciplinary procedures do not change placement and are generally not restricted by the courts. A significant restriction exists, however, against certain types of discipline that may result in a unilateral change in placement. To clarify which disciplinary practices are legal and which are not, disciplinary procedures may be placed into one of three categories: permitted, controlled, and prohibited (Yell, Cline, & Bradley, 1995; Yell & Peterson, 1995).

Permitted Procedures

Permitted disciplinary procedures include those practices that are part of a school district's disciplinary plan and are commonly used with all students. These procedures are unobtrusive and do not result in a change of placement or the denial of the right to a FAPE. Such procedures include verbal reprimands, warnings, contingent observation (a form of time-out where the student is briefly removed to a location where he or she can observe but not participate in an activity), exclusionary time-out, response cost (the removal of points or privileges when a student misbehaves), detention, and the temporary delay or withdrawal of goods, services, or activities (e.g., recess, lunch). As long as these procedures do not interfere significantly with the student's IEP goals and are not applied in a discriminatory manner, they are permitted. In general, if the disciplining of a student with disabilities does not result in a change of placement, the methods of discipline available to schools are the same for all students (Osborne & Russo, 2009). In fact, most courts have held that in-school discipline does not constitute a change of placement, and therefore does not trigger the due process protections of the IDEA against certain types of disciplinary procedures (Yu, 2009).

Controlled Procedures

Controlled procedures are those interventions that the courts have held to be permissible as long as they are used appropriately. The difficulty with these practices is that if they are used in an inappropriate manner, used excessively, or used in a discriminatory manner, these procedures can result in interference with IEP goals or objectives or in a unilateral change in placement. Controlled procedures include disciplinary techniques such as exclusionary time-out, in-school suspension, and out-of-school suspension.

Time-Out Time-out is a disciplinary procedure frequently used by teachers of students with disabilities. Time-out, which is actually time-out from positive reinforcement, is an intervention that involves removing a student from all sources of reinforcement following an inappropriate behavior (Yell, Meadows, Dragow, & Shriner, 2013). There are two major types of time-out: nonexclusionary time-out and exclusionary time-out (Yell, 1994). In nonexclusionary time-out, all sources of reinforcement are removed from a student. A common type of nonexclusionary time-out is contingent observation, in which a student is removed from an activity and allowed to watch but not participate. In exclusionary time-out, a student is removed from the potentially reinforcing activity and required to sit in an area devoid of reinforcement. As used in schools, exclusionary time-out generally involves placing a student in a less reinforcing environment for a period of time following inappropriate behavior. Exclusionary time-out should be considered a controlled procedure. Seclusion or isolation time-out, a type of exclusionary time-out, is definitely a controlled procedure and may be a prohibited procedure. Seclusion time-out is examined in this chapter's section on prohibited procedures. Two federal court cases and a ruling from the OCR considered the legality of exclusionary time-out, as discussed next.

In *Dickens v. Johnson County Board of Education* (1987), a federal district court ruled that the use of time-out with the plaintiff, Ronnie Dickens, was only a de minimis (trivial or minor) interference with the student's education. The use of time-out did not, therefore, violate the plaintiff's right to an education. While extremely harsh and abusive use of time-out may violate a student's rights, the court found that the legitimate and reasonable use of time-out was a particularly appropriate disciplinary procedure to use with students with disabilities because it would not deprive them of their right to an education.

Hayes v. Unified School District No. 377 (1987) involved the use of seclusion/isolation time-out with two students with behavioral disorders. The teacher used a system of written warnings to allow the students time to alter their behavior to escape time-out. If the students received three warnings, they were placed in a time-out room. The court ruled that the teacher had used time-out to ensure the safety of others, protect the educational environment from disruptive behavior, and teach the students more appropriate behavior. According to the court, the appropriate use of seclusion/isolation time-out is not prohibited by the IDEA.

The OCR affirmed the use of time-out following an investigation of a complaint against a school district's use of this procedure (*Marion County {FL} School District*, 1993). The investigation revealed that the school district properly followed state and local educational policies, established a disciplinary policy that included time-out procedures for students with and without disabilities, incorporated behavior management plans into students' IEPs that included the use of time-out, and kept records on the use of time-out. Furthermore, parents were informed about the possible use of time-out and agreed to its use. Concluding that the school district was not in violation of Section 504 or the Americans with Disabilities Act, the OCR stated that time-out prevented the necessity of using more restrictive measures to control behaviors. When time-out escalates to a level of punishment that infringes on a student's personal safety rights and appropriate education, however, it may be a violation of Section 504 or the IDEA (Cline, 1994). In a 1991 OCR ruling, for example, the excessive and prolonged use of time-out was ruled a violation of Section 504 (*McCracken County School District*, 1991).

In-School Suspension   In-school suspension (ISS) programs require the suspended student to serve the suspension period in the school, usually in a classroom isolated from schoolmates. During ISS, the student works on appropriate educational material provided by the teacher. Several advantages of using ISS are that (a) it avoids the possibility of the suspended student roaming the community unsupervised, (b) the student being disciplined is segregated from the general school population, and (c) the student continues to receive an education during the suspension period (Yell, 1990). In *Hayes v. Unified School District No. 377* (1987), a school district's use of ISS was challenged. The plaintiffs, who had not consented to its use, argued that ISS, which sometimes lasted as long as 5 days, constituted an illegal change of placement and a deprivation of due process. The court noted that the school had clearly specified the behaviors that would lead to ISS, thereby providing the students with adequate notice to protect themselves from being placed in ISS. The court also ruled that as long as the school continued to provide an appropriate education, ISS for 5 days did not constitute an illegal change of placement.

In a ruling regarding a school district's use of ISS, the OCR determined that ISS was being used appropriately (*Chester County {TN} School District*, 1990). The complainant alleged that the district had improperly placed special education students in ISS for periods in excess of 10 days and had failed to provide adequate notice of these disciplinary actions to parents. The OCR determined that the district had established formal procedures regarding its disciplinary policies (including the use of ISS), provided parents with written explanations of these procedures, and adequately notified parents prior to the use of ISS. The OCR also stated that the ISS program, when used for 10 days or more (in this case 28 days), did not constitute a change in placement because the school district provided a program that was "comparable, in nature and quality, to the educational services regularly provided to special education students" (p. 301). The ISS instructor was a certified special education teacher, usually the number of students in ISS was less than six, and lesson plans were sent daily or weekly from the student's regular and special education teachers. The OCR confirmed that the goals and objectives on the students' IEPs were followed when students were in ISS. Figure 13.2 lists the necessary components of a legally sound ISS program.

Despite the fact that ISS programs remove students with disabilities from their classrooms, the courts have not considered them either long-term suspensions, expulsions, or changes of placement as long as the programs are comparable to the educational program regularly offered to students (Norlin, 2007). Schools, however, must not use ISS as a de facto long-term suspension or expulsion. In such cases, ISS may be viewed as an illegal change of placement.

Out-of-School Suspension   Out-of-school suspension generally refers to a short-term exclusion from school for a specified period of time, accompanied by a cessation of educational services. Numerous cases have ruled on the use of out-of-school suspension with students with disabilities (*Doe v. Koger*, 1979; *Doe v. Maher*, 1986; *Honig v. Doe*, 1988; *Kaelin v. Grubbs*, 1982; *S-1 v. Turlington*, 1981; *Stuart v. Nappi*, 1978; *Victoria L. v. District School Board*, 1984). According to the courts, expulsion and indefinite out-of-school suspensions are changes in placement and cannot be made unilaterally even in cases where students present a danger to themselves or others. Courts have stated, however, that schools can use short-term suspensions of up to 10 days. Suspension from transportation to school, unless alternative means of transportation are available, should be treated as part of the 10 days (*Mobile County {AL} School District*, 1991). Sorenson (1993) suggests that schools adopt a 10-day suspension policy. The IDEA Amendments of 1997 specifically allow school officials to suspend students with disabilities for up to 10 school days. Suspensions for longer than 10 days constitute a change of placement under the IDEA, and if a student's parents do not agree to a change in placement, the IDEA procedural safeguards must be followed.

Conclusion   Time-out, in-school suspension, and out-of-school suspension are permitted if used appropriately. Basic due process rights, such as notice and hearing, must be given to students prior to the use of suspension. It is important in using such procedures that schools not abuse or overuse them, as these could be interpreted as unilateral changes of placement or discriminatory by the courts.

FIGURE 13.2 ■
Legally Sound In-School Suspension Policies

- Have a written policy informing students and parents of when violation of rules may result in a student being placed in ISS.
- Provide a warning to students when their behavior may lead to ISS.
- Inform parents when a student is placed in ISS.
- Supervise ISS with a paraprofessional or a teacher.
- Continue to provide an appropriate education (e.g., have student's teacher prepare lesson plans, provide materials).
- Document in-school suspension.

Prohibited Procedures

Disciplinary procedures that result in a unilateral change in placement are prohibited. Thus, expulsions (i.e., the exclusion from school for an indefinite period of time) and long-term suspensions are illegal if made without following the IDEA's procedural safeguards. In many states, corporal punishment is illegal and therefore a prohibited procedure. Additionally, it is important that school personnel follow state or federal laws that prohibit or restrict the use of certain disciplinary procedures.

Long-Term Suspension and Expulsion

If the IEP team determines that a student's misbehavior and his or her disability are not related, long-term suspensions and expulsions are legal. However, even when no relationship is found and an expulsion is made in accordance with procedural rules, there cannot be a complete cessation of educational services. If the IEP team determines that the misbehavior and disability are related, long-term suspensions and expulsions are not legal.

Attempts to bypass the suspension and expulsion rules have not been looked upon favorably by the courts or administrative agencies. The OCR has stated that a series of suspensions cumulatively totaling more than 10 days constitutes a change of placement if the results create a pattern of exclusion (*OCR Memorandum,* 1988). Serial and indefinite suspensions, therefore, are prohibited. A series of five suspensions totaling 22 days over a school year was found to be a pattern of exclusions that created a significant change of placement for a student with disabilities (*Cobb County {GA} School District,* 1993). In *Big Beaver Falls Area School District v. Jackson* (1993), a Pennsylvania court ruled that a school district, in violation of the IDEA and state law, had effectively suspended a student by continually assigning her to ISS. Rather than serve the ISS, the student was allowed to leave school, which she usually did. According to the court, the school continually assigned the ISS knowing that the student would leave school; therefore, the action amounted to a de facto expulsion in violation of the IDEA.

Corporal Punishment

One of the most controversial disciplinary procedures is corporal punishment. Courts have heard many challenges to the use of this type of disciplinary action in schools. In 1977 the U.S. Supreme Court, in *Ingraham v. Wright,* held that corporal punishment in public schools was a routine disciplinary procedure not prohibited by constitutional law. The U.S. Court of Appeals for the Fourth Circuit, in *Hall v. Tawney* (1980), stated that brutal, demeaning, or harmful corporal punishment would be a violation of a student's substantive due process rights. The court applied the standard of reasonableness in holding that corporal punishment that is reasonable is legitimate, but if it is not reasonable (e.g., excessive) it is illegal.

According to the Center for Effective Discipline, 31 states have banned the use of corporal punishment in schools and 19 states have laws permitting corporal punishment in schools. Furthermore, in states where corporal punishment is not prohibited, many local school districts prohibit its use. In many schools throughout the country, therefore, corporal punishment is not allowed.

Restraint and Seclusion

In 2009 the U.S. Government Accountability Office (GAO) issued a report on the use of seclusions and restraints in schools (U.S. Government Accountability Office, 2009). The report detailed hundreds of allegations of the inappropriate use of restraint and seclusion in schools, which had resulted in the abuse and even death of students. Furthermore, the GAO reported that these procedures were more likely to be used on students with disabilities. The GAO investigation also found that there were no federal laws restricting the use of seclusion and restraint in public or private schools. Additionally, state regulation and oversight of such seclusion and restraint in schools varied greatly.

According to Ryan, Peterson, and Rozalski (2007), seclusion is the placing of a student in a room or location where he or she is alone and prevented from leaving the room. Physical restraint is when one or more persons use their bodies to restrict the movement of the student (Peterson, Albrecht, & Johns, 2009). Seclusion and restraint are procedures that are generally used as a last-resort intervention for students who are out of control and posing a danger to themselves and others (Rozalski & Yell, 2004). Numerous professional organizations have taken positions on the use of seclusions and restraints in schools (Council for Children with Behavioral Disorders, 2009; Council for Exceptional Children, 2009; Council of Parent Attorneys and Advocates, 2009; National Disability Rights Network, 2009).

The issuance of the GAO report received considerable publicity. Congress and the White House held hearings on the abuse of these practices in schools. The Keeping All Students Safe Act, which was introduced in the House by Representative George Miller and in the Senate by Senator Tom Harkin, would allow restraint and seclusion to be used in schools only in situations when there is an imminent danger of injury and only when used by appropriately trained staff. The bill would also prohibit school personnel from including restraint or seclusion in the IEPs of students with disabilities. Furthermore, school administrators would be required to notify parents immediately following incidents where restraint or seclusion was used. School districts could establish schoolwide policies and procedures on the use of restraint and seclusion. Schools would also have to keep thorough records on the use of any seclusions or restraints. The legislation would also allow states flexibility in developing their own laws on restraints and seclusions as long as they met the minimum federal standards. Recent OCR data on seclusion and restraint showed that students with disabilities account for 58% of the students who were placed in secluded environments while at school and 75% of the students who were restrained while at school, even though they make up about 12% of the student population (U.S. Department of Education, 2012).

Many states have laws that control school personnel's use of restraint and seclusion. Prior to using such procedures, school officials should be aware of their states' laws, regulations, and policies regarding restrain and seclusion. A guide to state laws is available at www.autcom.org/pdf/HowSafeSchoolhouse.pdf. The guide, titled *How Safe is the Schoolhouse?* was compiled by Jessica Butler and covers laws, regulations, and policies that were in effect as of December 31, 2016 (Butler, 2017). Paige (2017) asserted that state laws usually disfavor the use of restrain and seclusion and that the use of such practices are antithetical to basic freedoms and the intent of special education.

In 2012, the U.S. Department of Education developed a document that addressed 15 guiding principles for stakeholders to consider when developing or revising policies and procedures on restraint and seclusion. Noting that there was no evidence that restraint or seclusion was effective in reducing problem behavior, the Department's principles emphasized the importance of school personnel ensuring that every effort would be made to prevent the need for the use of restraint and seclusion and that any interventions must be consistent with a student's rights to be treated with dignity and to be free from abuse. The Department's document was clear that restraint or seclusion should never be used except in situations where a student's behavior posed an imminent danger of serious physical harm to that student or others, and restraint and seclusion should be avoided to the greatest extent possible without endangering the safety of students and staff. The document, which is available at www2.ed.gov/policy/seclusion/restraints-and-seclusion-resources.pdf, includes the following 15 principles:

1. Every effort should be made to prevent the need for the use of restraint and for the use of seclusion.

2. Schools should never use mechanical restraints to restrict a child's freedom of movement, and schools should never use a drug or medicine to control behavior or restrict freedom of movement (except as authorized by a licensed physical or other qualified health professional).

3. Physical restraint or seclusion should not be used except in situations where the child's behavior poses imminent danger of serious physical harm to self or others and other interventions are ineffective and should be discontinued as soon as imminent danger of serious physical harm to self or others has dissipated.

4. Policies restricting the use of restraint and seclusion should apply to all children, not just children with disabilities.

5. Any interventions must be consistent with the child's rights to be treated with dignity and be free from abuse.

6. Restraint or seclusion should never be used as punishment or discipline (e.g., placing in seclusion for out-of-seat behavior), as a means of coercion or retaliation, or as a convenience.

7. Restraint or seclusion should never be used in a manner that restricts a child's breathing or harms the child.

8. The use of restraint or seclusion, particularly when there is repeated use for an individual child, multiple uses within the same classroom, or multiple uses by the same individual, should trigger a review and, if appropriate, revision of strategies currently in place to address dangerous behavior if positive behavioral strategies are not in place, staff should consider developing them.

9. Behavioral strategies to address dangerous behavior that results in the use of restraint or seclusion should address the underlying cause of purpose of the dangerous behavior.

10. Teachers and other personnel should be trained regularly on the use of effective alternatives to physical restraint and seclusion, such as positive behavioral interventions and supports and, only for cases involving imminent danger of physical harm, on the safe use of physical restraint and seclusion.

11. Every instance in which restraint or seclusion is used should be carefully and continuously and visually monitored to ensure the appropriateness of its use and safety of the child, other children, teachers, and other personnel.

12. Parents should be informed of the policies on restraint and seclusion at their child's school or other educational setting as well as applicable Federal, State, or local laws.

13. Parents should be notified as soon as possible following each instance in which restraint or seclusion is used with their child.

14. Policies regarding the use of restraint and seclusion should be reviewed regularly and updated as appropriate.

15. Policies regarding the use of restraint and seclusion should provide that each incident involving the use of restraint and seclusion should be documented in writing and provide for the collection of specific data that would enable teachers, staff, and other personnel to understand and implement the preceding principles.

Weapons

A topic that has received a great deal of attention recently is the issue of school officials' authority in disciplining students with disabilities who bring weapons to school. *The Gun-Free Schools Act* (GFSA), which was enacted as part of the *Goals 2000: Educate America Act* (20 U.S.C. § 5801 et seq.), essentially required school districts to expel any student who brings a gun to school. According to the statutory language,

> No assistance may be provided to any local educational agency under this Act unless such agency has in effect a policy requiring the expulsion from school for a period of not less than one year of any student who is determined to have brought a weapon to school under the jurisdiction of the agency except such policy may allow the chief administering officer of the agency to modify such expulsion requirement for a student on a case-by-case basis.

(*Gun-Free Schools Act*, 20 U.S.C.S. § 3351(a)(1))

The Gun-Free Schools Act and Students with Disabilities
A policy guidance statement issued by the U.S. Department of Education stated that the FAPE and stay-put requirements of the IDEA prohibited the automatic removal of any student with a disability for disability-related misbehavior (*Gun-Free Schools Act guidance*, 1995). This position appeared to be at odds with the expulsion requirement of the GFSA. According to the statement, no conflict between the laws existed because administrators were allowed to consider discipline on

a case-by-case basis; therefore, administrators could take the laws affecting students with disabilities into account. Congress sought to alter this apparent discrepancy by allowing schools to immediately and unilaterally remove students with disabilities who bring guns to school to an interim alternative setting for up to 45 days. The primary effect of the law was to modify the stay-put provision of the IDEA. During the 45-day period, the school and parents may decide on a permanent placement. The school may also convene a team to conduct a manifestation determination. If the result of the determination is that the misbehavior was not a manifestation of the disability, a student may be expelled or may receive a long-term suspension. If parents request a due process hearing to contest the placement in the interim setting or an expulsion, the school may keep the student in the alternative placement during the pendency of the hearing.

LESSONS FROM LITIGATION AND LEGISLATION

Principles extrapolated from the body of case law on discipline and the IDEA can provide guidance to school districts.

Principal 1: Formulate and disseminate discipline policies and procedures: School districts should develop policies and procedures for ensuring that schools maintain safe and orderly environments where teachers can teach and students can learn. Procedures for disciplining students to maintain safety and order, to reduce misbehavior, and to teach appropriate behavior are essential. Such policies must clearly delineate behavioral expectations of students and the consequences for not conforming to these expectations. If the consequences include suspension and expulsion, all students are entitled to basic due process rights before exclusion occurs. For suspensions of 10 days or less, students must be afforded oral or written notice of the charges and the opportunity to respond to these charges. For suspensions in excess of 10 days, in addition to a notice and hearing, students must be provided with the opportunity for a more formal hearing process. When students present a danger to themselves or others, they can be removed from the school immediately, with notice and hearing to follow. When students violate the law, the legal authorities should be informed.

School staff should also receive ongoing professional development in research-based procedures for (a) assessing problem behavior, (b) developing and implementing proactive programs to ameliorate problem behavior and teach socially appropriate replacement behaviors, and (c) monitoring student progress toward behavior goals. As OSEP has repeatedly emphasized it is critical that school district personnel take steps to address problem behavior in students' IEPs regardless of whether the behavior results in disciplinary sanctions (*Letter to Osterhout,* 2000). OSEP has funded the Technical Assistance Center of Positive Behavioral Interventions and Supports (www.pbis.org/). The center is a tremendous resource to school districts and individuals in establishing research-based programming to promote positive student behavior and reduce inappropriate behaviors on a schoolwide, classroom, or individual basis.

It is extremely important that school administrators, teachers, and other personnel understand the district's disciplinary policies and procedures. Steps should also be taken to ensure that parents have access to, and understand, information in the school district's discipline policy. Methods to ensure parental access include mailing discipline policy brochures to district parents and having teachers explain the procedures in parent-teacher conferences.

Principle 2: Recognize the dual disciplinary standard: Courts have repeatedly held that students with disabilities *are not immune* from a school's normal disciplinary procedures. Students with disabilities, however, have special protections against any procedures that result in a unilateral change of placement. Expulsions and long-term or indefinite suspensions, and suspensions exceeding 10 consecutive days are changes in placement and cannot be made without following the procedural safeguards of the IDEA or Section 504. If a school decides to use long-term suspension or expulsion, the IEP team must meet to conduct a manifestation determination, in which the team determines the relationship between the behavior and the student's disability. A school district cannot expel a student on the basis of misbehavior caused by the disability. Nothing in the IDEA prevents students with disabilities from being disciplined, rather the IDEA provides students with disabilities with procedural safeguards to ensure that they are not denied a FAPE when disciplined (Osborne & Russo, 2009; Yell, 2011). Figure 13.3 is a flowchart depicting decision-making points when disciplining students with disabilities.

Principle 3: Address problem behavior in the IEP: Because of these additional protections, it is crucial that school officials know which students are classified as having disabilities under the IDEA and Section 504. A disciplinary meeting may involve many issues and concerns.

Students with disabilities with problem behavior that impedes their learning or the learning of others should have behavior goals and a disciplinary plan included in their IEPs (Senate Report, 1997; Yell, 2011; U.S. Department of Education, 2016). This requirement, which applies to all students in special education, regardless of their disability category, was included in the IDEA Amendments of 1997. The plan must be based on an FBA and should cover strategies, including proactive positive behavioral interventions and supports, to address the behavior problems. Additionally, because these elements would be discussed at an IEP meeting, the plan would have an increased probability of success because of parental support and participation. The intervention plan would also be less likely to be legally challenged and more likely to pass legal muster if challenged. Figure 13.4 is a flowchart on appropriately addressing problem behavior in the IEP process.

FIGURE 13.3 ■ Flowchart for Disciplining Students with Disabilities

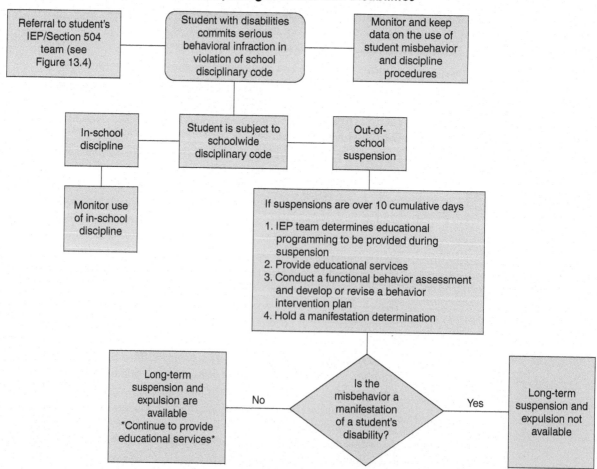

The discipline plan for each student should delineate expected behaviors, inappropriate behaviors, and positive and negative consequences for the behaviors (Hartwig & Reusch, 2000). The disciplinary process that will be followed, including intervention techniques, should be outlined in the plan. The plan should also include procedures for dealing with a behavioral crisis.

BIPs must be based on legitimate disciplinary procedures. To ensure that procedures are used reasonably, schools should use disciplinary methods in accordance with the principle of hierarchical application. According to Braaten, Simpson, Rosell, and Reilly (1988), this principle requires that school officials use more intrusive disciplinary procedures (e.g., in-school suspension) only after less intrusive procedures (e.g., warnings and reprimands) have failed.

Principle 4: Document disciplinary actions taken and interventions implemented, and evaluate their effectiveness: A common understanding in law is that if it isn't written down, it didn't happen. In disciplining students with disabilities, therefore, it is crucial to keep written records of all discussions and of all disciplinary actions taken. An examination of court cases and administrative rulings in disciplinary matters indicates that in many instances, decisions turned on the quality of the school's records. For example, in Cole v. Greenfield-Central Community Schools (1986), Dickens v. Johnson County Board of Education (1987), and Hayes v. Unified School District No. 377 (1987), the thoroughness of the schools' record keeping played a significant part in the court's decisions in favor of the schools. In *Oberti v. Board of Education of the Borough of Clementon*

FIGURE 13.4 ■ Flowchart on Addressing Problem Behavior in an IEP/Section 504 Plan

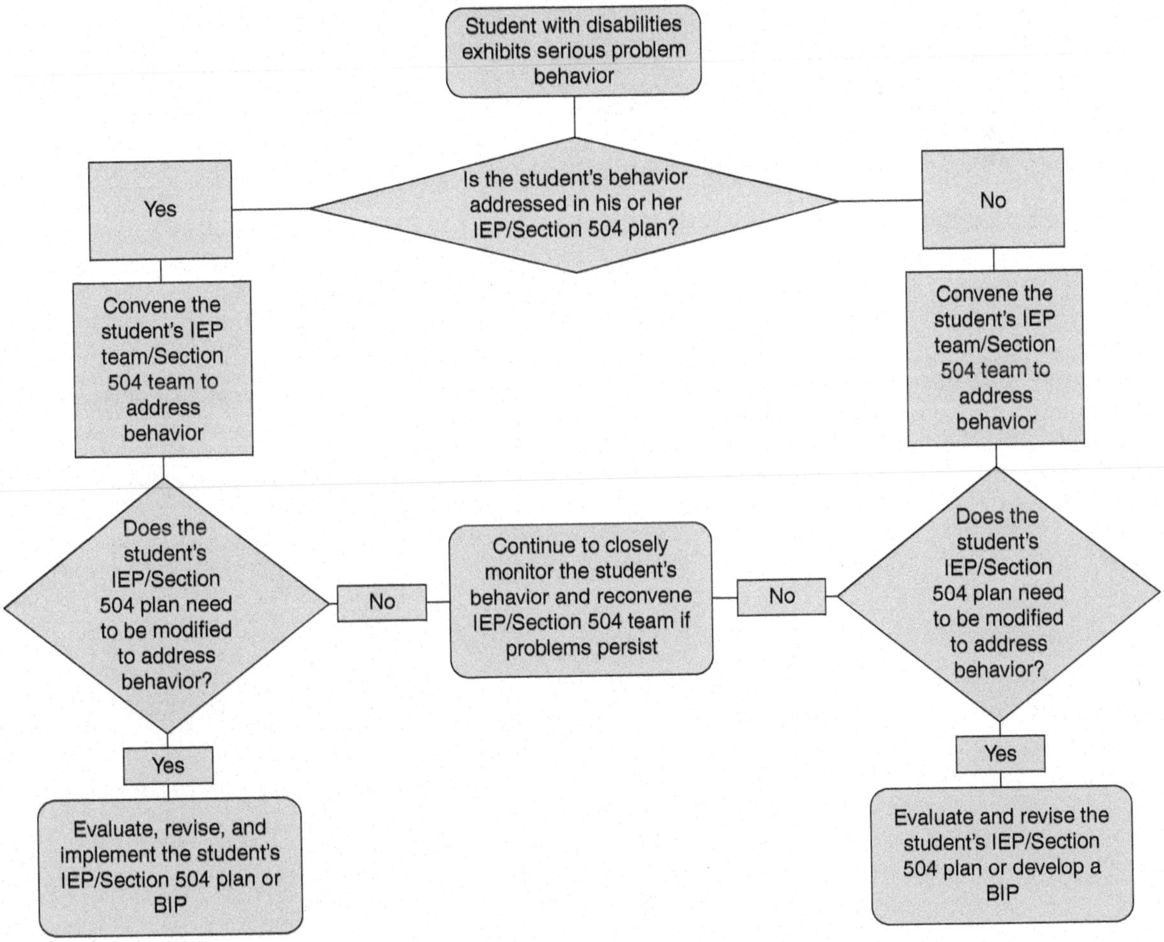

School District (1993), the court decided against the school district, partly because no BIP to improve the student's behavior in the regular classroom was included in the IEP. Although the school district maintained that it did have a BIP, it was not written down, and therefore it did not exist in the eyes of the court.

Records on emergency disciplinary actions are also important. Such records should contain an adequate description of the incident and disciplinary action taken, as well as the signatures of witnesses present. Figure 13.5 is an example of a behavior incident report.

Finally, it is important that teachers evaluate the effectiveness of disciplinary procedures used. There are a number of reasons for collecting data on an ongoing basis. To make decisions about whether an intervention is reducing target behaviors, teachers need data collected during the course of the intervention. If formative data are not collected, teachers will not know with certainty if a given procedure is achieving the desired results. Teachers are accountable to supervisors and parents, and data collection is useful for accountability purposes. From a legal standpoint, it is imperative that teachers collect such data. Courts do not readily accept anecdotal information, but data-based decisions certainly are viewed much more favorably.

FIGURE 13.5 ■ A Sample Behavior Incident Report

Behavior Incident Report

Student: _____   Date: _____
Teacher: _____   Time: _____

Observed behavior prior to the incident:

Description of the incident:

Parents notified: Yes   No
Description of positive approaches to correct behavior:

Did behavior endanger the safety of students or disrupt the learning environment? If yes, how?

SUMMARY

Specific guidelines regarding the discipline of students with disabilities were not written into federal law (e.g., the IDEA, Section 504) until the IDEA Amendments of 1997. Prior to that time, school districts had to operate on guidelines extrapolated from the decisions of administrative agencies (e.g., OSEP, OCR) and case law.

Students with disabilities are not immune from a school's disciplinary procedure. Schools may use procedures such as reprimands, detention, restriction of privileges, response cost, in-school suspension (if the student's education is continued), and out-of-school suspensions (10 days or less) as long as the procedures are not abused or applied in a discriminatory manner. Disciplinary procedures that effectively change a student's placement are, however, not legal if not done in accordance with the procedural safeguards afforded students with disabilities by the IDEA and Section 504. Such procedures include suspension (if over 10 days) and expulsion.

When determining whether or not to use a long-term suspension or expulsion, the school must convene the student's IEP team and other qualified personnel to determine the relationship between the student's misbehavior and the disability. If there is a relationship, the student cannot be expelled. If the team determines that no relationship exists, the student may be expelled. Even when an expulsion follows a determination of no relationship and is done in accordance with procedural safeguards, there cannot be a complete cessation of educational services.

A school district cannot unilaterally exclude a student with disabilities from school, regardless of the degree of danger or disruption. School districts may go to court, however, to obtain a temporary restraining order (TRO) to have the student removed from school. The school will bear the burden of proof when attempting to get a TRO. If students with disabilities bring weapons to school or use, possess, or sell illegal drugs, school officials may unilaterally remove them to an interim alternative setting for 45 school days. During this time, the IEP team should meet to consider appropriate actions.

Disciplining students with disabilities is a complex issue. In addition to observing the due process rights that protect all students, administrators and teachers must be aware of the additional safeguards afforded to students with disabilities by the IDEA. In using disciplinary procedures with students with disabilities, educators should be aware of state and local policies regarding discipline, develop and inform parents of school discipline policies, and continuously evaluate the effectiveness of disciplinary procedures. When disciplinary procedures are used, proper documentation is critical. Teachers must collect formative data to determine if the procedures are having the desired effect on student behavior. Finally, disciplinary procedures should be used reasonably and for legitimate educational purposes; they must not compromise a student's FAPE or be applied in a discriminatory manner.

> **Enhanced eText Application Exercise 13.1.** *Honig v. Doe,* 479 U.S. 1084 (1988).

FOR FURTHER INFORMATION

Norlin, J. W. (2007). *What do I do when: The answer book on discipline* (3rd ed.). Palm Beach Garden, FL: LRP Publications.

U.S. Department of Education, Office of Special Education and Rehabilitative Services (2016). Dear colleague letter on the inclusion of behavioral supports in individualized education programs.

Available at www2.ed.gov/policy/gen/guid/school.../dcl-on-pbis-in-ieps--08-01-2016.pdf

Yu, D. Y. (2009). *Discipline dilemmas: Your guide to avoiding the top IDEA and Section 504 mistakes.* Palm Beach Garden, FL: LRP Publications.

REFERENCES

Alexander, K., & Alexander, M. D. (2012). *American public school law* (8th ed.). Belmont, CA: Wadsworth Cengage Learning.

Baldwin Park Unified School District, 10 ECLRP 6 (SEA CA 2012).

Big Beaver Falls Area School District v. Jackson, 624 A.2d 806 (Pa. Cmwlth. 1993).

Binghamton City School District v. Borgna, 1991 WL 29985 (N.D.N.Y. 1991).

Board of Education of the Akron Central School District, 28 IDELR 909 (SEA 1998).

Board of Education of Township High School District No. 211 v. Corral, 441 EHLR Dec. 390 (N.D. Ill. 1989).

Board of Education of Township No. 211 v. Linda Kurtz-Imig, 16 EHLR Dec. 17 (N.D. Ill. 1989).

Braaten, S., Simpson, R., Rosell, J., & Reilly, T. (1988). Using punishment with exceptional children: A dilemma for educators. *Teaching Exceptional Children, 20,* 79–81.

Butler, J. (2017). *How safe is the schoolhouse? An analysis of state laws and policies* Available at www.autcom.org/pdf/HowSafeSchoolhouse.pdf.

Chester County (TN) School District, 17 EHLR 301 (OCR 1990).

Cline, D. (1994). *Fundamentals of special education law: Emphasis on discipline.* Arden Hills, MN: Behavioral Institute for Children and Adolescents.

Cobb County (GA) School District, 20 IDELR 1171 (OCR 1993).

Cole v. Greenfield-Central Community Schools, 657 F. Supp. 56 (S.D. Ind. 1986).

Concerned Parents and Citizens for Continuing Education at Malcolm X v. The New York City Board of Education, 629 F.2d 751 (2d Cir. 1980).

Council for Children with Behavioral Disorders. (2009). *Position paper on the use of physical restraint and seclusion.* Arlington, VA: Author. Available at http://www.ccbd.net/-advocacy/positionpa-pers.cfm?categoryID=D399524C-C09F-1D6F-F9ABEED1B%20 7D76FDD#.

Council for Exceptional Children. (2009). *Position paper on restraint and seclusion.* Arlington, VA: Author. Available at www.cec.sped.org/AM/ Template.cfm?Section=Home&TEMPLATE=/CM/ContentDisplay. cfm&CONTENTID=13031.

Council of Parent Attorneys and Advocates. (2009). *Unsafe in the schoolhouse: Abuse of children with disabilities.* Towson, MD: Author. Retrieved from www.copaa.org/news/unsafe.html.

Council Rock School District v. M.W., 59 IDELR 132, 59 IDELR 132 (E.D. Pa. 2012).

Curwin, R., & Mendler, A. (1999). *Discipline with dignity.* Alexandria, VA: Association for Supervision and Curriculum Development.

Dagley, D. L., McGuire, M. D., & Evans, C. W. (1994). The relationship test in the discipline of disabled students. *Education Law Reporter, 88,* 13–31.

Department of Education answers questions. (1997, November 21). *The Special Educator, 1.*

Dickens v. Johnson County Board of Education, 661 F. Supp. 155 (E.D. Tenn. 1987).

Doe v. Koger, 480 F. Supp. 225 (N.D. Ind. 1979).

Doe v. Maher, 793 F.2d 1470 (9th Cir. 1986).

Drasgow, E., & Yell, M. L. (2002). School-wide behavior support: Legal implications. *Child and Family Behavior Therapy, 24,* 129–145.

Drasgow, E., Yell, M. L., Bradley, R., & Shriner, J. G. (1999). The IDEA Amendments of 1997: A school-wide model for conducting functional behavioral assessments and developing behavior intervention plans. *Education and Treatment of Children, 22,* 244–266.

Dunlap, G., & Koegel, R. L. (1999). Welcoming introduction. *Journal of Positive Behavior Interventions, 1,* 2–3.

Endrew F., by and through his parents and next friends, Joseph and Jennifer F. v. Douglas County School District RE-1, Available at http://blogs.edweek.org/edweek/speced/Endrew%20Order.pdf

Farrin v. Maine School Administrative District No. 59, 35 IDELR 189 (D. Me. 2001).

Goals 2000: Educate America Act, 20 U.S.C.S. § 5801 *et seq.*

Goss v. Lopez, 419 U.S. 565 (1975).

Grannis v. Ordean, 234 U.S. 383 (1914).

Gun-Free Schools Act, 20 U.S.C. § 1415(e)(3).

Gun-Free Schools Act guidance. (1995, January 20). U.S. Department of Education, Office of Elementary and Secondary Education, Assistant Secretary, Thomas W. Payzant. Washington, DC: Author.

Hall v. Tawney, 621 F.2d 607 (4th Cir. 1980).

Hartwig, E. P., & Reusch, G. M. (2000). *Discipline in the schools* (2nd ed.). Horsham, PA: LRP Publications.

Hayes v. Unified School District No. 377, 669 F. Supp. 1519 (D. Kan. 1987).

Honig v. Doe, 479 U.S. 1084 (1988).

Horner, R., & Carr, E. (1997). Behavioral support for students with severe disabilities: Functional assessment and comprehensive intervention. *Journal of Special Education, 31,* 84–101.

Individuals with Disabilities Education Act (IDEA), 20 U.S.C. § 1400 *et seq.*

Individuals with Disabilities Education Act (IDEA) Regulations, 34 C.F.R. § 300.533 *et seq.*

Ingraham v. Wright, 430 U.S. 651 (1977).

Kaelin v. Grubbs, 682 F.2d 595 (6th Cir. 1982).

Katsiyannis, A., & Maag, J. W. (1998). Disciplining students with disabilities: Practice considerations for implementing IDEA '97. *Behavioral Disorders, 23,* 276–289.

Lake Travis Independent School District v. M. L., A-06-CA-046-SS, A-07-CA-626-SS (W.D. Tex. 2007).

Letter to Anonymous, 30 IDELR 707 (OSEP 1999).

Letter to Osterhout (OSEP 2000). Retrieved from https://www2.ed.gov/policy/ speced/guid/idea/letters/2000-3/osterhout72500mdreviewsec.pdf.

Light v. Parkway School District, 21 IDELR 933 (8th Cir. 1994).

Marion County (FL) School District, 20 IDELR 634 (OCR 1993).

Martin, J. L. (1999, May). Current legal issues in discipline of disabled students under IDEA: A section by section comment of § 1415(k), discipline regulations, and initial core law. Paper presented at LRP's Annual Conference on Special Education Law, San Francisco, CA.

McCracken County School District, 18 IDELR 482 (OCR 1991).

M.M. and C.M. v. District 0001 Lancaster County School, 60 IDELR 92 (8th Cir. 2012).

Mobile County (AL) School District, 18 IDELR 70 (OCR 1991).

National Disability Rights Network. (2009). School is not supposed to hurt: Investigative report on abusive restraint and seclusion in schools. Available at http://www.napas.org/sr/srjan10/Schoo-%20is-Not-Supposed-to-Hurt-(NDRN).pdf.

Neosho R-V School District v. Clark, 315 F.3d 1022, 38 IDELR 61 (8th Cir. 2012).

Norlin, J. W. *What do I do when: The answer book on discipline* (4th ed.). Horsham, PA: LRP Publications.

Oberti v. Board of Education of the Borough of Clementon School District, 995 F.2d 1204 (3d Cir. 1993).

OCR Memorandum, EHLR 307:05 (OCR 1988).

OSEP (2016). Dear Colleague Letter on discipline and positive behavior interventions and supports. Retrieved from

O'Neill, R. E., Horner, R. H., Albin, R. W., Sprague, J. R., Storey, K., & Newton, J. S. (1997). *Functional assessment and program development for problem behavior: A practical handbook.* Pacific Grove, CA: Brooks/Cole.

Osborne, A. G., & Russo, C. J. (2009). *Discipline in special education.* Thousand Oaks, CA: Corwin Press.

OSEP Memorandum 95-16, 22 IDELR 531 (OSEP 1995).

OSEP questions and answers (1999, March 12). *Federal Register, 64*(48), 12,617–12,632.

Paige, M.A. (2017). Disciplining students with disabilities. In E. A. Shaver & J. R. Decker (Eds.) *A guide to special education law* (pp. 137–151). Cleveland, OH: Education Law Association.

Peterson, R., Albrecht, S., & Johns, B. (2009) CCBD's position summary on physical restraint and seclusion procedures in school settings. Council for Children with Behavioral Disorders. Available at http://www.state.ky.us/agencies/behave/misc/CCBD%20Summary%20on%20Restraint%20and%20Seclusion%207-8-09.pdf.

Prince William County School Board v. Malone, 762 F.2d 1210 (4th Cir. 1985).

Prince William County School Board v. Willis, 16 EHLR 1109 (Va. Cir. Ct. 1989).

Richards, D., & Martin, J. (2005). *The IDEA amendments: What you need to know.* Horsham, PA: LRP Publications.

Rozalski, M. E., & Yell, M. L. (2004). The law and school safety. In J. Conoley & A. Goldstein (Eds.), *School violence intervention: A practical handbook* (2nd ed., pp. 507–526). New York: Guilford Publications.

Ryan, J. B., Peterson, R. L., & Rozalski, M. E. (2007). Review of state policies concerning the use of timeout in schools. *Education and Treatment of Children, 30,* 215–239.

S-1 v. Turlington, 635 F.2d 342 (5th Cir. 1981).

Section 504 of the Rehabilitation Act of 1973, 29 U.S.C. § 794 *et seq.*

Senate Report of the Individuals with Disabilities Act Amendments of 1997. Available at http://wais.access.gpo.gov.

Smith, S. W., & Yell, M. L (2013). *Preventing problem behavior in the classroom.* Upper Saddle River, NJ: Merrill/Pearson Education.

Sorenson, G. (1993). Update on legal issues in special education discipline. *Education Law Reporter, 81,* 399–411.

Stuart v. Nappi, 443 F. Supp. 1235 (D. Conn. 1978).

Tatgenhorst, A., Norlin, J. W., & Gorn, S. (2014). *What do I do when … The answer book on special education law* (6th ed.). Palm Beach Garden, FL: LRP Publications.

Telzrow, C. F., & Naidu, K. (2000). Interim alternative educational settings: Guidelines for prevention and intervention. In C. Telzrow & M. Tankersley (Eds.), *IDEA Amendments of 1997: Practice guidelines for school-based teams* (pp. 199–204). Bethesda, MD: National Association of School Psychologists.

Texas City Independent School District v. Jorstad, 752 F. Supp. 231 (S.D. Tex. 1990).

U.S. Department of Education, Office of Civil Rights, Civil Rights Data Collection, Data Snapshot: School Discipline (2012). Available at http://ocrdata.ed.gov/Downloads/CRDC-School-Discipline-Snapshot.pdf (2016).

U.S. Department of Education, Office of Special Education and Rehabilitative Services and the Office of Special Education Programs, Dear Colleague Letter on Positive Behavior Supports in student's IEPs. Available at www2.ed.gov/policy/gen/guid/school-discipline/files/dcl-on-pbis-in-ieps--08-01-2016.pdf

U.S. Government Accountability Office. (2009). Seclusions and restraints: Selected cases of death and abuse at public and private school and treatment centers. Available at www.gao.gov/new.items/d09719t.pdf.

Valente, W. D., & Valente, C. (2005). *Law in the schools* (6th ed.). Upper Saddle River, NJ: Merrill/Prentice Hall.

Victoria L. v. District School Board, 741 F.2d 369 (11th Cir. 1984).

Walker, H. M., Ramsey, E., & Gresham, F. M. (2004). *Antisocial behavior in school: Evidence-based practices.* Belmont, CA: Thomson/Wadsworth.

Walsh, J. (2009). *Manifestation determinations: Avoiding needless conflict and common mistakes.* Horsham, PA: LRP Publications.

Yell, M. L. (1990). The use of corporal punishment, suspension, expulsion, and timeout with behaviorally disordered students in public schools: Legal considerations. *Behavioral Disorders, 15,* 100–109.

Yell, M. L. (1994). Timeout and students with behavior disorders: A legal analysis. *Education and Treatment of Children, 17,* 293–301.

Yell, M. L. (2011). Disciplining students in the public schools: Legal considerations. In T. J. Zirpoli (Ed.), *Behavior management* (6th ed., pp. 688–734). Upper Saddle River, NJ: Merrill/Pearson Education.

Yell, M. L., Cline, D., & Bradley, R. (1995). Disciplining students with emotional and behavioral disorders: A legal update. *Education and Treatment of Children, 18,* 299–308.

Yell, M. L., Katsiyannis, A., Bradley, R., & Rozalski, M. E. (2000). Ensuring compliance with the discipline provisions of IDEA '97: Challenges and opportunities. *Journal of Special Education Leadership, 13,* 204–216.

Yell, M. L., Meadows, N. B., Drasgow, E., & Shriner, J. G. (2013). *Evidence based practices in educating students with emotional and behavioral disorders.* Upper Saddle River, NJ: Merrill/Pearson Education.

Yell, M. L., & Peterson, R. L. (1995). Disciplining students with disabilities and those at risk for school failure: Legal issues. *Preventing School Failure, 39*(2), 39–44.

Yell, M. L., Rozalski, M. E., & Drasgow, E. (2001). Disciplining students with disabilities. *Focus on Exceptional Children, 33*(9), 1–20.

Yu, D. Y. (2009). *Discipline dilemmas: Your guide to avoiding the top IDEA and Section 504 mistakes.* Horsham, PA: LRP Publications.

Zirkel, P.A. (2017). Judicial ruling specific to FBAs and BIPs under the IDEA and corollary state laws: An update. *The Journal of Special Education, 51,* 50–56.

Zvi D. v. Ambach, 694 F.2d 904 (1982).

Additional Issues: Bullying, Charter Schools, Response to Intervention, Educational Records, and Liability for Student Injury

While there is broad consensus that bullying is wrong and cannot be tolerated in our schools, the sad reality is that bullying persists in our schools today, and especially so for students with disabilities.

U.S. DEPARTMENT OF EDUCATION, OFFICE FOR CIVIL RIGHTS (2014, P. 1)

Learner Objectives

At the end of the chapter, students will be able to

14.1 Describe how bullying and school personnel's reaction to bullying can result in a violation of Section 504 of the Rehabilitation Act.

14.2 Describe how bullying and school personnel's reaction to bullying can result in a violation of the Individuals with Disabilities Education Act.

14.3 Describe the content of the Dear Colleague Letters on bullying from the U.S. Department of Education.

14.4 Describe charter schools and the responsibilities to student with disabilities.

14.5 Describe the basis of response to intervention in the Individuals with Disabilities Education Act.

14.6 Describe the Family Education Rights and Privacy Act.

14.7 Describe intentional torts and negligence torts as they may apply to educators.

14.8 Describe the four elements that must be proved for a negligence case to succeed.

Special education was born in the arena of advocacy, litigation, and legislation. Previous chapters have delineated many of these highly regulated and litigated issues. Other issues that may affect special education administrators and teachers have also been the subjects of hearings and court cases. The purpose of this chapter is to review the following issues: (a) bullying of students with disabilities, (b) charter schools and responsibilities to students with disabilities, (c) accessibility and confidentiality of student records, and (c) teachers' legal liability for student injury.

BULLYING AND HARASSMENT OF STUDENTS WITH DISABILITIES

"Bullying fosters a climate of fear and disrespect that can harm the physical and psychological health of victims and create conditions that negatively affect learning" (U.S. Department of Education, Office of Civil Rights, 2010, p. 1). Bullying is a common occurrence in America's schools and is currently at the forefront of national attention. The problem has become so serious that the Obama administration, the U.S. Department of Education, Congress, and the 50 states have sought ways to deal with this serious and growing problem. For example, in 2010 the Obama administration held a White House Summit on Bullying. The U.S. Department of Education developed a website at www.stopbullying.gov. The purpose of the website, which has been called a "one-stop comprehensive site for resources on bullying and prevention," is to assist administrators, teachers, and staff members in America's schools to have the tools needed to address this serious problem. The Department of Education also developed training materials on preventing bullying and included them on the Safe Supportive Learning website at http://safesupportive-learning.ed.gov/topic-research/safety/bullyingcyberbullying. Additionally, every state except Montana has enacted anti-bullying laws. Links to every state's anti-bullying law can be found at www.bullypolice.org.

In a speech at the first federal education summit on bullying Dr. Arnie Duncan, the U.S. Secretary of Education, stated:

> As educators, as state and local officials, and at the federal level, we simply have not taken the problem of bullying seriously enough. … It is an absolute travesty of our educational system when students fear for their safety at school, worry about being bullied or suffer discrimination and taunts because of their ethnicity, religion, sexual orientation, disability or a host of other reasons. The fact is that no school can be a great school until it is a safe school first.

(Arnie Duncan, 2010)

Enhanced eText Video Example 14.1
In this **video** Dr. Sheldon Horowitz addresses the problem of students with disabilities being bullied in schools at:
www.youtube.com/watch?v=ys57WmPWDeY&list=PLA56C5C658A236B31&index=2.

Students with disabilities are frequently the targets of peer-on-peer bullying. In fact, Blake, Lund, Zhou, Kwok, and Benz (2012) reported that 24.5% of students with disabilities in elementary schools, 34.1% of middle school students with disabilities, and 25.6% of high school students with disabilities regularly report being bullied while at school.

Courts have heard, and ruled on, cases in which students with disabilities have been bullied. These decisions have shown that it is very important that school personnel deal with the bullying of students with disabilities quickly and efficiently. Students are not the only ones at risk when bullying is not stopped; school district officials and personnel also subject themselves to legal risks. In fact, school attorneys Boyce and Manna (2011) wrote the following regarding school liability for bullying and harassment: "Think your school district cannot be held liable for student bullying? Think again. Victims of bullying and their families have a number of potential claims against school districts and officials" (p. 1).

The purpose of this section is to present (a) how bullying may be a potential violation of civil rights of students with disabilities, (b) how bullying may violate special education students' rights to a free appropriate public education (FAPE), and (c) ways in which school district administrators and teachers, individualized education program (IEP) team members, and Section 504 teams should address bullying and students with disabilities.

Bullying as a Violation of the Civil Rights of Students with Disabilities

In Chapters 5 and 6 we examined Section 504 of the Rehabilitation Act of 1973 and the Americans with Disabilities Act (ADA). Section 504 and the ADA are civil rights laws for persons with disabilities and like all civil rights laws, including Title VI of the Civil Rights Act of 1964, which prohibits discrimination based on race, color, or national origin, and Title IX of the Education Amendments of 1972, which prohibits discrimination based on sex, Section 504 and the ADA prohibit discrimination based on disability. With respect to students with disabilities in public schools, Section 504 requires that school districts prohibit discrimination by ensuring that students with disabilities have the opportunity to participate in and benefit from educational opportunities that are provided by the school.

Dear Colleague Letters on Bullying and Harassment from OCR   At the first White House Summit on Bullying, Dr. Arnie Duncan asserted that a reinvigorated Office of Civil Rights (OCR) would vigorously investigate complaints of bullying and harassment in schools (Duncan, 2010). To assist administrators and teachers in addressing bullying when it is directed toward students with disabilities, the OCR and the Office of Rehabilitative and Special Education Services (OSERS) have issued public policy guidance documents in the form of open letters, called Dear Colleague Letters (DCLs), addressing school district responses to the bullying of students with disabilities. (See Chapter 1 for an explanation of the importance of DCLs.)

In a DCL that was released on July 25, 2000, officials at OCR and OSERS noted that when students with disabilities are harassed[1] in a severe, persistent, and pervasive manner, a hostile school environment is created in which a student may be denied a FAPE and an opportunity to participate in or benefit from the educational program, thus potentially being a violation of the Individuals with Disabilities Education Act (IDEA) and Section 504. The DCL included examples of disability-based bullying, such as the following: (a) several students taunt a student with learning disabilities, calling him retarded or deaf and dumb out loud during class, which results in the student's grades declining in the class; (b) a student repeatedly places classroom furniture or other objects in the path of a classmate who uses a wheelchair, impeding the student's ability to enter the classroom; (c) a school administrator repeatedly denies a student with a disability access to lunch, field trips, assemblies, and extracurricular activities as punishment for taking time off from school, which is sometimes needed because of the student's disability; and (d) a teacher subjects a student to inappropriate physical restraint and seclusion because of conduct that is related to the student's disability, resulting in the student trying to avoid school. According to the DCLs these examples are disability harassment that results in a hostile environment in which a student is denied an equal opportunity to participate in a school's educational program. Note in these examples that the harassment targets a student's disability.

The DCL further warned that school officials and personnel are responsible for preventing and responding to disability-based harassment. According to the DCL it is critical that school officials develop and disseminate a school district policy on harassment and bullying. When incidences of disability-based harassment or bullying occur, school personnel should investigate the incidences promptly and respond accordingly. The 2000 DCL is available at www2.ed.gov/about/offices/list/ocr/docs/disabharassltr.html.

On October 26, 2010, OCR issued another DCL on bullying in which officials at OCR reminded school district officials that some student behavior that would be covered by the

---

[1] The DCLs refer to "harassment" rather that "bullying." According to Norlin (2014), OCR, OSERS, and state and federal courts frequently make no distinction between harassment and bullying, so the two terms often are used interchangeably.

school district's anti-bullying policy may also trigger a school district's responsibilities under Section 504, Title II of the ADA, Title IV of the Civil Rights Act of 1964, or Title IX of the Education Amendments of 1972. It is important, therefore, when harassment or bullying is based on disability, race, color, national origin, or sex that school personnel promptly investigate and respond to all such incidences. The actions of school district officials must go beyond the requirements of the school district anti-bullying policy to address potential discrimination under any of the aforementioned statutes. Moreover, if district officials fail to appropriately address the discriminatory aspects of the bullying, that failure, in and of itself, may constitute a violation of a student's civil rights.

The DCL also warned that school districts are responsible for addressing harassment "about which it knows or reasonably should have known" (OCR, 2010, p. 2). Obvious signs of bullying harassment, such as bullying that occurs in hallways, classrooms, at recess, or on the bus that are in plain sight are clearly sufficient to put school district personnel on notice that they need to act quickly to respond to the bullying. In other incidences, the bullying or harassment may be more covert and come to school personnel's attention through complaints by parents or students. When bullying or harassment or the suspicion of bullying and harassment come to the attention of school district personnel, they have a duty to respond by taking immediate and appropriate action to investigate or determine what occurred. The inquiry should be prompt, thorough, and impartial and if bullying or harassment is uncovered, school district officials should take immediate actions to end the harassment, eliminate the hostile environment, and prevent the harassment from recurring. This DCL is available at www2.ed.gov/about/offices/list/ocr/letters/colleague-201010.pdf.

A third DCL was issued by OCR on October 21, 2014. The letter began by noting that the sad reality in public schools is that even though awareness regarding bullying issues has increased, this serious problem persists in America's schools, especially for students with disabilities. It reiterated the possible violations of Section 504 and Title II of the ADA when a student is bullied or harassed or bullied based on his or her disability and addressed how school district officials should respond to disability-based bullying.

The DCL again elaborated on schools' obligations to address disability-based harassment noting that such harassment is a violation of Section 504 and Title II of the ADA when (a) a student is bullied based on a disability; (2) the bullying is sufficiently serious to create a hostile environment; (3) school officials know or should know about the bullying; and (4) the school does not respond appropriately" (OCR, 2014, p. 4).

This DCL, however, differed from the two previous DCLs because in it OCR officials wrote "bullying of a student with a disability on *any* basis can similarly result in a denial of FAPE under Section 504 that must be remedied" (U.S. Department of Education, Office of Civil Rights (2014), p. 2). OCR officials also noted that a student's IEP team or Section 504 team must address any denial of FAPE by reconvening the team and examining the plan to determine if it still provides FAPE. Moreover, OCR officials wrote that this obligation exists in cases in which a student is being bullied or harassed, regardless if the bullying is disability based or not. This DCL is available at www2.ed.gov/about/offices/list/ocr/letters/colleague-bullying-201410.pdf.

When OCR receives a complaint regarding bullying of a student with disabilities it will follow the standards announced in the DCLs to investigate the complaint. As the majority of Supreme Court Justices noted in their opinion in the case of *Davis v. Monroe County Board of Education* (1999), federal agencies, such as the U.S. Department of Education, have the power to promulgate and enforce requirements that enact the nondiscrimination mandate of the civil rights laws. Thus, the OCR will investigate complaints against school districts regarding bullying cases, and if the OCR investigation finds that (a) bullying of a student with disabilities did occur; (b) the bullying was sufficiently severe, pervasive, or persistent as to create a hostile educational environment; (c) the hostile environment interfered with or *limited a student's opportunity to participate*; and (d) school personnel *knew or reasonably should have known* but did nothing to prevent and address the bullying, it is likely that OCR will rule that the school district violated Section 504 and Title II of the ADA. In addition to filing an administrative complaint with the OCR, students who are bullied and their families can also sue school districts for damages over incidences of bullying. The standard for prevailing in a lawsuit are somewhat different from those for prevailing in an administrative complaint.

Litigation on Bullying as a Violation of a Student's Civil Rights

The leading case on bullying in the schools, *Davis v. Monroe County Board of Education* (hereafter *Davis*), was heard by the U.S. Supreme Court in 1999. Although the case did not involve a student with a disability it did involve an allegation of sexual harassment in violation of Title IX of the Education Amendments of 1972. In this case a fifth grade public school student was repeatedly sexually harassed while at school. The girl's mother filed a lawsuit against the school district seeking injunctive relief and monetary damages under Title IX. (Readers should note that monetary damages are also available under Section 504 and Title II of the ADA.) Norlin (2014) reported that the antidiscrimination provision of Title IX is very similar to that of Section 504 and courts have consistently applied the *Davis* standard to disability-based harassment and bullying lawsuits brought under Section 504 and Title II of the ADA.

The *Davis* case involved a fifth grade female student who was repeatedly subjected to sexually explicit comments and behavior by a male classmate. Over a 5-month period the girl's mother complained to various teachers about the misconduct. The girl's grades suffered. At the end of the school year, the mother reported the actions to the school's principal. Unfortunately, school district personnel took no action to address the sexual harassment. The girl's mother filed a lawsuit that eventually would end up in the Supreme Court. In a 5–4 decision the majority ruled that a school could be liable for damages in a harassment case in situations in which school personnel acted with deliberate indifference to known acts of harassment that were so severe, pervasive, and objectively offensive that they effectively barred the victim's access to educational opportunity or benefit. School district attorneys had argued that the school district could not be liable for the actions of a third party. The Court, however, rejected this argument and focused on the liability of school district personnel for the failure to take action. In *Davis*, school personnel knew about the harassment by the male student but did not act, the harassment was severe, and the student's academic performance suffered. Additionally, the Court noted that in order to find a district liable, the alleged harasser must be under some form of control by the school, which in *Davis* the male student was and all students in a school environment certainly are.

A federal district court in *Werth v. Board of Directors of the Public Schools of the City of Milwaukee* (2007) relied on the principles set forth by the Supreme Court in *Davis* when it developed the following five-part test for imposing liability for peer-on-peer harassment or bullying: (a) the plaintiff was a student with a disability, (b) he or she was harassed based on the disability, (c) the harassment was sufficiently severe or pervasive that it created an abusive educational environment, (d) the defendant school district knew about the harassment, and (e) the defendant school district was deliberately indifferent to the harassment. Boyce and Manna (2011) referred to this test as the five-part test of liability for peer bullying and harassment.

A federal district court in *K.M. ex rel. D.G. v. Hyde Park Central School District* (2005) refused to dismiss a claim against a school district for failing to react to incidences of disability-related bullying. In the case, the mother of a 13-year-old boy with pervasive developmental disorder and average intelligence sued the Hyde Park Central School District alleging that school district officials were deliberately indifferent to harassment of her son. The mother had reported that her son was repeatedly called "idiot," "retard," and other disability-related names and was physically abused while he was on the bus riding to and from school. The mother had met on numerous occasions with school administrators to complain, but no action was taken. The student became depressed and threatened to commit suicide. The boy's mother withdrew him from school and homeschooled him for the remainder of the school year. The court refused to dismiss the claims against the school district, finding that the school district could be liable for the alleged failure to react to the harassment that was severe enough to deny the student equal access to educational opportunity. When courts allow claims to go forward it is very likely that the attorney for the school district will attempt to settle the case with the plaintiff because it is likely that the school district will lose if the case continues. As Weatherly (2013) asserted, in such situations the conversation between the attorneys will usually be about how big the check that the school district writes needs to be!

Interestingly enough, the court in the *K.M.* case also included the following comment in the opinion: A student with disabilities is "probably not on equal footing to defend himself against harassment from his more able peers, leaving him vulnerable to abuse that the district should have anticipated and worked harder to prevent" (p. 42). Thus, according to this court, a school district may have a greater duty to prevent the bullying and harassment of students with disabilities (Jacobs, 2012).

In the case of *Estate of Lance v. Lewisville Independent School District* (2011), a claim for monetary damages was allowed to go forward when a court found that the evidence presented supported a finding that the school district acted with deliberate indifference because of a student's young age (9 years old) and vulnerability due to his disabilities (emotional disturbance, speech/language impairment, and Asperger's syndrome, which is now considered part of the autism spectrum). Despite the student making suicidal threats and being bullied, the school district had failed to inform the student's parents. He had also locked himself in a school restroom a number of times but was allowed to go unsupervised to the restroom, where he hanged himself.

School officials who fail to respond to reports of bullying, by teachers, students, or parents, may be found to have acted with bad faith, gross misjudgment, or deliberate indifference in cases involving bullying (Jacobs, 2012). Cases in which courts allowed parent claims to go forward because the school district officials were determined by courts to have acted in bad faith or with gross misjudgment include *C.L. v. Leander Independent School District* (2013), *M.P. v. Independent School District* (2003), *Kendall v. West Haven Department of Education* (2000), *Moore v. Chilton County Board of Education* (2013), *Sutherlin v. Independent School District No. 40* (2013), *D.A. v. Meridian School District* (2013), and *M.Y. v. Grand River Academy* (2010).

Norlin (2014) noted that a plaintiff suing a school district for damages faces a difficult burden in establishing that a school district is liable because its personnel acted with deliberate indifference, bad faith, or gross misjudgment. This is especially true when the school district had no awareness or reason to be aware of the bullying or that officials had been shown to take actions to prevent and respond to the incidences of bullying in an appropriate manner. The correct manner of responding to incidences of bullying is to investigate promptly and thoroughly and respond effectively to incidences of bullying. Cases in which courts have found that school district officials had acted in a reasonable manner to address the problems of bullying, thus defeating claims against the district, include the following cases: *Broaders v. Polk County School Board* (2011), *Doe v. Big Walnut Local School District Board of Education* (2013), *S.S. v. Eastern Kentucky University* (2008), *J.B. v. Mead School District No. 354* (2010), *Roquet v. Kelly* (2013), *S.S. v. Eastern Kentucky University* (2010), *Silano v. Board of Education of the City of Bridgeport* (2010), and *Wright v. Carroll County Board of Education* (2013).

Bullying as a Violation of a Free Appropriate Public Education

The Individuals with Disabilities Education Act (IDEA) and Section 504 both mandate that eligible students with disabilities receive a FAPE. The Office of Special Education Programs (OSEP) is an office within OSERS in the U.S. Department of Education. Officials at OSEP and at OCR have held that bullying of a student with disabilities can result in the denial of a FAPE under the IDEA and Section 504.

Dear Colleague Letters on Bullying and Harassment from OSERS and OSEP

In the previously discussed DCL of 2000, which was jointly issued by OSERS and OCR, it was clear that bullying could result in the denial of a FAPE. According to the DCL:

> States and school districts also have a responsibility under Section 504, Title II (of the ADA) and the Individuals with Disabilities Education Act (IDEA), which is enforced by OSERS, to ensure that a free appropriate public education (FAPE) is made available to eligible students with disabilities. Disability harassment may result in the denial of FAPE under these statutes. Parents may initiate administrative due process procedures under IDEA, Section 504, or Title II to address a denial of FAPE, including a denial that results from disability harassment. Individuals and organizations also may file complaints with OCR alleging a denial of FAPE that results from disability harassment. In addition, an individual or organization may file a complaint alleging a violation of IDEA under separate procedures with the state educational agency. State compliance with IDEA, including compliance with FAPE requirements, is monitored by OSERS's Office of Special Education Programs.

(U.S. Department of Education, Office of Civil Rights (2000), p. 1)

The clear implication is that there are a number of avenues that parents of bullied students with disabilities can pursue against school districts.

On August 20, 2013, OSERS issued a DCL on bullying. The purpose of the DCL was to remind school districts that bullying of students with disabilities that results in a student not receiving meaningful educational benefit from his or her program constitutes a denial of FAPE, a violation of the IDEA. This is true *whether or not the bullying is based on a student's disability* (see also DCL of October 2014). Additionally, the letter provided an overview of the school district's responsibilities under the IDEA to address the bullying of students with disabilities.

Officials at OSERS suggested that students' IEPs and Section 504 plans were the mechanism for responding to bullying of a student with disabilities. To address bullying in an appropriate manner, officials at OSERS suggested that school personnel convene a student's IEP or Section 504 team to determine whether, as a result of the effects of the bullying, the student's needs had changed so that the IEP or Section 504 plan no longer provided meaningful educational benefits. If the determination was that a student's needs had changed, the IEP or Section 504 team were to revise the IEP or Section 504 plan so that a FAPE would be provided. The DCL also included an enclosure titled "Effective Evidence-based Practices for Preventing and Addressing Bullying" with the letter. This enclosure identified practices, such as the use of a comprehensive multitiered behavioral framework, teaching appropriate behaviors, and how to respond appropriately including providing active adult supervision, training and providing ongoing support for staff and students, developing and implementing clear policies to address bullying, monitoring and tracking bullying behaviors, notifying parents when bullying occurs, addressing ongoing concerns, and sustaining bullying prevention efforts over time. The DCL is available at www2.ed.gov/policy/speced/guid/idea/memosdcltrs/bullyingdcl-8-20-13.pdf and the enclosure is available at www2.ed.gov/speced/guid/idea/memosdcltrs/bullyingdcl-enclosure-8-20-13.pdf.

Litigation on Bullying as a Violation of a Student's FAPE

Rulings by the U.S. Courts of Appeals and a number of lower courts have recognized that bullying can lead to a denial of a student's FAPE. In *Shore Regional High School Board of Education v. P.S.* (2004) a student with disabilities had been subjected to harassment and bullying from his peers for many years. The student's parents alleged a denial of a FAPE because the student had been inappropriately placed at a local high school. The setting, the parents asserted, was inappropriate because the students who attended the high school were many of the same students who harassed their son when he was in elementary and middle school. The parents sought a placement in a neighboring school district. The U.S. Court of Appeals for the Third Circuit ruled that the student would have been denied a FAPE by a placement at the local high school because of the presence of the students who bullied him. The circuit court thus ruled in favor of the parents and ordered a lower court to determine appropriate attorney's fees and reimbursement that the school district owed to the student's parents.

In *M.L. v. Federal Way School District* (2005) the parents of a young child with autism alleged that their child was denied a FAPE and removed him from school because the school personnel did not take actions to prevent other students from harassing their child despite their knowledge that such harassment was occurring. The court noted that if a teacher or principal is deliberately indifferent to the harassment of a student with disabilities and the harassment leads to a denial of education benefits, then the student would have been denied a FAPE. In this particular case the parents were unable to convince the court that bullying had resulted in the denial of a FAPE because the time between the parents' complaint and their removal of their child from school was only 5 days. According to the court this short amount of time did not give the school personnel a reasonable opportunity to address the harassment.

T.K. v. New York City Department of Education (2011) was a significant federal district court case out of New York on bullied students with disabilities and their right to receive a FAPE. The case involved a 12-year-old girl with a learning disability. The student's peers ostracized and ridiculed her on a daily basis, which resulted in emotional withdrawal and a denial of educational benefits. The parents repeatedly complained to the principal of the school who apparently ignored their complaints and refused to take any action. The principal decided to return the student to the same school during the next school year. The child's parents objected and enrolled their child in a private school and requested a due process hearing alleging a deprivation of a FAPE. A hearing officer and review officer concluded that the district provided a FAPE, so the parents sued in federal court. The district court found that the bullying caused a denial of a FAPE, even though the student's IEP offered the needed programs and services to her. Moreover, the court noted that to deny a student a FAPE because of bullying did not require that the bullying be based on a student's disability; rather, bullying for any reason could result in the denial of FAPE if it resulted in adverse effects to a student's education. Additionally, it was not necessary that the parents prove that the bullying deprived the student of all educational benefit or that the student regressed; the parents needed only to show that the bullying was likely to affect the student's opportunity to receive an appropriate education. The court cited the 2010 DCL from OCR in the decision and asserted that a school district had to take prompt and appropriate action to address the bullying. This decision may have signaled that the standard for liability for peer bullying and harassment may be getting easier for plaintiffs to meet because of the adoption of standard set out in the OCR DCL of 2010 (Leadership Insider, 2011).

LESSONS FROM LITIGATION AND LEGISLATION

Bullying and harassment of students with disabilities, whether based on a student's disability or not, is a serious problem. School district officials need to understand that when bullying or harassment of students with disabilities occurs it also may trigger further responsibilities under Section 504, Title II of the ADA, and the IDEA (Norlin, 2014). When such bullying occurs, therefore, school personnel must take immediate effective steps to address the problem. The following guidelines for school districts are extrapolated from the administrative guidance and court cases.

Principle 1: Develop and Publicize the School District's Policy for Preventing and Addressing Bullying School districts need to adopt strong policies for preventing and addressing bullying. A number of common characteristics are seen in the most effective discipline policies: (a) statements of purpose; (b) scope of the policy; (c) the behaviors that the policy prohibits; (d) specific procedures for reporting complaints, investigating complaints, and documenting actions taken; (e) consequences for the offending student, and actions directed to the bully victim (e.g., counseling, provision of services); and (f) monitoring procedures to ensure the policy is implemented correctly. Moreover, the policy must be publicized, and discussions about the policy with parents, teachers, students, and school staff should take place. Because of the possibility of bullying being a violation of state and federal law, if it is not addressed, special education directors and Section 504 coordinators as well as other involved officials (e.g., Title IX coordinator) should be involved in policy development.

Recommendation 2: Adopt a Research-Based Bullying Prevention Program School district officials should adopt a research-based bullying prevention programs. For a website of research programs see SAMHSA's National Registry of Evidence-based Programs and Practices at http://nrepp.samhsa.gov/ and www.samhsa.gov/?from=carousel&position=1&date=10142014. Websites such as the U.S. Department of Education's www.stopbullying.gov and OSEP's Technical Assistance Center on Positive Behavioral Interventions and Supports' www.pbis.org contain a wealth of information on anti-bullying programs. There is a growing body of research on effective anti-bullying programs (e.g., Merrell, Gueldner, Ross, & Isava, 2008; Rose, Swearer, & Espelage, 2012). If school districts use a program that has evidence of success and the program is communicated, publicized, and implemented with fidelity, the program will be more likely to prevent bullying rather than only having to deal with effects of bullying.

In a document by the U.S. Department of Education on evidence-based practices for preventing and addressing bullying (www2.ed.gov/policy/speced/guid/idea/memosdcltrs/bullyingdcl-enclosure-8-20-13.pdf), officials at the department asserted that efforts to address bullying behavior should be embedded within a comprehensive, multi-tiered behavioral framework used to establish a positive school environment, set high academic and behavioral standards, and guide delivery of evidence-based instruction and interventions that address the needs of all students, including those with disabilities. Moreover, in such a framework all behavioral policies, including policies to prevent and respond to bullying, would be implemented consistently on a schoolwide basis. Researchers, such as Ross and Horner (2009), have demonstrated positive effects on bullying when bullying programs were embedded with a schoolwide system of positive behavior support. (Information on such a system can be found at www.pbis.org, the website of the OSEP-funded Technical Assistance Center on Positive Behavioral Interventions and Supports.)

Principle 3: Provide Professional Development on Prevention of Bullying School districts should provide administrators, principals, teachers, staff, and the larger school community with up-to-date professional development activities to ensure that they use the research-based bully prevention programs with fidelity. School district staff should also understand the procedural aspects of the school district's bullying policy (e.g., recognizing anti-bullying, reporting bullying, responding to incidences of bullying). Professional development activities should also include familiarizing staff with the requirements of the IDEA, Section 504, Title II of the ADA, Title IV of the Civil Rights Act, and Title IX of the Education Amendments. Bullying is always a serious problem that needs to be addressed quickly and effectively. Furthermore, when bullying involves potential discrimination against students with disabilities, school districts may be at risk of legal action if their personnel do not address the problem in an appropriate manner. Most states have anti-bullying laws. School personnel should be aware of any unique requirements in their state laws.

Principle 4: Be on the Lookout for Incidences of Bullying Detecting and responding to bullying when it first occurs are extremely important. Bullying can take many forms, including verbal acts, physical acts, and written statements. Bullying may be in plain sight and well known (e.g., school hallways, at recess) or it may be surreptitious (e.g., threatening e-mails). It is important that staff be on the lookout for indications that bullying is occurring. This is critical if the victim is being bullied because of his or her disability, race, color, national origin, or sex. When there is a complaint from a student's parents, peers, or teaches, administrators need to act quickly to address the potential problem. School officials should remember that when students in a protected class (e.g., disability, race, color, national origin, sex) are the target of bullying, the school district is responsible for addressing bullying incidence about which it knows or *should have known*. Moreover, all investigations should be thoroughly documented. School administrators should never take the tack of the principal at the Grand River Academy who reportedly told parents of a bullied student that it was the school's policy to "look the other way" (*M.Y. v. Grand River Academy,* 2010), which resulted in the student's parents claim moving forward.

Principle 5: Respond to Incidences of Bullying Quickly and Effectively When there is evidence that a student with disabilities is being bullied, administrators need to respond quickly and effectively. In responding to bullying, school personnel should do more than simply discipline the offender. Although such an action will probably be necessary, it is usually an insufficient response. School personnel, including IEP and Section 504 teams, need to (a) eliminate the hostile environment created by the bullying, (b) address the effects of the bullying on the victim (e.g., providing counseling), and (c) take steps to ensure that the bullying does not recur.

If the student being bullied is in special education, his or her IEP team should meet to determine if the student's IEP still provides a FAPE, and if it doesn't, they must modify the IEP. Similarly, if a student with disabilities has a Section 504 plan, then that team should meet to determine if the plan still offers a FAPE.

Summary of Bullying and Harassment of Students with Disabilities

Bullying is a common occurrence in America's schools and is currently at the forefront of national attention. The problem has become so serious that the Obama administration, the U.S. Department of Education, Congress, and the 50 states have sought ways to deal with this serious and growing problem. Unfortunately, despite the increasing awareness of bullying, it remains a major problem in American schools. This is especially true for students with disabilities. The bullying and harassment of students with disabilities has been such a major concern to the U.S. Department of Education that officials in the department have issued four policy guidance statements in Dear Colleague Letters. The purpose of DCLs, when sent by officials in an agency of the federal government (e.g., U.S. Department of Education, U.S. Department of Justice), is to provide guidance on meeting obligations under a law and offer members of the public information about their rights under the laws that the agency enforces. DCLs are issued in the form of an open letter. Two DCLs have been issued by the OCR, which enforces Section 504; in the department, one DCL was issued by the OSERS, which enforces the IDEA; and OCR and OSERS issued one jointly. The three DCLs from OCR have emphasized that when a student with disabilities is bullied based on his or her disability that may constitute discrimination. In such a situation it is the responsibility of school personnel to react promptly and effectively to end the bullying.

Additionally, according to OCR officials bullying may also deny student with disabilities a FAPE. In that case, a student's Section 504 team must examine his or her Section 504 plan to determine if it needs to be modified. Similarly, the DCL issued by OSEP addressed students' educational programs. If bullying results in a student's failure to achieve meaningful educational benefit, a student will not receive a FAPE. In such cases a student's IEP team must be convened to modify his or her IEP so that the student continues to receive a FAPE.

These DCLs are important guidance documents, and school personnel must be familiar with them. Court cases have also been heard in which the parents of students with disabilities who were bullied have sued school districts. Although the standards by which courts decide such cases are somewhat different from the standards used by OCR and OSERS, the results can be very serious. In fact, parents can receive attorney's fees, tuition reimbursement, compensatory education, and monetary damages. Thus, it is important that school district officials and personnel investigate and react promptly and effectively when students with disabilities are bullied.

STUDENTS WITH DISABILITIES IN CHARTER SCHOOLS

Mitchell L. Yell, Ph.D.
University of South Carolina

David F. Bateman, Ph.D.
Shippensburg University

In 1991, the first charter school law was passed and signed in Minnesota. A year later, the first charter school opened in the state. In 2017, all but seven states had charter laws and there were almost 7000 charter schools in the United States serving over three million students (National Alliance of Charter Schools, 2017). New charter schools open every year but also a number of charter schools close. Most states allow profit and not-for-profit charter schools.

Charter schools were founded, in part, to allow for a combination of innovation, freedom, and to reform how public schools have provided education. Charter laws, which govern charter schools, vary from state to state. Charter schools are typically managed by a group or organization under a charter, or legislative contract, with a state or local school district (National Center on Educational Statistics, 2014). The operators of charter schools have greater flexibility and autonomy in exchange for meeting the accountability standards outlined in the charter, thus the schools are able to innovate and use experimental educational practices (Mulligan, 2011; National Center on Educational Statistics, 2014).

Because charter schools are free from certain state and local regulations, charter schools are seen as providing flexibility and a greater opportunity to innovate in how they educate students while still being held accountable to the public for improving students' achievement. Using public funds, charter schools are exempt from many state laws, but in turn are held accountable for student academic performance. Charter schools are allowed to adopt instructional practices that will provide for instructional gains for their students. These different instructional practices can include parents as board members, teachers as board members, focusing solely on reading and math, dress codes, meeting at different times, longer school days, or more technology or arts. Proponents of charter schools hope that these new and differing methods will change and improve traditional education.

Public charter schools can operate either as a school within a local education agency (LEA) or as an LEA itself. No charter is permanent, however, and the charter must be renewed regularly based on student enrollment and educational results.

The Every Student Succeeds Act defines a charter school as a public school meeting the following requirements:

- Is developed in accordance with a state's charter school laws.
- Is exempt from many State and local rules that inhibit the flexible operation and management of public schools.
- Is not exempt from federal laws, rules, and regulations, including the Age Discrimination Act of 1975 [42 U.S.C. 6101 et seq.], Title VI of the Civil Rights Act of 1964 [42 U.S.C. 2000d et seq.], Title IX of the Education Amendments of 1972 [20 U.S.C. 1681 et seq.], Section 504 of the Rehabilitation Act of 1973 [29 U.S.C. 794], the Americans with Disabilities Act of 1990 [42 U.S.C. 12101 et seq.], Family Educational Rights and Privacy Act of 1974 [20 U.S.C. 1232g], and Part B of the Individuals with Disabilities Education Act [20 U.S.C. 1411 et seq.]

- Is created by a developer as a public school, or is adapted by a developer from an existing public school, and is operated under public supervision and direction.
- Operates in pursuit of a specific set of educational objectives determined by the school's developer and agreed to by the authorized public chartering agency.
- Provides a program of elementary or secondary education, or both.
- Is nonsectarian in its programs, admissions policies, employment practices, and all other operations, and is not affiliated with a sectarian school or religious institution.
- Does not charge tuition.
- Is a school to which parents choose to send their children, and that (a) Admits students on the basis of a lottery if more students apply for admission than can be accommodated, or (b) In the case of a school that has an affiliated charter school (such as a school that is part of the same network of schools), automatically admits students who are enrolled in the immediate prior grade level of the affiliated charter school.
- Agrees to comply with the same Federal and State audit requirements as do other elementary schools and secondary schools in the State, unless such State audit requirements are waived by the State.
- Meets all applicable Federal, State, and local health and safety requirements
- Operates in accordance with State law.
- Has a written performance contract with the authorized public chartering agency in the State that includes a description of how student performance will be measured in charter schools pursuant to State assessments that are required of other schools and pursuant to any other assessments mutually agreeable to the authorized public chartering agency and the charter school.
- May serve students in early childhood education programs or postsecondary students.

According to Angelov and Bateman (2016) how a charter school is set up, either as an LEA or a school within an LEA, determines how a charter school operates and is funded regarding students with disabilities. As we previously noted, because charter schools are public schools, all charters schools must comply with federal education laws, such as the Every Student Succeeds Act (ESSA) of 2015, the Individuals with Disabilities Education Act (IDEA), Section 504, the American with Disabilities Act (ADA), and the Family Rights and Privacy Act (FERPA). How a charter school is classified under the applicable state law will affect how a charter school implements the rules and regulations for the school. If the charter school is considered a building within a larger charter school organization, the charter school district must ensure that the obligations under the law are met. If the charter school is considered a LEA, the charter school, as the LEA, is responsible for ensuring the requirements of the law are met. If a charter school is part of a public school district (i.e., the LEA), that school district is responsible for ensuring that the charter school fulfills its obligation under the law. Additionally, virtual charter schools are required to meet the same responsibilities under the various laws as are all charter schools.

IDEA and Charter Schools

With respect to the IDEA, charter schools are public schools and, therefore, are required to fulfill the same duties relating to student with disabilities as do all public schools. That is, charter school operators must (a) publicize and conduct child find activities, (b) evaluate students suspected of having a disability and needing special education services, (c) provide special education and related services to eligible students with disabilities that confers a free appropriate public education (FAPE), (d) collaborate with a student's parents to develop an individualized education programs that delineates his or her special education program, (e) place a student in the least restrictive environment (LRE) that is appropriate to the student's needs. Additionally, charter school operators must ensure the school meets all the IDEA's procedural mandates, such as notice and consent requirements. According to the Office of Special Education and Rehabilitation Services (U.S. Department of Education, Office of

Special Education and Rehabilitative Services, 2016), because a charter school is a public school, whether it operates as an LEA or part of an LEA, eligible students with disabilities and their parents retain all their rights and protections under Part B of the IDEA. In 2016, these rights and protections were described in a document titled *"Frequently Asked Questions about the Rights of Students with Disabilities in Public Charter Schools under the Individuals with Disabilities Education Act"* (U.S. Department of Education, Office of Special Education and Rehabilitative Services, 2016) The document is available at https://sites.ed.gov/idea/files/policy_speced_guid_idea_memosdcltrs_faq-idea-charter-school.pdf

The IDEA includes the rights mandated in FERPA to students with disabilities and their parents. Charter school must extend rights under FERPA to all students without disabilities and their parents. Charter school officials, therefore, must ensure (a) the charter establishes or adopts written policies regarding student records and inform parents of their rights under FERPA annually, (b) students' parents are guaranteed access to their children's educational records, (c) students' parents have the right to challenge the accuracy of the records, (d) educational records cannot be disclosed to third parties without parental consent, and (e) students' parents may file complaints regarding a charter school's failure to comply with the FERPA.

The following are the IDEA regulations related to charter schools (34 C.F.R. 300.33).

(a) Rights of children with disabilities. Children with disabilities who attend public charter schools and their parents retain all rights under this part.

(b) Charter schools that are public schools of the LEA.

(1) In carrying out Part B of the Act and these regulations with respect to charter schools that are public schools of the LEA, the LEA must—

(i) Serve children with disabilities attending those charter schools in the same manner as the LEA serves children with disabilities in its other schools, including providing supplementary and related services on site at the charter school to the same extent to which the LEA has a policy or practice of providing such services on the site to its other public schools; and

(ii) Provide funds under Part B of the Act to those charter schools—

(A) On the same basis as the LEA provides funds to the LEA's other public schools, including proportional distribution based on relative enrollment of children with disabilities; and

(B) At the same time as the LEA distributes other Federal funds to the LEA's other public schools, consistent with the State's charter school law.

(2) If the public charter school is a school of an LEA that receives funding under § 300.705 and includes other public schools—

(i) The LEA is responsible for ensuring that the requirements of this part are met, unless State law assigns that responsibility to some other entity; and

(ii) The LEA must meet the requirements of paragraph (b)(1) of this section.

(c) Public charter schools that are LEAs. If the public charter school is an LEA, consistent with § 300.28, that receives funding under § 300.705 that charter school is responsible for ensuring that the requirements of this part are met, unless State law assigns that responsibility to some other entity.

(d) Public charter schools that are not an LEA or a school that is part of an LEA.

(1) If the public charter school is not an LEA receiving funding under § 300.705 or a school that is part of an LEA receiving funding under § 300.705 the SEA is responsible for ensuring that the requirements of this part are met.

(2) Paragraph (d)(1) of this section does not preclude a State from assigning initial responsibility for ensuring the requirements of this part are met to another entity. However, the SEA must maintain the ultimate responsibility for ensuring compliance with this part, consistent with § 300.149 (Authority: 20 U.S.C. 1413(a)(5))

As noted above and in the chapter on IEPs, the IEP is a very important part of the process of providing education for students eligible for special education and related services. The only students who get an IEP are students receiving special education services and it is a team document developed after an evaluation is completed and the student has been determined to be eligible for special education.

The IEP serves as a tool for providing information to administration, teachers, and parents about the special education services a child is to receive. It is very important for charter schools officials and personnel keep parents informed about what is being provided to their child so the parents can be an informed part of the team that is making educational decisions.

Planning the amount of time a student requires as a part of his or her special education programming is an important part of the IEP process. Personnel in charter schools will need to review IEPs and determine from the various intensity levels listed for the student(s) and make decisions about whether additional staff will be required. Some of the services needed can be provided by a paraprofessional. The IEP will also list related services a student is expected to receive, which may include transportation, speech therapy, or physical therapy. Charter school administrators need to review IEPs for the related service requirements to administratively plan for coverage.

It is the responsibility of personnel in a charter school to ensure that the IEP is developed in an appropriate timeframe with all the necessary IEP team members contributing. IEPs are to be revised at least annually. In some cases, if the student is not making progress, the IEP should be revised more frequently depending upon the needs of the student. It is not the parents' responsibility to make sure their child's IEP is written in a timely fashion, is appropriate, or is implemented correctly. The burden is completely that of the charter school.

Once an IEP is written it is the charter school's responsibility to make sure the services written in the IEP are being delivered to the student. As noted above, the parents are a part of the team developing the IEP, however, they do not bear the burden of ensuring that the implemented as written. Additionally, the charter school cannot write into the IEP that the parents are expected to provide any of the services for the child.

Charter school administrators should periodically check to make sure the IEP is being implemented and the related services are being delivered. It is better for a charter school to determine an IEP is not being implemented than to have parents or outside compliance monitor make that determination. Obviously, the development and implementation is an extremely important requirement of a charter school, when the school services student eligible for special education.

Section 504 and Charter Schools

If a charter school is a school within a LEA or a charter school operating as a LEA and receives federal funding, the charter school must adhere to the requirements of Section 504 of the Rehabilitation Act. The charter school operators, administrators, teachers, staff, therefore, must not discriminate against students with disabilities, their parents, or employees with disabilities. That is, persons with disabilities must have an equal opportunity to access educational programs and facilities equivalent to the opportunities extended to persons without disabilities. According to the Office of Civil Rights (U.S. Department of Education, Office of Civil Rights, 2016) there is no difference between the Section 504 nondiscrimination rights that are extended to students with disabilities in public schools and students with disabilities in charter schools, including prospective charter school students. In 2016, the Office of Civil Rights in the U.S. Department of Education issued a document titled "*Frequently Asked Questions about the Rights of Students with Disabilities in Public Charter Schools under Section 504 of the Rehabilitation Act of 1973.*" The document is available at www2.ed.gov/about/offices/list/ocr/docs/dcl-faq-201612-504-charter-school.pdf.

Often educational services are provided to students with disabilities under Section 504 by having school district personnel develop a Section 504 plan. Although no standard Section

504 plan required by the federal law, SEAs and LEAs certainly can require that such plans be developed to ensure that students with disabilities receive an appropriate education under Section 504. A Section 504 plan is a way of ensuring that a student with disabilities who is covered only by Section 504 receives an appropriate education under the law. Typically, a Section 504 plan lists the accommodations a child is to receive as a part of his or her education. The purpose of a Section 504 plan is to prevent a student with a disability from being discriminated against and to allow the student to participate in the school. A student with a Section 504 plan typically spends the entire school day in a general education classroom because they are not eligible for special education.

LESSONS FROM LITIGATION AND LEGISLATION

Principle 1: Provide thorough professional development in federal education laws to charter school directors, administrators, teachers, and staff It is crucial that if charter schools are to meet federal education laws, that school directors, administrators, teachers, and staff receive thorough training in the requirements of the IDEA, Section 504, FERPA, and other federal education requirements. Moreover, frequent updates on changes in these laws should be provided. If charter school personnel understand the laws and act in accordance with them they have a higher likelihood of meeting their responsibilities to students with disabilities. It also minimizes the chances that personnel will violate the rights of students with disabilities. Most charter schools operate as a separate LEA or as a school within a LEA. In either case, the LEA is responsible for meeting all special education requirements.

Principle 2: Appoint a contact person in the charter school to address special education issues Angelov and Bateman (2016) suggested every charter school should identify a primary staff member who is ultimately responsible for issues regarding special education. If there is a contact person regarding special education issues, including monitoring compliance issues and being available to questions and concerns from parents, administrators, LEA administration, and community members, the likelihood of inadvertently violating procedural aspects of the IDEA and having staff members provide contradictory information to parents would be minimized (Angelov and Bateman, 2016).

Principle 3: Special education should be a foundational aspect of a charter school's educational program Angelov and Bateman (2016) asserted that a healthy special education program is vital to the overall health of the charter school. When charter schools have a positive learning environment that is sensitive to the needs of students with disabilities, all students will benefit. It is important charter schools develop and maintain strong special education programs. Charter schools are accountable for meeting their charters and providing effective services to all students, including students with disabilities. According to the Council of Exceptional Children, the charter school standards that apply to education children and youth with disabilities must be the same as the standards that apply to these students in public schools (Council for Exceptional Children, 2011).

Principle 4: Charter school must adhere to the IDEA regulations Many charter schools were founded as a way of providing education free of many state regulations. However, the requirement that students eligible for special education continue to review a free appropriate public education in the least restrictive environment must still be maintained. In exchange for federal financial assistance, states represent to the federal government that students with disabilities are receiving an appropriate education. Charter schools need make sure there is a designated point person ensuring state compliance with all forms and procedures.

Summary of Students with Disabilities and Charter Schools

A charter school is a public school, whether it operates as its own LEA, is part of a public school district, or operates within a number of charter schools. This is also true of virtual charter schools. States have charter school laws that govern how charter schools are to operate within a particular state. Charter school operators must write a charter, which is approved by state officials. Such charters must ensure that the school operates in accordance with state rules and regulations, although state charter laws may allow some state rules and regulations to be waived for charter schools. However, all charter schools must operate in accordance with federal laws such as the IDEA, Section 504, the ADA, and FERPA.

RESPONSE TO INTERVENTION

The Individuals with Disabilities Education Improvement Act (IDEIA) of 2004 made a number of significant changes to the federal special education law. One of the most significant of these changes was in the guidelines for identifying students with learning disabilities (LD). The 1999 regulations to the IDEA required states to use a discrepancy formula when determining if a student had a learning disability (*Analysis of Comments and Changes to 2006 IDEA Part B Regulations*, 2006, p. 626). Although there are different types of discrepancy formulas, one of the commonly used formulas typically involves administering a test of ability, usually an IQ test, and an achievement test to a student suspected of having a learning disability. A formula is then applied to the results of the two tests to determine if there is a performance discrepancy between ability and achievement. The discrepancy refers to an unexpected difference between a student's ability and his or her achievement. The discrepancy formula approach has been criticized on technical and conceptual grounds (Lyon et al., 2001; President's Commission, 2001).

The IDEIA prohibited state education agencies (SEAs) from requiring that local education agencies (LEAs) use a discrepancy model to identify students with learning disabilities, instead permitting SEAs and LEAs to use a process whereby students are identified as having learning disabilities if they have failed to respond to scientific, evidence-based instruction or some other alternative research-based procedure (IDEA Regulations, 34 C.F.R. § 300.307(a)). SEAs could, however, prohibit local school districts from using a discrepancy model and require that school districts use a response-to-intervention procedure. According to the U.S. Department of Education, the adoption of this regulation reflected that department's position that procedures to identify students with LDs should focus on assessments that are instructionally relevant (*Analysis of Comments and Changes to 2006 IDEA Part B Regulations*, 2006). This procedure became known as response to intervention or, more simply, RTI.

Comments to the regulations promulgated by the U.S. Department of Education explained how school-based teams should use RTI information when determining the existence of a learning disability. The comments require school-based teams to assemble information on strategies or interventions used in general education settings and collect data-based documentation on a student's response to these interventions (IDEA Regulations, 34 C.F.R. § 300.311(a)(7)). The regulations also required that when team members make their eligibility decision the team must consider data-based documentation of repeated assessments of achievement at reasonable intervals during intervention, which means that some form of progress monitoring must be conducted. Comments to the regulations indicated that the effectiveness of a response to intervention model would depend on repeated assessments of a student's progress, which will allow educators to make informed decisions about the need to change instruction when necessary to meet a student's needs (IDEA Regulations, Comment, p. 689).

In a policy letter, the OSEP in the U.S. Department of Education noted that the core characteristics of an RTI model include (a) high-quality, research-based instruction in general education; (b) continuous progress monitoring; (c) screening for academic and behavior problems; and (d) multiple tiers of progressively more intense instruction (*Memorandum to Chief State School Officers*, 2008). In the same policy letter, the OSEP allowed a percentage of IDEA Part B funds to be used for early intervening services (EIS) to be used for RTI systems as long as the funds also serve nondisabled students in need of additional academic or behavioral support and supplement, not supplant, any other funds that are used to fund RTI.

Early intervening services permits school districts to use up to 15% of the IDEA Part B funds that the district receives each year in combination with other funds (including funds from the *Elementary and Secondary Education Act*) to develop and implement EIS for students in kindergarten through grade 12, with an emphasis on students in kindergarten through grade 3, who have *not* been identified as needing special education or related services but who need additional academic and behavioral support to succeed in the general education environment (IDEIA 20 U.S.C. § 613(f)(1)). The purpose of EIS is to identify young students who are at risk for developing academic and behavioral problems while they are still in general education settings, and then to address these problems by delivering interventions in a systematic manner using research-based academic and behavioral interventions along with progress monitoring systems. The advantages of an early intervening model include (a) identifying students early in their school careers using a risk rather than a deficit model, (b) emphasizing research-based practices in intervention, and (c) focusing on student outcomes rather than services received (Yell & Walker, 2010).

The concept of RTI has moved far beyond a method for improving the identification of students with learning disabilities to a schoolwide approach to adapting instruction to meet the needs of students who are having problems learning in the general curriculum. The purpose of an RTI system, which combines evidence-based instruction and progress monitoring, is to increase the number of students who learn successfully before they are in need of special education services. According to Fuchs and Mellard (2007), advocates have suggested that RTI systems have the following advantages: (a) early identification of disabilities, which avoids the traditional "wait to fail" model for identifying students with academic disabilities; (b) a strong focus on providing effective instruction and improving student outcomes; and (c) a decision-making process supported by continuous progress monitoring of skills closely aligned with desired outcomes.

Although use of RTI systems in states and school districts is a relatively recent occurrence, there have been a few due process hearings and court cases that have addressed issues that may arise when RTI systems are used to identify students with disabilities. RTI practices could potentially pose problems to school districts in conducting child find activities and determining eligibility (Walker & Daves, 2010). Although these decisions did not directly address RTI (instead they examined areas such as prereferral interventions, child find, and evaluation), these decisions may have implications for school district RTI programs.

RTI and the IDEA: Administrative Guidance and Litigation

The IDEA only directly addresses RTI in the section of the law on identifying students with learning disabilities. The IDEA also allows school districts to expend Part B funds on EIS, which often take the form of RTI programs. Nonetheless, Dr. Melody Musgrove, the director of OSEP, issued administrative guidance on RTI in a letter to state directors of special education. The letter, which was dated January 21, 2011, was titled "A Response to Intervention (RTI) Process Cannot Be Used to Delay or Deny an Evaluation for Eligibility Under the Individuals with Disabilities Education Act" (*Memorandum to State Directors of Special Education*, 2011, p. 1).

According to Musgrove, it had come to the attention of officials at OSEP that some school districts had been using an RTI system to delay or deny a timely initial evaluation for children suspected of having a disability. Musgrove wrote that it is a state and school district's obligation to ensure that such delays or denials do not occur. Musgrove also noted that if a student's parents request an evaluation, and if school district personnel deny the parents' request, the school district personnel must provide prior written notice explaining their reason for refusing the request. Of course, the student's parents have the option of filing a state complaint or a request for a due process hearing. The OSEP memorandum is available online at www2.ed.gov/policy/speced/guid/idea/memosdcltrs/osep11-07rtimemo.pdf.

Litigation has not directly addressed RTI and the IDEA; however, a few decisions have addressed issues such as child find and evaluation that have implications for school districts that developed and implemented RTI systems. Some of these decisions are examined in this section.

In a case out of Wisconsin, *Marshall Joint School District No. 2 v. C.D. by Brian and Traci D.* (2009), a U.S. District Court ruled that even though a third grade student performed on the same level as his peers after receiving modifications in the general education classroom, school officials still had a responsibility to conduct an evaluation to determine if the student was eligible for special education. Similarly, in *El Paso Independent School District v. Richard R.* (2009; hereafter *El Paso Independent School District*), an LEA repeatedly referred a student with ADHD (attention deficit/hyperactivity disorder) for interventions in the LEA's general education classroom rather than evaluating the student for special education. At the hearing level, the state education hearing officer (SEHO) ruled that the LEA had violated child find regulations because the LEA's Student Teacher Assessment Team (STAT) had devolved from a body meant to "provide support and intervention" to "an obstacle to parents who want to access the special education referrals" (*El Paso Independent School District*, 2008, p. 18). The SEHO wrote that the STAT process, which consisted of a team of school-based personnel who suggested interventions in the general education setting prior to referral, "while a mandatory district requirement, is not a prerequisite to conducting a special education evaluation" (*El Paso Independent School District*, 2008, p. 18). The hearing officer also noted that after a parent makes a request for a special education evaluation, the LEA should begin the special education evaluation process while at the same time providing intervention strategies through the STAT process.

The El Paso Independent School District appealed the hearing officer's decision to the District Court of West Texas. In affirming the hearing officer's decision, the district court judge held that a two-prong process should be used to determine whether an LEA is in compliance with its child find responsibilities. The first prong involves an examination of whether the LEA had reason to suspect that the student had a disability, and whether there was reason to suspect that special education services might be needed to address that disability. If the first prong is answered in the affirmative, then the court should progress to the second prong. The second prong involves determining if the LEA evaluated the student within a reasonable time after having notice of the behavior likely to indicate a disability. In the *El Paso* case, the district court found that there was insufficient justification to overturn the finding by the SEHO, and that the school district failed to meet its child find requirements. Officials in the El Paso School District stated that the school delayed starting the evaluation process because it needed time to implement intervention strategies. The district court judge was not swayed by this argument, holding that "one of the factors used to measure whether a local educational agency has met its IDEA responsibility to provide a FAPE is whether the accommodations accorded to the student demonstrate positive academic benefits" (*El Paso Independent School District*, 2008, p. 22). The facts in this case showed that the student in question had failed the Texas Assessment of Knowledge and Skills (TAKS), a statewide achievement test, for 3 years in a row and continued to display significant academic difficulties in reading, math, and science despite the district's implementation of intervention strategies in the general education setting. According to the hearing officer, these signs should have been "clear signals that an evaluation was necessary and appropriate" (*El Paso Independent School District*, 2008, p. 22). The general education interventions that had been used over the past 3 years had been shown to be ineffective in helping the student achieve passing scores on the TAKS. To summarize the decision of the district court judge, "faced with three years of repeated failure, the Court agrees with the SEHO's finding that [a] special education evaluation would have clearly indicated whether RR had a disability that was affecting his educational progress" (*El Paso Independent School District*, 2008, p. 22).

The district court then turned to the second prong of the court's child find inquiry to determine if the LEA had evaluated the student within a reasonable time after suspecting the student might have a disability. The district court in this case pointed to other federal courts that had developed standards varying from a delay of 6 months (*A. W. v. Jersey City Public Schools*, 2007) to a delay of 12 months (*O. F. ex rel. N.S. v. Chester Upland School District*, 2002) from the time that a child's parents had informed a school district that the child was experiencing difficulties or the point at which school officials had reason to suspect a child had a disability. Therefore, when this length of time passes, a district should be scheduling a special education evaluation; if it does not, this could be a child find violation. In the *El Paso* case the court ruled that the 13 months that passed between the request for evaluation and the school's offer of evaluation was unreasonable.

Finally, in its ruling the court adopted the SEHO's finding that the IDEA "gives the parent a right to seek an evaluation and overrides local district policy concerning intervening procedures. ... In those instances where the STAT committee impedes the exercise of rights guaranteed by federal law, those practices violate the IDEA" (*El Paso Independent School District*, 2008, p. 18). These decisions should serve to caution school district officials that an RTI system should not delay a special education evaluation when a student's performance indicates such a need, as this could be found to violate the IDEA.

On the other hand, a few decisions have implications for how school districts may conduct RTI in ways that are consistent with the IDEA. For example, in *Baltimore City Public School System* (2007), state complaint resolution system officials noted that it was appropriate to attempt interventions in a general education setting before referring students for special education services as long as the "process does not delay or deny a student's access to special education services under IDEA (34 CFR § 300.111)" (*Baltimore City Public School System*, 2007, p. 4). A similar ruling was handed down by a federal district court in Connecticut in 2008 in *A. P. by Powers v. Woodstock Board of Education*. A. P. was a 14-year-old student diagnosed with a nonverbal learning disability who attended Woodstock schools from kindergarten through April of sixth grade. A. P.'s parents had filed a complaint that the district had not evaluated their child for special education. In ruling on this case, the district court wrote that the child find requirement of the IDEA applies to students who are suspected of having a qualifying disability *and* being in need of special education as a result of their disability. The court found that whereas the student was suspected of having a disability, he did not need special education services because he responded well to interventions and the teacher maintained regular contact with A. P.'s parents and informed them of their child's progress. In his decision, the district court judge wrote:

> This is decidedly not a case in which a school turned a blind eye to a child in need. To the contrary, [the teacher] acted conscientiously, communicating regularly with [the mother] and utilizing special strategies to help [the student] succeed. Given the student's response to interventions, however, the district did not err in failing to evaluate him sooner. There is nothing in either the IDEA or in the state or federal implementing regulations to indicate that a student would qualify as a "student with a disability," when the school voluntarily modifies the regular school program by providing differentiated instruction which allows the child to perform within his ability at an average achievement level.

(*A. P. by Powers v. Woodstock Board of Education*, 2008, p. 4)

In *Ashli and Gordon C. ex rel. Sidney C. v. State of Hawaii, Department of Education* (2007; hereafter *Ashli*), the U.S. District Court in Hawaii reached similar conclusions. Thus, the results of these decisions indicate that when a school district uses an RTI system and the district has data showing that the interventions are effective in helping a student who had previously displayed academic learning difficulties, the school district may be meeting its responsibilities under the IDEA. It is very important in such situations that school district personnel collect meaningful data regarding the effects of these interventions on their students. School district officials must always attend to parents' concerns and realize that if parents request that their child be evaluated for special education placement, this request overrides local school district policy concerning the use of interventions in the general education setting.

LESSONS FROM LITIGATION AND LEGISLATION

These decisions have several important implications for state and school district officials who implement an RTI system. The following guidelines are offered based on this information.

Principle 1: Ensure that school district administrators, teachers, and staff understand their responsibilities under the IDEA Due process hearings and court cases have been caused by disputes that could have been avoided if school district administrators and teachers understood their responsibilities under the law. School districts should implement professional development activities to keep administrators, teachers, and staff abreast of current developments in the law.

Principle 2: Develop an RTI/MTSS system based on best practices The widespread use of schoolwide RTI systems is a relatively new development in education. Nonetheless, there is a growing body of evidence on how schools and districts should structure and implement RTI. For example, the OSEP currently funds the National Center on Response to Intervention. The Center's mission is to provide technical support to states and schools districts in implementing proven RTI models. The Center's website, www. rti4success.org, contains excellent resources and information on RTI.

Principle 3: Use instructional practices and progress monitoring systems that are based on evidence and research There are three essential components to a well-functioning RTI system: (a) a schoolwide, multilevel instructional and behavioral system for preventing school failure, (b) evidence-based instructional and behavioral interventions, and (c) a data-based progress monitoring system for movement within the RTI tiers and for identifying students with disabilities. With respect to identifying students with disabilities, the data-based progress monitoring system is particularly important. As the previous cases and hearings indicate, when school district personnel use RTI as a prereferral system, they need to have meaningful data for decision making. A school's multidisciplinary team can then use this information to determine if a student is responding to intervention in the general education setting. If a student is failing to respond to instruction, the team can use this data to determine the student's eligibility for special education services.

Principle 4: Ensure that the RTI/MTSS system does not interfere with the IDEA's child find or evaluation requirements School districts that adopt or develop an RTI system must ensure that the system does not interfere with students' rights under the IDEA. Such rights will always trump school districts' RTI policies. Moreover, school officials must ensure that the RTI system is not an excuse for delaying or failing to conduct child find or evaluation activities when needed. For example, if the length of time that a student spends at various tiers is excessive, and a student is not making progress, the school district could be in violation of the IDEA. To ensure that school districts do not violate the IDEA, it is advisable that the RTI system should consist of no more than three or four tiers and that the top tier of intensive interventions for nonresponders should either be special education or result in immediate referral to special education.

It is much more likely that those school districts that have an excessive number of tiers (e.g., six or seven) in their RTI systems and insist that all students go through all tiers before making a referral to special education will likely be in violation of the child find and evaluation requirements of the IDEA. Additionally, when a student's parents or teachers make a referral to special education, school districts should act on the referral and not use RTI as an excuse to delay evaluation.

Summary of Response to Intervention

Response to intervention was first introduced as an alternative method to identify students with LDs in the reauthorization of the IDEA in 2004. The law prohibited SEAs from requiring that local school districts use a discrepancy formula to identify students with LDs. Instead states were allowed to require, or at least permit, school districts to adopt an identification method in which students' response to research-based instruction was used to determine if students had LDs. In the past few years, however, RTI has become much more than a method used to identify students with learning disabilities. In fact, RTI is more about making systematic changes in the ways that improve the education of all students. RTI certainly has the potential to transform education. The goal behind RTI is that by identifying students who are at risk of academic failure early in their school years and then providing increasing intensities of research-based instruction and progress monitoring, educators can prevent academic failure. School district officials who adopt and implement RTI models must be aware of their responsibilities under the IDEA and ensure that they do not violate the child find and evaluation requirements of the law.

STUDENT RECORDS

Prior to 1974, it was common for schools to deny parental access to educational records. Granting access was time consuming and costly and often was seen in a negative light because it increased a school's potential liability by opening up records to public scrutiny. Additionally, students' educational records, although denied to parents, were often made available to third parties without regard to student confidentiality (McCarthy, Cambron-McCabe, & Eckes, 2013).

In 1974, Congress enacted the Family Educational Rights and Privacy Act (FERPA) to address concerns regarding the confidentiality and accessibility of student records. Senator James Buckley of New York introduced the law, also known as the Buckley Amendment. Senator Buckley introduced this act to (a) ensure that parents and students would have access to their educational records and (b) protect students' right to privacy by not releasing records without consent. The law applies equally to both preschool-grade 12 school and institutions of higher education (Bathon, Gooden, & Plenty, 2017).

When the Education for All Handicapped Children Act (now the Individuals with Disabilities Education Act, or IDEA) was passed in 1975, the confidentiality and access provisions of FERPA were incorporated into the law. In 2014, the U.S. Department released a document titled *IDEA and FERPA Confidentiality Requirements*. The document is a table that compares the confidentiality requirements of IDEA-Part B, IDEA-Part C, and FAPE (Surprenant, Miller, Pasternak, 2014). This very useful document can be accessed at www2.ed.gov/policy/gen/guid/ptac/pdf/idea-ferpa.pdf. The regulations implementing the student records provisions of the IDEA can be found at 34 C.F.R. § 300.560–300.577.

State educational agencies must notify parents of students with disabilities about their rights under the IDEA's records provisions. Figure 14.1 notes the information that must be included in this notice.

FIGURE 14.1 ■
Confidentiality Notice

> The IDEA requires that public schools supply this information to parents of students with disabilities:
>
> 1. The extent to which the notice is provided in the native language of the different population groups within the state
> 2. The children and youth on whom the state maintains records that contain personally identifiable information
> 3. The types of information the state maintains
> 4. The methods the state uses to gather the information
> 5. The ways in which the information will be used
> 6. The policies and procedures schools follow with respect to storing, disclosing, retaining, and destroying records with personally identifiable information
> 7. The rights of parents, children, and youth regarding this information, including their rights under FERPA
>
> This confidentiality notice must be published or announced in newspapers and through other outlets before identification, location, or evaluation activities are undertaken.

Family Educational Rights and Privacy Act

The FERPA applies to all students who attend public schools that receive federal financial assistance. The law requires that these institutions adhere to the following requirements: (a) school districts must establish written policies regarding student records and inform parents of their rights under FERPA annually; (b) parents are guaranteed access to their children's educational records; (c) parents have the right to challenge the accuracy of the records; (d) disclosure of these records to third parties without parental consent is prohibited; and (e) parents may file complaints under FERPA regarding a school's failure to comply with the law.

Definition of Educational Records
FERPA and the IDEA cover all records, files, documents, and other materials that contain personally identifiable information directly related to a student and that are maintained by the school district or by a person acting for the district. Records not covered by the FERPA disclosure rules include (a) those records made by educational personnel that are in sole possession of the maker and are not accessible or revealed to other persons except substitutes (e.g., personal notes made by a child's teacher, a school psychologist's interview records) and (b) records of the law enforcement unit of an educational agency (e.g., a school's police liaison officer) that are maintained solely for law enforcement purposes. Additionally, schools need not obtain parental consent when records are made available to correctional facilities (*Alexander v. Boyd,* 1995), school attorneys, or special education service providers (*Marshfield School District,* 1995), or when disclosure of information is related to child find activities under the IDEA (*Letter to Schipp,* 1995). A school district's release of confidential information to a family doctor without parental permission, however, was ruled a violation of FERPA (*Irvine Unified School District,* 1995).

The IDEA adopted the definition of educational records found in FERPA. The U.S. Department of Education has determined that educational records include (a) IEPs and treatment plans; (b) test forms, providing that the school district retains personally identifiable test forms; (c) school evaluations, medical evaluations, independent evaluations, and any other documents that pertain to a student's educational performance; (d) recordings of IEP meetings; (e) transcripts of due process hearings; (f) complaints filed with the SEA; and (g) correspondence and investigative findings regarding a complaint if they contain personally identifiable information and are maintained by the school district. The following items are not considered educational records by the Department of Education: (a) personal notes or teacher papers, and other records of instructional, supervisory, and educational personnel that are not revealed to others; (b) test protocols that do not contain personally identifiable information; and (c) documents, such as tests, instruments, and interpretive materials, that do not contain a student's name (Pitasky, 2000).

Accessibility Rights

Parents and eligible students over 18 years of age have the right to see, inspect, reproduce, and challenge the accuracy of educational records. These rights extend to custodial and noncustodial parents, unless a court order has been issued that denies the noncustodial parent access rights. Additionally, schools must explain and interpret records to parents if they ask school officials to do so. School officials must comply promptly with parental requests to inspect educational records. The response must be made "in a reasonable time frame"—within 45 days of the parent's request.

Similarly, the IDEA requires that upon request a school district must allow parents of students with disabilities to inspect and review educational records related to their child that are collected and maintained by the school district. Moreover, they are required to reply to any requests in less than 45 days. The access rights apply to educational records and not to classroom visits because state and school district rules govern access to classrooms (Pitasky, 2000).

Amending Records

If parents believe educational records are misleading or incorrect, they may request that the school amend the records. The school may deny the parents' request. The parents may contest this refusal in a due process hearing. The task of the hearing officer in this situation is to determine whether the information in the file is accurate and appropriate. If the officer determines that the information is not accurate or does not belong in the file, it must be removed from the file immediately. If the hearing officer determines that the files are accurate and appropriate, the school does not need to amend the records. The parents, however, may attach a statement regarding their objection to the educational record. This statement must be kept in the student's records.

Confidentiality of Information

Third-party access to educational records is permitted only if the parents provide written consent. The exceptions to these confidentiality provisions include (a) school personnel with legitimate educational interests, (b) officials representing schools to which the student has applied, (c) persons responsible for determining eligibility for financial aid, (d) judicial orders for release, and (e) in emergency situations, persons who act to protect the student's health and safety. Additionally, FERPA allows a school to use and make public directory information, including the name and address of a student, if the school gives parents prior notice of the type of information to be released and gives them adequate time to respond if they disagree. The content of directory information is left to school districts. Courts have held that the directory information provision of the law is the one significant exception to FERPA's confidentiality requirements (Johnson, 1993).

Destruction of Records

Finally, when the LEA no longer needs the records, it must notify the parents. The parents may request copies of the file or may request that the records be destroyed. If destruction is requested, the LEA may retain a permanent record of the student's name, address, telephone number, grades, attendance, grade level, and the last year of school the student completed.

The IDEA also gives parents the right to request the destruction of personally identifiable educational records. Additionally, the school has to inform parents when the records are no longer needed to provide educational services to the student. The school may retain permanent records of students, including information such as name, address, phone number, grades, attendance record, classes, and grade level completed. Also, records that are used to demonstrate compliance with the IDEA, including IEPs, evaluations, and other records that prove a FAPE has been provided, must be kept for at least 3 years. When parents of students in special education request the destruction of records, they should be informed that the records may be useful at a later date.

Enforcement of FERPA   Schools receiving federal financial assistance are in violation of FERPA when they deny parents their rights to inspect and review records or if third parties that are not exempt from FERPA's requirements are allowed to view records without parental permission. If a school district does not take steps to voluntarily remedy the violation, the Department of Education may terminate federal aid to the district. Under FERPA, however, there is no private right of action, which means that a person cannot sue a school under the law (Johnson, 1993; Mawdsley, 1996). In fact, in 2002 the U.S. Supreme Court in *Gonzaga University v. Doe* (2002) ruled that individuals could not file private lawsuits against schools or colleges for violations of FERPA. If schools and colleges violate FERPA, individuals can only file a complaint with the U.S. Department of Education. If a FERPA violation occurs with a student also covered by the IDEA, however, the parent may, following exhaustion of due process remedies, initiate a lawsuit under the latter law. The Department of Education is empowered to withhold federal funds if a school or college violates FERPA and fails to correct the violation.

LESSONS FROM LITIGATION AND LEGISLATION

Principle 1: School district officials should develop and publicize clear policies regarding students' educational records School district officials need to develop clear and unambiguous policies regarding the handling of student records. Moreover, these policies should be publicized widely to personnel working in the district and to the public who reside in the school district. Of course, the IDEA requires that information regarding procedural safeguards, including requirements regarding student records, be made available to the public.

Principle 2: Ensure that school district administrators, teachers, and staff understand their responsibilities regarding student records The IDEA and FERPA contain very specific requirements that school district personnel must understand and follow regarding the educational records of their students. Although such information is important for all educators, because special education teachers have constant access to their students' educational records, especially IEPs and evaluation records, it is especially crucial that they understand the importance of maintaining confidentiality (e.g., counselors, administrative assistants, paraeducators). It is also important that school district officials not overreact to confidentiality requirements by withholding important information from persons with a legitimate reason to access it (e.g., paraeducators, substitute teachers).

Principle 3: Appoint a case manager to keep a student's special education and section 504 records It is advisable to assign one person, probably either the student's primary service provider or administrator, to maintain a student's special education or Section 504 records. These records should be locked, and if other school personnel with a legitimate reason to access the records need to review them, the service provider or administrator should maintain an access file.

Summary of Student Records

The IDEA contains all of the components of FERPA, and both laws apply to the educational records of students with disabilities. The IDEA requires that state and local education agencies formulate policies that are consistent with FERPA regarding the educational records of students with disabilities. Furthermore, school districts must inform parents of students with disabilities of district policies on educational record access, confidentiality, and maintenance and destruction of records, and explain to parents their rights regarding their children's records.

Additionally, the IDEA requires that school districts assign a qualified person at each school to protect the confidentiality of all personally identifiable educational records. Persons who have access to these records must be trained in the policies and procedures of the state as well as FERPA requirements. The school must also keep a record of persons obtaining access to educational records. The information that must be collected for accessing records includes the name of the party reading the records, the date of access, and the purpose.

LIABILITY FOR STUDENT INJURY

In the past few years, there has been a substantial increase in the number of lawsuits filed on behalf of students with disabilities injured while at school. These suits are usually filed against the schools and school personnel (Pitasky, 1995). Typically these cases involve injuries, either physical or emotional, that occur either accidentally or intentionally. Often these suits involve tort claims of negligence.

Tort Laws

Tort laws are laws that offer remedies to individuals harmed by the unreasonable actions of others. Tort claims usually involve state law and are based on the legal premise that individuals are liable for the consequences of their conduct if it results in injury to others (McCarthy, Cambron-McCabe, & Eckes, 2013). Tort claims involve civil suits, which are actions brought to protect an individual's private rights. Civil suits are different from criminal prosecutions. Criminal prosecutions are actions brought by the state to redress violations of the law. Two major categories of torts are typically seen in education-related cases: intentional torts and negligence.

Intentional Torts
Intentional torts are usually committed when a person attempts or intends to do harm. For intent to exist, the individual must know with reasonable certainty that injury will be the result of the act (Alexander & Alexander, 2012). A common type of intentional tort is assault. Assault refers to an overt attempt to physically injure a person or to create a feeling of fear and apprehension of injury. No actual physical contact need take place for an assault to occur. Battery, however, is an intentional tort that results from physical contact. For example, if a person picks up a chair and threatens to hit another person, assault has occurred; if the person then actually hits the second person, battery has occurred. Both assault and battery can occur if a person threatens another, causing apprehension and fear, and then actually strikes the other, resulting in injury. According to Alexander and Alexander (2012), teachers accused of assault and battery are typically given considerable leeway by the courts. This is because assault and battery cases often result from attempts to discipline a child, usually by some manner of corporal punishment, and courts are generally reluctant to interfere with a teacher's authority to discipline students (Alexander & Alexander, 2012; McCarthy, Cambron-McCabe, & Eckes, 2013).

Courts have found teachers guilty of assault and battery, however, when a teacher's discipline has been cruel, brutal, excessive, or administered with malice, anger, or intent to injure. In determining if a teacher's discipline constitutes excessive and unreasonable punishment, courts will often examine the age of the student; the instrument, if any, used to administer the discipline; the extent of the discipline; the nature and gravity of the student's offense; the history of the student's previous conduct; and the temper and conduct of the teacher. For example, a teacher in Louisiana was sued and lost a case for assault and battery for picking up a student, slamming him against bleachers, and then dropping the student to the floor, breaking his arm (*Frank v. New Orleans Parish School Board*, 1967). In Connecticut, a student was awarded damages when a teacher slammed the student against a chalkboard and then a wall, breaking the student's clavicle (*Sansone v. Bechtel*, 1980). Clearly, teachers may be held personally liable for injuries that occur to students because of teachers' behavior. The legal principles that apply to teachers whose behavior causes injury are the same principles that apply to all citizens (Fischer, Schimmel, & Kelly, 1994).

A small body of case law also indicates that school districts and school officials may be liable for damages in cases alleging teacher abuse of students. In *C. M. v. Southeast Delco School District* (1993), the federal district court for the Eastern District of Pennsylvania ruled that a student could proceed with a suit for damages against a school district and school officials because of injuries incurred as a result of alleged abuse perpetrated by a special education teacher. The abuse in this case included verbal harassment (e.g., name calling, ridiculing, profanity), physical abuse (e.g., slapping, hitting, grabbing and slamming into a locker, spraying with water and Lysol), and sexual abuse. The court ruled that the state had an affirmative duty to protect people from its own employees. Furthermore, the court stated that this was particularly true of teachers, because they are in positions of great sensitivity and responsibility. Later that year, the same court heard another damage claim against the same school district and teacher for sexual, physical, and verbal abuse. In *K. L. v. Southeast Delco School District* (1993), the court reiterated that the student had an appropriate claim for damages based on the school district's actions or inaction that resulted in injuries to the student. Again, the court noted that school districts and school officials have a heightened duty to supervise and monitor teachers. Pitasky (1995) posited that these cases, although legally binding only in their districts, have created a potential for damages to be imposed on school districts and school officials for liability claims against teachers and other school personnel.

Teachers have also won assault and damage suits against students. A Wisconsin court awarded a teacher compensatory and punitive damages for a battery case he brought against a student who physically attacked and injured him as he brought the student to the principal's office for a rule violation (*Anello v. Savignac,* 1983). An Oregon court assessed damages against a student who struck and injured his teacher for not allowing him to leave the classroom during a class period (*Garret v. Olson,* 1984).

Negligence The second type of tort seen most frequently in education-related cases is negligence. The difference between negligence and an intentional tort is that in negligence the acts leading to injury are neither expected nor intended (Alexander & Alexander, 2012). Negligence arises in instances where conduct falls below an acceptable standard of care, thereby resulting in injury. For negligence to occur, an injury must have been avoidable by the exercise of reasonable care. The ability to foresee injury or harm is an important factor in determining negligence. Unforeseeable accidents that could not have been prevented by reasonable care do not constitute negligence.

Four elements must be present for negligence to occur:

1. The teacher must have a duty to protect another from unreasonable risks.
2. The teacher must have failed in that duty by failing to exercise a reasonable standard of care.
3. There must be a causal connection between the breach of the duty to care and the resulting injury.
4. There must be an actual physical or mental injury resulting from the negligence.

In a court, all four elements must be proved before a court will award damages for negligence (Freedman, 1995; McCarthy, Cambron-McCabe, & Eckes, 2013).

Duty to Protect The first element, the duty to protect, is clearly part of a teacher's responsibilities. Teachers have a duty to anticipate foreseeable dangers and take necessary precautions to protect students in their care from such dangers (McCarthy, Cambron-McCabe, & Eckes, 2013). Specifically, teachers' duties include adequate supervision, maintenance of equipment and facilities, and heightened supervision of high-risk activities. In the majority of cases of negligence against teachers, the duty to protect is easily proved (Fischer et al., 1994). Clearly, this duty applies to activities during the school day; however, courts have also held that this duty may extend beyond regular school hours and away from school grounds (e.g., after-school activities, summer activities, field trips, bus rides).

Failure to Exercise a Reasonable Standard of Care   The second element occurs when teachers fail to exercise a reasonable standard of care in their duties to students. If a teacher fails to exercise reasonable care to protect students from injury, then the teacher is negligent. In negligence cases, courts will gauge a teacher's conduct on how a "reasonable" teacher in a similar situation might have acted (Alexander & Alexander, 2012). The degree of care exercised by a "reasonable" teacher is determined by factors such as (a) the training and experience of the teacher in charge, (b) the student's age, (c) the environment in which the injury occurred, (d) the type of instructional activity, (e) the presence or absence of the supervising teacher, and (f) a student's disability, if one exists (Mawdsley, 1993; McCarthy, Cambron-McCabe, & Eckes, 2013). For example, a primary grade student will require closer supervision than a secondary school student; a physical education class in a gymnasium or an industrial arts class in a school woodshop will require closer supervision than a reading class in the school library; and a student with a mental disability will require closer supervision than a student with average intelligence. In *Foster v. Houston General* (1981), a student with a moderate mental disability was struck and fatally injured when she darted into traffic while being escorted, along with nine other students, from her special education class to a park three blocks from the school. The court held that the teacher had failed to select the safest route to the park and to maintain the close supervisory duties required in this situation. The court also found that the general level of care required for all students becomes greater when the student body is composed of students with mental retardation. Finally, the court stated that the standard of care was heightened because the children were being taken off the school campus. A number of cases have held that the student's IEP, disability, and unique needs are all relevant factors in determining a reasonable level of supervision (Daggett, 1995). Additionally, school officials may be liable for damage claims resulting from a failure to supervise a student with a disability when that student injures another student. In *Cohen v. School District* (1992), a federal district court ruled that a liability claim could go forward when a behaviorally disordered student with known violent tendencies was placed in a general education classroom without adequate supervision and subsequently attacked and injured another student.

Proximate Cause   The third element that must be proved in a negligence case is a connection between the breach of duty by the teacher (element 2) and the subsequent injury to the student (element 4). This element, referred to as *proximate cause*, often hinges on the concept of foreseeability; that is, was the student's injury something that a teacher could have anticipated? If the injury could have been foreseen and prevented by a teacher if a reasonable standard of care had been exercised, a logical connection and, therefore, negligence may exist. To answer questions regarding proximate cause, courts will ask, "Was the injury a natural and probable cause of the wrongful act (i.e., failure to supervise), and ought [it] to have been foreseen in light of the attendant circumstances?" (*Scott v. Greenville*, 1965). Negligence claims will not be successful if the accident could not have been foreseen. In *Sheehan v. St. Peter's Catholic School* (1971), a teacher was supervising a group of students at recess when some of the students began throwing rocks. The rock throwing had continued for almost 10 minutes when a student was struck in the eye and injured. The court found the supervising teacher liable for negligence because a reasonable teacher would have anticipated or foreseen potential harm arising from the incident and stopped it. In a Wyoming case, *Fagan v. Summers* (1978), a teacher's aide was determined not to be the proximate cause of a playground-related injury that occurred during her supervision. Immediately after the aide walked by a group of students, one child threw a rock, which was deflected and hit another child. The court concluded that the injury was unforeseen and could not have been prevented even with the aide providing stricter supervision.

Actual Injury   The final element that must be proved in negligence cases is that there was an actual physical or mental injury. Even in instances in which there is negligence, damage suits will not be successful unless there is provable injury.

Monetary Damages in Personal Injury Suits

In Chapter 12 I addressed Section 1983, and monetary or damage claims under Section 504 and Title II of the ADA. Section 1983 of the Civil Rights Act is an option that parents may use when their child's rights are violated because they can collect monetary awards in a situation in which they can prove their child's rights were violated by a person or entity acting for the local, state, or federal government. So, for example, if an administrator, teacher, or other school personnel injured a student, ether intentionally or through negligence, they could possibly be sued under Section 1983 and, if they lose, could be required to pay monetary damages. Furthermore, a school district could be similarly sued for the actions or inaction of school personnel.

In *Herrera v. Hillsborough County School Board* (2013) the parents of young girl, called I.H. by the court, with a neuromuscular disability filed claims under Section 1983, Section 504, and Title II of the ADA. The student's parents alleged that school district personnel knew that their child had difficulty holding her head upright and needed proper positioning. The child's need for proper positioning had to been included in her IEP because I.H. was having difficulty holding her head up. This could be dangerous because failing to position I.H. correctly could lead to an obstructed airway. The parents also said that they had repeatedly warned of problems that occurred with staff members failing to properly position I.H. when she was riding the school bus.

When placing I.H. on the bus for a ride home, staff members failed to properly position her. At some point during the ride, I.H. had difficulty holding her head upright and developed an obstructed airway. The bus aide noticed that I.H. was unable to breathe but made no effort to check her airway or begin resuscitation efforts. Instead, the bus aide called the girl's mother and told her to come to the bus. The bus driver pulled to the side of the road to wait for I.H.'s mother but made no efforts to resuscitate the girl or call 911. When the mother arrived, I.H. was not breathing and was unresponsive. Although she was air-lifted to a hospital, I.H. died. The parents brought a lawsuit against the Hillsborough School District and Hillsborough School Board. Among other allegations, the parents claimed that the school district had failed to properly train the staff and unresponsiveness to complaints supported a cause of action because of the school district's deliberate indifference. The court allowed the claims to go forward. As previously mentioned when a court allows a claim to go forward, it is very likely followed by the school district settling the case.

Hatfield v. O'Neill (2013) was an unpublished case out of the U.S. Court of Appeals for the Sixth Circuit. A school nurse had become particularly concerned when a number of students with profound disabilities in a particular teacher's classroom were being sent to the nurse for medical care. She asked two paraeducators in the teacher's classroom if they would document the teacher's behavior toward her students. In the situation that led to this particular case, the special education teacher, who was aware that a student with profound disabilities had undergone brain surgery, struck the student during feeding. The two paraeducators went to the principal and reported that the teacher struck the student out of frustration and this had happened on many occasions. The principal confronted the teacher, who maintained that all her actions were done for educational reasons. The principal fired the teacher, who was arrested and charged with aggravated child abuse. The teacher was acquitted of all charges. The student's parents then filed an action against the school district and the teacher. They sued under Section 1983. The court found the teacher's behavior an egregious use of force and allowed the claim to go forward.

Attempts to cover up abuse can also put school districts, administrators, and personnel at legal risk. In *Hamilton v. Spriggle* (2013), a student, K.H., was diagnosed with autism and cognitive impairments. K.H.'s teacher had repeatedly abused the students in her classroom. Three paraeducators in the teacher's classroom were very alarmed at the abuse they were witnessing and reported the teacher to the principal of the school and the district's supervisor of special education. The school district's director was also told about the abuse. The reports, however, were seemingly discounted and little was done. This reaction occurred despite evidence to show previous abuse on the teacher's part that previously had resulted in a letter of reprimand being placed in her file. When the paraeducators brought forth additional allegations of abuse the director interviewed two other paraeducators who also expressed concern about the abuse. The director of special education told the paraeducators that they were not to report the incidences to the student's parents. One of the paraeducators felt compelled to resign over the incidents. She also wrote a number of letters. Eventually the matter came to the attention of the police, who charged the teacher with abuse and harassment. The teacher was convicted, given probation, and required to perform community service. Also, her teaching license was revoked.

The student's parents also sued the school district, the teacher, and eight additional defendants under Section 1983, Section 504, and the constitution of the state. They asked for punitive damages. The cases were dismissed against all the individuals except the teacher, school principal, district supervisor of special education, and the district director of special education. These claims were allowed to proceed. Additionally, the three administrators who had attempted to hide the reports of abuse against the special education teacher actively created a dangerous situation for K.H. This "state-created danger" theory of liability allows parents to hold administrators responsible for an employee's misconduct if the administrators used their authority in such a way as to create an opportunity for harm that would not have otherwise existed. Because the three administrators attempted to suppress allegations of abuse and did not contact the student's parents or the police the case could proceed to trial. Although no public record exists, this case was probably settled before it could go to trial.

Teachers' Defenses Against Liability

If it can be shown that a student contributed to the injury, the teacher may use a defense of contributory negligence. If the court finds that contributory negligence was present, the teacher will not be held liable. With younger students (i.e., under age 6), it is difficult to prove contributory negligence because the tort laws in many states hold that young children are incapable of contributory negligence. In these instances, therefore, students can collect damages even if they did contribute to the injury. Additionally, if students are between the ages of 7 and 14, contributory negligence can be difficult to prove, unless it can be shown that they are quite intelligent and mature. When actions involve students with disabilities, contributory negligence is also difficult to prove.

With older students, assumption of risk can also be used as a defense against negligence claims. Assumption of risk has been recognized as a defense against claims of liability in activities such as competitive sports (Fischer et al., 1994). If a student is mature enough to recognize the dangers of certain activities and still volunteers to participate, the student assumes a certain amount of risk. For example, in *Kluka v. Livingston Parish Board* (1983), an 11th grade student challenged his basketball coach to a wrestling match. The student was injured during the match and subsequently sued the coach for damages. The student testified that he had not contributed to the injury because he had not known he could be injured wrestling. The court found the teacher not liable for damages, stating that there were some risks that everyone must appreciate. As is the case with contributory negligence, it is unlikely that young and less mature students would be found by a court to assume the risk in activities, since they are often seen as not able to understand or appreciate the consequences of high-risk activities.

Finally, it is often assumed that teachers and schools can release themselves from damages by having parents sign waivers or releases. This is untrue, because parents cannot waive their children's claims for damages (Fischer et al., 1994; Freedman, 1995; McCarthy, Cambron-McCabe, & Eckes, 2013). Teachers always have a duty to their students to supervise them to prevent foreseeable injury. Parental releases, waivers, and permission slips do not relieve teachers or schools of liability if they fail to appropriately discharge their duties. According to Fischer, Schimmel, and Kelly (1994), such waivers may be useful for public relations purposes, but they will not relieve teachers or school officials of possible liability for negligence.

LESSONS FROM LITIGATION AND LEGISLATION

Schools, school officials, and teachers may have a heightened standard of care for students with disabilities (Mawdsley, 1993). School districts should take actions to make certain that administrators, special education and regular education teachers, and other personnel are aware of their care and supervisory duties under the law (Daggett, 1995; Freedman, 1995; Mawdsley, 1993). (These responsibilities are listed in Figure 14.2.)

The following are suggestions to assist administrators and teachers in meeting these responsibilities:

Principle 1: Develop policies and procedures School districts should develop policies regarding standards of care and supervision. These policies should be in writing. Because this area of law changes rapidly, legal developments should be monitored and school policies should be updated when necessary. Additionally, tort laws vary by state, so it is extremely important that school district officials understand tort laws in their states prior to developing policies.

Principle 2: Provide professional development Special education and regular education teachers, as well as administrators and other staff, should be trained in their responsibilities under the law. The training should emphasize school personnel's responsibilities regarding student safety and protection. Training may be important in convincing a court that a school district acted with care and good faith.

Principle 3: Involve students' IEP teams or section 504 teams A student's IEP team or Section 504 team should address potential safety risks and plan for them when appropriate. The IEP or Section 504 plan should include actions that will be taken to minimize these risks. The listing of precautionary procedures in the IEP or Section 504 plan could provide very convincing evidence that a school district has made an effort to prevent student injury. If, however, procedures listed in the IEP or Section 504 plan are not followed and an injury results, the school's negligence can be more easily proved (Daggett, 1995).

Principle 4: if you see something occurring that you know to be wrong, report it to your supervisors If a teacher, administrator, or any school employee sees something occur that he or she thinks is wrong, it should be reported to school district officials. *Never* attempt to hide or cover up a wrong. Be certain to document any reports or e-mails. Act with common sense! Additionally, administrators should take any reports of possible abuse or negligence very seriously and promptly investigate any such reports.

FIGURE 14.2 ■
Avoiding Liability for Student Injury

- Develop written school district policies regarding care and supervision of students.
- Train administrators, teachers, paraprofessionals, and other staff in responsibilities for care and supervision of students.
- Have the IEP team address potential safety risks for students with disabilities.

Summary of Liability for Student Injury

In addition to the responsibility of special education teachers and administrators to provide a FAPE for students with disabilities, educators also have a duty to maintain a safe environment and to protect students from harm. Although there are instances of teachers committing violations of the law by abusing and neglecting students, the most likely area in which teachers can violate students' rights is through negligence. School districts, school administrators, teachers, and other school personnel can put themselves at legal risk through either intentional or unintentional actions in which students are harmed. International torts, negligence torts, and Section 1983 can be legal avenues to address such problems.

> Enhanced eText **Application Exercise 14.1.** *Davis v. Monroe County Board of Education,* 526 U.S. 629 (1999).

FOR FURTHER INFORMATION

Bullying

Norlin, J. W. (2012). *Disability-based bullying and harassment in schools: Legal requirements for identifying, investigating, and responding.* Palm Garden, FL: LRP Publications.

U.S. Department of Education website on bullying, www.stopbullying .com.

Charter Schools

Angelov, A.D.S., & Bateman, D.F. (2016). *Charting the course: Special education in charter schools.* Arlington, VA: Council for Exceptional Children.

Center for Parent Information & Resources (2011). *The facts on charter schools and students with disabilities.* Available at www.parentcenterhub. org/charters/

The Council of Exceptional Children policy on educating children and youth with exceptionalities in charter schools (N.D.). Available at www.cec.sped.org/~/media/Files/Policy/CEC%20Professional%20 Policies%20and%20Positions/charterschoolspolicy.pdf

U.S. Department of Education, Office of Civil Rights (2016). Frequently Asked Questions about the Rights of Students with Disabilities in Public Charter Schools under Section 504 of the Rehabilitation Act of 1973." Available at www2.ed.gov/about/offices/list/ocr/docs/dcl-faq-201612-504-charter-school.pdf

U.S. Department of Education, Office of Special Education and Rehabilitative Services (2016). Frequently Asked Questions about the Rights of Students with Disabilities in Public Charter Schools under the Individuals with Disabilities Education Act. Available at https:// sites.ed.gov/idea/files/policy_speced_guid_idea_memosdcltrs_faq-idea-charter-school.pdf

Response to Intervention

Yell, M. L., & Walker, D. W. (2010). The legal basis of response to intervention: Analysis and implications. *Exceptionality, 18,* 109–124.

FERPA

Norlin, J. W. (2011). *From the FERPA files: Quick tips on student education records.* Palm Beach Garden, FL: LRP Publications.

Norlin, J. W. (2012). *Beyond FERPA: A guide to student records under the IDEA.* Palm Beach Garden, FL: LRP Publications.

Teacher Liability

Pitasky, V. M. (1995). *Liability for injury to special education students.* Palm Beach Garden, FL: LRP Publications.

REFERENCES

Alexander, K., & Alexander, M. D. (2012). *American public school law* (8th ed.). Clifton Park, NY: Cengage Learning.

Alexander v. Boyd, 22 IDELR 139 (D.S.C. 1995).

Analysis of Comments and Changes to 2006 IDEA Part B Regulations, 71 Fed. Reg. 46,647 (2006).

Anello v. Savignac, 342 N.W. 2d 440 (Wis. Ct. App. 1983).

Angelov, A.D.S., & Bateman, D.F. (2016). *Charting the course: Special education in charter schools.* Arlington, VA: Council for Exceptional Children.

A. P. by Powers v. Woodstock Board of Education, 572 F. Supp. 2d 221 (2008).

A. W. v. Jersey City Public Schools, 486 F.3d 791 (3d Cir. 2007).

Ashli and Gordon C. ex rel. Sidney C. v. State of Hawaii, Department of Education, 47 IDELR 65 (D. Haw. 2007).

Baltimore City Public School System, 49 IDELR § 206 (Md. SEA 2007).

Bathon, J., Gooden, J.S., & Plenty, J.A. (2017). Student record. In J.R. Decker, M.M. Lewis, E.A. Shaver, A.E. Blankenship-Know, & M.A. Paige (Eds.) *The principal's legal handbook* (6th. Ed), pp. A103-A116. Cleveland, OH: Education Law Association.

Blake, J. J., Lund, M. E., Zhou, Q., Kwok, O., & Benz, M. R. (2012) National prevalence rates of bullying victimization among students with disabilities in the United States. *School Psychology Quarterly, 27,* 210–222.

Board of Education of the Hendrick Hudson Central School District v. Rowley, 458 U.S. 176 (1982).

Boyce, S. P., & Manna, A. A. (2011). School liability for bullying & harassment. *Leadership Insider: Practical Perspectives on School Law & Policy & policy, 2011,* 1–3.

Broaders v. Polk County School Board 57 IDELR 46, 111 LRP 46063 (M.D.FL 2011).

C.L. v. Leander Independent School District, 61 IDELR 194, 113 LRP 30097 (W.D.TX 2013).

C. M. v. Southeast Delco School District, 19 IDELR 1084 (E.D. Pa. 1993).

Cohen v. School District, 18 IDELR 911 (1992).

Council of Exceptional Children (2016). CEC's on children with exceptionalities in charter schools. Retrieved from www.cec.sped.org/~/media/Files/Policy/CEC%20Professional%20Policies%20and%20Positions/charterschoolspolicy.pdf on October 12, 2017.

D.A. v. Meridian School District, 60 IDELR 192, 113 LRP 6930 (ID 2013).

Daggett, L. M. (1995, April). Reasonable schools and special students: Tort liability of school districts and employees for injuries to, or caused by, students with disabilities. Paper presented at the International Conference of the Council for Exceptional Children, Indianapolis, IN.

Davis v. Monroe County Board of Education, 526 U.S. 629 (1999).

Doe v. Big Walnut Local School District Board of Education 57 IDELR 74,111 LRP 51476 (S.D. Ohio 2013).

Duncan, A. (2010). The myths about bullying: Secretary Arne Duncan's remarks at the bullying prevention summit. Retrieved from www.ed.gov/news/speeches/myths-about-bullying-secretary-arne-duncans-remarks-bullying-prevention-summit on March 11, 2012.

El Paso Independent School District v. Richard R. 53 IDELR 175 (5th Cir. 2009).

Estate of Lance v. Lewisville Independent School District, 58 IDELR 277, 112 LRP 24543 (E.D. TX 2011).

Fagan v. Summers, 498 P.2d 457, 1227 (1978).

Family Educational Rights and Privacy Act (FERPA), 20 U.S.C. § 1232 *et seq.*

Fischer, L., Schimmel, D., & Kelly, C. (1994). *Teachers and the law* (3rd ed.). White Plains, NY: Longman.

Foster v. Houston General, 407 So. 2d 758 (1981).

Frank v. New Orleans Parish School Board, 195 So. 2d 451 (La. Ct. App. 1967).

Freedman, M. (1995, August). Substance and shadows: Potential liability of schools and school personnel in special education cases. Paper presented at the Seventh Utah Institute on Special Education Law and Practice, Salt Lake City, UT.

Fuchs, L. S., & Mellard, D. F. (2007). *Helping educators discuss responsiveness to intervention with parents and students.* [Brochure]. Lawrence, KS: National Research Center on Learning Disabilities.

Garret v. Olson, 691 P.2d 123 (Or. Ct. App. 1984).

Gonzaga University v. Doe, 536 U.S. 273 (2002).

Hatfield v. O'Neill, 113 LRP 32934 (11th Cir. 2013) (unpublished).

Hamilton v. Spriggle, 113 LRP 33094 (M.D. Pa. 2013).

Herrera v. Hillsborough County School Board, 61 IDELR 137 (M.D. Fla. 2013).

Individuals with Disabilities Education Act (IDEA), 20 U.S.C. § 1401 *et seq.*

Individuals with Disabilities Education Act Regulations, 34 C.F.R. § 300.1 *et seq.*

Irvine Unified School District, 23 IDELR 911 (FPCO 1995).

J.B. v. Mead School District No. 354, 55 IDELR 250, 110 LRP 72692 (E.D. 2010).

Jacobs, M. (2012, November). The year in review 2013-2014. Tri-State Special Education Law Conference. Omaha, NE.

Johnson, T. P. (1993). Managing student records: The courts and the Family Educational Rights and Privacy Act of 1974. *Education Law Reporter, 79,* 1–16.

K. L. v. Southeast Delco School District, 20 IDELR 244 (E.D. Pa. 1993).

Kendall v. West Haven Department of Education, 33 IDELR 270, 33 6342 (CT Superior Ct. 2000).

Kluka v. Livingston Parish Board, 433 So. 2d 213 (1983).

K.M. ex rel. D.G v. Hyde Park Central School District, 44 IDELR 37, 381 F. Supp. 2d 343 (S.D.N.Y. 2005)

Leadership Insider (2011). White House and U.S. Department of Education focus on bullying and harassment in schools. *Leadership Insider: Practical Perspectives on School Law & Policy, 2011, August,* 2.

Letter to Schipp, 23 IDELR 442 (OSEP 1995).

Lyon, G. R., Fletcher, J. M., Shaywitz, S. E., Shaywitz, B. A., Torgeson, J. A., Wood, F. B., Shulte, A., & Olson, R. (2001). Rethinking learning disabilities. In C. E. Finn, A. J. Rotherham, & C. R. Hokanson (Eds.), *Rethinking special education for a new century.* Washington, DC: Thomas B. Fordham Foundation and Progressive Policy Institute. Available from www.ppionline.org/documents/SpecialEd_complete_volume.pdf.

Marshall Joint School District No. 2 v. C.D. by Brian and Traci D., 592 F. Supp. 2d 1059 (W.D. Wis. 2009).

Marshfield School District, 23 IDELR 198 (SEA Me. 1995).

Mawdsley, R. D. (1993). Supervisory standard of care for students with disabilities. *Education Law Reporter, 80,* 779–791.

Mawdsley, R. D. (1996). Litigation involving FERPA. *Education Law Reporter, 110,* 897–914.

McCarthy, M. M., Cambron-McCabe, N. H., & Eckes, S. E. (2013). *Public school law: Teachers' and students' rights* (7th ed.). Upper Saddle River, NJ: Merrill/Pearson Education.

Memorandum to Chief State School Officers, 51 IDELR 49 (OSEP 2008).

Merrell, K. W., Gueldner, B. A., Ross, S. W., & Isava, D. M. (2008). How effective are school bullying interventions? A meta-analysis of intervention research. *School Psychology Quarterly, 23,* 26–42.

M.L. v. Federal Way School District, 105 LRP 13966 (9th Cir. 2005).

Moore v. Chilton County Board of Education, 60 IDELR 274, 936 F. Supp 2d 1300 (M.D. AL 2013).

M.P. v. Independent School District, 38 IDELR 262, 103 LRP 15159 (8th Cir 2003).

Mulligan, E. (2011). The facts on charter schools and students with disabilities. Retrieved on March, 2016 from www.parentcenterhub.org/charters/.

Musgrove, M. *Memorandum to State Directors of Special Education* (OSEP 2011). Available at www2.ed.gov/policy/.../memosdcltrs/osep11-07rtimemo.pdf.

M. Y. v. Grand River Academy, 54 IDELR 255,110 LRP 33246 (N.D. Ohio 2010).

National Center on Educational Statistics (2014). *Fast facts on charter schools*. Retrieved from https://nces.ed.gov/fastfacts/display.asp?id=30 on 9/11/217.

Norlin, J. W. (2012). *Beyond FERPA: A guide to student records under the IDEA*. Palm Beach Garden, FL: LRP Publications.

Norlin, J. W. (2014). *Disability-based bullying and harassment in schools: Legal requirements for identifying, investigating, and responding*. Palm Beach Garden, FL: LRP Publications.

O. F. ex rel. N.S. v. Chester Upland School District, 246. F. Supp. 2d 409 (E.D. Pa. 2002).

OSEP policy letter, 17 IDELR 1117 (OSEP 1991).

People v. Overton, 249 N.E. 2d 366 (NY 1969).

Pitasky, V. M. (1995). *Liability for injury to special education students*. Horsham, PA: LRP Publications.

Pitasky, V. M. (2000). *The complete OSEP handbook*. Horsham, PA: LRP Publications.

President's Commission on Excellence in Special Education. (2001). A new era: Revitalizing special education for children and their families. Retrieved from www2.ed.gov/inits/commissionsboards/whspecialeducation/reports/index.html.

Rose, C. A., Swearer, S. M., & Espelage, D. L. (2012). Bullying and students with disabilities: The untold narrative. *Focus on Exceptional Children*, 45 (2), 1–11.

Roquet v. Kelly 62 IDELR 46, 113 LRP 41154 (M.D. PA 2013).

Ross, S. W., & Horner, R. H. (2009). Bully prevention in positive behavior support. *Journal of Applied Behavior Analysis*, 42, 747–759.

Sansone v. Bechtel, 429 A.2d 820 (Conn. 1980).

Scott v. Greenville, 48 S.E. 2d 324 (1965).

Sheehan v. St. Peter's Catholic School, 188 N.W. 2d 868 (Minn. 1971).

Shore Regional High School Board of Education v. P.S., 41 IDELR 234 (3rd Cir. 2004).

Silano v. Board of Education of the City of Bridgeport, 54 IDELR 199, 110 LRP 27171 (Conn. Superior Ct. 2010).

S.S. v. Eastern Kentucky University 110 LRP 62749 (6th Cir. 2008).

Surprenant, Miller, Pasternak, 2014

Sutherlin v. Independent School District No. 40, 61 IDELR 69, 960 F. Supp. 2d 1254 (N.D. OK 2013),

T.K. v. New York City Department of Education, 56 IDELR 228 E.D.N.Y. 2011).

U.S Department of Education, Office of Civil Rights (2000). Dear Colleague Letter on Bullying. Available at www2.ed.gov/about/offices/list/ocr/docs/disabharassltr.html

U.S. Department of Education, Office of Civil Rights (2010). Dear Colleague letter on Bulling. Available at www2.ed.gov/about/offices/list/ocr/letters/colleague-201010.html

U.S. Department of Education, Office of Civil Rights (2014). Dear Colleague Letter on Bullying. Available at www2.ed.gov/about/offices/list/ocr/letters/colleague-bullying-201410.pdf

U.S. Department of Education, Office of Civil Rights (2016). Frequently Asked Questions about the Rights of Students with Disabilities in Public Charter Schools under Section 504 of the Rehabilitation Act of 1973. Available at www2.ed.gov/about/offices/list/ocr/docs/dcl-faq-201612-504-charter-school.pdf

U.S. Department of Education, Office of Special Education and Rehabilitative Services (2016). Frequently Asked Questions about the Rights of Students with Disabilities in Public Charter Schools under the Individuals with Disabilities Education Act. Available at https://sites.ed.gov/idea/files/policy_speced_guid_idea_memosdcltrs_faq-idea-charter-school.pdf

Walker, D. W., & Daves, D. (2010). Response to intervention and the courts: Litigation-based guidance. *Journal of Disability Policy Studies*, 21, 40–46.

Weatherly, J. (2013, November). *What the courts are saying: 2013*. Tri-State Regional Law Conference. Omaha, NE.

Werth v. Board of Directors of the Public Schools of the City of Milwaukee, 47 IDELR 67, 422 F. Supp. 2nd 1113 (E.D. Wisc. 2007).

Wright v. Carroll County Board of Education, 59 IDELR 5, 112 LRP 27373 (D.C. MY 2013).

Yell, M. L., & Walker, D. W. (2010). Response to intervention: The legal basis and current litigation. *Exceptionality*, 18, 124–136.

Appendix A
Major Changes of IDEA 2004

Title & Part	Area of Change	Description
Title I, Part A	Assistive technology device	• Adds language to clarify that the term does not include surgically implanted medical device or replacement of that device.
	Core academic subjects	• Adds the definition from NCLB that core academic subjects are English, reading, language arts, mathematics, science, foreign language, civics and government, economics, arts, history, and geography.
	Homeless children	• Adds the definition of homeless children from the McKinney-Vento Homeless Assistance Act: "Children who don't have a regular night time residence, including children (a) sharing others' housing due to loss of housing, economic hardship, or similar reason; living in motels, hotels, trailer parks, or campgrounds due to lack of alternative adequate accommodations; living in emergency or transitional shelters; abandoned in hospitals; or awaiting foster care placement."
	Limited English proficient	• Adds definition of limited English proficient from NCLB: "An individual, aged 3–21, enrolled or preparing to enroll in an elementary or secondary school, 1. (a) who wasn't born in the U.S. or whose native language isn't English; (b) who is a Native American or Alaskan Native, or native resident of the outlying areas and comes from an environment where a language other than English has significantly impacted level of English language proficiency; or (c) who is migratory, with a native language other than English, from an environment where a language other than English is dominant; and 2. whose difficulties in speaking, reading, writing, or understanding English may be sufficient to deny the child (a) ability to meet proficiency level of achievement on State assessments; (b) ability to successfully achieve in class where instruction is in English; or (c) opportunity to participate fully in society."
	Parent	• Adds natural, adoptive, or foster parent; guardian (but not the state if child is a ward of the state); or a person acting in place of a natural or adoptive parent with whom the child lives or who is legally responsible for the child.
	Related services	• Adds school nurse services and interpreting services to the list of related services.
	Transition services	• Adds that services must be focused on improving academic and functional achievement, and that students' strengths must be taken into account.

Title & Part	Area of Change	Description
	Universal design	• Adds definition from the Assistive Technology Act of 1998: "A concept or philosophy for designing and delivering products and services that are usable by people with the widest possible range of functional capabilities, which includes products and services that are directly usable (without requiring assistive technology) and products and services that are made usable with assistive technologies."
	Highly qualified special education teachers	• The new highly qualified special education teacher requirements do not create a right of action if a teacher is not highly qualified. • All special educator teachers must: a) Be certified by the state to teach in special education. b) Hold at least a bachelor's degree. c) Demonstrate competency in all core academic subjects in which they teach. • Special education teachers teaching students with significant cognitive disabilities, who are assessed on alternative achievement standards, must: a) Be certified by the state to teach in special education. b) Hold at least a bachelor's degree. c) Demonstrate competency in (a) all core academic subjects they teach or (b) in subject knowledge appropriate to the level of instruction. • Currently teaching special education teachers who teach two or more academic subjects may meet the highly qualified standards of the NCLB by passing a single, multi-subject, highly objective, uniform state standard of evaluation (HOUSSE). • New special education teachers who teach two or more academic subjects and are highly qualified in math, language arts, or science may meet the highly qualified standards by passing a state's HOUSSE within 2 years of the date they were hired. • Certification/licensure requirements cannot be waived on emergency, temporary, or provisional basis.
	Paperwork reduction	• Fifteen states can apply to a pilot program in which states may develop and implement 3-year IEPs. States that are in the program may offer parents the option of developing a comprehensive 3-year IEP designed to coincide with natural transition points in their child's education (e.g., preschool to kindergarten, elementary school to middle school, middle school to high school). Parents have to agree to this option. • Pilot programs must also include a process for reviewing and revising the IEP, including (a) review at natural transition points, (b) annual review to determine levels of progress and whether progress is sufficient for goals to be met, and (c) a requirement to review and amend the IEP if the student is not making sufficient progress to meet his or her goals.
Title I, Part B	Local educational agency risk pool	• Adds language that every year allows states to reserve 10% of funds reserved for state-level activities to establish a high-cost fund and to support innovative ways of cost sharing.

Title & Part	Area of Change	Description
	Prohibition on mandatory medication	• Adds language that prohibits state and local educational agency personnel from requiring a child to obtain a prescription for medications covered by the Controlled Substances Act (e.g., Ritalin) as a condition of school attendance or receiving an evaluation or services.
	Individualized Education Programs (IEPs)	• Special education services must be based on peer-reviewed research.
	Initial evaluation	• Parent, school district, state educational agency, or other state agency may request initial evaluation. • Although IDEA 2004 requires school districts to obtain parental consent before conducting an initial evaluation, there are circumstances in which an initial evaluation can be completed without parental consent. Unless parental consent is required by a state, a school district may use mediation or due process to conduct an initial evaluation even when parents refuse to provide their consent or fail to respond to a request to evaluate. • Eligibility determination must be made within 60 days of consent for evaluation or within the timeframe set by the state if it is less than 60 days. • Timeframe does not apply if the child's parents repeatedly fail to produce the child for evaluation or if the parents refuse to provide consent to evaluate. • If a school screens a student to determine appropriate instructional strategies, it is not considered evaluation for special education eligibility.
	Evaluation procedures	• Assessments of a student who has transferred from another school district must be coordinated between prior and new school. • An evaluation is not required before dismissing a student from special education if the dismissal was due to graduation with a regular diploma or if he or she exceeds the state age at which a free appropriate education (FAPE) is no longer required (usually 21). • If a student ages out of special education, a school district is required to provide a summary of the student's academic achievement and functional performance. This includes recommendations on how to assist the student to meet his or her postsecondary goals. • A student cannot be determined to have a disability if the student's primary problem is a lack of appropriate instruction in reading, including instruction in the essential components of reading instruction.
	Identification of students with learning disabilities	• When determining if a student has a learning disability, a state cannot require a school district to use a discrepancy formula. • A school district may use a process, referred to as a response-to-intervention model, in which an IEP team is used to determine if a student responds to scientific, research-based intervention.

Title & Part	Area of Change	Description
	IEPs	• Parents and educators can agree to change an IEP without holding a formal IEP meeting. Annual IEP reviews are still required. If a meeting is not held, parents and teachers may develop a written document to amend or modify the current IEP.
		• The IEP team can agree to conduct IEP meetings by conference calls, video conferencing, or other means instead of face-to-face meetings.
		• A member of the IEP team won't be required to attend the IEP meeting or other meetings if the student's parents and the local education agency personnel agree that the person's attendance is not necessary because his or her area of curriculum or related services is not being modified or discussed at a meeting. To be excused the team member must submit a request in writing to the parents and the IEP team, and the parents and IEP team must agree to excuse the team member.
		• For transfer students in the same state who had an IEP in that year, a school district shall provide services comparable to the previous IEP until the district adopts the previous IEP or develops a new one.
		• IDEA 2004 no longer requires that benchmarks or short-term objectives be included in the IEP, except for students with severe disabilities who take alternate assessments.
		• IDEA 2004 emphasizes the importance of writing measurable annual goals and then measuring progress toward each goal during the course of the year. The IEP must describe how the student's progress toward the annual goals will be measured. The IEP must also include the schedule for reporting a student's progress. A student's parents must be informed of their child's progress at least every 9 weeks.
		• When an IEP is developed for a child who was in a Part C program, the parent may request that the Part C service coordinator shall be invited to the IEP team meeting.
		• After a student reaches 16 years of age, his or her IEP must include (a) measurable postsecondary transition goals based on age-appropriate transition assessments related to training, education, employment, and, when appropriate, independent living skills; and (b) transition services, including courses, needed to assist a student to reach his or her goals.
	Providing a special education	• A school district shall seek to obtain parental consent before providing special education services.
		• A school district shall not be required to develop an IEP or provide special education and related services to a child in the absence of parental consent. If a parent doesn't consent to placement, the school district cannot be held liable under the IDEA for failing to provide special education and related services.
	Scientifically based instruction	• Special education services must be grounded in scientifically based research.

Title & Part	Area of Change	Description
	Discipline	• A school district may remove a student who violates a student code of conduct from his or her current placement to an interim alternative educational setting (IAES) or another setting, or suspend him or her for not more than 10 school days, to the extent that similar procedures would be used with a student who does not have a disability.
		• If a school district wants to order a disciplinary change of placement that exceeds 10 school days, the district must conduct a manifestation determination.
		• When conducting a manifestation determination, the misbehavior can be determined to be a manifestation of a student's disability only if the conduct in question was "caused by" or had a "direct and substantial relationship" or if a school fails to implement a student's IEP as written.
		• If a student's misbehavior was not a manifestation of his or her disability, the school may use disciplinary procedures that are used with students who do not have a disability. These procedures may also be used for the same duration of time, although educational services must continue for any period beyond 10 school days.
		• A student with a disability who is removed from his or her current placement in excess of 10 school days must continue to receive educational services that enable him or her to progress toward IEP goals and continue to participate in the general education curriculum. Additionally, a functional behavioral assessment must be conducted as appropriate, and the student must continue to receive behavioral interventions and supports.
		• Students can be moved to an IAES if they possess or use weapons or drugs in school or at a school function or if they inflict serious bodily injury on another person while at school or a school function, without regard to whether the behavior was a manifestation of the student's disability.
		• Students can be placed in an IAES for up to 45 school days (this is longer than the previously allowed 45 calendar days).
		• The stay-put placement during hearings in which a disciplinary sanction is challenged will be the IAES, not the setting the student was in before the dispute.
		• Children or youth who are not currently in special education can receive protections under the disciplinary provisions of the IDEA if (a) the child's parents expressed their concern that their child needed special education services, in writing, to an administrator, supervisor, or teacher; or (b) the child's teacher or other school personnel expressed concerns about the child's behavior directly to the special education director or other supervisory personnel.
	Mediation	• If at the conclusion of mediation, both parties agree to and sign a legally binding agreement, that agreement will be enforceable in state or federal court.

Title & Part	Area of Change	Description
	Personnel qualifications	• Related services personnel must meet state-approved certification or licensure requirements. • Certification or licensure cannot be waived on an emergency, temporary, or provisional basis. • Special education teachers must be highly qualified by the NCLB deadline of no later than the 2005–2006 school year. • States must have policies that require school districts to take measurable steps to recruit, hire, train, and retain highly qualified personnel. • Parents may file a complaint with the state regarding a teacher's qualifications.
	Overidentification of minority students	• School districts that have high rates of minority students in special education are required to implement early identification services and eliminate the IQ discrepancy model to reduce overidentification of minority students.
	Parental empowerment	• School districts may use state IDEA funds to support supplemental services chosen by parents for their children with disabilities in schools that are identified as needing improvement under No Child Left Behind.
	Attorneys' fees	• State educational agencies and school districts that are prevailing parties in hearings and court cases may collect reasonable attorneys' fees when parents' attorneys file or litigate cases found to be frivolous, unreasonable, or without foundation. • Courts may levy a fine against parents if they bring actions against school districts for improper purposes such as harassment, causing unnecessary delay, protracting the final resolution, or increasing the cost of litigation. • Attorneys' fees are not available for prehearing resolution sessions.
	Administrative proceedings	• If either the parents or school district decide to bring a civil action following a due process hearing, they will have 90 days from the date of the decision to file the action.
	State performance plans	• States must develop performance plans that evaluate the state educational agency's efforts to implement the IDEA and describe how implementation will be improved. The plan must be approved by the Secretary of the U.S. Department of Education and reviewed at least once every 6 years. • In this plan the state must: a) Establish measurable goals and rigorous targets regarding the provision of FAPE in the least restrictive environment, the state's general supervisory authority, and disproportionate representation of racial and ethnic minorities, and collect data on these goals. b) Collect data on these goals and targets, analyze the data, report to the public annually on school districts' performance, and file a report with the U.S. Department of Education. The U.S. Department of Education will review these reports annually and determine if the state needs assistance, intervention, or substantial intervention to implement the IDEA.

Title & Part	Area of Change	Description
		• The U.S. Department of Education will enforce this plan to determine the state's status in implementing the IDEA.
		• If for 2 consecutive years the Department of Education determines that the state needs assistance in implementing the IDEA, the Secretary may (a) advise the state of technical assistance sources, (b) direct use of state funds to where the assistance is needed, or (c) identify the state as high risk and impose conditions on the state's grant under Part B.
		• If for 3 consecutive years the Department of Education determines that the state needs intervention, the Secretary may (a) require a new improvement plan or that the state take corrective action, (b) require a compliance agreement, (c) withhold state funds until the problem is corrected, (d) seek to recover funds, (e) withhold some or all IDEA payments to the state, or (f) refer the state to an appropriate agency for enforcement.
		• If the Department of Education determines that the state needs substantial intervention, the Secretary may: (a) recover funds, (b) withhold some or all IDEA payments to the state, (c) refer to the U.S. Department of Education Inspector General, or (d) refer the state to an appropriate agency for enforcement.
	Education of students with autism	• Part D authorizes support for developing and improving programs to train special education teachers to work with students who have autism spectrum disorders.
	Funding	• Schools may redirect a share of their local resources for activities consistent with NCLB. • The Individuals with Disabilities Education Improvement Act (IDEIA) of 2004 establishes a 6-year path to reach the 40% funding goals originally set in 1975.
Title I, Part C	Scientifically based research	• Early childhood special education services must be grounded in scientifically based research.
	Early childhood special education	• Children with disabilities who are served under Part C can continue in the same program from birth to kindergarten.
Title I, Part D	State personnel development grants	• In years when appropriations for this category of grants are less than $100 million, competitive grants are awarded to states for personnel development. Priority will be given to states that demonstrate the greatest difficulty in meeting personnel needs. • In years when appropriations for this category of grants exceed $100 million, formula grants will be awarded to all states. • To receive a grant, a state must have a personnel development plan and spend at least 90% of the grant for professional development.
	Accountability for alternative achievement standards	• National studies are authorized to examine the (a) criteria that states use to determine eligibility for alternative assessments, (b) reliability and validity of states' instruments and procedures, (c) alignments with a state's content standards, and (d) effectiveness of measuring progress on outcomes specific to instructional needs.

Title & Part	Area of Change	Description
	IAES, behavioral supports, and systemic schoolwide interventions	• Authorizes grants to support safe learning environments that foster academic achievement by improving quality in IAESs and providing behavioral supports and systemic schoolwide interventions.
		• Funds from these grants must be used to support activities such as staff training on: (a) identification, prereferral, and referral procedures; (b) positive behavioral supports and interventions; (c) classroom management; (d) linkages between school-based and community-based mental health services; and (e) using behavioral specialists and related services personnel to implement behavioral supports.
		• Funds may also be used to improve IAESs through (a) staff training, (b) referrals for counseling, (c) instructional technology, and (d) interagency coordination.
Title II	National Center for Special Education Research	• Establishes the National Center for Special Education Research within the Institute for Education Sciences.
		• The center's mission is to (a) expand the knowledge base in special education, (b) improve services under the IDEA, and (c) evaluate the implementation and effectiveness of the IDEA.
		• A commissioner of special education research will direct the center.

Appendix B
Relevant Sections of the
U.S. Constitution

PREAMBLE

We the people of the United States, in order to form a more perfect union, establish justice, insure domestic tranquility, provide for the common defense, promote the general welfare, and secure the blessings of liberty to ourselves and our posterity, do ordain and establish this Constitution for the United States of America.

* * *

ARTICLE 1

Section 8. [1] The Congress shall have the power to lay and collect taxes, duties, imposts and excises, to pay the debts and provide for the common defense and general welfare of the United States; ...

Section 8. [3] [Congress shall have the power] To regulate commerce with foreign nations, and among the several states, and with Indian tribes ...

* * *

ARTICLE III

Section 1. The judicial power of the United States shall be vested in one supreme Court, and in such inferior Courts as the Congress may from time to time ordain and establish ...

* * *

ARTICLE VI

This constitution, and the laws of the United States which shall be made in pursuance thereof; ... shall be the supreme law of the land; and the judges in every state shall be bound thereby, any thing in the Constitution or laws of any state to the contrary not withstanding.

* * *

AMENDMENT I

Congress shall make no law respecting an establishment of religion, or prohibiting the free exercise thereof; or abridging the freedom of speech, or of the press; or the right of the people peaceably to assemble, and to petition the Government for a redress of grievances.

* * *

AMENDMENT IV

The right of the people to be secure in their persons, houses, papers, and effects, against unreasonable searches and seizures, shall not be violated, and no warrants shall issue, but upon probable cause, supported by oath or affirmation, and particularly describing the place to be searched, and the persons or things to be seized.

*   *   *

AMENDMENT V

No person shall be ... compelled in any criminal case to be a witness against himself, nor be deprived of life, liberty, or property, without due process of law; nor shall private property be taken for public use, without just compensation.

*   *   *

AMENDMENT X

The powers not delegated to the United States by the Constitution, nor prohibited by it to the states, are reserved to the states respectively, or to the people.

*   *   *

AMENDMENT XIV

Section 1. All persons born or naturalized in the United States, and subject to the jurisdiction thereof, are citizens of the United States and of the state wherein they reside. No state shall make or enforce any law which shall abridge the privileges or immunities of citizens of the United States; nor shall any state deprive any person of life, liberty, or property, without due process of law, nor deny to any person within its jurisdiction the equal protection of the laws.

Glossary of Key Terms and Acronyms

ADA Americans with Disabilities Act.

Affirm To ratify or confirm, such as when a higher court upholds the opinion of a lower court in an appeal.

Amicus curiae "Friend of the court"; a person or organization that is allowed to appear in court or file arguments with the court even though the person or group is not a party to the suit.

Appeal A request to a higher court for a review of the decision of a lower court to correct mistakes or an improper ruling.

Appellate court A court that has jurisdiction to review decisions by lower courts but that does not have the power to hear a case initially.

BIP Behavior Intervention Plan. A plan developed for a student with disabilities who exhibits problem behavior. Required by the IDEA when a students is suspended from school for more than 10 days.

Case law Law developed by courts; also called *common law*.

Certiorari A request to a higher court to review a decision of a lower court; the request can be refused.

C.F.R. Code of Federal Regulations.

Civil cases All lawsuits other than criminal proceedings; usually brought by one person against another and usually involving monetary damages.

Class action A lawsuit brought by a person on behalf of all persons in similar situations as well as him- or herself; to bring such a suit, the person must meet certain statutory criteria.

Concurring opinion A statement by a judge or judges separate from the majority opinion, in which the results of the majority opinion are endorsed but the judge or judges provide their own rationale for reaching the decision.

Consent decree An agreement by the parties in a lawsuit, sanctioned by the court, that settles the matter.

De minimis Trivial or unimportant matter.

Defendant The person against whom a legal action is brought; at the appeals stage this person is the appellee.

Dicta The part of an opinion in which the court discusses the reasoning behind the court's ruling; it is not binding. The singular is *dictum*.

Dissenting opinion A statement by a judge or judges who disagree with the majority opinion and ruling.

DOE Department of Education.

EAHCA Education for All Handicapped Children Act; in 1990, renamed the Individuals with Disabilities Education Act.

En banc "In the bench"; when a full panel of judges hears a case.

ESEA Elementary and Secondary Education Act.

ESSA Every Student Succeeds Act

Et seq. "And following"; it is used in a legal citation to indicate the sections that follow the cited section.

F.2d Federal Reporter, second series; the reporter contains selected rulings of the U.S. Courts of Appeals. Published by West Publishing Company.

F.3d Federal Reporter, third series; the reporter contains selected rulings of the U.S. Courts of Appeals. Published by West Publishing Company.

F. Supp. The *Federal Supplement*; the supplement contains selected decisions of federal district courts. Published by West Publishing Company.

FAPE Free appropriate public education. The primary charge of the IDEA; eligible students are to receive a FAPE, which consists of special education and related services that are (a) provided at public expense, (b) meet the standards of the SEA, and are provided in conformity with a student's IEP.

FERPA Family Educational Rights and Privacy Act.

HCPA Handicapped Children's Protection Act.

Holding The part of a judicial opinion in which the law is applied to the facts of the case; the ruling.

IDEA Individuals with Disabilities Education Act.

IEP Individualized Education Program. All students who receive services under the IDEA must have an IEP, which is designed by a school based team along with a student's parents.

IFSP Individualized Family Services Program. All students, between the ages of 3 and 6, who receive services under the IDEA must have an IFSP.

Informed consent When a person agrees to let an action take place; the decision must be based on a full disclosure of the relevant facts.

Injunction A court order requiring a person or entity to do something or refrain from taking a particular action.

In re "In the matter of"; this prefix is often used in a case in which a child is involved.

LEA Local Education Agency.

LRE Least Restrictive Environment. Students with disabilities must be educated in integrated setting with their nondisabled peers to the maximum extent appropriate.

NCLB No Child Left Behind Act of 2001.

Negligence The failure to exercise the degree of care that a reasonable person would exercise in a similar situation. This lower standard of care falls below the standard of care required by law to protect a person from injury or harm.

OCR Office of Civil Rights.

Opinion Judges' statement of a decision reached in a case, consisting of the dicta and the ruling.

OSEP Office of Special Education Programs.

OSERS Office of Special Education and Rehabilitative Services.

P.L. 94-142 The number of the Education of All Handicapped Children Act of 1975; the bill was a public law, the 142nd bill passed by the 94th Congress.

PLAAFP Present Levels of Academic Achievement and Functional Performance. Statements in a student's IEP that reflect his or her academic and functional needs. The IEP is based on these individualized need statements.

Plaintiff A person who initiates a lawsuit.

Precedent A court decision that gives direction to lower courts on how to decide similar questions of law in cases with similar facts.

PRR Peer-reviewed research. A student's special education services, related services, and supplementary services in his or her IEP should be based on peer-reviewed research to the extent practicable. PRR is research that is published in a peer-reviewed journal or approved by an independent panel of experts.

Punitive damages A monetary punishment given when a defendant has acted with malice or deliberate indifference.

Remand To send back; a higher court may send back a ruling to a lower court with directions from the higher court.

RTI Response to intervention. The IDEA allows school district to use a method to identify a student with disabilities based on how a student responds to research based interventions. A state may not require a school district to use a discrepancy formula to determine the existence of a learning disability. RTI also refers to a schoolwide approach to adapting instruction to meet the needs of all students through the use of (a) high quality, research based instruction; (b) screening for academic and behavior problems; (c) continuous progress-monitoring; and (d) multiple tiers of progressively more intense instruction.

SEA State Education Agency.

Section 504 Section 504 of the Rehabilitation Act of 1973.

Stare decisis "To stand by that which was decided"; similar to precedence.

Tort A civil wrong done by one person to another.

U.S.C. United States Code.

Vacate To cancel or rescind, such as when a higher court overturns or sets aside the opinion of a lower court in an appeal.

Case Index

Author Index

Subject Index